The
Roman Inquisition
and the
Venetian Press,
1540–1605

The fire of the Holy Spirit operating through Sts. Peter and Paul, patrons of the Church, burns bad books. Source: *Index librorum prohibitorum usque ad annum MDCCXI regnante Clemente XI P. O. M.* (Romae, Ex Typographia Rev. Cam. Apost., 1711).

The Roman Inquisition and the Venetian Press, 1540-1605

Paul F. Grendler

PRINCETON UNIVERSITY PRESS
Princeton, New Jersey

Library of Congress Cataloging in Publication Data will
be found on the last printed page of this book

Publication of this book has been aided by a grant from
The Andrew W. Mellon Foundation

This book has been composed in Linotype Granjon

Printed in the United States of America
by Princeton University Press, Princeton, New Jersey

For Peter and Jean

CONTENTS

Contents

LIST OF ILLUSTRATIONS AND TABLES

TABLES

ACKNOWLEDGMENTS

ONE of the pleasures of completing a book is thanking those who helped write it. My greatest debt is to Martin Lowry, who cheerfully read the entire manuscript and prohibited many errors in the area of Venetian history. Antonio Rotondò and John Tedeschi read substantial portions of the manuscript and expurgated additional mistakes. Others graciously checked a source, contributed good advice, or offered a valuable reference: Peter Bietenholz, William Archer Brown, Gaetano Cozzi, Robert Finlay, Frederic C. Lane, Oliver Logan, Julius Molinaro, Reinhold Mueller, Antonio Santosuosso, Joseph Shatzmiller, Malcolm Smith, Frank Talmage, Maria Francesca Tiepolo, James Williamson, Daniel Williman, and William Wurthmann. Charles Schmitt put his immense knowledge of the period at my disposal on a number of occasions, and he and Anthony Molho have broadened my understanding of the Renaissance through our discussions over the years. The staffs of many archives and libraries have aided my work, especially those of the Archivio di Stato, Biblioteca Marciana, Museo Civico Correr, and Fondazione Giorgio Cini in Venice, the Archivio Segreto Vaticano and Biblioteca Apostolica Vaticana, and the Biblioteca Nazionale Centrale in Florence. William O'Sullivan, manuscript curator of Trinity College, Dublin, was also very helpful. I thank them all.

Since I began to read the Venetian Inquisition trials in the summer of 1967, generous financial support from the American Council of Learned Societies, the American Philosophical Society, the Canada Council, the Harvard Center for Italian Renaissance Studies, the Leopold Schepp Foundation, and the Society for the Humanities of Cornell University has made the research and writing possible. My wife and I are particularly grateful for the hospitality shown us by Myron and Sheila Gilmore at Villa I Tatti during 1970–72 and by Henry and Rita Guerlac at the Society for the Humanities during 1973–74.

The illustrations are reproduced through the courtesy of the Biblioteca Marciana, Museo Civico Correr, Biblioteca Apostolica Vaticana, and The Pierpont Morgan Library.

My wife, Marcella, cheerfully read every chapter, helped edit Appendix I, and occasionally aided in the research. To our children, Peter and Jean, this book is dedicated.

University of Toronto   PAUL F. GRENDLER
March, 1975

ABBREVIATIONS

Archival and Library

ASV: Archivio di Stato, Venice. Unless otherwise indicated, all archival references are to ASV. Some ASV series are abbreviated as follows:
Bestemmia Esecutori contro la bestemmia
CX Consiglio dei Dieci
SU Santo Uffizio
ASVa: Archivio Segreto Vaticano
BAVa: Biblioteca Apostolica Vaticana
BM: British Museum
BNF: Biblioteca Nazionale Centrale, Florence
DTC: Dublin, Trinity College
VC: Venice, Museo Civico Correr
VM: Venice, Biblioteca Marciana
Bu.: Busta
F.: Filza
R.: Registro

Printed Sources

BHR: *Bibliothèque d'Humanisme et Renaissance*
BSV: *Bollettino dell'Istituto di Storia della Società e dello Stato Veneziano*
Brown, *Venetian Press*: Brown, Horatio. *The Venetian Printing Press 1469–1800: An Historical Study Based upon Documents for the Most Part hitherto Unpublished.* London, 1891; rpt. Amsterdam, 1969.
Cambridge Catalogue: Catalogue of Books printed on the Continent of Europe, 1501–1600, in Cambridge Libraries. Compiled by H. M. Adams. 2 vols. Cambridge, 1967.
DBI: *Dizionario biografico degli Italiani.* Rome, 1960–.
HC: *Hierarchia Catholica medii et recentioris aevi.* Ed. C. Eubel et al. 6 vols. Munich, 1913–35; Pavia, 1952–58; rpt. Padua, 1960–68.
Nunziature I: *Nunziature di Venezia.* Vol. I (1533–35), ed. Franco Gaeta. Rome, 1958.
Nunziature II: *Ibid.,* Vol. II (1536–1542), ed. Franco Gaeta. Rome, 1960.
Nunziature V: *Ibid.,* Vol. V (1550–1551), ed. Franco Gaeta. Rome, 1967.
Nunziature VI: *Ibid.,* Vol. VI (1552–1554), ed. Franco Gaeta. Rome, 1967.
Nunziature VIII: *Ibid.,* Vol. VIII (1566–1569), ed. Aldo Stella. Rome, 1963.

Nunziature IX: *Ibid.*, Vol. IX (1569–1571), ed. Aldo Stella. Rome, 1972.

Nunziature XI: *Ibid.*, Vol. XI (1573–1576), ed. Adriana Buffardi. Rome, 1972.

Pastor: Pastor, Ludwig von. *The History of the Popes.* Trans. F. I. Antrobus et al. 40 vols. London and St. Louis, 1898–1953.

Pastorello: Pastorello, Ester. *Tipografi, editori, librai a Venezia nel secolo XVI.* Florence, 1924.

Reusch, *Index*: Reusch, Franz Heinrich. *Der Index der Verbotenen Bücher. Ein Beitrag zur Kirchen- und literaturgeschichte.* 2 vols. in 3 parts. Bonn, 1883–85; rpt. Darmstadt, 1967.

Reusch, *Indices*: Reusch, Franz Heinrich, ed. *Die Indices Librorum Prohibitorum des Sechzehnten Jahrhunderts.* Tübingen, 1886; rpt. Nieuwkoop, 1961.

STC French: Short-title Catalogue of Books printed in France and of French Books printed in other countries from 1470 to 1600 in the British Museum. London, 1924; rpt. London, 1966.

STC German: Short-title Catalogue of Books printed in the German-speaking countries and German Books printed in other countries from 1455 to 1600 now in the British Museum. London, 1962.

STC Italian: Short-title Catalogue of Books printed in Italy and of Italian Books printed in other countries from 1465 to 1600 now in the British Museum. London, 1958.

Stella I: Stella, Aldo. *Dall'Anabattismo al Socinianesimo nel Cinquecento veneto. Ricerche storiche.* Padua, 1967.

Stella II: Stella, Aldo. *Anabattismo e antitrinitarismo in Italia nel XVI secolo. Nuove ricerche storiche.* Padua, 1969.

NOTE

References to the Inquisition trials. Because the trials frequently consist of loose or unpaginated documents, making a precise citation is sometimes a problem. For very short trials (one to three folios), I cite the trial as a whole with a date: SU, Bu. 59, Gioachino Brugnolo, April 9, 1587. For longer trials, I try to supply enough information (adding foliation, giving the name of the witness and the date of his testimony) to locate the reference.

Dating. mv = modo veneziano. The Venetian calendar initiated the new year on March 1. I give all dates in the modern style in the text, but follow the original form, adding mv when appropriate, in the notes. Hence, a Venetian governmental document of February 20, 1558 mv is 1559. On the other hand, the Venetian Holy Office, like the papacy, used the modern calendar.

Orthography. For names, I employ modern spelling and avoid Venetian usage (i.e., Giovanni Donà rather than Zuanne Donato.) For the bookmen, I usually follow Pastorello, who gives the modern, vernacular, or customary form.

However, for a few obscure figures, and for quotations in the footnotes, I follow the original form given in the sources.

Money. The following monetary values are used throughout: 20 soldi = 1 lira; 124 soldi or 6 lire 4 soldi = 1 ducat of account. Indeed, the Inquisition sometimes specified this value when levying a fine. A ducat, a florin, and a scudo were roughly equivalent.

INTRODUCTION

Antonio Rotondò commented in 1963 that little is known of the internal history of the Index of Prohibited Books.[1] The monumental works of Franz Heinrich Reusch and Joseph Hilgers in the late nineteenth and early twentieth centuries provide a great deal of information on its external history, including reliable editions of the early Indices, information on how they were compiled, identifications of banned books, and reprints of individual prohibitory decrees. But they offer little information on enforcement, especially at the level of the bookstores. Although Firpo and, recently, Rotondò, Prodi, and Tedeschi, have done some work in that area, Rotondò's observation is still valid.[2] How effective *in practice* were the Index and its enforcing agency, the Roman Inquisition? To what extent and when were its decrees enforced? Why were they enforced or not, as the case might be? Above all, how did the Index and Inquisition affect the book trade?

This study attempts to provide answers for one Italian city. Venice, one of the great European publishing centers, produced half or more of all the books printed in cinquecento Italy. Equally important, the Inquisition records there are almost complete and are fully available to scholars.[3]

---

[1] Antonio Rotondò, "Nuovi documenti per la storia dell'Indice dei libri proibiti (1572–1638)," *Rinascimento*, ser. 2, vol. 3 (1963), pp. 145–46. The works referred to next are Franz Heinrich Reusch, ed., *Die Indices Librorum Prohibitorum des Sechzehnten Jahrhunderts* (Tübingen, 1886; rpt. Nieuwkoop, 1961), and *Der Index der Verbotenen Bücher: Ein Beitrag zur Kirchen- und Literaturgeschichte*, 2 vols. in 3 pts. (Bonn, 1883–85; rpt. Darmstadt, 1967); and Joseph Hilgers, *Der Index der Verboten Bücher* (Freiburg, 1905).

[2] Luigi Firpo, "Filosofia italiana e Controriforma," *Rivista di filosofia* 41 (1950), 150–73, 390–401; 42 (1951), 30–47; Rotondò, "Nuovi documenti"; and "La censura ecclesiastica e la cultura," in *Storia d'Italia*, vol. v, *I documenti* (Turin: Einaudi, 1973), pp. 1,397–1,492; Paolo Prodi, *Il Cardinale Gabriele Paleotti (1522–1597)*, vol. II (Rome, 1967), pp. 235–43, 252–62; John A. Tedeschi, "Florentine Documents for a History of the *Index of Prohibited Books*," in Anthony Molho and John A. Tedeschi, eds., *Renaissance Studies in Honor of Hans Baron* (Florence and De Kalb, Ill., 1971), pp. 577–605.

[3] The archives of the Roman Congregations of the Holy Office and of the Index are housed in the Palazzo del Santo Uffizio, Piazza S. Offizio 11, Rome, just outside the walls of the Vatican, now the home of the Congregation for the Doctrine of the Faith. However, scholars have always been denied access, even Pastor, who criticized the policy years ago. Pastor, xii, 507–08. Only Firpo has gained entry in recent years, and he found some significant materials, which he used in "Filosofia

With these one can follow the inquisitorial inspectors into the bookstores as they pursued prohibited books and the men who sold them. From Venetian governmental records and papal documents in the Vatican Archive and Library, one can trace the controversies that arose as the Venetian patriciate debated whether to enforce the Index or to support the disobedient printers. A Venetian proverb has it, "Una parte veneziana dura una settimana" (A Venetian law lasts only a week).[4] Throughout this book an attempt has been made to ascertain how long and how strongly the Index was enforced and, conversely, the extent of violation.

Scholarship on Venetian press censorship is meager. Horatio Brown's study of the Venetian press (1891) presents much valuable information and many documents, and it seldom errs factually. Brown did not always succeed in uncovering all the relevant information on particular incidents, and he tended to confine himself to legislation without determining enforcement; nevertheless, he authored an indispensable book. As a historian he was far superior to John Addington Symonds, his long-time friend, who is better remembered today.[5] Giovanni Sforza authored a

italiana e Controriforma," and a few less important papers on Bruno for his "Il processo di Giordano Bruno," *Rivista storica italiana* 60 (1948), 542-97; 61 (1949), 5-59. Recently Paul Kristeller obtained from the Holy Office archive a microfilm of a document, first noted by Firpo, which he edited as "Francesco Patrizi da Cherso, 'Emendatio in libros suos novae philosophiae,'" *Rinascimento*, ser. 2, vol. 10 (1970), pp. 215-18. How much sixteenth-century documentation survives is problematical because of the sack of the Holy Office at the death of Paul IV in 1559, and the unfortunate destruction in 1815-17 of the bulk of the inquisitorial records taken to Paris by Napoleon. Firpo was disappointed with what remained. "Il processo di Bruno," pp. 544-45. However, some dispersed documents have survived, notably the DTC mss., and a few others have turned up as BAVa mss. On this subject generally, see especially John A. Tedeschi, "La dispersione degli archivi della Inquisizione Romana," *Rivista di storia e letteratura religiosa* 9 (1973), 298-312; Angelo Mercati, *Il sommario del processo di Giordano Bruno*, Studi e Testi, 101 (Vatican City, 1942), pp. 3-4; and Leonard E. Boyle, *A Survey of the Vatican Archives and of Its Medieval Holdings* (Toronto, 1972), 85-86.

[4] *I diarii di Girolamo Priuli*, vol. 4, ed. Roberto Cessi (Bologna, 1938), p. 115, entry of June 29, 1509.

[5] On Brown (1854-1926), see T. W. Allen, in *The Dictionary of National Biography: 1922-1930* (Oxford, 1937), pp. 120-23. Brown's other historical works include *Venice: An Historical Sketch of the Republic* (first ed. 1893); his collected *Studies in the History of Venice* (the two vol. ed. of 1907 is the most complete); chapters, for the most part on medieval and Renaissance Venice, in *The Cambridge Modern History*, I, ch. viii; IV, ch. ii; and in *The Cambridge Medieval History*, IV, ch. xiii. He edited the *Calendar of State Papers, Venice* for 1581-1613, wrote a biography of Symonds (first ed. 1895), *Life on the Lagoons* (1884), poetry, and other works. For his friendship with Symonds, see Phyllis Grosskurth, *John Addington Symonds: A Biography* (London, 1964), passim.

long article (published posthumously in 1935) on the introduction of the Counter Reformation in Venice containing information on press censorship.[6] A number of other studies, to be cited as they are used, provide bits and pieces of information, but Brown and Sforza made the only substantial contributions.

Chapters I and II of this study introduce the protagonists, the bookmen and their trade, and then the members of the Inquisition, who moved within the web of Venetian links with God, church, and papacy. The detailed narrative of Venetian censorship begins with Chapter III. Following the directives of the Bible and classical antiquity, church and state had traditionally met heresy with suppression.

When Protestant literature began to appear in Italy about 1520, some zealots very early sought an Index of Prohibited Books. But both pope and secular leaders held back until reconciliation efforts with the Protestants failed. The Republic renewed its Inquisition and authorized the preparation of an Index in the late 1540s. The leaders of the Venetian state still were not wholly convinced of the gravity of the threat of heretics and their books, and they refused to put the weight of the state behind the Inquisition.

From 1549 through 1559, the bookmen resisted papal attempts to impose an Index on the Venetian press. The patriciate came to the aid of the bookmen eventually, and together they defeated the Indices of 1549, 1554/55, and 1559. Lacking an Index and the full support of the government, the Venetian Holy Office could only prosecute heretical books and their owners to a limited extent. A few sympathetic bookmen even assisted in providing prohibited titles to the Protestant conventicles that flourished in the 1550s and early 1560s.

The bookmen delayed, but could not halt, the Counter Reformation, for the patriciate slowly moved toward suppression of heretics and their books. The Inquisition, whose activity always reflected what the highest levels of government permitted, arrested Anabaptists initially, and orthodox Protestants subsequently. A civil court, rather than the Holy Office, destroyed large quantities of Hebrew books in 1553 and 1568, during a period of rising anti-Semitism. By the 1560s a reformed papacy had led a genuine religious revival that swept all before it—and put money in the pockets of bookmen who published religious titles. A combination of political and religious motives persuaded the Venetian patriciate to support the Counter Reformation wholeheartedly. Above all, the discovery that Protestantism had won converts among the younger members of the

[6] Giovanni Sforza, "Riflessi della Controriforma nella Repubblica di Venezia," *Archivio storico italiano* 93 (1935); pt. 1, pp. 5-34, 189-216; pt. 2, pp. 25-52, 173-86.

nobility aroused the Republic to implement and enforce strong censorship measures.

In the 1560s the Venetians erected an effective prepublication censorship system that provided for religious and political scrutiny. The government then tightened the inspection of imported books by stationing an inquisitorial representative at the customs house. At the end of the decade, the Inquisition began to make surprise visits to the bookstores, apprehending twenty-two bookmen in possession of prohibited titles. Church and state now cooperated in the pursuit and destruction of forbidden books.

At this moment of full acceptance of Index and Inquisition, Republic and papacy disagreed over what might appear to be an insignificant matter: the papal practice of issuing exclusive printing rights for the Tridentine breviary and missal. These privileges (copyrights) provoked lengthy quarreling and eventual papal withdrawal. The dispute helped to delimit Venetian support for ecclesiastical press controls, and it planted the seeds of future strife. So long as the state perceived ecclesiastical restrictions of the press as necessary to fight heretical books, it accepted them, even at the expense of clerical incursions into lay jurisdictional territory and financial losses to the book trade. But if the issue was not clearly heresy, the state again worried about the economic health of the book industry and lay jurisdictional rights.

From about 1570 until the early 1590s, the Inquisition strongly enforced the Index, halting the printing of all but a very few prohibited titles and continuing its surveillance of the bookstores. The bookmen retaliated by organizing clandestine networks to smuggle banned titles from northern Europe into the city. The Holy Office made arrests, but could not halt the illicit traffic. If a reader knew whom to ask—a bookseller who specialized in contraband, a Protestant Nicodemite, or a foreign merchant—he could obtain any prohibited title; he had only to avoid detection.

In the 1590s the cooperation between Rome and Venice, upon which successful enforcement of the Index had rested, disintegrated. Just as an identity of interests had earlier brought the two powers together, so differences now drove them apart. The Venetian government determined to enlarge its control over the resources of the state and over the religious, moral, and social lives of its citizens, at the expense of the church. The Republic encouraged lay ownership of ecclesiastical lands, asserted civil jurisdiction in areas where the church also claimed a voice, and curtailed the powers of the Holy Office.

The Republic took similar action in defense of the press when the bookmen persuaded the government that papal restrictions threatened their economic viability. The Republic argued the case of the bookmen in Rome in dispute after dispute in the 1590s, gradually formulating a policy of protecting the press. Although these conflicts seldom touched censorship, they kindled Venetian hostility toward ecclesiastical regulation.

The clash over the Clementine Index of 1596 ended in much reduced inquisitorial power over the press. All areas of censorship except political weakened as Venetian-papal relations deteriorated on the eve of the interdict. Probably more prohibited books entered Venice between 1590 and 1605 than at any time since the 1550s. During the interdict of 1606–07, the clandestine traffic in prohibited books became almost open because the Holy Office could do nothing. After Venetian-papal reconciliation, the Index and Inquisition failed to regain their former effectiveness; the bookmen openly, even mockingly, ignored them in the first half of the seicento. The stern Counter Reformation had passed in Venice.

Practical consequences rather than historiographical questions dominate this monograph, but since it discusses the Counter Reformation throughout, perhaps the author's understanding of that issue should be outlined. This study accepts Hubert Jedin's definitions of, and distinctions between, Catholic Reformation and Counter Reformation.[7] Jedin defines the former as the quest for internal renewal of the church. According to Jedin, the Catholic Reformation began before 1517 with the efforts of individuals to rekindle spiritual fervor in themselves and their neighbors. The Catholic Reformation developed independently of the Protestant Reformation, but Luther's revolt aided it by emphasizing the dangers of continuing in the old, unreformed ways. In the years between 1534 and 1555, the Catholic Reformation spread until it won over a majority of the church's lead-

---

[7] Hubert Jedin, *Riforma cattolica o Controriforma? Tentativo di chiarimento dei concetti con riflessioni sul Concilio di Trento*, trans. Marola Guarducci, 2nd ed. (Brescia, 1967), esp. pp. 35–53. First published in German in 1946, this is the fundamental study. No attempt is made to list all the literature on the interpretation of the Catholic Reformation and Counter Reformation in Italy, but the reader's attention is directed to the following recent surveys, each with ample bibliographies: Pier Giorgio Camaiani, "Interpretazioni della Riforma cattolica e della Controriforma," in M. F. Sciacca, ed., *Grande antologia filosofica. Parte III: Il pensiero della Rinascenza e della Riforma (Protestantesimo e Riforma cattolica)*. Vol. VI (Milan, 1964), pp. 329–490; Paolo Prodi, "Riforma cattolica e Controriforma," in *Nuove Questioni di Storia Moderna*, vol. I (Milan, 1964), pp. 357–418; Gaetano Cozzi, "Rinascimento Riforma Controriforma," in *La storiografia italiana negli ultimi vent'anni*, vol. II (Milan, 1970), pp. 1,219–40; Giuseppe Alberigo, "Studi e problemi relativi all'applicazione del Concilio di Trento in Italia (1945-1958)," *Rivista storica italiana* 70 (1958), 239–98. Alberigo's article is particularly valuable because it lists many unpublished laureate theses. Also see the discussions of Delio Cantimori in *Studi di storia* (Turin, 1959), pp. 537–53; and in *Storici e storia* (Turin, 1971), pp. 657–74.

ers. The Council of Trent affirmed its principles in the disciplinary reform decrees, especially in the concluding session of 1562–63. The attempt to implement the Tridentine measures and the program of sacred scholarship marked the last phase of the Catholic Reformation.

From apostolic times, Christians like St. Augustine have alternated between two approaches to the dissenter. The New Testament overwhelmingly exhorts Christians to love and convert the wrong-headed, but in a few passages it endorses expulsion, lest the heretic corrupt the community of believers. Jedin points out that the Counter Reformation embodied the latter approach, for the institutional church took up spiritual and temporal arms to defend the souls under its care. Apologists first tried to refute Protestant doctrines. Then, as conciliation efforts failed, the papacy brought to bear coercive weapons such as the Inquisition and Index. A bellicose spirit animated the major figures of the Counter Reformation, crusaders against Protestantism such as Paul IV and Pius V. Papal nuncios carried the war into distant places and prodded governments to take action against heretics.

Jedin's distinction offers a useful analytical tool, so long as one does not see the Catholic Reformation and the Counter Reformation as mutually exclusive, nor as completely separate after 1542. As Jedin states, the two movements shared the goal of the salvation of souls and had points of contact. The Council of Trent and prelates like Cardinal Girolamo Seripando adopted the procedures of both at one time or another. Since the two movements met in Rome, most popes after mid-century simultaneously promoted both.

Perhaps neither Jedin nor other scholars stress enough that princes and prelates acted together to suppress heretics and their books. Scholars tend to see the Counter Reformation as a result of the efforts of clerical leaders to persuade lay powers to eradicate Protestantism. Pastor, for example, constantly portrays individual popes exhorting balky civil rulers to act. Certainly after mid-century the papacy took the lead in urging upon princes measures to safeguard the faith, and civil rulers sometimes only reluctantly relinquished political and economic benefits to do so. Nevertheless, agreement on the essentials united prince and prelate, despite frequent disputes over timing or the degree of severity. The papacy did not force the Counter Reformation on indifferent civil governments; both powers moved together to suppress Protestantism.

The Venetian Republic was not an unqualified champion of civil autonomy against clerical pretensions.[8] The Venetian leaders carefully weighed

[8] This is a persistent and, in my judgment, somewhat exaggerated theme in Venetian historiography. Examples are Bartolomeo Cecchetti, *La Repubblica di Venezia e la Corte di Roma nei rapporti della religione*, 2 vols. (Venice, 1874); Antonio

each censorship issue and altered their stance to accommodate the constantly shifting political and religious realities. They judged the claims of God and mammon from the perspective of their times, sometimes strongly supporting the Index, sometimes rejecting it. The Republic probably acted no differently than any other Italian state.

This monograph ignores the many achievements of the Catholic Reformation, as well as those of the Protestant Reformation, except when they touch censorship and violation. Its goal is to examine Venetian enforcement of the Index of Prohibited Books in the hope of deepening our understanding of cinquecento Italy, a turbulent era in some ways similar to our own.

Battistella, "La Politica ecclesiastica della Repubblica Veneta," *Archivio veneto*, ser. 2, vol. 16 (1898), pp. 386–420; and William J. Bouwsma, *Venice and the Defense of Republican Liberty: Renaissance Values in the Age of the Counter Reformation* (Berkeley and Los Angeles, 1968).

The
Roman Inquisition
and the
Venetian Press,
1540–1605

I

THE VENETIAN BOOKMEN

THOSE seeking to regulate the Venetian press faced a formidable task. The first Venetian printed book did not appear until about 1469, but the press grew so rapidly that it became the largest in Europe by the end of the incunabular period.[1] The city's commercial preeminence and its distribution network (the best in the world) attracted the merchants of the new craft. In the early cinquecento Aldo Manuzio and other Venetian printers greatly aided the diffusion of humanistic learning by editing and publishing numerous editions of classical texts and modern humanist authors. After 1525 the enthusiasm for the vernacular, encouraged by such publishers as Gabriel Giolito, produced further growth. Northern rivals such as Lyons, Paris, and Basel challenged Venetian supremacy, but the Queen of the Adriatic probably still produced and sold more books than any other city at mid-century.[2]

1. PUBLISHERS, PRINTERS, AND SELLERS

A Venetian patrician estimated in 1596 that the press employed 400 to 500 men.[3] Publishers, printers, and booksellers, with much overlapping, comprised the book industry. The publisher, the man who placed his name

[1] Rudolf Hirsch, *Printing, Selling and Reading 1450–1550*, 2nd printing with a supplemental annotated bibliographical introduction (Wiesbaden, 1974), pp. 58–60. I wish only to introduce the bookmen in this chapter, not to discuss in detail the commercial history of the Venetian press. In general, the new information presented here confirms the picture presented by the able surveys of Lucien Febvre and Henri-Jean Martin et al., *L'apparition du livre*, 2nd ed. rev. (Paris, 1971); and Hirsch.

[2] This is my estimate; I do not know any studies providing enough statistical data for a census. The *Index Aureliensis. Catalogus librorum sedecimo saeculo impressorum* (Baden-Baden, 1962–) is now finishing the letter *B*. When it is completed sometime in the twenty-first century, comparisons among cities will be possible.

[3] Speech of Leonardo Donà in Collegio, Esp. Roma, R. 6, f. 123^r, July 12, 1596; also printed in Federico Seneca, *Il Doge Leonardo Donà: la sua vita e la sua preparazione politica prima del Dogado* (Padua, 1959), p. 252 n. 1. Since the press had declined a little by this date, one can estimate that at its peak (1550–74) it employed 500 to 600 persons.

on the title page, led the industry. Giolito, Giunti, and Manuzio, the most famous names in Venetian printing, published, but they also had a hand in every other phase of the trade. They printed, they marketed their product throughout Europe, and they owned retail stores in Venice and elsewhere from which they offered the public domestic and foreign imprints. The publisher might place a manuscript with a printer, one whose name appeared only on the colophon if at all. But the printer eagerly shed his anonymity when the opportunity arose to publish a profitable manuscript. The greatest exclusiveness appeared at the base of the industry; the independent bookseller probably lacked the capital to do more than sell books. Contemporaries, with some justification, used the terms *libraio, stampatore*, and *bibliopola* interchangeably.

At mid-century, 30 to 50 publishers produced at least one title in any given year.[4] The size of the firms varied greatly, from the giants—Giolito, Giunti, and Manuzio—down to individuals who published a single edition. Gabriel Giolito published c. 900 editions (originals and reprints) from 1541 through 1578, an average of nearly 24 per year, and his heirs added another 150 through 1599.[5] The Giunti and Aldine presses spanned the century, the former producing a few more than 1,000 editions, the latter about 950, for an average of about 10 per year.[6]

Many other very active publishers followed the giants. The Venetian

---

[4] Checking Pastorello, one finds 36 publishers in 1550, 30 in 1560, and 53 in 1570, exclusive of Giolito, Marcolini, and Manuzio, who also published in those years.

[5] When describing the production of a cinquecento press, it is difficult to use "edition," "reprint," "impression," and "printing" with twentieth-century precision. For the count of a firm's output, I (like Ester Pastorello) call every publication large enough to be called a book an edition, whether it is the first printing, a textually unchanged reprint carrying a new date, or a printing with small or large textual alterations. The figures for Giolito are my conservative count based on Salvatore Bongi, *Annali di Gabriel Giolito de' Ferrari da Trino di Monferrato, stampatore in Venezia*, 2 vols. (Rome, 1890–97; rpt. Rome, n.d.); and Paolo Camerini, "Notizia sugli Annali Giolitini di Salvatore Bongi," *Atti e memorie della R. Accademia di scienze, lettere ed arte in Padova. Memorie della Classe di scienze morali*, n. s., 51 (1934–35), 103–238. Camerini puts the total higher by counting sections of works with individual title pages. I prefer to combine sections into one title and to omit pamphlets and broadsides. But no system can be entirely precise, and all counts are only approximations. It should also be remembered that only surviving works can be counted. Hirsch, *Printing*, 11, estimates that 10 percent to 25 percent or more of sixteenth-century printings have disappeared completely.

[6] Paolo Camerini, *Annali dei Giunti. Volume I, Venezia, Parte I e II.* Biblioteca Bibliografica Italica, nos. 26, 28 (Florence, 1962–63); and A. A. Renouard, *Annales de l'imprimerie des Alde, ou Histoire des trois Manuce et de leurs éditions*, 3rd ed. (Paris, 1834; rpt. Bologna, 1953).

· 4 ·

press enjoyed strength through numbers and avoided dependence on one or two great firms.[7] Girolamo Scoto published 197 editions between 1540 and 1573, Vincenzo Valgrisi published 202 works from 1540 to 1572, Michele Tramezzino 190 from 1536 to 1574, Comin da Trino 170 from 1540 to 1573, and Francesco Ziletti 103 during the short period 1569–1587. Each of these individual publishers averaged at least 5 or 6 imprints a year. Smaller firms produced 3 to 4 titles annually: Domenico and Giovanni Battista Guerra published 160 between 1560 and 1598, Melchiorre Sessa (the Elder) 151 from 1506 to 1555, Giordano Ziletti 121 from 1549 to 1583, Damiano Zenaro 84 from 1573 to 1599, and Francesco Rampazetto 78 from 1553 to 1576. Others averaged about two editions a year: Andrea Arrivabene published 82 from 1536 to 1570, Nicolò Bevilacqua 48 from 1554 to 1572. A number of firms spanned the century or came within a few years of doing so. In addition to Manuzio and Giunti, the Scoto family published 362 works, the Sessa 298, and the Bindoni 234, in the century. Behind these well-known firms were a host of others, down to individuals who published a single title and disappeared.[8] The names of about 500 publishers appeared on the title pages and colophons of cinquecento Venetian printings.[9]

The majority of the bookmen located their shops in an area in the center of the city bounded by the districts of San Marco, Sant'Angelo, the Rialto bridge, Santi Apostoli, San Zanipolo (Giovanni e Paolo), and Santa Maria Formosa. The Mercerie, stretching from the Torre dell'Orologio to Campo San Bartolomeo, and the Frezzeria, from San Moisè to San Fantin, were lined with bookstores. The parishes of San Zulian (Giuliano), San Salvatore, San Bartolomeo, San Moisè, Sant'Angelo, and San Canciano contained many shops and homes of the bookmen. The church of San Zanipolo had a large warehouse used by many bookmen, and served as the meeting place of their guild. Other shops and homes were scattered across the city, as far away as the district of San Pietro in Castello. Books were also sold in outdoor stands, especially on and near the Rialto bridge, and were hawked in Piazza San Marco.

The preferred subject matter varied considerably from publisher to publisher. All published a little bit of everything, but the larger firms tended to specialize. The Giunti press printed large numbers of breviaries, missals, and other liturgical manuals, enabling the Venetian press to lead

[7] The following figures are based on Pastorello and, as noted below, may be as much as 50 percent underestimated. The figures include those editions published jointly with other firms.

[8] Among others were Giovanni Britto in 1543, Ferdinando Bertelli in 1563, Giovanni Bari in 1567, and Vittorio Baldini in 1582.

[9] Pastorello's figure is 493, exclusive of Manuzio, Giolito, and Marcolini.

Europe in the production of canonical works. The Aldine press enjoyed wide recognition for its editions of the classics and humanist commentaries. Tramezzino specialized in vernacular chivalric romances, vernacular history, and legal texts, but he also published significant amounts of vernacular translations of the classics, religious titles, and maps. Completely absent from his list were contemporary vernacular literature and science. Marcolini promoted exactly the vernacular literature that Tramezzino avoided, specializing in such authors as Pietro Aretino and Anton Francesco Doni. Gabriel Giolito published all manner of vernacular literature—dialogues, plays, treatises, histories, sermons, devotional matter, and poetry—and avoided law, philosophy, science, mathematics, and Latin titles generally. The Gardano family, especially Antonio (active 1539–69) and Angelo (1576–99), published music almost exclusively. Smaller publishers were more eclectic; with smaller financial resources and less reputation, they probably were more willing to publish whatever came their way.

The publishers sold their books in Italy and abroad, and accumulated capital. But the book industry included many humbler members: master printers and their assistants who printed on contract; employees of the bookstores owned by the publishers, from the manager down to his youngest shop boy; couriers who regularly shepherded their cargoes to and from the book-fairs of Frankfurt and elsewhere; and the lowly tradesmen who bought and sold used books from outdoor benches at the Rialto or hawked devotional pamphlets at the doors of San Marco. Too poor to appear on tax records, most members of the book trade have disappeared without trace except when they ran afoul of the Holy Office.

2. THE SIZE OF THE PRESS

The Venetian presses published an enormous number of editions in the sixteenth century; a conservative estimate suggests from 15,000 to 17,500. The higher number is arrived at by adjusting the survey made by Ester Pastorello in the light of more recent studies. Pastorello examined the holdings of three libraries: the Marciana in Venice, the Braidense in Milan, and the University of Padua.[10] She counted 7,000 editions carrying a publisher's name and 560 anonymous editions, excluding the output of the Aldine, Giolito, and Marcolini presses, which had already been surveyed.[11] She did not examine the holdings of such major repositories as the National Central Library in Florence, the Vatican Library, and the

[10] Ester Pastorello, *Tipografi, editori, librai a Venezia nel secolo XVI* (Florence, 1924), esp. pp. vii–viii.

[11] Scipione Casali, *Annali della tipografia veneziana di Francesco Marcolini da Forlì* (Forlì, 1861; rpt. Bologna, 1953, with a new introd. by Luigi Servolini).

LA BEAT.^{MA.} VERGINE DEL ROSARIO, E S.TOMASO D' AQUINO
PROTETTORI DELL'UNIVERSITÁ DE LIBRAJ, E STAMPATORI.

1. Our Lady of the Rosary and St. Thomas Aquinas, protectors of the guild of the bookmen. Source: VC, Ms. Cicogna 3044

British Museum. Recent studies of three presses demonstrate how incomplete her survey was. Pastorello counted 360 Giunti editions, whereas Camerini noted over 1,000. Pastorello counted 93 Venetian Tramezzino editions; Tinto noted over 200.[12] Pastorello's figure should be doubled. If her count of 7,200 (7,560 less the 360 Giunti editions) is doubled, and the 950 Aldine, 1,050 Giolito, 1,000 Giunti, and 150 Marcolini editions are added, an estimate of about 17,500 individual editions seems reasonable.

An analysis of the imprimaturs (permissions to print) issued by the Venetian government for new or substantially revised titles supports a lower conjecture of about 15,000 titles in the century. Between 1550 and 1599 the government granted an average of 71 imprimaturs annually.[13] For every new title, however, there were one or more reprints that did not need an imprimatur. Castiglione's *Courtier* and Ariosto's *Orlando Furioso*, as well as the works of less well-known authors, were often reprinted. To cite a modest example, Francesco Sansovino's *Delle cose notabili che sono in Venetia* (1561), a historical guide, was reprinted 12 times in 45 years.[14] The Giolito press published a few more than 1,000 titles, of which slightly over one-half were reprints of their own previous publications (1.09 reprints for every new title).[15] Vernacular literary titles, devotional works, and classics in the original and in translation were reprinted more often than legal, medical, mathematical, and scientific works.

When the average annual Venetian total of 71 imprimaturs granted in the second half of the cinquecento is multiplied by 2.09, an average annual production of 148.4 new and reprinted books can be projected. This means that about 7,420 (148.4 x 50) editions were published from 1550 through 1599. Since it is likely that the presses were a little more active in the second half of the century than in the first,[16] perhaps only c. 6,000 editions were produced between 1500 and 1550. Thus, the total editions for the century projected on the basis of known imprimaturs is c. 13,420 edi-

[12] Alberto Tinto, *Annali tipografici dei Tramezzino* (Venice-Rome, 1968).

[13] The imprimaturs are found in Capi del Consiglio dei Dieci, Notatorio, R. 14–31, F. 1–13. For an explanation of the imprimaturs and their count, see Ch. IV, sec. 1, and Ch. VIII, sec. 1.

[14] Paul F. Grendler, "Francesco Sansovino and Italian Popular History 1560–1600," *Studies in the Renaissance* 16 (1969), 167, n. 66.

[15] This is based on my analysis of the editions in Bongi, *Giolito*; and Camerini, "Notizia."

[16] An examination of Pastorello and *STC Italian* shows that fewer titles were published in the first quarter of the cinquecento. The press then entered upon rapid expansion, which probably reached its height in the period c. 1540 to 1575. The plague of 1575–77 caused a ten-year depression in the book industry. The press rebounded in the last fifteen years of the century, but never regained all the lost ground. For more on this, see Chs. IV, sec. 1, and VIII, sec. 1.

tions (6,000 + 7,420). But publishers did not obtain an imprimatur for every title; especially in the first two-thirds of the century, they often ignored the law.[17] Possibly for every 10 titles for which an imprimatur was granted, one title was published in first edition and subsequent reprint without an imprimatur. If the total number of editions for the century is increased by 10% to allow for the works published without imprimaturs, the total for the century was c. 14,800 (13,420 + 1,342).[18]

A Venetian press run varied according to the anticipated demand for the book and the size of the publisher. The normal press run of a title of ordinary or modest sales potential was about 1,000 copies; a major publisher with a title of assured high demand ordered press runs of 2,000 or 3,000 copies. Financial considerations probably dictated the average press run of 1,000 copies. In 1548 the papal nuncio, Giovanni Della Casa, investigated the possibility of publishing an unidentified book of history. He learned that the government would not issue a *privilegio* (copyright) unless the Venetian press run was at least 400 copies, and that a publisher preferred for reasons of cost to print 1,000.[19]

[17] In reading the imprimaturs c. 1550 to c. 1565, I did not find several titles of authors such as Anton Francesco Doni, Nicolò Franco, Ortensio Lando, and Ludovico Domenichi, whose bibliography I have studied.

[18] Peter Bietenholz has suggested to me another method, based on the catalogues of the Frankfurt book-fairs, for counting the number of editions. One counts the number of Venetian imprints offered for sale at the fair during a period of years and then estimates what percentage this was of the total Venetian production for those years. For example, during the decade 1565 through 1574, the Frankfurt catalogues listed a total of 578 Venetian imprints, an annual average of 57.8. (See the table in Peter G. Bietenholz, *Basle and France in the Sixteenth Cenury: The Basle Humanists and Printers in Their Contacts with Francophone Culture* [Geneva and Toronto, 1971], pp. 46–47.) Bietenholz (p. 45) points out that about one-third of the annual production of the Geneva presses, which has been analyzed by Hans Joachim Bremme, *Buchdrucker und Buchhändler zur Zeit der Glaubenskämpfe: Studien zur Genfer Druckgeschichte 1565–1580* (Geneva, 1969), appeared in the Frankfurt fair catalogues. If it is estimated that Venetian imprints at the fairs also comprised one-third of annual production, then the annual production for the decade 1565–74 was 173 editions (57.8 x 3). This estimate for the decade 1565–74 is 8.5 percent lower than my count of 189 based on the imprimaturs. (Please see Tables 4 and 5.) Unfortunately, estimating Venetian production for the whole half-century 1550–99 by this method is very difficult because only eleven other fair catalogues survive for this period. Nevertheless, the crests and troughs of Venetian imprints listed in the surviving catalogues of the Frankfurt fairs correspond roughly to the rise and fall of imprimaturs.

[19] Letter of Carlo Gualteruzzi to Giovanni Della Casa, July 28, 1548, printed in Lorenzo Campana, "Monsignor Giovanni della Casa e i suoi tempi," *Studi storici* 18 (1909), 465. The publisher was Tramezzino of Rome, i.e., Francesco Tramezzino, who published jointly with his brother Michele in Venice. For identification, see Tinto, *Tramezzino*, pp. ix–xvii.

In 1559 the Aldine press published a number of titles for the Accademia Venetiana, a learned group subsidized by some Venetian nobles. Nine of the editions had press runs of 825 copies, another nine of 1,100 or 1,125, one of 1,250, and one of 1,700.[20] In 1554 Plinio Pietrasanto printed Girolamo Ruscelli's *Il capitolo delle lodi del fuso*; according to the author, the press run was 800 to 1,000 copies. Part of the genre of poetry praising lowly subjects (a *fuso* is a spindle), the work was not of great significance and may not have been reprinted.[21] In 1581 the heirs of Tramezzino contracted with Luc'Antonio Giunti and Giovanni Varisco to print a new edition of the five-volume *Delle historie del mondo* of Giovanni Tarcagnota, Mambrino Roseo da Fabriano, and Bartolomeo Dionigi da Fano, and specified a press run of 1,125, less those spoiled in printing.[22] In 1590 Girolamo Polo, a small publisher, printed 1,125 copies of a new edition of the frequently published *Vitae pontificum* by the quattrocento author, Bartolomeo Sacchi (called il Platina).[23] In Rome, the 1570 edition of the *opera omnia* of St. Thomas Aquinas had a press run of 1,000.[24] The first volumes of Cesare Baronius's *Annales Ecclesiastici*, published in Rome, 1588, had press runs of 800 copies.[25]

Indirect evidence also suggests that press runs of around 1,000 copies were common. In January 1562, Michele Tramezzino inventoried the published titles still in his possession. The remaining copies of titles recently published in single editions provide a basis for projecting the size of a Tramezzino press run. He had 900 remaining copies of a chivalric romance, 796 of an anonymous vernacular hagiography, and 720 of a Latin defense of papal authority.[26] All three were published in 1560 or 1561.

[20] Renouard, *Annales des Alde*, 270–76. On the Accademia Venetiana, the most recent study is Paul Lawrence Rose, "The Accademia Venetiana: Science and Culture in Renaissance Venice," *Studi veneziani* 11 (1969), 191–242.

[21] SU, Bu. 159, "Acta S. Officij Venetiarum 1554–1555," parte 5, 27ʳ, August 23, 1555. Pietrasanta, who published 29 titles from 1553 to 1557, was paid 5 ducats per month for his work, but the printing time is not stated. The *STC Italian*, 592, lists only the 1554 edition.

[22] The contract is printed in Tinto, *Tramezzino*, pp. 117–19; also see pp. 90–92. The first four volumes were reprints; vol. 5 was new. Varisco published alone or in association 72 editions from 1558 to 1590.

[23] SU, Bu. 66, Girolamo Polo, no pag., his testimony of January 18, 1590. Polo published 25 editions from 1573 to 1598.

[24] Pastor, XVII, 200, n. 1. It was published by a consortium of Roman publishers headed by the heirs of Antonio Blado. See *STC Italian*, 669.

[25] Generoso Calenzio, *La vita e gli scritti del Cardinale Cesare Baronio della Congregazione dell'Oratorio, Bibliotecario di Santa Romana Chiesa* (Rome, 1907), p. 245.

[26] The three works were *Dell'historia del valorosissimo cavalliero don Florambello di Lucea, Vite di dodici gloriosi confessori*, and the *Summa de Ecclesia* by Juan de Torquemada, a fifteenth-century Spanish theologian. See Tinto, *Tramezzino*, nos. 177, 185, and 192. The inventory of January 10, 1562, is published in

Assuming that some, but not many, copies had been sold and distributed to bookstores, press runs of about 1,000, perhaps a little higher for the romance and slightly lower for the Latin religious work, can be estimated. Press runs of less than 1,000 also appeared. In 1554 Arrivabene published 500 copies of a book of vernacular poetry by a little-known author.[27] In 1582 the Roman heirs of Tramezzino let a contract to print 750 copies of a vernacular devotional title.[28] Again in Rome, a Latin work of 1592 meant for essentially private distribution had a press run of 504 copies.[29]

The major publishers also printed larger press runs. A concordance of Boccaccio by Francesco Alunno published by the Aldine press in 1543 had a printing of more than 2,000.[30] In 1543 Giolito published Ludovico Dolce's translation of Ovid's *Metamorphoseos* with a dedicatory letter of May 1. Having sold 1,800 copies in four months, Giolito hastened to issue another printing before the end of the year.[31] In 1572 the Aldine press printed six press runs of 3,300 copies, each in various formats of a liturgical work, the Little Office of Our Lady.[32] By comparison, the ordinary print-

---

Tinto, pp. 102–6. It listed stocks of 800 to 864 of seven other titles, but since they were all published more than once within the previous 12 years, it is impossible to estimate the original press runs.

[27] SU, Bu. 159, "Acta S. Officij Venetiarum 1554–1555," parte 2, f. 24^r, January 10, 1555. The book was Marco Pagani, *Delle rime libro primo*, printed by Stefano Griffio for Arrivabene. *STC Italian*, 484. Stefano is not listed in Pastorello, but there are several other Griffio publishers.

[28] Tinto, *Tramezzino*, p. xxxv. The book was Bonsignore Cacciaguerra, *Pie e devote meditazioni* (Rome, 1583). Fernanda Ascarelli, *Le cinquecentine romane: "Censimento delle edizioni romane del XVI secolo possedute dalle biblioteche di Roma"* (Milan, 1972), p. 41.

[29] This was the *De sacri consistorii consultationibus* of Gabriele Paleotti, published by Domenico Basa at the author's expense; it cost 548 scudi. Paolo Prodi, *Il Cardinale Gabriele Paleotti (1522–1597)*, vol. II (Rome, 1967), pp. 490–91.

[30] *Le ricchezze della lingua volgare . . . di sopra il Boccaccio novamente ristampate. . . .* (In Vinegia nell'anno MDLI. In Casa de' Figliuoli di Aldo), f. 2.

[31] *Le trasformationi di M. Lodovico Dolce di nuovo stampate. . . .* (In Venetia, Appresso Gabriel Giolito de' Ferrari e Fratelli, MDLIII), "Ai Nobili e Sinceri Lettori. Gabriel Giolito," ff. x–xi. The two editions are described in Bongi, *Giolito*, I, 395–401, 404; and the work was reprinted by Giolito in 1555, 1557, 1558, 1561, and by Domenico Farri in 1570.

[32] SU, Bu. 156, "Librai e libri proibiti 1545–1571," ff. 42^v–43^r, July 29, 31, 1572. For more on this, see Ch. v, sec. 2. Other less precise information suggests that press runs of 2,000 were not rare. The author of a famed commentary on the *Materia medica* of Dioscorides, Pietro Andrea Mattioli, boasted in 1568 that 30,000 copies had been sold since first publication in 1544. I have noted 16 editions (9 Latin, 6 Italian, and 1 French), at least 7 published by Vincenzo Valgrisi, before 1568. If nearly all copies were sold, average editions consisted of 2,000 copies. *De i discorsi . . . nelli sei libri di Pedacio Dioscoride Anazarbeo, della materia medicinale. . . .* (MDLXXXV, In Venetia, Appresso Felice Valgrisio), sig. *7, dedication letter dated 1568. In Paul F. Grendler, *Critics of the Italian World 1530–*

ing of the Plantin press of Antwerp in the second half of the sixteenth century was 1,250 to 1,500 copies, but it could be as high as 2,500 or as low as 800.[33] On the basis of the number of Venetian editions and the size of their press runs, church and state faced the mountainous task of regulating an industry that printed an estimated 15–20 million books in the cinquecento.[34]

3. PRINTING AND SELLING

The bookmen offered volumes to suit every taste and purse. For 4, 6, or 8 soldi the reader could purchase from Giolito a short vernacular comedy, a book of poetry, or a devotional treatise in 12° or 8°. For 1 lira he might buy a larger volume, such as the vernacular translation of Cicero's *De Oratore* (1554, 12°, 400 pp.); for 1 lira 10 soldi, he might buy Domenichi's *Dialoghi* (1562, 8°, 435 pp.). The large cinquecento appetite for history might be appeased for 2 lire with a popular history, such as Ludovico Dolce's *Vita di Ferdinando I* (1566, 4°, 278 pp.) or one of the titles in the *Collana historica*, the series of vernacular translations of ancient Greek histories published in the 1560s, always in 4°.[35]

The retail price of a book varied greatly according to its size and length. Table 1 indicates the range of Giolito retail prices.

Aldine retail prices demonstrated the same wide range: in 1590 one could purchase a vernacular comedy by Annibale Caro (1589) in 12° for 6 soldi, or a folio volume of Cicero, *Epistolae ad Atticum*, with commentary by Paolo Manuzio, for 9 lire 6 soldi.[36] The customer could get a ver-

---

1560: Anton Francesco Doni, Nicolò Franco, & Ortensio Lando (Madison, Milwaukee, and London, 1969), p. 179; the first edition is erroneously cited as 1557.

[33] Febvre and Martin, *L'apparition du livre*, p. 311.

[34] This figure is arrived at by estimating that 12,500 editions had press runs of 1,000, that 2,500 editions had press runs of 500, and that 2,500 had press runs of 2,000. The number of individual books printed would be 18,750,000.

[35] For a description of the *Collana historica* and its accompanying "historical jewels," see Grendler, "Sansovino," pp. 158–61.

[36] The Aldine prices are based on five price lists appended to Aldine editions of 1588 to 1592 examined in the Houghton Library (Harvard). Renouard, *Annales des Alde*, p. 341, noted 23 such catalogues from 1586 to 1598. The price lists used here are in the following:

C. *Iulii Caesaris Commentarii ab Aldo Manuccio* . . . (1588), Houghton Ald 1588.4
De Fascino libri tres, Auctore Leonardo Vairo Beneventano . . . (1589), Houghton Ald 1589.8
Niccolò Vito di Gozzi, *Dello stato delle Repubbliche secondo la mente di Aristotele* (1591), Houghton Ga 112.715*
Livy, *Historiarum ab urbe condita* (1592), Houghton Ll 16.117*F
Louis Le Roy, *Della vicissitudine o' mutabile varietà delle cose* . . . (1952),

TABLE 1

RETAIL PRICES AND SIZE OF GIOLITO BOOKS, 1549–91

Price in soldi	Format 12°. Pp.	Number of examples	Format 8°. Pp.	Number of examples	Format 4°. Pp.	Number of examples
2	56	1				
4	81	5	52	2	28	1
6	118	10	79	6	37	2
8	165	1	114	7		
10	264	4	147	5		
12			179	4		
16[a]	316	3	278	8	124	1
20[b]	399	2	288	3	150	1
24	572	1	318	1	205	1
30			433	9	212	5
36			610	1		
40			700	1	269	7
50[c]	700	1	748	1	256	1
60			872	1	480	4
70					552	2
80					601	4
90					555	3
100					666	2
110					880	1
120					688	1
180					1528	2

[a] one of 15   [b] one of 19   [c] one of 48

SOURCE: The prices, size, and length of the works have been collated from Bongi, *Giolito,* who based them on the only known extant Giolito catalogue: *Indice copioso, e particolare, di tutti li libri stampi dalli Gioliti in Venetia, fino all'anno 1592* (n.p., n.d.), in VM, 193. D. 443, and described by Bongi, *Giolito,* II, pp. 456–57. Omitted from the table are three folio titles published in 1579, 1587, and 1590, and priced at 6, 8, and 7 lire respectively. I have also excluded a handful of other titles because they comprise multiple volumes, are profusely illustrated (and therefore more expensive), or because information on size and length are lacking. The catalogue is, of course, only a sampling of Giolito prices.

nacular translation of the letters to Atticus in 8° for 2 lire 10 soldi. As with Giolito, the format made a difference. In 1592 Aldine offered two illustrated editions of Torquato Tasso's *Aminta*: the one of 1589, in 12°, sold for 6 soldi; the other of 1590, in 4°, for 1 lira.

Houghton *FC5.L5627.Ei 585cb. This list precedes the text, Sig. b3 verso–b4 verso.

The prices quoted are in all five lists, with the exception of the Tasso, *Aminta* comparison, missing from the Caesar and Vairo lists.

The average price per book was between 1 and 2 lire. For example, a 1576 valuation of 95 miscellaneous titles (most in Latin) ranged from 15 soldi to 6 lire per volume, with the average price at 1 lire 16 soldi.[37] The Giolito average price (1549–91) was exactly the same. The Aldine average in 1592 was considerably higher, 3 lire 8 soldi, to be accounted for by the larger number of folio volumes.[38]

Books were priced within the reach of the lowest as well as the highest economic strata. During the second half of the cinquecento a master mason or carpenter earned from 30 to 50 soldi per day, while a semi-skilled workman in the building trades earned from 20 to 37.[39] If they had the inclination to read and the cost of living permitted any surplus, these craftsmen and laborers could easily buy the less expensive titles. A folio volume retailing for 6 or 8 lire, i.e., the equivalent of 3 to 6 days' pay for a master, would be difficult but not impossible to buy. A merchant or professional could afford a library of moderate size, and a patrician could support hundreds or thousands of volumes.

The financial arrangements for the publication and sale of a single title could be intricate and involve substantial sums. In 1580 or 1581 the two heirs of Tramezzino, Michele (the Younger) of Venice and Venturino of Rome, contracted with Luc'Antonio Giunti and Giovanni Varisco for a new edition of Giovanni Tarcagnota et al., *Delle historie del mondo*, in five volumes. As previous publishers for the first four volumes, the Tramezzino held privilegi (copyrights) from the Venetian Senate, the Duke of Tuscany, Pius IV, the King of France, and the Emperor. They also possessed the manuscript for volume 5, which carried the history forward to 1579, although Varisco secured the Venetian privilegio for the latter. The contract specified a press run of 1,125 copies, less those spoiled in printing, and that two presses must operate continuously until the work was completed. It would carry the names of the heirs of Tramezzino on the title pages. The completed copies were to be deposited under lock in

[37] VC, Ms. P D C 2118, "Ricevuto 1571–1580"; these are miscellaneous business records of Giulio Michiel, unnumbered and bound chronologically. The book inventory is a single folio dated 1576, lacking further identification.

[38] The Giolito average price has been computed from the *Indice copioso*, the Aldine average price from the above price lists. I have not had the opportunity to consult the Italian price lists, 1591–1605, in the Broxbourne Library. See Graham Pollard and Albert Ehrman, *The Distribution of Books by Catalogue from the Invention of Printing to A.D. 1800 Based on Material in the Broxbourne Library* (Cambridge, 1965), pp. 49–51, 286–92.

[39] Brian Pullan, "Wage-Earners and the Venetian Economy, 1550–1630," in Brian Pullan, ed., *Crisis and Change in the Venetian Economy in the Sixteenth and Seventeenth Centuries* (London, 1968), p. 158. For additional daily wages, see Frederic C. Lane, *Venice: A Maritime Republic* (Baltimore and London, 1973), pp. 333–34.

a rented warehouse until removal for sale. Strict regulations for the removal of copies were laid down, and Giunti and Varisco held the key for alternating six-month periods. Giunti and Varisco each bore three-eighths of the printing expenses, and each Tramezzino one-eighth. Warehouse rental was portioned equally to all four, and Giunti and Varisco received a small compensation for the care of the books in the warehouse. The completed press run was split equally among the four partners.[40] The five volumes were published in 1581 and 1582. However, Michele Tramezzino and Luc'Antonio Giunti quarreled; as was customary, three other bookmen arbitrated. They decided that Michele had defaulted on his one-eighth share of the costs, and ordered him to pay 240 ducats.[41]

The resolution of the quarrel provides an opportunity to estimate roughly the unit cost and profit. Based on Michele's one-eighth, the total printing cost was 2,720 ducats for about 5,500 volumes, assuming that some 25 copies of each volume were spoiled in printing. Hence, the cost per volume was slightly over 3 lire. The retail price of these 4° volumes of 750 to 900 pages was probably 6 or 7 lire per volume, giving the bookmen a unit profit of 50 per cent or more before the deduction of selling expenses, trade discounts, and other charges. The gross profit per unit was the same as that which the Plantin press in Antwerp earned.[42]

Other examples confirm this level of economic activity. If a medium-sized publisher produced five titles a year with an average press run of 1,000, to be sold at an average price of 1 lira 16 soldi, the value of his annual production was 1,450 ducats. Of course, this was only part of his business; he also bought and sold other books in Venice and elsewhere. Again, the sums involved were substantial; single business transactions concerned with selling books in the Kingdom of Naples frequently involved hundreds of ducats, and occasionally one or two thousand.[43] A bookman also had large sums tied up in inventory. In 1562 Michele Tramezzino (the Elder) had on hand 28,234 unsold volumes from his own press.[44] This inventory was worth approximately 8,200 ducats, assuming the above average retail price. Other titles, printed in Venice, France, and Germany, were not included in this inventory. Similarly, in 1578 Fran-

[40] The contract, January 7, 1580 (whether mv or modern style is not clear), is printed in Tinto, *Tramezzino*, pp. 117-19.

[41] Tinto, *Tramezzino*, p. xxxv, n. 2.

[42] Raymond De Roover, "The Business Organisation of the Plantin Press in the Setting of Sixteenth-Century Antwerp," *De Gulden Passer* 34 (1956), 109. Also see William A. Pettas, "The Cost of Printing a Florentine Incunable," *La Bibliofilia* 75 (1973), 67-85.

[43] Corrado Marciani, "Editori, tipografi, librai veneti nel Regno di Napoli nel Cinquecento," *Studi veneziani* 10 (1968), 457-554, passim.

[44] Tinto, *Tramezzino*, pp. 102-6.

cesco Ziletti purchased the inventory of a bookseller who was not a publisher for 1,114 ducats, agreeing to pay the sum within one year.[45]

The distribution of books involved a large commercial network and large sums of money. Upon assuming leadership of the Giunti press in 1564, Luc'Antonio Giunti plunged into commercial activity that in its scope and diversity was reminiscent of the fourteenth-century Prato merchant, Francesco di Marco Datini. Luc'Antonio sold books everywhere in Italy, in large cities and small towns, from Turin to Palermo. His business in Spain was possibly even greater; he owned bookstores in Salamanca and Medina del Campo, and had a representative at the court of Phillip II, where business was so brisk that the representative in 1583 owed Luc'Antonio over 6,500 ducats, mostly for breviaries and missals. Luc'Antonio sold books at the usual European centers, like Lyons, but also as far away as Cracow, where his trade amounted to 1,000 ducats per year. Nor did he limit himself to books; he also bought and sold sugar, pepper, tin, and salted fish across Europe.[46]

The scale of activity of Luc'Antonio may have been extraordinary, but the pattern was typical. The bookstores of a Venetian publishing house stocked its own publications, other Venetian imprints, and imports from Lyons, Basel, and elsewhere. The Venetian bookmen were probably the major suppliers for Italy, and they plied their trade the length of the peninsula. In the second half of the cinquecento about 100 Venetians—publishers, printers, and sellers, large and small—distributed and sold in the Kingdom of Naples.[47] Gabriel Giolito in 1565 had bookstores in Ferrara, Bologna, and Naples,[48] and Vincenzo Valgrisi owned bookstores in Padua, Bologna, Macerata, Foligno, Recanati, and Lanciano in Italy, as well as in Frankfurt and Lyons.[49]

4. ECONOMIC AND SOCIAL WORLD OF THE BOOKMEN

The publishers fitted snugly into the middle-class world of merchants and professionals, comfortably above the struggle of lower-class life but far beneath the opulent nobility. The lesser members of the book industry shared the status of small shopkeepers and artisans. Family enterprises featuring matrimonial alliances and intricate business ties characterized the industry.

Bookmen from all over Italy and a few from foreign lands left their

[45] Marciani, "Editori veneti in Napoli," p. 507.

[46] Alberto Tenenti, "Luc'Antonio Giunti il giovane, stampatore e mercante," in *Studi in onore di Armando Sapori* (Milan, 1957), II, 1,021–60.

[47] Marciani, "Editori veneti in Napoli," p. 467.

[48] Bongi, *Giolito*, I, ciii, from an Inquisition document.

[49] SU, Bu. 14, Vincenzo Valgrisi et al., f. [24r], Valgrisi's testimony of August 9, 1559.

birthplaces to come to Venice. In the 1530s, Venetian peace and prosperity, in contrast to political and economic dislocation elsewhere, beckoned them. Immigrants such as Giolito from Trino in Piedmont, Marcolini from Forlì and Michele Tramezzino from Rome, founded publishing firms in that decade. But bookmen came throughout the century: Giorgio Dei Rusconi, whose name first appeared on a work in 1501, came from Milan; Nicolò Bevilacqua, from the Trentino toward mid-century; Francesco Ziletti, from Brescia in 1569; and Giovanni Battista Ciotti, from Siena in 1583. Nearly all the Venetian bookmen were immigrants or the descendants of immigrants, the largest number of them coming from Brescia and its territory.[50]

The family ties within publishing firms provided continuity; for example, eleven different members of the Bindoni family published in the century. Other members of the family contributed by printing, managing a bookstore, or traveling to the fairs. The guild reinforced the familial character of the industry by waiving the entrance fee for the sons of members.[51] Brother partnerships and father to son, or uncle to nephew, devolutions were common. There were exceptions; when Melchiorre Sessa died in 1565, his wife Veronica assumed leadership of the firm (although Sessa publications did not carry her name), and led it to prosperity.[52]

The success of a publishing house depended to a great extent upon the initiative and acumen of its head, and if the heir lacked ability, the firm could disappear. Upon the deaths of Michele Tramezzino of Venice and Francesco Tramezzino of Rome, the firm passed into the hands of the closest relatives, Michele's nephew and Francesco's natural daughter. The daughter married a printer who took the name of Tramezzino, and he and the nephew attempted to continue. The house declined in both cities. After a few printings, the Venetian branch ceased publishing; the Roman bookstore was eventually sold.[53] The disappearance of a name, however, did not always mean the dispersal of the assets. The name of Andrea Arrivabene (al segno del Pozzo) disappeared at his death in 1570, but his store was sold to Francesco Ziletti, who operated it under the same sign.[54]

[50] Often the pressmark indicated the place of origin; in addition to the above, Pastorello lists many others whose birthplace was not Venice. See also Bongi, *Giolito*, I, xi–xviii, and Tinto, *Tramezzino*, pp. xi–xii. On Ziletti, see Marciani, "Editori veneti in Napoli," p. 513. See also a list of 64 bookmen of September 13, 1567, in which father's name, place of origin, and Venetian location of the press or store is given. SU, Bu. 156, "Librai e libri proibiti, 1545–1571," ff. [76^{r-v}].

[51] Regulation of April, 1572. Brown, *Venetian Press*, 88, 253–54.

[52] Veronica directed affairs at least through 1582. Marciani, "Editori veneti in Napoli," pp. 468, 500–505.

[53] Tinto, *Tramezzino*, pp. xi, xxvii–xxxi.

[54] SU, Bu. 30, Francesco Ziletto e Giulio Bonfadio, ff. 1^{v}, 2^{v}, testimony of Ziletti of February 1, 1571.

Intricate commercial relations bound the bookmen together like a clan. And like a clan, they frequently quarreled among themselves. Internal arbitration was the normal procedure for resolving conflicts. Each party named another bookman, and those named chose a third. The three arbiters rendered a binding decision.[55]

The bookmen tended to marry within the industry or with the sons and daughters of other members of the middle class; the dowries involved help to illustrate their economic status. Francesco Ziletti promised in 1569 to marry the second daughter of Nicolò Bevilacqua, a small publisher and cautious father, who would provide a dowry of 1,000 ducats in books and printing within three years. Ziletti was obliged to settle upon his betrothed 300 ducats, to be increased to 500 if he did not remain with her in Venice for at least six years.[56] Whether Ziletti was faithful is not known, but ten years later he married the daughter of the late Vincenzo Valgrisi and received a larger dowry of 2,500 ducats—1,000 in law books left her by her father and the rest provided by her two brothers.[57] In 1592 Giovanni Varisco provided a dowry of 3,000 ducats for his daughter, who married a merchant.[58] Wealthier bookmen provided larger dowries. In his testament of 1559, Federico Torresani of the Aldine press left 5,000 ducats to each of his two daughters for their dowries.[59] At the lower end of the scale, an employee of the Sessa firm in 1577 received a dowry of 300 ducats from his bride, and he settled 100 ducats on her.[60] The dowries clearly differentiated the bookmen from the nobility and the lower classes. In 1561, patrician dowries were at the level of 20,000 to 25,000 ducats; during the century they sometimes reached 40,000 to 60,000 ducats.[61] Lower-class dowries could be less than 100 ducats: Veronica Sessa provided a dowry of 83 ducats for a former maid, and the Scuola di San Marco dispensed dowries of 10 to 18 ducats to impoverished girls in the 1550s.[62]

---

[55] Marciani, "Editori veneti in Napoli," lists a number of disputes.

[56] Marciani, "Editori veneti in Napoli," p. 513.

[57] The brothers were Felice, who published 26 editions between 1583 and 1591, and Giorgio, whose name does not appear as a publisher, although the heirs of Vincenzo Valgrisi published seven editions between 1573 and 1580. Marciani, "Editori veneti in Napoli," pp. 508, 515.

[58] Marciani, "Editori veneti in Napoli," p. 510.

[59] Corrado Marciani, "Il testamento, e altre notizie, di Federico Torresani," *La Bibliofilia* 72 (1971), 166, 174.

[60] Marciani, "Editori veneti in Napoli," p. 504.

[61] Brian Pullan, "Service to the Venetian State: Aspects of Myth and Reality in the Early Seventeenth Century," *Studi secenteschi* 5 (1964), 138; Pompeo Molmenti, *La storia di Venezia nella vita privata*, 5th ed. (Bergamo, 1911), II, 512.

[62] Marciani, "Editori veneti in Napoli," p. 503; Brian Pullan, *Rich and Poor in Renaissance Venice: The Social Institutions of a Catholic State, to 1620* (Cambridge, Mass., 1971), p. 188.

The guild played but a small role in the book industry and the lives of its members. Not formed until 1549, it enrolled only 66 to 75 printers and booksellers, considerably fewer than those active in the industry. Nor did the major figures consider it important; Luc'Antonio Giunti was elected prior three times but accepted only once.[63] The government used the guild to raise money for armaments, but the bookmen understandably felt that it offered them little. Because the guild lacked the power to compel membership, many bookmen, especially the lesser members of the industry, were able to resist enrollment. Those who did lead the guild chronically mismanaged its finances. The government legislated reform but did not provide for enforcement, and nothing improved.[64] The guild played a minor charitable[65] and social role, and served occasionally as a vehicle for collective protest, but did little more.

Publishers and authors shared an intellectual world in which roles were not always exclusive. Francesco Sansovino (1521–83) and Anton Francesco Doni (1513–74), two prolific authors and editors, operated presses in Venice and Florence respectively. Publishers such as Gabriel Giolito, Marcolini, and successive members of the Manuzio family had close intellectual ties with their authors. The prefatory letters of other publishers offer additional evidence that many of them kept abreast of intellectual developments. Moreover, if a son did not follow his father into the book trade, he sometimes entered the learned professions. Francesco Tramezzino's son read Greek, Arabic, Turkish, and other languages, published a translation of Cicero, and held various secretarial positions of some importance in the Venetian government.[66]

Like other Venetians, nobles and commoners, the bookmen hastened to invest their capital in cultivated land and in residential property in Venice. In 1566 and again in 1582 the state levied a tax on the income from this property, and the bookmen necessarily listed their holdings in their declarations.[67]

[63] He refused in 1581 and 1587 but accepted in 1596. Tenenti, "Luc'Antonio Giunti," p. 1,057, n. 201.

[64] Brown, *Venetian Press*, pp. 83–91.

[65] For example, on March 28, 1596, the guild granted a 20-ducat dowry to Lucia, age 18 and the orphan of Francesco Ciscut stampatore, who wished to marry a poor but worthy young man from the Arsenal. Arte dei libreri, stampatori e ligadori, Bu. 163, Registro Atti 1 (1578–1597 mv), ff. 116[r–v].

[66] Tinto, *Tramezzino*, pp. x–xi.

[67] The tax was collected by the Dieci Savii sopra le decime in Rialto in 1514, 1537, 1566, 1581 (actually 1582), and 1661. The declarer was taxed on the income from his investment property within the Venetian Dominion; the house in which he lived, his shop, property outside the state, and other income were exempt. The tax was regressive, varying from 20 percent for those of less than about 200 ducats

In 1566 Andrea Arrivabene reported that he had a shop in the Mercerie in the district of San Salvatore that he rented for 9 ducats 1 lira annually. He lived in one part of a house in Sant'Angelo leased from a patrician; the other part he sublet for 45 ducats annually. Arrivabene also owned 5 fields and rented 3 more near Padua. His taxable income from the fields was 20 lire 20 soldi, on which he paid 4 lire 2 soldi tax.[68]

A number of small- to medium-sized publishers and other bookmen declared similar or slightly greater investment property and income. In 1566 Gasparo Bindoni in San Salvatore enjoyed an annual income of 95 ducats from the rental of a house in Venice (60 ducats) and the income from his wife's dowry, which consisted of 3 small houses in Venice and 10 fields. His brother Francesco of Sant'Angelo had an income of 42 ducats 5 lire from half a house in Venice and 50 fields near Mestre, all of which came from his wife's dowry. He also had a villa near Mestre—of no value, according to Francesco. A third brother, Alessandro of Sant'-Angelo, earned 41 ducats annually from the rent of five and one-quarter houses in Venice.[69] Domenico and Giovanni Battista Guerra in the district of San Paternian received income of 24 ducats 5 lire from 2 houses and 8 fields in Valvasone (Friuli), their native land.[70] Giovanni Domenico Micheli, a small publisher, of San Moisè, declared income of 30 ducats from land near Treviso.[71]

Non-publishers tended to have a little less property. A bookseller in San Maurizio owned 2 fields, which yielded 10 ducats' worth of grain. Another bookseller in San Marco earned 10 ducats from fields. A binder in the Mercerie paid 20 ducats annually to rent his shop and 24 ducats for his home, and earned 36 ducats' income from his fields.[72]

The above bookmen enjoyed investment income comparable to that of

income to 1 percent for incomes of thousands of ducats. It is not known how honest the declarations were or how much documentation the tax gatherers demanded.

[68] Dieci Savii sopra le Decime in Rialto. Condizione di Decima, 1566, San Marco, Bu. 126, no. 290 (hereafter abbreviated as Decima, 1566, etc.). Arrivabene also stated that he paid 500 ducats' rent for a warehouse, a figure that strains credulity.

[69] Decima, 1566, Bu. 127, no. 753 (Gasparo); Bu. 126, no. 315 (Francesco); and Bu. 126, no. 311 (Alessandro). All were sons of Francesco, who published 113 editions from 1523 to 1553. Francesco (the son) and Gasparo published 25 editions separately and together (1558–89). Although he did not publish, Alessandro's profession was listed as *libraio*.

[70] Decima, 1566, Bu. 127, no. 432.

[71] Decima, 1581, Bu. 157bis, no. 458. He published nine editions between 1575 and 1584 in association with the heirs of Luigi Valvassori.

[72] Decima, 1566, Bu. 127, no. 782 (Piero di Lorenzo); Decima, 1581, Bu. 158, no. 1068 (Zuanmaria de Zulianis, i.e., Giovanni Maria di Giuliano); Decima, 1581, Bu. 157, no. 3 (Nicolò Pasini).

CAPITOLI
DELL'VNIVERSITA
DELLI STAMPATORI,
ET LIBRARI,

Approbati, laudati, & confermati dalli Clariſſimi
Signori Proueditori di Comune.

IN ESSECVTIONE DELLA PARTE
dell'Illuſtriſſimo, & Eccelſo Conſiglio di X.
ſotto di 18. Genaro 1548.

Stampati per Gio: Pietro Pinelli
Stampator Ducale.

2. The law of January 18, 1549, establishing the guild of the bookmen. Source:
VC, Ms. Cicogna 3044

retail merchants or skilled craftsmen with their own shops, such as a spice retailer or a master tailor. Members of the professional class, such as physicians, lawyers, and secretaries, especially those employed in the ducal palace, owned enough property to generate 100 to 150 ducats' income annually. A number of publishers enjoyed comparable investment income. Michele and Francesco Tramezzino received an income of 168 ducats from the rental of 12 houses in 1566.[73] The author, editor, and publisher Francesco Sansovino declared an income of 199 ducats from 4 houses and 40 fields.[74]

The simple ownership of property indicated sizeable financial assets. For example, in 1575 the publisher Giovanni Varisco and his cousins, the brothers Camillo, Orazio, and Scipione Paganini, bookmen but not publishers, purchased 134 fields in Friuli for 5,000 ducats.[75] The ownership of income-producing property placed the bookmen in the upper ranks of a Renaissance city, specifically in the upper 14 to 19 percent of Venetian society.[76] But the income of the bookmen did not approach that of wealthy patricians, who owned hundreds of fields and houses, and declared income from these sources of 2,000 to 3,000 ducats.[77] Luc'Antonio Giunti was an exception. From 140 fields in 1566, he increased his holdings to

[73] Tinto, *Tramezzino*, p. xv, n. 2.

[74] Decima, 1581, Bu. 157, no. 340. He published 47 editions, including those issued under the name of Jacopo Sansovino, his young son, from 1560 through 1581. Part of this property was probably the result of an annual stipend of 60 ducats wrung from the Venetian government in 1570 for unpaid fees owed to his father, the sculptor Jacopo.

[75] Marciani, "Editori veneti in Napoli," pp. 495–96, 510. Varisco alone and in association published 73 editions between 1558 and 1590.

[76] In 1566 there were 6,164 declarations in a population of 183,000 (1563 census). If each declaration represented a household of four, 13.5 percent of the population made declarations. Similarly, in 1582 there were 6,335 declarations in a population of 142,000 (1581 census), or 17.8 percent. On Venetian population, see Julius Beloch, "La popolazione di Venezia nei secoli XVI e XVII," *Nuovo archivio veneto*, n.s., 3 (1902), 44. Population figures of 169,000 in 1563 and 135,000 in 1581 are given by Beltrami. With these figures, the declarations would represent 14.5 percent and 18.8 percent of the population respectively. Daniele Beltrami, "Lineamenti di storia della popolazione di Venezia dal Cinquecento al Settecento," in *Storia dell'economia italiana*, vol. 1, *Secoli settimodiciassettesimo*, ed. Carlo M. Cipolla (Turin, 1959), pp. 506–7. Lane, *Venice*, pp. 19, 462, believes that both Beloch and Beltrami have slightly underestimated the population, and that it reached nearly 190,000 before the plague of 1575–77. This figure would move the bookmen who filed *decime* returns slightly higher in the economic scale.

[77] For example, Alvise Tiepolo, Procurator of St. Mark, declared income of 2,180 ducats, and Giacomo and Giovanni Soranzo 2,560 ducats, in 1582. Decima, 1581, Bu. 157bis, nos. 671, 702. Of course, not all patrician investment incomes were this large.

220 fields (yielding nearly 600 ducats' income) in 1582, to over 400 in 1601. He also purchased for 15,000 ducats a large house on the Grand Canal.[78]

Scattered evidence argues that the bookmen maintained and increased their wealth in the second half of the cinquecento. Luc'Antonio Giunti was one example, the Scoto and Gardano families were others. In 1566 the brothers Girolamo and Ottaviano Scoto, who operated two presses in their house in Sant'Angelo, made their declarations. They owned 3 houses in Padua and 57 fields and 1 woodland elsewhere, on which they reported a total income of 99 ducats. But they were experiencing great financial difficulties "because the book trade is very depressed as usual, and the other trades are all fallacious." Moreover, they had to support two indigent brothers in Milan with 8 sons and 9 unmarried daughters.[79] Somehow the family survived and became wealthier. Melchiorre Scoto, nephew and heir to Girolamo and Ottaviano, reported in 1582 that he paid 120 ducats' rent for his house in Sant'Angelo, but still managed to own 2 houses in Padua and from 110 to 120 fields, which yielded 276 ducats' income.[80] Antonio Gardano on the Mercerie in the district of San Salvatore owned 26 fields, which produced income of 13 ducats in 1566. His son Angelo declared income of 54 ducats from 50 fields in 1582.[81]

The Venetian nobility participated in the book industry only in a limited way. Pier Francesco Barbarigo, the son of Doge Agostino (1486–1501), contracted with Aldo Manuzio and Andrea Torresani in 1495 to publish "Latin and Greek books," and his heirs maintained some connection with the Aldine press until 1542. The amount of the investment and the nature of the participation are unknown.[82] Alvise (later Giovanni)

---

[78] Tenenti, "Luc'Antonio Giunti," pp. 1,047–55. Also Decima, 1581, Bu. 157bis, no. 783.

[79] "Perchè l'arte della stampa è molto declinata del solito, et le altre mercantie sono tutte fallaci. . . ." Decima, 1566, Bu. 126, no. 115. One hundred ninety-seven editions were published under the name of Girolamo Scoto from 1540 to 1573.

[80] Decima, 1581, Bu. 158, no. 859. Forty-two editions were published under the name of heirs of Girolamo Scoto from 1573 to 1599, and the Scoto name continued in the following century. Other commercial activity of Melchiorre is described by Marciani, "Editori veneti in Napoli," p. 500.

[81] Decima, 1566, Bu. 126, no. 56; Decima, 1581, Bu. 157bis, no. 767. The additional financial documents printed and analyzed by Claudio Sartori, "Una dinastia di editori musicale. Documenti inediti sui Gardano e i loro congiunti Stefano Bindoni e Alessandro Raverii," *La Bibliofilia* 58 (1956), 176–208, confirm this level of ownership and income. Antonio published 29 editions between 1539 and 1569; the sons of Antonio, 12 editions between 1570 and 1575, and Angelo, 30 editions between 1576 and 1599. It is also Marciani's judgment, "Editori veneti in Napoli," 470, that the bookmen grew wealthier in this half-century. Unfortunately, the next *decima* was not levied until 1661, making impossible further comparisons in the cinquecento.

[82] Ester Pastorello, "Di Aldo Pio Manuzio: Testimonianze e Documenti," *La Bibliofilia* 67 (1965), 167 and passim.

Bragadino and Marc'Antonio Giustiniani published Hebrew books. Some indirect patrician interest in the press has also come to light: the Ca' Grande Cornaro family enjoyed a monopoly of paper sales in Padua and its territory from 1475 through 1530.[83] And Federigo Badoer financed the Accademia Venetiana, whose publisher was the Aldine press, from 1557 through 1561.[84] But this is all that has been found. Probably such traditional activities as maritime commerce, communal officeholding, and *terraferma* agriculture attracted the nobility far more than did the press.

In a 1552 dialogue on the press, one speaker remarked that he had heard that bookmen such as Robert Estienne of Paris, Gryphius of Lyons, Froben of Basel, and "many of our Italians in Venice" had earned thousands of ducats by operating presses. The second speaker retorted that many others had gone bankrupt.[85] Both were probably correct. This survey has necessarily ignored those who published one or a handful of editions before disappearing. Those who survived and prospered made up the large and vital industry that Church and state tried to control.

[83] Antonio Sartori, "Documenti padovani sull'arte della stampa nel sec. XV," in *Libri e stampatori in Padova. Miscellanea di studi storici in onore di Mons. G. Bellini—tipografo editore libraio* (Padua, 1959), pp. 131–34.

[84] Rose, "Accademia Venetiana."

[85] Anton Francesco Doni, *I Marmi* . . . . (In Vinegia per Francesco Marcolini MDLII), pt. 2, p. 20.

II

THE INQUISITION

VENETIAN religion was a complex phenomenon. Redeeming a sinful Republic, worshiping God through church and creed, and obeying the spiritual authority of the pope were sometimes viewed as contradictory, rather than complementary, activities. The operation and staffing of the local church, and Venetian expectations of ecclesiastical officers added further complexity. The discrepancy between the proclaimed Venetian view of state supremacy in religious matters and the pragmatic reality generated controversy. When the Venetians revived the Holy Office at mid-century, all these factors helped to determine the tribunal's role.

1. GOD, CHURCH, PAPACY, AND REPUBLIC

The Venetians believed that the Republic had been founded with God's aid, and that it had survived and prospered only through his continuing favor. The historian Bernardo Giustiniani (1408–89) related the traditional account of the construction of the first Venetian church. For some time after they had settled in the safety of the lagoon, the early inhabitants had neglected to build a church. When fire threatened to devastate the colony, a pious settler, sensing divine retribution, prayed to God for forgiveness, vowing that the settlers would erect a church. God sent rain to douse the flames, and in 421 the Venetians built and dedicated a church. By common consent, wrote Giustiniani, this event marked the origin of Venice.[1] Future Venetian rulers took the lesson to heart, calling upon God's aid to stave off calamity in other centuries. The churches of Il Redentore and Santa Maria della Salute were built to fulfill vows made by the Senate in thanksgiving for deliverance from the plagues of 1575–77 and 1630 respectively.

Like other Renaissance rulers, the Venetian nobility held that political and military disasters were God's punishment for sin and corruption, and they legislated against sin to save the state. The widespread disasters of the sixteenth century generated a wave of such legislation. Ordinances

---

[1] Patricia H. Labalme, *Bernardo Giustiniani: A Venetian of the Quattrocento* (Rome, 1969), pp. 266–68.

against blasphemy were typical. In 1510 Louis XII of France promulgated an ordinance against blasphemers that specifically linked war, famine, and pestilence to this "enormous and detestable" offence. He and his successors issued five more such edicts through 1546, and another five after 1560, when civil war convulsed France. When the Council of Ten learned on August 29, 1500, that the Turks had taken Modon, a strategic outpost in the Ionian Sea, it passed, amidst sorrow and lamentation, stern legislation against blasphemers, sodomites, prostitutes, and procuresses. During the struggle against the League of Cambrai (1509–13), the view that immorality was the basic cause for Venetian difficulty was officially held.[2] But defiance of Julius II's excommunication was not among the sins for which the Venetians sought God's forgiveness.

Neither disaster nor sin abated. As the tiny Venetian ship of state struggled to stay afloat in the storms generated by the great powers, the Council of Ten issued additional decrees with heavier penalties against sinners, including dissolute friars, who in Venetian eyes bore heavy responsibility for divine wrath. These laws, passed in 1514, 1517, and 1534, were not backed by enforcement; they were cries for mercy and warnings to the populace. In December 1537, after an autumn of severe political travail, a tribunal of morality with enforcement authority, the Esecutori contro la bestemmia, was established. The preamble explicitly invoked "the fear of God, on which depends the public and private good of the Republic."[3] At first the tribunal had jurisdiction only over blasphemy, but gambling and sacrilege were immediately added to its charge; to be followed by violation of the press laws in 1543, and other crimes later in the century. The Counter Reformation approach of working with the state to extirpate heresy and punish moral offenders, including the vendors of lascivious literature, was rooted in the practice of Renaissance states.

The majority of Venetians, nobles and commoners, probably held Catholic views in varying degrees of fervor without concerning themselves with doctrinal subtleties.[4] Fundamental conviction and historical tradition com-

---

[2] Gaetano Cozzi, *Religione, moralità e giustizia a Venezia: vicende della magistratura degli Esecutori contro la bestemmia* (Padua, [1969]), pp. 1–9; Felix Gilbert, "Venice in the Crisis of the League of Cambrai," in J. R. Hale, ed., *Renaissance Venice* (London, 1972), pp. 274–80.

[3] Cozzi, *Religione, moralità a Venezia*, p. 1.

[4] Bouwsma finds that a distinctive Venetian spirituality, which he calls "Venetian Evangelism," prevails from the fifteenth century through the first quarter of the seventeenth century. His most complete definition (*Venice*, p. 41) includes Augustinianism, neglect of doctrine, individual spiritual insight, grace rather than sacerdotal mediation, distrust of formalism and hierarchy, involvement in politics, "profound affinities with republicanism," and lay status. He finds Gasparo Contarini, Paolo Paruta (less so), Leonardo Donà, Nicolò Contarini, the *giovani* (a group of patricians of the 1580s and later who held antipapal and other political

bined to render the Venetians as orthodox as any other group of Italians. And, as in other cities, a few Venetians participated in either Catholic or Protestant renewal.

---

views), Fra Fulgenzio Micanzio, and Fra Paolo Sarpi to be exemplars. (Ibid., pp. 41, 82, 113, 122–32, 153, 208–9, 254–59, 457–60, 497–500, 528–34, 572, 583–85.)

One of the very few studies of Venetian spirituality is that of Logan (cited below), who finds in Venetian testaments a vague Augustinian spirituality. But he does not argue that it was peculiar to Venice or a distinctive element in the Venetian *Weltanshauung*. Carlo Borromeo, who visited Venice in 1580, and nuncios throughout the century saw nothing spiritually unusual in Venice. They noted widespread reception of the sacraments among the laity and carnality among the clergy, but these traits were hardly uniquely Venetian. In his large study of Venetian social welfare, a subject closely related to religious attitudes, Pullan in *Rich and Poor* noted little that was unique in Venetian spirituality. One can perhaps make a case for Gasparo Contarini, Tommaso Giustiniani, and Vincenzo Querini, who were remarkable by any standard, but their spiritual influence on later Venetians appears to have been slight. Bouwsma's evidence for the other Venetian figures is not extensive.

Bouwsma sought to find in Venetian Evangelism a partial cause for the traditional Venetian attitude, often articulated but not always observed, of lay supremacy in local church affairs and independence toward the papacy. Lay supremacy was hardly unique to Venice; every Italian lay ruler attempted to control the local church and to keep the papacy at a distance. (See also the comments of John A. Tedeschi in his review of Bouwsma's book in the *Journal of Modern History* 44 [1972], 259–62.) And one does not need to find a spiritual explanation, for the Venetians, like other rulers, clearly acknowledged the concrete financial and political benefits to be derived from state supremacy.

Bouwsma also believes that Venetian Evangelism was very similar to the Evangelism described by Cantimori and other scholars. But significant differences separate the two. Cantimori described Evangelism as a search for salvation featuring the primacy of justification through faith without denying good works, emphasis on Scripture, and the desire to reform abuses. Bouwsma's formulation ignores Scripture and pays little attention to faith and the reform of abuses. Moreover, besides Contarini, few Evangelicals (Juan Valdés, Bernardino Ochino, Reginald Pole, etc.) manifested an interest in politics or were laymen. Obviously scholars will differ on such a complex topic, but until more evidence is available, I prefer to avoid projecting a unique Venetian spirituality.

The essential bibliography is Oliver Logan, "Grace and Justification: Some Italian Views of the Sixteenth and Early Seventeenth Centuries," *Journal of Ecclesiastical History* 20 (1969), 67–78; Delio Cantimori, "La Riforma in Italia," in Ettore Rota, ed., *Questioni di storia moderna* (Milan, 1948), pp. 181–208, esp. pp. 183–87; and *Prospettive di storia ereticale italiana del Cinquecento* (Bari, 1960), pp. 28, 33–34; Hubert Jedin, *Papal Legate at the Council of Trent: Cardinal Seripando*, trans. F. C. Eckhoff (St. Louis and London, 1947), pp. 104–7; and *A History of the Council of Trent*, trans. E. Graf, vol. 1 (London, 1957), pp. 363–67, 370; Eva-Maria Jung, "On the Nature of Evangelism in 16th-Century Italy," *Journal of the History of Ideas* 14 (1953), 511–27; Phillip McNair, *Peter Martyr in Italy* (Oxford, 1967), pp. 1–50; Dermot Fenlon, *Heresy and Obedience in Tridentine Italy: Cardinal Pole and the Counter Reformation* (Cambridge, 1972), pp. 1–23. Also see Grendler, *Critics*, pp. 104–35.

A group of young nobles met together for prayer and study between 1510 and 1512. Of this group Tommaso Giustiniani and Vincenzo Querini sought ordination, and both dedicated themselves to Catholic renewal.[5] Giustiniani entered the monastery of Camaldoli (near Arezzo). Gasparo Contarini, another member of the group, was named a cardinal in 1535, and immediately provided curial support for the Catholic Reformation. The three carried on the bulk of their reform activity far from Venice, and had little influence on the spiritual life of the city. One nuncio after another lamented the failure of the Venetian hierarchy to improve the morals and education of the clergy—a central goal of Giustiniani, Querini, and Contarini.

Some heresy existed among the nobility and commonalty at mid-century, although it is sometimes difficult to be certain that some men or ideas were truly Protestant in this period of spiritual ferment. In 1545 Baldassarre Altieri, secretary to the English ambassador in Venice and a Protestant, wrote to Martin Bucer that the younger senators were so filled with the gospel that one could soon expect it to be freely preached, i.e., Protestant doctrine openly promulgated. The following year he reported that philo-Protestantism was widespread enough among the nobility that the Protestant Schmalkalden League might expect diplomatic support from the Republic.[6] Although Altieri mistook political sympathy for religious conviction, and magnified the political sympathy, some Venetians did hold Protestant views. From the late 1540s until the 1560s, several conventicles, whose membership included nobles as well as commoners and foreigners, flourished.[7] But none of these nobles carried sufficient political weight to move the government to make any overt move favoring the Protestant cause. The international political situation through most of the 1540s prompted the Republic to adopt a cautious, noncommittal policy that ignored Protestantism in the city. In the last years of the 1540s and in the following two decades, the government gradually moved against local dissenters.

Had the Counter Reformation not appeared, Protestantism still would

[5] There is a large literature on Giustiniani (Father Paolo), 1476–1528, Querini (Father Pietro), c. 1479–1514, and Contarini, 1483–1542. See the recent studies of Gigliola Fragnito, "Cultura umanistica e riforma religiosa: il *De officio boni viri ac probi episcopi* di Gasparo Contarini," *Studi veneziani* 11 (1969), 75–189; James B. Ross, "Gasparo Contarini and His Friends," *Studies in the Renaissance* 17 (1970), 192–232; and "The Emergence of Gasparo Contarini: A Bibliographical Essay," *Church History* 31 (1972), 1–24; and their respective bibliographies.

[6] Aldo Stella, *Chiesa e stato nelle relazioni dei nunzi pontifici a Venezia. Ricerche sul giurisdizionalismo veneziano dal XVI al XVIII secolo.* Studi e testi, 239 (Vatican City, 1964), p. 3.

[7] See Ch. III, sec. 7, and Ch. IV, sec. 2, for further information and documentation.

have had little chance in Venice. In addition to their fundamental Catholicism, the majority of the nobility accepted the widely held view that a change in religion led to the overthrow of the state. The increasingly turbulent French scene seemed to confirm this judgment. One contemporary Italian historian commented on French affairs of the late 1550s: "Heresies are a pretext by men determined on innovation and change in governments."[8] The Venetian ambassador to France, upon his return to Venice in 1561, predicted that the religious divisions in France would lead to civil war and the destruction of the kingdom.[9] The Republic willingly tolerated heterodox foreigners, from Greek Orthodox communicants from the east to German Protestant merchants; Venetians thus had more opportunity than most Italians for contact with men of different religious views. But the leaders of the Republic would never permit any significant portion of their subjects to embrace heresy.

Neither God's attitude toward the Republic nor the spiritual health of the citizenry preoccupied the Venetian nobility nearly as much as the political role of the papacy and the staffing of the local church. Cinquecento Venetians inherited the Republic's traditional view that papacy and church were separate bodies necessitating different policies: the papacy was a foreign political power whose policies frequently ran contrary to the Republic's best interests, but the church within Venetian borders was essentially a state church to be managed for the benefit of the Republic and the profit of the nobility.

Venice and the politically resurgent papacy contested territory in the Romagna, navigation on the Adriatic, and other issues in the first half of the century. The long Habsburg-Valois conflict usually found them on opposite sides. The war against the League of Cambrai confirmed Venetian suspicions of papal hostility, and no community of interests, like that between Medici popes and princes of Florence, existed to smooth over differences. Venice acknowledged the pope to be the spiritual head of Christendom, but had no choice than to fight back when Sixtus IV in 1483 and Julius II in 1509 laid Venice under interdict in political disputes. Only an overriding common political and spiritual cause, like the struggle against the Turks, could bring the two powers together.

As in the past, distrust of Rome led the Venetian government to legislate against nobles with close papal connections. In July 1550 the Senate

---

[8] "Le heresie sono un pretesto da gli huomini escogitato per innovatione e mutatione de gli stati." Printed marginal summary in *Delle historie de' suoi tempi di Natale Conti. Parte Prima.* (In Venetia, Apresso Damian Zenaro, 1589), p. 289^v. Also see the further analysis in the text, 289^v–90^r.

[9] See the *relazione* of Giovanni Michiel in E. Albèri, *Le relazioni degli ambasciadori veneti al Senato,* ser. 1, vol. 3 (Florence, 1853), p. 428.

barred nobles with relatives in the Roman Curia—called *papalisti*—from the highest offices of the state, for fear that Rome would learn too much about Venetian affairs. The action displeased many, including Doge Francesco Donà (1545–53), who ordered the decree suspended. Shortly thereafter, with Rome also applying pressure, the decree was revoked,[10] but the concern continued. In October 1554 a motion to bar the *papalisti* during Senate discussions of papal relations carried half the Council of Ten, not enough to sustain the motion.[11] Two years later the proposal carried almost unanimously, and for the rest of the century the *papalisti* left the chamber when the Senate and Council of Ten discussed policy toward Rome.[12] This law typified the official Venetian attitude at mid-century and later: the papacy was a foreign power to be kept at arm's length to the point that senators with relatives in papal service were not to be trusted. The legislative reversals demonstrated that many patricians did not share this view.

The Venetians tended to see the local church as a department of state whose responsibility was saving souls and promoting social discipline. The Venetians argued that since many bishoprics in the Republic's extended empire contained diverse peoples or bordered on hostile lands politically reliable bishops were needed. Experienced nobles could best fulfill this requirement; and, indeed, some nobles moved directly from civil posts to *terraferma* bishoprics. But the Venetians drew a line between a local bishopric and any post more closely connected to the Vatican, such as a papal diplomatic appointment or a cardinalate. Many senators worried that a noble who accepted such preferment would become the pope's man.

The Venetians were by no means unanimous in their attitude toward high ecclesiastical office, nor did they always succeed in separating the papacy and the Venetian church. A Senate debate in early December 1588 revealed some of the ambiguities as well as fears and expectations.[13] React-

[10] Letters of Nuncio Ludovico Beccadelli of July 12, 19, 26, Venice, and Girolamo Dandino of July 19, 1550, Rome, in *Nunziature* v, 87, 89–91, 93–94.

[11] The motion failed twice. With two-thirds approval needed, the first vote was 14 yes, 11 no, 2 abstentions; the second was 13 yes, 11 no, 3 abstentions. CX, Secrete, R. 6, f. 127ʳ, October 20, 1554.

[12] The vote was 24 yes, 1 no, 1 abstention. CX, Secrete, R. 6, f. 167ʳ, December 28, 1556. Perhaps it is significant that the reigning pope, Paul IV, was considered anti-Venetian.

[13] VM, Mss. Italiani, Classe vii, 1279 (8886), "Avisi notabili del Mondo, et deliberazioni più importanti di Pregadi, dal 4 marzo 1588 al 25 febbraio 1588," (mv), ff. 120ᵛ–24ᵛ, December 7, 1588. All the three speakers were Savii Grandi at the time of the debate and were of the approximately thirty patricians who dominated the government. For brief résumés of their political careers and some economic data, see Martin J. C. Lowry, "The Church and Venetian Political Change in the

ing to a rumor that Sixtus V planned to create new cardinals at Christmas, the Senate pondered requesting the pontiff to consider some Venetians. Leonardo Donà vigorously opposed this measure on the traditional grounds that Republic and papacy were two separate political entities, each entitled to claim exclusive allegiance from its servants. Not only did honor bind a prelate to serve the papacy, but also the financial comforts of his benefices softened him to the papal will. Donà maintained that nobles would become so entangled in "le cose di Roma" that the Republic would become a papal dependency. He felt that the city could not afford the loss of her ablest sons; and, since no man could serve two masters, Venetian nobles must spurn ecclesiastical preferment in favor of serving the Republic. He closed by calling to mind how the Medici popes had sealed the doom of the Florentine Republic, the fate that befell a state whose citizens became too involved with the papacy. Venetian cardinals would lead to a Venetian pope, and the destruction of the Republic.[14]

Gabriel Cornaro and Alvise Zorzi, two senators as influential as Donà, answered that nobles could serve the papacy and the Republic to the particular advantage of the latter. They professed astonishment at Donà's speech, and leveled the weighty charge that he wished to depart from past practice. The Republic had always found Venetian cardinals extremely useful: Cardinal Domenico Grimani had prevailed upon Julius II to lift his interdict, Cardinal Giovanni Francesco Commendone had softened Pius V on the bull *Coena Domini* and had been useful in the Holy League negotiations, all the Venetian cardinals had interceded with Gregory XIII over the vexing affair of the Patriarchate of Aquileia, and Cardinal Agostino Valier had helped to resolve in Venetian favor the most recent dispute, the presentation to the abbacy of San Cipriano di Murano

---

Later Cinquecento," Ph.D. thesis, University of Warwick, 1970–71, pp. 340–41, 343–44, 365–66. Donà (1536–1612) was the leader of the *giovani*. See especially Seneca, *Donà*, who, however, did not note this debate. Gabriel Cornaro (died c. 1589) is considered to be a *vecchio*, or propapal senator, on the basis of this incident by Gaetano Cozzi, *Il doge Nicolò Contarini: Ricerche sul patriziato veneziano agli inizi del Seicento* (Venice-Rome, 1958), 38. Alvise Zorzi (d. 1593—not the antipapist who flourished during the interdict of 1606–7) adopted both propapal and antipapal positions at various times. Perhaps the "spirit of contradiction" noted by a contemporary was the key to his character. Cozzi, *Contarini*, p. 38 n. 1; Lowry, "Church and Venetian Political Change," p. 269, n. 55, and pp. 270, 287.

[14] Donà's concluding argument was unhistorical. Three Venetian popes in the fifteenth century, Gregory XII (1406–9), Eugenius IV (1431–47), and Paul II (1464–71), did not reduce Venetian liberty. Moreover, although Leo X and Clement VII, with the all-important aid of imperial troops, destroyed Florentine Republican regimes, they themselves had attained the cardinalate, the springboard to the papacy, only as a consequence of prior Medici ascendancy in Florence.

in 1586–87.[15] Cornaro and Zorzi asked whether anyone could serve Venice's interests better than its own subjects. In the past the Republic had gone so far as to put two unnamed cardinals on the state payroll in recognition of their services. Cardinals were particularly useful in Rome because a pope hesitated to offend a cardinal lest the cardinal retaliate against the papal nephews when their protector was dead.

Cornaro and Zorzi responded to the question of divided allegiance as well. One could not argue that a prelate was the subject of a foreign prince because the pope's temporal power and worldly wealth were Christ's. Venetian nobles admittedly profited from the acquisition of prelacies, but should they be deprived of them simply because they became "part foreign"? Are we jealous of the faith? To the charge that a noble prelate could not honorably serve both doge and pope, they cited the example of Cardinal Valier, "huomo da bene, gran Prelato, et grande amico della sua Patria." Had not Sixtus V publicly acclaimed him an ornament of the College of Cardinals? Was not this also a compliment to Venice? O Clarissimo Donà, they demanded, why do you hate the prelacy so much?

The debate concluded, and the letter instructing the ambassador to ask for additional Venetian cardinals was approved, 101 senators voting yes, 43 voting no, and 33 abstaining. However, on December 14, before the ambassador could have advanced his case very far, the pontiff created two new cardinals: a Florentine and a Milanese.[16]

Donà bluntly, and Cornaro and Zorzi more delicately, touched the primary ecclesiastical consideration for many noble families: the acquisition of benefices. The Venetians tried to maintain a de facto territorial church in order to harvest the church's wealth. The government held the papacy at arm's length so that it could staff the major episcopal sees with the nominees of its choice. The Venetians managed to achieve their goal even though the Senate enjoyed the right of presentation to only one see, the Patriarchate of Venice, and the additional right to present four candidates, from whom the pope would make the selection, to the Archbishopric of Crete. They often used the *renuncia cum regressu*, in which an ageing incumbent resigned in favor of a younger relative, who took the office and eventually obtained papal confirmation. In this way some posts, like the Patriarchate of Aquileia, which the Grimani family held throughout the century, became family benefices. The bishoprics were not distributed evenly. Certain family groups, like the Barbaro, Grimani, Cornaro, and Pisani, held many sees while others, like the Da Ponte and

---

[15] For the details of the San Cipriano dispute, see Lowry, "Church and Venetian Political Change," pp. 265–70. The other disputes are fairly well known.

[16] Pastor, XXI, 239–40.

Donà, held few if any. The nobility's interest in a see rose and declined with its revenue. The powerful families monopolized the richest sees, those of the *terraferma* cities such as Aquileia, Padua, Verona, Vicenza, Bergamo, and Brescia (Padua yielded 15,000 ducats annually, the others 5,000 to 10,000).[17] These noble bishops discharged their debt to the Republic; a chronicler proudly noted that in 1570 ten patrician incumbents of the richest sees contributed 1,000 scudi to 4,000 ducats each to the war against the Turks.[18] Commoners, who were almost always Venetian subjects, might hold the poorer sees, such as the Dalmatian bishoprics.

Some pontiffs refused to accept gracefully the Republic's control over the local church, and, like the Venetians, manipulated the levers of power to get their way. For example, Pietro Barbarigo, Bishop of Curzola and Stagno in Dalmatia and the holder of other benefices, died in 1566. The Collegio urged upon Rome the appointment of his brother Agostino as his successor, on the grounds that he had two unmarried daughters and had advanced to his late brother the funds to purchase ecclesiastical offices. Pius V assured the Venetians of his warm regard for the Barbarigo family, but made no move to accede to the request. A long and complex dispute broke out over who should get the late bishop's benefices. At the same time, the pope was vexed by the Venetian threat to tax the property of the mendicant orders; though he never directly linked the two issues, he obviously kept both in mind. Agostino Barbarigo failed to obtain the bishopric, and the Apostolic Camera denied his claim to the benefices, but the pope did promise him some compensation.[19]

Only unusual political circumstances prevented the nobility from collecting the rich *terraferma* sees. In exchange for his support in the league against the Turks in 1570, Pius V succeeded in appointing his associate, the dedicated reformer Niccolò Ormaneto, to the Paduan see.[20] This was the only occasion in the century that the Paduan revenues escaped the Venetian nobles, who could still console themselves in the knowledge that Ormaneto was a native of Verona and a subject of the Republic. Few pontiffs were as skillful in plying worldly weapons for spiritual ends as the saintly and tough Pius V, nor did such an opportunity to extract

[17] Pullan, "Service to the Venetian State," pp. 125–34; Oliver Logan, *Culture and Society in Venice 1470–1790: The Renaissance and its Heritage* (London, 1972), pp. 30–33.

[18] VM, Mss. Italiani, Classe VII, 519 (8438), Niccolò Trevisan, "Cronaca di Venezia al 1585," f. 327ʳ.

[19] Letters of Nuncio Giovanni Antonio Facchinetti of December 7, 14, 28, 1566, January 11, 25, May 3, 1567, Venice, and of Cardinal Michele Bonelli of December 14, 21, 1566, February 1, May 10, 1567, Rome, in *Nunziature* VIII, 142–43, 146–47, 149–51, 157, 163–64, 168, 210, 216.

[20] Stella, *Chiesa e stato*, pp. 202, 218–19.

concessions occur again. With few exceptions the Venetian nobility harvested the important and wealthy *terraferma* bishoprics—and occasionally resided in them.

Individual or family interests magnified the complexity of Venetian-papal disputes. The nuncio observed in 1571 that the Venetian government handled affairs of state dispassionately enough unless a noble's personal interests were involved, but then the resulting intrigue produced "incredible difficulty."[21] Ten years later, another nuncio charged that the nobility were more solicitous for their private advantage than for the welfare of the Republic.[22] The same charge could have been leveled at more than one Vatican prelate or curial official who used a dispute to advance a private goal.

Both the Senate and the Curia distrusted the political influence exerted through families, but both sought to profit from it. Since a bishop could restore the family's fortunes, the other members found it difficult to withstand pressure channeled through him. Aware of this, the papacy in 1576 instructed a new nuncio to caress the noble bishops, who would speak to their relatives in the government.[23] A Venetian cardinal or bishop likewise solicited concessions from Rome for his poor relatives. Even if one was a senator and the other a cardinal, the loyalty between brothers could transcend other claims to allegiance.

The complexity of the issues and the multiplicity of concerns dictated the pattern of Venetian-papal negotiations. The disputants staked out apparently rigid initial positions, bargained interminably, and brought to bear every available weapon. Each sought to take advantage of the other's internal problems and dragged out disputes in the hope that time would produce a favorable change of circumstances or personalities. Doge and pope bartered political, economic, and even spiritual commodities, carefully observing their fluctuation in value from month to month. Both sides agreed that substance was more important than form. One nuncio reported that if he closed one eye and did not insist on an agreement in writing he often got what he wanted.[24] But the reluctance to commit a pact to paper left the door open for future disputes. At the same time, both parties recognized that some prerogatives could not be bartered. The Republic accepted the pope's right to proclaim doctrine, and the papacy

---

[21] "Ma le cause nelle quali i gentilhuomini venetiani hanno interesse sono piene di molto maggior difficultà che le publiche, perchè queste le trattano senza particolar passione, ma le proprie, se ben private, le fanno in questi casi publiche, et ciascuno poi tanto broglio, che se ne vede con incredibile difficultà il fine." Letter of Nuncio Giovanni Antonio Facchinetti of May 19, 1571, Venice, in *Nunziature* IX, 503–4.

[22] Stella, *Chiesa e stato*, p. 212.   [23] Stella, *Chiesa e stato*, p. 9.

[24] Stella, *Chiesa e stato*, p. 216.

usually did not challenge the system that enabled the Republic to control the local church.

Finally, common interests often brought Republic and papacy together. Doge, pope, senator, and cardinal recognized circumstances, such as the salvation of souls or the security of the state, that transcended minor differences. As everywhere else in Catholic Europe, prelates and princes were the co-rulers of a society where the lines demarcating their respective spheres of authority were blurred. In practice, pragmatic arrangements and subtle understandings guided relations between the papacy and Venice. When the papacy initiated the Counter Reformation, the Venetian nobles weighed it in the context of their responsibilities to God, the local church, their families, and other political powers. Last, but not least, they kept in mind the current dispute with Rome.

2. ESTABLISHMENT OF THE INQUISITION

Much of the meager information available on the medieval Inquisition in Venice comes from Paolo Sarpi, who wrote that in the thirteenth century the government established a lay magistracy of three nobles, who with the assistance of the bishops were to investigate heresy.[25] On one occasion he gave the date of origin as 1220; on another as 1249. He always insisted that the state, not the papacy or the local church, had founded the Venetian Inquisition, that it was a lay body, and that it exercised lay supremacy in its operations. Recently discovered documents show that a magistracy with jurisdiction over heresy and usury existed in 1256, and that it expanded to include additional offenses in the second half of the century. These documents confirm Sarpi's outline of the medieval Inquisition in Venice, but little more. In 1289 Pope Nicholas IV reached an accord with the Venetian government in which he formally installed a Franciscan who, as inquisitor for the Venetian state, would travel from place to place as his services were required, with the state paying his salary. Sarpi insisted that the inquisitor in no way superseded the lay magistracy. When in 1301 the inquisitor came to Venice to assert papal jurisdiction over heresy, the government rebuked him. In the fourteenth century, according to Sarpi, the Venetian Inquisition gradually declined for lack of something to do. In 1385 the inquisitor's stipend was cut, and in 1423, eliminated entirely, on the grounds that it was a superfluous ex-

[25] Sarpi's accounts of the origins of the Venetian Inquisition are found in his *Sopra l'officio dell'inquisizione* (1613), in *Scritti giurisdizionalistici*, ed. Giovanni Gambarin (Bari, 1958), pp. 138–41; and "In materia di crear novo inquisitor di Venezia" (1622), in *Opere*, ed. Gaetano and Luisa Cozzi (Milan-Naples, 1969), pp. 1,202–6. The latter account is enriched in the notes by the research of Reinhold Mueller and by the comments of Gaetano Cozzi.

pense. From 1423 until the Protestant Reformation, the Venetian Inquisition, in Sarpi's words, "existed more in name than in fact."

The Inquisition resumed activity by 1540.[26] In August of that year the nuncio wished to arrest Fra Giulio della Rovere, a Milanese Augustinian, but because Fra Giulio enjoyed the support of the "first gentlemen" of Venice, he proceeded with caution. Eventually the nuncio arrested Fra Giulio, who abjured and was sentenced to a year in prison. In late 1541 or early 1542 Giulio fled to Switzerland and became a Calvinist.[27] Sarpi states, and the trial documents confirm, the absence of lay participation in the proceedings of the early 1540s. The inquisitor and nuncio were free of lay intervention but powerless. If they wished to make an arrest, they had to beg the assistance of the Council of Ten, and they met delay or rebuff as often as not.[28]

The era of the Counter Reformation began on July 4, 1542, when Paul III created the so-called Roman Inquisition in *Licet ab initio*. Roman centralization and universal jurisdiction marked the reconstituted tribunal. All appointments of inquisitors as well as overall direction were to come from Rome, and the tribunal was empowered to proceed, independent of existing clerical and lay authorities, against anyone, regardless of rank.[29] The bull signaled that the pontiff had lost hope of reunion with Protestantism, and wanted concerted action against heresy.

Paul III urged the Venetians to take stronger action against heretics and their books. He had heard that Venice harbored open dissenters, and he recommended strong action lest these rebels against God become traitors to Caesar.[30] Members of the papal court became increasingly

[26] For the 1533 Roman trial of a Venetian heretical group, see Franco Gaeta, "Documenti da codici vaticani per la storia della Riforma in Venezia," *Annuario dell'istituto storico italiano per l'età moderna e contemporanea* 7 (1955), 5–53. Also for heresy in the 1530s, see Gaeta, *Un nunzio pontificio a Venezia nel Cinquecento (Girolamo Aleandro)* (Venice-Rome, 1960); and *Nunziature* I (1533–1535).

[27] Letter of the nuncio, Giorgio Andrassi, of August 13, 1540, Venice, in *Nunziature* II, 261–62. Also see Pio Paschini, *Venezia e l'inquisizione romana da Giulio III a Pio IV* (Padua, 1959), pp. 11–17.

[28] Sarpi, "In materia di crear novo inquisitor di Venezia," in *Opere*, p. 1,206. Antonio Santosuosso, "Religious Orthodoxy, Dissent and Suppression in Venice in the 1540s," *Church History* 42 (1973), 477–78, 480. The same author's "The Life and Thought of Giovanni Della Casa, 1503–1556," Ph.D. thesis, University of Toronto, 1972, ch. v, pp. 182–302, is the best discussion of Della Casa's inquisitorial activity while nuncio to Venice.

[29] Pastor, XII, 503–7. Because of its centralization, the reconstituted Inquisition is usually termed the Roman Inquisition. Unless otherwise indicated, in this study "Inquisition" is understood to mean the Roman Inquisition rather than one of the medieval Inquisitions or the Spanish Inquisition.

[30] Letter of Ambassador Francesco Venier of March 1, 1544, Rome, in Archivio

pointed in their criticism of Venetian tolerance. In January 1546 the learned Cardinal Jacopo Sadoleto had a long talk with the Venetian ambassador.[31] Sadoleto lamented that Venice, once so truly Christian, had become "very infected" by the Lutheran pestilence, to the point that the plague had spread even to "governing circles" and writers. The ambassador's anger showed in his reply. Just as not everything one sees in Rome is consistent with the "sublime name of Rome," so what is said of Venice is not necessarily true. He characterized Venice as "a city of the world, free and open to all"; even if some of the people who came to Venice were evil, one could not attribute a *peccatum civitatis*. He then launched into a vigorous rendition of the religious myth of Venice, i.e., that the Catholic faith had been implanted with the foundation of the city, and that the Republic had remained faithful to the point of shedding the blood of her citizens for the faith. His harangue moved both to tears, but did not dissuade Sadoleto, who urged that the Venetians give some sign of their devotion. They might at least prohibit the importation and holding of Lutheran books. Instead of worrying about offending Protestant authors and princes, they should realize that they risked the vengeance of other Italian states for permitting heresy easy entry into the peninsula.

The Venetians turned a deaf ear to papal pleas, and tried to chart a neutral course throughout the 1540s. In Germany the conflict between the Protestant princes and Emperor Charles V reached a critical point, and each desired the Republic's support. The Venetians favored the political aims of the German princes because defeat in Germany would loosen Charles's grip on Italy. Protestant observers sometimes believed or hoped that Venetian political empathy was founded on religious sympathy. With the election of Doge Francesco Donà (November 24, 1545), by reputation anti-imperial and antipapal, Italian philo-Protestants sought a favorable response from the Republic. Pier Paolo Vergerio, soon to flee to the Protestant north, addressed a letter to Doge Donà at his election exhorting the Republic to take the lead in reforming the church by eliminating abuses and emphasizing Scripture.[32] The government made no moves in this direction, but it also refrained from a crackdown on local Protestants.

Proprio Roma, F. 6, ff. 39ʳ⁻ᵛ. I am indebted to Antonio Santosuosso for bringing this and the following letter to my attention.

[31] Letter of Ambassador Giovanni Antonio Venier of February 6, 1545 mv, Rome, in Capi del CX, Lettere di ambasciatori a Roma, Bu. 23, documents 117–18.

[32] See Aldo Stella, "L'orazione di Pier Paolo Vergerio al Doge Francesco Donà sulla riforma della chiesa (1545)," *Atti dell'Istituto Veneto di scienze, lettere ed arti: Classe di scienze morali, lettere ed arti* 128 (1970), 1–39. For diplomacy at this time, see Stella, "Utopie e velleità insurrezionali dei filoprotestanti italiani (1545–1547)," BHR, 27 (1965), 133–82.

In June 1546 the anti-imperial forces asked the Republic to take the first step toward active support. Baldassarre Altieri presented letters from Henry VIII and the princes of the Schmalkalden League requesting that he be recognized as the League's representative in Venice. The request posed a delicate political and moral problem. Although a positive response might have far-reaching consequences, it would serve Venetian political interests. Moreover, the alliance of Protestant princes and English and French monarchs appeared to be winning the war against Charles V. But if the Republic acquiesced, it would be conferring de facto recognition on princes banded together for the purpose of consolidating Protestantism and waging war against Europe's preeminent Catholic monarch. It was much easier to justify continuing relations with the schismatic English, who might return to the faith, than to initiate ties with Protestant rebels. Moreover, official diplomatic status would facilitate the efforts of Altieri and his confederates to raise soldiers for the Schmalkalden League among sympathetic Italians. How would the emperor and other Italian states view such a step?

The request provoked an intense debate in the Senate.[33] Those in favor of granting Altieri diplomatic recognition argued that the matter was one of state, not of faith. They began by invoking tradition that suited their purpose: a commercial Republic like Venice sought friendship with all nations. They stressed the political nature and broad structure of the Schmalkalden League. The League included three imperial electors and all the free territories, and was more interested in defending liberty than in spreading Protestantism. Since its foundation in 1517 it had acted only in self-defense. The monarchs of England and France had aided the League despite religious differences. Also, strong Protestant princes who ruled most of Germany wanted to check the emperor's power, a most useful contribution to Venetian welfare. Proponents of the measure took the offensive against those with spiritual doubts by playing on Venetian anticlericalism and the Republic's spirit of independence toward the papacy. They argued that real concern for the faith would require them to halt priestly simony rather than to vote against this political measure. A negative response to the Protestants would indicate that the Republic dare not act contrary to the wishes of Rome.

Those who opposed granting Altieri recognition feared for the Republic if it defied God. The princes of the Schmalkalden League were Luther-

[33] VM, Mss. Italiani, Classe VII, 808 (7296), "Annali di 1545–1546," no pag., entries of June 7, 8, 1546; the same material is in VC, Ms. Cicogna 2552, "Annali delle cose della Repubblica di Venezia dall'anno 1541–1548," same dates, no pag. at this point. S. Romanin, *Storia documentata di Venezia*, 2nd ed., vol. VI (Venice, 1914), pp. 214–16; and Stella, "Utopie," p. 153, provide brief accounts.

ans; receiving their representative would aid heretics in Germany and in
Venice, and the spread of heresy locally would lead to sedition. Granting
a Protestant diplomatic status and official favor would cause a grave scandal among the people. One speaker stressed that Altieri's real aim was
to promote Protestantism in Venice; diplomatic recognition would enable
him to propagate Protestant books and views with immunity.[34]

The Senate split. Two motions failed to gain the necessary two-thirds
support, and Altieri was denied recognition. He continued to act as the
unofficial representative of the Protestant princes, and the Schmalkalden
League continued to court Venice, but the emperor also applied pressure.
The Venetians offered friendship to all and active support to none. In October Altieri asked on behalf of Elector John Frederick of Saxony and
Landgrave Phillip of Hesse for a loan of 100,000 ducats. The Venetians
declined, but assured the Protestants that German merchants would always be welcome in Venice and that the city would not prosecute them
for their beliefs.[35]

Events proved the wisdom of caution. From the end of 1546 through
the defeat of the League of Schmalkalden at Mühlberg on April 24, 1547,
Charles V again imposed his authority, at least temporarily, over Germany. The deaths of Henry VIII (January 27, 1547), and Francis I (March
31, 1547), and the different policies of their successors, further increased
the desirability of staying on the best possible terms with the emperor
and the pope.[36] The Venetians swiftly adjusted to the new balance of
power. Upon Henry VIII's death, they withdrew their ambassador from
England, and covered all traces of their negotiations with the dead monarch. In May they executed a prominent Italian philo-Protestant agent of
the Schmalkalden League for his complicity in the assassination of a patrician, a legitimate, but also convenient, removal of a troublesome man.[37]

The Venetians chose this period to establish a new magistracy to deal
with heresy. On March 19, 1547, Nuncio Giovanni Della Casa reported
that the Venetians were ready to take strong action.[38] The apprehension
of an Augustinian friar preaching heresy in the Church of San Barnabà
may have provided the occasion, for the Venetians seldom acted except in

[34] Whatever Altieri's motives, this assessment of his activity was completely accurate; it demonstrated that, although the patriciate might feign ignorance, they
were well aware of local proselytizing. Leandro Perini, "Note e documenti su
Pietro Perna libraio-tipografo a Basilea," *Nuova rivista storica* 50 (1966), 148.

[35] Stella, "Utopie," pp. 153–55, 176–77.

[36] Despite temporary ruptures, such as that caused by the murder of Pier Luigi
Farnese in September 10, 1547, the political and religious situation normally made
allies of emperor and pope.

[37] Stella, "Utopie," pp. 157–58.

[38] The letter is quoted in Sforza, "Controriforma," pt. 1, 194–95.

response to an immediate stimulus.[39] A month later, remarkably quick by Venetian standards, the doge appointed three nobles to assist the inquisitor, nuncio, and patriarch in the suppression of heresy.

The decree of April 22, 1547, read as follows. We, Francesco Donà Doge of Venice, recognizing that there is nothing more worthy of a Christian prince than to defend the faith, and that this is part of our ducal commission, have elected with the Collegio you three nobles, Nicolò Tiepolo, Francesco Contarini, and Antonio Venier, "probi, discreti e cattolici uomini," to investigate diligently heretics in our city and to take action against them, acting together at all times and in everything that happens in the "formation of the trials" with the Reverends Legate, Patriarch, and Inquisitor. As assistants you will execute the sentences that are passed against the guilty, and from time to time you will inform us of everything that has taken place.[40] The government named the new magistracy the Tre Savii sopra eresia.

Very little comment and no visible controversy accompanied the action. The same chronicle that provided a detailed account of the debate over Altieri's recognition offered only one uninformative sentence on the Tre Savii.[41] The only semiofficial Venetian explanation appeared years later in the unpublished history of Alvise Contarini, who was elected public historiographer in March 1577, but died two years later leaving his "De-

---

[39] VC, Ms. Cicogna 2552, "Annali 1541–1548," ff. 10[r], 22[v], c. March 21, March 28, 1547.

[40] The decree is printed by Sforza, "Controriforma," pt. 1, pp. 195–96, from ASV, Compilazione di leggi, Bu. 204, E, Eresie e Eretici, f. 442. It is also printed in Francesco Albizzi, *Risposta all'Historia della Sacra Inquisitione composta già dal R. P. Paolo Servita.* . . . Edizione seconda corretta . . . [Rome, 1678], pp. 40–41; and in Cesare Cantù, *Gli eretici d'Italia. Discorsi storici.* Vol. 3 (Turin, 1866), p. 134. But Sarpi's sole reference to the 1547 decree completely misrepresented it. He reported only the final clause, in which the doge instructed the lay assistants to give him information on the tribunal's activities, and used this as a platform for an argument for lay supremacy. *Sopra l'officio dell'inquisizione* in *Scritti giurisdizionalistici*, pp. 122, 152–54. The reason for Sarpi's fraud is that the decree damaged his case. It did not state that the Tre Savii were a continuation or a revival of a thirteenth-century lay magistracy, nor did the decree claim lay supremacy either by the government or the lay deputies. Practically speaking, the creation of the Tre Savii was a new departure that Sarpi did not wish to admit. In general, Sarpi is not a reliable historical source for the operations of the Inquisition and of censorship in the cinquecento and early seicento, and his works have not been used in that way in this study.

[41] "Fù proposto di fare provisione sopra l'Inquisitione contro li Heretici, et contra li redutti di quelli che parlano publico in tal materia. Fù poi con l'auttorità del Serenissimo et del Consiglio dato il carico à 3 gentilhuomini, et per il Consiglio dei Dieci si rimettono le cose alli detti." VC, Ms. Cicogna 2552, "Annali di 1541–1548," ff. 15[r-v], no date but c. March 20, 1547.

lineatio Historiae," a narrative of the events from 1513 to 1570, incomplete. Shortly thereafter, Agostino Valier, Bishop of Verona and cardinal from 1583, repeated Contarini's account in a history of Venice from its origins through 1581, a work that remained in manuscript until the eighteenth century. According to Contarini and Valier, the Venetians were worried about heretical preachers who attacked the morals of clergymen, denied free will, and induced the people to libertinage. At the same time, they were concerned about others being falsely accused of spreading heresy and heretical books. After consultation, they asked Pope Julius III (not elected until 1550) to allow three senators to participate in the activities of the Holy Office, without vote in the decisions. The request was granted, with the result that heresy was totally extirpated.[42] Whether by design or accident, Contarini and Valier confused the establishment of the Tre Savii in Venice in 1547 with the agreement of 1551 that permitted the two Venetian governors of Dominion cities to participate in the operations of the local Inquisitions.[43] Their evaluation of Venetian motives may contain a grain of truth, but their account of what transpired was a whitewash.

The lack of information on the discussion within the government makes it difficult to determine the precise reason for the establishment of the Tre Savii. Political considerations helped determine the timing. Altieri and Vergerio had mistaken political benevolence for religious sympathy; the Venetians wished to make certain that the victorious emperor would not make the same error. Manifesting their commitment to religious orthodoxy through the reorganization of the Holy Office clearly signaled Venetian adjustment. Political considerations, however, cannot provide the fundamental reason for the formation of the Tre Savii; this has to have been the fear of heresy. Defense of the faith was part of Venetian tradition, and the flirtation with the Schmalkalden League had troubled the consciences of many patricians. The defeat of the Protestant princes and change of rulers in France and England eliminated the diplomatic obstacles to a move against heresy. All Italian states took the initial steps to suppress heresy in the 1540s, Venice as decisively as the others, if more slowly.

[42] VM, Mss. Latini, Classe x, 285 (3180), Alvise Contarini, "Delineatio Historiae, quae res gestas Venetorum complectitur, nulla diligentia contexta, iterum expolienda et debitis coloribus exornanda in quatuordecim libris distincta," f. 76^r; *Dell'utilità che si puo ritrarre dalle cose operate dai veneziani libri xiv, del Cardinale Agostino Valerio Vescovo di Verona*, tradotti dal latino ed illustrata da Monsignor Niccolò Antonio Giustiniani (Padua, 1787), pp. 328–29. Valier's work appears to have been written c. 1581. For Contarini, Valier, and their histories, see Gaetano Cozzi, "Cultura politica e religione nella 'pubblica storiografia' veneziana del '500," BSV, 5–6 (1963–64), 242–55.

[43] See Ch. VII, sec. 2 for details.

A small group of Venetian leaders was able to establish the Tre Savii swiftly and without controversy because the constitution empowered the doge and his council, rather than Senate or Council of Ten, to guard the faith. It is likely that the doge and a few others took the matter into their own hands. The next nuncio reported in 1551 that without the warm support of Doge Donà it would have been difficult to establish the Tre Savii because of the "diversity of views" in the Republic.[44] The patriciate was no more unanimous on this question than on any other. Such outspoken anticlericals as Nicolò Da Ponte might have objected that the creation of the Tre Savii moved the Republic too close to Rome.

The magistracy of the Tre Savii had immediate impact. Within a few days, Nuncio Della Casa met with the three nobles. He found them to be "very favorably disposed" and predicted that the tribunal would be effective.[45] His optimism was not misplaced; an immediate increase in the number of trials occurred, from 7 in 1544–46, to 25 in 1547, 51 in 1548, and 41 in 1549, according to the surviving records. The level of prosecution did not approach that of later years, but the increase was significant enough to discourage Altieri, who reported in March 1549 that "persecution is every day harsher."[46]

3. OPERATION OF THE INQUISITION

The most important political feature of the Venetian Inquisition was the participation of the elected representatives of the Venetian government, the Tre Savii, who were also called lay assistants, lay deputies, or simply assistants or deputies. The Great Council ratified the procedure for their election in 1554, but altered it significantly in 1556, by legislating that the Great Council would elect one of two ducal nominees. This law was not implemented, however, and the choice remained in the hands of the doge and Collegio until 1595, when it passed to the Senate.[47]

The office of lay deputy became part of the highest level of the Venetian political structure. The base of the governmental pyramid was the Great Council, which at mid-century had about 2,500 male nobles over the age

[44] Nuncio Ludovico Beccadelli's letter of September 5, 1551, Venice, in *Nunziature* v, 279.

[45] Sforza, "Controriforma," pt. 1, p. 196.

[46] Santosuosso, "Orthodoxy, Dissent and Suppression," p. 481.

[47] The laws of June 5, 1554, and June 7, 1556, are in Maggior Consiglio Deliberazioni, F. 7, anno 1554–1558, and are cited here from the copies in SU, Bu. 154, a miscellaneous collection entitled "Collazione delle missive universali alli punti singolari contenziosi tra la Corte di Roma e la Repubblica di Venezia," arranged chronologically, and in VC, Ms. P D C 808, "Copie di documenti tratti dall'Archivio di Stato relative all'Inquisizione a Venezia (secc. xiii–xviii)," docs. 17 and 18. The 1595 change in election procedure is discussed in Ch. vii, sec. 2.

of 25 (and a handful between the ages of 20 and 25); above the Great Council stood the Senate, which had about 300 members. The greatest power resided in the smaller group of men who filled approximately 60 major administrative offices of a total of about 800 posts allotted to the nobility. Included in the major offices were the doge, nine Procurators of St. Mark,[48] six Savii del Consiglio (or Savii Grandi), six members of the Pieno Collegio (or Collegio, the doge's cabinet), the Council of Ten, fifteen members of the Zonta (a committee attached to the Council of Ten charged with financial affairs—abolished in 1583), five resident ambassadors (to Rome, Vienna, Madrid, Paris, and Constantinople), and governors of the most important Dominion cities and islands.[49] A patrician worked his way through lower offices until he became a member of the Council of Ten or a Savio Grande in his forties or fifties, the former office often preceding the latter by a few years. A few of these successful and powerful politicians were elected to the lifetime post of Procurator at the age of sixty or later, and one very fortunate survivor became doge. James C. Davis estimates that, after allowing for the period of ineligibility before a patrician could resume a major post, a constitutional provision sometimes breached, about 100 patricians were needed for the above major offices.[50] Martin Lowry, after tabulating the number of men who monopolized the major offices, concludes that a smaller group of great office-holders, perhaps 30 in number, dominated the government in a given chronological span—from a decade to a generation.[51] These 30 senior men held the top posts of Procurator and Savio Grande, and seats in the Council of Ten, either in alternation, or moving to a lesser post before returning, or succeeding themselves in spite of the rules.

[48] The office of Procurator did not carry important administrative authority, but granted entry to some other councils and conferred great prestige on the holder. Almost all doges were chosen from the ranks of the Procurators. Incidentally, there were two cinquecento exceptions to the limitation of nine Procurators, both occurring in time of great crisis. In June 1537, when the Turks besieged Corfu, seven nobles were permitted to purchase the office with large contributions (14,000 ducats in one case), and in January 1571, during the Cyprus War, six nobles purchased the office with loans of 20,000 ducats to the Republic.

[49] Lane believes that the inner group was slightly smaller. He states that sixteen officers (doge, six Savii Grandi, three Heads of the Council of Ten, and six Ducal Councillors) constituted the inner circle, and another twenty-four officers were "on the outer edge of the inner circle." *Venice*, p. 257; see also pp. 96–97, 253–57, 429.

[50] James C. Davis, *The Decline of the Venetian Nobility as a Ruling Class* (Baltimore, 1962), pp. 15–33, esp. p. 23.

[51] Lowry, "Church and Venetian Political Change," pp. 140–200, esp. p. 157. Some of his data has been published in his article, "The Reform of the Council of Ten, 1582–83: An Unsettled Problem?" *Studi veneziani* 13 (1971), 307–10.

The lay deputies were chosen from the ranks of the great officeholders or, rather, these powerful, experienced men elected themselves to the office.[52] Marchio (or Melchiorre) di Tommaso Michiel (c. 1489–1572) was first elected a Savio Grande in 1551, and was reelected 20 times; he served almost annually in the Council of Ten or the Zonta from mid-century, and was elected a Procurator in 1558. He was a lay deputy in 1552, 1557, 1560, 1562–65, 1567, and 1570. Alvise di Tommaso Mocenigo (1507–77) was a lay deputy in 1562, 1565, and 1568–70. He steadily ascended the ladder, from the Council of Ten and Zonta frequently in the 1550s, to Savio Grande in 1559, to Procurator in 1566, and doge in 1570. Election as a lay assistant tended to coincide with a noble's arrival at the high plateau of Council of Ten and Savio Grande. Pasquale Cicogna (1509–95) was first elected to the Council of Ten in 1577, the same year that he first served on the Inquisition. He became a Savio Grande in 1580, repeated the following four years, became a Procurator in 1583, and doge in 1585.

The papacy found some of the lay deputies to be cooperative in the suppression of heresy and sympathetic to ecclesiastical jurisdictional claims, and sought to keep them in a favorable frame of mind through commendations and favors. Procurator Giulio di Zorzi Contarini (c. 1498–c. 1577) served as a lay deputy in 1553, 1555, 1559–62, 1565–67, and 1570–71, and was present during some of the delicate trials of Venetian nobles in the 1560s. Twice in 1566 the papacy praised him for his zeal in defense of the faith, as a "warm protector of ecclesiastical immunity and jurisdiction," and for his "great devotion toward the Holy See." Contarini was particularly useful in persuading the government to extradite Guido Giannetti da Fano.[53] The nuncio judged Girolamo di Marin Grimani, a lay assistant in 1560–62 and 1565–67, as "very devoted to the Apostolic See

---

[52] Because the doge and Collegio elected the Tre Savii, their names are not included with other officeholders in the Segretario alle voci *fondo* until 1595. Some names are to be found in Collegio, Notatorio. I have been able to compile a list of the lay deputies from the trials themselves, since their names are normally listed at the top of the transcript of the day's testimony. I hope to publish this list. To ascertain which other major offices the lay deputies held, I have used the data compiled from the Segretario alle voci by Lowry, "Church and Venetian Political Change," pp. 145–52, 301–66, as well as his additional research, which he graciously showed me, and my own research. Additional biographical data on the lay assistants can be found in ASV, Marco Barbaro, "Arbori dei Patritii veneti." A convenient list of the Procurators can be compiled from Raimondo Morozzo della Rocca and Maria Francesca Tiepolo, "Cronologia veneziana del Cinquecento," in *La civiltà veneziana del Rinascimento* (Florence, 1958), pp. 197–249.

[53] This was on the advice of the nuncio who also dictated the wording of the commendations. Letters of Giovanni Antonio Facchinetti and Michele Bonelli of May 21, Venice; June 1, Rome; August 24, Venice; August 31, 1566, Rome; in *Nunziature* VIII, 46–47, 49, 55–56, 96, 102.

and protector of ecclesiastical things." To retain Grimani's "customary devotion," the nuncio vigorously interceded with Rome on his behalf in a case involving taxes in Ravenna.[54] Similarly, the nuncio intervened on behalf of Grimani, Lorenzo di Agostino Da Mula, lay assistant in 1567–68 and described as "most zealous" in defense of God's honor, and Andrea Barbarigo, a lay assistant in 1558–59, 1561, 1563, and 1569, so that they might export grain from Ravenna.[55]

Whether some lay assistants sought the post as a consequence of their zeal to suppress heresy, or whether they acquired their zeal in the course of their duties, is impossible to determine. No evidence concerning the qualities sought in a lay deputy by the doge and Collegio beyond Doge Donà's praise of the original trio as "upright, discrete, and Catholic men" has come to light. Since the leaders of the government chose themselves, it is clear that they sought experienced, influential and reliable men. Pope and nuncio probably did not urge the appointment of nobles "devoted to the Apostolic See." All patricians at least paid lip service to the tradition of separation between Republic and papacy, and any overt move by the papacy would have been counterproductive. More subtle lobbying that may have occurred has escaped detection. Doubtlessly, doge and Collegio freely chose the men that they wanted. But some of the great officeholders must have been temperamentally more suited to the job, or more convinced of the necessity of extirpating heresy. Nomination and renomination came their way frequently. The doge and Collegio very seldom selected notorious anticlericals and antipapists. Nicolò di Antonio Da Ponte (1491–1585), whose long and distinguished career culminated in a Procuratorship in 1570 and dogate in 1577, opposed every papal initiative that came within his purview; the newly elected Pius V refused to receive him as one of the envoys sent to offer the Republic's homage. Da Ponte appeared as a lay deputy no more than twice, in November 1562, at the trial of some Anabaptists, and in September 1564.[56] Giovanni di Bernardo Donà (1510–91), a ferocious anticlerical throughout his public life, may have served on the Holy Office for a single day in May 1573.[57] Leonardo di

---

[54] Letter of Giovanni Antonio Facchinetti, June 11, 1566, Venice, in *Nunziature* VIII, 62. Although the nuncio repeatedly asked for action, the matter dragged on and on without a clear decision.

[55] Letter of Giovanni Antonio Facchinetti, November 20, 1568, Venice, in *Nunziature* VIII, 462–63. Da Mula was described as *zelantissimo* in Facchinetti's letter of April 3, 1568, Venice (ibid., p. 369).

[56] Stella, *Chiesa e stato*, p. 14. For his appearance with the Holy Office, see Stella I, 129 n. 31; SU, Bu. 20, Francesco Lazzaro, testimony of September 7, 1564.

[57] SU, Bu. 34, Alessandro Mantica, testimony of May 29, 1573. Since the SU documents do not list patronymics of the Tre Savii, this may also have been Giovanni di Benedetto Donà, a less prominent figure.

Giovanni Battista Donà (1536–1612), who as doge led Venetian resistance against Paul V in 1606–07, was appointed to the Holy Office once in his long career, in October 1604, and it is not certain that he actually served.[58]

The tribunal did not vacillate according to whether the Tre Savii were "devoted to the Holy See" or antipapal. Individual lay deputies were not consistent on either religious or church-state issues. The antipapal Da Ponte by his own admission had argued in favor of the death penalty for several heretics when a lay deputy and during his tenure with the Council of Ten.[59] And Girolamo Grimani, the defender of ecclesiastical rights while with the Holy Office, stood with Da Ponte to oppose a papal request that the mendicant orders be granted a tax exemption for their property in 1566.[60] Paolo di Marin Corner (Cornaro), a lay deputy whom the nuncio called his good friend, did not hesitate to differ publicly with the nuncio over a benefice.[61] More important than the views of individual lay deputies was the policy expressed by the major organs of the government. The great officeholders were not themselves of one mind on religious policy, but they were generally able to reach a consensus, which the Inquisition reflected.

The lay deputies assisted the Inquisition by representing the authority of the Council of Ten, the chief judicial organ of the state. They authorized warrants for arrest, assisted at the trials, and gave their opinions; but they submitted to the judgment of the three ecclesiastics, who alone were authorized to pronounce sentence. During the trial, the inquisitor questioned the accused and witnesses; the patriarch and the nuncio spoke infrequently, and the deputies almost never. When the sentence had been decided, the deputies issued it, and the Council of Ten deputized a captain to execute it. The trials show that from mid-century at least one noble was present at every formal session of every trial, although not at every preliminary denunciation; all three nobles normally attended trials of importance. Indeed, their insistence on being present at every session

---

[58] Segretario alle voci, Elezioni del Senato, R. 7 (1600–1606), f. 104ᵛ, elected on October 2, 1604. Because there are no extant trials for that time, I have been unable to confirm that he served. I suspect that he did not, or that he served only for a very limited time, because he was named to many other offices during the years 1603–5, one of them on the same date. (Seneca, *Donà*, 245, n. 1.) This supposition is supported by the fact that another lay deputy was elected on January 19, 1605, and two more on April 23, 1605. It was a period of rapid turnover in the office.

[59] Stella, *Chiesa e stato*, p. 14, n. 37.

[60] Letter of Nuncio Facchinetti of December 14, 1566, Venice, in *Nunziature* VIII, 145.

[61] Letters of December 6, 13, 1567, in *Nunziature* VIII, 312, 318. Corner (d. 1580), a very distinguished patrician who reached the Procuratorship in 1567, was a lay deputy from 1562 to 1567.

slowed the work of the tribunal and inflicted great boredom on all, in the opinion of an ex-nuncio in 1581. He felt that the inquisitor and either the nuncio's auditor or the patriarch's vicar should hear the minor cases, and the lay assistants read the accounts. In that way the accused would not have to remain in prison as long, and all members of the court would not have to listen to trifles. But he did not advocate any alteration, and the tribunal did not change its ways.[62]

Although the nuncio in 1551 reported to Rome that the lay assistants did not impose their will on the ecclesiastical members of the tribunal,[63] there can be little doubt that they had great influence. The support of the Tre Savii was so essential to the functioning of the Holy Office that the ecclesiastical members would have been unlikely to risk serious disagreement. The Tre Savii spoke for the Inquisition in the Council of Ten and other organs of government.[64] If an inquisitor incurred the displeasure of the lay deputies or the ruling patricians, the government could press Rome for his removal, as it did, successfully, in the case of Fra Felice Peretti da Montalto in 1560.[65] Nor were all the ecclesiastical members in a position to ignore government pressure: the patriarch was a noble elected by the Senate and about half the inquisitors were Venetian subjects who might hope for preferment within the Dominion. Yet it is unlikely that the lay members consistently disagreed with ecclesiastical members. Although no records survive to describe internal debates, there is every reason to believe that the six members were normally in agreement. Cleric and layman hated and feared heresy for the same reasons, whatever differences might occur over individual cases.

The liaison with the major governmental bodies provided by the Tre Savii was a channel used by both the Republic and the papacy to get favorable action. In 1568, for example, the nuncio unsuccessfully pressed the government to pursue fleeing Inquisition suspects more vigorously. After Lorenzo Da Mula, a lay deputy "most zealous" in defense of God's honor, became a Head of the Council of Ten, the nuncio anticipated action.[66] In 1569 the Capi of the Council of Ten sanctioned the interven-

---

[62] Letter of Nuncio Ludovico Beccadelli of September 5, 1551, Venice, in *Nunziature* v, 279–80; Stella, *Chiesa e stato*, pp. 290–91.

[63] Letter of Nuncio Beccadelli of September 5, 1551, in *Nunziature* v, 279.

[64] For one example of the many appearances made by the Tre Savii before the Council of Ten (this time accompanied by the nuncio), see CX, Secrete, R. 7, ff. 63ᵛ–64ʳ, October 29, 1561.

[65] See Ch. iii, sec. 8. Also, in 1558 the Council of Ten instructed the podestà of Rovigo that Gian Maria Beati (or Beato) of Rovigo, an Anabaptist, was to be granted a new trial under a new inquisitor to be sent there. CX, Secrete, R. 6, ff. 193ᵛ–94ʳ, August 18, 1558. For more on Beati, see Stella ii, 66, 74, 158.

[66] "Il clar.mo messer Lorenzo Da Mula, il quale è uno degli assistenti et dell'honor

tion of laymen into a Dominion Inquisition, an action contrary to the agreement of 1551, which banned laymen except on the inquisitor's request. The nuncio protested, and when he got little satisfaction from the Collegio, he spoke to the lay deputies, who promised to help. Eventually the doge barred the laymen; possibly the lay assistants were able to persuade him.[67] No doubt powerful nobles asked the Tre Savii to deliver messages to the nuncio and Rome as well.

Rome conceded no canonical privileges to the lay deputies. In 1552 the papacy refused them permission to read heretical books because experience had shown that the practice had injurious results and, moreover, one permission opened the door to others.[68] The refusal was consistent with papal policy; Rome had revoked previous permissions and refused new ones in the 1540s and 1550s.[69] It meant that the laymen were dependent upon the inquisitor and theological experts to judge books. It also pointed to an Index as a practical necessity.

The ecclesiastical component of the Inquisition included the father inquisitor, the nuncio, and the patriarch; these three alone had decisive votes. The nuncio's auditor and the patriarch's vicar, who often substituted for their superiors at trials, had consultative votes only. In addition, the personnel included a fiscal, a notary, and one or more commissaries, who might have particular duties, such as overseeing the printing industry, and who were sometimes attached to the nuncio's household. The Venetian inquisitor was a Franciscan until 1560, when the charge passed to the Dominicans.[70] Appointed by Rome to an unlimited term of office, an in-

---

di Dio zelantissimo, si trova di presente capo de' X, onde si può sperare qualche bene." Letter of Facchinetti of April 3, 1568, Venice, in *Nunziature* VIII, 369.

[67] Letters of Nuncio Facchinetti and Cardinal Michele Bonelli of September 3, Venice; September 10, Rome; September 14, Venice; September 24, Rome; October 1, 1569, Venice; and February 21, 1570, Venice; in *Nunziature* IX, 119–20, 122–24, 127, 132, 214.

[68] Letter of Cardinal Marcello Cervini, answering on behalf of the Congregation of the Inquisition, December 3, 1552, Rome, in *Nunziature* VI, 184–85.

[69] See letters and decrees to Gian Matteo Giberti, bishop of Verona, of February 17, 1542; to a Benedictine Congregation in Padua of July 31, 1544; a general prohibition revoking all previous permissions and denying prohibited books to everyone excepting inquisitors, of April 29, 1550; and another of December 29, 1558, in Bartolomeo Fontana, "Documenti vaticani contro l'eresia luterana in Italia," *Archivio della R. Società Romana di Storia Patria* 15 (Rome, 1892), 385, 396, 412–14, 448–50.

[70] By 1645, the Venetian state had 14 inquisitors, half of them Dominicans (Venice, Vicenza, Verona, Brescia, Bergamo, Crema, and Zara [in Dalmatia], the others Franciscans (Padua, Adria, Treviso, Ceneda, Aquileia, Belluno, and Capo d'Istria). BAVa, Ms. Vaticanus Latinus 10945, "Anima del Sant'Offitio spirata dal Sopremo Tribunale della Sacra Congregatione raccolta dal Padre Predicatore

quisitor was required to give an oath that he would obey the laws of the Republic. Periods of office averaged five years. Of the twelve men who held the office of Venetian inquisitor from 1560 through 1622, six came from the Dominion and six from elsewhere in Italy. Limited evidence suggests that the office was a stepping stone to preferment within the Venetian church, as three of the six inquisitors who were Venetian subjects moved directly from their post as Venetian inquisitor to minor bishoprics in the Dominion.[71]

The functionaries, such as the nuncio's auditor and the commissaries, played important roles in the Inquisition. They carried out directives and provided continuity when the upper clerical and lay personnel experienced rapid turnover. A good example is Monsignor Annibale Grisonio, a native of Capo d'Istria. Attached to the household of Nuncio Giovanni Della Casa (1544–49), Grisonio aided him and the inquisitor, especially with the trial and negotiations concerning Pier Paolo Vergerio. In late 1548 and early 1549, the Council of Ten authorized Grisonio to go to Capo d'Istria to assist the local inquisitor. Pleased with the results, the Council next sent him as Apostolic Commissioner to root out heresy in Pirano and Pola on the Dalmatian coast.[72]

Grisonio's zeal sometimes exceeded his judgment. In 1551 the lay deputies sharply rebuked him for wishing to change the venue for some trials of alleged heretics, informing him that violating local jurisdiction contravened the laws of the Republic and would "turn everything upside down."[73] In 1552 the nuncio heard a rumor that Rome had sent Grisonio a list of about 200 Venetian nobles, including leading figures of the government, accused of being Protestants. The horror-struck nuncio frantically inquired, and Rome assured him that, although the names of many nobles had appeared in Inquisition trials, no list had been sent to anyone. The nuncio's fears were little eased. Because of the "immoderate zeal" and "little judgment" of Grisonio and others, he warned, the papacy ran a grave risk of provoking the Venetians "to hate the pope." He was certain

---

F. Giacomo Angarano da Vicenza l'anno del Signore MDCXLIV," f. 162[r]. Despite its date, the ms. contains some material of 1645 and 1646.

[71] Adriano Valentino da Vicenza, inquisitor from 1564 to 1566, became Bishop of Capo d'Istria; Marco Medici da Verona, inquisitor from 1574 to 1578, became Bishop of Chioggia; and Giovanni Vicenzo Arrigoni (or Arrijoni), inquisitor from 1595 to 1599, became Bishop of Sebenico (or Sibenik) in Dalmatia. See SU, Bu. 153, "Elenco degli Inquisitori Domenicani 1560–1755," and HC, III, 216, 170; IV, 314.

[72] Gottfried Buschbell, *Reformation und Inquisition in Italien um die Mitte des XVI Jahrhunderts* (Paderborn, 1910), pp. 144–54, and passim; CX, Comune, R. 18, ff. 179[r], 199[r]–200[r], November 13, 1548, and January 16, 1548 mv.

[73] Letter of Nuncio Beccadelli of January 16, 1551, Venice, in *Nunziature* v, 198.

that the Venetians had not learned of the list; one can almost hear him adding a fervent "Thank God!" Should anything develop, he begged to be informed. If any nobles were suspected of heresy, they should be tried singly, not in a group. Otherwise the patriciate would be greatly agitated, and those nobles inclined to prosecute heretics would not dare do so. Apparently the papacy heeded the nuncio, for the list was not mentioned again.[74]

From mid-century the Inquisition met month after month, year after year, every Tuesday, Thursday, and Saturday (chosen to avoid conflict with civil courts) with few missed or altered dates. In summer they met in the small church of San Teodoro, contiguous with San Marco,[75] and in winter in an unnamed presbytery, probably a Franciscan house before 1560 and a Dominican canonry later. The tribunal looked forward in 1581 to the construction of its own quarters, including a prison, at a cost of 2,000 ducats, but apparently it was never built.[76]

The Holy Office had some financial difficulties, partly because according to Venetian law the confiscated property of convicted heretics (with the exception of Judaizing Christians) reverted to the state, which normally passed it on to the heirs.[77] The Council of Ten occasionally helped, but expenses kept rising.[78] In 1573 the Venetian tribunal enjoyed an annual income of 200 ducats—but still begged for help from Rome.[79] In the late 1570s the papacy put the Venetian tribunal on a more secure finan-

[74] Letters of Nuncio Beccadelli of February 27, 1552, Venice; of Cardinal Marcello Cervini, March 5, Rome; and Beccadelli, March 12, in *Nunziature* VI, 57–59, 64, 69. It is interesting that Grisonio and other unnamed commissaries of the Holy Office were at least partly independent of the nuncio's control and maintained their own communications with Rome. Padre Alvise Scortica played a role similar to Grisonio's in the 1560s, but avoided controversy.

[75] San Teodoro was located behind and to the left of the high altar of San Marco, approximately where the Sagrestia dei Canonici now stands.

[76] Stella, *Chiesa e stato*, p. 294.

[77] See the letters of the Council of Ten to the rectors of Bergamo and Brescia of November 8, 1568, and to the rector of Padua of February 20, 1577. They ordered the rectors to search out the heirs if necessary, but in no circumstances should the property revert to the guilty because it was not just that they should enjoy it. SU, Bu. 153, "Editti, lettere pubbliche e private, esposizione del Nunzio, estratti di processi, ecc. riguardanti il Santo Uffizio. Sec. XVI–XVIII," a packet of material organized chronologically. Also Stella, *Chiesa e stato*, p. 294. The Bolognese Inquisition also suffered financial difficulties despite sometimes receiving the confiscated goods of heretics. See Antonio Battistella, *Il S. Officio e la riforma religiosa in Bologna* (Bologna, 1905), pp. 34–41.

[78] CX, Comune, R. 21, ff. 91^v–92^r (March 13, 1554); R. 24, ff. 46^v, 159^r (September 22, 1559; December 19, 1560). The Council of Ten also turned down the Tre Savii at least once: R. 22, f. 2^v, March 16, 1555. The sum was 25 ducats in all cases.

[79] Letter of Cardinal Scipione Rebiba of December 5, 1573, Rome, in *Nunziature* XI, 105.

cial basis by diverting to it 300 ducats' income from Dominion benefices; that amount was increased. In 1645 the Venetian Holy Office spent 505 scudi annually on salaries for the notary and other personnel, maintenance of the church of San Teodoro and the father inquisitor's quarters, food for the prisoners, and maintenance of the prisons, including the rooms of the captain.[80] Although the Inquisition had considerably less to do than in the 1570s, inflation undoubtedly more than offset the decline in activity.

The Venetian Inquisition followed a regular procedure throughout the century.[81] On receipt of a denunciation, or evidence from a confessing heretic or witness, the tribunal held a hearing to question one or more of these. If the charges lacked foundation, the Holy Office dropped the matter, with the accused possibly unaware that he had been discussed. If the evidence warranted, the tribunal issued a summons for his arrest; if denouncer or witness had mentioned prohibited titles, the suspect's books were impounded. The tribunal then imprisoned the suspect, confined him in a monastery, or extracted an oath to appear upon request. The Inquisition occasionally tried *in absentia* a suspect who could not be found.

The trial began either with the questioning of additional witnesses or with the initial interrogation of the accused. The inquisitor normally asked the accused whether he knew why he had been arrested, and whether he had any known enemies? Rarely did the suspect blurt his culpability or give new information. The suspect should have been completely unaware of the nature of the charges and from whom they came, because all participants in trials were sworn to secrecy. But suspects frequently knew both, and it is probable that secrecy was often violated. Realizing that nothing could stop gossip, the father inquisitor was not

[80] Vaticanus Latinus 10945, ff. 74ʳ–77ʳ, 162ʳ–65ʳ.

[81] The following brief description of the operation of the Venetian Inquisition is based on my reading of all the trials in the sixteenth century and the first third of the seventeenth century dealing with books, and many heresy trials, but no more than a handful of trials dealing with demonology, witchcraft, judaizing Christians, etc. I focus on the practice in typical trials; no attempt is made to encompass extraordinary cases, or to define precisely the legal aspects. This should be done by means of a detailed comparison of the actual procedure with guides such as Giulio Masini, *Sacro arsenale overo prattica dell'Officio della Santa Inquisitione* (first published in Genoa, 1621, and many times reprinted). The Venetian Inquisition did not differ in procedure from the Bolognese Inquisition. See Battistella, *S. Officio in Bologna*, pp. 58–63, 196–97. The similarity in Inquisition procedure from city to city was the result not only of standardized guides, but also of a steady exchange of information between the Congregation in Rome and local tribunals. With a few exceptions, this correspondence does not survive in Venice, but some of the Vatican side of it is to be found in BAVa mss., *viz.* Vaticanus Latinus 10945, Barberino Latino 1369, 1370, 5195, 5205, and Borginum Latinum 558.

visibly upset. The initial questions gave the accused the opportunity to make an opening statement. He might immediately confess to all or part of the, as yet unread, charges. He could also name his personal enemies; if the accusation came from one of them, the tribunal treated it more cautiously. The Holy Office sometimes confronted an accuser with a counter-accusation and punished a false witness.[82]

The father inquisitor then systematically questioned the accused. Normally he did not reveal immediately the full extent of the charges, but proceeded step by step with questions designed to uncover specific information. He might first ask if the accused were acquainted with a heretic or a witness, or if he had lived in Protestant lands. If heretical books had been found, the accused was asked to identify them and to explain how they had come into his possession. The heart of inquisitorial procedure was shrewd and persistent interrogation. The Inquisition had the advantage of possessing information initially denied to the suspect and the right to prolong the trial until it was satisfied with the answers. The accused did not have defense counsel present, although he might request a transcript of the interrogation to prepare a written defense.[83]

The defendant had three choices: complete denial, limited and gradual admission of guilt as the father inquisitor brought new evidence to bear, or immediate confession. The most common reaction was complete denial, usually by claiming ignorance. The defendant protested that he was unacquainted with a religious dissident, that he had never visited the place where the conventicle had met, or that he had no idea how a heretical title had come into his possession. Often at this point the tribunal broke off the questioning; the suspect was escorted back to confinement, and the Holy Office went on to another case. The tribunal did not complete a trial in one sitting unless the charge was minor and easily resolved; it would return to a suspect after two or three days or a week had passed. In a complex trial where many additional witnesses had to be questioned, the Inquisition might not return to the accused for two, three, or four weeks. He normally remained in prison or other confinement during the interval.

When the interrogation resumed after the first pause, the accused often confessed complete or partial guilt, especially in minor cases, even

---

[82] Albizzi, *Risposta*, p. 336, gives five examples (1567–94) of the punishment of false witnesses by three to five years of banishment, three years in the galleys, and lesser penalties.

[83] I can find no evidence that defense counsel was present at the formal interrogations, although it is possible that the accused could discuss his case with counsel in prison.

though he had previously denied everything. Although there is no indication in the documents that in the interim the father inquisitor had visited the accused in prison to point out the evidence against him and to advise him to confess, at least to a reduced charge, it is possible that this happened. With the exception of contrite heretics who were apprehensively seeking to exchange information for clemency, the vast majority of defendants at this point still offered information grudgingly, admitting only what the tribunal already knew. The bookmen in particular continued to profess great ignorance about such fundamental points as the identity of those with whom they did business.

The case against a bookman with prohibited titles tended to be straightforward; if the tribunal possessed the evidence (i.e., the volumes), conviction and punishment followed quickly. The court was satisfied even if the bookman's explanations were implausible and were filled with lacunae (at least, the responses seem inadequate to this twentieth-century reader; it is difficult to determine how the members of the Inquisition judged them). In minor cases the tribunal seems to have wanted a quick, uncomplicated conviction and destruction of the prohibited volumes, even when it suspected that there was more to be learned. Perhaps it weighed the time and trouble involved in further probing against the probable results and decided to rest. If the evidence had disappeared, the tribunal had to be content with issuing a warning and vowing to watch the bookman in the future. Of course, when the tribunal suspected that the accused harbored heretical views in addition to books, the trial was more thorough and lengthy.

Often toward the end of the testimony, but before the decision and sentencing, the tribunal asked the defendant whether he obeyed the laws of the church. He would answer when and where he had last confessed and communicated or why he had been neglectful. The tribunal might then question his confessor or parish priest about his reception of the sacraments and his moral reputation; the confessor and pastor normally gave defendants favorable recommendations or, at least, the benefit of the doubt.

When the defendant had confessed to a minor offense, such as the possession of prohibited, but not necessarily Protestant, books, or mild heresy (i.e., had held limited heretical views but shown contrition), the trial would end without further ado. The possessor of prohibited books would be sentenced without the formality of an abjuration. For heresy, an abjuration was drawn up for the guilty person to sign. If a defendant stubbornly denied heresy in the face of damning evidence, the tribunal continued to question him. Despite his denials, a defendant could be found guilty if the evidence was strong enough.

The Inquisition could use torture, but only if various conditions were met. In 1575 the Venetian tribunal had in custody a *relapsus* who, in the opinion of the tribunal, still had not confessed all in his second abjuration. The local tribunal wrote to Rome to inquire whether torture might be used, and the Congregation of the Holy Office responded with guidelines. If a heretic spontaneously confessed his errors and named some of his accomplices, especially the major ones, he could not be tortured. But since this person in his first abjuration had repeatedly denied the truth until he saw himself convicted by letters and his own writings, he could, by law and custom, now be tortured, "but lightly," to get the whole truth of his own beliefs, the names of his confederates, and evidence against them. If the accused was so weak or ill that torture would imperil his life, it would be enough to frighten him by showing him the instrument of torture, tying him into it, and then pretending to be ready to proceed. If he was gravely ill, he could not even be frightened. As for the place and necessary personnel for torture, the Congregation advised that the Venetians had provided these in the past and would presumably do so again.[84]

In effect, the Congregation ruled that torture might be used only when substantial evidence indicated that the accused was holding back information, and only if several conditions were satisfied. Although the local tribunal could on its own initiative inflict torture, it continued to seek the advice of Rome.[85] In practice, the Venetian Inquisition used

[84] "Et che se il Donzelino da sè havesse confessato spontaneamente gli errori suoi et nominato alcuni complici, quelli massime che verissimilmente potevano esserli complici, o dei quali se n'haveva inditio, non s'esporrebbe a tormenti, *nec pro ulteriori veritate, nec pro complicibus, nec ut afficeret nominatos*, ma non havendo ciò fatto, anzi alla prima abiuratione *de vehementi* tacciuto la verità de gli errori et de' complici, et doppo piú volte negato, et finalmente vistosi convitto dalle lettere et scritture sue, haver confessato, in tal caso per ragione et per consuetudine se le deve dar corda, legiermente però, *pro ulteriori veritate, complicibus et ut dictum suum afficiat complices et nominatos ab eo.* È ben vero che, s'el reo fusse decrepito o infermo talmente che non si potesse tormentare senza pericolo, basterebbe quanto *terreretur*, presentandolo alla corda, et legandoglielo, et mostrando di volergliela dare senza levarlo, et senza procedere più oltra, et essendo gravemente infermo lasciarlo star et non minacciargliela; il che si lascia all'arbitrio de' giudici et de' periti, facendo apparer in processo la causa perchè non è stato tormentato, nè bisogna far fondamento sopra i voti di quella Congregatione che siano contrarii alle determinationi di questa, perchè quella s'ha da governar da questa et non è contra; che non s'habbiano birri nè luogo da tormentar ci par duro, però che per il passato quelli Signori sempre hanno accomodato il Santo Officio de l'un et l'altro a tal effetto, et se crede faranno il medesimo adesso, essendo ricercati." Letter of Cardinal Scipione Rebiba of January 29, 1575, Rome, in *Nunziature* XI, 318–19. For more on Girolamo Donzellini, see Ch. III, sec. 7, and Ch. VI, sec. 1.

[85] In six additional cases (five involving heresy and the other sacrilege) the

torture sparingly, perhaps in no more than 2 to 3 percent of the trials.[86] Torture was not inflicted on an ordinary heretic, but only on an unusually obstinate one, a *relapsus,* the leader of a conventicle, or a combination of all three.

The only torture employed by the Venetian Inquisition in the cinquecento was the strappado, usually called *la corda* (the rope), the standard judicial torture of both civil and ecclesiastical courts.[87] The victim's hands were tied behind his back, and he was hoisted above the ground by means of a rope fastened to his wrists. He was then abruptly dropped to a point short of the ground, wrenching and probably dislocating his shoulders. It was painful; the meticulously recorded screams of the victims testify to this. Yet, torture rarely induced the victim to change his testimony.[88] Undoubtedly the courage of the dissenters was the major reason, but there were others as well. Torture was inflicted for limited periods of time, typically from 30 to 90 minutes, although it might be repeated on the following day or days.[89] The victim realized that he did not have to hold out indefinitely. Also, men of the sixteenth century were probably more accustomed to pain than those of the twentieth

Congregation when asked for advice permitted the Inquisitions of Venice and Vicenza to use torture. The five heresy cases, unfortunately noted without the names of the accused, were similar to that of Donzellini, i.e., the heretics were *relapsi* who in the judgment of the Inquisition were holding back important information on their beliefs and confederates. Vaticanus Latinus 10945, ff. 45[r] (July 23, 1611, Venice); 58[r-v] (April 9, 11, 1579, Venice; August 20, 1588, Vicenza; April 26, 1597, Vicenza; July 10, 1599, Vicenza); 80[r] (November 14, 1587, Venice).

[86] This statement is based on my reading of the trials, although I did not make a count. The nuncio in 1585 also reported that torture had been used "rarissime volte" in the past. Nor was his hope that it might be used more frequently in the future realized. Letter of Nuncio Cesare Costa of September 21, 1585, in ASVa, Segretario di Stato, Venezia, F. 10, ff. 439[r-v]. Comba narrates the torture of a number of suspects to make the point that it was frequent. However, this was simply not the case. Emilio Comba, *I nostri Protestanti*, vol. II, *Durante la Riforma nel Veneto e nell'Istria* (Florence, 1897), pp. 617–25.

[87] For example, Machiavelli suffered six drops of the strappado at the hands of his Florentine jailors in 1513. Roberto Ridolfi, *The Life of Niccolò Machiavelli,* trans. Cecil Grayson (Chicago, 1963), p. 136. Masini, *Sacro arsenale overo prattica dell'Officiò della Santa Inquisitione* (In Bologna, MDCLXXIX, Per Gioseffo Longhi), pp. 159–62, discusses other forms of torture. But in 1635 and 1638 Rome denied permission to the Holy Office of Vicenza to use anything except the strappado. Vaticanus Latinus 10945, f. 58[v].

[88] Of course, one cannot tell how often the unspoken threat of torture prompted a confession.

[89] See, for example, the trial of Franco in Rome. Angelo Mercati, *I costituti di Niccolò Franco (1568–1570) dinanzi l'Inquisizione di Roma esistenti nell'Archivio Segreto Vaticano* (Vatican City, 1955), p. 6.

century and better able to bear it. In an age in which there was little remedy for the excruciating pain of a toothache, except the possibly greater pain of extraction, men must have built up endurance to pain. Finally, the victim might cling to the knowledge that if he withstood the torture his defense was strengthened and his trial was over. He might still be subject to severe penalty for his beliefs and deeds, but he need no longer fear betraying himself or his comrades.

Reading the trials, even from the distance of four centuries, supports the conclusion that the Venetian Inquisition was a fair-minded tribunal whose verdicts were accurate and reasonable—if not by twentieth-century standards of legal procedure and views on the rights of the defendant, certainly by sixteenth-century norms.[90] The inquisitors were persistent and thorough, but not deceitful in their questioning; they succumbed only to the temptation to lecture defendants and witnesses. Venetian nobles were treated more politely and carefully than commoners, but the difference was slight. The conclusions reached by the tribunal appear to have been supported by the evidence. Much of this concurrence stemmed from the nature of a judicial system heavily oriented toward confession. It was a system built upon the verbal testimony of witnesses who had heard the defendant speak heresy or seen him consort with heretics; once the tribunal was convinced that the witnesses spoke the truth, the accused gained little by maintaining innocence if he was culpable. Moreover, confession and contrition generated mercy; obstinacy, possibly great severity. If the defendant did stubbornly maintain his innocence, he could hope to make the tribunal uncertain. Then the trial could continue for a long time while the Inquisition sought to determine who was lying or mistaken. Even with the qualification that inquisitorial procedure was oriented toward obtaining a confession, the impression remains that the Holy Office seldom reached an unjust verdict.[91] In many trials greater guilt may have existed than what the defendant confessed. One often has the impression that the Inquisition was satisfied with a reduced plea when more could have been uncovered. Notably in the 1560s, when the tribunal had a large number of heretics and the enforcement of the Tridentine Index to deal with, it did not follow up every name uttered by a confessing heretic. Inquisition resources

[90] A comparison with a civil court, such as the Esecutori contro la bestemmia, would be interesting, but unfortunately only the conclusions survive for this tribunal.

[91] On one occasion, a man from Brescia appealed to the Venetian Inquisition, claiming that the Brescian inquisitor had unjustly confiscated his books. The Venetian tribunal agreed, and asked the Brescian inquisitor to restore them. The latter refused and appealed to Rome. The result is unknown. SU, Bu. 50, Theodoro Graziolo (June 1583).

were limited, and political considerations may also have dictated caution in some cases.

The Venetian Inquisition pronounced and executed death sentences very infrequently. Of 1,560 surviving complete and partial trials in the sixteenth century, fourteen are known to have resulted in death sentences for heresy, always by drowning.[92] These were sentences handed down and executed in Venice; the figure does not include the unknown number of death sentences emanating from Dominion Inquisitions. To the fourteen executions should be added at least four heretics who died in prison, and possibly a handful of other executions that have escaped notice.[93] Partial responsibility might be laid on Venetian shoulders for the execution in Rome of four heretics who were extradited by the Council of Ten.[94] It seems reasonable to conclude that the Venetian Inqui-

[92] The count of 1,560 trials is for the period 1541–92, and is from ASV, Indice 303, "Indici alfabetico, cronologico, e geografico dei Processi del Santo Uffizio 1541–1794."
The following executions have been noted: 1553, "un grisone annabatista" (Letter of Nuncio Ludovico Beccadelli of November 11, 1553, Venice, in *Nunziature* VI, 285); 1556, Baldo Lupetino (a well-known execution); 1562, Bartolomeo Fonzio, Giulio Gherlandi; 1565, Antonio Rizzetto, Francesco Della Sega (Stella II, 110, n. 35; Stella I, 112, 134); 1567, Publio Francesco Spinola (Letter of Nuncio Giovanni Antonio Facchinetti of February 1, 1567, Venice, in *Nunziature* VIII, 166–67); 1568, Giovanni Sambeni of Brescia (Stella II, 198); 1584, "Marco calzolaro da Dignano, Cesare cremonese stracciarolo, et Giorgio greco heretici relapsi" (Letter of Nuncio Lorenzo Campeggi of March 10, 1584, Venice, in ASVa, Segretario di Stato, Venezia, F. 25, f. 80r); 1587, Claudio Textor, Girolamo Donzellini (Stella I, 185; Bongi, *Giolito*, I, 351); 1588, Pietro Longo (see Ch. VI, sec. 1).

[93] Francesco Spiera died in prison of natural causes and remorse in 1548, and Gian Giorgio Patrizi was reported dead shortly after an interrogation of December 27, 1570, but whether he was executed or died of natural causes is unknown. Stella I, 74; II, 213. Girolamo Galateo died in 1541 at the age of about 50 after imprisonment of seven years and house confinement of four. Pietro Speziali died in prison in 1554 at the age of 76, and Fedele Vico (or Vigo) died in prison in August 1568 after undergoing torture. Comba, *I nostri Protestanti*, II, 78–79, 251, 617.

[94] Pomponio de Algerio da Nola was arrested in Padua in 1555, extradited, and burned alive in Rome in 1556. M. Rosa, "P. de A.," DBI, 2, p. 361. Teofilo Panarelli was imprisoned in Venice and hanged in Rome in 1572, but I have not located the extradition documentation. Domenico Orano, *Liberi pensatori bruciati in Roma dal xvi al xviii secolo. (Da documenti inediti dell'Arcivio di Stato in Roma)* (Rome, 1904; rpt. Livorno, 1971), pp. 45–49. Alessandro di Giacomo da Bassano was imprisoned in Gorizia, extadited in 1573, and burned alive in Rome in 1574. For the extradition, see BAVa, Ms. Barberino Latino 5195, "Raccolta di alcuni negotij, e cause spettanti alla Santa Inquisitione nella Città e Dominio Veneto. Dal principio di Clemente VIII sino al presente mese di luglio MDCXXV," f. 18r; and Albizzi, *Risposta*, p. 152; execution noted in Orano, *Liberi pensatori*, p. 54. Giordano Bruno was extradited in 1593 and burned alive in 1600.

sition was directly responsible for the deaths of at least eighteen persons, and possibly for twenty to twenty-five, in the sixteenth century.

Exact quantitative comparison with other tribunals is impossible because of the scarcity or inaccessibility of documentation, but it appears that the Venetian Holy Office dealt with heretics no more and no less severely than the Inquisitions of other Italian states outside of Rome. The figure of eighteen to twenty-five deaths can be compared with the seven known executions for heresy in Milan between 1568 and 1630, a period that excluded most of the relatively severe 1550s and 1560s.[95] In the Venetian Dominion, the Inquisition of Adria and Rovigo condemned three heretics in the second half of the cinquecento.[96] The Holy Office in Rome executed about 135 persons between 1553 and 1601,[97] but, though the Roman tribunal undoubtedly was more severe, the figure is inflated by two factors: the papacy often insisted on extradition to Rome of heretics more likely to be executed (recidivists and the obstinate), and executions for crimes other than heresy are included.[98] Neither the papacy nor the Republic were notably severe by sixteenth-century standards. Their combined annual total of executions for heresy, and perhaps the annual total for all of Italy, did not equal the number of executions that occurred when Thomas Cromwell enforced Henry VIII's religious settlement and Mary Tudor tried to undo it.[99]

Italian Inquisitions exercised great restraint compared to civil tribunals. The Council of Ten and various other Venetian civil courts executed 168 persons in the cinquecento, always through decapitation or hanging. Nobles and commoners, local residents and other Italians, suffered the extreme penalty. Convicted thieves and murderers accounted

[95] Mario Bendiscioli, "Fermenti ereticali e repressione controriformista. Gli ebrei," in *Storia di Milano*, vol. x (Milan, 1957), p. 298.

[96] Adria is near the mouth of the Po river, Rovigo is 20 kilometers west. Gino Marchi, *La Riforma Tridentina in diocesi di Adria nel secolo XVI col sussidio di fonti inedite* (Rovigo, 1946), p. 259.

[97] See the documents printed by Orano, *Liberi pensatori*, and Luigi Firpo, "Esecuzioni capitali in Roma (1567–1671)," in *Eresia e Riforma nell'Italia del Cinquecento* (Florence and Chicago, 1974), 309–42.

[98] The documents list executions for homicide, necromancy, sacrilege, falsifying apostolic bulls, and pasquinades against a pope, as well as many without clear charges.

[99] For the period 1542–50, Elton counts 308 executions for treason in England, Wales, and Calais. Disputing the king's religious settlement was defined as treason by the Treason Act of 1534, and was the primary cause of executions. Nearly 300 victims lost their lives for religious reasons during Mary's reign, 1553–58. G. R. Elton, *Policy and Police: The Enforcement of the Reformation in the Age of Thomas Cromwell* (Cambridge, 1972), p. 388; J. D. Mackie, *The Earlier Tudors 1485–1558* (Oxford, 1952), p. 552.

for the largest number of Venetian executions, followed by rebels and traitors, a dozen sodomites (including several clergymen), and a few blasphemers. A handful suffered death for other reasons; one man and his wife were hanged for stealing clothes from the dead during the Great Plague of 1575–77.[100] Yet, Venetian courts were far from harsh by Renaissance standards. The much smaller princedom of Ferrara carried out 293 executions between 1441 and 1500, when the city's population ranged from 30,000 to 35,000.[101] Geneva, with a population of 18,000 to 20,000, put to death twelve men and two women in 1562: three men for raping children, three murderers, three thieves, two homosexuals, one counterfeiter, and two witches.[102]

The Venetian Holy Office drowned its victims secretly. The condemned person was taken out to sea at night, bound, and dropped into the water. In this way the Venetians hoped to avoid antagonizing Protestant rulers; secret executions attracted no attention and easily could be denied. In November 1553 the Inquisition condemned to death an unrepentant Anabaptist from the Grisons. Some members of the government hesitated for fear of offending the Grisons, but, as a result of the persuasive efforts of the lay deputies, the Anabaptist was drowned secretly by night.[103] Similarly, in February 1567, the nuncio requested a public execution by fire of a relapsed and obstinate heretic from Milan.

[100] Newberry Library, Chicago, Case/MS/6A/34, "Vollume de' Giustiziati in Venezia," ff. 10–22. (Essentially the same information can be found in VM, Mss. Italiani, Classe VII, 437[7678]; 1596[7712]; 1717[8683]; 1794[7678]; 2499[11906]; but a detailed comparison has not been made.) E. W. Monter, "La sodomie à l'époque moderne en Suisse romande," *Annales: Économies, Sociétés, Civilisations* 29 (1974), 1,025, n. 8, brought the Newberry manuscript to my attention. It gives a brief summary of Venetian civil executions (but no Inquisition executions) from 803 through 1775, listing the victim's name, sometimes his age, and always the date, method of execution, and sentencing body, most often the Council of Ten. However, because the charge is not always given, a complete analysis of the reasons for condemnation is not possible. Although I have not made a systematic search, enough executions have been confirmed from other sources to suggest that the ms. is reasonably complete for the second half of the cinquecento. But this may not be true for earlier periods. For example, the ms. lists only 33 executions in the trecento in comparison to 29 for homicide and theft alone in the 1350s and 1360s noted by Stanley Chojnacki, "Crime, Punishment, and the Trecento Venetian State," in Lauro Martines ed., *Violence and Civil Disorder in Italian Cities 1200–1500* (Berkeley, Los Angeles, and London, 1972), pp. 224–25.

[101] Werner L. Gundersheimer, "Crime and Punishment in Ferrara, 1440–1500," in Martines ed., *Violence and Civil Disorder*, pp. 110–113.

[102] E. William Monter, "Crime and Punishment in Calvin's Geneva, 1562," *Archiv für Reformationsgeschichte* 64 (1973), 283.

[103] Letter of Nuncio Beccadelli, November 11, 1553, Venice, in *Nunziature* VI, 285.

He addressed a shrewd appeal to the Venetians, arguing that a public execution would hearten the Catholics of Flanders and France and disprove the Huguenot claim that Venice was a friend of Protestants. The appeal found support, but not enough; the nuncio accepted the counsel of a patrician who warned that a dispute would take weeks and months to settle, during which time the prisoner might escape, and advised that immediate drowning was better.[104]

Light punishment and commutation, rather than severity, marked the Venetian Inquisition. Public penances, forced donations to charity, imprisonment for a few years, or a combination of all three were common; the tribunal only occasionally issued long or perpetual prison terms. Although governmental press legislation often specified heavy penalties of 50 to 100 ducats for violations, the Inquisition almost always assessed lighter fines, such as 10 ducats. Humanitarianism often moved both the tribunal and the government. In 1566, for example, Rome desired the public execution in Brescia of a relapsed heretic to frighten others. The Venetians resisted, arguing that God had preserved the life of the old man through ten years' imprisonment and would not want him executed. After six months of negotiations, it was agreed that if the heretic would recant for a second time, his sentence would be commuted to life imprisonment. He did, and his life was spared.[105] Commutation was frequent; a long prison sentence might be shortened, and a short one commuted to house arrest. For example, an abjured heretic sentenced to perpetual imprisonment in 1580 was free within three years and, perhaps conscience-stricken, openly professing heresy again within six. Arrested again in 1587, he refused to recant and went willingly to death by drowning.[106]

The insecurity of prisons also mitigated the tribunal's severity; within eighteen months in 1567–68, Inquisition prisoners escaped from civil or church prisons in Conegliano, Udine, and Venice itself. The Venetians had no more success in holding their prisoners than Inquisitions elsewhere in Italy.[107]

[104] The condemned heretic was Publio Francesco Spinola. Letter of Nuncio Facchinetti, February 1, 1567, Venice, in *Nunziature* VIII, 166–67.

[105] Letters of July 6 through December 21, 1566, Venice and Rome, in *Nunziature* VIII, 71, 99, 103, 105, 110, 113, 115, 121–22, 126–27, 130–32, 137, 139, 149. The heretic's name is not given.

[106] This was Claudio Textor; Stella I, 158–85.

[107] See letters of Nuncio Facchinetti of February 14, May 3, 1567, and October 30, 1568, Venice, in *Nunziature* VIII, 173, 208–9, 451. Two additional escapes from prisons in Venice and Verona are noted by Cardinal Scipione Rebiba in his letter of September 3, 1575, Rome, in *Nunziature* XI, 412. The Bolognese Inquisition also mitigated sentences frequently and had the same problem of insecure prisons.

Requests for extradition of Inquisition prisoners seldom failed to provoke dissent within the government and to manifest the political, religious, and personal factors that marked religious policy and relations with the papacy. A few examples will have to suffice for a large topic. In May 1558 Paul IV requested the extradition of Francesco Stella of Portobuffolè (a small village near Pordenone, north of Treviso), a physician with a long history of involvement with Protestantism in Friuli. In four motions the Council of Ten could not agree either to extradite or to hold him. A week later another motion for extradition, which hinted that additional information had been received, passed. Nevertheless, Stella was not extradited but held in prison. Two years later, Pius IV, whose relations with Venice were more cordial, tried again, and after much correspondence may have succeeded.[108] Suspects with blood ties to the nobility were normally not extradited. In June 1567 Rome requested extradition of a Paduan monk, one Francesco Contarini, a bastard nephew of the late Cardinal Gasparo, who was accused of denying the immortality of the soul. His relatives successfully intervened so that he might be tried by the Paduan Inquisition.[109]

In extradition as in other aspects of Venetian religious policy, circumstances were as important as jurisdictional principles. In 1561, on behalf of the Inquisition in Rome, the Venetians arrested Guido Giannetti da Fano, who for many years was in the service of the English crown. Elizabeth I asked the Venetians not to extradite, threatening commercial reprisals. Caught between the queen and the pope, the Venetians wrote to Rome that Giannetti was ill and could not be moved; eventually he was released. In July 1566, with fresh evidence, Rome requested that Giannetti, now living in Padua, be arrested and extradited. After sharp exchanges and vigorous negotiation, he was extradited in August to Rome, where he abjured and was sentenced to perpetual imprisonment.

Different circumstances explain why Giannetti was not extradited in 1561 but was in 1566. Powerful Venetian nobles supported and opposed

---

Battistella, *S. Officio in Bologna*, pp. 77–83, 33. For escapes in Milan and Ferrara, as well as the recognition of the problem by the authorities, see Domenico Maselli, "Per la storia religiosa dello Stato di Milano durante il dominio di Filippo II: l'eresia e la sua repressione dal 1555 al 1584," *Nuova rivista storica* 54 (1970), 356–57.

[108] CX, Secrete, R. 6, f. 192^r; Paschini, *L'Inquisizione*, pp. 123–24. Albizzi, whose information on extradition is generally accurate, reports that Stella was extradited, but his eventual fate is unknown. *Risposta*, p. 152.

[109] CX, Secrete, R. 8, f. 88^{r-v} (June 16, 1567); and letters of June 7, 14, 21, Venice, and June 14, Rome, in *Nunziature* VIII, 226–27, 231–33. Also see Paschini, *L'Inquisizione*, pp. 22–23; and Stella II, 107, n. 30; I, 32, n. 86.

extradition on both occasions. The Venetians argued that if they permitted a subject to be deported others would not feel secure; the papacy held that Giannetti, born in Fano, should be considered a papal subject. However, Pius V and his nuncio had more damaging evidence against Giannetti and pursued the matter more vigorously than had Pius IV and his nuncio. Also, in 1566, Elizabeth was no longer believed to be wavering between Catholic and Protestant worlds, and Venetian diplomatic relations with England had lapsed.[110]

By mid-century a renewed Venetian Inquisition had been established and was in operation. Papacy and Republic had worked out the terms of reference for a tribunal that would satisfy the papal demand for effective prosecution of heresy and the Venetian insistence on local control. Paul III conceived the Roman Inquisition to be a tribunal guided by Rome and assisted by the state, an unrealizeable goal unless church and state were in substantial agreement. At mid-century, as at every point in the following fifty years, the Inquisition's vigor reflected the support that the patriciate was willing to grant it. This, in turn, depended on how the Venetians balanced the imperatives of God, papacy, local church, and the world. The Venetians had left behind the relative unconcern for heresy of the 1530s and early 1540s, and had authorized moderate Inquisitorial prosecution; they still had not attained the zeal of the 1560s.

[110] Aldo Stella, "Guido da Fano eretico del secolo XVI al servizio dei re d'Inghilterra," *Rivista di storia della chiesa in Italia* 13 (1959), 196–238. Another complex extradition dispute concerned Raffaele Maffei, Servite prior to the monastery of S. Giacomo della Giudecca, who was eventually extradited. See letters of June 21, 28, July 12, 19, 1567, Venice, and July 5, Rome, in *Nunziature* VIII, 234, 238–39, 245, 246, 249. Two other cases in which extradition was denied are in CX, Secrete, R. 6, f. 193ᵛ, July 28, 1558, and R. 7, ff. 36ʳ⁻ᵛ, October 30, 1560. Also see Carlo De Frede, "L'estradizione degli eretici dal Dominio veneziano nel Cinquecento," *Atti dell' Accademia Pontaniana*, n. s., 20 (1970–71), 255–86.

III

THE GROWTH OF CENSORSHIP

1. RENAISSANCE ATTITUDES TOWARD CENSORSHIP

CENSORSHIP is an old question. Italians in the cinquecento considered it against a background of discussion that went back to both classical and Christian antiquity. That censorship is necessary to prevent man from straying from the paths of truth and goodness and that a tribunal is needed to punish the unbeliever are ideas found in ancient Greece. Plato worried that poets might lead men away from the true and good, with resultant harm to individuals and society. The state judged what was good and exercised prepublication censorship to insure that only poetry that praised the good appeared. Plato also held that since belief in the gods was both demonstrable and fundamental to the welfare of the community those who denied their existence must be punished, with perpetual incarceration or death in some circumstances. He urged citizens to aid the authorities in repressing the wrongdoing of others.[1]

In the New Testament the only mention of book burning occurs in the story of the new Christians of Ephesus, who voluntarily burned their books of magic (Acts 19:19). A number of passages attack false teachers and exhort church leaders to guard against false doctrines; these could be used to justify censorship as a defense against error.[2] But they are few in comparison to the many that teach God's love of all sinners and urge man to forgive his erring neighbor.

As the church emerged from patristic times into the Middle Ages, it concluded that heresy had no rights, and that souls had to be protected against pernicious doctrine—by force if necessary. St. Augustine's advocacy of coercion against the Donatists lent support to this position. Theologians held that the church had the right to prohibit books; although in practice the church condemned titles and authors only infrequently, and then normally only when confronted by an active heresy.[3] But Christians did

---

[1] *Republic*, Bk. II, 377 through III, 396; *Laws*, II, 662; V, 730; VII, 801–2, 817; X, 907–9. The Loeb Classical Library texts are used.

[2] Galatians 1: 6–9; I Timothy 1: 3–7, 19–20; 4: 1–3; Titus 1: 10–16; II Peter 2: 1–22; II John 1: 7–11; Jude, passim.

[3] Surveys of censorship during the patristic and medieval periods are found in

not necessarily hold the Platonic view that the true and the good were one, so there was room for discussion on alleged immoral literature. Was a particular book, indeed, vicious, or did its beneficial effect balance or outweigh its evil influence? Much depended on how the reader understood what he read.

Italians of the early Renaissance inherited these views. They would not have advocated reading heretical literature had the question arisen, but the pressing issue was different: should pagan literature that portrayed vice attractively and might have a harmful moral effect on the reader be permitted? Humanists and others leaped to refute the charge that pagan classical literature endangered souls. From the clash of opinion developed two approaches toward censorship that ultimately influenced the Indices of the cinquecento.

Giovanni Boccaccio (1313–75) in Books XIV and XV of his *Genealogia deorum gentilium* rejected Plato's banishment of poets and the argument from Christian antiquity (especially from St. Jerome) that poetry was sinful. Nevertheless, he suggested some caution in his long and eloquent defense. He acknowledged that it was better to read sacred literature and that those who did so were more acceptable to God and the church. In defending the poets against Plato, he opined that some unnamed lascivious "comic poets" should be condemned. Boccaccio also believed that not everyone could emerge unscathed from reading about pagan superstitions and sacrilegious cults, but he called upon the church's authority to ban harmful literature to justify the reading of such books. If it were necessary for everyone to avoid this subject matter, the church would have issued a perpetual prohibition. Indeed, the early church had banned it for fear that Christians would slip back into paganism. Since that danger was past, and the church strong, these topics could be studied freely.[4]

Humanists began to refer to the *Exhortation to Youths as to How They Shall Best Profit by the Writings of Pagan Authors* of St. Basil the Great (c. 330–79).[5] St. Basil warmly endorsed pagan literature because it taught virtue and prepared the mind for the study of Holy Scripture. He believed that the study of the pagan classics was generally morally beneficial; to

---

Reusch, *Index*, I, 8–45; and Francescantonio Zaccaria, *Storia polemica della proibizioni de' libri* (Rome, 1777), pp. 1–130.

[4] The English translation is used: *Boccaccio on Poetry: Being the Preface and the Fourteenth and Fifteenth Books of Boccaccio's 'Genealogia Deorum Gentilium' in an English Version with Introductory Essay and Commentary*, trans. Charles S. Osgood (Princeton, N. J., 1930), Bk. XIV, ch. 18, p. 82; XIV, 19, pp. 93–94; XV, ch. 9, pp. 123–24. Since the *Genealogia* was composed over a long period, it is impossible to give it a precise date.

[5] St. Basil, *Letters* (Loeb ed.), IV, pp. 363–435.

illustrate, he demonstrated how they taught virtue through allegory. The latter part of his treatise exhorted men to reject sensual pleasure in favor of virtue; again he made copious references to the pagan authors to support his argument. Basil pleaded for the pagan authors chiefly on ethical grounds, but he also communicated his deep love for their intrinsic beauty. His only caution was selectivity; the reader should cherish and imitate the pagans when they taught virtue, but not when they elevated wickedness. Leonardo Bruni (c. 1370–1444) translated the treatise into Latin between 1400 and 1403, with a dedication to Coluccio Salutati.[6] Humanists and others warmly received Basil's message, both in Bruni's translation and the original Greek, in the following two centuries.

St. Basil's treatise provided quattrocento humanists with the terms of reference for their defense of pagan literature. Coluccio Salutati (c. 1330–1406) defended the reading of the pagan classics with the argument that ancient letters clearly condemned vice and encouraged virtue. One should read Old Testament adulteries and murders allegorically, so also the poets. Salutati emphasized the importance of the reader's attitude. There was nothing in human action so pure that man could not turn it to an evil end, and conversely, Salutati implied, one could learn virtue from the most lascivious poet.[7] In his *De liberorum educatione* (1449) Aeneas Sylvius Piccolomini (1405–64) held the same view. Closely following St. Basil, he argued that when one reads the ancient authors one should "absorb the things of life and beauty, leaving that which is but idolatry, error, or lust, to pass to its natural decay." Erroneous beliefs and defective morals should be ignored and exhortations to virtue heeded. To be sure, the works of authors like Juvenal, and some works of Ovid, were not suitable for young minds. But Piccolomini advocated an open approach. He asked rhetorically, "If we are to reject the great writers of antiquity for the errors they contain, how shall we treat the masters of theology? From them proceeded the heresies."[8]

Battista Guarino (1425–1513) argued similarly in his *De ordine docendi et studendi* (1459): one should focus on the underlying truths of the

---

[6] Hans Baron, ed., *Leonardo Bruni Aretino Humanistisch-Philosophische Schriften mit einer Chronologie seiner Werke und Briefe* (Leipzig-Berlin, 1928), pp. 99–100, 160–61.

[7] Letter to Fra Giovanni da San Miniato of January 25, 1406, in *Epistolario di Coluccio Salutati*, ed. Francesco Novati (Fonti per la Storia d'Italia, Epistolari secolo xiv–xv), vol. IV, pt. I (Rome, 1905), pp. 170–205, esp. pp. 195–98. English translation in Ephraim Emerton, *Humanism and Tyranny: Studies in the Italian Trecento* (Cambridge, Mass., 1925), pp. 312–41, esp. pp. 331–35.

[8] As translated in William H. Woodward, *Vittorino da Feltre and Other Humanist Educators* (Cambridge, 1897; rpt. New York, 1963, with a foreword by Eugene F. Rice, Jr.), pp. 149–50.

classical authors and not be disturbed by the surface cruelties and impieties. Like Piccolomini, Guarino did not think that Ovid, with the exception of the *Metamorphoseos*, was suitable for the classroom, but he defended Juvenal's *Satires* as acceptable.[9] Maffeo Vegio da Lodi (1407–58), a humanist who joined the Augustinian Order in 1455, voiced the usual cautions about the possible moral dangers of some classical literature in his *De educatione liberorum* (composed, 1445–48). He suggested that the teacher carefully check poets and historians before assigning them to students. He warned against the violence and corrupting amusements in Vergil and, similarly, suggested caution with regard to modern poets.[10]

Although not a humanist, the great preacher San Bernardino da Siena (1380–1444) shared humanistic views. In a sermon delivered in Florence on February 20, 1425, he advised students to avoid "dishonest books," like those of Ovid, and *Il Corbaccio* and other unnamed titles of Boccaccio, recommending in their place Dante, Petrarch, and Salutati, as well as Scripture and the church fathers. The reason for the caution was the usual one: to avoid imitating the vice attractively described. Yet, these were minor cautions in a long sermon that endorsed scholarship and showed a favorable attitude toward humanistic studies.[11]

Quattrocento humanists held that learning led to virtue. The aim of much humanistic writing was to stimulate the positive moral development of the individual, especially the young person. The humanists had an optimistic view of human potentiality: man would normally do what was right if powerful enough verbal imagery moved his will.[12] They universally believed that the pagan authors taken as a whole exercised an enormously beneficial moral influence, although a few individual titles raised occasional doubts. It was the responsibility of teachers and parents to protect the young by denying them some texts. The humanists did not prescribe censorship for adults and, after Boccaccio, did not defer to ecclesiastical authority when the question arose. Since the humanists held that divine and secular studies were basically complementary, they did not fear pagan literature and saw small cause for censorship.

Although dominant, the humanist approach was not the only one. Giovanni Dominici (1356–1420), a Dominican cardinal and Salutati's

---

[9] Woodward, *Vittorino da Feltre*, pp. 170–71.

[10] Mapheus Vegius, *Maphei Vegii Laudensis . . . opera . . . quarum prior de educatione liberorum lib. vi. . . . Pars prima.* (Laudae [Lodi], Ex Typographia Bertoeti, MDCXIII), Bk. II, ch. 19, p. 74; Bk. III, ch. 2, pp. 82–83.

[11] His sermon, "Lo studio," in St. Bernardino da Siena, *Le prediche volgari inedite, Firenze 1424, 1425–Siena 1425*, ed. P. Dionisio, O.F.M. (Siena, 1935), pp. 197–98.

[12] Charles Trinkaus, *In Our Image and Likeness: Humanity and Divinity in Italian Humanist Thought* (Chicago, 1970), II, 771.

antagonist, argued that pagan literature had no value in comparison to Holy Scripture and could be harmful. He warned against Ovid and Vergil because they seduced young readers away from virtue to carnality, from the one God to false gods. Read Holy Scripture and ignore the rest, he advised.[13]

Dominici's specific prohibitions were less significant than his attitude. If secular learning was valueless and pagan literature harmful, it followed that some books ought to be prohibited and destroyed. At the end of the quattrocento, Girolamo Savonarola and his Florentine supporters reached this conclusion and acted on it. For Savonarola, all human knowledge paled in comparison to the knowledge of God. He judged some contemporary poetry as vain and vicious, and he distrusted the humanistic enthusiasm for the classics. At the "burning of vanities" in Florence on February 7, 1497, Savonarola's followers destroyed works of Boccaccio and Petrarch, Pulci's *Morgante* and other chivalric works, books of magic and superstition, and books containing obscene pictures.[14] The Florentine book-burning was short-lived but significant for future censorship. Savonarola joined uncompromising reformist zeal with distrust for secular learning, and he and his followers acted against what they considered to be offensive books.

At the same time that he burnt morally objectionable books, Savonarola skillfully used the press to spread his own message. The Florentine printers produced at least 150 editions of his pamphlets and manifestoes in the years between his arrival in Florence in 1489 and his execution in 1498. Before Erasmus and Luther, Savonarola seized the opportunity offered by the press to challenge the papacy and disseminate a program of religious reform.

Desire for reform and distrust of secular learning produced a recommendation for prepublication press censorship from Tommaso Giustiniani and Vincenzo Querini. In a joint memorandum addressed to the newly elected Leo X (March 11, 1513), they condemned the failure of church leadership and aired other problems, including the low educational level of the clergy.[15] They charged that thousands of clergymen did not know

---

[13] From his *Regola del governo di cura familiare*, as cited in the selection in *Prosatori volgari del Quattrocento*, ed. Claudio Varese, La Letteratura Italiana, Storia e Testi, vol. 14 (Milan and Naples, 1955), pp. 27–29. Varese provides no date for the treatise.

[14] Joseph Schnitzer, *Savonarola*, trans., Ernesto Rutili (Milan, 1931), II, 342, 345–46; I, 443–44. For Savonarola's use of the press for his own purposes, see Victor Scholderer, "Printers and Readers in Italy in the Fifteenth Century," *Proceedings of the British Academy* 35 (1949), 34–35.

[15] Their "Libellus ad Leonem X" is in *Annales Camaldulenses*, ed. J. B. Mittarelli and A. Costadini, vol. 9 (Venice, 1773), pp. 612–719, esp. pp. 675–81. These

how to read or write and that only a handful knew any Latin. They thought the learned clergy too occupied with the lies of the poets and the impieties of the philosophers. Giustiniani and Querini urged priests to acquire enough Latin to study Holy Scripture and then to limit themselves to sacred studies in the original texts, avoiding modern commentaries and humanistic studies. The two reformers distrusted the printing press and believed that the publication of fewer books would help to advance their objectives. They urged the pope to appoint a committee of learned men to grant, and restrict, permissions to publish.

Gianfrancesco Pico (1469–1533) held views similar to those of Giustiniani and Querini. His famous uncle, Giovanni Pico, had under the influence of Savonarola turned increasingly to Scripture and prayer, and away from secular intellectual pursuits, in the last years of his life. Gianfrancesco, a devoted follower of Savonarola, launched a general attack on secular learning. In his view, there was "an unbridgeable chasm between the truth of the Christian religion and the falsehoods of all other religions, philosophies, arts, and sciences. Non-Christian attempts at knowledge in no way approach[ed] the truth, but [were] completely misdirected."[16] In his early work, *De studio divinae et humanae philosophiae* (1496), he argued that philosophy and the liberal arts were in no way necessary for salvation, and were of limited value generally. One might try to convince heretics by the learned way of his uncle, but one would have more success by teaching them the path of Christian simplicity described by Savonarola. In his *Examen vanitatis doctrinae gentium* (1520), Gianfrancesco discredited all knowledge except Scripture. Philosophy was useful only to destroy arguments against Christianity. The liberal arts, instead of leading to truth, certitude, and wisdom, produced falsity, ambiguity, and controversy. Gianfrancesco desperately wanted a divine learning uncontaminated by secular studies. In his judgment, heresy had intruded itself into the history of Christianity because the Scriptures had been adulterated by pagan learning and because vanity had turned men away from the faith. Gianfrancesco recommended simple faith, and believed that only divine revelation guided by Scripture could lead men to God. Like Giustiniani and Querini, Gianfrancesco was dedicated to church reform; he addressed an oration on the subject to the Fifth Lateran Council.

---

passages are also summarized by Felix Gilbert, "Cristianesimo, Umanesimo e la Bolla 'Apostolici Regiminis' del 1513," *Rivista storica italiana* 79 (1967), 985–86. Gilbert gives no date but notes that it was for the newly elected pope.

[16] Charles B. Schmitt, "Gianfrancesco Pico della Mirandola and the Fifth Lateran Council," *Archiv für Reformationsgeschichte* 61 (1970), 161–78, quote on p. 163. For the following, see Schmitt, *Gianfrancesco Pico della Mirandola (1469–1533) and His Critique of Aristotle* (The Hague, 1967), pp. 37–54.

The Council heeded the criticism of secular learning and pleas for censorship. The bull *Apostolici regiminis* of December 19, 1513, condemned the opinion that the soul is mortal, as well as other propositions of secular Aristotelianism. *Inter sollicitudines* of May 3, 1515, proclaimed a universal, but vague, press censorship.[17] The bull noted that books containing doctrinal error and material contrary to Christian religion, or against the good names of individuals, had been published. Therefore, a system of universal prepublication censorship would be exercised in Rome by the Master of the Sacred Palace (the pope's personal theologian) and the cardinal-vicar, and by local bishops and inquisitors elsewhere. Printers who failed to obtain permission before publishing were liable to excommunication and fines of 100 ducats, the proceeds to go toward the building of St. Peter's. Since the bull was an expression of concern rather than a serious attempt to initiate censorship, it is highly unlikely that it aided St. Peter's.

Contrasting attitudes of broad tolerance for all secular learning and concern that the pagan classics might seduce men from Christian paths sometimes existed uneasily in the same minds. Neither Querini, Giustiniani, nor Gianfrancesco Pico were ignorant of the classics that they distrusted, and Savonarola's call for reform attracted some prominent humanists. Many Europeans hailed the invention of the printing press as an aid to the dissemination of learning, but some worried about its enormous power to propagate error as well as truth.

Whether such unease about the press would have led to effective press censorship without the Protesant Reformation is conjectural, for within a few months of the conclusion of the Fifth Lateran Council, Luther posted his theses on the door of a Wittenberg church. His condemnation as a heretic followed; and, when Italians eventually perceived that heresy was spreading in Italy, they agreed to destroy Protestant books. No one argued that heretical books should be read by any believer except the theologian authorized to refute them.

Nevertheless, the contrasting humanist and reformist positions toward pagan literature and secular learning touched censorship discussions. The two attitudes influenced the resolution of such practical questions as whether an individual title should be banned, and what general principles should guide the drafting of an Index? Both the internal contra-

[17] *Conciliorum oecumenicorum decreta*, ed. J. Alberigo, P-P. Joannow et al. (Freiburg im Breisgau, 1962), pp. 581–82, 608–09. Also see Rudolf Hirsch, "Bulla Super Impressione Librorum, 1515," *Gutenberg-Jahrbuch 1973*, pp. 248–51. Pico certainly, and Giustiniani and Querini probably, had a hand in *Apostolici regiminis* (Gilbert, "Cristianesimo, Umanesimo," pp. 979–80, 986–87), but it is not known what role, if any, the three played in drafting *Inter sollicitudines*.

dictions within Indices and the manner of enforcement were partially traceable to the differing approaches.

Clergy and laymen more persuaded by the tolerant humanistic view tended to permit the individual to read almost anything short of unequivocal heresy. They agreed that the reader could extract what was good from a text, and they protested what they perceived to be censorial excess. Inquisition defendants trying to explain why they possessed banned titles and bookmen protesting the restrictions of a new Index echoed humanistic arguments. Leading churchmen of pronounced humanist outlook judged the Index and Inquisition to be of limited efficacy in saving souls. Cardinal Girolamo Seripando (1492/3–1563) did not believe that the Index and Inquisition could restore lost lands to the church or by themselves maintain its position. Catholics would, in his opinion, have to prove their superiority in such areas as biblical studies and church history.[18]

Still a minority at the time of the Fifth Lateran Council, but growing in strength in the succeeding decades, reformers inclined toward strict censorship. Not humanistic studies, but personal sanctification and the dedicated practice of works of charity were at the center of the programs of the religious societies founded or renewed in the early cinquecento. The successors of Querini and Giustiniani favored a restrictive Index and a severe Inquisition, and were insensitive to the damage that these might do to learning. Paul IV was well acquainted with the Latin and Greek classics, but promulgated an Index that denied Italians many northern European humanistic and scientific titles, not because they were heretical, but because they were authored by Protestants. The pleas of Italian scholars that his Index would do great harm to their work failed to move him. Once it was accepted that "Erasmus laid the egg that Luther hatched," the works of the Dutch humanist were prohibited and destroyed with a vengeance. The stern moralism and dedication to church renewal of early cinquecento reformers tended to become the puritanical censorship of the post-Tridentine period.

At the same time, the contrast between humanistic and reformist approaches to censorship should not be exaggerated or viewed as mutually exclusive. Major figures in church reform like Cardinal Seripando adopted both as circumstances warranted. Dedicated popes wanted both to destroy heretical books and to wrest leadership in religious and secular scholarship from the Protestants. In the second half of the cinquecento, the papacy reformed the calendar, prepared critical editions of the Greek fathers— and expurgated Castiglione's *Courtier*. Events overshadowed all, and moved Italians to promulgate and accept relatively severe censorship, but the more tolerant attitude never disappeared.

[18] Jedin, *Seripando*, pp. 554–55.

2. EARLY ATTEMPTS AT PRESS CENSORSHIP

German ecclesiastical and civil authorities first attempted to censor the press. In 1475 an anti-Semitic tract printed in Esslingen carried the notation that it had been submitted to the bishop of Regensburg for corrections and approval. The first prosecution for alleged misuse of the press was instigated in 1478 by the city council of Cologne in an effort to punish a printer for publishing a book critical of the council. The archbishop of Mainz followed in 1485 with a general decree authorizing the establishment of prepublication censorship by professors at the universities of Mainz and Erfurt of all translations from Greek and Latin. Violators would be excommunicated and fined 100 guilders, and the books confiscated. He also decreed a presale inspection of the books exhibited at the Frankfurt book fair. The decree was repeated in 1486 and 1487, but the degree of implementation, if any, is unknown.[19]

The papacy, acting in its role of spiritual leader, alerted Europe to the dangers of misuse of the new invention. In 1479 Sixtus IV addressed a letter to the rectors of the University of Cologne authorizing them to use ecclesiastical censures against the printers, purchasers, and readers of heretical and erroneous books. In a bull of 1487 Innocent VIII judged the printer's art to be useful when it multiplied good books but perverse when it spread wicked doctrine. He warned the Master of the Sacred Palace and diocesan ordinaries in all Christian lands to watch diligently lest heretical, impious, and scandalous books be published. He decreed excommunication, fines, and book burning as punishments for evildoers, and asked the secular arm for support.[20] He banned Pedro de Gui's *Ianua artis Raimundi Lulli* (Barcelona, 1482) in 1483,[21] and the nine hundred theses (Rome, 1486) of Giovanni Pico della Mirandola in 1487. Alexander VI in 1501 and, as previously noted, Leo X in 1515, issued additional bulls authorizing universal censorship. There was no sense of alarm or urgency in any of these proclamations. In its approach to the press, the papacy followed the medieval pattern of exercising censorship over the expression of doctrine by issuing general guidelines and by occasionally banning a work.

Local Venetian ecclesiastical authorities engaged in a few acts of censorship limited in scope. Niccolò Franco, Bishop of Treviso and papal legate to the Republic, ordered in 1491 that books dealing with doctrine and

[19] Rudolf Hirsch, "Pre-Reformation Censorship of Printed Books," *Library Chronicle* 21 (1955), 100–105; and *Printing*, pp. 87–90. Pasquale Lopez, *Sul libro a stampa e le origini della censura ecclesiastica* (Naples, 1972), surveys early examples of censorship.

[20] Hilgers, *Index*, pp. 479–82, prints the letter of 1479 and the bull of 1487.

[21] Pierina Fontana, "Per la storia della censura pontificia. Il primo caso di sequestro di un libro a stampa," *Accademie e biblioteche d'Italia* 5 (1932), 470–75.

ecclesiastical matters had to have the permission of the ordinary or his vicar. He also ordered two titles burnt: Antonio Roselli's *Monarchia sive de potestate imperatoris et papae* (Venice, 1487) and Pico's nine hundred theses. There is no evidence that his decrees were put into effect.[22] On the other hand, Patriarch Tommaso Donà in 1497 threatened Luc'Antonio Giunti (the elder) with excommunication if he would not modify nude figures in his new edition of Ovid's *Metamorphoseos*. Giunti complied by retouching genital organs and coloring the figures; subsequent printings of 1501 and 1508 carried more modest illustrations. In 1510 Patriarch Antonio Contarini issued a general decree to the bookmen prohibiting immoral illustrations and demanding that Scriptural commentaries be shown to him before publication.[23]

Despite the book burning of Savonarola and the concern of church reformers, the traditional approach of limited censorship seemed adequate for the press. Ecclesiastical and civil authorities were content to see the new invention as a more efficient copier of manuscripts—until Martin Luther demonstrated its revolutionary capability.

From the early days of the Reformation, Italians and foreigners imported Protestant books into Italy. Scholars procured them in northern Europe and brought them back. The books of the Reformers entered Lucca c. 1525 in the baggage of the city's silk merchants, and helped to found and nourish a heretical community that endured until the mid-1560s. Foreign merchants and students carried heretical literature, and Protestant mercenary soldiers sometimes bore books as well as arms. Soon Italian enthusiasts translated Protestant works into the vernacular; in 1529 Ortensio Lando, a Milanese popular writer, reported that he had translated "many writings" of Luther into Italian.[24]

Luther's books entered Venice very early. In September 1520 a German monk reported that he had carried some of Luther's works to Venice and sold them immediately.[25] Possibly these included the three great treatises of the summer of 1520: the *Appeal to the Christian Nobility of the German Nation, On the Babylonian Captivity of the Church*, and *On the Freedom of the Christian Man*. On August 25, 1520, the diarist

---

[22] Brown, *Venetian Press*, pp. 123–24, although Brown overemphasizes its uniqueness and importance.

[23] Antonio Niero, "Decreti pretridentini di due patriarchi di Venezia su stampa di libri," *Rivista di storia della Chiesa in Italia* 14 (1960), 450–52.

[24] On the mercenaries, see the letter of Nuncio Beccadelli of June 16, 1554, in *Nunziature* VI, 364–65. It is likely that mercenaries spread Protestant books in Italy long before this date. On Lando, see Grendler, *Critics*, p. 24.

[25] Pietro Tacchi Venturi, *Storia della Compagnia di Gesù in Italia narrata col sussidio di fonti inedite*, vol. I, pt. I: *La vita religiosa in Italia durante la prima età della Compagnia di Gesù*, 2nd ed. enlarged (Rome, 1930), p. 434.

Marino Sanudo recorded that the patriarch's vicar had appeared before the Collegio to present a papal brief (possibly *Exsurge Domine* of June 15) condemning Luther's books. The vicar asked the government to act against one "Zordan todesco merchadante di libri" who sold Lutheran titles at his house in San Maurizio. The government seized the books. "Nevertheless," Sanudo exulted, "I got one of them, and I have it in my study."[26]

A few months later, a certain Fra Andrea di Ferrara was preaching Luther's doctrines to a crowded Campo San Stefano (now Campo Francesco Morosini), one of the largest in the city. The pope protested, and also asked that Fra Andrea be forbidden to publish his book. Three weeks later, the Venetians assured the pope that Fra Andrea had departed, his manuscript unpublished.[27]

No consistent censorship policy followed these early Venetian actions, and two figures with opposite points of view confirmed that Lutheran believers and books circulated freely. Patriarch Girolamo Querini asked the Collegio in 1526 to investigate the large number of heretics in the city, and Martin Luther was happy to be informed in 1528 that the Venetians were hearing the word of God. A similar situation existed in the Dominion. Clement VII warned the nuncio in January 1524 that Lutheran books were being bought and sold in Brescia and Verona. At the same time he informed the bishop of Trent that Lutheran books were clandestinely entering and circulating in the city.[28] From Trent books could easily enter the Venetian Republic.

The first Italian civil ruler to go beyond a very occasional seizure of volumes upon the request of ecclesiastical authorities was Francesco II Sforza, who in March 1523 legislated against Protestant books. Upon learning that Lutheran books from Germany were entering Milan clandestinely, he ordered anyone in possession of a Lutheran title to give it to the civil authorities within four days under penalty of confiscation of his property. Milan passed under Spanish rule, and in 1538 the Milanese Senate established another precedent by issuing the first Italian Index of Prohibited Books. Compiled by the local Dominican inquisitor, it listed forty-two titles of such authors as Bucer, Calvin, Melanchthon, Oecolampadius, Otto Brunfels, Antonius Corvinus, Johann Gast, Ulrich von Hutten, Os-

[26] "Tamen Io ne havia auto una e l'ho nel mio studio." *I Diarii di Marino Sanuto*, vol. 29 (Venice, 1890), col. 135, August 25, 1520. "Zordan todesco" may be Giordano de Dislach, a longtime associate of Aldus Manutius. See Pastorello, "Di Aldo Pio Manuzio," pp. 170, 190, 191.

[27] *I Diarii di Sanuto*, vol. 29, cols. 492, 552, 615, December 25, 1520, January 12, February 2, 1521.

[28] Tacchi Venturi, *La Compagnia di Gesù*, pp. 434–35; for the Dominion, Fontana, "Documenti vaticani," documents ii, iii, vii, pp. 77–78, 81–82.

wald Myconius, and Erasmus Sarcerius, as well as the *Sommario de la Sacra Scrittura*, and the opera omnia of John Hus and John Wycliffe. Luther, previously banned, was omitted. The books dealt almost exclusively with theology and scriptural commentary, although the *Defensor pacis* of Marsilio of Padua was also listed. Booksellers and others within the Milanese state had to consign these books to the episcopal vicar within three days, under penalty of confiscation of property. In addition, merchants and bookmen importing books were ordered to present inventories to the vicar.[29] The Milanese statutes were significant initiatives, for not even the papacy had, as yet, promulgated a list of heretical authors. It is unlikely that much, if any, enforcement supported the decrees.

The Venetians did not go so far as the Milanese in the 1520s and 1530s, but they did establish a largely nominal prepublication censorship. In the early years of the cinquecento, the Venetian government had occasionally practiced prepublication censorship. When an author or publisher sought a *privilegio*, the Council of Ten in a few cases asked someone to read the work to make sure that it was free of religious, moral, or political error. In 1527 the government passed a law to regularize this process. The Heads (Capi) of the Council of Ten had to grant an imprimatur before the Senate would issue a *privilegio* protecting the rights of publisher or author. The Heads appointed two readers to examine texts and ascertain that they contained nothing politically, morally, or religiously offensive; when the approval of a reader had been secured, the imprimatur was granted. But no machinery existed to force publishers to apply for an imprimatur and *privilegio*. A large majority of books were published without them at this time, for a *privilegio* had, at best, only local effectiveness. Postpublication censorship was even less common; it occurred only on the very few occasions when a person or group persuaded the Heads to punish the author or publisher of a title that had given offense.[30]

The Republic made little or no effort to halt the entry of foreign Protestant books in the 1530s, and those books circulated freely. Giampietro Carafa, who had lived mostly in Venice since 1527, wrote in October 1532 that many clergy and laymen purchased heretical writings openly offered for sale.[31] In February of the same year, Rome lamented that nothing

[29] Luigi Fiumi, "L'Inquisizione Romana e lo Stato di Milano. Saggio di ricerche nell'Archivio di Stato," *Archivio storico lombardo*, Anno 37, ser. 4, vol. 14 (1910), pp. 340–42. The Milanese Index of December 18, 1538, missed by Reusch, is printed by Josef Hilgers, "Bücherverbot und Bücherzensur des sechszehnten Jahrhunderts in Italien," *Zentralblatt für Bibliothekswesen* 28 (1911), 114–16.

[30] Brown, *Venetian Press*, pp. 60–78, 207–10; Sforza, "Controriforma," pt. 1, pp. 5–8.

[31] Pastor, x, 312–13; Gaeta, *Un nunzio pontificio*, pp. 87–89.

seemed able to halt the influx of heretical books, which came into Venice hidden in bales of wool, clothing, and other merchandise.[32]

Luther had demonstrated the effectiveness of the alliance between heretic and printer, but only to a northern audience. Italian civil and ecclesiastical leaders viewed heresy as an abstract and distant phenomenon, not a real and present danger. Why should Italians pay more than passing attention to the works of a German monk? Aside from a few zealots like Carafa, only firsthand witnesses to northern events took alarm at the circulation of Lutheran books in Venice. One of these was the new nuncio, Cardinal Girolamo Aleandro (1480–1542), a veteran of the religious struggle of the north.[33] In the spring of 1533 he made forceful representations to the Venetians. The circulation of two titles in particular worried him: an Italian translation of Luther's *Address to the German Nobility*, entitled *Il libro de la emendatione e correctione dil* [*sic*] *stato Christiano*, which carried the date 1533 but lacked other information,[34] and a 1532 Venetian printing of the *Unio dissidentium dogmatum* of "Hermannus Bodius."[35]

According to the nuncio, Luther's book circulated in many copies and was read with gusto in the house of an unnamed patrician. Possibly Luther's vigorous antipapal polemic and call to the nobility to reform the church appealed more than his doctrine. The nuncio demanded that the book be suppressed. The Council of Ten promised that it would be destroyed and that in the future the nuncio might read religious manuscripts before publication. But a year later he learned that the title had not been burned and was still in circulation. Again he protested, but was rebuffed; one noble argued that the book was not even heretical. Stung, Aleandro

---

[32] Gaeta, *Un nunzio pontificio*, 26–27. Also see Fontana, "Documenti vaticani," document xxxvi, p. 128, February 16, 1532.

[33] Giuseppe Alberigo, "Girolamo Aleandro," DBI, 2, pp. 128–35.

[34] *STC Italian*, 171, lists an edition of Luther's book fitting Aleandro's description, with publication attributed to G. Ulricher, Strasburg.

[35] Unable to locate the Venetian printing, Gaeta, *Un nunzio pontificio*, p. 135 n. 1, opined that the imprint may have been fictitious. There is a copy in the Bayerische Staatsbibliothek, Munich: *Unio Hermani Bodii in unum corpus redacta et diligenter recognita.* (MDXXXII. Colophon: Venetiis apud Augustinum de Bindonis Impensis Io. Baptiste Pederzani Anno a Virginali Partu MDXXXII). It is listed in *Index Aureliensis*, 120.877. Marcella Grendler examined this copy and compared it with other imprints of Agostino Bindoni and Giovanni Battista Pederzano (active 1528–50 and 1524–55, respectively, and sometimes in collaboration) and could see no reason to doubt its authenticity. The work was one of the early successes of the Reformation. Basically a collection of passages from Scripture and the church fathers, it appeared first in 1527, was reprinted 24 times through 1562 according to the *Index Aureliensis*, and was banned by some of the earliest European Indices. But the identity of "Bodius," who authored only this title, eludes scholars. It has been suggested that "Bodius" was a pseudonym of Bucer.

asked the papacy to compile a list of heretical books that would include assurances from the imperial court that certain German authors were heretics. The papacy did nothing, and the nuncio's additional efforts to persuade the Venetians to pass stern legislation against heretics and their books were ignored.[36]

Aleandro's demands were much too strong for either the Republic or the papacy. Even if Clement VII had not been struggling with such grave problems as the Habsburg-Valois wars and Henry's divorce case, he would not have been resolute enough to do anything as decisive as compiling an Index. Paul III (October 1534–1549) pursued reconciliation with the heretics through the first half of his pontificate, and thus necessarily refrained from taking strong action against them. Lacking papal leadership, civil governments failed to move. Most important of all, few ecclesiastical or civil leaders saw Lutheranism as a real threat in Italy; only when they realized that Protestantism had won Italian converts would they take action.

There were a few Venetian affirmations of loyalty to the faith during this period of indifference to heresy. Although some enjoyed Luther's books, others burned their Lutheran titles and tearfully sought absolution from the ecclesiastical censures.[37]

3. EDICTS AND INDICES OF THE 1540S

When the papacy and civil leaders became aware of the existence of Italian heretics and their works, they moved beyond isolated acts of confiscation and issued edicts and Indices that were to a limited degree enforced. The clamorous events of 1541 and 1542—the failure of the Ratisbon colloquy, the death of Gasparo Contarini, the establishment of the Roman Inquisition, and the apostasy of Bernardino Ochino, Celio Secondo Curione, and Peter Martyr Vermigli—profoundly altered Italian religious history. Perhaps the apostasy of Ochino, Curione, and Vermigli within a few days of one another in late August 1542 had the greatest impact, for their flight made Italian leaders and people aware of the strength of native dissent. The apostasy of Ochino, general of the Capuchin Order and Italy's most famous preacher, shocked Italians. Claudio Tolomei (1492–1557), a Sienese vernacular author and later a bishop, addressed a letter to his departed countryman that summarized the reaction. Tolomei believed that no good could possibly result from apostasy, nor could an apostate be reckoned good. If Ochino had fled because of bad advice, or mistaken fear

[36] Letters of Aleandro of May 9-10, 1533, February 29, March 14, April 23, 30, June 26, 1534, in *Nunziature* I, 45, 173–74, 190–92, 208–9, 214, 251–52.
[37] Aleandro's letters of May 5, 24, 1533, April 23, 1534, in *Nunziature*, I, 41, 55, 208.

of ecclesiastical censure, he should return and submit himself to the judgment of the church. But if he had freely chosen heresy, "those embers of love that still live in many hearts will be everywhere extinguished; and in their place will enter hatred, scorn, and anger against you."[38]

Ochino was not only a mesmerizing preacher but also an esteemed author. His *Dialogi* and *Prediche* had enjoyed a combined total of at least seven Venetian printings between 1540 and 1542.[39] Almost immediately after Ochino's apostasy, Genevan presses began to publish these and new works in Italian and Latin, and other Swiss presses followed with titles of Curione and Vermigli. Within a few months Italian governments had enacted censorship laws whose primary purpose was to halt the circulation of these works.

On January 8, 1543, the imperial governor proclaimed a multiple censorship for the city and state of Milan to halt heresy, condemned as offensive to God and harmful to the state.[40] The decree forbade bookmen to publish a title without an imprimatur, and ordered them to present within four days inventories of their stock to the diocesan vicar or the local inquisitor, who would authorize the sale of innocent titles. Inspection of imported merchandise to uncover Protestant literature was ordered, again under the direction of the vicar or inquisitor. Finally, because the *Prediche* and other titles of Ochino had been entering the city, it was decreed that possessors of these works surrender them to the same ecclesiastical authorities and report the existence of other known copies. Penalties of 500 scudi were to be assessed for all infractions.

The Venetians needed prodding, but they also moved to halt the distribution of the works of the apostates. Nuncio Fabio Mignanelli asked the Venetians to halt the extensive circulation of Ochino's *Prediche*, Curione's *Pasquino in estasi*, anonymous "Antechristi," and "impious and abusive" placards. He was happy to report on February 1, 1543, that the Republic had imprisoned an unnamed bookman who had confessed to selling the *Prediche* and *Pasquino in estasi*. A little later he noted that the Republic had, on his recommendation, imprisoned one "messer Vincentio Napole-

---

[38] "Ma seguendo voi il secondo, si spegneranno in tutti quelle reliquie d'amore ch'ancor in molti cuori si mantengon calde: e in lor luogo, v'entranno l'odio, e lo sdegno, e l'ira contra di voi." *De le lettere di M. Claudio Tolomei* (Vinegia, Appresso Gabriel Giolito de' Ferrari, MDXLVII), 189r-91v (quote 191v), October 20, 1542.

[39] Philip McNair and John Tedeschi, "New Light on Ochino," BHR, 35 (1973), 289–301.

[40] The edict is printed by Benedetto Nicolini, "Una polemica tra Girolamo Muzio e Bernardino Ochino," in his *Ideali e passioni nell'Italia religiosa del Cinquecento* (Bologna, 1962), pp. 77–78.

tano" for distributing the Curione title. The Venetians also promised legislation.[41]

On February 12, 1543, the Council of Ten ordered the Esecutori contro la bestemmia to punish presses for infractions of the law. The measure's preamble lamented that in violation of previous statutes bookmen printed and sold many unlicensed books that were immodest and offensive to God and the Christian faith. Therefore, heavier penalties were to be introduced: printers of unlicensed books were to be fined 50 ducats; sellers, 25. Those who hawked the books in the piazza were to be flogged from San Marco to the Rialto and imprisoned for six months. Publishers using false imprints were to be imprisoned for one year and then banned from the Venetian state. If unanimous, the three Esecutori could at their discretion levy heavier penalties. Typical of the Venetian judicial system, the court could use and reward secret denouncers.[42]

The Venetian legislation of 1543 was similar to that of Milan except that the Venetians kept censorship prosecution wholly in lay hands and neglected to provide for the punishment of those who imported heretical books. Four years later, the Council of Ten noted its oversight and enacted a supplemental law levying fines of 50 ducats for this offense. It granted jurisdiction to both the Esecutori and the newly reorganized Holy Office.[43] As far as legislation was concerned, the Republic reacted in the same way as the papacy and other Italian states to the new threat posed by the works of Ochino and the other apostates.

The papacy and other Italian states followed with censorship legislation similar to that of Milan and Venice. On July 12, 1543, the Congregation of the Holy Office issued a comprehensive edict valid for Rome, Bologna, Ferrara, and Modena. Bookmen and customs officials were threatened with high penalties of 1,000 or 2,000 ducats, and excommunication, for publishing, buying, selling, or permitting the entry of erroneous, heretical, scandalous, or seditious books. The edict specifically referred to the sermons of Ochino and the Latin version of Curione's *Pasquino in estasi*.[44] A Mantuan decree of April 1544 ordered the inhabitants to present to the civil authorities for examination all books written by "new authors" within

---

[41] Benedetto Nicolini, "Il frate osservante Bonaventura De Centi e il nunzio Fabio Mignanelli. Episodio di vita religiosa veneziana," in his *Aspetti della vita religiosa politica e letteraria del Cinquecento* (Bologna, 1963), pp. 67–68.

[42] CX, Comune, R. 15, ff. 110^{r-v}, February 12, 1542 mv. It is also printed in Brown, *Venetian Press*, pp. 210–11, and summarized on p. 78. Both Cozzi, *Religione, moralità a Venezia*, p. 9, and Giulio Pesenti, "Libri censurati a Venezia nei secoli XVI-XVII," *La Bibliofilia* 58 (1956), 16, assign the erroneous date 1542 to the law.

[43] CX, Comune, R. 18, f. 24^v, May 17, 1547.

[44] The edict is printed in Hilgers, *Index*, pp. 483–86.

the past 20 years, and anonymous works, if their subject matter was "spiritual," under pain of the galleys.[45] The Luccan government promulgated a short Index in 1545 that condemned the opera omnia of about 25 northern Protestant authors as well as works of Ochino, Vermigli, and Curione.[46]

One edict served as an example for others. On June 12, 1545, the archbishop of Siena, then at the Council of Trent, wrote to the Sienese government urging them to promulgate a "very serious edict" against those who discussed or possessed heretical books. He noted that Lucca, Ferrara, and Florence had already issued similar laws, and he enclosed copies for guidance. The Sienese government did as he urged.[47]

Three years later, the Sienese went a step further by providing an Index and limited implementation personnel. On April 2, 1548, the government appointed three priests to oversee the book industry, without specifying the scope of their authority, and ordered the bookmen to carry their prohibited books to the priests for burning. On April 9, the Signoria issued a general edict against heresy that forbade holding, selling, giving, reading, or listening to prohibited books. For the first offense the penalty was 100 gold scudi, with the accuser receiving 25; for the second offense, the galleys. The Sienese Index was similar to earlier ones; it included the opera omnia of Bucer, Luther, Melanchthon, Oecolampadius, Zwingli, Ochino, and Vermigli, as well as Curione's *Pasquino*, Alfonso Valdés' *Due dialoghi. L'uno di Mercurio et Caronte, l'altro di Lattantio et di uno archidiacono*, an anonymous *Tragedia di Bertuccio*, and "the greater part" of Erasmus, especially the *Colloquies*.[48]

The Viceroy of Naples, Don Pedro da Toledo, prohibited anonymous and heretical books and ordered close supervision of religious works in several proclamations from 1544 to 1550.[49] In Florence, an edict of November 1549 ordered the holders of Protestant books to present them to the vicar within 15 days under penalty of 100 scudi and 10 years in the galleys (the edict made specific reference to Ochino and Vermigli).[50]

[45] Stefano Davari, "Cenni storici intorno al Tribunale dell'Inquisizione in Mantova," *Archivio storico lombardo* Anno 6 (1879), 563–64.

[46] It is printed in Reusch, *Indices*, pp. 136–37.

[47] Letters of June 12, 19, 1545, printed in Paolo Piccolomini, "Documenti del R. Archivio di Stato in Siena sull'eresia in questa città durante il secolo XVI," *Bullettino senese di storia patria* 17 (1910), 20–21. Unfortunately, the texts of the decrees are not included.

[48] Piccolomini, "Documenti del R. Archivio di Stato in Siena," pp. 25–27. I have not identified the *Tragedia di Bertuccio*.

[49] Hilgers, *Index*, pp. 486–87.

[50] BNF, Ms. Magliabecchiana II. IV. 19, "Diario di Firenze dal 1536 al 1555," ff. 149–50; also noted in Hilgers, "Bücherverbot und Bücherzensur," p. 109.

The governments of Italy promulgated an impressive battery of decrees as well as some local Indices, but probably very little civil or ecclesiastical enforcement accompanied the laws in the 1540s. The decrees seldom offered concrete provision for civil enforcement. Eventually local Inquisitions would provide the investigative force to make the laws at least partially effective, but they would not do so until individual states and the papacy had worked out the terms of reference for the reorganized Roman Inquisition. In later decades, inquisitorial investigations confirmed the existence of much heretical activity and wide circulation of heretical books in the 1540s, but during that decade they went on virtually unthreatened.

A similar situation of light enforcement existed in Venice until the creation of the Tre Savii in the spring of 1547. With Council of Ten legislation to regulate the press, and the Esecutori contro la bestemmia to enforce it, the Venetians appeared to have organized effective censorship. They had not. In the 1540s the Esecutori levied penalties for press offenses only three times and to limited effect. In 1544 the publication without an imprimatur of the *Paradossi* of Ortensio Lando resulted in a fine of ten ducats for the printer and five ducats for the seller. One of the three Esecutori wanted the book burned because of its "mala qualità," but was overruled by the other two. Possibly he objected to Lando's description of how Luther, "armed only with Holy Scripture," routed the Scholastic theologians of Leipzig, Louvain, and Cologne. The book was reprinted, unaltered, in 1545.[51] In the same year a book entitled *Il dio priapo* was burned, and the publisher, printer, and seller fined five, three, and three ducats respectively.[52] The following year an action that began as a quarrel between bookmen over rival printings of the *Rime* of Francesco Berni resulted in the decision that the book was lascivious, and should not be printed or sold in the future. Eleven bookmen were called in to hear the decision. Again the action had limited effect, for subsequent Venetian printings of Berni appeared in 1550 and 1565–66.[53] Although the Esecutori punished a large number of moral offenders, they paid little attention to

[51] The printer was Bernardino Bindoni and the seller Giulio Danza; the publishers, Andrea Arrivabene and Pasqualin da S. Sebastian (not identified further) were exonerated. Bestemmia, Bu. 56, Notatorio Terminazioni, R. 1542–1560, f. 41ᵛ, August 2, 5, September 5, 1544. Also see Grendler, *Critics*, pp. 120, 223–24. Pesenti, "Libri censurati," notes some of these actions against press law offenders.

[52] Vielmo da Monferà (probably Guglielmo Da Fontaneto di Monferrato) was the publisher, Zuan Padoan (Giovanni Padovano) the printer, and Francesco Faencino the seller. The title has not been identified. Bestemmia, Bu. 56, R. 1542–1560, f. 49ʳ, August 7, 1545.

[53] Bestemmia, Bu. 56, R. 1542–1560, f. 64ʳ, September 3, 1546. Also see *STC Italian*, 88.

press law violators and ignored those who imported heretical books.[54] The Esecutori had neither the authority nor the staff to police the printing industry, and probably acted only on the rare occasions when they received a denunciation.

The Venetian bookmen were slightly less free to publish what they pleased after 1543, not because they feared the Esecutori contro la bestemmia, but because Ochino, Vermigli, and Curione were known apostates. In 1543 Ortensio Lando mocked Venetian censors for forbidding the sermons of Ochino and the books of Luther and the Anabaptists, while permitting the lascivious, immoral *Decameron* of Boccaccio.[55] His assessment was accurate; although widely available, titles of Italian exiles and northern Protestants were not published in Venice after 1542; vernacular books that guilefully professed Evangelism and heresy were. Between 1533 and 1546, Antonio Brucioli published a number of commentaries on Scripture that were translations and paraphrases of Bucer's commentaries. In 1544 Ambrogio Catarino (or Lancellotto) Politi pointed out Brucioli's use of Bucer, but the books were not burned, and Brucioli was not molested for his beliefs at this time.[56] Similarly, the *Alphabeto Christiano* of Juan Valdés and the *Mercurio et Caronte* of Alfonso Valdés were granted privilegi by the Senate in 1544, and were subsequently published.[57] The *Beneficio di Christo*, with many passages paraphrased from Calvin and Luther, appeared in at least three Venetian editions at this time. Politi denounced it also, but to no avail, doubtlessly

---

[54] I have not counted the number of convictions in the 1540s, but of the c. 100 folios of sentences for that decade, the above three press convictions cover less than one and one-half folios. In the period 1550-70, Cozzi found three press offense convictions, as opposed to 110 for blasphemy, of a total of 273 sentences. *Religione, moralitià a Venezia*, p. 11.

[55] Ortensio Lando, *Paradossi cioè, sententie fuori del comune parere . . .* (In Venetia, MDXLV), p. 73.

[56] They were published by Bartolomeo Zanetti, Aurelio Pincio, and Brucioli himself. On Brucioli (c. 1490-1566) and his commentaries, see Giorgio Spini, *Tra rinascimento e riforma: Antonio Brucioli* (Florence, 1940), pp. 97-98, 228-40; for the editions, see Spini, "Bibliografia delle opere di Antonio Brucioli," *La Bibliofilia* 42 (1940), 156-63. Politi's works are listed in Tinto, *Tramezzino*, pp. 14-16.

[57] The privilegi, dated October 29 and December 29, 1544, are in VM, Mss. Italiani, Classe VII, 2500 (12077), "Privilegi veneziani per la stampa concessi dal 1527 al 1597, copiati da Horatio Brown," arranged chronologically. Unfortunately, the printers are not listed. The *Cambridge Catalogue*, 26, lists an edition of the *Alphabeto Christiano* of Venice, "per Nicolo Bascarini, ad instantia di Marco Antonio Magno, 1545." Bascarini, from Brescia, published 23 editions between 1543 and 1554; Magno has not been identified. A Venetian edition of the *Mercurio et Caronte*, no printer, possibly 1545, and a possible Venetian edition of the *Alphabeto Christiano*, no printer, 1546? are listed in STC Italian, 171, 435.

because some prominent churchmen could find nothing wrong with the book.[58]

After its reorganization in 1547, the Venetian Inquisition began to confiscate and burn books. In July 1548, several bales of books valued at 400 scudi (possibly close to 1,400 volumes), found in the house of an unidentified clandestine bookseller who had fled, were burned publicly in Piazza San Marco and at the Rialto.[59] The father inquisitor for the period 1542-50 stated that he had burned an "infinite number" of books during his tenure.[60]

Trials in 1548 and 1549 involving heretical books show that the Inquisition normally investigated only upon receipt of a denunciation and that it burned the books and fined the owner but did not investigate the religious opinions of the accused, who frequently did not appear personally at the trial. Acting upon a denunciation in July 1548, the tribunal discovered three bales of heretical books belonging to Antonio Brucioli, including titles of Luther, Bibliander, Andreas Osiander, Erasmus Sarcerius, Urbanus Rhegius, and others. The books were burned on July 12, and on November 21, Brucioli—conveniently absent from the city the whole time—was fined 50 ducats and exiled for two years. Neither his opinions nor his writings were examined. Having paid the fine, he returned to Venice in early 1549, and resumed printing in 1551.[61]

---

[58] No imprimatur or privilegio has been located for the *Beneficio di Christo*. Venetian editions that have survived include those published by Bernardino Bindoni in 1543 (which described itself as the second edition); Filippo Stagnino, 1546; and another lacking publisher and date. "The *Beneficio di Cristo*," trans. and intro. Ruth Prelowski, in John A. Tedeschi ed., *Italian Reformation Studies in Honor of Laelius Socinus* (Florence, 1965), p. 95. Pier Paolo Vergerio reported that the book sold 40,000 copies in Venice between 1543 and 1549 (ibid., p. 23). Although the work undoubtedly existed in many copies, this figure seems exaggerated, for twenty large press runs would be required to produce that number. Ten thousand copies seems more realistic. The latest analysis of its authorship is in Fenlon, *Heresy and Obedience*, pp. 69–88.

[59] Campana, "Giovanni della Casa," 17 (1908), 267. Since a scudo was approximately equivalent to a ducat, and the average retail price per book was 1 lira 16 soldi unless a high percentage were folio size (see Ch. 1, sec. 3), 400 scudi worth of books could have been c. 1,375 volumes.

[60] SU, Bu. 12, Padre Marin da Venezia, f. 3ᵛ, August 9, 1555.

[61] The titles were Luther, *De servo arbitrio* and *Annotationes in aliquot cap. Matthaei*; Bibliander, *Ad omnium ordinum Reip. Christianae Principes . . .* ; Osiander, *Coniecturae de ultimus temporibus*; Sarcerius, *Expositiones in Epistolas dominicales* and *In Evangelia dominicalia*; an Italian translation of Rhegius' *Novae doctrinae ad veterem collatio*; Giulio Rovere da Milano, *Prediche*; and the anonymous *Pie et christiane epistole di un servo di G. C.* (noted in Reusch, *Index*, 1, 377). See SU, Bu. 13, Antonio Brucioli, ff. 2ʳ-3ᵛ, July 5, 12, 1548, for the list and the

D V E
❧DIALOGHI❧

LVNO DI MERCVRIO ET CARONTE.

*Nelquale, oltre molte cose belle, gratiose, & di
buona dottrina si raconta quel, che accade
nella guerra dopo lanno. M.D.XXI.*

LALTRO DI LATTANTIO ET DI
VNO ARCHIDIACONO.

*Nelquale puntalmente si trattano le cose
auenute in Roma nellano.*
M. D. XXVII.

Di Spagnuolo in Italiano con molta acutezza
& tradotti, & reuisti,

IN VINEGIA

CON GRATIA ET PRIVILEGIO
PER ANNI DIECI.

3. Alfonso de Valdés, *Due dialoghi, l'uno di Mercurio et Caronte*. . . . (In Vinegia, [1545?]). Source: VM, 217. C. 160

Similarly, in 1549, the Inquisition received a denunciation involving heretical books, opinions, and associates of Francesco Stella. The investigation uncovered a library of 59 titles, including works of Luther, Melanchthon, Bullinger, and Joachim Vadianus, among northern Protestants; and Ochino, Curione, Vergerio, Vermigli, Giulio della Rovere, and Francesco Negri, among Italian apostates, with the majority of the books having been published in Basel and Geneva in the 1540s. Ignoring the other accusations, the tribunal fined Stella *in absentia* 50 ducats and burned the books.[62] Also in 1549, a young scribe was discovered to possess Ochino's sermons and commentary on Paul to the Galatians, which he claimed had been given him by acquaintances. He admitted to having purchased the *Beneficio di Christo, Sommario della Sacra Scrittura,* and *Il capo finto* from Venetian bookstores in 1547 and 1548. He argued that if these were bad books the bookmen ought to be prohibited from selling them. The Inquisition released him into his father's custody, but did not question his acquaintances or the booksellers.[63]

Like other Italian states, the Republic had partially changed its view on censorship during the 1540s. In 1541 the inquisitor and vicar of Brescia had apprehended a local bookseller with many Protestant titles, but the Venetian governors constrained them to return the books.[64] At the end of the decade, the Venetian Holy Office was burning books, although it was not prosecuting exhaustively; it destroyed Protestant books when their existence was brought to its attention. The tribunal was far from establishing prepublication censorship, from halting the importation of northern Protestant publications, and from policing the book trade. The Venetian Republic was probably doing as much as, or a little more than, other Italian states, including the papacy. The Venetian Inquisition did not have an official Index of banned books—but neither did Rome.

Nevertheless, the reorganization of the Holy Office in 1547 generated more book burning and marked at least a small turning-point. The Holy Office had the authority and a greater will to destroy heretical books

---

order to burn the books. This trial of Brucioli and his movements are summarized in Spini, *Brucioli*, pp. 99–108, 115, with a partial list of the books.

[62] SU, Bu. 7, Francesco Stella. The trial is paraphrased by Brown, *Venetian Press*, pp. 112–21, and the annotated inventory is published by Leandro Perini, "Ancora sul libraio-tipografo Pietro Perna e su alcune figure di eretici italiani in rapporto con lui negli anni 1549–1555," *Nuova rivista storica* 51 (1967), 392–94.

[63] SU, Bu. 7, Angelo Leono, testimony of May 22, 23, 1549. The Ochino titles are in *STC Italian*, 472. The complete title of *Il capo finto*, but no additional information, is noted in Perini, "Ancora sul Pietro Perna," p. 387, n. 7.

[64] Letter of Cardinal Alessandro Farnese to the nuncio, February 19, 1541, Rome, in *Nunziature* II, 280–81.

than had the preoccupied Heads of the Council of Ten or Esecutori contro la bestemmia. The growth of censorship from the early 1540s through the implementation of the Tridentine Index was a gradual process. The Venetians had not yet decided that complete and effective censorship was necessary, but the destruction of heretical books no longer depended on whether the nuncio could persuade the Council of Ten to engage in an isolated punitive action.

4. THE *CATALOGO* OF 1549

At the end of the decade, the Republic moved to draft an Index of Prohibited Books, as Milan, Lucca, and Siena had earlier done. Reacting to the discovery of the large cache of contraband books earlier in the month, the Council of Ten on July 18, 1548, ordered bookmen and others holding books containing "anything against the Catholic faith" to present them within eight days to the Tre Savii. At the expiration of this period, the lay assistants would be authorized to search out and punish the holders according to the previous laws. Denouncers were promised secrecy and a share of the fines.[65]

The decree alarmed the bookmen because it authorized the Holy Office to search out and destroy heretical books, defined in the broadest terms. The bookmen feared that the government might be abandoning empty decrees in favor of action. On July 24, 1548, Tommaso Giunti presented to the lay deputies a polite memorandum that asked for clarification and criticized the decree from the standpoints of humanistic tolerance of non-Christian authors and the potential threat to scholarship from censorship.[66] The memorandum noted that many ancient and modern pagan, Mohammedan, and Hebrew authors had written books containing criticism of the faith. These books had circulated freely before the appearance of the Protestant heresy and were still being sold openly. Philosophers, astrologers, physicians, and linguists used them extensively. Were they to be banned along with the new Protestant works?

By underlining the extreme vagueness of the decree, the bookmen obviously hoped to persuade the government not to enforce it except for manifestly heretical titles. They succeeded; the decree was ignored, and the Holy Office continued to conduct limited investigations upon receipt of denunciations.[67]

[65] CX, Comune, R. 18, f. 136ʳ. The vote was 20 yes, 5 no, 5 abstentions. It is printed in Brown, *Venetian Press*, p. 212; and Sforza, "Controriforma," pt. 2, pp. 27–28.

[66] For the text of this memorandum from SU, Bu. 156, "Librai e libri proibiti 1545–1571," see App. I.

[67] I cannot find any evidence in the Inquisition records that this decree stimulated greater activity.

The Council of Ten soon answered the objections of the bookmen by authorizing the drafting of the first Venetian Index. Noting that the previous decree had lacked the titles of books against the faith, the Council on January 16, 1549, ordered the nuncio, inquisitor, and lay deputies, with the advice of "many masters of theology," to compose "a catalogue or summary of all the heretical books, and of other suspect books," as well as those "containing things against good morals." The Council of Ten ordered this catalogue printed, with the inclusion of the decrees of July 18, 1548, and January 16, 1549, and distributed to every bookman in the city. It was also to be proclaimed throughout the Dominion and sold publicly.[68]

Compiled exactly as the Council of Ten ordered, the catalogue was printed by Vincenzo Valgrisi with an exclusive privilege of May 7, 1549.[69] It banned the opera omnia of 47 authors, the vast majority of whom were northern Protestants (Ochino, Vermigli, and Giulio della Rovere were included as well).[70] The catalogue also listed about 100 individual titles, many of them anonymous. By contrast, the Lucca Index of 1545 banned the opera omnia of only 30 authors, and a handful of individual titles. The *Catalogo* was the first Index to prohibit the *Beneficio di Christo* and Valdés's *Alphabeto christiano*; it gave no indication of the authors. It ventured into general prohibitory rules by condemning all anonymous works, i.e., those lacking author, printer, or place of publication, published since 1525. Bibles with prefaces and glosses attacking the faith were banned, as were titles critical of the saints and the church. The 1549 *Catalogo* was the most extensive and accurate Italian Index to

[68] CX, Comune, R. 18, ff. 194ᵛ–95ʳ. The vote was 25 yes, 3 no, 2 abstentions. The decree is printed in Brown, *Venetian Press*, pp. 212–13; and Sforza, "Controriforma," pt. 2, p. 28.

[69] See figure 4. It is a small 8°, 13.6 x 19.7 cms., of six leaves with the last verso blank. The only known extant copy is VM, Miscellanea 128. 9. It was first discovered (with an incomplete shelf mark) and announced by Horatio Brown. "The *Index Librorum Prohibitorum* and the Censorship of the Venetian Press," in his *Studies in the History of Venice*, 2 vols. (London, 1907), II, 64–67, 85–87, reproduces the documents included with the catalogue. Brown's find has been completely ignored by scholars; with his notice and the assistance of the VM staff, I rediscovered it in September 1970. The 1549 catalogue, usually named for Della Casa, was immediately counterfeited by Vergerio in exile. Copies of the counterfeit are to be found in VC, Opus. P.D. 92, and *STC Italian*, 153; also see Georges Bonnant, "Les index prohibitifs et expurgatoires contrefaits par des protestants au XVIᵉ et au XVIIᵉ siècle," BHR, 31 (1969), 613, 622, 624. Reusch, *Indices*, pp. 138–42, reprinted it from Vergerio's counterfeit.

[70] Because Reusch in his *Indices* prints almost all sixteenth-century Indices, and in his *Index* analyzes them, I am providing only brief summaries of the 1549 *Catalogo* and subsequent Indices.

CATALOGO
DI DIVERSE OPERE,
COMPOSITIONI, ET LIBRI;
*li quali come heretici, sospetti, impij, & scandalosi si dichiarano dannati, & prohibiti in questa inclita citta di Vinegia, &
in tutto l'Illustrissimo dominio Vinitiano, sì da
mare, come da terra:*

Composto dal Reuerendo padre maestro M A R I N O Vinitiano, del
monastero de frati Minori di Vinegia, dell'ordine di San Francesco, de
conuentuali, Inquisitore dell'heretica prauita; con maturo cõsiglio, essa
minatione, & comprobatione di molti Reuerendi Primarij maestri in
Theologia di diuerse religioni, & monasteri di detta citta di Vinegia:
d'ordine, & cõmissione del Reuerendissimo Monsignor G I O V A N N I
D E L L A C A S A, eletto di Beneuento, Decano della camera Aposto=
lica di sua S A N T I T A, & della Santa sede Apostolica in tutto l'Illustriss. Dominio predetto Legato Apostolico: aggiūtoui anchora il con
siglio de i clarissimi Signori Deputati contra gli heretici: stampato in
essecutione della parte presa nell'eccellentissimo Consiglio de Dieci
con la giunta; à laude del Signore I D D I O, conseruation della sede
Christiana, & felicita di esso Illustrissimo Dominio.

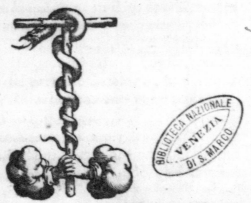

In Vinegia, alla bottega d'Erasmo di Vincenzo Valgrisi.
M. D. X L I X.

4. Title page of the original printing of *Catalogo di diverse opere.* . . . (In Vinegia,
alla bottega d'Erasmo di Vincenzo Valgrisi, MDXLIX). Source: VM, Miscellanea 128.9

date, but it fell short of the comprehensiveness and accuracy of the Indices drafted by the theological faculties of Louvain and Paris at this time. The latter listed many of the major titles of heresiarchs such as Luther, included special sections on Scripture and vernacular titles, and displayed more knowledge of the books that they condemned.

No sooner was the *Catalogo* completed than the Venetians drew back. Nuncio Giovanni Della Casa sent a manuscript copy to Rome on May 18, lamenting that even though preparation had required great labor promulgation was not assured. On May 25, he reported that the catalogue was printed, but "one of the principal men" of the Senate opposed it because it listed a work composed by a friend.[71] The lay deputies argued in favor of the catalogue in the Collegio, but Della Casa feared that they were losing.[72]

Nicolò Da Ponte, recently returned from Rome, where he had served as ambassador, led the opposition with the argument that in Rome itself no Index existed and every sort of book was sold publicly. He charged that the lay deputies were asking the Republic to take measures against heresy stronger than those taken by the pope. The nuncio tried to answer by citing the stern punishments meted out to heretics in Rome and by arguing that proximity to German lands made a Venetian Index necessary. Other patricians objected that the *Catalogo* lacked precision because it failed to take into account the confusing and varied names (pseudonyms, latinized forms, etc.) employed by the German heretics. By the end of June the battle was lost, and the catalogue was suppressed.[73]

The episode showed that the leaders of the Republic were not yet convinced of the necessity of going beyond unenforced decrees. Some, perhaps a majority, supported more effective action, but this front disinte-

[71] Possibly the work composed by the senator's friend was *Espositione letterale del testo di Matteo Evangelista di M. Bernardin Tomitano* (In Venetia, per Gio. dal Griffo, nel 1547). Location: BNF, Guicciardini 11-7-56. Tomitano, a professor of logic at Padua, enjoyed Venetian favor. For his encounter with the Inquisition over this work, see sec. 6 of this ch.

[72] Letters of Della Casa as quoted in Campana, "Giovanni della Casa," *Studi storici* 17 (1908), 272–73. The Collegio discussion cannot be followed at first hand because the ASV, Collegio, Esposizioni Roma *fondo* does not survive before 1567, and there is no record of the debate in Collegio, Esposizioni Principi.

[73] Letters of Della Casa of June 8, 15, 1549, as quoted in Campana, "Giovanni della Casa," *Studi storici* 17 (1908), 273–74. The final mention of the *Catalogo*—that it had not been promulgated because of Venetian opposition—is in a letter to Rome of Annibale Grisonio of the nuncio's household of June 29, 1549, Venice, in Archivio di Stato, Parma, Carteggio Farnesiano e Borbonico Estero, Venezia, F. 510/2 (1547–1555), letter no. 64, ff. 192–93 (consulted on microfilm at the Fondazione Giorgio Cini in Venice).

grated when powerful nobles opposed the *Catalogo* because of traditional antagonism toward Rome and personal considerations. The lack of a papal Index, a minor example of the general inadequacy of papal religious leadership at this time, was an unanswerable argument and probably the crushing blow.

5. THE BURNING OF THE TALMUD IN 1553

Immediately after mid-century, limited Venetian toleration of diversity began to give way to persecution. The Republic arrested Anabaptists in 1551, and zealously joined the papacy and other Italian states in burning the Talmud. The rejection of an Index did not protect the large and important Hebrew press.

The Republic, like nearly all European states, feared and hated Anabaptists more than other heretics because they seemed a threat to civil authority. A voluntary confession of October 17, 1551, to the Bolognese Inquisition disclosed the names of dozens of Anabaptists and "Lutherans," i.e., orthodox Protestants, all over Italy. In particular, the repentant heretic revealed the existence of Anabaptist conventicles in the Republic; the Anabaptists had held a synod in Venice in September 1550, and they were especially numerous in Padua and Vicenza. Copies of the confession were sent to Inquisitions throughout Italy. In Venice, on the advice of the lay assistants, the Holy Office presented the information on Anabaptist activity to the Collegio in a secret session on December 18, 1551. Shocked by "this conspiracy of scoundrels against the governments of heaven and earth," and no doubt embarrassed that the synod had been held in Venice, the Council of Ten ordered wide-scale secret arrests. They netted only about twenty Anabaptists, far fewer than expected, but over the next few years they did succeed in destroying Anabaptist conventicles. On the other hand, the Venetian Inquisition suppressed the confession's denunciation of several Venetian residents, including three nobles, as Lutherans.[74]

Girolamo Muzio (1496–1576), a fervent Catholic apologist then in Venice, cited the prosecution of Anabaptists as evidence of the growth

---

[74] This was the confession of Don Pietro Manelfi, now published in entirety by Carlo Ginzburg, *I costituti di Don Pietro Manelfi* (Florence and Chicago, 1970). For the Venetian reaction, see the letters of Nuncio Beccadelli of December 19, 26, 1551, and January 2, 1552, Venice, in *Nunziature* v, 330 (quote), 332; vi, 29. For some of the results of the arrests and trials, see Stella i, 87–103. The Venetian nobles were the brothers Bernardo and Gerolamo Navagero, and Giovan Battista Tagliapietra, but their names were canceled in the Venetian copy of the confession, and they were not arrested. *I costituti*, pp. 16–17, 49, 70.

of the Catholic faith there.[75] The action also demonstrated that the patriciate was becoming less tolerant of diversity, as the Hebrew publishers were next to discover.

From about 1515 to 1553 the Hebrew press in Venice flourished; it was the most important in Europe. The key figure was Daniel Bomberg (c. 1483–1553), a Christian from Antwerp who had great sympathy for Jewish learning. He established a Hebrew press in 1516 and, until his retirement in 1548, published about 200 titles, including such landmarks in the history of Hebrew printing as the complete Talmud (1519–23). In the 1540s other publishers entered the field, including Giovanni de Farri e fratelli, and Francesco Brucioli, brother of Antonio. Although Jews could serve as editors and printers, they were forbidden to publish. Nevertheless, Me'ir Parenzo published at least 10 titles from 1545 through 1552. Two patricians, Marc'Antonio Giustiniani (beginning in 1545) and Alvise Bragadino (beginning in 1550) published about 85 and 15 titles respectively through 1553.[76]

The Venetian patriciate at mid-century was not noticeably more tolerant toward the Jews than were other Italian civil and ecclesiastical leaders.[77] The Venetians distinguished between three groups of Jews: Levantine, Ponentine (Western), and German (local Jews, most of whom had come from other Italian cities). Levantine Jews had for some time enjoyed trading and other privileges within the maritime Empire; German and Ponentine Jews, especially the newly arrived refugees from Iberian persecution, were most often the target of anti-Semitism. The Venetians placed Jews living in Venice into a ghetto in 1516, and forced them to pay large sums of money for permission (*condotta*) to reside in the city for a specified term of years. But beginning in the 1540s, Venetian hostility toward the hapless infidel at home steadily mounted, sometimes anticipating papal anti-Semitism. The Venetians did little to punish those who incited pogroms in the Veneto in the 1540s. In 1550 the Senate ordered the expulsion of the Marranos, i.e., forcibly converted Christians from Iberia believed to be secretly practicing their

[75] *Lettere catholiche del Mutio Iustinopolitano* (In Venetia, Appresso Gio. Andrea Valvassori, detto Guadagnino, MDLXXI), p. 146, February 16, 1552.

[76] David W. Amram, *The Makers of Hebrew Books in Italy. Being Chapters in the History of the Hebrew Printing Press* (Philadelphia, 1909), pp. 146–224; Joshua Bloch, "Venetian Printers of Hebrew Books," *Bulletin of the New York Public Library* 36 (1932), 71–92; Cecil Roth, *History of the Jews in Venice* (Philadelphia, 1930), pp. 245–55; and *The History of the Jews in Italy* (Philadelphia, 1946), pp. 225–26; Brown, *Venetian Press*, 105–06; Alfredo Cioni, "Daniel Bomberg," DBI, 11 (1969), 382–87.

[77] Lane, *Venice*, pp. 300–304; Pullan, *Rich and Poor*, pp. 431–537; Roth, *Jews in Venice*, pp. 1–71, 105–211.

ancient faith, but did not implement the order when Venetian merchants protested that expulsion would disrupt commerce.[78] And the Republic demanded increasing sums of money for renewal of the *condotta*.

The Republic treated the Hebrew press in similar fashion, suffering its existence in exchange for large payments early in the cinquecento, but turning on it later. When in October 1525 Bomberg offered 100 ducats for an extension of his permission to print Hebrew books, he was opposed on the grounds that his publications attacked the faith, and the Senate turned him down. Three votes later, in March 1526, his offer of 500 ducats was accepted.[79] But at mid-century, the Hebrew press was visible and vulnerable, and anti-Semitism was rising.

Rome became worried about the danger to the faith of Hebrew books just before mid-century, and in November 1548 directed Nuncio Della Casa to expurgate Hebrew publications. With the support of the lay deputies to the Inquisition, Della Casa readily obtained the consent of Marc'Antonio Giustiniani, but Bomberg objected on scholarly grounds. Because of the lack of Christian experts in Hebrew, Della Casa hesitated.[80] In December 1550, Cardinal Girolamo Verallo in Rome complained vigorously to the Venetian ambassador that a printing of over 800 copies of the Talmud was more than half finished and that many other Hebrew books "of the greatest perniciousness" to the Christian religion were being printed in Venice.[81] Nevertheless, the Giustiniani printing of the Babylonian Talmud was completed in 1551.

In February 1551 the Collegio became concerned. Believing the Talmud to be filled with blasphemy it charged the Esecutori contro la bestemmia to arrange for Christian experts in Hebrew to examine the book and note the blasphemies and passages against the faith. The results of the investigation were to be communicated to the Collegio.[82]

A bitter dispute between the Giustiniani and Bragadino presses over rival editions of a title generated denunciations and charges that, when translated to Rome, provided the immediate justification for a general

---

[78] David Kaufmann, "Die Vertreibung der Marranen aus Venedig im Jahre 1550," *Jewish Quarterly Review* 13 (1901), 521–32.

[79] Bloch, "Venetian Printers of Hebrew Books," 77.

[80] Correspondence between the nuncio and Rome from November 24, 1548, through February 23, 1549, as quoted in Campana, "Giovanni della Casa," 17 (1908), 269–71.

[81] Letter of Ambassador Matteo Dandolo in Capi del CX, Lettere di Ambasciatori a Roma, Bu. 23, no. 159, December 26, 1550. Paschini, *L'Inquisizione*, p. 66, quotes the letter.

[82] Collegio, Notatorio, R. 27, f. 138^v, February 23, 1550 mv. The vote was 20 yes, 1 no.

attack on Hebrew literature.[83] A papal order of August 12, 1553, condemned the Talmud and similar books to burning. On September 12, after the order had been executed in Rome, the Congregation of the Holy Office ruled that the same action be taken throughout Italy. The Council of Ten unanimously endorsed the order. On October 18, having learned from the report of the Esecutori contro la bestemmia that the Talmud was filled with blasphemies against God the Father, Jesus, and Mary, the Council ordered the Esecutori to burn all the Talmuds collected to date, and to search in the ghetto and elsewhere, in the houses of Jews, Christians, and bookmen, for other copies. Originally scheduled for Thursday, the fire was postponed until the Sabbath, Saturday, October 21. On that morning, the burning of the Talmud made "a good fire" (in the nuncio's words) in Piazza San Marco. In the next few months the Talmud and other works were destroyed as far away as Crete in the Venetian Dominion; across Italy possibly hundreds of thousands of Hebrew books were burned.[84] The Venetian government burned the Talmud before all parts of the papal state had complied with Rome's order.[85]

The Venetians needed little persuasion to join in burning the Talmud. As the nuncio noted, no one spoke against the decree condemning the book, and the Esecutori contro la bestemmia, rather than the Holy Office,

[83] Amram, *Makers of Hebrew Books*, pp. 252–76; Kenneth R. Stow, "The Burning of the Talmud in 1553, in the Light of Sixteenth Century Catholic Attitudes toward the Talmud," BHR, 34 (1972), 435–59.

[84] CX, Comune, R. 21, ff. 58ᵛ–59ʳ. The votes on three decrees ordering confiscation and destruction were 19 yes, 0 no, 0 abstentions; 26 yes, 0 no, 2 abstentions; and 26 yes, 0 no, 0 abstentions. The general decree of October 21 is published in David Kaufmann, "Die Verbrennung der Talmudischen Litteratur in der Republik Venedig," *Jewish Quarterly Review* 13 (1901), 537–38; in Sforza, "Controriforma," pt. 2, pp. 44–45; and in C. Castellani, "Documenti circa la persecuzione dei libri ebraici a Venezia," *La Bibliofilia* 7 (1905–6), 304–7, with documents relating to Crete as well. See the letters of Nuncio Beccadelli of August 19, 26, September 23, October 14, 21, 1553, in *Nunziature* VI, 255, 258, 267, 274–75, 277 (quote on 277). Some of this correspondence is also in Paschini, *L'Inquisizione*, pp. 108–11. Also see Pastor, XIII, 214–15; Roth, *Jews in Venice*, pp. 255–59; Roth, *Jews in Italy*, pp. 290–93; William Popper, *The Censorship of Hebrew Books* (New York, 1899), pp. 29–37; Salo Wittmayer Baron, *A Social and Religious History of the Jews*, 2nd ed. rev., vol. XIV, *Catholic Restoration and Wars of Religion* (New York, London, and Philadelphia, 1969), pp. 29–31, 127–28, 141–42.

[85] See the letter of Girolamo Muzio to Fra Michele Ghislieri of December 16, 1553, Pesaro, in which he reported that the Talmud had just been burned in the Dukedom of Urbino, while in nearby Ancona no action had yet been taken. Muzio also reported how broadly officials interpreted their mandate; they burned even biblical commentaries if they thought that they contained antichristian sentiments. *Lettere catholiche del Mutio*, pp. 185–86.

executed it. Economic considerations failed to sway the patriciate in the face of alleged blasphemy against the faith. It was to be expected that the government would be insensitive to the spiritual and financial distress of the Jews, but the Republic's leaders were equally unmoved by the losses sustained by the two patrician Hebrew presses. Giustiniani worked behind the scenes to stop the destruction of Hebrew books, and then to prevent the confiscation of his recently printed Talmud. When it was apparent that the Republic intended to proceed, he appealed to the papacy for financial compensation. He got nothing. The government simply seized the Giustiniani publications, and presumably those of Bragadino as well. Twenty years later, Antonio Giustiniani, the son and successor of Marc'Antonio, reported that his father had lost 24,000 ducats' worth of books in 1553.[86]

In response to Jewish pleas, the pope on May 29 and December 18, 1554, issued modifying decrees permitting Hebrew books (except for the Talmud) to be held if they had been expurgated.[87] But Hebrew publishing in Venice halted in 1553. It moved to Cremona, Ferrara, Mantua, Sabbioneta, and Riva di Trento, and sometimes flourished in these northern Italian cities through the dark days of the pontificate of Paul IV (1555–59), until the resumption of Venetian Hebrew publishing in 1563. For example, Cristoforo Madruzzo (1512–78), the Cardinal of Trent, founded and patronized a Hebrew press at Riva di Trento (about 50 kilometers southwest of his episcopal seat) that lasted from 1558 through 1562.[88] The Jews did not publish in Venice, perhaps because the Republic forbade them to, but more likely because they feared further destruction of their books. The Venetians ignored the damage to the economy from the emigration of Hebrew publishing as well as the loss of revenue from taxes levied on paper and books entering and leaving the city. On this occasion, guarding the faith was more important than money.

6. THE INDEX OF 1554/55

Although local Indices had been issued across Europe, the papacy did not address itself to the task of drafting one until the late 1540s. Because

---

[86] Letters of Nuncio Beccadelli of August 26, September 23, October 14, 21, 1553, in *Nunziature* VI, 258, 267, 274–75, 277; SU, Bu. 37, Antonio Giustiniani, f. [6ᵛ], his testimony of November 4, 1574. Antonio may have exaggerated the loss, for his father in 1553 estimated before the fire that the cost of paper and printing for the confiscated books was 3,000 ducats. *Nunziature* VI, 275, October 14, 1553. On the other hand, the loss calculated on the basis of the retail price would have been at least twice 3,000 ducats. Moreover, additional books may have been confiscated after October 14.

[87] Pastor, XIII, 215; Roth, *Jews in Venice*, pp. 259–60.

[88] Amram, *Makers of Hebrew Books*, pp. 277–337.

of the enormous amount of time and effort required to draft an original Index based on examination of all suspect authors and titles, Fra Michele Ghislieri initially resolved simply to reprint together the two most recent Indices of the Sorbonne (1547) and Louvain (1546). The Congregation of the Inquisition reluctantly concluded that this approach would not be adequate. Sometime between April 1547 and May 1550, the cardinals commissioned two Dominicans, Egidio Foscarari, Master of the Sacred Palace, and Pietro Bertano, Bishop (later Cardinal) of Fano to draft a new Index. The pair completed a two part Index listing "heretical" and "suspect" titles, probably sometime in 1552; but the cautious cardinals refrained from promulgation in order to improve it. When the Florentine vicar and the Venetian nuncio asked for Indices to guide them, the Congregation sent this Index in manuscript form (to Florence in the first months of 1553, and to Venice in late 1554 or early 1555).[89] They also sent it to Milan (in 1554 or 1555).[90]

[89] "Per il che mandai à dimandar il sudetto Rev. Padre [Michele Ghislieri], co'l quale ragionai à lungo, et quanto mi disse fù che già alcuni anni egli si deliberò di fare un catalogo, et perche bisognava lungo tempo, et molta fatica à veder gli libri, deliberò di torre il catalogo, che era stato fatto dalla università di Lovania, et quello fatto dalla università di Paris, et stamparli tutti due insieme, et intimarli alli librari. Di poi parendo che questo non bastasse, fù dato il carico al mastro di sacro palazzo, che hora è vescovo di Modena, et al Rev. Cardinal di Fano, che all'hora non era cardinale. Li quali fecero un catalogo delli libri, che chiaramarano heretici, et un'altro di quelli, che loro haveano per dubij. Questi non furono stampati, nè intimati alli librari, deliberando di considerarli anchora meglio. Occorse poi ch'l Rev. Vicario del vescovo di Fiorenza ricercasse dalli Rev. Inquisitori, che facesseno un catalogo de libri per poter sapere come proceder nelle cause di heresia, et esso Frate gli mandò quello, che fù fatto dal mastro di sacro palazzo, et sopra nominati, che non era stampato, et havendo il presente Rev. Nontio di Vinetia ricercato che se facesse un catalogo de libri per poter meglio conoscer i libri heretici, egli gli mandò lo istesso che havea mandato al vicario di Fiorenza, il qual è questo, che è stato hora stampato à Vinetia. . . ." Letter of Ambassador Domenico Morosini to the Tre Savii, of July 2, 1555, Rome, in SU, Bu. 156, "Librai e libri proibiti, 1545-1571," ff. [64ʳ⁻ᵛ]. With the information in the letter and knowledge of the careers of the two Dominicans, one can determine when the Index was drafted. Both Foscarari (1512-64) and Bertano (1501-58) were moderates who fell under suspicion during the pontificate of Paul IV. The former was imprisoned by the Inquisition for several months in 1558, and the latter narrowly avoided the same fate. See G. Rill, "Pietro Bertano," DBI, 9, pp. 467-71; for Foscarari, *Enciclopedia cattolica*, v, 1545. Also see HC, III, 32, 194, 252.

For the approximate date when this Index was sent to Florence, see Friedrich Hubert, *Vergerios publizistische Thätigkeit nebst einer bibliographischen Übersicht* (Gottingen, 1893), pp. 257-58. But no Florentine copy of the Index has come to light, suggesting that it may not have been printed or promulgated there.

[90] The 1554 Milanese Index is a few authors and titles shorter than the Venetian version, but otherwise identical. Its *fortuna* is unkown.

In Venice Gabriel Giolito published the new Index in a printing that carried the date 1554, but probably was done in the first two months of the following year.[91] Both the Venetian and Milanese printings dropped the category of suspect books and banned outright a considerably larger number of authors and books than had the 1549 *Catalogo*. The Venetian version of the new Index banned the opera omnia of about 290 authors, over four times as many as its predecessor, as well as many more individual titles. Part of the growth in size resulted from the increasing number of Protestant authors and from greater papal awareness of them. Among Italian apostates whose opera omnia were banned for the first time were Curione, Francesco Stancaro, and Pier Paolo Vergerio (many of Vergerio's anonymous works were listed separately). However, the major reason for the greater number of authors and titles was the inclusion of many northern Protestant scholarly authors. These scholars had usually written at least one Protestant religious title, but they had authored many more works in such fields as law, medicine, and the humanities. Nevertheless, the new Index banned their opera omnia.

The 1554 Index was the first of a new family of Indices that adopted the principle of banning the opera omnia of a broad range of Protestant authors, scholars as well as theologians. Earlier northern Indices, such as those of Louvain and Paris, had listed the individual titles of heresiarchs and other Protestant religious figures; previous Italian Indices promulgated by city governments had tended to ban the opera omnia of authors, but only those universally considered to be heretics. Occasionally, previous Indices had ventured beyond a narrow definition of heresy to ban works that were anticlerical or antipapal, such as Marsilius of Padua's *De defensor pacis*; the 1554 Index did so more frequently and more significantly.

The new Index manifested greater hostility toward dissent in a variety of ways. It was the first Index to adopt the principle, for a small handful of titles, that a few heretical pages could contaminate an entire book. For this reason it intruded upon current Italian literature for the first time,

---

[91] At least two original copies survive. One is in the BAVa, Z. 1020. J554, first noted by Mario Scaduto, "Lainez e l'indice del 1559: Lullo, Sabunde, Savonarola, Erasmo," *Archivum historicum societatis Jesu* 24 (1955), 6, n. 25. Another original copy, to my knowledge previously unnoticed, is in VC, Opusc. P. D. 92. In a single volume are bound together (1) the Vergerio counterfeit of the 1549 *Catalogo*, (2) Vergerio's counterfeit of the 1554 Index, and (3) the original Giolito printing of the 1554 Index. The title page with the Giolito pressmark and the type, clearly identify it as the original. It is a small 12°, 9.5 by 14.8 cms., of 32 pages with the list of titles on pp. 3–31. For comparison with the counterfeit, please see figures 5 and 6. There are minor textual differences between the original and the counterfeit. Other copies examined turned out to be the more common Vergerio counterfeit, which Reusch used for his *Indices*.

banning Giambattista Gelli's *I capricci del bottaio* and two works of Ortensio Lando published under pseudonyms. It banned antipapal works of the past such as Dante's *De monarchia* and Lorenzo Valla's *De falso donatione Constantini*, and philosophical and theological works such as the opera omnia of William of Occam and Valla's *De libero arbitrio*. Rejecting humanistic tolerance for the ancient pagan authors, the new Index also banned Lucian of Samosata. The *Catalogo* of 1549 had, with one exception,[92] omitted Erasmus, but the new Index banned ten of his titles (still fewer than the number condemned by the Louvain and Paris Indices). The Talmud and books of necromancy were also banned for the first time. On the other hand, the Index of 1554 lacked the general prohibitions and regulations found in the 1549 *Catalogo*.

The 1554 Index presented the contradictory aspects of severity of form and, as will be seen, moderation in promulgation. The reasons are to be found in the Congregation of the Inquisition and the reform leadership offered by Julius III. The pontiff's initial appointees to the Holy Office in 1550 were a diverse group, ranging from the moderate Giovanni Morone and Reginald Pole to the stern Carafa. A year later, Morone and Pole had withdrawn, but Cardinal Verallo, who took a severe position against the Talmud, had been added, and Fra Michele Ghislieri had been appointed commissioner general of the body. Although the membership continued to fluctuate, Carafa and Ghislieri were fixtures, and the sterner reformers dominated.[93] The shifting membership suggests an evolving Index. The various kinds of nondoctrinal works probably were classified as "suspect" in the original draft; the moderates may have felt that it was sufficient to warn readers of them. The final version probably reflected the views of the sterner group, who saw a threat to the faith in a variety of subject matter. The ultimate form of this Index indicated that Carafa, Ghislieri, and those who agreed with them had attained some influence in Rome. The reigning pope, however, was an indecisive man who vacillated between reform and frivolity. Julius III initiated many reform projects at the inauguration of his pontificate, but most came to little.[94] As determined as Carafa and Ghislieri were to eradicate heretical books, they were still dependent on a wavering pontiff for support.

On March 12, 1555, the Venetian Holy Office announced to the bookmen that the new Index was ready, and offered them three months in which to comment on it.[95] At the end of that period it would go into

---

[92] This was the Tomitano translation of Erasmus's *Paraphrasis in evangelium Matthaei*, which was listed under the translator's name. For more on this, see below.

[93] Pastor, XIII, 210, 217.

[94] Jedin, *Seripando*, pp. 491–94; Pastor, XIII, 155–70.

[95] SU, Bu. 159, "Acta S. Officij Venetiarum 1554–1555," parte 2, f. 48ᵛ.

J. C. M.

CATHALOGVS
LIBRORVM
HAERETICORVM,

QVI HACTENVS COLLIGI
potuerunt à uiris Catholicis suppleudus in dies
si qui alij ad notitiam deuenerit de
commissione Tribunalis,

SANCTISSIME INQVISITIO-
NIS VENETIARVM.

VENETIIS APVD GABRIELEM
IVLITVM DE FERRARIS, ET
FRATRES. MDLIIII.

5. Title page of the original printing of *Cathalogus librorum haereticorum.* . . .
(Venetiis Apud Gabrielem Iulitum de Ferraris, et Fratres, MDLIIII). Source: VC,
Opusc P D 92

CATHALO-
GVS LIBRORVM
HAERETICORVM.

* *

*

QVI HACTENVS
colligi potuerūt à uiris Catholicis, sup-
plendus in dies, si qui alij ad noti-
tiam deuenerint, de commis-
sione Tribuna-
lis,

Sanctiſſimæ inquiſitionis Ve-
netiarum.

VENETIIS APVD GABRIELEM
IVLITVM DE FERRARIS,
ET FRATRES, MDLIIII.

6. Title page of the counterfeit of *Cathalogus librorum haereticorum.* . . . (Venetiis Apud Gabrielem Iulitum de Ferraris, et Fratres, MDLIIII). Source: VC, Opusc P D 92

effect, and violators would be liable to fines of 100 ducats. Clearly the Congregation viewed Venetian promulgation as a trial run.

The bookmen took advantage of this invitation in order to present three memoranda to the Holy Office.[96] In the first they began by complaining about the prohibition of nonreligious works. The bookmen regretted that the opera omnia of authors who had written many books on topics other than religion had been condemned. To illustrate their point, they listed a number of authors and their titles in law, medicine, and philosophy: Konrad Gesner, Janus Cornarius, Joannes Oldendorpius, Hieronymus Schiurpff of St. Gall, Christoph Hegendorff, Jacob Ziegler, Joannes Velcurio, Sebastian Muenster, and Otto Brunfels. (The bookmen avoided mentioning that these men had usually written one or more religious titles as well.) Depriving the world of their books would serve no useful purpose and would disappoint many. In addition, the bookmen pointed to a practical difficulty. Since legal works of various authors (i.e., diverse glosses on a single text) were often bound together in a single volume, banning Protestant legists would necessarily result in the destruction of innocent titles.

The bookmen next pointed to the confusion and inadequacy of the entries. Who could identify "Amaricus," "Alnordus," and many more? Who were "Antonius Anglus" and "Petrus de Anglia"? English Catholics might also bear these names; such imprecise entries risked offending the citizens of a kingdom recently returned to the faith. The bookmen concluded that an Index should list only individual works with complete author and title citations, except in the case of heresiarchs like Luther.

A second memorandum repeated the previous arguments and added new ones. The bookmen touched briefly on the financial losses and subsequent suffering that the Index would cause among the families of the printers. Then they objected to the prohibition of Lucian; the church had tolerated him and similar authors for over 1,400 years. The world of learning was filled with copies of this ancient, who was very useful in teaching Greek. The bookmen asked for moderation and a complete reappraisal. Noting that the papacy had moderated the prohibitions against Hebrew books in the decrees of May 29 and December 18, 1554, the bookmen asked Rome to convoke a commission of theologians, jurists, and other experts to review all book condemnations. The inference was that this Index was not the product of careful study.

On June 22, nineteen bookmen, including major publishers like Tommaso Giunti, Vincenzo Valgrisi, Michele Tramezzino, Andrea Arrivabene, Ottaviano Scoto, and Giorando Ziletti appeared on behalf of the

---

[96] For the texts and dating of these memoranda, please see App. 1.

guild to read another statement. Previously humble and petitioning, they had become angry and importunate. Addressing primarily the lay members of the tribunal, they began by noting that they had appeared many times to discuss the Index. They complained of being subjected to an Index and rules not in effect in Rome, and asked how the tribunal could permit those who had been "born and raised under the most just and clement government of this holiest Republic" to be treated worse than the Roman booksellers who live under the very eyes of the cardinals of the Holy Office? They requested that the tribunal write to the ambassador in Rome to ascertain that this measure was not in force there, and the tribunal agreed to do so.[97]

Ambassador Domenico Morosini immediately took up the Index with Commissioner General Ghislieri, who told him that the Congregation was already aware of the objections and had decided to reconsider the prohibitions of nonreligious titles. The ambassador also checked with Roman bookmen, who confirmed that no Index was in effect within the city. The Congregation studied the question for the rest of the summer without reaching a decision. On July 6 Fra Ghislieri informed the Venetian Inquisition that four theologians had been deputized to examine the nonreligious titles on the Index. In the meantime, however, those titles should not be sold without the approval of the local Holy Office. On August 3 he retreated a little more; books written by acceptable authors but carrying prefatory material, glosses, and the like authored by Protestants might be sold after the objectionable pages had been replaced with blank sheets.[98] On September 28, however, the Venetian Inquisition suspended the 1554 Index, no doubt with the approval of Rome, and nothing more was heard of it.[99] Very few copies of the original Giolito printing survive, suggesting that it was destroyed.

Again an Index had been drafted, printed, and suppressed, this time because the Congregation of the Holy Office drew back. The cardinals were not yet sure of the principles for condemnation, nor confident in their leadership. Illness and death also deprived the Congregation of papal support at the moment of promulgation. Julius III was already bedridden in February, and he died on March 23, 1555. Marcellus II succeeded him on April 10, but he died on May 1. Giampietro Carafa was

---

[97] SU, Bu. 159, "Acta S. Officij Venetiarum 1554–1555," parte 3, f. 42ᵛ. The ambassador acknowledged the request of the Tre Savii in a letter of June 29, 1555, Rome. SU, Bu. 156, "Librai e libri proibiti, 1545–1571," ff. [66ʳ–ᵛ].

[98] Letters of Ambassador Morosini to the Tre Savii, July 2, 1555, Rome; of Fra Ghislieri to the nuncio's auditor, Rev. Brugnatello, of July 6, and August 3, 1555, Rome, in SU, Bu. 156, "Librai e libri proibiti, 1545–1571," ff. [64ᵛ–65ʳ, 55ʳ–ᵛ].

[99] SU, Bu. 159, "Acta S. Officij Venetiarum 1554–1555," parte 5, ff. 5ʳ–ᵛ.

elected on May 23. Paul IV would prove to be an imperious leader and an implacable foe of heretical literature, but he was not ready to promulgate this Index. Possibly he ordered the Congregation to withdraw the 1554 Index, and then sent the cardinals back to draft a sterner one.

In Venice the Index was not implemented, and things went on as before. The Inquisition prosecuted only upon receipt of a denunciation, and the bookmen sold Protestant literature until they were caught. Yet, the Index of 1554/55 did create difficulties for one Paduan professor. Bernardino Tomitano (1517?–76) taught logic from 1539 to 1563 and later medicine, participated in the Paduan literary academies, and basked in the praises of students and the Venetian Senate. In 1547 he published as his own work a vernacular translation of Erasmus's *Paraphrasis in evangelium Matthaei*; both the 1549 *Catalogo* and the 1554 Index accepted his authorship and banned the work. While the bookmen were criticizing the new Index, Tomitano spontaneously appeared before the Venetian Holy Office to exculpate himself. He testified that he had translated the work for a third party, who had borne the publication cost, and that the Venetian inquisitor had approved it with minor corrections. The former inquisitor contradicted him, however. He claimed that he had refused to approve the work because of its "logico caviloso et molto astuto." When he had protested to the secretary of the Riformatori dello Studio di Padova about Tomitano's going ahead with the printing, the secretary had shrugged his shoulders.[100]

Tomitano declared that he had never given his assent to Erasmus's doctrines. The Holy Office accepted his declaration, but ordered him to prepare an expiatory oration. Tomitano defended himself and attacked Erasmus in his oration, but not vehemently. Certain passages could be read as double entendres; for example, Tomitano noted that Erasmus's books had earlier been approved by the learned, read by everyone, and printed "with the privileges that ordinarily are given to good works." Perhaps the Holy Office was not entirely satisfied with him, for Tomitano wrote a second oration, published in 1556, which lauded religious orthodoxy in general terms.[101] The Inquisition did not question Tomitano

---

[100] SU, Bu. 12, Padre Marin da Venezia, ff. 2^{r-v}, his testimony of August 9, 1555. See footnote 71 of this ch. for the Tomitano title and a location.

[101] SU, Bu. 11, Bernardino Tomitano (which includes an autograph copy of the first oration, delivered to the Holy Office on August 22, 1555). Also SU, Bu. 159, "Acta S. Officij Venetiarum 1554-1555," parte 3, ff. 24^v-25^v (May 21, 1555), 33^v-34^r (June 14, 1555). Also see Luigi De Benedictis, *Della vita e delle opere di Bernardino Tomitano: studio* (Padua, 1903), although he was unaware of the SU, Bu. 159 material; and E. Riondato, "Bernardino Tomitano," *Enciclopedia filosofica*, IV, 1,228-30. I have not found a printed version of the 1555 oration, although De

again, although the translation of Erasmus was again listed as his work in the 1559 Index. The Tridentine Index correctly cited it as a translation.

7. HERETICAL BOOKS AND BOOKMEN

While Indices were printed and suppressed, conventicle leaders and the merely curious found a wide assortment of heretical titles in Venice. Protestant literature from the north entered the city in a variety of ways and was distributed by religious dissenters and sympathetic bookmen. Those engaged in this trade could not carry on their activities as openly as in the past, but they found efficient clandestine ways to conduct business. Much remains unknown, but enough information has come to light to suggest the existence of a flourishing commerce in heretical books in the 1550s and the first half of the following decade.

The libraries of two abjured heretics illustrate the availability of Protestant literature in 1551. Lucio Paolo Rosello (or Roselli), a Paduan priest, author, and scholar, had Calvin's *Institutes* and titles of Luther, Zwingli, Johannes Brenz, and others in a library of about thirty-five northern Protestant titles. His associate, Pietro Cocco, a minor Venetian nobleman, had many titles of Italian heretics, such as Brucioli, Ochino, Stancaro, Vergerio, and Vermigli, as well as Melanchthon's *Loci communes theologici*, in a library of about forty banned titles.[102]

By the early 1550s, some bookmen had organized clandestine routes to bring Protestant books from Switzerland to Venice. What little is known of them came to light on the rare occasions when a denunciation brought them to the attention of the Holy Office. In 1550, for example, the tribunal learned of an organization that smuggled Protestant books from Switzerland into the Republic through the northwestern frontier. In the Swiss Protestant town of Poschiavo, the northern terminus, Dolfin Landolfo, a Protestant publisher of Vergerio, was the key figure. His Italian collaborators included an unidentified Brescian bookman and one of the Zanetti, a family of Venetian printers who originally came from Brescia. Zanetti, whose Christian name was not revealed, journeyed to Poschiavo to meet Landolfo under the pretext of arranging a printing contract. He then returned to Brescia with his contraband. From there the books were transhipped to Verona, Mantua, and Venice, probably with the aid of the

---

Benedictis (p. 95), writes that it is sometimes printed with the second one. The second oration is *Oratione seconda de l'eccellente M. Bernardino Tomitano, alli medesimi signori* (n.p., n.d., but with a dedicatory letter of March 20, 1556, Padua). There is a copy in the VM, Misc. 2380.–.5.

[102] SU, Bu. 10, Lucio Paolo Rosello & Pietro Cocco, docs. of June 22 and 23, 1551. These inventories are printed and annotated by Perini, "Ancora sul Pietro Perna," pp. 387–91.

Brescian bookman. Landolfo went to Brescia annually, ostensibly on business, but undoubtedly to supervise the operation. The Brescian Holy Office reportedly acted to halt the illicit traffic, but the Venetian tribunal does not appear to have investigated Zanetti.[103]

Pietro Perna, a bookman from Lucca who went to Basel in 1543 and became a Protestant, established a network for shipping prohibited books that flourished from c. 1546 through 1558, and possibly longer. Under the cover of legitimate commercial transactions, he established contacts for the delivery of prohibited books in Venice, Padua, Bergamo, Bologna, and Lucca. Perna journeyed back and forth from Basel to Italy, including Venice, to carry on his clandestine trade. As the growing vigilance of the authorities imperiled his trips, Perna concentrated on publishing Italian Protestant titles in Basel, but he continued to ship contraband south until his death in 1582.[104]

The smugglers had the initial advantage of several years to organize and operate their clandestine networks before church and state authorities made any effort to intercept them. Throughout the 1550s and early 1560s, the Venetian Holy Office did little; it was not empowered to police the book trade, and not until the mid-1560s did it prosecute enough local heretics (as opposed to Anabaptists from the Dominion) to uncover much information on the traffic in Protestant books. Until then the Holy Office was dependent on denunciations for leads to the clandestine activity. More than likely, there was greater illegal traffic in these two decades than what the tribunal discovered.

Interrelated conventicles with membership drawn from a cross section of Venetian society received the Protestant literature. Humanist schoolmasters who taught the children of the patriciate held heretical views, as did lawyers and physicians who had studied at Padua. Young nobles, both legitimate sons who enjoyed the right to sit in the Great Council and bastards who carried the name but not the privileges of nobility, partici-

[103] SU, Bu. 8, Dolfin Landolfo, anonymous denunciation of April 22, 1550, and testimony of Antonio Moretti of Poschiavo, October 20, 1550. These are documents of the Brescian Inquisition sent to the Venetian Holy Office. Some of this material has been noted by Edouard Pommier, "Notes sur la propagande protestante dans la République de Venise au milieu du XVIe siècle," in *Aspects de la propagande religieuse* (Geneva, 1957), p. 242. "Zanetti" could be one of several of that family who were active as publishers from 1535 to 1596, including Bartolomeo, who published several editions of Antonio Brucioli's vernacular Bible, commentaries on Scripture, and *Dialogi* between 1536 and 1540. For Zanetti family chronology, see Roberto Cessi, "Bartolomeo e Camillo Zanetti, tipografi e calligrafi del '500," *Archivio veneto-tridentino* 8 (1925), 174–82. The Brescian bookseller was identified only as at the sign of the Gallo near the church of San Agata.

[104] Perini, "Pietro Perna," and "Ancora sul Pietro Perna." For his later activities, see Ch. VI, sec. 1, and Antonio Rotondò's forthcoming study.

pated in the conventicles. Merchants from Venice and abroad, especially the Germans who lived in the sanctuary of the Fondaco dei Tedeschi, joined conventicles. Membership extended as far down the social ladder as petty shopkeepers, and included a goldsmith, a druggist, and a street vendor of shoes. By and large, these dissidents were oriented toward the doctrines of Calvin and Luther rather than toward those of the Anabaptists. They professed the sole authority of Scripture and faith alone, and denied purgatory, the efficacy of works, and the intercession of saints.[105]

Teofilo Panarelli was the leader of one conventicle. He had first been taught heretical views by Fra Bartolomeo Fonzio in Fonzio's school in Padua in 1550 and 1551.[106] Panarelli studied medicine at Padua from 1554 to 1559 and, upon receiving his degree, went to Venice. With an autographed copy of Fonzio's "Catechism" as his guide, Panarelli became, in turn, the teacher of Venetian dissidents, who included merchants, lawyers, nobles, and at least one bookman. They met in a bookstore or a pharmacy, and then went to the gardens of the Giudecca or the Isola di San Giorgio, where they walked and talked, or sat in the shade while Panarelli instructed them from a text. At other times they met in the houses of adherents like Marc'Antonio Da Canale, a noble of some importance, or in the Fondaco dei Tedeschi. After listening to music, Panarelli read and interpreted the New Testament, Ochino's *Prediche*, and Calvin's *Catechism*. In their meetings the dissenters agonized over whether they should flee to Geneva to avoid committing "idolatry." A handful left, but the majority remained, only to be denounced and arrested. Beginning in 1565, when the Inquisition acted, some fled, others abjured, and some were questioned and released; for still others who were accused, the records are silent. Panarelli continued his teaching until denounced in June 1567; he was hanged in Rome in 1572.

[105] The fate of the noble members of the conventicles, and the government's reaction upon learning of their involvement, is discussed in Ch. IV, sec. 2. Here the trials are examined for what they indicate of the availability of prohibited books from c. 1555 to c. 1567 and the role of the bookmen. The most informative trial is SU, Bu. 32, Teofilo Panarelli e Ludovico Abioso. Also see Bu. 32, Teofilo, Virginia, e Catherina Panarelli, Francesco Rocca libraro, Giulio Gemma, e Hieronimo de Padua; Bu. 11, Giovan Andrea Ugone; Bu. 20, Antonio Loredano e Alvise Malipiero; Bu. 20, Pietro Agusto; Bu. 20, Michele De Basili, Carlo Corner, e Venturino Dalle Madonette; Bu. 22, Francesco Emo; Bu 22; Matteo e Alessandro degli Avogari, Andrea Pasqualigo; Bu. 23, Silvestro, Cipriano, et Stefano Semprini, Andrea Dandolo, Marc'Antonio Da Canale, Luigi Mocenigo et al.

[106] There is a large literature on Fonzio. See Achille Olivieri, "Il *Catechismo* e la *Fidei et doctrinae . . . ratio* di Bartolomeo Fonzio, eretico veneziano del Cinquecento," *Studi veneziani* 9 (1967), 339–452; Ester Zille, *Gli eretici a Cittadella nel Cinquecento* (Cittadella, 1971), pp. 141–221; and the works cited therein.

A series of trials between 1565 and 1572 revealed that members of the conventicles held an impressive assortment of orthodox Protestant titles, but few Anabaptist, Antitrinitarian, and Socinian works. They possessed Calvin's *Catechism* and *Institutes*, and titles of northern heresiarchs such as Bèze, Brenz, Bucer, Bullinger, Luther, Melanchthon, and Oecolampadius. They read the works of Italian exiles such as Francesco Betti, Brucioli, Giulio della Rovere, Ochino, Vergerio, and Vermigli. The Geneva New Testament was their Bible. Fonzio's "Catechism" and excerpts from heretical works circulated in manuscript.[107]

In addition to the smuggling networks of the bookmen, the dissenters had several means of acquiring and distributing Protestant titles. One Venetian follower of Panarelli, a merchant who dealt in waxes and hempen rope, imported "many copies" of Calvin's *Catechism* from Lyons for dissemination.[108] The Protestants at the Fondaco dei Tedeschi had a supply of heretical literature to distribute. On the eve of his departure, one German merchant gave Panarelli copies of Bucer, Luther, and John Hus. Dissenters also exchanged titles; for example, Panarelli gave a holograph copy of Fonzio's "Catechism" to a Venetian goldsmith in exchange for a *Beneficio di Christo*.[109]

The heretics were adept at disposing of their forbidden titles when danger threatened; they habitually left the Inquisition one step behind. Of the many titles that the heretics around Panarelli admitted holding, the tribunal did not lay its hands on a single copy. The abjuring heretic always testified that the books were no longer in his possession because he had sold them to a foreigner since departed from Venice, because he had burned them upon his reconversion to Catholicism, or even because the books had been stolen. The tribunal had its hands full dealing with the heretics and probably could not spare additional effort for the books. Thus, the books survived, perhaps to inspire and serve other conventicles.

A few bookmen distributed heretical books, aided the local dissidents, and perhaps shared their views. Andrea Arrivabene was the target of a series of accusations from the mid-1540s until his death in 1570. A detailed review of his activities and associations strongly suggests, but does not conclusively prove, that he held Protestant beliefs.

Giorgio Arrivabene from Mantua published in Venice from 1483 through 1515, followed by Cesare from 1517 to 1528. Most of Cesare's

---

[107] For a detailed list, see App. II.

[108] "Cathechismo del Calvino l'hebbi da Ludovico Abioso quale me disse che ne haveva fatto venire molti da Lione per distribuirle." SU, Bu. 32, Teofilo Panarelli e Ludovico Abioso, f. [3^r], Panarelli's testimony of November 23, 1571.

[109] SU, Bu. 32, Panarelli e Abioso, ff. [2^v–3^v], Panarelli's testimony of November 23, 1571.

publications were religious titles—several were by Savonarola. After a short hiatus, Andrea di Giorgio began publishing in 1534 in his shop al segno del Pozzo (at the sign of the well) in the Mercerie.[110]

Between 1544 and 1549, Arrivabene supplied books to, corresponded with, and visited a group of heretics from Viadana, a village on the Po between Parma and Mantua. The titles supplied included the *Beneficio di Christo*, Urbanus Rhegius' *Medicina dell'anima*, and the *Sommario della Scrittura*. In one letter Arrivabene judged the *Medicina dell'-anima* to be good and Christian. In another he praised some unnamed books as being "full of the fire of love of those benefits that have been won for us ingrates by our benign Jesus Christ." The passage was perfectly orthodox, but it perhaps echoed the *Beneficio di Christo*. The Inquisition of Reggio Emilia in 1570 uncovered seven Viadana heretics and burned one of them. In its investigation the tribunal questioned Arrivabene's correspondent concerning the behavior and beliefs of the bookman, but learned nothing of consequence. The Inquisition of Reggio Emilia sent the material on Arrivabene, including the letters, to the Venetian Inquisition in late 1570, but Arrivabene had died in the first half of the year.[111]

Two sources linked Arrivabene to heretical associations and accused him of heterodox beliefs in Venice in 1549. Giovanni Osimanno of Viterbo, who had been condemned to the Venetian galleys for ten years for heresy, posted letters begging for help whenever his galley entered port in the spring of 1549. He addressed the letters to Francesco Stella in care of Arrivabene's bookstore.[112] In November of that year, an

---

[110] Of twenty-eight titles of Cesare Arrivabene noted in *STC Italian*, 765, and *Cambridge Catalogue*, II, 368, twenty-two were religious, including six of Savonarola. On Giorgio Arrivabene, see P. Tentori, "Giorgio Arrivabene," DBI, 4, pp. 324–25. Andrea is described as the son of "Zorzi mantovano in marzaria all'insegna del pozzo," in SU, Bu. 156, "Librai e libri proibiti, 1545–1571," f. [76ʳ], September 13, 1567.

[111] SU, Bu. 30, Andrea Arrivabene. The documents include an excerpt from the trial of Viano de Viani of October 24, 1570, letters of October 28 and December 4, 1570, from the inquisitor of Reggio Emilia to the Venetian inquisitor, and five autograph letters of Arrivabene to Viano de Viani of May 31, 1544; June 6, 1547; June 5, July 31, and August 27, 1549. All mention books; that of May 31, 1544, the *Medicina dell'anima*. The quoted passage is in the letter of August 29, 1549: "Voglio siatj contento accettare queste belle opere: laquale è tutto pieno di focho [fuoco] da amore di quelli beneficij che noi ingratj havemo conseguitj dal nostro benigno Giesù Cristo." The Arrivabene material of Bu. 30 is also printed by Carlo de Frede, *La prima traduzione italiana del Corano sullo sfondo dei rapporti tra Cristianità e Islam nel Cinquecento*, Studi e materiali sulla conoscenza dell'oriente in Italia, 2 (Naples, 1967), pp. 63–73. My references, however, are to the originals.

[112] Eight letters of Giovanni Osimanno to Stella "alla libraria del pozzo in Merzaria," from March 21 through June 9, 1549, in SU, Bu. 7, Girolamo

anonymous denouncer accused Stella of heresy and of holding prohibited books; the accuser added that Arrivabene shared the heretical views of Vergerio and that he had heretical books in his house.[113] The Inquisition searched Arrivabene's house and shop but found nothing.[114]

In June 1551 the Venetian Holy Office questioned Arrivabene about his relationship with Lucio Paolo Rosello and Pietro Cocco; it was particularly eager to discover what connection, if any, Arrivabene had had with the prohibited books in the possession of those men. The tribunal established that Arrivabene was acquainted with Rosello and Cocco; for the latter he had bound two heretical works: the anonymous *Il capo finto* (1544) and a *Libretto consolatorio a li perseguitati per la confessione della verità evangelica* (Milan, 1545) attributed to Urbanus Rhegius.[115] Arrivabene claimed that he could not recall other heretical titles that might have passed through his hands, and the tribunal seemed unaware of the fact that Arrivabene was in the process of publishing two, apparently innocent, titles of Rosello.[116] Nevertheless, the tribunal was suspicious enough to order Arrivabene to deposit a bond of 100 ducats as a guarantee of his future good conduct.[117]

Dall'Avogaria, Simeone De Cattanei, Girolamo Dalla Crosette, Camillo Orsino, e Giuliano Tagliapietra, no pag.

[113] Denunciation of November 16, 1549, quoted by Brown, *Venetian Press*, p. 113, from SU, Bu. 7, Francesco Stella. The inventory of Stella's prohibited books is printed and annotated by Perini, "Ancora sul Pietro Perna," pp. 392–94.

[114] "Domandato che lui debba dir la verita [illegible word] il tempo che esso constituto mando diti libri come di sopra.

Rispose: in verita io ho dito il tempo, et fu pocho dopo che mi fu cercato in case se ge [?] era libri per la denuntia che mi fu data contra heresia, et li mandai coj dir guarda [?] che se mi cerchavano in bottega, et haveseno trovato tal libri mi havriano ruinato, et certo come vi ho dito sendo era, che mi fu cercato come di sopra, non mi ricordava nianche del diti libri." Testimony of Arrivabene of June 27, 1551, in SU, Bu. 158, Processi Registro 1551, libro secondo, f. 1ʳ. His testimony begins in mid-sentence and is undated, but can easily be dated because the following testimony (f. 2ʳ) is of Tuesday, June 30. Since the tribunal normally sat on Tuesday, Thursday, and Saturday, the date of June 27, Saturday, is logical.

[115] SU, Bu. 158, Processi Registro 1551, libro secondo, ff. 1ʳ–3ʳ, testimony of Arrivabene of June 27 and of Lucio Paolo Rosello of July 1, 1551. Also, SU, Bu. 10, Lucio Paolo Rosello e Pietro Cocco, testimony of Cocco of July 27, 1551, no pag. Both works were listed in the 1549 *Catalogo* and the Venetian Index of 1554. Also see Reusch, *Index*, I, 122, 383. Incidentally, another dissenter testified in 1551 that he had purchased a Vergerio title at Arrivabene's shop. Perini, "Ancora sul Pietro Perna," p. 365, n. 11.

[116] They were an Italian translation of the Greek sermons of Bishop Theodoret of Cyprus in 1551, and *Il ritratto del vero governo del prencipe dal essempio vivo del gran Cosimo* of 1552. Perini, "Ancora sul Pietro Perna," p. 370, n. 41; *STC Italian*, 587, 752.

[117] SU, Bu. 158, Processi Registro 1551, libro secondo, ff. 2ʳ (sentence of June

The confession of October 17, 1551, that revealed many Anabaptists across Italy also denounced Arrivabene and his unnamed brother as "Lutherans."[118] Although the Venetian Inquisition and government arrested the Anabaptists, they did not at this time pursue many of the Venetians accused of orthodox Protestantism. Besides, the Holy Office had recently questioned Arrivabene, searched his home and shop, and found nothing.

Arrivabene may have been a terminus in Pietro Perna's network for smuggling Protestant literature into Venice. On October 30, 1552, an Inquisition commissioner discovered in Arrivabene's store Giovanni Francesco Virginio's *Le dotte e pie parafrasi sopra le pistole di Paolo a Romani, Galati, et Hebrei, non mai piu veduti in luce* (Lyons, 1551). "Virginio" is thought to be a pseudonym for Cornelio Donzellini, an Italian Protestant. The Holy Office questioned Arrivabene, who responded that he had purchased the book from "Messer Piero," a bookseller in the Mercerie at the sign of Santi Pietro e Paolo. Upon interrogation, Messer Piero reported that the work was from three bales of books that Girolamo Donzellini, brother of Cornelio, had brought him to sell. Donzellini had told him that he had gotten the books at the customs house from Tommaso Giunti. Piero was unable to recall the titles; he had had a list, but lost it, and he could only remember that the majority had been medical and philosophical titles. He did remember that he had sold Arrivabene eight or nine ducats' worth, an amount that could represent as few as five or as many as thirty volumes, depending on format and size. The Holy Office ordered Piero to bring in the remaining books, but the documents do not indicate whether this was done or whether the tribunal took further action.[119]

The significant point of this testimony is Arrivabene's possible link with the smuggling network of Perna and Girolamo Donzellini. A physician from Brescia, Girolamo came to Venice in 1546; Baldassarre Altieri introduced him to Protestant literature. Cornelio Donzellini, a monk and theologian already persuaded by the new views, encouraged Girolamo's Prot-

---

30, 1551), 12^v (receipt for a deposit of 15 ducats by Arrivabene on November 5, 1551).

[118] Ginzburg, *I costituti di Manelfi*, 49, 70.

[119] SU, Bu. 158, Processi Registro 1553, libro quarto, ff. 54^r–55^r, October 31, 1552. On the title and Virginio's identity, see John A. Tedeschi, "Genevan Books of the Sixteenth Century," BHR, 31 (1969), 174–76. The work was reprinted in an enlarged edition in Geneva, 1555, but does not appear to have been listed in the Index. Eugénie Droz, *Chemins de l'hérésie. Textes et documents*, vol. II (Geneva, 1971), pp. 236–37, suggests on limited evidence another identity for Virginio. In this volume, pp. 229–93, and in vol. III (Geneva, 1974), pp. 75–207, she offers additional information on northern printings of Italian Protestant works.

estant inclinations. Cornelio soon left Italy, but Girolamo remained in Venice, where he continued his Protestant studies, passing from Melanchthon to Johannes Brenz, Curione, and Francesco Negri, with books furnished by Perna.

Girolamo also distributed contraband in Venice for Perna. In November 1550, Perna, then in Basel, sent Girolamo detailed instructions on how to sell a bale of books being sent to him in Venice. The bale, which included a "grammatica" by Cornelio, would be sent in care of a merchant, and then some unnamed "gentlemen" would help him get it through customs. Perna instructed Girolamo to take the books to "quello di Ss. Pietro e Paulo" to sell. On his next trip to Padua, Perna would pick up the unsold volumes. He warned Girolamo not to mention Perna's name at any time.[120] Girolamo's actions in 1552 closely matched Perna's instructions of 1550.

It is impossible to determine from the testimony of Arrivabene and Messer Piero whether the former was a regular or occasional purchaser of Perna-Donzellini contraband, but the poor memories of the two suggest that they had something to hide. Neither Arrivabene nor Piero could recall which titles had been sold; yet it is unlikely that neither of them knew. They were businessmen, and the transaction involved eight or nine ducats. In light of the above testimony, and the number of heretics who knew of Arrivabene's store, it is possible that he was an important retail distributor of heretical books.[121]

Since Perna sent Girolamo Donzellini one bale of books in late 1550, but Donzellini had three bales in 1552, it appears that Donzellini was an active agent, at least until 1553, when he was denounced for heresy. He fled, and traveled widely in Italy, Switzerland, and Germany, where he consorted with Vergerio. Returning to Venice, he abjured in 1560 and began to practice medicine in Brescia, Verona, and Venice. Denounced again, he abjured before the Venetian Holy Office a second time, in 1574; he was released in 1576 when the prisons were emptied because of the

---

[120] Letter of Perna of November 13, 1550, Basel, to Donzellini in Venice, printed by Perini, "Pietro Perna," p. 159.

[121] Another question remains unresolved: Was Tommaso Giunti (1494–1566), head of the publishing house, in league with Perna? In November 1551, the Holy Office questioned Giunti about Perna, who, although forbidden entry into the Venetian state, had come, ostensibly for business reasons, with a twenty-day pass obtained for him by Giunti. The Inquisition was disappointed that it could not lay its hands on Perna, but honored the pass. SU, Bu. 158, Processi Registro 1551, libro secondo, ff. 19^{r-v}, November 14, 1551. A year later Girolamo Donzellini reportedly obtained books, which more than likely originated with Perna in Basel, from Giunti at the customs house. Giunti may have been a collaborator of Perna. On the other hand, he may only have unwittingly provided Perna with a legitimate commercial shield for his smuggling.

plague. He remained in Venice and possibly continued to play a role in the distribution of prohibited books until he was executed in 1587 as a relapsed and obstinate heretic.[122]

Inquisition witnesses testified that Arrivabene held heretical beliefs throughout the 1550s, and that he continued to offer his shop as a meeting place and post office for dissenters. A Florentine testifying on his heretical acquaintances in Venice in the period c. 1555 to c. 1562 judged Arrivabene to be "in part" a heretic. He added that he had delivered letters from Francesco Stella and Giovanni Bernardino Bonifacio, the Marchese d'Oria, to Arrivabene. Bonifacio, a southern nobleman of Protestant sympathies who fled Italy for Basel in 1557 but visited Venice in 1558 and again in 1560, also judged Arrivabene to be a heretic, according to the Florentine.[123] Another witness testified that Teofilo Panarelli frequented Arrivabene's bookstore between 1554 and 1559.[124]

[122] On the Donzellini brothers, see SU, Bu. 39, Girolamo Donzellino; Bongi, *Giolito*, I, 345–52; Perini, "Pietro Perna," pp. 147–51, 158–59, and "Ancora sul Pietro Perna," pp. 368–75; Stella I, 178; Stella II, 38–39, n. 75; *Nunziature* XI, 346–47, n. I; Ch. VI, sec. I.

[123] "In Venetia ho havuto cognoscenza con messer Andrea Arrivabene libraro il quale se mostrava in parte heretico et favorevole a queste." And elsewhere: "Andrea Arrivabene libraro lo cognobi parecchi anni sono credo otto anni in circa per mezzo de Francesco Stella quale dovendo io andare a Venetia me dette una lettera che la portasse a detto Andrea. . . . al quale Andrea portai lettere dal Marchese d'Oria, che una andava ad un gentilhomo venetiano del quale non me ricordo il nome al quale condotto dal detto Andrea portai la sua lettera et detto Marchese me diceva che giudicava detto Andrea per heretico se ben diceva che non si era scoperto in tutto." SU, Bu. 24, Francesco Boroni, Giuseppe Cingano, Gabriele De Stringari, e Luigi De Colti, a two-folio copy of a (Roman?) trial entitled "Ex processu Petri tornaquinci florentini" addressed to the Venetian nuncio and dated April 14, 1569. Tornaquinci confessed to a wide acquaintance with major and minor Venetian heretics of this period, including Antonio Brucioli, Andrea Da Ponte, Francesco Stella, and Bartolomeo Fonzio, whom he visited in prison. Although his testimony is a little unclear chronologically, one can ascertain generally the period of Arrivabene's involvement by Tornaquinci's references to the other heretics. Brucioli died in 1556; Stella was active in Venice, Gorizia, and Trieste until imprisoned in the summer of 1558; Andrea Da Ponte fled to Geneva about 1560; and Fonzio was imprisoned in 1558, and drowned on August 4, 1562. Bonifacio (1517–97), was in Venice in 1557 before fleeing to Basel in August; he returned to Venice in April 1558, and was visited by Stella, but fled to Trieste in July after he was denounced to the Inquisition. (Incidentally, his flight possibly was welcomed by the Venetian government, for the Council of Ten did not want to arrest and extradite him. CX, Secrete, R. 6, f. 193^v, July 28, 1558.) Bonifacio returned secretly to Venice in April and May 1560, possibly to recover his beloved books, before leaving Italy for the last time. On Bonifacio, see Frederic C. Church, *The Italian Reformers 1534–1564* (New York, 1932), pp. 273–303, and passim.

[124] "Io l'ho conosciuto avanti che'l si vestisse a manega comedo [i.e., manica

No evidence linking Arrivabene to heretics and heretical books after c. 1562 has come to light. He may have cut his associations with Protestants, or he may have been careful enough to escape notice. When Arrivabene died in the first half of 1570, Francesco Ziletti took over his shop at the sign of the Pozzo. The Holy Office soon discovered a stock of prohibited books in the store, but Ziletti protested that they had come into his hands unknowingly with his purchase of the store.[125] Ziletti's protestation was typical of the alibi used by bookmen when caught with contraband, and it is impossible to determine if it contained any truth.

Although Arrivabene exercised caution in his publishing, he did publish the works of religious dissenters, and these contained some unorthodox passages. Between 1545 and 1552, Arrivabene published seven different titles of Ortensio Lando, including *Dialogo della Sacra Scrittura* (1552), which presented Evangelical views and at times strayed beyond orthodoxy, and *Ragionamenti familiari* (1550), which proposed an Evangelical view of faith and works, and sharply criticized the clergy. Indeed, Lando may have been propagating in disguised form the same religious ideas circulating in Venetian Anabaptist conventicles at mid-century. Arrivabene also published in 1547 the first Italian translation of the Koran.[126]

The chain of accusations and associations argues that from the mid-1540s to c. 1560 Arrivabene was at least a Protestant sympathizer and probably a heretic. The accumulated evidence was enough to warrant a thorough investigation by the Holy Office. He escaped such probing primarily because of his discretion. Arrivabene was always circumspect; he never committed himself in writing or spoke carelessly. When questioned by the Inquisition, he offered just enough information to give his answers bare plausibility and to avoid arousing the suspicion that he was holding back too much. If Arrivabene was a Protestant, he probably was an extremely discreet and solitary one. When the Inquisition broke up the conventicles in the 1560s, Arrivabene was not identified as a participant. However large a role he played in smuggling Protestant literature, Arrivabene avoided drawing attention to himself in other ways. For example, he

---

comodo] nella libraria di Messer Andrea dal pozzo dove esso soleva pratticare." SU, Bu. 32, Teofilo Panarelli e Ludovico Abioso, f. 6ʳ, testimony of Abioso about Panarelli of May 24, 1568. The phrase, "vestirsi a maniche comode" in the plural, means to receive an academic degree. Hence, Panarelli frequented Arrivabene's shop while still a medical student in Padua (1554–59).

[125] See Ch. v, sec. 1.

[126] Grendler, *Critics*, pp. 120–27; App. ii, items 12, 18, 19, 22, 23, 26, 27, and 53; Silvana Seidel Menchi, "Spiritualismo radicale nelle opere di Ortensio Lando attorno al 1550," *Archiv für Reformationsgeschichte* 65 (1974), 210–77; De Frede, *La prima traduzione italiana del Corano*, pp. 31–48.

joined, but did not play a prominent role, in the opposition to the various Indices. Arrivabene was also fortunate in his encounters with the Inquisition, or perhaps he had a keen sense of how exhaustively the tribunal intended to investigate. When the tribunal interrogated him in 1551 and 1552, it was not yet vigorously and thoroughly prosecuting people like himself. To find out more about his commerce in prohibited books and his beliefs, the Inquisition would have had to devote much more time and energy than his possible offense seemed to warrant at that time. In the 1560s, when the tribunal investigated more vigorously, Arrivabene avoided detection. He may simply have been fortunate, in that no confessing heretic volunteered any incriminating information about him. Where much evidence is lacking, a final assessment of the beliefs and activities of someone who lived four centuries ago ultimately depends in part on the researcher's intuition, and must be offered tentatively. Yet, even with all the qualifications, there is strong reason to believe that Arrivabene was a Protestant and was deeply involved in the clandestine traffic in prohibited books.

A humbler bookman was also accused of heresy and of trafficking in prohibited books at this time. Paolo Avanzo (or degli Avanzi), born c. 1540, was described as a "bresciano" and as a native of Salò on Lake Garda, about thirty kilometers northeast of Brescia. It is likely that Paolo was related to the small publisher Ludovico Avanzo at the sign of the Albero in the Mercerie, who was also described as a Brescian.[127] Paolo was not a publisher, nor did he ever have his own shop. He worked for the Aldine Press and Gabriel Giolito, and he also bound books and sold manuscripts. Like many bookmen, he had traveled abroad, to Geneva, Lyons, and Naples.

Several confessing heretics identified Paolo Avanzo as a Calvinist. Panarelli admitted teaching Avanzo, whom he described as an uneducated man, about "le cose di Ginevra" at the meetings in the gardens of the Isola di San Giorgio in late 1559 or early 1560. Bartolomeo Bartocci, an Italian Calvinist exile who subsequently was burned alive in Rome in May 1569, testified that Avanzo was a Calvinist. These and other witnesses added a few scraps of information about Avanzo's convictions, i.e., that he had praised the anti-Catholic preaching that he had heard in Lyons and that he possessed a Genevan New Testament.[128]

[127] SU, Bu. 156, "Librai e libri proibiti, 1545–1571," f. [76ʳ]. Ludovico Avanzo published 30 editions between 1556 and 1576.

[128] SU, Bu. 11, Giovanni Andrea Ugone, f. 45ʳ, testimony of Michel Schiavor of March 30, 1565, in which he named as a heretic "un Paolo stava alla libraria dell'anchora in mazzeria, il quale fu in Geneva, et è ritornato al questo libraro dell'anchora." SU, Bu. 32, Teofilo Panarelli e Ludovico Abioso, testimony of Panarelli of November 19, and December 6, 1571, no pag., and Abioso's testimony on

Avanzo may have played an important role in the clandestine book traffic between Geneva and Venice. When Bartocci lived in Geneva, from 1555 or 1556 to 1567, he sent Calvinist titles into Venice and other Italian cities with the aid of Avanzo. Bartocci testified that he had sent Avanzo a printed copy of Théodore de Bèze's speech(es) at the Colloquy of Poissy of September 1561 and a printed letter of exhortation composed by Peter Martyr Vermigli.[129] Another member of the Bartocci family testified that he had carried a *Catechism* (probably Calvin's) to Vicenza, where he had passed it on to Avanzo. Neither explained the means by which the books were smuggled into Venetian territory. These Bartocci depositions, made in Rome, were forwarded to the Venetian Inquisition, which questioned Avanzo in January 1570. He denied everything, and his name disappeared from the tribunal's records. However, Panarelli testified in 1571 that he had heard that Avanzo was imprisoned in Rome. His fate is unknown.

Fragmentary evidence suggests that another bookman shared the views of the Venetian heretics. Panarelli testified that when his arrest seemed imminent (c. June 1567) another heretic had arranged for an unnamed bookman to come and examine his books for possible purchase. This bookman had a shop at San Polo, and was described to Panarelli as a heretic and the friend of the merchant Ludovico Abioso, a prominent member of the Panarelli conventicle. According to Panarelli, the bookman came but declined to take the books on the grounds that he would be unable to find a buyer for them.[130]

---

ff. 23ᵛ, 25ᵛ (July 31, 1568), and 27ʳ (August 2, 1568). SU, Bu. 29, Paolo Avanzo. This trial also contains excerpts of testimony before the Inquisition in Rome concerning Avanzo; see ff. 16ʳ⁻ᵛ, 19ʳ⁻ᵛ (Bartolomeo Bartocci's testimony of September 7, 1568 and January 28, 1569), 20ᵛ (Alessandro Bartocci's testimony of August 15, 1568). On January 28, 1570 (f. 21ᵛ), the Venetian tribunal questioned Avanzo, who was described as a "ligador giovane nella bottega insegna del Capello." On Bartolomeo Bartocci, see Carlo Ginzburg, "Bartolomeo Bartocci," DBI, 6, pp. 547–49.

[129] In Bartolomeo Bartocci's words, the books were "una lettera essortativa stampata, composta da Pietro Martire Vermiglio & il parlamento che fece il Bezza avanti il Re di Franza." SU, Bu. 29, Paolo Avanzo, f. 19ᵛ, January 19, 1569. Several French editions of Bèze's speeches and one Italian translation whose title exactly matched Bartocci's description were printed in Geneva in 1561. Paul Chaix, Alain Dufour, and Gustave Moeckli, *Les livres imprimés à Genève de 1550 à 1600*, rev. ed. by Gustave Moeckli (Geneva, 1966), pp. 45–46. I have been unable to identify the Vermigli title.

[130] "Quando la corte venne per prendermi, io havevo ascoso i libri miei prohibiti in una botte vacua in cantina, et per far danari, questo Gio. Stella me menò un libraro a casa, accio che quel libraro me le vendesse, dicendo che quel libraro era heretico anco lui, io non so il suo nome, ma fu bottega de libraro a San Polo, et era questo libraro amico anco di Ludovico Abioso, et gli ligava i libri." SU, Bu. 32, Teofilo Panarelli e Ludovico Abioso, ff. [5ʳ⁻ᵛ], November 23, 1571.

This sketchy information points to Francesco Rocca at the sign of the Castello in the parish of San Polo. Rocca published seventeen works between 1550 and 1576, including two suspect titles: an Italian translation of Erasmus' *Institutio Christiani matrimonii* (1550), which was banned by the 1554 Venetian, the Pauline, and the Tridentine Indices,[131] and a 1551 printing of a vernacular New Testament derived from Brucioli's Protestant version.[132] In 1572 Abioso told the Inquisition that Rocca had been a heretic at one time. The tribunal questioned Rocca about his religious opinions and asked whether he had ever dealt in prohibited books with Panarelli. Rocca denied ever having sold prohibited titles or discussed the faith (a way of assuring the Inquisition of his unquestioning acceptance of Catholicism) and the Inquisition dismissed him.[133]

The final reference to Rocca is a posthumous one. In 1588 the Holy Office questioned Oswaldo (or Ubaldo) Venzoni, who published a handful of titles and operated a bookstore under the sign of the Castello, now in San Moisè. The tribunal asked him about three prohibited titles discovered in his shop: Calvin's *Responsio ad Balduini* (1562), Mathurin Cordier's *De corrupti sermonis emendatione*, and Erasmus' *Paraphrasis in epistolas Pauli* (a work permitted if expurgated). Venzoni testified that all three had come to him as part of his wife's dowry from his late father-in-law, Francesco Rocca, who had died during the Great Plague of 1575–77.[134] These bits of information are insufficient to establish that Rocca was a Protestant or a sympathizer, or even that he dealt in prohibited books. But he may have leaned toward Protestantism at one time, and he may have helped his heretical friends obtain and dispose of banned works.

Initially, the desire for profit probably motivated some of the bookmen as much as, or more than, sympathy for Protestantism. They were accustomed to seeing a book simply as a piece of merchandise to be bought and sold at a price. When the Inquisition began to burn heretical books in the late 1540s, it probably drove up their price. The temptation to exploit the shortage at a time when the risks were not great must have been over-

[131] *Ordinatione del Matrimonio de Christiani, per Desiderio Erasmo Roterodamo, opera veramente utile non solo ai maritati, ma a tutti quelli, che desiderano vivere secondo la christiana dottrina; hora del latino tradotta, e primieramente stampata.* (In fine: In Vinetia per Francesco Rocca et fratelli, 1550.) 8°. Not listed in *Bibliotheca Erasmiana*, it can be found in BNF, Guicciardini 23-3-11, and VM, 218. c. 149, where Marcella Grendler noted these copies.

[132] Spini, "Bibliografia di Brucioli," p. 153; *STC Italian*, 102.

[133] SU, Bu. 32, Teofilo, Virginia, e Catherina Panarelli, Francesco Rocca libraro, Giulio Gemma, e Hieronimo de Padua, ff. 26v–27v, testimony of Rocca of February 27, of Abioso of March 4, 1572.

[134] SU, Bu. 62, Oswaldo Venzoni, Giulio Rizzo, e Girolamo Zennaro, ff. 1r–v, 3v (testimony of Venzoni of October 8, and sentence of October 11, 1588). Venzoni was imprisoned for three days, then released with a warning.

whelming in a few cases. A bookman could have imported and sold clandestinely titles such as Ochino's *Prediche* in the early 1550s solely for financial motives. Throughout the century, some bookmen sold a few prohibited books for financial gain, but close association with local or foreign heretics, and traffic in the major works of northern heresiarchs in the late 1550s and subsequent decades, definitely suggested Protestant sympathies. Arrivabene's continuing use of his shop as a post office and meeting place for heretics and Avanzo's reported trafficking in Calvin's works argue Protestant beliefs or, at least, persevering sympathy for the Protestant cause.

One can only speculate about how Arrivabene and Avanzo, if they were heretics, arrived at Protestant beliefs. Possibly foreign experience played a major role. The bookmen had more opportunities for travel to Protestant lands, or to cities where Protestant preaching might be heard, than did members of most other trades. Avanzo reportedly traveled to Geneva and was moved by Protestant preaching in Lyons; as an "uneducated man" he would have been more likely to be swayed by the oral word than by his own study. The very discreet Arrivabene offered no clues about the origins of his beliefs; a generation older than Avanzo, he may have been a product of the Evangelism of the 1530s and 1540s. Nor is it possible to gauge the strength of their commitment to Protestantism. Even if their belief was strong and deep, they remained in Venice and conformed outwardly. They did not flee to Geneva to avoid "living in idolatry," but neither did very many other Venetians. Except for wealthy laymen and unencumbered monks, few could leave behind family and livelihood for the dangers of the unknown. Bookmen with heretical sympathies contributed to the Protestant cause through their trade: they imported and distributed banned literature, transported books and messages, volunteered their shops as post offices and meeting places, and occasionally published titles containing heterodox passages.

8. THE INDEX OF PAUL IV

The 1554/55 Index having been withdrawn, the Venetian Holy Office resorted to individual decrees, especially after the appointment of Fra Felice Peretti da Montalto (1521–90) of the Franciscan Conventuals, a zealous reformer and the future Sixtus V, as inquisitor in January 1557.[135] On June 22, 1557, the local tribunal forbade the sale of Erasmus' *Colloquies* and Valdés' *Mercurio et Caronte*, apparently on its own authority rather than on papal instruction. Fifty-seven bookmen appeared before the Holy

---

[135] Montalto is a small hill town in the March of Ancona. BAVa, Vaticanus Latinus 12141, "Sixtus Quintus Pontifex Maximus," f. 65^r. Pastor, xxi, 431–38, gives excerpts from this anonymous biography.

Office on August 22, 1558, to be informed that they were forbidden to print the Bible in any vernacular. Again the Venetian court had acted on its own authority, but it anticipated the stringent controls on vernacular Bibles to appear in the next Index.[136] On February 9, 1558, the Holy Office decreed that anyone importing books into the city had to deposit an inventory with the tribunal before the books might clear customs.[137] It received at least a few inventories, but possibly none earlier than December 1559.[138] The Holy Office also questioned a number of authors and bookmen who had avoided or disobeyed the prepublication scrutiny decreed by the Heads of the Council of Ten in 1527. The tribunal found that this limited prepublication censorship was often ignored, and occasionally levied a small fine.[139] The Holy Office was attempting to compensate for the failure of the Esecutori contro la bestemmia to enforce the press laws of the state.

A Roman commission had begun work on a new Index in 1556, but Paul IV's war against Spain delayed completion until December 1558. The new Index was printed and promulgated in Rome in January 1559.[140] Paul IV's Index condemned the opera omnia of about 550 authors, nearly twice the number listed in the 1554/55 Index, as well as many more individual titles.[141] It was the first to manifest the puritanism characteristic of Counter Reformation censorship, with the result that it vastly enlarged prohibitions in the field of vernacular literature. Newly prohibited were a number of authors and works that were not heretical, but were judged to be anticlerical, immoral, lascivious, or obscene. They included the opera omnia of Aretino, Machiavelli, and Rabelais, the poems of Francesco Berni and Giovanni Della Casa, and the *Facetie* of Poggio Bracciolini; Boccaccio's *Decameron* was ordered expurgated. With these prohibitions Paul IV

---

[136] SU, Bu. 156, "Librai e libri proibiti, 1545-1571," ff. [56^{r-v}, 97^{r-v}, 98^v].

[137] For the decree, see Brown, *Venetian Press*, pp. 127, 213 (text), 364, although he overestimates its impact. It is also noted in Barberino Latino 5195, f. 54^r. Sforza, "Controriforma," pt. 2, p. 174, mistakenly dates it as 1559 in the belief that the original date was mv. However, the Holy Office did not use mv dating.

[138] An inventory of "Libri venuti da Lione" of Tommaso Giunti, and four of Michele Tramezzino, carrying dates of December 9, 1559 through January 14, 1560, with the notation that they had been presented to the Inquisition in March 1560, are found in SU, Bu. 156, "Librai e libri proibiti, 1545-1571," ff. [91^r-95^v].

[139] SU, Bu. 14, Vincenzo Valgrisi et al., ff. 1^r-5^v, and additional unpaginated material not in chronological order, of March 3, 14, 22, December 17, July 9, August 20, September 20, and August 3, 1558.

[140] Pastor, xiv, 277-78; Hilgers, *Index*, pp. 488-89; Scaduto, "Lainez e l'indice del 1559," pp. 6-17.

[141] The 1559 Index lists 583 authors, but this includes a number of dual listings, such as "Calvinus" under "C" and "Joannes Calvinus" under "J," as well as many pseudonyms entered separately.

sought to excise some of the vibrant worldliness in Renaissance literature. The new Index expanded prohibitions in other areas as well. The 1554/55 Index had banned ten of Erasmus's titles but none of Savonarola's; the new Index condemned all of Erasmus's titles and many of Savonarola's. The Talmud was again banned along with works based on it. On the other hand, Paul IV's Index prohibited only two dialogues of Lucian and selected titles of William of Occam in contrast to the complete ban of the 1554/55 Index.

Paul IV's Index introduced into Italy a feature of earlier northern European Indices; it specifically condemned nearly sixty editions and printings of the Bible. It also banned the printing and possession of Bibles in any vernacular except with the permission of the Inquisition. The papacy's goal was to remove from circulation such works as Antonio Brucioli's Bible. Another innovation was the listing of about sixty publishers whose total output was proscribed. Publishers of Basel, Geneva, Nuremberg, Strasbourg, and Wittenberg predominated, but one Italian, Francesco Brucioli of Venice, the brother and publisher of Antonio, was also banned.[142] The new Index added some general rules but did not give directions for implementing them. All anonymous works published within the past forty years were banned, as were all books of magic, necromancy, etc., and books lacking the imprimaturs of diocesan ordinary and inquisitor.

Paul IV's Index was much larger than its predecessors and included some new categories of prohibitions, but its greatest significance derived from the fact that it was the first Index to be promulgated unequivocally by the papacy in its capacity as spiritual leader of Catholic Christendom. Paul IV did not invite the bookmen of Venice or any other city to comment on his Index, but demanded immediate implementation and enforcement.

In Paul IV's Rome, where even cardinals held their tongues for fear of the Inquisition, the new Index produced great consternation and caused large numbers of books to be destroyed. In the words of a contemporary historian, Paul IV wanted to "expunge from human memory the names of heretics."[143] When the Index appeared, the Roman bookmen offered to sell prohibited volumes as scrap paper in order to realize a minimal return on their investment, but were turned down. The pope's uncompromising severity displeased even the cardinals of the Congregation of the Inquisi-

---

[142] Francesco Brucioli published about ten editions and printings of his brother's works and a handful of other titles between 1540 and 1546.

[143] *Delle istorie del mondo, parte terza. Aggiunte da M. Mambrino Roseo da Fabriano alle istorie di M. Giovanni Tarcagnota* (In Venezia, Appresso i Giunti, MDLXXXV), Bk. VII, 603–04. The first edition was 1562.

tion, but they dared not protest. It was estimated that every reader lost some books, and that humanists, legists, and medical scholars were particularly hard hit.

From all over Italy laymen and clergy, especially the Jesuits, protested the new Index.[144] Readers and bookmen were dismayed, not only because the Index was comprehensive, but also because the pope intended to enforce it vigorously. In the middle of the swirling controversy was Cardinal Michele Ghislieri, who had been Grand Inquisitor since December 1558. Ghislieri skillfully played the political and spiritual cards at his disposal to obtain enforcement the length of the peninsula.

On December 31, 1558, Cardinal Ghislieri sent a manuscript of the new Index to the Venetian inquisitor to be published.[145] He included detailed instructions for its enforcement: the bookmen were to present inventories of the volumes they had on hand and wait upon inquisitorial permission before selling titles needing correction. Confessors were to be instructed to refuse absolution to anyone holding prohibited books.

The bookmen faced a grave threat. A fiery pope and strong-willed Grand Inquisitor had promulgated a papal Index and had placed in the hands of the local inquisition the weaponry for enforcement. If the bookmen could be coerced into providing inventories, the Holy Office would for the first time have limited entry into the bookstores themselves. If confessors could be mobilized, the potent spiritual force of the sacrament of penance would bear down upon Venetians of all classes. The pope and Cardinal Ghislieri could rely upon Fra Peretti to exert maximum pressure on bookmen, lay deputies, and government. Reacting quickly to the threat, the priors of the guild (Tommaso Giunti, Marchio Sessa, and Michele Tramezzino) called a January meeting in Giunti's store. The assembled bookmen resolved to disobey the Index in order to avoid heavy financial losses, and in the hope that they could force the papacy to moderate it. Pressure was put on guild members to present a united front.[146]

[144] For reactions and enforcement, see especially Scaduto, "Lainez e l'indice del 1559"; Reusch, *Index*, I, 294–300; Pastor, XIV, 280–81, 482–83; Hilgers, *Index*, pp. 488–96; Prodi, *Paleotti*, II, 236–37; Jedin, *Seripando*, pp. 551–52.

[145] Letters of Ghislieri to the Venetian inquisitor of December 31, 1558, January 19, 25, 28, February 4, 1559, Rome, in SU, Bu. 160, "Dispacci ai Capi del Consiglio dei Dieci, 1500–1560," organized chronologically. These and subsequent letters cited from this *busta* include originals and contemporary copies probably prepared for the Capi, from whose archive they were removed to be placed in the SU *fondo* at the end of the nineteenth-century. Unfortunately, some other sources are lacking. There are no dispatches of the nuncio because Paul IV recalled his nuncio in April 1557 when the Venetians declined to support his war against Spain. And none of the few extant letters of 1559 of the Venetian ambassador to the Holy See deals with the Index.

[146] SU, Bu. 14, Vincenzo Valgrisi et al., no pag., testimony of Valgrisi and of

Although summoned to obedience by the Holy Office twice in January, the bookmen would neither print the Index nor submit inventories. Upon learning of the situation in early February, Cardinal Ghislieri exploded in rage. It was monstrous that the Index could not be printed and promulgated in a Catholic city under a most Catholic prince! He repeated his instructions that confessors not absolve the holders of prohibited books. He demanded three times in February and March that the Venetian Inquisition send him the names of the disobedient bookmen. To assist the inquisitor he arranged for five copies of the Index to be sent to him.[147]

The Inquisition and the bookmen were deadlocked throughout February and March. At first the Venetian government aided the bookmen by temporizing: it would not use its power to force the bookmen to comply but neither would it suppress the Index.[148] Fra Peretti, a brusque man at any time, pursued implementation in a manner that angered some patricians. On March 16, as he was entering the room in the ducal palace where the Collegio met, a member of the Donà family spat in his face. At this time, the Collegio defied Rome and supported the bookmen by ruling that they were free to sell all their books, even the prohibited ones. If the tribunal wished to burn volumes, it would first have to buy them. In addition, the Holy Office was not to destroy books published in Venice with the proper governmental privilegi.[149] This order put the titles of most Italian authors, as well as some scholarly works authored by northern Protestants, beyond the reach of the Inquisition.

Cardinal Ghislieri made some concessions on individual titles, permitting Venetians and other Italians to retain some humanistic and scientific titles of ultramontane Protestants if they were corrected.[150] It is very un-

---

Zaccaria Zenaro of August 9, and of Zuanne Guarisco (Varisco) of August 11, 1559. Part of this is quoted by Sforza, "Controriforma," pt. 2, pp. 175–77.

[147] Letters of Ghislieri to the Venetian inquisitor of February 11, 18, 25, March 4, 11, 1559, in SU, Bu. 160, "Dispacci ai Capi del Consiglio dei Dieci, 1500–1560."

[148] In addition to Ghislieri's angry letters, see the dispatches of the Florentine ambassador to the Holy See, who reported on March 10 and 11, upon the authority of the secretary to the Venetian ambassador to Rome, that the Venetians were temporizing. Antonio Panella, "L'introduzione in Firenze dell'Indice di Paolo IV," *Rivista storica degli archivi toscani* 1 (1929), 16.

[149] Letter of Girolamo Feruffini, Este ambassador to Venice, of March 18, 1559, as quoted in Rotondò, "Nuovi documenti," p. 147, n. 1.

[150] He permitted Marco Corner, Bishop of Spalato, to hold for six months a botanical title, Leonhard Fuchs, *De historia stirpium commentarii*, and gave general permissions for Etienne Dolet, *Commentariorum linguae Latinae* and Sebastian Muenster, *Horologiographia*. Letter of Ghislieri to Fra Peretti of March 11, 1559, in SU, Bu. 160, "Dispacci ai Capi del Consiglio dei Dieci, 1500–1560." For Ghislieri's concessions to the Jesuits, see Scaduto, "Lainez e l'indice del 1559," pp. 28–31. As Scaduto points out, the *Moderatio indicis librorum prohibitorum* of June 24, 1561,

likely that he offered any financial compensation to the bookmen. When the Florentine ambassador raised the question, Ghislieri rejected the idea. When plague struck, he pointed out, princes ordered the contents of infected houses burned. They willingly suffered this loss of goods in order to save the city; it ought to be with the plague of heresy. Moreover, he believed that the bookmen would recoup their losses by selling Catholic books.[151]

The government did not prevent Fra Peretti and the local clergy from using the pulpit and confessional to persuade the inhabitants of the city to purge their libraries. The patriciate might justify their protection of the bookmen on economic and humanitarian grounds, but ordering the clergy not to carry out their spiritual duty was another matter. Besides, as the persecution of the Anabaptists and the burning of the Talmud demonstrated, the patriciate also feared heretics and infidels, and their books. By early March the Inquisition had gathered over 7,000 volumes, enough for Rome to order a public fire. On March 18, the Saturday before Palm Sunday, 10,000 to 12,000 volumes were burned, and more were accumulating.[152]

In similar fashion Italians up and down the peninsula granted the Index at least partial obedience. In Florence the Index was published on March 15, and books were publicly burned in front of the cathedral and in Piazza

---

was at least partially in effect from early 1559. Also see Hilgers, "Bücherverbot und Bücherzensur," pp. 118–21.

[151] Letters of the Florentine ambassador to the Holy See of March 10 and 11 as quoted by Panella, "L'introduzione in Firenze," p. 17. Another Florentine source reports that in March books were burned all over Italy, including Florence, but not in Venice because the Venetians demanded compensation for books to be destroyed. The pope promised to pay and to send appraisers to estimate their value. The Venetians waited and waited, but the appraisers never came. Florence, Biblioteca Riccardiana, Ms. 2131, "Ricordi istorici di Michelangelo Tenagli," f. 12ʳ. The passage is also quoted in Giovanni Lami, *Catalogus codicum manuscriptorum qui in Bibliotheca Riccardiana adservantur* (Livorno, 1756), p. 47, and copied by Bongi, *Giolito*, I, xliv. This ms. is a political diary covering Italian events from 1557 to 1566. But I have been unable to confirm the story or to identify Tenagli. On the contrary, books were burned in Venice in March, and I cannot find any evidence that the bookmen were promised compensation. It is possible that the pope mollified the Venetians in this way while he sought by other means to force the bookmen to obey.

[152] The figure of 7,000 comes from Ghislieri speaking to the Florentine ambassador, as quoted in Panella, "L'introduzione in Firenze," p. 17; the order for the fire came from a letter of Fra Thomaso di Vigorio to Fra Peretti of March 4, 1559, Rome, in SU, Bu. 160, "Dispacci ai Capi del Consiglio dei Dieci, 1500–1560." Ghislieri confirmed that the fire took place and gave the number of volumes destroyed in his letter to the Genoese inquisitor of March 31, 1559, Rome, in Pastor, XIV, 281, 482.

Santa Croce on the eighteenth. Yet Duke Cosimo I heeded the protests of local bookmen and scholars, and instructed that the fire should produce "more demonstration than effect"; he wanted a "fire for show" to satisfy Rome but protect the "poor booksellers." The volumes burned probably included heretical and occult works but not the nonreligious titles of heretical authors.[153] Similarly, the Index was printed in Naples, Bologna, Genoa, Novara, and Rimini, and books were burned in Naples and probably elsewhere. In Milan the inquisitor published the Index with a series of regulations in March. This was followed by stern civil legislation against heretics, as well as measures later in the year designed to halt the importation of prohibited books.[154]

The papacy secured a certain degree of voluntary obedience to the Index from Venetian readers through the assertion of spiritual authority. But the bookmen, with the support of the government, would continue to resist unless the papacy could bring to bear a weapon beyond Venetian jurisdiction. The papacy turned to economic reprisal: it initiated action to confiscate the contents of bookstores owned by Venetians but located in the papal state. And it barred the bookmen from attending book fairs within its boundaries.

Greatly alarmed, the members of the guild met again in Tommaso Giunti's shop at the end of March or the beginning of April. They addressed a joint letter asking the Commune of Foligno to obtain from the papacy safe conducts so that they might attend the bookfair in that city.[155] The answer is unknown, but it is unlikely that the Commune could help. The bookmen went to the doge for assistance against the threat of confiscation, but there was little that he could do.[156] It is unlikely that the Roman publishers, a small group of firms of limited size, owned stores in Venice that might be seized in turn. Moreover, a commercial nation

[153] See the letter of Bartolomeo Concino to Alessandro Strozzi of March 11, as quoted in Panella, "L'introduzione in Firenze," p. 19, as well as pp. 24–25.

[154] For printings of the Index, see Reusch, *Index*, I, 259–61; and Hilgers, *Index*, pp. 492–96; for book burning in Naples, see Pastor, XIV, 482–83; for Milan, see Luigi Fiumi, "L'Inquisizione Romana e lo Stato di Milano," fasc. XXVI, p. 374. For implementation in Bologna, see Scaduto, "Lainez e l'indice del 1559," pp. 19–20.

[155] SU, Bu. 14, Vincenzo Valgrisi et al., testimony of Valgrisi of August 9, 1559 (also printed in Sforza, "Controriforma," pt. 2, p. 176), of Zaccaria Zenaro of August 9, and of Zuanne Guarisco of August 11.

[156] "Et perche il Papa ci fece inten [intendere] tenir in Recanati, in Foligno, in Bologna et altri luoghi delle sue terre tutte le botteghe et creditj, noi librari tutti radunatj insieme se presentassemo al serenissimo Dominio per chiamar suffraggio da sua Serenità et anco se presentassemo a questo santo tribunale, et non me ricordo in specie qualche succedesse nel sacro tribunale." SU, Bu. 14, Vincenzo Valgrisi et al., f. 14v, testimony of Valgrisi of September 1, 1570.

like the Republic was much more vulnerable than the papacy to economic reprisal. Besides, what economic or political considerations would deflect the fiery old pontiff from his goal of the destruction of heretical books?

In April the united front of the guild began to disintegrate. Zaccaria Zenaro submitted an inventory and three bales of prohibited books on April 1. He also wrote to the other bookstores that he owned or operated, instructing his correspondents to obey.[157] Marchio Sessa, one of the priors, censured him for his defection. Vincenzo Valgrisi, who owned stores in Bologna, Foligno, and Recanati within the papal state, submitted the desired inventory in April or early May, and was censured. Valgrisi also took the precaution of changing his insignia from the sign of Erasmus to the sign of Tau at this time.[158] Bernardino Bosello, Alvise Valvassori (called Guadagnino), Giovanni Varisco (or Guarisco), and Giordano Ziletti submitted inventories and prohibited books in June and July.[159]

The Venetian government finally accepted Paul IV's Index, and the Heads of the Council of Ten authorized its publication on July 8. It was printed with the date of July 21 by Girolamo Giglio (or Lilio)—see figures 7 and 8.[160] With this and instructions from Cardinal Ghislieri, the Holy Office punished Zenaro, Valgrisi, Bosello, Valvassori, and Varisco for their disobedience, sentencing them on August 11 to prayers and almsgiving.[161] The remaining holdouts understood that the struggle had ended in defeat. Three days later, Tommaso and Giovanni Maria Giunti, Gabriel Giolito, Michele Tramezzino, Marchio Sessa, Francesco Bindoni,

---

[157] SU, Bu. 14, Vincenzo Valgrisi et al., Zenaro's testimony of August 9, 1559. The inventory is in SU, Bu. 156, "Librai e libri proibiti, 1545–1571," ff. [89^r–90^v], dated April 1, 1559.

[158] SU, Bu. 14, Vincenzo Valgrisi et al., Valgrisi's testimony of August 9, 1559; also quoted in Sforza, "Controriforma," pt. 2, pp. 175–76.

[159] SU, Bu. 14, Vincenzo Valgrisi et al., testimony of Bosello, Valvassori, and Varisco of August 9, 11, 1559. For Ziletti's testimony and inventory, both dated June 10, 1559, see SU, Bu. 156, "Librai e libri proibiti, 1545–1571," ff. [72^{r-v}, 86^{r-v}].

[160] It is a 12°, 9.9 x 15.1 cms., of thirty-two unpaginated folios. The colophon carries the permission to print of the Heads of the Council of Ten and the date. On Sig. h2 recto is the notation that Fra Peretti collated it with a Roman printing. The only copy of the Venetian printing known to me is VC, Cicogna, P D 6842. The only other notice of the Venetian printing is in Reusch, *Index*, 1, 260, n. 2, although he did not claim to have seen it. Extant copies of the Roman printings are more numerous.

[161] SU, Bu. 14, Vincenzo Valgrisi et al., sentence of August 11, 1559, also printed in Sforza, "Controriforma," pt. 2, pp. 177–78. One of the lay deputies who authorized the sentence was Bernardo Zorzi, who as a Head of the Council of Ten had licensed the publication of the Index a month earlier—another example of the integration of the office of the Tre Savii into the apex of the governmental pyramid.

INDEX

AVCTORVM, ET LIBRORVM,
Q̃ V I   A B   O F F I C I O   S.   R O M.
& uniuerſalis Inquiſitionis caueri ab
omnibus, et ſingulis in uniuer
ſa Chriſtiana Republica
mandantur;
Sub cenſuris contra legentes, uel tenentes Libros
probibitos in Bulla, quæ lecta eſt in Cœnâ
Domini, expreſſis, & ſub alijs pœnis
in Decreto eiuſdem Sacri
Officij contentis.

V E N E T I I S
Presb. Hieronymus Lilius, & ſocij excudebant.
Die XXI Iulij. M. D. LIX.

7. Title page of *Index auctorum, et librorum, qui ab Officio S. Rom. & universalis Inquisitionis caveri ab omnibus, et singulis in universa Christiana Republica mandantur.* . . . (Venetiis, Presb. Hieronymus Lilius, & socij excudebant. Die XXI Iulij, MDLIX). Source: VC, Cicogna P D 6842

LA LICENTIA DELLI ECCELI.
Sig. Capi sopra l'impressione dell'Indice.

GLI infrascritti Eccellentiß. Signori Capi dell'Illustriß. Conseglio de i Dieci, concedono licentia, che l'Indice delli libri prohibiti, uenuto da Roma, possa essere stampato in questa Città nostra.   Dat. die 8. Iulij. 1559.

D. Antonius Iustiniano
D. Hieronymus de Lege
D. Bernardus Georgio

Capita Illustriß.
Cons. X.

Illustriß. Cons. X.
Secret. Ricius.

LABI

VIRTVS   NESCIT

VENETIIS
Presb. Hieronymus Lilius, & socij excudebant.

8. Colophon of *Index auctorum, et librorum, qui ab Officio S. Rom. & universalis Inquisitionis caveri ab omnibus, et singulis in universa Christiana Republica mandantur. . . .* (Venetiis, Presb. Hieronymus Lilius, & socij excudebant. Die XXI Iulij, MDLIX). Source: VC, Cicogna P D 6842

Andrea di Obici, and Andrea Arrivabene, leading publishers and priors of the guild, spontaneously appeared before the tribunal to present inventories and from one-half to ten bales of books each, a total of twenty-one bales.[162]

But how fully did the bookmen comply when they offered inventories and prohibited books? Gabriel Giolito's inventory (see App. II) listed twenty-nine titles without specifying the quantity of each. With one possible exception, all were banned by Paul IV's Index.

Giolito surrendered to the Holy Office some Protestant biblical works, several titles of Erasmus, and a few nonreligious works authored by Protestants. Nearly all these books were published in northern Europe. Although Giolito's inventory did not give places of publication, the majority of the titles listed never had a Venetian or Italian printing, and Erasmus, with the exception of the *Moriae encomium*, was infrequently printed in Venice in comparison to the abundant northern European printings. Giolito gave up very few Venetian imprints of banned Italian authors and works. He failed to hand over his stock of Aretino even though he had published many of his titles, including the *Lettere*, as recently as 1557. Nor did he surrender any copies of Machiavelli, although he had published the *Prince, Discourses, Art of War*, and *Florentine Histories* in 1550. Copies of the Venetian printings of the *Beneficio di Christo* and Valdés' *Mercurio et Caronte* still circulated, but Giolito did not concede that he held any. Among prohibited cinquecento Italian authors published in Venice, Giolito volunteered only titles of Antonio Brucioli and Federigo Fregoso, the latter a composite work including Italian translations of two of Luther's works. Giolito offered the Holy Office partial obedience by yielding some banned works published abroad, while retaining most of his prohibited Venetian imprints, which he undoubtedly held in greater number. He sought to minimize his losses by generally following the Collegio's ruling that books bearing the Republic's privilegi might not be destroyed by the Holy Office. Other bookmen did the same.[163]

The Holy Office was surely aware of the omissions, and it might have pursued the bookmen further, but for the fact that on August 18 Paul IV died. Fra Peretti fled Venice; the Roman populace celebrated by setting

[162] SU, Bu. 14, Vincenzo Valgrisi et al., testimony of August 14, 17, 19, 1559; also summarized in Sforza, "Controriforma," pt. 2, p. 178. I have been unable to identify Obici (or Obiti).

[163] Zaccaria Zenaro's inventory of April 1 contained mostly Latin legal titles published abroad, and Giordano Ziletti's inventory of June 10 listed a preponderance of Latin humanist works, also published in the north. SU, Bu. 156, "Librai e libri proibiti, 1545-1571," ff. [89ʳ-90ᵛ, 86ʳ⁻ᵛ]. Other inventories submitted in 1559 have not been located.

fire to the Holy Office buildings and freeing the prisoners.[164] During the riots and interregnum, the enforcement of the Index halted in Venice; no more inventories were submitted and no more bookmen were prosecuted. The almost total disappearance of the Venetian printing of Paul IV's Index suggests that it was suppressed and destroyed. After a long conclave, Pius IV (Gian Angelo Medici) was elected on December 25. A reformer, but a tactful and practical man, he reined in the zealots. His relations with Venice were cordial from the beginning.[165] In March 1560 he announced his intention to moderate Paul IV's Index, and soon a commission began work anew.[166]

Even though Paul IV's death deprived the Holy Office of a full triumph over the bookmen, Cardinal Ghislieri and the Congregation of the Inquisition could be well satisfied with the results obtained. Although unable to force Venetians and other Italians to comply fully, they had succeeded in destroying a substantial number of volumes. They had gone much further than in the past, and had accomplished as much as could be expected with the weapons at hand, which did not include the power of making surprise inspections of the bookstores. The Venetian bookmen had maintained a lengthy and stubborn resistance, but in the end been forced into partial capitulation.

Outmaneuvered by the pope and Cardinal Ghislieri, the Venetians vented their anger on the departed Fra Peretti. In early February 1560, the Republic informed the pope that it did not want him back. It charged that he had published the Index prematurely (although it bore the permission of the Heads of the Council of Ten), that he was ambitious, and that he had conducted irregular Inquisition trials. The Venetians argued that he had held *processi informativi* (preliminary hearings to determine whether there was enough evidence to proceed) without the presence of a lay assistant. Some friars in his convent, where he was director of studies, attacked him because he was severe and because he was a foreigner. Eventually a compromise was reached. The Venetians rid themselves of Peretti at the price of permitting the office of inquisitor to pass to the Dominicans, a goal first sought by the papacy in 1550. Pius IV named a Dominican in mid-summer of 1560, and all future inquisitors came from the ranks of the Order of Preachers.[167] After a hiatus of nearly a year, the

[164] Vaticanus Latinus 12141, f. 65[r]; Pastor, xiv, 414–16; xxi, 33.
[165] Pastor, xvi, 91–93.
[166] Scaduto, "Lainez e l'indice del 1559," pp. 31–32; Pastor, xvi, 12–13.
[167] Paschini, *L'Inquisizione*, pp. 126–30, tends to see the matter purely as a monastic dispute. But governmental hostility on broader grounds is documented in CX, Secrete, R. 7, ff. 19[v]–20[r] (February 9, 1559 mv), 22[v], 23[r-v] (February 23, 1559 mv), 24[v] (April 2, 1560), 25[r-v] (May 7), 27[v]–28[r] (June 7). Also see Vaticanus Latinus 12141, ff. 65[r-v]; and Pastor, xxi, 33–34.

Venetian Inquisition resumed its work, although the Venetians were still suspicious and hostile. The Council of Ten charged in September that the tribunal was "neither just nor intelligent," and in the following year it warned the nuncio against any procedural novelties.[168]

Like other Italians, the Venetian nobility had moved a long way between 1540 and 1560. At first unconcerned, they had come to accept, grudgingly and partially, the necessity of prosecuting heretics and burning their books. However hostile the patriciate might be to an individual pontiff or inquisitor, they were not immune either as individuals or as a public authority to the changed attitude. Another decade would pass before full implementation of Counter Reformation measures against prohibited books would succeed, but open opposition was no longer possible after 1559. Those who best perceived the change were the bookmen who had fought the successive Indices. They would have to adapt to the new conditions.

[168] CX, Secrete, R. 7, ff. 35ᵛ–36ʳ (September 16, 1560), 48ʳ⁻ᵛ (June 16, 1561).

IV

THE COUNTER REFORMATION IMPLEMENTED

In the 1560s the Italians reached the conclusion that their religious consciences were fundamentally Catholic and that heretics and heretical books should be suppressed. The attempt to implement effective censorship had been slowly gathering momentum since the 1540s. The bookmen had fought skillfully and had achieved notable victories, but they had not been able to hold back the tide of orthodox fervor. After decades of uncertainty, the Italian religious revival emerged strong, unified, and sure of its means and goals. The intense search to discover whether man was saved through faith alone, or by faith that manifested itself through works as a sign of love, or by faith and works in tandem had ended for most Italians with the Tridentine decrees. Princes and people agreed that salvation, as well as important temporal benefits, were to be found in the old church. But the old church was also a new one, pledged to the elimination of abuses and to pastoral reform.

Most Italian lay and ecclesiastical rulers were freer to turn their attention to domestic religious concerns than they had been for decades. The long series of wars on Italian soil had ended with Paul IV's gallant, though ill-advised, stand against the Spanish and the Peace of Cateau-Cambrésis in 1559. Liberated from the imperial incubus, the fathers of Trent completed their work in 1562-63 with a stream of doctrinal decrees and reform legislation. Pius IV (1559-65) and Pius V (1566-72), though opposites in temperament and *modus operandi*, shared a dedication to renewal and provided the leadership that in previous pontificates had been either lacking or so intemperate as to be counterproductive.

It was a troubled decade for the leaders of the Venetian Republic, for the Protestant heretic seemed to threaten the state from within; and the infidel Turk, from afar. The government had for a decade ignored hints that heretics had infiltrated the populace and had won converts even among the nobility. In the 1560s the overwhelming evidence demanded action. Externally, the threat of the Turk overshadowed the later years of the decade. As the infidel encroached on the Christian Mediterranean, Pius V preached a crusade. Italian captains hoping to restore their tarnished military reputations in a war that would protect, rather than destroy, Italy joined the pontiff, as did the populace, who saw the crusade as God's will. But the Venetian patriciate had to weigh the very complex commercial and political costs before joining the eager papacy and reluctant Spanish in the Holy League.

Complicated religious and political motives spurred the Venetians to make a powerful effort to apply effective controls on the press. For the bookmen, the 1560s were fraught with peril and, paradoxically, bright with opportunity. The reformed papacy issued an authoritative Index in 1564, and it no longer needed to soften prohibitions; the government now supported the Holy Office. At the same time, the religiosity of these years offered a commercial opportunity of large magnitude. Many writers took up their pens to express religious fervor, and great numbers of readers waited for the Venetian bookmen to print and distribute this fare.

1. EXPANSION OF THE RELIGIOUS PRESS

Although the bookmen catered to nearly every interest, some subject areas claimed the major part of their production. Religious literature, doctrinal and devotional, was one of the largest. Doctrinal titles embraced theology, Scripture and commentaries, patristic literature, confessors' manuals, catechisms, liturgical guides, and works dealing with clerical discipline, all intended primarily for the theologian, abbot, bishop, or other reader with a professional, as well as a spiritual, interest. Devotional titles, such as inspirational treatises, sermons, meditations, and hagiography, were offered to the average clerical or lay believer. Devotional titles, normally in the vernacular, made up two-thirds of the religious production; doctrinal works, usually in Latin, claimed the rest.

Secular vernacular literature also claimed a large share of the printers' efforts. Included in this category were poetry, drama, courtly and Platonic love tracts, chivalric romances such as the *Amadis di Gaula*, courtesy books, collections of letters, eclectic dialogues, vernacular grammars, and much else. The vernacular classics of Dante, Petrarch, Boccaccio, and Ariosto, as well as most of the works of such prolific authors as Aretino, Della Casa, Doni, and many others, appeared on publishers' lists.

The products of Renaissance humanism were a distinctive part of the trade. The ancient Latin and Greek classics and their Italian translations were the heart of this group. Commentaries and treatises, almost always in Latin, on grammar, rhetoric, moral philosophy, and poetry, directly related to the ancient classics and authored by such figures as Leonardo Bruni, Lorenzo Valla, and Giovanni Pontano, as well as a few titles of Renaissance Latin poetry, completed the humanist sector. Vernacular translations of the classics comprised nearly 33 percent of this group until about 1575; thereafter they fell off sharply to 10 percent or less of the humanist sector, suggesting that the great work of making the classics accessible to Italians lacking Latin and Greek had largely been completed. The decreasing number of vernacular translations and the passing of leadership in classical studies to northern Europe may have accounted for the Venetian decline in the printing of classics and humanism, from about 10 percent of the total production in the 1560s and early 1570s to about 5 percent at the end of the century.

The printers satisfied the intense Italian interest in history and politics with a variety of books. Italians were particularly interested in their own century, and political narratives by such historians as Guicciardini, Paolo Giovio, and Giovanni Tarcagnota were often reprinted. Other authors called upon ancient history, political philosophy, military science, geography (especially the descriptions of the New World), and other disciplines to fill out the picture. Some authors wrote monographs, and some ranged widely to produce composite works, such as Giovanni Botero's *Relationi universali* (1591 and later), and Francesco Sansovino's two works on the Turks, *Dell'historia universale dell'origine et imperio de' Turchi* (1560) and *Gl'annali overo le vite de' Principi et Signori della Casa Othomana* (1570). The ties between history and the analysis of contemporary politics were also very close. As historians increasingly came under the influence of Machiavelli, Guicciardini, Polybius, and Tacitus, history's ties to rhetoric became weaker and the tendency to mine history for political science applicable to the contemporary world grew. Even ancient history came to be used in this way. Machiavelli's *Discourses on the First Ten Books of Livy*, ostensibly a commentary on an ancient work, was, in reality, an analysis of the nature of politics with particular reference to the Florence in which he lived.[1]

The bookmen printed many learned works intended primarily for professional and scholarly readers. Groups of works in related subject areas appealed to different parts of the professional and scholarly market. Readers studying the physical world sought titles in mathematics, physics,

---

[1] Placing history with politics, instead of within the cycle of humanistic disciplines, is, like any classification, arguable. Yet this link seems to be appropriate for Venetian book production in the second half of the cinquecento because the bookmen printed so much contemporary history allied with political analysis. The tendency was particularly noticeable in the great amount of popular history the Venetian press offered; for more on this, see Grendler, "Francesco Sansovino and Italian Popular History." Grouping history with the *studia humanitatis* might be the proper classification for another chronological period, such as the quattrocento, or for the production of another press, such as that of Basel, but would distort the Venetian picture in the second half of the cinquecento, I believe.

astronomy, and astrology, as well as treatises on the reform of the calendar, a study that embraced more than one discipline. Physicians and medical scholars gravitated toward works of medicine (anatomies and books of diseases and cures), biology, botany, and alchemy. Lawyers sought theoretical and practical treatises in law and jurisprudence. In the 1590s, treatises arguing for secular or ecclesiastical jurisdiction appeared in increasing number, and probably found purchasers beyond the circle of lawyers. Perhaps as a result of the jurisdictional tracts, perhaps for other reasons, the number of legal works published gradually increased. Philosophers wanted formal treatises on such topics as logic and metaphysics; the bookmen offered them everything from commentaries on Aristotle's *Metaphysics* to Bernardino Telesio's *De rerum natura*.[2] The majority of works in all these professional and scholarly disciplines were in Latin.

The presses also issued a few titles (annually or once every several years) in a wide range of other subjects: agriculture, architecture, business practice, the culinary arts, falconry, and much else. The presses published Hebrew works, a good deal of music, and some maps, engravings, and woodcuts, but the publisher, composer, or artist ordinarily did not seek an imprimatur for these. One who did was "Tician pittor," who in 1567 received an imprimatur for "diverse stampe et rame" on the condition that they avoided obscenity.[3]

In the 1560s publishers adapted to the changing public consciousness, and profited from the religious revival, by diverting part of their production from secular vernacular literature to a comparable religious field. The imprimaturs issued by the government for new titles, i.e., titles not published previously in Venice, show the extent of the change.[4]

[2] Aristotle's works and commentaries on them have been classified according to their subject, i.e., the *Rhetoric* with classics and humanism, the *Physics* with mathematics, physics, astronomy, and astrology, and so on.

[3] Capi del CX, Notatorio, R. 21, f. 68r, January 22, 1566 mv. The Heads granted only a few imprimaturs for Hebrew books because the Esecutori contro la bestemmia normally censored the Hebrew press. See sec. 3 of this ch.

[4] The imprimaturs contain the name of the applicant and a brief identification of the book, i.e., a much abbreviated or summarized title and usually, but not always, the name of the author, translator, or editor. Upon receipt of an imprimatur, the publisher or author might petition the Senate for a privilegio specifying duration and penalty for infringment. Once an imprimatur had been granted, a title could be printed as often as wished, subject to the terms of the privilegio. As noted previously, the 1527 law of the Council of Ten demanding imprimaturs was initially often ignored, but gradually compliance became more common until it was nearly universal in the last third of the century. Brown examined the privilegi and published his count in *Venetian Press*, pp. 96–98, 240–42. His notes, which are copies of imprimaturs and privilegi, partly in his hand, are in VM, Mss. Italiani, Classe VII, 2500–502 (12077–79), "Privilegi veneziani per la stampa concessi dal 1527 al

TABLE 2

Imprimatures for New Titles, 1551–1607, Grouped by Subject

Subject Areas	Mar. 1551–Feb. 1555	Mar. 1555–Feb. 1558	Mar. 1562–Feb. 1570	Mar. 1572–Feb. 1575	Mar. 1578–Feb. 1582	Mar. 1585–Dec. 1589	Jan. 1590–Feb. 1595	Mar. 1597–Dec. 1599	Jan. 1600–Dec. 1604	Jan. 1605–Feb. 1607
Religion	15.6%	12.8%	24.1%	21.5%	28.8%	33.3%	35.7%	28.3%	30.5%	34.9%
Secular Vernacular Literature	31.3%	25.6%	20.9%	21.8%	16.7%	21.3%	17.3%	18.4%	17.6%	22.4%
Classics and Humanism	9.4%	18.6%	10 %	11.2%	7 %	6.7%	17.3%	18.4%	5.9%	5 %
Politics and History	11.2%	13.1%	10.6%	9.9%	5.8%	6.1%	7.7%	8.6%	5.4%	7.9%
Mathematics, Astronomy, Astrology, Physics	3.6%	4.8%	5 %	3.3%	5.1%	5.6%	5.9%	2.8%	2.5%	3.7%
Medicine, Biology, Botany, Alchemy	7.1%	7.7%	4.4%	5 %	4.5%	4.4%	4 %	3.3%	5.6%	3.7%
Civil and Canon Law	6.3%	5.1%	7.4%	11.2%	8.3%	5.4%	10.8%	10.4%	14 %	10.4%
Philosophy	4 %	2.6%	3.1%	5.9%	7.1%	3.1%	2.2%	6.4%	4.7%	3.3%
Other: Hebrew, miscellaneous, music, engravings, unidentified	11.6%	9.9%	14.6%	10.2%	16.7%	14.1%	12.9%	16.3%	15 %	8.7%
Total imprimaturs	224	274	701	303	156	390	325	212	408	241

SOURCE: Capi del CX, Notatorio, R. 14–33 and F. 1–14. While the imprimaturs are repeated in the Registri and Filze, thus compensating for most gaps, no imprimaturs survive for March 1584 through February 1585, and March 1595 through February 1597. Many titles were immediately recognizable and easily classified; others were checked against standard bibliographies to get a complete title. Nevertheless, some titles were impossible to identify, and these are included in the "Other" category. Possibly one title in twenty has been erroneously identified or classified. Hence, a 5 percent margin of error should be kept in mind when reading the table. For example, the 10 percent figure for Classics and Humanism from 1562 to 1570 could be between 9.5 and 10.5 percent.

In the 1550s, religious titles accounted for only 13 to 15 percent of the total new titles, but the share expanded to about 25 percent during the years 1562 to 1582, and about 33 percent the rest of the century. Secular vernacular literature made up 25 to 31 percent of the total in the 1550s, but only about 20 percent in the 1560s, and the same or a little less for the duration of the century. Instead of printing secular titles, some of which were anticlerical, irreverent, and obscene, the bookmen published devotional works. The combined total of the two areas remained approximately the same throughout the second half of the century, ranging from 43 to 57 percent, and averaging 49 percent, of the titles granted imprimaturs.

In the 1560s the bookmen also reprinted fewer older secular works. For twenty years more than half of the Giolito imprints, new titles and reprints, had been secular vernacular works. In 1557 Giolito reprinted Aretino for the last time; in the following decade, new and reprinted religious titles took the largest share of the Giolito publishing list. A keen observer and shrewd businessman, Gabriel completely changed the subject emphasis of his list, though he continued to publish almost exclusively in the vernacular. Instead of Aretino, he offered the devotional works of Luis de Granada in Italian translation, which he reprinted again and again.

The bookmen expanded production when they made the changeover. The total number of imprimaturs rose in the 1560s, and remained at a high level until the Great Plague of 1575–77. Publishing then fell off sharply, as did all economic activity, and did not fully recover for nearly a decade. After 1585 the number of imprimaturs again rose until it approached, but did not equal, the pre-plague level.[5]

The battle over Paul IV's Index and the stronger censorship of the 1560s were persuasive reasons for the bookmen to alter the direction of their publishing. But their perception of the changing market also played a role; just as Cardinal Ghislieri had predicted, a large market for religious works had developed. In 1567 a priest charged with the implementation of the Tridentine press regulations in Milan reported to Archbishop Carlo Borromeo the happy results of the religious revival for one Milanese

---

1597, copiati da Horatio Brown." The copies are accurate but very incomplete, for Brown or his assistant overlooked a great deal, as many as half of the privilegi in some years in the last two decades of the century. But from this incomplete count, Brown concluded that the Index caused a "ruinous" quantitative decline in the press. I suspect that Brown missed so much because he approached the titles through the privilegi, which are sometimes difficult to locate in the voluminous Senato Terra records, instead of through the imprimaturs, which are easier to find in the smaller Capi del CX, Notatorio, file. In addition, not every imprimatur was followed by a privilegio.

[5] For documentation and a discussion of the economic vicissitudes of the Venetian press in the later years of the century, see Ch. VIII, sec. 1.

TABLE 3

Giolito Publications, New Titles and Reprints, Grouped by Subject

	Religion	Secular vernacular literature	Other	Total titles
1541–1550	7.1%	53.3%	39.6%	240
1551–1560	12.6%	52.4%	35 %	326
1561–1570	39.3%	24.4%	36.3%	234
1571–1580	69 %	11.5%	19.5%	113
1581–1590	57.1%	13.2%	29.7%	98

Source: Bongi, *Giolito*, and Camerini, "Notizia."

bookman. In the past this bookman had had annual sales of about 3,000 scudi, the greater part derived from vernacular titles, romances, and "other vanities." Now he sold the fathers and doctors of the church, Bibles, catechisms, the Tridentine decrees, theological *Summae*, and "libri spirituali"; by October his sales for 1567 had already reached 4,000 scudi.[6]

2. PATRICIAN HERETICS

In 1560 the Council of Ten charged that the Holy Office was "neither just nor intelligent." Twelve years later, the nuncio confidently reported that the leaders of the Republic supported the Inquisition as strongly as any government in Italy, because they held pious beliefs and because they feared heresy as a threat to the state.[7] The Republic had discovered that Protestantism had won converts among the younger nobility. Throughout the 1550s and early 1560s, some thirty to forty nobles and commoners, loosely joined through a series of conventicles led by dedicated Protestants, had met periodically to explore Protestant beliefs. A major figure was Andrea di Antonio Da Ponte (1509–85), brother of the future doge Nicolò. Andrea led a conventicle that included several young patricians. A fervent Protestant who talked constantly about "le cose della fede" even during

---

[6] Mario Bendiscioli, "Vita sociale e culturale," in *Storia di Milano*, vol. x, *L'età della Riforma Cattolica (1559–1630)* (Milan, 1957), p. 467.

[7] "Et quanto al favorire le cose del Santo Offitio, trovai questi Signori cosi saldi et confermati che Sua Santità si può prometter che le favoriranno al pari di qualsivoglia Prencipe d'Italia. Molti si muoveno per la pietà et debito; altri per interesse di stato, che veggiono chiaramente che nessuna peste è tanto contagiosa et pericolosa come è questa della heresia." Letter of Giovanni Antonio Facchinetti, July 5, 1572, in ASVa, Segretario di Stato, Venezia, F. 12, f. 22ʳ. This is also quoted in Pastor, xix, 300, n. 3.

meetings of the Great Council,[8] he fled to Geneva in or about 1560, but persuaded only one other noble, Nicolò Paruta, to accompany him.[9] Humanist schoolmasters employed as tutors in noble households, and Teofilo Panarelli, were other conventicle leaders.

A spontaneous confession in February 1565 that disclosed that the conventicles had enrolled nobles undoubtedly caused anguish among the leaders of the Republic. They probably had known that Andrea Da Ponte had gone to Geneva, but they had for years ignored hints of links between local heretics and the nobility. But now the Inquisition acted, no doubt only after secret (and unrecorded) discussion with the doge and Council of Ten. As painful as the decision must have been, the Republic's leaders had no choice if they were to be faithful to their own principles as well as to their faith. Solicitude for the future security of the Republic impelled them, for few matters were of higher priority than safeguarding the moral character and spiritual health of their heirs. Venetian practice was to deny publicly any criticism of the nobility—and then to act swiftly to eliminate the defect. Moreover, Venetian tradition taught that all men, even the doge, were subject to the law. It was a situation made to order for a powerful Council of Ten. A handful of men resolved a delicate problem swiftly and secretly by ordering the Holy Office to proceed. But few knew of the trials, since the papacy also maintained silence.

Fifteen nobles were accused of heresy, and eight abjured, from early 1565 through 1569. Carlo di Francesco Corner (1532–84), a lawyer,[10] Antonio di Zuanne Loredano (1542–76),[11] Francesco di Girolamo Emo

---

[8] SU, Bu. 11, Giovanni Andrea Ugone, f. 36^r, testimony of Carlo Corner of March 26, 1565. For Da Ponte's dates, see ASV, Barbaro, "Arbori," VI, 204.

[9] J.B.G. Galiffe, *Le refuge italien de Genève aux XVIme et XVIIme siècles* (Geneva, 1881), p. 79, reports that about thirty Venetians fled to Geneva, including four nobles: Da Ponte, Nicolò Paruta (1560), Giulio Barbaro (1559), and Beniamino Priuli (1638). There are references to "quel Paruta" and "uno Paruta," who accompanied Da Ponte to Geneva in SU, Bu. 11, Giovanni Andrea Ugone, ff. 19^v (testimony of Ugone of February 27, 1565), 38^v (testimony of Carlo Corner of March 22, 1565).

[10] SU, Bu. 20, Michele De Basili, Carlo Corner, e Venturino Dalle Modonette, Corner's abjuration of March 14, and sentence of March 23, 1565. VM, Mss. Italiani, Classe VII, 926 (8595), Marco Barbaro, "Arbori dei Patritii veneti," p. 19. The only study of these patrician heretics is Edouard Pommier, "La société vénitienne et la Réforme protestante au XVIe siècle," BSV, I (1959), 7–14, who sees these Protestant nobles as moved by "une sorte de dillettantisme religieux" (p. 10). Perhaps he underestimates the seriousness of their commitment, for they engaged in several years of clandestine activity, and some of them considered following Da Ponte to Geneva.

[11] SU, Bu. 20, Antonio Loredano e Alvise Malipiero, Loredano's abjuration and sentence of July 3, 1565. ASV, Barbaro, "Arbori," IV, 353, with the notation that he died of the plague.

(1533–77), a *nipote* of Andrea Da Ponte,[12] Alvise di Anzollo Malipiero (1529/35–68), another lawyer,[13] Andrea di Francesco Dandolo (1548–71),[14] and Giacomo di Zuanne Malipiero (c. 1543–?), a lawyer at the Ducal Palace but a bastard without the right of entry into the Great Council,[15] abjured orthodox Protestant beliefs. They admitted to having denied all or some of a number of Catholic articles: the Real Presence in the Eucharist, purgatory, the necessity of oral confession, priestly celibacy, papal primacy, indulgences, the intercession of saints, and the veneration of images. Giacomo Malipiero also confessed to having held that only faith, not works, was necessary for salvation. Most of the nobles affirmed that they had been led astray by an unnamed notorious heretic (Andrea Da Ponte) or by one of the humanist schoolmasters (for example, Publio Francesco Spinola in the case of Giacomo Malipiero). They admitted to having read such titles as Calvin's *Catechism* and *Institutes*, and titles of Ochino, Vergerio, and Vermigli. The Holy Office sentenced Giacomo to one year of imprisonment on bread and water, and three years of penances. The others received lesser penalties of one to four years of penances.

Not all the abjurees were young men under the spell of a persuasive teacher. When the Holy Office arrested Marc'Antonio di Giacomo da Canale on or about July 1, 1568, the nuncio wrote that this seizure of a "gentleman of some quality" showed that the Inquisition was no respecter of rank.[16] Canale (1519–87) had married a Bembo and had been elected one of the 120 members of the Quarantia, the judges who presided over the civil and criminal courts of the Republic.[17] The tutor for Canale's

[12] SU, Bu. 22, Francesco Emo, abjuration and sentence of October 20, 21, 1567. Panarelli called him a *nipote* of Da Ponte in his testimony of November 23, 1571, in SU, Bu. 32, Teofilo Panarelli e Ludovico Abioso, no pag. VM, Ital., VII, 926 (8595), "Arbori," p. 100.

[13] SU, Bu. 20, Antonio Loredano e Alvise Malipiero, the latter's abjuration and sentence of March 26, 1565. ASV, Barbaro, "Arbori," IV, 408, notes that he married a Pesaro and gives his dates as 1535–68. But Ugone testified on March 2, 1565, that he was 36 years old. SU, Bu. 11, Giovanni Andrea Ugone, f. 20r.

[14] SU, Bu. 23, Silvestro, Cipriano, e Stefano Semprini, Andrea Dandolo, Marc'Antonio Canale et al., ff. 1r–2v, testimony of Dandolo of September 2, 1568. His abjuration and sentence are missing, but he freely admitted the same heretical beliefs as the others and was sentenced to some kind of confinement within the city. In the following year, the Holy Office, noting the neglect of his affairs, permitted Dandolo to spend the month of September in his villa. Ibid., document of July 19, 1569. ASV, Barbaro, "Arbori," III, 184, with the notation "fu ammazzato."

[15] SU, Bu. 20, Antonio Loredano e Alvise Malipiero, ff. 3v–8r, testimony of Giacomo Malipiero of June 14, 19, 26, and his abjuration and sentence of July 7, 1565. Several witnesses described him as 23 years old and illegitimate.

[16] Letter of Nuncio Facchinetti of July 3, 1568, in *Nunziature* VIII, 404.

[17] ASV, Barbaro, "Arbori," II, 214. It is likely that Canale reached the Quarantia before his abjuration.

three sons, a confessed Protestant and conventicle leader, named Canale as a heretic. Other witnesses testified that Canale had been a conventicle participant for a decade or more.

The trial suggested that Canale had for years been torn by conflicting loyalties. The evidence was sufficient to demonstrate his Protestant beliefs, but he had not chosen exile. At one point in the interrogation, Canale testified that he had advised a heretical acquaintance to stay in Venice lest his flight lead to disgrace and ruin for the family left behind. Concern for his family was undoubtedly the basis for Canale's own decision. As the trial dragged on through summer and fall, Canale begged for a speedy verdict because his neglected affairs were suffering grievously. The tribunal, in turn, faced a dilemma: several witnesses had testified to Canale's heresy, but Canale himself would admit very little. During the sessions of July 15 and August 3, in an effort to break the impasse, all six members of the tribunal rose to their feet and implored Canale to tell the truth lest he damn his soul and bring ruin on his posterity. The weeping Canale continued to protest his innocence. Finally, on October 9, 1568, he abjured, confessing that he had denied purgatory, indulgences, and the intercession of the saints, and that he had read Ochino's *Catechismo* (Basel: Pietro Perna, 1561) and *Prediche*. The Inquisition sentenced him to monastic confinement for four years and penances.[18]

The final noble abjuree, Alvise (or Luigi) di Marino Mocenigo (possibly a bastard) was an ecclesiastic who enjoyed an income of 300 scudi annually from benefices. He had tutored the sons of Girolamo Grimani and had participated in conventicles for years. In December 1565, he abjured and was sentenced to a year of penances. Arrested again in July 1568, he abjured again, confessing that he had denied transubstantiation, purgatory, the intercession of the saints, and papal supremacy, and that he had held and read heretical books for years.[19] He was turned over to the secular arm as a *relapsus*, but escaped death; in 1578 he broke out of prison and

---

[18] SU, Bu. 23, Silvestro, Cipriano, e Stefano Semprini, Andrea Dandolo, Marc'Antonio Canale et al., ff. 56[r-v] (testimony of Prete Fedele [Vico] of July 1, 1568), 58[v]-65[r], 69[r]-75[r], 77[r-v], 78[v] (testimony of Canale of July 3, 10, 13, 15, 29, August 3, September 6, October 2, abjuration and sentence of October 9). In addition, several other witnesses in this group of trials testified to Canale's heretical associations and beliefs.

[19] He was described a "persona ecclesiastica et figlio d'un mons. Marino Mocenigo" by Nuncio Facchinetti on July 10, 1568, in *Nunziature* VIII, 408. He is also often referred to as "monsignor" in the trials. My inability to locate Luigi in Barbaro, "Arbori," suggests illegitimacy, although I may have overlooked him, since the Mocenigo were an enormous clan with many sons of that name. For his trial, see SU, Bu. 23, Silvestro, Cipriano, e Stefano Semprini, Andrea Dandolo, Marc'Antonio Canale et al., ff. 65[v]-68[v], 78[r] (testimony of Mocenigo of July 12 and September 19, 1568), abjuration and sentence of March 12, 1569 (no. pag.), and sentence on December 17, 1565 (no. pag.).

disappeared.[20] Of the other seven nobles accused of heresy, only one was questioned.[21]

As a consequence of the trials, the Venetians took two steps immediately. The leaders of the government assured the papacy that they would deny public office to any patrician "suspect in the faith,"[22] and the government and the Holy Office arranged to test the orthodoxy of the humanist schoolmasters. Anyone wishing to teach publicly or privately had to undergo examination by the patriarch and profess his faith according to the norms of Trent. The ordinance was extended to the Dominion, where local bishops approved the teachers.[23] Before long the Republic would also tighten press censorship and permit the Holy Office to search the bookstores for contraband.

Other forces besides the fear of Protestantism within the nobility induced the Venetians to accept the Counter Reformation. Popular sentiment had changed. To demonstrate that the public endorsed stern measures against heretics, the nuncio persuaded the government to permit a public penance. An abjured heretic dressed in the penitential habit and holding a lighted candle was made to stand in front of the church of San Geminiano (where the Ala Napoleonica now stands) in Piazza San Marco for an entire Sunday morning in October 1566. Hidden observers

[20] SU, Bu. 43, Luigi Mocenigo, testimony of the jailor and others of January 7, 9, 14, 28, 1578.

[21] Carlo Corner named Piero di Antonio Calbo (1524–74) and Agostino di Nicolò Tiepolo (c. 1543–92) as associates of Andrea Da Ponte. Tiepolo was questioned, but he denied acquaintance with Da Ponte. SU, Bu. 11, Giovanni Andrea Ugone, ff. 37^v (testimony of Corner of March 20, 1565), 47^v–48^v (testimony of Tiepolo of March 31, 1565). VM, Mss. Ital., vii, 925 (8594), Barbaro, "Arbori," p. 199; ms. 928 (8597), p. 128. Matteo da Riva named Andrea Pasqualigo as a heretic. SU, Bu. 22, Matteo e Alessandro degli Avogari, Andrea Pasqualigo, testimony of April 19, 1567. Prete Fedele Vico named Domenico Contarini detto Roncinetto. SU, Bu. 23, Silvestro, Cipriano, e Stefano Semprini, Andrea Dandolo, Marc'Antonio da Canale et al., f. 52^r, June 29, 1568. One Francesco di Michele Priuli reported that he had heard Alvise Malipiero (who did abjure) and his brother Polo discussing heretical subjects. He also suspected Nicolò di Marco da Molin of heresy. SU, Bu. 20, Antonio Loredano e Alvise Malipiero, deposition of March 20, 1565.

[22] "Quanto all'oprar con questi signori che i sospetti della fede non siano eletti ad uffici et amministrationi, essi me hanno detto più d'una volta che servano questa intelligentia tra loro: di tener con le pallotte sempre esclusi questi de' quali s'ha sospitione; onde io non havrò da far altro se non confermarli in questa risolutione, et V. S. ill.ma stia certa che nessun gentilhuomo, per grande che fusse, osaria adesso scoprirsi punto alieno dalla via catholica." Letters of Michele Bonelli of August 31, Rome, and Giovanni Antonio Facchinetti, September 7, 1566, Venice, in *Nunziature* viii, 102–3 (quote).

[23] Letters of Giovanni Antonio Facchinetti and Michele Bonelli of May 24, 1567, Venice; May 31, Rome; January 8, 1569, Rome; January 15, Venice; January 26, Rome, in *Nunziature* viii, 220, 225, 480–82, 488.

noted that the throng cried out for burning and stoning.[24] It is likely that the crowd included both nobles and commoners, for they listened to the same preachers and read the same books. As a result of his experiment, the nuncio looked forward to public executions, for it was obvious that the reason advanced by the government against them, that they would kindle sympathy for the heretic and his doctrines, was not true. The cautious government did authorize a few more public penances, but it continued to insist on secret executions.

Finally, the Holy League against the Turks brought Venice and the papacy into closer collaboration than at any other time in the century. The Venetian position in the Mediterranean steadily eroded in the 1560s, but commercial and political restraints kept the Venetians from war for some time. Pius V did not hesitate; he urged an alliance on the Venetians and the even more reluctant Spanish from the beginning of his pontificate. The painfully slow negotiations occupied the three powers from 1567 on, and only in 1570 did Venice formally declare war. The Turkish invasion of Cyprus in July 1570 spurred the Venetians to action; the long siege of Famagusta and the fall of Nicosia on September 9 underlined the desperate situation. The Venetians frantically armed for war, and the negotiations between the three powers proceeded, notwithstanding disputes. On May 25, 1571, the Holy League was formally concluded, setting the stage for the allied armada that won the great battle of Lepanto on October 7.

Inevitably, alliance with the pope in an atmosphere of crusade helped create a climate of opinion favorable to greater inquisitorial vigor. In the common view, infidel, heretic, and Jew were linked together: the infidel attacked the Christian state by waging war; the heretic, by poisoning the minds of the people; and the Jew, by aiding the Turk from within. Pius V was unrelenting in his opposition to all three, and the Venetians for a few years shared his views and matched his zeal. The first press victim in this time of crusade would be the Hebrew press.

The Venetians did not, however, change their position on clerical reform and ecclesiastical jurisdiction. In October 1564 the Senate voted overwhelmingly to publish the Tridentine decrees, making the Republic one of the first states to accept them.[25] But the government made no move toward implementation. Five years later, the nuncio lamented that neither doge nor patriarch, despite their promises, had taken the first step toward halting clerical concubinage.[26] Similarly, the Venetians rejected Pius V's attempt to strengthen ecclesiastical authority through promulgation of a

---

[24] Letters of Facchinetti of October 5, 12, 1566, in *Nunziature* VIII, 115–16, 119.

[25] Senato, Deliberazioni Roma, R. 1, ff. 131^v–32^r (October 6, 1564), with a vote of 135 yes, 4 no, 1 abstention.

[26] Letter of Nuncio Facchinetti of September 7, 1569, in *Nunziature* IX, 122.

strong version of the bull *In coena domini*.[27] The Venetians endorsed the suppression of heresy, the heart of the Counter Reformation, but continued to reject most of the Catholic Reformation.

3. THE REPUBLIC BURNS HEBREW BOOKS AGAIN

After a four-year delay, the Republic followed the lead of the papacy and permitted the resumption of Hebrew publishing. Referring to edicts of Julius III of May 29, 1554, and Paul IV of March 26, 1555, the Esecutori contro la bestemmia in 1559 ruled that Hebrew books, except for the Talmud and its commentaries, might again be published in expurgated form. The Esecutori appointed two experts in Hebrew to expurgate titles according to papal guidelines, and also permitted, after correction, the return to their owners of the remaining Hebrew titles seized in October 1553.[28]

The bookmen and their Jewish patrons did not immediately resume publishing, probably because they were awaiting the outcome of the Tridentine discussions on Hebrew books. Failing to reach a decision on either Hebrew works or the Index as a whole in 1562 and 1563, the fathers referred all censorship matters to Pius IV, a result that heartened the Jews, who expected kinder treatment from the pope than from any other source.[29] They were not disappointed; the Tridentine Index of 1564 permitted the Talmud, and its commentaries and glosses, as long as the name "Talmud" and antichristian passages were omitted. No further restrictions, beyond the censorship required of all titles, were laid down. With this assurance, Alvise Bragadino, Me'ir ben Jacob Parenzo, and four newcomers began to publish Hebrew books in 1564 and 1565. Bragadino, Giorgio de' Cavalli, Giovanni di Gara (who acquired much of Bomberg's type and was sometimes called his heir), Giovanni Griffio, Parenzo, and Cristoforo Zanetti each published a handful to fourteen or more works through 1568.[30]

The times did not favor the Jews in Venice or elsewhere in Italy. Pius V (1566–73) provided an example of persecution for the entire peninsula, but the Venetians had their own reasons, which focused on Don Joseph

---

[27] *Nunziature* IX, is filled with the negotiations concerning *In coena domini*.

[28] Bestemmia, Bu. 56, R. 1542–1560, ff. 161ᵛ–64ʳ, July 24, 1559.

[29] Salo Wittmayer Baron, "The Council of Trent and Rabbinic Literature," in his *Ancient and Medieval Jewish History*, ed. Leon A. Feldman (New Brunswick, N.J., 1972), pp. 353–71, 555–64; Baron, *Social and Religious History of the Jews*, XIV, pp. 19–23, 310–13.

[30] *STC Italian*, 796, 806, 830–32, 856, 906–7, 985. Of course, it is unlikely that the British Museum has a complete collection of Venetian Hebrew editions. Amram, *Makers of Hebrew Books*, pp. 338–71.

Nasi (João Miquez), a wealthy merchant from Portugal. In 1550 Nasi asked the Republic to sell him an island that he might turn into a haven for Jewish refugees. The Venetians rebuffed him, and in 1553 the Council of Ten instigated kidnapping charges against him and his associates for what apparently was the rescue of his aunt from a Venetian prison. Sentenced *in absentia* to hanging, Nasi made his way to the Turkish court in 1554 and soon became the leading financier and tax farmer for the sultan. Now very anti-Venetian, Nasi organized a commercial network for East-West trade in direct competition with the Republic. In the late 1560s the Venetians believed that he wished to become King of Cyprus; when the Turkish invasion came, they held him responsible.[31]

A series of incidents in the last years of the 1560s convinced many Venetians that local Jews were Turkish agents attempting to sabotage the Republic from within. In 1567 the government intercepted coded Hebrew letters giving the details of a joint plot by Jews in Constantinople and Venice to bribe a Venetian ambassador extraordinary.[32] In April 1568 a fire in Constantinople endangered the life of the *bailo* (the Republic's resident ambassador), and the Venetians again held the Jews responsible.[33] Public opinion held Nasi's Jewish agents in Venice culpable for the devastating fire of September 13, 1569, in the Arsenal.

In this period of rising anti-Semitism, the Hebrew publishers faced increasing harassment from the government. Venetian Hebrew publishers, like their counterparts elsewhere in Italy, had always taken care to delete antichristian sentiments, although some derogatory remarks about Gentiles appeared in imprints of the first half of the century.[34] In the 1560s, the Esecutori and their *conversos* advisers exercised keen vigilance over Hebrew works. In 1561 the Esecutori discovered several bales of books lacking the proper corrections at the Bomberg press and in the hands of various booksellers. Since Hebrew publishing had not yet resumed, these

---

[31] Constance H. Rose, "New Information on the Life of Joseph Nasi, Duke of Naxos: The Venetian Phase," *Jewish Quarterly Review* 60 (1969–70), 330–44. However, the identity of the rescued lady is disputed by P. Grunebaum-Ballin, *Joseph Naci, duc de Naxos* (Paris, 1968), p. 52, a work that I have been unable to consult. I thank Benjamin Ravid for this information. Also see Lane, *Venice*, pp. 301–2; Romanin, *Storia di Venezia*, VI, 270–74.

[32] Arrested on account of the letters, which may have been counterfeit, the ambassador was tried and eventually absolved by the Senate. See the letters of Nuncio Facchinetti of July 19, August 16, October 18, 1567, May 22, 1568, in *Nunziature* VIII, 251, 260–61, 290, 388.

[33] Letter of Facchinetti of April 10, 1568, in *Nunziature* VIII, 372.

[34] Meir Benayahu, *Haskamah u-reshut bi-defuse Venetsi'ah (Copyright, Authorization and Imprimatur for Hebrew Books Printed in Venice)* (Jerusalem, 1971), pp. 160–90. I wish to thank Joseph Shatzmiller for reading this book for me.

works had to be older Venetian imprints or imports. The Esecutori ordered the titles expurgated, but levied no penalties.[35] Upon the resumption of Hebrew publishing, the Esecutori severely censored the texts; inked-out passages and blank spaces abounded in works published between 1564 and 1568.[36]

Despite the prepublication censorship, the Esecutori believed that Jews and their printers were guilty of publishing objectionable works. Alleging that Venetian Jews had sponsored the publication of many titles, of which "nearly all were uncorrected and unexpurgated," the Esecutori in September 1568 seized at least sixteen or seventeen titles (about 20,000 volumes) published between 1566 and 1568.[37] The books embraced a wide range of Jewish thought and worship; included were a polyglot Old Testament, liturgical manuals, Midrash titles, and Kabbalistic tracts. The Esecutori ordered about 7,000 to 8,000 volumes burned, perhaps destroying nearly complete press runs. For example, 800 copies of the *Midrash Rabboth* (Giorgio de' Cavalli, 1566), in folio, were confiscated and ordered burned. Other titles had to be exported out of Venice and Italy or, in a few cases, could be retained after correction. The Esecutori fined the eleven Jews held responsible for commissioning the works 5 to 500 ducats each for a total of 1,805 ducats. They also fined the publishers Cavalli, Gara, Griffio, and Zanetti, as well as Nicolò Bevilacqua, who had done some of the printing, 50 or 100 ducats each for a total of 400 ducats. Almost all the money went to the Arsenal.

The proximate cause for this wholesale destruction is difficult to determine. The papacy had issued no new decrees against Hebrew books. Nor had the Council of Ten given new instructions, although the Esecutori probably secured the approval of the Council before acting. The Esecutori implied that the Hebrew publishers had systematically ignored censorship regulations; although possible, it seems unlikely that the publishers would have risked massive deception in a period of anti-Semitism. It is also possible that the government cynically raised money for the coming war by punishing the Jews for censorship infractions that had in the past been ignored. Yet, the Venetians normally honored their pacts with the Jews until the pacts expired, and then raised the price for renewal. It is more likely that in a period of mounting hostility the Esecutori and their experts became more sensitive to alleged antichristian passages. They

---

[35] Bestemmia, Bu. 56, R. 1561–1582, ff. 4ᵛ–5ʳ, September 25, 1561. Unfortunately, no titles are given.

[36] Benayahu, pp. 198–207; Popper, *Censorship of Hebrew Books*, p. 54.

[37] Bestemmia, Bu. 56, R. 1561–1582, ff. 41bisʳ–47ᵛ, September 22, 24, 27, October 29, 1568. For the titles of the Hebrew books and other details, please see my article, "The Destruction of Hebrew Books in Venice, 1568," in *Proceedings of the American Academy for Jewish Research*, vol. 45.

may have become increasingly suspicious of the Hebrew press, seeing it as another internal threat. The Republic felt that it had granted the Jews a haven from persecution, and been repaid with treachery. Retroactive censorship and heavy fines seemed just retribution.

Although not prohibited, open Hebrew publishing in Venice nearly ceased, and clandestine activity developed. In April 1570 a priest came to the Holy Office to denounce Marc'Antonio Giustiniani, a patrician who had published Hebrew titles until 1553.[38] Having been appointed governor of Cephalonia, a Venetian island stronghold in the Ionian Sea, Giustiniani had turned it into a distribution center for Hebrew books, and perhaps a printing center as well. According to the denouncer, Giustiniani had, since 1565, imported twelve chests of Hebrew books, including some titles identical to those confiscated in 1568, from Venice for redistribution. He had brought in a bookbinder and an engraver-printer skilled in Arabic, and then had set up a press in the governor's palace. The Arabic printing project had not materialized, but Giustiniani had carried on a thriving commerce in Hebrew books, selling them in Asia Minor and Venice.

The denouncer and other witnesses, all of whom had been with Giustiniani in Cephalonia, supplied enough concordant information to confirm that Giustiniani was trafficking in Hebrew books. But either they were unwilling to reveal all they knew, or they had been unable to penetrate the veil of secrecy around the press in the governor's palace. They did not know if Giustiniani was printing Hebrew titles. Nor did they know for certain whether the twelve chests of books shipped from Venice to Cephalonia were volumes ordered destroyed or exported by the Esecutori in 1568. The Inquisition did its best to avoid discovering additional evidence. The priest in his original denunciation had urged the Holy Office to seize immediately a chest of allegedly uncensored Hebrew books from Cephalonia resting in a ship docked in Venice. The tribunal delayed at least three days; when the chest was opened before the eyes of the priestly accuser, it contained only pelts and sponges.[39] The Holy Office also neglected to question two nobles who reportedly were fully informed of

[38] SU, Bu. 28, Marco Antonio Giustiniani, no pag., consisting of the denunciation and questioning of Don Angelo Fasoli of April 8, 1570, the testimony of other witnesses, and additional material, from April 11 though May 25, 1570. Again see my article, "The Destruction of Hebrew Books in Venice, 1568," for a fuller account.

[39] Don Fasoli delivered his denunciation on April 8. After questioning three soldiers formerly stationed in Cephalonia, the lay assistants on the eleventh ordered the box seized. On the ninteenth it was noted that the order had been carried out. Although it is unclear whether the order was executed on the eleventh or later, it made little difference once the tribunal failed to act on the eighth. Ample time existed for someone, e.g., one of the soldiers, to warn Giustiniani.

Giustiniani's activities. A few days later Giustiniani sent a denunciation of the priest as a scandalmonger, and the investigation ended.

The clandestine movement of uncensored Hebrew books between Cephalonia and Venice continued. In 1574 Antonio Giustiniani, the son of Marc'Antonio, who had died on the Ionian island, brought into Venice fourteen chests of Hebrew books; the Inquisition sealed two chests at the customs house pending expurgation.[40] When the two chests disappeared, Antonio claimed to have sold them to a Ferrara Jew. After a fruitless quest for the buyer and a Rialto broker, the Holy Office fined Antonio 100 ducats. Whatever the truth behind this episode, it demonstrates that uncensored Hebrew books continued to enter Venice. The Giustiniani and their Jewish confederates evidently found ways to distribute, and perhaps even to print, uncensored Hebrew books in the most difficult of times.

After 1568 the situation of the Venetian Jews became perilous. Crowds celebrated the victory of Lepanto by freeing prisoners and harassing Levantine Jews.[41] But the victory was followed by the fall of Cyprus, and anti-Semitism increased. In this fateful time the *condotta* expired, and the Senate met to decide the fate of the Jews. Many senators felt that the moment had come to rid the city of their presence.[42] One senator depicted the Jews as "the scum of the earth, spies for the Turks, [and] internal enemies," holding them responsible for the grain shortage and the Arsenal fire. He went on to charge that their moneylending led youths to vice and reduced noble families to penury. The older arguments for tolerance carried little weight on this occasion. Another senator asked rhetorically whether anyone would deny that the Jews were perfidious, usurious, miserly, and politically unreliable. However, he pointed out that the Jews contributed significantly to the ducal treasury and made it possible for Christians to avoid staining themselves with the sin of usury. He urged the Republic to maintain its traditional policy on the grounds of economic utility and in the hope that, someday, the Jews would become Christians. But the Senate, expressing thanks to God for Lepanto and vowing vengeance for Jewish treachery, voted on December 18, 1571, to expel them.[43]

[40] SU, Bu. 37, Antonio Giustiniani, no. pag., the questioning of Giustiniani and others from October 22, 1574, through April 19, 1575. It appears that Giustiniani did pay the fine.

[41] "Li Turchi hebrei Levantinj ch'erano in rialto per esser l'hora di negocij de rialto et in altri luochi della citta fugissero alle lor' case. . . ." VM, Mss. Italiani, Classe VII, 134 (8035), "Cronaca veneta di Girolamo Savina sino al MDCXV," f. 358r.

[42] The speeches are summarized by Agostino Valier, *Dell'utilità che si può ritrarre dalle cose operate dai veneziani*, Bk. XIII, ch. 1, pp. 358–60.

[43] The preamble of the expulsion act is given by Pullan, *Rich and Poor*, p. 537.

Within a few days the Venetians reconsidered: they calculated the effects of the loss of the *condotta* payment and the disruption of the monetary exchange. The Senate canceled the expulsion order, but did not renew the *condotta*, leaving the Jews suspended between acceptance and exile while secret peace negotiations with the Turks got under way. It is likely that peace was conditional upon a reprieve for the Jews; in the summer of 1573 the Republic renewed the *condotta* on the condition that the Jews would operate loan banks for the poor on terms reminiscent of the Monti di Pietà. After this crisis, the lot of the Venetian Jews steadily improved; their indispensable role in the Republic's commercial and social life grew and was acknowledged.[44]

The easing of anti-Semitism led to a revival of Hebrew publishing. Only Giovanni di Gara published Hebrew titles (three) between 1569 and 1573, but in 1574 Alvise Bragadino and Me'ir Parenzo joined him. After the Great Plague of 1575–77, Gara, by far the most active, and the respective Bragadino and Parenzo heirs, published Hebrew titles in greater quantity. A handful of other publishers later joined them—especially in the 1590s.

4. EFFECTIVE PREPUBLICATION CENSORSHIP

Although a more fervent but worried Republic persecuted heretics and Jews at home, and fought the Turks abroad, the Catholic world lacked an authoritative Index to guide it in the struggle against dissent. When the Council of Trent turned to the question of an Index at the end of January 1562, the fathers expressed a variety of opinions, the Venetian participants as divided in their counsel as the rest. Daniele Barbaro (1514–70), diplomat, humanist, and Patriarch of Aquileia, argued for a restricted Index.[45] He began with a reiteration of the Republic's basic position: heretical titles, attacks against princes, and works that corrupted public morality should be banned. He pleaded that all other titles be permitted. "Libri omnes scientiarum et artium" containing neither impiety, slander, nor depravity, but authored by heretics, should be allowed after deletion of the authors' names. Lascivious poetry that was the product of indiscreet

[44] Pullan, *Rich and Poor*, pp. 537–40, for the events of 1571–73, and pp. 541–78 for the later history.

[45] For the Tridentine discussions, January 30 through February 26, 1562, see *Concilium Tridentinum: diariorum, actorum, epistularum. Nova Collectio edidit Societas Goerresiana*, vol. VIII, *Actorum Pars Quinta*, ed. Stephan Ehses (Freiburg im Breisgau, 1964), pp. 306–14, 348–50, 358–59, esp. pp. 308–9 for Barbaro; and vol. III, *Diariorum pars tertia, volumen Prius*, ed. Sebastian Merkle, 2nd ed. (Freiburg im Breisgau, 1967), pp. 250–74, esp. p. 261 for Contarini. On Barbaro, see Pio Paschini, "Daniele Barbaro letterato e prelato veneziano nel Cinquecento," *Rivista di storia della Chiesa in Italia* 16 (1962), 73–107; and Giuseppe Alberigo, "Daniele Barbaro," DBI, VI, 89–95. On Contarini, see HC, III, 269.

youth rather than malice should not be banned (Barbaro may have had in mind the early poetry of his late friend, Giovanni Della Casa, banned by the Pauline Index). Barbaro also believed that good books should not be banned simply because the printer was a heretic. Although Barbaro did not indicate that he spoke for anyone but himself, the Venetian bookmen and some patricians would have endorsed his position. Other Venetian prelates did not share his view. Pietro Contarini, Bishop of Paphos (or Baffo) in Cyprus and a friend of the late Paul IV, wanted the Pauline Index reissued unchanged; the Venetian patriarch, Giovanni Trevisan, made ineffectual noises as usual.

After the opening speeches, the council appointed a commission to draft a new Index, empowering it to revise, if necessary, the Pauline entries. The commission spent months at its task, debating controversial authors such as Erasmus. One of the most important products of its work was a proposal for general rules for censorship, formulated in November 1563.[46] When the council ended before the Index commission could finish its task, the work was turned over to the papacy.

Pius IV promulgated the so-called Tridentine Index in the spring of 1564. A union of discordant parts, the new Index mirrored the diversity of views expressed at Trent and the split between moderate and stern reformers generally. With a handful of significant exceptions, the author and title entries reproduced the Pauline Index in full severity. But the few changes were toward moderation, and they encompassed some of the most important authors of the century. The Erasmus entry was less restrictive than it had been in previous papal Indices. The 1554/55 Index had banned ten of Erasmus's works; the Pauline Index, all of them. The Tridentine Index banned six titles: the *Colloquia, Moriae encomium, Lingua, Institutio christiani matrimonii, Epistola . . . de interdicto esu carnium,* and the Tomitano translation of the *Paraphrasis in evangelium Matthaei.* But it also insisted upon expurgation by a Catholic theological faculty of all his other religious works. The Pauline Index had banned a long list of Savonarola's sermons; the Tridentine Index wanted them expurgated. The 1554/55 Index had banned works on the New Testament of Jacques Lefèvre d'Étaples, and the Pauline Index had condemned an additional title; the Tridentine Index permitted all of them in expurgated form. Giovanni Battista Gelli's *Capricci del bottaio,* banned in 1559, was also allowed if expurgated. The Tridentine Index dropped the specific condemnations of nearly sixty printings of the Bible and the proscription of an

---

[46] For the Index commission's discussions, February 1562 through November 1563, see *Concilium Tridentinum,* vol. XIII, *Tractatuum pars altera prius ex collectionibus Vincentii Schweitzer,* ed. Hubert Jedin, 2nd ed. (Freiburg im Breisgau, 1967), pp. 587–607, esp. pp. 603–6 for the general rules.

equal number of printers. However, 99 percent of the entries, including the prohibitions of the opera omnia of Aretino, Machiavelli, and hundreds of others, were reaffirmations of the Pauline condemnations.

The Tridentine Index promulgated in altered form the rules or guidelines for censorship prepared by the council's commission. Their effect was to mitigate the sweeping condemnations of Paul IV, whose Index had condemned everything published by a heretical author, whatever the subject matter and however slight the author's contribution to a particular volume. The Tridentine Index attempted to make some distinctions. It condemned all the works of heresiarchs (without offering a clear definition), but allowed a bishop or inquisitor to permit the nonreligious works of other heretics (Rule II).[47] Books free of error, but containing concordances, indices, or other material authored by heretics could be held after expurgation (Rule V). Books that contained some error, but "whose chief matter" was "good," could also be held in expurgated form (Rule VIII).

The Tridentine Index replaced Paul IV's condemnation of Scripture in the vernacular and his list of proscribed editions of the Bible with a series of qualified permissions and prohibitions. Rule III authorized bishops to permit editions of the Old Testament edited by heretics as long as the editions themselves were free of heresy, but it prohibited editions of the New Testament prepared by heretics of the first class, i.e., those whose entire corpus was banned. The Index also authorized bishops and inquisitors to issue permissions to hold and read vernacular Bibles and works of religious controversy (Rules IV and VI).

Rule VII banned obscene works and cautioned that some ancient classics admired as models of style should be kept out of the hands of young people. Since this rule carefully avoided condemning lascivious classics, it can be inferred that adults were permitted to read them. Rule IX reaffirmed the Pauline ban of all titles of magic and the occult, but permitted works of judicial astrology as long as they did not deny free will. Finally, Rule I reiterated a Pauline prohibition of all books condemned by the pope or council before 1515.

These nine rules reflected the influence of moderate reformers like Cardinal Seripando and attempted to meet some of the objections to the Pauline Index.[48] But the amelioration was more apparent than real because the rules did not provide for implementation. Much of the moderation depended upon substituting expurgation for outright prohibition, but the rules neither offered guidelines for expurgation nor permitted individuals to expurgate their own books. Instead, they insisted that the task

[47] For the rules, see Reusch, *Indices*, 247–51.

[48] Jedin, *Seripando*, p. 589, believes that the Tridentine Index was largely Seripando's work.

be done by theologians acting under the auspices of the local bishop and inquisitor. Very few dioceses had the theological expertise or manpower for such a task, even if Rome were willing to countenance local expurgation and its inevitable inconsistencies. In 1571 the papacy established a Congregation of the Index to expurgate books, but very few expurgated titles were published before the 1590s.

Other difficulties stemmed from the contradictions between the rules and the entries of the Tridentine Index. The rules attempted to make a distinction between heresiarchs and ordinary heretics, and to authorize a bishop or inquisitor to permit the holding of nonreligious works of the latter. The intent was to make available the humanistic and scientific titles of such authors as the polymath scientist Konrad Gesner, the jurist Joannes Oldendorpius, and other learned heretics who had published little religious matter. But like the two previous papal Indices, the Tridentine Index banned the opera omnia of these writers and many others like them, in effect classifying them as heresiarchs. Local inquisitors would inevitably follow the definite prohibitions of the entries rather than the vague rules.

By contrast, Rule X of the Tridentine Index promulgated detailed instructions for prepublication censorship and control of book distribution. Inquisitors and bishops (or bishops' delegates) were given the power to examine each manuscript and issue an approval, which had to be included in the printed volume, to inspect bookstores, to examine imported volumes, and to forbid titles not on the Index. Booksellers were required to submit inventories to the inquisitor and bishop, as were persons who inherited books. If implemented, Rule X would have great impact on the book trade and the reading public.

The Tridentine Index was published in Venice by the Aldine Press and at least one other printer in 1564 (see figures 9 and 10) and was frequently reprinted in subsequent years. Its appearance ignited no controversy in Venice or elsewhere in Italy because it was the joint product of council and pope and because it had eliminated some of the most objectionable features of its predecessor. Moreover, it was promulgated at a time of substantial Italian agreement on the importance of defending orthodoxy.

Rule X had two goals: ecclesiastical prepublication censorship and ecclesiastical control of book distribution. The Republic had already granted the first; in 1562 the Venetians had established a system of prepublication censorship that formally empowered the inquisitor to read all new manuscripts before they were printed.[49]

---

[49] The rest of this section discusses the prepublication censorship; see Ch. v, sec. 1 for an analysis of how the Venetian Holy Office sought to implement the rest of Rule X.

INDEX LIBRORVM

PROHIBITORVM,

CVM REGVLIS CONFECTIS

per Patres a Tridentina Synodo delectos,
auctoritate Sanctiss. D.N. Pij IIII,
Pont. Max. comprobatus.

AL DVS

VENETIIS, M. D. LXIIII.

9. Title page of the Aldine printing of the Tridentine Index: *Index librorum prohibitorum . . . per Patres a Tridentina Synodo delectos, auctoritate . . . Pij IIII. . . .* (Venetiis, MDLXIIII). Source: VM, Aldine 768 (38437)

INDEX LIBRORVM

PROHIBITORVM,

CVM REGVLIS CONFECTIS
per Patres à Tridentina Synodo delectos,
auctoritate Sanctiff. D. N. Pij IIII.
Pont. Max. comprobatus.

VENETIIS, M. D. LXIIII.

10. Title page of another Venetian printing of the Tridentine Index: *Index librorum prohibitorum . . . per Patres a Tridentina Synodo delectos, auctoritate . . . Pij IIII. . . .* (Venetiis, MDLXIIII). Source: VM, Miscellanea 2228.2

In 1527 the Council of Ten had established a state prepublication censorship that excluded the Holy Office at a time when the tribunal was dormant. However, by mid-century the inquisitor and other clergymen were participating—whether regularly or occasionally is not clear—in prepublication censorship, probably because the Riformatori dello Studio di Padova had delegated some power to them. It is likely that bookmen seeking imprimaturs were obliged to obtain a *testamur* or *fede* (certificate of approval) from a clergyman, at least for religious titles. But the obligation was often ignored, and the entire system was haphazard. (It will be recalled that the inquisitor had refused to approve the Tomitano translation of Erasmus's *Paraphrasis in evangelium Matthaei* but had been ignored by both the author and the secretary of the Riformatori.) The Holy Office discovered in 1558 that the bookmen often neglected to obtain a clerical fede. The preamble to the regulation of 1562 justified the new decree on the grounds that the bookmen were in the habit of obtaining fedi from whomever they pleased.

In its decree of March 19, 1562, the Riformatori dello Studio di Padova laid down a multiple procedure for prepublication censorship that gave the Holy Office a major role.[50] The decree required that manuscripts be examined by three readers. Each reader was empowered to correct or reject a manuscript, and each had to issue a fede testifying that the manuscript contained nothing "contrary to religion, princes, or public morality," and that it merited publication. The Riformatori hoped that if one censor missed erring passages, another would excise them. In practice each censor tended to take responsibility for a different kind of censorship.[51] The author, editor, or bookman wishing to publish a new title first presented his manuscript to the inquisitor or his designate, who read it carefully for doctrinal and moral error. Next, the applicant took the manuscript to a public reader, who examined it primarily for political content.[52] Then he took it to a ducal secretary, who gave it a final scrutiny in the light of current Venetian policy and made sure that it did not offend a friendly monarch or upset delicate negotiations. In practice the ducal secretary

[50] The decree is printed by Brown, *Venetian Press*, pp. 213–14; and by Sforza, "Controriforma," pt. 2, p. 179. The testamurs and imprimaturs are to be found in Capi del CX, Notatorio, R. 14–33, and F. 1–13.

[51] This statement is based on an analysis of the few cases in which the corrections ordered by a particular censor are known. See below.

[52] The 1562 decree named one public reader, Marc'Antonio Mocenigo, a noble described as "Lettor in Filosofia." Another public reader who frequently censored books until he left for Rome in 1585 was Aldo Manuzio il Giovane (1547–97), publisher and author. Fabio Paolini (c. 1535–1605), who taught Greek at the library of St. Mark and authored many humanistic and medical works, frequently acted as censor in the 1580s and 1590s.

approved the vast majority of titles that reached his desk with no more than a cursory glance.[53]

The petitioner then took the three testamurs to the Riformatori dello Studio di Padova, which issued a certificate attesting to their existence. With this certificate he went to the Heads of the Council of Ten, who granted the imprimatur, thus completing the censorship process. The bookman might then request a Senate privilegio, if he wished. The Heads (i.e., their secretaries) determined the duration of a privilegio (ten to thirty years) and the penalty for infringement (100 to 300 ducats' fine and confiscation of illegally printed volumes), and presented the privilegio applications for the formality of Senate approval. After printing, but prior to public sale, the publisher had to present a copy of the book to the Riformatori.

Additional laws plugged small loopholes. On September 17, 1566, the Council of Ten ruled that the imprimatur and privilegio had to be registered with the Esecutori contro la bestemmia, obviously in order to facilitate the apprehension of violators.[54] The Council of Ten also noted that the bookmen sometimes introduced antireligious passages into their books and made other alterations after obtaining the testamurs of the censors. It decreed in 1569 that the successful applicant must deposit a bound copy of the manuscript with the Riformatori so that comparisons between the approved manuscript and the printed book could be made.[55]

The entire censorship process probably took one to three months. The Holy Office reader possibly needed one to four weeks to read a manuscript, depending on its length and on how busy he was; the other testamurs normally followed within three to eight weeks.[56] The printer could save time by setting type and printing proofs before the imprimatur was granted, but he ran the risk of being forced to make changes.[57] The

[53] The dated testamur of the ducal secretary normally followed within 24 to 48 hours that of the public reader.

[54] The law is printed in Brown, *Venetian Press*, pp. 214–15; and Sforza, "Controriforma," pt. 2, p. 180, although the latter misdates it as 1562.

[55] CX, Comune, R. 59, ff. 30ʳ⁻ᵛ, June 28, 1569. The text of this law is printed in App. 1; other provisions are discussed in Ch. v, sec. 1. Incidentally, the few extant Riformatori documents of the cinquecento include no book manuscripts. Either they have disappeared over the years, or else this costly provision of the law was ignored.

[56] For example, in the fall of 1597 one title received the inquisitorial testamur on October 25, that of the public reader on October 29, of the ducal secretary on October 31, and imprimatur of the Heads on November 10. Another book took longer, from August 12 for the testamur of the Inquisition reader to October 9 for the imprimatur of the Heads. Capi del CX, Notatorio, F. 13, no pag., documents of the above dates.

[57] Possibly the charge that the bookmen were introducing alterations after re-

GLI Eccellentiſſimi Signori Capi dell'Illuſtriſſimo Conſeglio di Dieci infraſcritti, hauuta fede
dalli Signori Reformatori dello Studio di Padoa,
per relatione delli doi à ciò deputati, cioè del Re-
uer. P. Inquiſitor, & del circonſpetto Secretario del
Senato Zuanne Meraueglia con giuramento, che
nel Libro intitolato Theatro vniuerſale de' Prencipi, & di tutte le Hiſtorie del Mondo di Gio. Nicolo Doglioni, diſtinto in otto Parti, non ſi troua
coſa contra le leggi, & è degno di ſtampa; concedono licentia, che poſſi eſſere ſtampato in que-
ſta Città.

Dat. die 4. Aprilis, 1605.

D. Nicolo Querini.
D. Z. Battiſta Contarini. } Cap. Ill.ᵐⁱ Cons. X.
D. Lunardo Mocenigo.

Illuſtriſs. Cons. X. Secret.
Leonardus Otthobonus.

---

11. Imprimatur from Giovanni Nicolò Doglione, *Del theatro universale de' prencipi,
et di tutte l'historie del mondo.* . . . . Vol. 1. (In Venetia, Appresso Nicolò Misserini,
MDCVI)

process was also expensive. Each of the three censors was allowed to charge a fee of one *bezzo* (1/160th of a ducat) per manuscript folio; censorship of a manuscript of 160 folios would thus cost three ducats, equivalent to the gross from the retail sale of about ten copies of an average book.[58] The author or bookman also had to bear the cost of the bound manuscript deposited with the Riformatori.

With the 1562 decree, the Venetians had made participation by the Holy Office in prepublication censorship formal and legal. They had done so in order to attain the effective censorship that they felt was necessary to guard the spiritual health of the Republic. However, the process was jurisdictionally predominantly civil, for the three testamurs of the censors were civil documents leading to the issuance of a state imprimatur. The Venetians had willingly conceded great power to the Holy Office, but they were as determined as ever to manifest outwardly the priority of secular jurisdiction.

From the 1560s through the end of the century, the prepublication censorship machinery prevented the publication of books that were religiously, politically, or morally objectionable. The inquisitorial reader was the first, and probably the most careful, censor for the vast majority of manuscripts. He was in a position to make certain that no title on the Index slipped through, and he had the power to eliminate heretical religious content from new titles. But the system provided even stronger controls over political content. The two censors appointed by the state ensured that no criticism of the Republic or of friendly princes slipped through. Church and state agreed on the necessity of strict and effective censorship, and shared the responsibility.[59]

---

ceiving the testamurs stemmed from a practice of setting type before the censorship process was completed, and then failing to take the trouble of making changes ordered by the censors.

[58] The value of the *bezzo* is given by Brown, *Venetian Press*, p. 93, n. 2, and the average price of 36 soldi has been used for the calculation.

[59] Commenting on the decrees of 1562 and 1566, Brown generalized that (1) "it was hardly possible to have invented a more irritating and cumbersome process"; (2) the government was aware that this legislation was ruinous to the industry but went ahead in order to check the clandestine press, i.e., publications lacking imprimaturs and privilegi; and (3) although state enforcement remained "an empty letter," "every priest, every friar, was a policeman," *Venetian Press*, pp. 94–95. Brown was certainly correct on (1) but not on (2) and (3). There was no reason for the government to concern itself with financial losses to the industry because there was, as yet, no economic decline. Moreover, by its burning of the Talmud in 1553 and of other Hebrew books in 1568, and in its response to the Pauline and Tridentine Indices, the government demonstrated that suppressing objectionable literature was more important than economic considerations. The clandestine press was a minor irritant in comparison to the spread of heretical

The surviving testamurs and imprimaturs reveal in a handful of cases the precise corrections or excisions ordered by inquisitor, public reader, or ducal secretary. In 1567 the inquisitorial reader objected to one novella in the *Sei giornate* of Sebastiano Erizzo.[60] A noble whose career took him to the Senate, Council of Ten, and Savii di Terraferma, Erizzo (1525–85) also authored works of literature, numismatics, and politics. The *Sei giornate* was an early work (c. 1554) in the style of Boccaccio but with moralizing tendencies. According to the title page, six youthful Paduan scholars had met in 1542 to relate tales that by means of "diverse fortunate and unhappy events" taught "noble and useful precepts of moral philosophy." In the thirty-six stories, the characters suffer accidents, shipwrecks, and miraculous recoveries until virtue triumphs. Sometimes borrowing from Valerius Maximus, the author underlined the moral of each story with a long oration placed in the mouth of the chief character and with concluding remarks. Published but once in the cinquecento, by Giovanni Varisco & Compagni in 1567, the work does not enjoy a high reputation among historians of Italian literature.

The novella that the inquisitorial reader objected to dealt with the "dog of Attila," and the Heads ordered its elimination. Another was put in its place to complete the thirty-six, but the missing story survived in manuscript until discovered and published at the end of the eighteenth century.[61] In the tale Ostrubaldo, King of Hungary, has a beautiful but very lustful daughter who carries on many amours. Angry at his dishonorable daughter, the king refuses to find her a husband and shuts her up in a tower with only a dog for companionship. The lonely girl lies with the dog and becomes pregnant. Despairing, Ostrubaldo comes to kill her. She meets him with a long impassioned defense in which she blamed him for her bestiality on the grounds that he has prevented her from satisfying her appetites naturally. She argues that women have the same desires as men;

---

ideas. Nor was Brown correct on (3). The new regulations were effective *because* the state enforced the prepublication censorship machinery and soon permitted the Holy Office to inspect the bookstores. The Venetian clergy played an insignificant role in this, and even clerical denunciations of bookmen and those who held prohibited titles were infrequent.

[60] Capi del CX, Notatorio, R. 21, f. 90ʳ, April 29, 1567. For a succinct biography of Erizzo, see Tommaso Bozza, *Scrittori politici italiani dal 1550 al 1650. Saggio di bibliografia* (Rome, 1949), pp. 45–46.

[61] "Del nascimento di Attila re degli Ungheri," in *Le sei giornate di messer Sebastiano Erizzo*, ed. Gaetano Poggiali (Londra [Livorno], 1794), pp. 407–22. Poggiali was unaware that it had been suppressed. The best modern edition of the *Sei giornate* is in *Novellieri minori del Cinquecento: G. Parabosco—S. Erizzo*, ed. Giuseppe Gigli and Fausto Nicolini (Bari, 1912), with the missing tale on pp. 429–35.

just as men claim that one woman cannot satisfy them, so women have the same need and right to a multiplicity of partners. Moved, her father spares her life and arranges a marriage with a compliant baron. In time she gives birth to a son of human physique but canine countenance. He is named Attila, the dog-man who becomes the "Scourge of God." The tale ends with a repetition of its moral: women are driven by carnal appetites equal to, or greater than, those of a man; if denied natural fulfillment, they will find an unnatural outlet.

The testamur does not list the inquisitor's reasons for censorship, but more than likely he objected to the tale's strong advocacy of uninhibited sexual gratification. In contrast to the other tales in the collection, the story of Ostrubaldo inverts virtue and vice to propound a naturalistic ethic contrary to Christian norms. The inquisitorial reader had little choice but to condemn it on moral grounds. The Heads of the Council of Ten endorsed his decision even though the author was a noble.

In 1597 the public reader, Fabio Paolini, ordered cuts for political reasons in a new printing of Giovanni Botero's *Reason of State*.[62] Botero (1543/44–1617) continually revised his famous work. The first edition, published by the Gioliti press (heirs of Gabriel Giolito) in Venice in 1589 concluded with book 10, chapter 8; the edition published in Rome in 1590 added a chapter 9, entitled "The purpose for which military forces should be used," a discussion of the conditions under which a Catholic ruler was justified in waging war on internal heretics and external infidels. Botero disapproved of toleration of heresy within the state, but acknowledged (with the French situation obviously in mind) that a monarch should sometimes refrain from making war on heretics. He vigorously called on Christian rulers to take up arms against the grave Turkish menace, and lamented that Christian rulers sometimes forged alliances with the infidel, instead of uniting with other Christian princes against the common foe. Botero concluded by praising the Venetians for spurning Turkish assistance in 1509, their hour of gravest peril; God, in return, had granted the Republic a miraculous recovery.

In the Milan and Turin editions of 1596, Botero appended to chapter 9 a slashing attack on Francis I and Henry II for their alliances with the infidel against Emperor Charles V. The Christians captured by the Turks as a result of these infamous alliances had called down upon the Valois rulers horrifying curses, which God had heard. He extinguished their house, inflicted an early and painful death on Henry II, and plunged

[62] The imprimatur was granted ". . . (levate via dell'opra quanto può offender nominatamente la Corona di Francia). . . ." Capi del CX, Notatorio, F. 13, no pag., document of July 1, 1597.

France into ruin. Botero concluded with another incident that demonstrated God's vengeance on the French who had allied with the infidel.

When the Gioliti press in 1597 wished to print a new Venetian edition, the imprimatur was granted on the condition that the material that criticized the French crown by name be excised. The publisher obeyed. The Gioliti edition of 1598 omitted the sharp attack on the Valois monarchs, and offered a chapter 9 identical with the earlier version in the Rome, 1590, edition.[63]

In addition to their habitual caution lest any criticism of foreign monarchs appearing in the press be construed as an official view, the Venetians may have had an immediate reason for the censorship. In February 1596 Henry IV had been acutely displeased by the Republic's refusal of his request for financial aid. The Venetian ambassador needed time to mollify him.[64] Since good rapport with France was essential to the anti-Spanish counterweight that Venetian policy sought to establish at the time, the Heads of the Council of Ten did not want to see anti-French sentiments appear in a Venetian printing of Botero's widely read book.

Other works were censored. In 1603 the Heads granted an imprimatur for the first edition of Botero's *Relatione della Repubblica Venetiana* subject to the "removal of the many things canceled out by the . . . [ducal] secretary."[65] Not surprisingly, the version published by Giorgio Varisco in 1605 presented a favorable portrait of the Republic. The exact nature and extent of the excisions are unknown because no uncensored version has come to light. In the same year, changes were ordered in a work of casuistry, Giovanni Battista' Corrado's *Quaesita 400 pro examinandis qui ad animarum curam vel confessiones.*[66]

Only a few of the thousands of imprimaturs granted contained indica-

---

[63] The modern critical edition prepared by Luigi Firpo is used: *Della ragion di stato di Giovanni Botero con tre libri Delle cause della grandezza della città, due Aggiunte e un Discorso sulla popolazione di Roma* (Turin, 1948). Firpo based his edition on the 1598 Venetian printing on the grounds that it embodied the author's last thoughts. Nevertheless, with sure editorial instinct, he included the suppressed material although he did not know why it had been omitted (pp. 338–40). Seicento Venetian printings of Botero's work that I have seen continued to omit the conclusion of ch. 9.

[64] Romanin, *Storia di Venetia*, VI, 413–14.

[65] Capi del CX, Notatorio, R. 32, ff. 152^v–53^r, March 16, 1603.

[66] Capi del CX, R. 32, f. 164^v, April 5, 1603. Corrado (Perugia 1530–c. 1606) was a Dominican theologian. First published in Venice, 1598, the work appeared in 1603 appended to an earlier title, *Responsa ad cuiuscunque pene generis casuum conscientiae*, but I have not attempted to locate copies to make a comparison. *New Catholic Encyclopedia*, vol. 4, p. 348; *Dictionnaire de théologie catholique*, vol. 3, pt. 2, pp. 1,906–7.

tions that the readers had ordered corrections or cuts. How frequently one of the readers canceled or emendated passages, or returned a manuscript for revisions, is impossible to tell. Certainly the readers were thorough, both in excising offensive passages and in rejecting titles and authors on the Tridentine Index. Nevertheless, a work slipped through occasionally. The Tridentine Index had banned the opera omnia of Ortensio Lando in an entry that took into account his aliases. Yet in 1569 his *Commentario delle più notabili & mostruose cose d'Italia* was published by Giovanni Bariletto. Like the earlier Venetian editions of 1548, 1550, 1553, and 1554 in content, it was published anonymously but with very obvious clues to Lando's authorship.[67]

The knowledge that effective prepublication censorship existed quickly begot self-censorship.[68] Authors began to weigh their words more carefully. They deleted anticlericalism, allegorized immorality, and veiled criticism with laughter. References to Protestant authors were suppressed. An author might refer to an anonymous Florentine history instead of Machiavelli's *History of Florence*, or mention a certain author of comedies instead of naming Aretino. Although such caution tended to encourage blandness, it left intact fundamental content. The heavy-handed expurgation typical of the Congregation of the Index was still in the future.

Yet, self-censorship was neither limited to religious matter nor a cinquecento innovation. Quattrocento humanists in the employ of cities and princes had sometimes held their pens on political matters and praised extravagantly those whom they had to praise. In the following century authors seldom used the local press to attack the government. Most states were quick to suppress criticism of themselves or foreign powers published within their borders.[69] Like other states, the Republic had always practiced political censorship and would continue to do so. In 1565 the Council of Ten discovered that a leaflet criticizing the emperor was circu-

[67] The clues were a concluding anagram "SUISNETROH SUDNAL ROTUA TSE," which read backward is "Hortensius Landus autor est," and a brief apology for the author signed by Lando. For the full citation, see Grendler, *Critics*, p. 231, no. 54. Bariletto, who had his shop at the sign of La Prudenza in the Calle dei Stagneri (now della Fava), which is very near Santa Maria della Fava, published twenty-two works between 1560 and 1575. He also sold prohibited books; see Ch. VI, sec. 1.

[68] I am only touching a complex phenomenon. For a conceptualization of the issues involved, see Luigi Firpo, "Correzioni d'autore coatte," in *Studi e problemi di critica testuale*, Convegno di studi di filologia italiana nel centenario della Commissione per i Testi di Lingua, 7–9 aprile 1960. (Bologna, 1961), 143–57.

[69] For example, the Florentine government expurgated Guicciardini's *Storia d'Italia* before its first publication in 1561. As Bongi notes, this kind of censorship was common. *Giolito*, II, 258–59.

lating in Venice. Although it bore a Milan imprint, the Council discovered that it had been printed in Padua and ordered the arrest of the bookman and confiscation of all copies.[70] In 1571 the Council of Ten directed the rectors of Bergamo to find out who had printed a pamphlet attacking a cardinal.[71] And when a bastard of the Soranzo family authored a book, published in Ferrara and Milan, containing references to the Turks of which the Venetians disapproved, the Republic ordered the book banned and the author arrested.[72] The area of free speech contracted noticeably in the 1560s because the new prepublication censorship machinery added tight religious and moral censorship to political censorship.

The insertion of the Holy Office into the censorship process gave the papacy the opportunity to engage in occasional extraordinary acts of censorship. If it wished to stop the printing of a work not on the Tridentine Index, or to impose changes, the papacy wrote the nuncio, who instructed the inquisitorial reader. The pope intervened to obtain in-press corrections in a work of Fra Antonio de Cordova (or Corduba) (1485–1578), a Spanish theologian and casuist. The pontiff objected to his defense of bullfighting in defiance of a recent papal decree (1567) banning the sport.[73] In 1575 the Senate promised Cardinal Alessandro Farnese that it would not permit the publication of a historical work "full of slanders" against Paul III. The author and an unidentified bookman did attempt to print it, but Rome stopped them through the Venetian Inquisition.[74] On another occasion Rome informed the nuncio that a furtive attempt to publish the works of Onofrio Panvinio (1530–68), a historian of ancient Rome and ecclesiastical antiquity, as well as a biographer of cinquecento

[70] The bookman was Pietro Antonio Alciati, who published three works between 1566 and 1569. CX, Secrete, R. 8, f. 21ʳ, January 12, 1564 mv.

[71] CX, Secrete, R. 9, ff. 128ʳ–29ʳ, February 3, 1570 mv. I have not found any evidence to suggest that this order was in response to a papal complaint.

[72] The book was *L'Ottomanno* by Lorenzo di Benetto Soranzo. Letter of Nuncio Anton Maria Graziani of August 12, 1598, in ASVa, Segretario di Stato, Venezia, F. 33, ff. 108ʳ⁻ᵛ. *STC Italian*, 634.

[73] The only title mentioned was "De difficilibus quaestionibus," which may have been his *Quaestionarium theologicum sive Sylva amplissima decisionum et variarum resolutionum casuum conscientiae*, his often printed book on casuistry. Giordano Ziletti published his *Opera libris quinque digesta*, which may have contained the emendated material, in 1569 and 1570. Letters of Nuncio Facchinetti and Cardinal Bonelli of January 24, 1568, through May 4, 1569, in *Nunziature* VIII, 341, 342, 386, 497, 502; IX, 46, 48, 53–54, 56. Pastor, XVII, 206–8. Incidentally, although Pius V could correct Fra Antonio's book, he could not halt bullfighting, partly because the Spanish episcopate lacked the courage to publish his decree.

[74] Senato, Deliberazioni Roma, R. 4, f. 97ᵛ, November 5, 1575; letters of Cardinal Tolomeo Galli of February 4, 1576, Rome, and Nuncio Giambattista Castagna of February 11, Venice, in *Nunziature* XI, 490–91, 493.

pontiffs, was under way. The papacy asked the nuncio to halt publication pending correction of the works; the nuncio spoke to the inquisitor, who promised not to issue a testamur. The nuncio then reported to Rome that it was easy to stop a new printing, but he could do nothing about earlier editions because the law did not cover them.[75] A bookman might continue to publish reprints of a work without submitting it to the censors for the duration of an earlier imprimatur and privilegio.

Some interventions exceeded the jurisdictional limits imposed on the Holy Office and violated Venetian press law. Yet, when the complaints of the bookmen reached the ears of the Council of Ten, its response was mild. The Council did not berate the nuncio or file a protest with Rome, but merely warned the nuncio to consult the government before acting. And it assured him of a sympathetic hearing.[76] Convinced of the importance of censorship, the leaders of the Republic were not inclined to make an issue of jurisdictional incursions.

The Republic's desire to achieve effective censorship of the book industry resulted in more vigorous enforcement of the civil press laws by the Esecutori contro la bestemmia, as well as cooperation between the civil court and the Holy Office for the first time. In contrast to their relative inactivity in the past, the Esecutori between 1566 and 1568 sentenced a half-dozen bookmen to fines of up to twenty-five ducats and a month's imprisonment for imprimatur violations.[77] This number of sentences within a short time suggests that the goal was to persuade the bookmen to obey the new press laws. The Esecutori also took another step to ensure compliance. Noting that false histories, poetry, and prophecies were printed without imprimaturs, and then sold at the Rialto bridge, the Esecutori appointed a former printer, Alvise Zio, to search for violators.[78] In the past the Esecutori had waited for denunciations; now they sought to patrol the industry.

Within a few days of his appointment, Alvise Zio and the Esecutori were aiding the Holy Office. In 1566 the Esecutori had fined Girolamo (or Troian) Calepin for printing a *Tariffa delle puttane*, a catalogue of Vene-

---

[75] It is not clear which of Panvinio's many titles were involved. Letters of Nuncio Facchinetti and Cardinal Michele Bonelli of January 12, Rome; January 19, Venice; January 26, Rome, and February 2, 1569, Venice, in *Nunziature* VIII, 481, 484 (esp.), 488–89, 491.

[76] CX, Secrete, R. 8, f. 143ʳ, February 8, 1568 mv.

[77] Esecutori, Bu. 56, Registro 1561–82, ff. 24ᵛ (July 23, August 9, 1566), 28ʳ (April 7, 1567), 31ᵛ (May 28, 1567), 33ʳ (July 16, 1567), 40ᵛ–41ᵛ (August 2, 19, September 9, 1568). Also see Pesenti, "Libri censurati," pp. 21–24.

[78] Esecutori, Bu. 56, Registro 1561–82, f. 38ᵛ, March 7, 1568. Alvise Zio published one title in 1564, and the firm of Domenico Zio e Fratelli published five works in 1538.

tian prostitutes with names, addresses, and fees.[79] In March 1568, the Esecutori ordered Zio to visit Calepin's store. He found the *Tariffa delle puttane*, as well as a number of prohibited books. He reported his discovery to the Holy Office, undoubtedly with the approval of the Esecutori. The Inquisition commissioned Zio and the nuncio's auditor to examine Calepin's books. They went to his house and were told by neighbors that Calepin no longer lived there. Returning the next morning, they learned that Calepin had cut the cord to the doorbell, had asked his neighbors to announce that he had moved away, and had used the night hours to spirit away a large number of books. Subsequent questioning of neighbors, employees, and other bookmen revealed the names of Calepin's prohibited titles: various works of Aretino, Berni, Machiavelli, Agrippa, Valdés' *Mercurio et Caronte,* and several works of geomancy. One bookman testified that it was common knowledge that Calepin sold Aretino titles because Calepin had been a distributor for the late Francesco Marcolini (d. 1559), Aretino's major publisher.[80] Calepin obviously still held a number of Aretino volumes, and had escaped with them. The Inquisition could do nothing.

In the 1560s the Republic had come to believe that close regulation of the book industry was essential to the security of the state. Political and religious motives had persuaded the leaders of the Republic to set up prepublication censorship that would guarantee that neither heresy, nor immorality, nor political dissent would be printed in Venice. The Republic had granted to the Holy Office directly, and the papacy indirectly, major roles in censorship; doge and pope, noble and nuncio, had worked in close cooperation to achieve a mutual goal. They had stopped the publication of dissenting works; next they would try to arrest the flow of contraband from abroad and purge the shelves of the bookstores.

[79] Calepin, at the Calle Fiubera in San Zulian, published at least four works between 1550 and 1554. Esecutori, Bu. 56, Registro 1561–82, f. 24ᵛ, July 23, 1566. This is also accurately noted in Pesenti, "Libri censurati," pp. 20–21. The *Tariffa* is identified in Molmenti, *La Storia di Venezia,* ii, 578.

[80] SU, Bu. 25, Girolamo Calepin, testimony of Zio of March 20, and of other witnesses of February 3, 4, March 27, 31, April 6, 8, May 14, 1568.

V

THE COUNTER REFORMATION ENFORCED

1. INSPECTION OF THE BOOKSTORES

THE Republic had halted the printing of prohibited books but had made no provision for the censorship of banned volumes printed abroad. The papacy and Inquisition had a double goal: preventing the importation of foreign contraband and destroying the titles already in the bookstores.

The Holy Office alone could not deal effectively with foreign books. Its demand in 1558 that the bookmen present inventories of all imported titles had not worked because no control ensured that the bookmen submitted true lists. Moreover, by 1567 northern Protestant publishers had adopted the expedient of prefacing heretical volumes with false title pages and innocent prefatory matter.[1] Rule X of the Tridentine Index had proposed two measures to deal with the problem: inquisitorial scrutiny of imported volumes at the customs house, and inspection visits to the bookstores. The Holy Office attempted to establish customs scrutiny on August 26, 1567, with a decree that all imported books had to be shown to the inquisitor, patriarch, or their designates before sale, under penalty of twenty-five ducats.[2] However, the decree contained no instructions for implementation—a clear sign that it was only hortatory. Stationing an inquisitorial official to look over the shoulders of bookmen and customs officials as they unpacked books was the only realistic means of enforcement, but the state's permission for the intervention of the Holy Office in customs regulation was obviously lacking. The Inquisition's largely futile effort to find and destroy foreign prohibited books still depended on denunciations, chance discoveries, and voluntary compliance by the bookmen.

The nuncio's complaints to the government at a time when the leaders were keenly aware of the dangers of heresy eventually produced action.[3]

---

[1] Letters of Nuncio Facchinetti of August 16, 23, and of Cardinal Bonelli of August 30, 1567, in *Nunziature* VIII, 260, 264, 267.

[2] SU, Bu. 156, "Librai e libri proibiti, 1545–1571," ff. [76ʳ–78ʳ], September 13, 1567. Sforza, "Controriforma," pt. 2, p. 181, prints the decree but without a citation.

[3] The following papal instruction to the Venetian Holy Office describes the background to the law of June 28, 1569: "Nel tempo, che Monsignor Illustrissimo

In an omnibus law of June 28, 1569, the Council of Ten established integrated church-state machinery similar to the prepublication apparatus for the censorship of foreign prohibited books. Anyone wishing to sell or otherwise dispose of any new book bearing a foreign imprint was to obtain a certificate of approval from the Riformatori dello Studio di Padova, which was directed to use "all those means and the same conditions" employed in the prepublication censorship. The inquisitorial censor, the public reader, and the ducal secretary were to approve the imported title before the Riformatori would permit its sale. Violators were threatened with fines of 100 ducats.

The law also established inquisitorial inspection at the customs house. All books entering the city through the customs house, or anywhere else, were to be opened in the presence of the inquisitor and one of the priors of the guild. The latter was ordered under pain of twenty-five ducats to compile in the inquisitor's presence an inventory of the "quality" and "quantity" of the books. This inventory was to be deposited immediately with a secretary of the Riformatori, and presumably the books were to be bonded, although the law did not mention it, until permission to sell was granted.

Pius V indicated that he was pleased to learn of the new law—and would be even more pleased if it were executed.[4] His scepticism was unfounded, for the Republic implemented the law's substance, although not all its forms. By August 1570 inquisitorial inspectors drawn from the regular clergy were checking incoming books at the customs house.[5] In-

---

Cardinale Santiquattro [Giovanni Antonio Facchinetti] fu Nuntio in Venetia, fece sapere al Doge che gl' Heretici in qualsivoglia sorte de libri, o con epistole premiali, o con scolie, o annotationi, che vi facessero asserivano heresie. Et si vede, che ne i Platoni, ne gl'Aristoteli, ne i libri di Cosmografia, di medicina, e di legge, et in somma in qualsivoglia sorte di libri gl'Heretici si erano ingegnati d'inserire il veleno dell'Heresie o in un modo o in un'altro. Onde quella Republica certificata di questo fece prohibitione che per l'avvenire non si potessero più vendere libri stampati fuori di qualsivoglia sorte, se non fussero riveduti da quell'huomini, et con quella medesima diligenza, che si faceva alli libri che si stampavano in Venetia. Et perchè essendo la quantità molto grande, acciò non s'impedisse il commercio, fu ordinato, che l'Inquisitore dovesse eleggere quattro Religiosi per ogni Monastero d'ogni Religione, nelle quali vi fussero letterati, e ciascuno di essi Religiosi havesse facultà di vedere, et approvare questa tal sorte di libri. Sarà a proposito per rimediare alli disordini, che occorrono costì in questa materia, di trovare questa prohibitione, et ordine fatto all'hora, et metterli in uso, facendo osservarli. 15 novembre 1586." Vaticanus Latinus 10945, ff. 118^{r-v} For the text of the law, see App. 1, document 3.

[4] Letter of Cardinal Bonelli of July 16, 1569, in *Nunziature* IX, 95.

[5] For example, one day in August 1570, Girolamo Scoto, upon seeing an Inquisition inspector checking books at the customs house, complained that the tribunal

ventories were compiled, probably by the importing bookman rather than the prior, while the inspector looked at the volumes and then gave his consent for their removal from the customs dock. Whether inventories were deposited and formal permissions to sell the books were granted is not clear. Probably the bookmen simply removed and sold the books after the inspection without further documents.

The customs house inspection presented little difficulty in implementation, but how could the foreign titles in the shops be censored without disrupting the book trade? If the bookmen stripped their shelves to carry the foreign titles to the three censors, they would have only domestic works to sell. And how long would three readers need to examine thousands of titles?

The government and Holy Office found a way. For the first time the Republic empowered the Inquisition to make surprise visits to the bookstores. Nothing so emphasized the seriousness with which the Venetians viewed the threat of heretical literature as this. The tribunal deputized about fifty priests, all regular clergy from the local monasteries and expert in such fields as Greek, Hebrew, history, law, philosophy, and theology.[6] It then sent them in pairs to visit the bookstores during July and August 1570. Index in hand, they examined the shelves, making inventories and seizing prohibited titles.

The bookmen were caught off guard. In one of the first visits, the inspectors entered the store of Francesco Ziletti at the sign of the Pozzo. Ziletti, after stalling the inspectors for over two hours, finally ordered an employee to conduct them into his magazine at or near the church of Sts. Zanipolo.[7] The employee attempted to divert attention from prohibited titles of Erasmus and others hidden on high shelves. Having seen through the ruse, the inspectors had begun noting the titles when the proprietor appeared. Ziletti asked innocently whether the titles were prohibited. As-

---

sold, rather than destroyed, confiscated volumes. (No evidence to support the charge has come to light.) SU, Bu. 159, Registro Processi 1569, 1570, 1571, ff. 75ᵛ–76ʳ, testimony of the inspector of September 2, 5, 1570. For further notice of the customs check, see Ch. VI, sec. 1.

[6] Lists, one of them dated December 1, 1571, with the names of about fifty priests, each identified by monastery and field of competence, are appended to SU, Bu. 30, Andrea Arrivabene. "Padre Appolinario" of the Augustinian monastery of San Salvatore, who came to examine Francesco Ziletti's books (see below) surely was the "Fra Appolinario" of San Salvatore, an expert in Greek, in the lists.

[7] SU, Bu. 14, Vincenzo Valgrisi et al., material entitled "Contra Vincentium Vadrisium et non nullos alios venditores librorum prohibitorum. 1570," ff. 1ʳ–10ʳ, esp. 8ʳ⁻ᵛ for Ziletti, August 19, 22, 1570. This is also briefly summarized in SU, Bu. 159, Registro Processi 1569, 1570, 1571, f. 73ᵛ, August 19, 1570. Sforza, "Controriforma," pt. 2, pp. 181–82, quotes brief passages from SU, Bu. 14.

sured that they were, he suggested that the inspectors simply select examples and leave the rest. The inspectors replied that their instructions were to carry away all prohibited volumes. "Almost resisting," Ziletti refused to sign the inventory that they were preparing. Unable to complete their survey, the priests sought a future appointment; Ziletti refused. The priests took the books and placed them in a storage area at the monastery of San Salvatore. However, the next morning the monks discovered that the seals on the confiscated books of Ziletti, and of Vincenzo Valgrisi and Giovanni di Gara, had been broken.

As news of the visits circulated, at least some bookmen took preventive action. Gilio Bonfadio (or Bonfadino), a bookseller at the sign of the Diamante in San Moisè, removed about eighty titles, some in multiple copies, from his store before it was inspected. He left them in care of a neighbor—who reported them to the Holy Office.[8] The volumes included four distinct groups of banned titles. Scripture dominated the religious group. Bonfadio had hidden Brucioli's vernacular New Testament as well as his editions of, and commentaries on, various books of the Old Testament, also in the vernacular; Erasmus's New Testament, which the Tridentine Index had ordered expurgated; and a Hebrew-Latin Bible edited by the banned Sebastian Muenster. Other religious titles included Juan Valdés's *Alphabeto Christiano*; Alfonso Valdés's *Dialoghi di Mercurio et Caronte*; many of Savonarola's sermons, which had been ordered expurgated; and the religious titles of Aretino. Bonfadio had also removed a number of vernacular works, most of them literary: Aretino's *Lettere* and *Ragionamenti*; Machiavelli's *Discorsi, Historie fiorentine*, and unnamed titles; Masuccio Salernitano's *Novelle*; and Boccaccio's *Decameron* and Gelli's *I capricci del bottaio*, both of which had been ordered expurgated. The third group consisted of learned works authored mostly by northern Protestants: Melanchthon's "Dialettica" (possibly his *Compendiaria dialectices ratio*); Mathurin Cordier's *De corrupti sermonis*; Francesco Stancaro's *Ebreae grammaticae compendium*; Jacob Ziegler's and Wolfgang Weissenberger's *Terrae sanctae quam Palestinam . . . descriptio*; and Erasmus's *Colloquia*, and other titles that had been ordered expurgated. Finally, Bonfadio had hidden some occult titles, such as the geomancy manuals of Peter of Abano and Bartholomaeus Cocles, which fell under the prohibition of Rule IX of the Tridentine Index.

Many bookmen did not act quickly and were caught with both foreign and local banned titles. In early September 1570 the Holy Office ordered

[8] SU, Bu. 30, Francesco Ziletti e Gilio Bonfadio, ff. 2^v–7^v, Bonfadio's testimony of February 6, 13, plus his unpaginated inventory, abjuration, and sentence of April 2, 1571. Also SU, Bu. 156, "Librai e libri proibiti, 1545–1571," ff. [79^{r-v}], August 23, 1570.

the confiscated volumes burned publicly in Piazza San Marco.[9] Then the tribunal questioned twenty-eight disobedient bookmen, a process that took over a year.

The tribunal began with Vincenzo Valgrisi, who had been found in possession of over 1,150 prohibited volumes.[10] The Holy Office had uncovered in his storehouse over 400 copies of a work that he had published in 1545 entitled *Simulachri, historie, e figure de la morte*, which collected in one volume the Dance of Death woodcuts of Hans Holbein, *La medicina dell' anima* of the Protestant Urbanus Rhegius (1489–1541), sermons of Saints Cyprian and John Chrysostom, and other devotional tracts.[11] A Lyons publisher had originally printed the Holbein woodcuts in 1538 along with a Catholic devotional essay. In 1542 another Lyons publisher had brought out a version that included the Protestant tract of Rhegius; Valgrisi had printed an Italian translation of this version. The Tridentine Index prohibited the Italian edition, undoubtedly because of Rhegius's essay; Valgrisi was selling it under the title *Le Epistole di Cicerone*. The Inquisition discovered 300 copies with the counterfeit title, as well as 104 in the original format. Other prohibited books included Valgrisi's printings of Italian translations of Erasmus's *Colloquia* (1545 and 1549) and Johann Schoener's *De iudiciis nativitatem* (1554). Valgrisi also possessed works of Aretino and Machiavelli, Juan Valdés's *Alphabeto Christiano*, and many banned French and German imprints.

Valgrisi pleaded that his large family would suffer if he had to bear the heavy financial loss of the destruction of the many prohibited books in his store. His parish priest and others testified that he and his family were good Christians and practicing Catholics. Nevertheless, the tribunal fined him fifty ducats and ordered him to perform penances.[12]

The Holy Office questioned the other twenty-seven bookmen in February and in August through October, 1571. Referring frequently to the law of June 28, 1569, the Inquisition demanded to know why the bookmen

[9] SU, Bu. 159, Registro Processi 1569, 1570, 1571, ff. 76ᵛ–77ʳ, September 9, 12, 1570.

[10] SU, Bu. 14, Vincenzo Valgrisi et al., "Contro Vincentium Vadrisium," ff. 11ʳ–19ʳ [20ʳ–22ʳ, 29ʳ–34ᵛ], testimony of Valgrisi and other documents of August 20, September 1, 2, 7, 12, October 24, 27, November 4, 5, 1570. The inventory of August 18, is in ff. [37ʳ–41ᵛ], and is reproduced in App. II. Sforza, "Controriforma," pt. 2, pp. 182–86, prints excerpts from the trial, as does Carlo De Frede, "Tipografi, editori, librai, editori del Cinquecento coinvolti in processi d'eresia," *Rivista di storia della Chiesa in Italia*, 23 (1969), 39–47.

[11] The Valgrisi printing is noted in *STC Italian*, 208. Also see Natalie Z. Davis, "Holbein's *Pictures of Death* and the Reformation at Lyons," *Studies in the Renaissance* 3 (1956), 97–130.

[12] SU, Bu. 159, Registro Processi 1569, 1570, 1571, ff. 128ᵛ–30ʳ, December 18, 1570. Sforza, "Controriforma," pt. 2, p. 186, is in error when he writes that the Inquisition failed to punish Valgrisi.

held prohibited titles or why their stores had escaped inspection. The bookmen offered excuses such as absence from the city, illness, and, most frequently, ignorance. They were unaware of the law of the Council of Ten or had no copy of the Index. Only once did a bookman manifest his real motive for disobedience. The inquisitor asked Pietro da Fino at the sign of the Gallo, a small publisher, to account for titles of Aretino, Fra Battista da Crema, Anton Francesco Doni, Machiavelli, and Cordier discovered in his store. After a series of evasions, Fino admitted that he had deliberately disobeyed. Why? Because "I live more for work than for books," he defiantly averred.[13] Earning a living was more important to him than obeying the Index. The Holy Office fined him two ducats for hostility.

Two other bookmen were also fined. A first inspection had netted two bales of prohibited books at the store of Alvise Valvassori (called Guadagnino); a second trip uncovered Aretino's *Ragionamenti* and a certain "De fisionomia" in great quantity. The Holy Office fined Valvassori ten ducats. The tribunal questioned Gabriele Giolito about two inventories of prohibited books, one beginning with Machiavelli's *Discorsi*, and also fined him ten ducats.[14] Francesco Ziletti, asked to account for unnamed titles of Agrippa, Antonio Brucioli, Joachim Camerarius, and Dolet, for the *Dialogues* of Lucian, and for unidentified authors, explained that they had come into his hands less than a year ago when he had become the proprietor of the bookstore at the sign of the Pozzo, previously owned by Andrea Arrivabene. Whether the Holy Office punished Ziletti is not clear, but twenty other bookmen were warned and released, and Bonfadio was sentenced to penances.[15] All suffered the destruction of the prohibited volumes found in their possession.

[13] "Io vivo più de' lavorar che de' libri," and again "Io vivo più presto de' lavorar, che de' libri." SU, Bu. 156, "Librai e libri proibiti," ff. 18ᵛ, 19ʳ (quotes August 25, 1571), 33ᵛ–34ʳ (sentence and payment October 11, 15, 1571). Fino published eight titles between 1556 and 1569. For the condemnation of the writings of Fra Battista da Crema (c. 1460–1534) of July 29, 1552, see Pastor, XIII, 212–13, 441 (doc. 16). Only Doni's *Lettere* were condemned by the Tridentine Index.

[14] SU, Bu. 156, "Librai e libri proibiti, 1545–1571," ff. 16ʳ–17ʳ, 20ʳ (Valvassori, August 23, 30), 23ᵛ–25ʳ (Giolito, September 18, 1571). Not a publisher, Alvise managed a store for Giovanni Andrea Valvassori (active as publisher 1541–72), who paid the fine. I have been unable to identify the "De fisionomia."

[15] Although no penalty was levied, Ziletti's trial may be incomplete. SU, Bu. 30, Francesco Ziletti e Gilio Bonfadio, ff. 1ʳ–2ᵛ, February 1, 1571. The following publishers were warned and released: Giovanni Barileto al segno della Prudenza, Giovanni Francesco Camocio (or Camozza) al segno del Piramide, Francesco dei Franceschi al segno della Pace, Francesco Rocca al segno del Castello, Giovanni Battista Somasco al segno del Centauro, Bolognino Zaltieri and Giordano Ziletti, both al segno della Stella, Damiano Zenaro al segno della Salamandra, and Fabio

The number of volumes destroyed is not known, but it must have been large; the inquisitor often referred to titles found "in quantity," or to several bales of books belonging to one bookman. The figure undoubtedly reached the thousands, and probably equaled or surpassed the number destroyed in 1559 and 1568. Although the inquisitor discussed the inventories compiled by the inspectors, only Valgrisi's has survived. The other titles mentioned in the trials encompassed a broad range of prohibited foreign and domestic imprints, including, in addition to the authors and titles previously noted, Ochino's *Dialoghi* and unnamed titles of Guillaume Postel, Olimpia de Sassoferrato, and Joannes Sleidanus. In 1559 the bookmen had suffered the loss of substantial numbers of foreign imprints; in 1570 they lost Venetian imprints of such authors as Aretino and Machiavelli as well. To conclude the purge, the Inquisition on December 1, 1571, summoned the entire guild to hear again the law of June 28, 1569. Only twenty-nine unhappy souls appeared.[16]

With the inspection of the bookstores and the inquisitorial check at the customs house, the Republic had been able to enforce the Tridentine Index. All major features of Rule X had been implemented; only the submission of inventories of inherited titles had been ignored. The Republic had authorized the insertion of the Holy Office into every phase of the censorship while retaining overall control of the process, which was jurisdictionally mostly lay. Civil and ecclesiastical censors worked in harmony while the bookmen murmured in discontent.

The bookmen had held on to their prohibited titles because they had been able to sell them. Many Italian readers wanted the orthodox spiritual works coming from the presses in increasing number, but some continued to buy the older banned works. When the inquisitor asked Bonfadio which prohibited titles his customers most often sought, Bonfadio mentioned vernacular Scripture, the works of Machiavelli, and the "cento novelle," i.e., the *Decameron* of Boccaccio and similar literary works.[17]

Zoppini al segno del Zotto. The booksellers were Gasparo Albara and Domenico Fossani al segno della Speranza, the store recently inherited from Giovanni della Speranza, Giacomo de Berechi (or Berichia), who was employed al segno della Gatta, the store of the Heirs of Melchiorre Sessa, Marco Bindoni al segno della Giustizia, Bernardino del Bò al segno dello Zio, Matteo del Bò, *nipote* of Bernardino, Carolus Bombello, who had a counter near San Moisè, Piero de Nicolo al segno di Giesù (whose chief activity was painting and selling holy cards for school use), Giulio Rizzo (or Rizzio) al segno della Donzella, Domenico Splendor al segno della Madonna, Giacomo da Trin, who had a counter on the Rialto bridge, and Zaccaria Zenaro al segno della Fontana. SU, Bu. 156, "Librai e libri proibiti, 1545–1571," ff. 6ʳ–9ᵛ, 15ᵛ–34ʳ, August 9 through October 24, 1571.

[16] SU, Bu. 156, "Librai e libri proibiti, 1545–1571," ff. 34ᵛ–37ʳ.

[17] SU, Bu. 30, Francesco Ziletti e Gilio Bonfadio, f. 7ᵛ, February 13, 1571.

Until the purge of 1570, the bookmen had sold all except the religious titles of northern heresiarchs more or less openly. Soon the bookmen would resort to clandestine methods to satisfy their customers.

2. THE QUARREL OVER THE REFORMED CANONICAL TEXTS

Zealous Catholics could be well-satisfied with Venetian enforcement of the Index. Yet, at this moment of accord, the Republic and the papacy quarreled over what might appear to be a trivial issue: papal privileges issued for the canonical books of worship. The publication of these religious titles provoked intense disputes resulting in papal discomfiture and hearalding future discord.

In its concluding decrees of 1563, the Council of Trent directed the papacy to revise Catholicism's two most important liturgical manuals, the breviary and the missal.[18] The breviary contains the entire canonical office, i.e., the prayers that at first by custom, then by canonical law, priests, monks, and nuns were obliged to recite daily at different times. The psalms are the heart of the breviary, but also included are a number of prayers arranged according to the liturgical seasons. When a priest reads his office, or a congregation of monks or nuns chants matins or lauds, they read and chant prayers as collected and organized in the breviary. The Roman breviary was the most circulated and authoritative version, but others, especially the Little Office of Our Lady, were also in widespread use. The missal contains the fixed and changing prayers that a priest reads at the sacrifice of the mass. In addition, the papacy promulgated the Tridentine Catechism, an instructional manual for pastors in Latin and the vernacular, containing basic doctrine as formulated at Trent.

Upon completion of the revisions, the papacy was in a position to promulgate authorized standard versions purged of historical accretions. Thanks to the printing press, every clergyman and layman would be able to worship from the same text, each with his own copy. It was a historic opportunity. As the various commissions completed their work, the reformed versions of the catechism, breviary, and missal appeared, the first in 1566 (usually these editons were designated by their title pages as having been prepared in response to the decree of the Council of Trent and published by the authority of Pius V). The papacy sent each work forth with a bull that rejoiced in its appearance, prescribed its use throughout Catholic Christendom, and banned most older versions.

---

[18] For succinct description and further bibliography, see Fernand Gabrol, "Breviary," and "Divine Office," in *The Catholic Encyclopedia*, ii, 768–77; xi, 219–20; and Herbert Thurston, "Missal," ibid., x, 354–57.

The promulgation bull, or sometimes a *motu proprio*,[19] also gave directions for the publication of each new work. The papacy usually granted a universal privilege for a period of years to a Roman printer and threatened violators with excommunication and fines. The papacy believed that exclusive privileges were needed to ensure accurate printing and widespread promulgation and that its spiritual authority embraced the right to issue them. It is unlikely that Pius V and his advisers anticipated opposition. The recipient of the exclusive privilege, normally Paolo Manuzio, who had been persuaded to move to Rome partially for this reason, printed the first edition. He then sold printing rights for the rest of the Catholic world to other bookmen, who were expected to reproduce faithfully the reformed version.

Bookmen all over Europe instantly realized that the reformed canonical works had a commercial dimension of great magnitude. The market for these books would be enormous! Every priest and most religious would have to have a new breviary; a new missal would be necessary for the celebration of every mass. In addition, many pious laymen and laywomen used a breviary or another formulation of the office.

Canonical texts had for some time been an essential part of the production of the major publishing centers, especially of Venice. For example, from 1501 until the appearance of the Tridentine breviary in 1568, Venetian bookmen published 107 known printings of the Roman breviary (64 of them by the Giunti press); Parisian bookmen, 63 printings; the Lyons publishers, 62; and eleven other cities, 29.[20] Humanist texts and vernacular classics garnered prestige for the bookmen, but liturgical manuals paid the bills. Christophe Plantin of Antwerp printed only 1,200 copies of the Polyglot Bible, and never sold them all, but when he secured exclusive rights in the Spanish Empire for the Tridentine breviary and missal, he published thousands of them and made a fortune.[21] In Venice, Luc'Antonio

---

[19] A *motu proprio* is a more personal form of decree, signifying that the pope has issued it not necessarily on the advice of others, but for reasons he deems sufficient.

[20] Hanns Bohatta, *Bibliographie der Breviere 1501–1850* (Leipzig, 1937, rpt. Stuttgart-Neiuwkoop, 1963), pp. 1–30. Bohatta's count is undoubtedly conservative; printings missed by him appear in booksellers' catalogues from time to time. It is also likely that some printings have disappeared completely.

[21] On the financial importance of the breviary to the presses, see Robert M. Kingdon, "Patronage, Piety, and Printing in Sixteenth-Century Europe," in *A Festschrift for Frederick B. Artz*, ed. David H. Pinkney and Theodore Ropp (Durham, N. C., 1964), pp. 19–36; and the same author's "The Plantin Breviaries: A Case Study in the Sixteenth-Century Business Operations of a Publishing House," *BHR*, 22 (1960), 133–50. The conflicts described in this section support two of Kingdon's major generalizations, *viz.*, that publishing empires were built on privi-

Giunti's commercial network and his expensive palace were built from the profits earned from canonical works. For smaller bookmen, whose participation might be limited to printing part of a breviary under contract to a major publisher, these books could mean the difference between survival and failure. Protestant printers similarly depended on the psalter. The papal privileges on the reformed canonical works precipitated a wild scramble among bookmen in Venice and elsewhere, and ignited disputes that took years to resolve.

The papacy promulgated the Tridentine (or Roman) Cathechism first. Pius V in a *motu proprio* of September 25, 1566, granted Paolo Manuzio an exclusive universal privilege for five years, for both Latin and Italian editions; violators were threatened with excommunication and fines of 500 ducats.[22] When Manuzio published both first editions in Rome in late 1566, the papacy instructed Nuncio Facchinetti to obtain Venetian adherence to the *motu proprio*. Despite some grumbling that the *motu proprio* violated Venetian law, which did not recognize foreign copyrights, the Venetians promised to consider it. In the meantime they would grant no privilege, in effect forbidding anyone else to publish the work.[23]

Domenico Farri quickly seized the opportunity to bring out an illegal vernacular edition.[24] The papacy learned of it while he was still printing, probably from Manuzio, and protested. The nuncio went to the Collegio, which told him that a *motu proprio* should be limited to the papal state. The nuncio answered that the pope was pope in Venice as well, that he had jurisdiction over ecclesiastical works, and that an excommunication decree was universally valid. The Venetians conceded, forbidding the disobedient bookman to sell his work and issuing a twenty-year privilege to Aldo Manuzio il Giovane; violators were to be fined 10 ducats for every illegally printed copy.[25] With both papal and Venetian privileges, the Aldine press had a secure monopoly.

The maneuvering to secure Venetian rights for the new breviary began

---

leges and concessions secured through intense intrigue, and that the privileges on liturgical works were worth fighting for.

[22] The *motu proprio* is in *Catechismo, cioè istruttione, secondo il decreto del Concilio di Trento, a' parocchi* . . . (In Venetia, MDLXVII, Appresso Aldo Manutio), Sigs. 2^v–3^v, cited from the copy in BNF, Palat. 14. x. 1. 6. 49. Other Aldine editions of the catechism are listed in Renouard, *Annales des Alde*.

[23] Letter of Nuncio Facchinetti of December 21, 1566, in *Nunziature* VIII, 148–49.

[24] *STC Italian*, 679.

[25] Letters of Cardinal Michele Bonelli and Nuncio Facchinetti of February 22 and March 1, 1567, in *Nunziature* VIII, 179, 182. The Senate privilege of February 19, 1566 mv, is printed in the 1567 *Catechismo* edition cited in note 22, Sig. 4^r; and copied in VM, Ms. Ital., Classe VII, 2501 (12078), "Privilegi veneziani," f. 583.

long before the work appeared. Again Pius V granted to Paolo Manuzio universal and exclusive rights, with violators under pain of excommunication. Manuzio ceded Venetian rights to a close associate, Domenico Basa. On September 6, 1567, Basa secured a Senate privilege that gave him the right to publish the reformed breviary for twenty years, with violators subject to 300 ducats' penalty.[26] The fact that this was a typical Venetian privilege suggests that the ducal secretaries had no notion of the work's commercial significance. In May 1568 Basa made preliminary arrangements with Luc'Antonio Giunti for Venetian publication; the papacy approved the arrangements, and a contract between Basa and Giunti was signed in February 1569. Four other Venetian bookmen were brought in, and the consortium employed fourteen presses.[27] To ensure accuracy, the nuncio in August 1568 deputized two correctors to oversee the printing.

Pius V promulgated the reformed breviary in *Quod a nobis* of July 9, 1568, while simultaneous printings were under way in Rome and Venice. But in August 1568, when the Roman printing failed to meet papal standards of accuracy, the pope ordered it and the Venetian printing, now well advanced, halted. The nuncio sympathized with the Venetian bookmen, and informed Rome that they would suffer serious financial losses. The new, more correct printings were completed in Rome and Venice in 1569, and subsequent editons in various formats quickly followed.[28] Luc'Antonio Giunti reported in October 1570 that he had printed "nine kinds of breviaries," i.e., press runs in different formats.[29] At this time the Venetian Inquisition ordered Giunti to suspend publication on the grounds that he had inserted unauthorized material into the breviary. Giunti pleaded that he had "thousands" of ducats tied up in the work, and that his enemies would be only too happy to see him in difficulty.

---

[26] I have been unable to discover the duration of the papal privilege, but years later, a Vatican official reported that it was ten years. Giovanni Mercati, "Vecchi lamenti contro il monopolio de' libri ecclesiastici, speci liturgici," in *Opere minori*, vol. II (Vatican City, 1937), p. 485. See Cioni, "Domenico Basa," pp. 46–47, for the Manuzio-Basa association. The Senate privilege is in Capi del CX, Notatorio, R. 21, f. 104ᵛ; and VM, Ms. Ital., Classe VII, 2501 (12078), "Privilegi veneziani," f. 597. Curiously, none of the several copies of the Giunti breviary printings of 1569–71 that I have examined carry either the papal or the Senate privilege.

[27] Tenenti, "Luc'Antonio Giunti," p. 1,027; Marciani, "Editori veneti in Napoli," pp. 515–16, notarial act of January 7, 1580.

[28] Letters of Cardinal Bonelli of July 24, August 7, 28, September 11, and of Nuncio Facchinetti of July 31, August 14, and September 4, 1568, in *Nunziature* VIII, 417, 421, 425–27, 432–34, 436–37.

[29] However, only one edition of 1569, two of 1570, and three of 1571 are noted in Camerini, *Annali dei Giunti*, suggesting that some printings have disappeared.

The matter was cleared up, probably through corrections, and Giunti continued to publish the work.[30]

The papal privilege, supported by the Senate privilege, enabled Manuzio, Basa, Giunti, and their confederates to establish a monopoly. Other Venetian bookmen were excluded from the profitable enterprise unless they were willing to risk both excommunication and Venetian civil penalties. A few did run that risk. Upon discovery of illegal breviaries, the papacy appealed to the Venetian government, which ordered the disobedient bookmen to stop.[31] As with the catechism, the Republic enforced a papal privilege over the objections of the excluded bookmen. The Giunti-Basa partnership enjoyed the fruits of the monopoly until the dissolution of their association in 1576.[32]

When the reformed Roman missal was ready in 1569, Pius V, much to Paolo Manuzio's chagrin, conferred an exclusive universal privilege for ten years on Bartolomeo Faletti, a Venetian bookbinder in Manuzio's employ (violators were subject to excommunication and fines of 1,000 ducats).[33] Faletti died before he could capitalize on it, but his heirs formed an association with Giovanni Varisco, a Venetian publisher, who obtained a Senate privilege. The heirs of the Faletti-Varisco association produced two Roman printings in 1570, four Venetian printings in 1571, and three more Venetian printings in 1572.[34] Once again, a small group used a papal priv-

---

[30] SU, Bu. 156, "Librai e libri proibiti, 1545–1571," ff. [53ʳ–54ʳ], interrogation of Giunti of October 12, 1570.

[31] Letters of Cardinal Bonelli of January 14, 1570, in ASVa, Segretario di Stato, Venezia, F. 7, ff. 77ᵛ–78ᵛ (not in *Nunziature* ix), and of Nuncio Facchinetti of January 21, 1570, in *Nunziature* ix, 186. Giunti also alluded to the illegal printings: SU, Bu. 156, "Librai e libri proibiti, 1545–1571," f. [53ʳ], October 12, 1570. The names of the disobedient bookmen are not given, but illicit Venetian printings of the breviary at this time by Nicolò Misserini (1568) and "Varisco-Faletti" (i.e., probably Giovanni Varisco and the heirs of Bartolomeo Faletti) are noted in Francesco Barberi, *Paolo Manuzio e la Stamperia del Popolo Romano (1561–1570) con documenti inediti* (Rome, 1942), p. 158, n. 1.

[32] See Camerini, *Annali dei Giunti*, passim, and Bohatta, *Bibliographie der Breviere*, pp. 34–41, for the printings; and Tenenti, "Luc'Antonio Giunti," pp. 1,027–28, for the commercial details.

[33] Pius V's *motu proprio* of February 8, 1569, is in *Missale Romanum Ex Decreto Sacrosancti Concilij Tridentini restitutim Pii V. Pont. Max. iussu editum*, Cum Privilegiis (Venetiis, Apud Ioannem Variscum, Haeredes Bartholomei Faleti, & Socios, MDLXXI), Sigs. +3ᵛ–+4ʳ. I cite an 8° copy of this work in the Pontificio Istituto Biblico library, Rome, Liturgica xxix–29. On Faletti, see Barberi, *Paolo Manuzio*, p. 84.

[34] Varisco (or Guarisco, and also called Giovanni della Serena), at the sign of the Serena in the "Mercerie," i.e., somewhere between Piazza San Marco and Campo San Bartolomeo, was originally from Brescia. He published 71 titles from 1558 to

ilege to establish a monopoly that excluded the vast majority of the book-men.

The bookmen dug in their heels, however, over the reformed Little Office of Our Lady (*Officium Beatae Mariae Virginis, nuper reformatum, & Pij V. Pont. Max. iussu editum*). The work had originated in the sixth century, and its popularity had spread quickly; by the fourteenth century it was regarded as obligatory for the regular clergy, and it was widely used by the laity, including children.[35] Pius V promulgated the reformed version as part of the breviary reform in *Quod a nobis*. Although obliga-tory recitation was lifted, the Little Office retained its popularity and con-tinued to serve as a substitute for the larger office for monks and nuns of many orders.

In a bull of March 11, 1571, Pius V banned all previous Little Offices on the grounds that printers were in the habit of including superfluous and superstitious material. He specifically condemned the Venetian Giunti printing of 1570, which falsely advertised itself as being revised according to the Tridentine decree. The pontiff conferred upon the Popolo Romano press (now directed by Fabrizio Galletti) an exclusive and universal six-year privilege with violators under pain of excommunication and fines of 500 ducats.[36] In anticipation, Girolamo Torresano, head of the Aldine press in Venice, and his brother Bernardino, on January 30, 1571, had obtained from the Senate a twenty-year Venetian privilege, with violators to be fined 300 ducats.[37] Having arranged with the Popolo Romano press

---

1588, most of them in association with other bookmen. I have been unable to locate a copy of his Venetian privilege; in view of the charges of fraud leveled against him (see below), this is not surprising. For his printings of the missal, see W. H. Iacobus Weale and Hanns Bohatta, *Bibliographia Liturgica. Catalogus Missalium Ritus Latini ab anno MCCCCLXXIV Impressorum* (London, 1928), pp. 199–201.

[35] "Ma in particolare di questi offitiuoli della Madonna . . . sendo comuni non solo a' religiosi, ma ad ogni altra sorte di persone, laici, donne, et putti." Letter of Nuncio Facchinetti, August 9, 1572, in ASVa, Segretario di Stato, F. 12, f. 47^r. For a brief history and description, see Leslie A. St. L. Toke, "Little Office of Our Lady," *The Catholic Encyclopedia*, IX, 294–95.

[36] A copy of this bull, *Superni omnipotentis Dei*, can be found in *Officium B. Mariae Virgines nuper reformatum et Pii V. Pont. Max. iussu editum . . .* (Romae, In Aedibus Populi Romani, MDLXXI), Sigs. t2^r–t6^v, cited from a presentation copy in 16° to the pontiff in the J. Pierpont Morgan Library, New York, E. 11. C. See figure 12. It is also to be found in *Bullarium Diplomatum et Privilegiorum Summorum Romanorum Pontificum*, vol. VII (Naples, 1882), pp. 896–901. I have not located a copy of the Giunti counterfeit, nor is it listed in Camerini, *Annali dei Giunti*, or Hanns Bohatta, *Bibliographie des livres d'heures (Horae B.M.V.) Officia, Hortuli Animae, Coronae B.M.V., Rosaria und Cursus B.M.V. des XV und XVI Jahrhunderts* (Vienna, 1909).

[37] The Senate privilege is printed in *Officium hebdomadae sanctae ad Missalis, &*

12. Title page of a presentation copy for Pius V of the *Officium B. Mariae Virginis nuper reformatum et Pii V Pont. Max. iussu editum.* . . . (Romae In Aedibus Populi Romani, MDLXXI). Source: The Pierpont Morgan Library, New York

to share printing of the Little Office, Girolamo Torresano moved to exploit his privilege. With the support of Vatican officials and others, he obtained permission from the archbishops of Milan and Naples to sell the Little Office in their dioceses. He printed six press runs of 3,300 copies each (a total of 19,800 copies) within seven or eight months in the latter part of 1571 and the first half of 1572.[38]

The other Venetian bookmen were acutely unhappy. The majority of them had had no part in printing the catechism, breviary, or missal, and now they saw the Aldine Press monopolizing the Little Office. The guild launched a collective challenge by authorizing a group of ten to twelve bookmen to publish the Little Office. The Inquisition learned of this in August 1571, no doubt from Torresano or his Roman supporters, and began to interrogate the disobedient bookmen. Angry, defiant, and even desperate, they showed no fear of excommunication. Nevertheless, the Inquisition forbade them to print or sell the Little Office.

The prohibition had little effect. In January 1572 the Inquisition discovered that the Giunti press continued to print and sell the older version of the Little Office.[39] In the summer of 1572 other bookmen drafted a letter of protest to Rome and began anew to print the work. The dispute reached the ears of a few patricians, who murmured that the pope was aiding the Roman press at the expense of the Venetian bookmen.

Nuncio Facchinetti reported these developments, and clearly hinted that lifting the exclusive privilege shared by the Popolo Romano press and Torresano would be the wisest course to follow. But Rome instructed him to enforce the privilege. In August 1572, the Venetian Holy Office again forbade other bookmen to print the Little Office. The nuncio went to the Collegio to obtain governmental enforcement of Torresano's Venetian

---

Breviarij reformatorum rationem. Pii V. Pont. Max. iussu restitutum (Venetiis, Ex bibliotheca Aldina, 1573), Sig. A2^{r-v}. I cite the copy in the VM, Aldine 837. There is a copy of the privilege in VM, Ms. Ital., Classe vii, 2501 (12078), "Privilegi veneziani," f. 656.

[38] According to Torresano's printer, the printings were one in 12°, another in 12° *lettera grossa*, two in 24°, and two in 32°. However, Renouard, *Annales des Alde*, lists only one edition of 1572, in 24°, and no others until 1581. The other printings may have disappeared. SU, Bu. 156, "Librai e libri proibiti, 1545–1571," f. 40^r, testimony of Piero de Vechino, Torresano's printer, of July 26, 1572. For the following, see ibid., ff. 9^v–10^v, 12^r–15^v, 19^r–20^r (testimony of Girolamo Torresano, Onofrio Farri, and Pietro Da Fino, all bookmen, of August 18, 23, 25, 28, 30, 1571), 39^v–45^v (testimony of Giovanni Griffio, Piero de Vechino, and Torresano of July 26, 29, 31, 1572, and excerpts from letters of various Vatican officials). Also see the letters of Nuncio Facchinetti of July 26, August 2, 9, 1572, in ASVa, Segretario di Stato, Venezia, F. 12, ff. 40^v–41^r, 43^{r-v}, 46^r–47^r.

[39] SU, Bu. 156, "Librai e libri proibiti, 1545–1571," ff. 37^v–38^v, decree of January 3, testimony of Bernardino Mazorin, the Giunti factor, of January 31, 1572.

privilege. He encountered opposition from Doge Alvise Mocenigo and Nicolò Da Ponte who objected to papal interference in Venetian affairs. The nuncio reasserted papal claims over the breviary, missal, catechism, and Index, and carried the Collegio.[40]

As the Little Office conflict grew, divisions appeared everywhere, even within the Holy Office. The guild opposed Torresano, although the patriarch supported him for unknown reasons. The nuncio, who saw the acute economic distress of the bookmen and feared that the dispute would jeopardize the enforcement of the Index, sided with the bookmen. In Rome, the Stamperia del Popolo Romano and its curial supporters intrigued to support Torresano. The Secretary of State, Cardinal Tolomeo Galli, realized that the privilege was being used for financial ends and wished to lift it.[41] The Venetian government had endorsed Torresano's privilege, but some nobles now argued for a change in policy.

By the end of October 1572, the disobedient bookmen were again printing the Little Office. The Inquisition summoned five of them, Domenico Farri, Girolamo della Barba, Giacomo Leoncini, Domenico Nicolini, and Francesco Rampazetto, to explain why they had disobeyed *motu proprii* of both Pius V and Gregory XIII. The nuncio in his letter to Rome repeated the answer: they risked excommunication and eternal damnation because of financial necessity. Their livelihood depended on their printing the Little Office.[42]

In addition to trying to persuade Rome to change its position, the nuncio aided the disobedient bookmen by neglecting to carry out orders. Patriarch Giovanni Trevisan complained to Rome that although the nuncio had received instructions authorizing Torresano to proceed he had

[40] Torresano's privilege was confirmed by a letter of Cardinal Tolomeo Galli, the Secretary of State, to the patriarch of August 9, 1572, Rome, quoted in SU, Bu. 156, "Librai e libri proibiti, 1545-1571," ff. 45ᵛ-46ʳ. For the Collegio appearance, see the letter of Nuncio Facchinetti of August 23, 1572, in ASVa, Segretario di Stato, Venezia, F. 12, f. 56ʳ. There is no record of this appearance in the extant Collegio documents.

[41] Although Galli (1526-1607), usually called the Cardinal of Como, carried out papal instructions supporting Torresano, later developments showed that he disapproved of the privileges. Galli served Pius V, who preferred his own counsel, and Gregory XIII, who sometimes heeded Galli's advice.

[42] SU, Bu. 156, "Librai e libri proibiti, 1545-1571," ff. 46ᵛ-47ʳ (order of October 30 that the five should appear on November 4, 1572). Girolamo della Barba has not been further identified; the other four are publishers to be found in Pastorello. "Potrà ben S. B.ne. parendole, considerar la natura del negotio in sè, perchè sendo il libro tanto frequente, et commune a tutti, conosco che alcuni poveri non per disprezzo, ma per necessità, et per essere soliti a guardagnarsi il vivere con lo stampar questi offitiuoli, gli stamperanno, et con pregiudicio delle anime loro persevararanno nella scommunica." Letter of Nuncio Facchinetti of October 25, 1572, in ASVa, Segretario di Stato, Venezia, F. 12, f. 98ʳ-ᵛ.

not shown these papal orders to the Inquisition, alleging that they were the result of misinformation. The patriarch asked the pope to spur the nuncio into action.[43]

Thereafter, the nuncio followed orders. In November 1572, he threatened the recalcitrant bookmen, badly frightening them, according to his report. However, they were not so frightened as to give up, for they immediately went to the Heads of the Council of Ten, who referred the dispute to the Venetian ambassador in Rome. The nuncio advised the pope, now Gregory XIII, to defend papal jurisdiction over the Index, catechism, missal, and office when meeting with the ambassador, and then to send the matter back to him for resolution. The nuncio promised to find a *modus vivendi* that would satisfy the papacy, for experience had shown that the bookmen could be brought around. More had been achieved with them with regard to prohibited books than one would have believed possible in Venice.[44] The nuncio was both justifying his conduct and hinting broadly that Rome should not insist on the Little Office privilege while Index enforcement went so well.

Gregory XIII took the nuncio's advice. On January 27, 1573, he issued a letter authorizing Luc'Antonio Giunti to print the Little Office notwithstanding the exclusive privilege granted by his predecessor to the Popolo Romano press.[45] With the monopoly broken, seven Venetian publishers brought out at least fifteen printings between 1573 and 1596.[46]

Encouraged by this success, the bookmen began to ignore papal privileges on other liturgical works. Even though Giovanni Varisco and the heirs of Faletti held both papal and Venetian privileges for the missal,

[43] Letter of Patriarch Giovanni Trevisan of November 1, 1572, in ASVa, Segretario di Stato, Venezia, F. 12, f. 100ʳ.

[44] "Che se Vostra Illustrissima saprà tutto quello, che si è fatto per conto dei libri prohibiti con questi librari, ella conoscerà che si è operato più di quel, che si sarà creduto, che si potesse fare in questa città." Letters of Nuncio Facchinetti of November 15, 29, 1572, in ASVa, Segretario di Stato, Venezia, F. 12, ff. 119ᵛ–20ʳ, 129ᵛ–30ʳ (quote). In the last months of his office, Nuncio Facchinetti openly advised Gregory XIII in a way that he had never dared with Pius V. Also see his claim at the end of his nunciate that the bookmen had always obeyed the Holy Office during his tenure and that he expected them to continue to do so for his successor. Letter of June 27, 1573, in ibid., f. 272ᵛ. There is a hint of self-congratulation in both these letters.

[45] For a copy of the letter, see BAVa, Barb. C. 1. 24, *Officium Beatae Mariae Virginis nuper reformatum Pij V Pont. Max. iussu editum* (Venetiis Apud Iunctam, Permittente Sede Apostolica, MDLXXXI), Sigs. +iᵛ–+iiʳ. A gap in the Senato, Dispacci da Roma, *fondo* from May 11, 1572, to March 7, 1573, makes it impossible to follow the concluding negotiations.

[46] Bohatta, *Bibliographie des livres d'heures*, pp. 59–61; and *Cambridge Catalogue*, items L 1061–62, for two additional printings.

Gratioso Perchacino and Francesco Rampazetto each produced a printing in 1573, thereby igniting another controversy.[47] The Stamperia del Popolo Romano, now in the hands of Domenico Basa and a consortium of Roman printers, asked the pope to enforce the missal privilege. The pontiff referred the matter to the nuncio, now Monsignor Giambattista Castagna, who soon discovered why the papal privilege had been ignored. Some unnamed Venetian bookmen had accused Varisco and the heirs of Faletti of fraud, alleging that the group had obtained a Senate privilege for only a small part of the missal but had published the entire volume. In addition, the missal had been printed outside of Venice (i.e., in Rome). Agreeing that violations had occurred, the government revoked the privilege, thus permitting anyone to print the work in Venice. Supported by this decision, Perchacino and Rampazetto continued to violate the papal privilege by printing the missal. Now on papal orders, Nuncio Castagna requested the Republic to uphold the papal privilege granted to Varisco, in effect giving the papal privilege precedence over Venetian copyright law. He was not optimistic.[48]

The nuncio took his case to the Collegio in November 1573.[49] He requested that the government proceed against Perchacino and Rampazetto who had earned excommunication by contravening the exclusive papal privilege. The lawyer for the pair objected to the papal privilege on economic and jurisdictional grounds. The duo would lose two thousand ducats if the printing were halted, and readers would be hurt by having to pay Varisco's inflated price of eight lire for the missal, rather than the five lire being charged by other Venetian bookmen.[50] The lawyer believed that this was a material, not a spiritual, matter. He conceded papal jurisdiction over heretical books, but argued that the welfare of the book industry was the central issue here. Indeed, the pope had created a monopoly, something forbidden by the Old Testament, as well as by canonical and civil law.

The nuncio charged the lawyer with exaggeration. How could one speak of a monopoly when the pope claimed jurisdiction over only the breviary, catechism, Index, and missal, among millions of titles? In discharging his responsibility, the pope had granted an exclusive privilege to a publisher known to be accurate and diligent. The lawyer interjected

---

[47] Weale and Bohatta, *Bibliographia Liturgica*, p. 201.

[48] Letters of Nuncio Castagna (1521–90, the future Urban VII) of October 31, November 14, and of Cardinal Filippo Boncompagni of November 7, 1573, in *Nunziature* XI, 92–93, 97.

[49] For the following, see Collegio, Esposizioni Roma, R. 1, ff. 75ʳ–76ᵛ, November 20, 1573; and the nuncio's letter of November 28, 1573, in *Nunziature* XI, 103–4.

[50] Both prices were high in comparison to most books.

that the pope should correct books, not printers. The nuncio responded by asserting that papal authority had been accepted in the rest of the Catholic world, even in Spain and Germany, but Venice disobeyed.

The nuncio's assertion was a tactical error. Doge Alvise Mocenigo rose to defend Venetian honor. For the love of God, do not say such a thing, he told the nuncio, for no other state was so obedient to the Holy See. The exclusive privilege, however, enriched one and deprived others. The nuncio answered that the disobedient bookmen had printed a missal with grave errors and on bad paper. If not stopped, they would flood the world with these illegal and faulty copies.

The Collegio rebuffed the nuncio. The next day the Senate sent a letter to the ambassador in Rome that stressed Varisco's fraud, the high price that he was charging, the illegality of monopolies, and the financial plight of the bookmen ("questi poveri artigiani").[51] Ambassador Paolo Tiepolo, considered one of the most able Venetian diplomats, met with the pope on November 27. The pontiff contended that it was customary and within the papal prerogative when reforming a sacred text to issue an exclusive privilege for a limited time to ensure accuracy. Tiepolo readily conceded papal authority to correct texts, but shrewdly argued that Varisco and his collaborators had perverted the privilege by using it to realize illicit profits. The Holy Office might punish those who printed error, but the secular authority had jurisdiction over price. The pontiff expressed surprise at the high price that Varisco was charging, and the interview ended inconclusively.

Tiepolo next found an ally in the Secretary of State, Cardinal Galli, who clearly perceived that the privileges were being used for financial ends. He abhorred them and regretted that the pope had initially ignored his advice on the Little Office privilege. He added that Cardinal Granvelle, who had intrigued so successfully for the Plantin Press in the past, had in his capacity as viceroy of Naples persuaded Gregory XIII to halt the sale of Venetian printings of the breviary and missal in the Kingdom of Naples.[52]

In the next audience, the pope maintained that since a great deal of time, labor, and expense went into a reformed edition some compensation for the publisher was just. Tiepolo readily agreed, but added that one person should not enjoy all the profit. With this the pope conceded, probably on the advice of Cardinal Galli. He would instruct the cardinals of

---

[51] Senato, Deliberazioni Roma, R. 4, ff. 39r–40v, November 21, 1573. For the negotiations in Rome, see the letters of Ambassador Tiepolo (d. 1585) of November 28 and December 5, 1573, in Senato, Dispacci da Roma, F. 9, ff. 504r–5r, 514r–v.

[52] Cardinal Granvelle was Antoine Perrenot de Granvelle (1517–86), Bishop of Arras and servant of Phillip II in a number of important posts.

the Congregation of the Index to find a formula that would permit the disobedient bookmen to print and sell the missal without formal revocation of the papal privileges.

The battle over the Tridentine editions of the canonical texts ended with the complete victory of the majority of the bookmen. Bookmen other than the privilege holders published the breviary, catechism, Little Office, and missal in subsequent years, although the Giunti press published the most. These printings sometimes carried the impressive but meaningless formula "Permittente Sede Apostolica," sometimes simply "Cum privilegiis," and sometimes no privilege notice at all. The Venetian press soon regained its dominant position in the European production of canonical works.

Gregory XIII had finally reached the correct decision. Although he had initially resisted, he conceded when the Republic raised the disputes to the ambassadorial level. Indeed, Pius V and Gregory XIII should not have tried to halt privilege violators outside the papal state because they could do so only by brandishing spiritual weaponry in an area perceived by many as secular. Since the threat of excommunication had little effect, the papacy was forced to ask the civil government to rule against the financial interests of its own subjects. It is not surprising that the Republic eventually refused.

Had the papacy not attempted to impose privileges on foreign printers, it would have had to endure slower promulgation of the reformed versions. Some bookmen would not have printed the new version until older copies had been sold, and others would have defrauded buyers by selling older copies with fresh new title pages. Yet, reader demand would have eventually forced the bookmen to provide the new texts, and perhaps slower promulgation would have been preferable to arousing the patriciate.

Although at first unconcerned, the patriciate had eventually responded to the pleas of the bookmen. Individuals like Nicolò Da Ponte had led the way, until a majority of the leaders supported the press. The nobility justified their stance on economic grounds primarily and jurisdictional grounds secondarily. The government's action should not be weighed too heavily, for the Republic came to the defense of the bookmen only when it was apparent to nearly everyone in Rome and Venice that profit, rather than piety, lay at the bottom of the disputes. Nevertheless, the patriciate had opposed a papal claim to regulate the press, and established a precedent for the future.

The disputes taught the bookmen that if they could find secular grounds on which to base their protest, and hold out long enough, the government would eventually take up their cause. By the end of the century the bookmen would put this knowledge to use in censorship disputes.

VI

THE CLANDESTINE BOOK TRADE

THE famous preacher Francesco Panigarola (1548–94) expressed the prevailing acceptance of the Counter Reformation by the majority of Italians: the Inquisition and Index guaranteed Italian peace and security in the midst of a world torn by strife.[1] While England, Flanders, and Germany suffered discord and war as a consequence of abandoning the faith, Italy preserved true liberty under the paternal care of the holy inquisitors. Panigarola asked Italians why they would want to read prohibited books, if not to infect themselves with heresy. They would not eat food that the doctor advised against; why, then, would they wish to kill their souls with bad books? Those countries that accepted the Tridentine decrees and did not permit their people to read indiscriminately were those that were happy.

The Venetian state gave the Holy Office its full support, as Republic and papacy collaborated amicably in the effort to extirpate heretics and their books. Noisy but short-lived disputes, such as the Apostolic visit in 1581 and the Republic's recognition of Henry of Navarre in 1589, did not weaken the cooperation.[2] The bookmen adjusted. They found ways of circumventing the Index, and enjoyed surprising success until harsh retri-

[1] *Lettioni sopra dogmi fatta da F. Francesco Panigarola minore osservante alla presenza, e per commandamento del Ser.mo Carlo Emanuelle Duca di Savoia, l'anno MDLXXXII in Turino. . . .* (In Venetia, Presso Pietro Dusinelli, MDLXXXIIII), 323ᵛ–25ᵛ. Much the same is to be found in his *Prediche quadragesimali . . . predicate da lui in San Pietro di Roma, l'anno 1577. . . .* (In Venetia, Appresso Pietro Miloco, MDCXVII), pp. 510–14.

[2] See Silvio Tramontin, "La visita apostolica del 1581 a Venezia," *Studi veneziani* 9 (1967), 453–533; and Seneca, *Donà*, pp. 172–91. The disputes have distracted historians from the great measure of agreement between the papacy and the Republic in the 1570s and 1580s. The Inquisition trials confirm it, and the nuncios' dispatches give much additional evidence. For example, within an eighteen-month period the government authorized the execution of three heretics, permitted the arrest of a nobleman, and refused to intervene on behalf of some confessed Portuguese Marranos. Letters of Nuncio Lorenzo Campeggi of March 10, 1584, and of Nuncio Cesare Costa of August 3, October 12, 19, 1585, in ASVa, Segretario di Stato, Venezia, F. 25, f. 80ʳ, F. 10, ff. 393ᵛ, 455ʳ⁻ᵛ, and 458ʳ.

bution spelled tragedy for one of them, and a stern warning for the rest, at the end of the 1580s.

1. THE SMUGGLING NETWORK

Although many Venetians accepted the Index, some continued to want banned titles. Both direct and circumstantial evidence points to the existence through the greater part of the 1570s and 1580s of a clandestine organization that imported prohibited titles to meet this demand. Through visitations and denunciations the Inquisition discovered that members of the book trade offered for sale a wide assortment of prohibited titles, particularly northern European imprints. When questioned, the bookmen offered ingenious explanations, all of which led the tribunal into dead ends. Nevertheless, the outline of a smuggling network can be reconstructed by piecing together numerous fragments of information.

The Inquisition found in the shop of the bookseller and occasional publisher Gioachino Brugnolo twenty-six prohibited items, including four titles of Luther. Brugnolo possessed the *Freedom of the Christian Man*, a religious title of Vadianus, a variety of humanistic and scriptural studies, the banned *Colloquia*, and seven New Testament paraphrases and patristic commentaries of Erasmus, which were prohibited unless expurgated by the theological faculties of Louvain or Paris. Brugnolo told the tribunal that he had gotten the titles from a lawyer's estate.[3]

As a result of a tip from the Esecutori contro la bestemmia, the Holy Office searched the storehouse of Stefano Bindoni, a bookseller, and found the anonymous Italian translation of Luther's *Address to the German Nobility*, the sermons of Ochino, and the *Sommario della Sacra Scrittura*. In Bindoni's house two or three copies of the *Mercurio et Caronte*, Erasmus's *Praise of Folly*, and some pasquinades were found. Apparently unaware of the true authorship of the Luther title, the Holy Office sentenced Bindoni to penances, including a bread-and-water fast every Friday for a year.[4]

Another minor bookseller, binder, and occasional publisher possessed Calvin's *Responsio ad Balduini*, a humanistic work of Mathurin Cordier, and Erasmus's *Paraphrasis in epistolas Pauli*, which he claimed had come to him through his wife's dowry from his late father-in-law, the publisher

---

[3] SU, Bu. 59, Gioachino Brugnolo, April 9, 1587. The documentation appears to be incomplete. See App. II for the inventory of his prohibited titles.

[4] SU, Bu. 46, Stefano Bindoni, containing the testimony of Bindoni and others before the Esecutori, December 14, 1579, through January 26, 1579 mv, and the Holy Office investigation of January 28 through March 1, 1580. Also see Bestemmia, Bu. 56, Notatorio Terminazioni, R. 1561–1582, ff. 159ᵛ–60ʳ, January 26, 1579 mv.

Francesco Rocca.[5] An Oecolampadius scriptural commentary was discovered in the shop of another bookseller, who testified that he had purchased it from an unidentified foreign priest.[6] Another bookseller claimed that the *Dialoghi* of Ochino in his possession was from a batch of books purchased from a widow.[7] Other banned ultramontane titles, such as Andreas Osiander's *Harmoniae evangelicae*, Erasmus Sarcerius's *Loci communes theologici*, legal volumes of Charles Du Moulin, works of Christoph Hegendorff, and the ubiquitous titles in the occult arts, were on sale in small bookshops and turned up in the Inquisition inspections or through occasional denunciations.[8] The Holy Office punished the booksellers with penances, a few days' imprisonment, a year's house arrest, and, of course, destruction of the books.

Even clergymen continued to hold banned titles, and sometimes were exposed in unlikely places. A valise of books belonging to a Parma priest was opened by accident in the patriarch's palace. It contained the banned *Colloquia* and *Ratio verae theologiae* of Erasmus and Aretino's *La Cortegiana*. The priest offered no concrete information on where he had obtained the books, although he acknowledged having purchased an innocent title of Erasmus at a local bookstore. The Holy Office sentenced him to penances.[9]

[5] SU, Bu. 62, Oswaldo Venzoni, Giulio Rizzo, e Girolamo Zennaro, ff. 1r–v, October 8, 1588. Venzoni, at the sign of the Castello in San Moisè, published three works between 1578 and 1582.

[6] Ibid., ff. 1v–2v, testimony of Giulio Rizzo at the sign of the Domicella in San Salvatore of October 8, 1588.

[7] SU, Bu. 50, Guidone Simottini, October 13, 15, 27, 1583. Simottini, at the sign of the Sole in San Moisè, was probably sentenced to one year's house arrest (the sentence is difficult to read).

[8] SU, Bu. 37, Bartolomeo de Sabio, ff. 1r–3v, October 2, 9, and November 9, 1574. Sabio, who had a bookstand on the Rialto bridge, and Giovanni Bariletto, a small publisher, were convicted. A year earlier, the Holy Office deposited a sealed bag of thirty volumes discovered in Bariletto's store with the priors of the guild. But the seal was broken, the prohibited titles gone, and the tribunal could only warn Bariletto. SU, Bu. 25, Girolamo Calepin, ff. 6v–8r, testimony of July 9 and August 4, 1573. SU, Bu. 50, Giovanni De Putei, July 16, 30, 1583. Putei was a binder who worked for Marco Bindoni. SU, Bu. 62, Oswaldo Venzoni, Giulio Rizzo, e Girolamo Zennaro, ff. 2v–3v, October 8, 11, 1588. Zennaro (or Zenaro), at the sign of the Aquila in San Moisè, was not a publisher although several members of his family were. SU, Bu. 62, Orazio Bozzuola, October 20, 25, November 17, 1588. Bozzuola was custodian of the guild's warehouse.

[9] The bookseller was identified only as "Messer Aurelio." SU, Bu. 59, Brocardo Boroni, April 28, 30, May 2, 12, 1587. More material concerning Venetian monks who held prohibited books is in SU, Bu. 49, Libri prohibiti, testimony of various monks of May 19, 22, 26, 31, June 7, 1582. Because the documents are incomplete and crumbling, it is impossible to determine exactly what transpired.

Not only minor booksellers, but also important publishers trafficked in prohibited titles. The roving Inquisition commissioner found a Franciscan monk with a copy of Erasmus's Greek and Latin New Testament and learned from the monk that, although all the booksellers carried the work, he had purchased his copy from Francesco Ziletti. The commissioner went incognito to Ziletti's shop and asked for it by name. Ziletti brought out an armload of banned editions of Scripture, including three different printings of Erasmus's New Testament (all published in Basel by Nikolaus Brylinger), the *Parafrasi sopra le Epistole di San Paulo* of "Virginio" (Cornelio Donzellini), and Brucioli's vernacular translation of the Epistles of St. Paul. Brought before the Holy Office, Ziletti stammered out the customary litany of excuses and ignorance, and was fined thirty ducats.[10] Similarly, the commissioner found a Melanchthon *Grammatica* and other unnamed prohibited books in the warehouse of Giovanni Giolito, son and successor to the late Gabriel. The commissioner locked and sealed the books in Giolito's warehouse, but, somehow, they disappeared. Giovanni told the Inquisition that one of his employees had stolen them and fled, and the tribunal did nothing.[11]

The Inquisition had been destroying prohibited books since the late 1540s, but still the bookmen offered for sale a wide assortment of banned titles. Volumes that escaped the purge of 1570 undoubtedly accounted for some of the illegal books, and estate sales possibly provided others. But the Holy Office also uncovered recent northern imprints. The Inquisition's discovery that major bookmen were eluding the customs inspection led it to suspect that contraband was entering Venice. In 1582 one of Luc'Antonio Giunti's employees removed some unexamined books from the customs house without obtaining permission from the Inquisition inspector. In the following year the Holy Office questioned Melchiorre Scoto about three or four bales of books from Lyons that had gone through customs without an inventory. Scoto claimed that an Inquisition commissioner—whose name he did not recall—had authorized their removal without the inventory.[12] Felice Valgrisi removed, unopened, from customs some books from Germany and Lyons. When the roving Inquisition commissioner caught up with him in the shop of Francesco Ziletti and

[10] SU, Bu. 49, Francesco Ziletti e Felice Valgrisi, ff. [5^r–9^r], December 4, 11, 1582. Ziletti's shop at the sign of the Stella was in the parish of San Zulian.

[11] SU, Bu. 49, Giovanni Antonio del Pavese [the employee], testimony of Giovanni Giolito of April 21, 1582.

[12] SU, Bu. 50, Bonifacio Ciera, Luc'Antonio Giunti, Melchiorre Scoto, e Antonio Bragia, August 9, 11, 20, 1583. Melchiorre, at the sign of the Albero in Santi Apostoli, was the nephew of Girolamo Scoto and an active bookseller but not a publisher.

informed him that his action was unlawful, Valgrisi turned to his employees and smiled! The Holy Office called him in, and Valgrisi testified that he had received permission from a priest to take the books home without inspection. Unconvinced, but lacking further evidence, the Inquisition fined him eight ducats.[13]

The Holy Office questioned a bookseller about an inaccurate inventory of some prohibited books imported from Frankfurt. The tribunal had discovered some of these volumes in his store, including a four-volume New Testament edited by Erasmus but bearing the name Théodore Bèze on the last volume. Most bookmen offered the tribunal ingenuous deference, but this one was defiant. He asserted that these prohibited books were sold daily in Venice and that the inventory regulation was impossible to obey. Angered, the inquisitor fined him six ducats.[14]

These cases show that the bookmen had found ways to slip prohibited titles through the inspection at the customs house. The career of Pietro (or Piero) Longo provides more information on what was happening. Longo's background is unknown. The first mention of him in the book trade occurred in 1570, when he quarreled with his brother. Both were carriers, i.e., transporters of books. In 1580 arbiters found Pietro guilty of negligence in allowing two bales of books that he was bringing from Frankfurt for two Milanese bookmen to get wet.[15] He probably made the long trip between northern Italy and Frankfurt throughout the 1570s and first half of the 1580s for other bookmen and private clients. From 1573 through 1582 Longo acted on behalf of two Paduan professors and Pietro Perna. He carried the manuscripts of Girolamo Mercuriale (1530–1606), who held the chair of medicine, and Antonio Riccobono (1541–99), who held the chair of rhetoric, to Basel for Perna to publish.[16] He also brought back books ordered by the professors, including at least one banned title,

---

[13] SU, Bu. 49, Francesco Ziletti e Felice Valgrisi, ff. [1ʳ–4ᵛ], November 4, December 2, 11, 20, 1582. Felice, the son of Vincenzo, published twenty-six titles between 1583 and 1591.

[14] SU, Bu. 48, Bartolomeo Chemer, his testimony of November 4, 1581, and July 10, 24, 26, 31, August 4, 1582. See App. II for a list of his prohibited books.

[15] Marciani, "Librai veneti in Napoli," pp. 511, 516, 545.

[16] See the letters of Mercuriale to Theodore Zwinger (1533–88), professor of medicine at Basel, Protestant, and friend of Perna, in Basel, Universitätsbibliothek, Mss. Frey-Grynaeus, II. 4, letters 163, 164, 166, 169, 171, 176, 179, 182; II. 19/II, letters 45, 47, 56; II. 23 1/II, letters 302, 304, 305. I am indebted to Antonio Rotondò, who found these letters and graciously provided me with photocopies. He reports briefly on his findings in "La censura ecclesiastica e la cultura," pp. 1,449–50. Also see the letter of Perna of May 2, 1579, Basel, to Riccobono printed in Perini, "Pietro Perna," pp. 181–82. Perna published Mercuriale's *Variarum lectionum libri* in 1576, his *De peste praesertim de Veneta & Patavina* in 1577, and Riccobono's *De Historia* in 1579.

Gesner's *Bibliotheca universalis*.[17] There is no sign that Longo ever operated a bookstore in Venice, and his name appeared on the title page of only one book, a scriptural allegory published in association with Gaspare Bindoni in 1575.[18] In May and July 1586 he attended meetings of the bookmen's guild but was never an officer.[19] In the same year Longo sold an unidentified Agrippa title to a Bolognese visiting Venice,[20] and sometime in the following year he sold Agrippa's *Opere* to a Venetian.[21]

The Inquisition had Longo in custody in late August 1587.[22] Two weeks later, a witness in another trial relayed some gossip about Longo told to him by Gaspare Bindoni, a small publisher in a prominent family of printers.[23] The Holy Office questioned Bindoni and learned a great deal. Gaspare had journeyed to and from Frankfurt many times in Longo's company. He testified that Longo had lived with Pietro Perna in Basel and had managed a bookstore for Perna in Protestant Strasburg for an indefinite period. Indeed, Longo had openly called himself "a citizen of Strasburg" in Gaspare's presence. On one occasion at an inn in that city, a group of Protestants came over to Longo and said, "How are you, our Messer Piero? You are one of us." And when religious arguments broke out at the inn, Longo would not take the Catholic side. When reproved by Bindoni, Longo responded that he had stayed with Perna to learn German, and that he called himself a citizen of Strasburg because it was good for business. He shrugged off his failure to defend Catholicism. Gaspare mentioned that, on their return from Frankfurt, the bookmen

[17] Letters of Mercuriale to Zwinger of November 24, 1574, and June 4, 1575, Padua, in Frey-Grynaeus, II. 4, letters 169 and 176. Mercuriale indicated the specific edition desired: *Bibliotheca instituta a C. Gesnero, in epitomen redacta & locupletata per I. Simlerum* (Apud C. Froschoverus: Tiguri, 1574).

[18] The book was Hieronymus Lauretus, *Sylva allegoriarum totius sacrae Scripturae. STC Italian*, 372. Further editions were published in Paris, 1583; and by Gaspare Bindoni, Venice, 1587. *Cambridge Catalogue*, items L286–87. I have been unable to identify author or title.

[19] Arte dei libreri, stampatori e ligadori, Bu. 163, R. 1 (Atti 1578–1598), ff. 67ʳ (May 6, 1586), 72ʳ (July 24, 1586).

[20] SU, Bu. 61, Pietro Longo, testimony of Giovanni Antonio Isolani of Bologna of January 26, 1588, copy of an interrogation of the Bologna Holy Office forwarded to Venice. The Longo folder contains one other brief document, mentioned below.

[21] SU, Bu. 66, Orazio Agostino e Raimondo de Grassi, f. [2ʳ], May 5, 1590. Thanks to an unusually detailed description, the edition can be securely identified as Agrippa's *Opere* (2 vols. [Lugduni, per Beringeros fratres], [1580?]). *Index Aureliensis*, no. 101.901.

[22] "Ragionai l'altro giorno col Mariano sudetto, credo fosse lunedi mattina in piazza, parlando detto Giorgio [Valgrisi] circa heretici et in proposito lui mi disse, che quel Piero Longo era in preson." SU, Bu. 59, Giorgio Valgrisi, f. 2ʳ, testimony of witness Father Alvise Ferro of August 27, 1587.

[23] Ibid., ff. 2ᵛ–3ʳ, testimony of Mariano Torre d'Nencitijs of September 10, 1587.

would stop in Basel to take on additional books. But Longo always packed his barrels apart from the others, so that his companions could not determine what titles he carried. Finally, Bindoni had heard that Longo had been imprisoned in Rome and elsewhere.[24]

Upon receipt of this damaging testimony, the Holy Office undoubtedly questioned Longo at length, but the trial has not come to light. It is known that an Inquisition official talked with Longo in prison on the night of January 27, 1588. Longo said that he wished to speak about an Inquisition matter, and the official obtained permission to receive the confidence. Longo admitted to having given a work of Agrippa to Alvise Michiel, a noble, and a title of Peter of Abano to a ducal secretary.[25]

Three different reports confirm that the Holy Office put Longo to death a few days later. On February 19, 1588, a Protestant scholar traveling in Venice wrote: "Pietro Longo was thrown into prison at the command of the Venetian magistracy and drowned at night twenty days ago for the same reason that the physician Girolamo Donzellini was executed last year."[26] Thus, Longo went to his death on the night of January 31, 1588. A Venetian chronicler stated that the Holy Office drowned Longo for bringing in prohibited books from "distant lands."[27] And in 1609 the Venetian ambassador to the Holy See confirmed the execution. During an audience in which Paul V taxed the Republic for failing to halt the traffic in prohibited books, the ambassador protested that the government had a few years ago ordered the drowning of a bookman who had tried

[24] Ibid., ff. 3ᵛ–4ᵛ, September 16, 1587. Bindoni's shop was in Piazza San Marco.

[25] SU, Bu. 61, Pietro Longo, testimony of Franciscus Julius di Guinzano. Michiel may have been Alvise di Marc'Antonio (1534–89) of the Rio Marin branch of the family. Although elected Savio di Terraferma six times, he never reached the inner circle of the most powerful patricians, but is remembered as the author of an important political diary. For his career see Lowry, "Church and Venetian Political Change," pp. 353–54, 367–73.

[26] "Petrus Longus, mandatu magistratus Veneti in carcerem coniectus, et ante dies viginti, noctu aquas submersus vitam finiit, eandem penem ob causam, propter quam anno superiori Hier. Donzelini Medicus eodem supplicii genere affectus fuit." Letter of Ludwig Iselin a. d. XI Cal. Mart. (February 19), 1588, Venice, to Basil Amerbach, Basel, in Basel, Universitätsbibliothek, Ms. G. 1. 70, ff. 60ʳ (quote)–60ᵛ. (Antonio Rotondò announced his discovery of this letter in a review in *Rivista storica italiana* 72 [1970], 755.) Amerbach (1535–91) was professor of law at the university in Basel 1564–89, while his nephew Iselin (1559–1612) also taught law at the gymnasium and later at the university.

[27] "Nell'anno 1588, nel mese di gennaio, per il S. Offizio fu fatto affogare annegato Pietro Longo libraro, quale fu quello portò dai paesi lontani dei libri proibiti." An anonymous VC ms. quoted by F. Albanese, *L'inquisizione religiosa nella Repubblica di Venezia* (Venice, 1875), p. 136. The shelf mark given by Albanese does not correspond to the present system, and I was unable to locate the ms.

to import heretical books.[28] It seems likely that he referred to the un-fortunate Longo.

Longo paid with his life for smuggling prohibited books and, possibly, for holding Protestant beliefs.[29] So far as can be determined, the Inquisition did not punish other bookmen for smuggling at this time. Yet, it would have been very difficult for Longo to have performed the multifarious tasks of a smuggling operation by himself. The appearance of prohibited titles in several different stores argues that he had help, at least in distributing the books. Who were his associates? A suggestive pattern of direct and circumstantial evidence points to members of the Ziletti and Valgrisi firms. Indeed, those bookmen may have been perpetuating or renewing clandestine networks initiated by their fathers and uncles years earlier.

Accusations of trafficking in prohibited books pursued the Ziletti across Italy. The Bolognese Inquisition arrested Giordano di Gianfrancesco from Brescia,[30] the first of the Ziletti family to publish, when he purchased a bookstore, including a stock of prohibited books, in 1548. Giordano convinced the tribunal that he had contracted to purchase only the "good" books, and was released three weeks later, according to the account of the incident that he gave years later.[31] Giordano managed a bookstore in Rome from 1548 to 1556, and suffered arrest in 1550 because two employees were selling prohibited books in the store. The Roman Holy Office released him after a day and a night in prison. Giordano persuaded the court that he had been granted permission to obtain prohibited books for the use of the prelates preparing for the Council of Trent. His employees

[28] Letter of Cardinal Scipione (Caffarelli) Borghese to the Venetian nuncio of March 21, 1609, in ASVa, Segretario di Stato, Venezia, F. 39, ff. 197^v–98^r; also quoted by Pietro Savio, ed., "Per L'epistolario di Paolo Sarpi," *Aevum* 13 (1939), 576, n. 3.

[29] Death was an extraordinarily severe penalty for smuggling prohibited books. Longo may also have been a fervent Protestant, perhaps a relapsus, who chose death rather than recantation. Iselin wrote that Longo was executed for the same reason as Donzellini, who was executed as a relapsus in April 1587; perhaps a combination of years of smuggling and fervent Protestantism cost Longo his life. Both the Longo and the last Donzellini trials are missing. Nor is there any mention of Longo in governmental records, such as the Council of Ten, but a reference would be expected only if a political issue, such as extradition, had been involved.

[30] SU, Bu. 156, "Librai e libri proibiti, 1545-1571," f. [76^v].

[31] There are two accounts of this episode. See L. Carcereri, "Cristoforo Dossena, Francesco Linguardo e un Giordano, librai processati per eresia a Bologna (1548)," "*L'Archiginnasio* 5 (1910), 177-92; and SU, Bu. 39, Girolamo Donzellino, f. 98^r, Ziletti's testimony of November 20, 1574. Perini, "Ancora sul Pietro Perna," pp. 372-73, pulls the two accounts together.

had sold the volumes to unauthorized persons while he was away, attending a book fair. Again, this version of events is Giordano's, given in 1574.[32]

Although he had issued at least one title in Venice in 1549, Giordano did not settle there until 1556, when he began to publish at the sign of the Stella in the Mercerie. He joined the general resistance to the Pauline Index, but did not go to extraordinary lengths; he submitted his inventory before some of the other bookmen did. After the purge of 1570 the Inquisition warned him for possessing prohibited titles.

Giordano maintained relations with foreign and Italian heretics over several decades. He spoke with Perna at Frankfurt in 1560 and had further contact with him there in 1568.[33] Giordano kept up an acquaintance with Girolamo Donzellini, also a Brescian, for many years. Donzellini, it will be recalled, was denounced for heresy in Rome in the 1540s, trafficked in prohibited books in Venice at mid-century, consorted with Protestants abroad, and abjured before the Venetian Holy Office in 1560 and 1574. During the latter trial, Ziletti was accused of having been Donzellini's comrade in Rome with full knowledge of the latter's views. Giordano admitted an acquaintance of many years, but denied that Donzellini had ever tried to persuade him to heresy. He added that he had no idea that Donzellini was a heretic, and that he himself had no interest in religion and had never read the Bible in his life. The Venetian Inquisition took no action against Ziletti.[34]

Giordano published 140 titles alone or in association, the vast majority between 1556 and 1578, an additional handful in 1582 and 1583. Latin learned works in diverse subjects dominated his list, and included non-religious titles of at least three Italian heretics. In 1563 he published the Latin poetry of the Milanese humanist and heretic Publio Francesco Spinola, who was drowned by the Venetian Inquisition in 1567. Also in 1563 he published a work of logic of Agostino Curione, son of Celio Secondo, at a time when the author was accused of spreading heresy in Venice and Padua. And in 1574 he printed a collection of Latin letters of Donzellini. Religious works comprised about one-seventh of the total, including Cardinal Reginald Pole's prolegomenon to the Tridentine Council (written in 1545, published in 1562), which outlined views on faith and works that failed to win acceptance from either Catholics or Protes-

---

[32] SU, Bu. 39, Girolamo Donzellino, f. 98[r], Ziletti's testimony of November 20, 1574.

[33] Perini, "Pietro Perna," p. 177; Perini, "Ancora sul Pietro Perna," p. 373.

[34] SU, Bu. 39, Girolamo Donzellino, ff. 14[r] (accusation of August 27, 1563), 98[v] (Ziletti's testimony of November 20, 1574).

tants. Giordano ceased publication in 1583 and probably died in or about that year.[35]

Francesco di Ludovico Ziletti, a nephew of Giordano, continued in the same paths. He began publishing in 1569, and by mid-1570 he was the proprietor of the shop that had been Andrea Arrivabene's. Francesco resisted the Inquisition inspectors who found banned titles there in 1570, and continued to sell prohibited books, including Pier Paolo Vergerio's *Instruttione christiana* in the late 1570s, and Brucioli, Erasmus, and Cornelio Donzellini editions of the Bible in 1582.[36] By 1578 he was publishing at the sign of the Stella in San Zulian, perhaps in partnership with his uncle.[37] Francesco published the bulk of his 103 titles between 1578 and 1587. His list demonstrated the same preference for Latin and the same diversity of subject matter as his uncle's, but he published fewer religious works. Francesco maintained the connection with Donzellini by publishing a medical title of his in 1586.[38] He died between 1587 and 1590.[39]

Marriage ties linked the Ziletti with the Valgrisi, another family that sold prohibited books. Giordano Ziletti was the son-in-law of Vincenzo Valgrisi, who was sentenced to penances for his opposition to the Pauline Index, and fined fifty ducats in 1570 for selling prohibited books. Felicità Vincenzo's daughter, married Francesco Ziletti in October 1579; her brothers Felice and Giorgio provided her dowry of 2,500 ducats.[40] Although not as active as their father, the heirs of Vincenzo Valgrisi published seven works from 1573 to 1580, and Felice alone published twenty-six titles from 1583 to 1591. In 1590 Felice published a posthumous work of Bernardino Telesio, his *Varii de naturalibus rebus libelli*. The 1596 Index ordered the expurgation of two of these short anti-Aristotelian pieces.[41] Two generations of the Ziletti and Valgrisi families lived in the parish of San Zulian.

Felice and Giorgio Valgrisi may have been deeply involved in illicit activities and beliefs. Felice, it will be recalled, was amused when the Inquisition official told him that imported books had to be inspected. The Holy Office fined him, but did not pursue the matter further. In August 1587 a priest denounced Giorgio, a bookseller at the sign of the Serpente

[35] *STC Italian*, 206, 226, 529, 637, 989–90; Stella 1, 126.

[36] SU, Bu. 47, Fra Clemente Valvassore, no pag., his written defense of February 13, 1581.

[37] Marciani, "Editori veneti in Napoli," pp. 513–16.

[38] *STC Italian*, 226.

[39] On January 18, 1590, publisher Domenico Farri testified that Ziletti had recently died. SU, Bu. 65, Domenico Farri.

[40] Marciani, "Editori veneti in Napoli," 508, 515, 529.

[41] *STC Italian*, 662; Reusch, *Indices*, 542.

in the Mercerie, for heresy.[42] Although he had been Giorgio's friend for ten or twelve years, the priest believed that Valgrisi had become a heretic. Valgrisi allegedly had laughed at indulgences, devotions, processions, and miracles, and had critcized the mass, saying at one point: "The heretics have written about the errors of the mass." The priest further testified that Giorgio had spent many years in Germany and had returned praising the northern Reformers.[43]

Giorgio had been a good friend of Donzellini and Claudio Textor, who were executed together in the spring of 1587. Donzellini had frequented Giorgio's bookstore, and once the priest had heard the two of them discussing prohibited books, Donzellini boasting that he held on to his, despite the Holy Office. Frowning, Giorgio had put his finger to his mouth to silence him. After Donzellini had left the store, the priest had remarked to Giorgio that Donzellini had spoken "molta licentiosamente." Sighing, Giorgio had agreed. He had told Donzellini that in this land one had to live according to the ways of others, and, if he did not wish to do so, he could go elsewhere. After Donzellini's execution, Giorgio lamented that his warnings to be more careful had been ignored. Giorgio had also been friendly with Textor and had criticized the members of the Holy Office as "ignoramuses" after his execution, but the priest could offer no details on the relationship. Finally, the accuser testified that Giorgio had dined with an unidentified Huguenot, and then had shown him St. Mark's Basilica, an action that affronted the priest.

The Holy Office questioned one of Valgrisi's neighbors immediately, suspended the investigation while it presumably dealt with Longo, and then resumed the questioning in February 1588.[44] Valgrisi's neighbors confirmed the provocative talk, the association with Donzellini and Textor, and the years in Germany. But they also testified that Valgrisi was a man of good reputation who occasionally frequented mass and received the sacraments. The pastor of San Zulian, who had known Giorgio for twenty-five years, explained that Giorgio avoided the sacraments because he was linked in a common-law union that he would not, or could not, regularize by marriage. With this the Holy Office dropped the matter, apparently without interrogating Valgrisi. Perhaps the tribunal was satisfied that Giorgio was not a heretic.

[42] SU, Bu. 59, Giorgio Valgrisi, ff. 1r–2v, testimony of Padre Alvise Ferro of August 27, 1587.

[43] Giorgio had also enrolled at the University of Basel during the academic year 1557–58, but neither the priest nor the Holy Office was aware of this. Giovanni Busino, "Italiani all'Università di Basilea dal 1460 al 1601," BHR, 20 (1958), 525–26.

[44] SU, Bu. 59, Giorgio Valgrisi, ff. 3r–v, testimony of Mariano Torre of September 10, 1587, 5r–8v, testimony of two tradesmen and the pastor of San Zulian of February 6, 1588.

Pietro Longo, Giordano and Francesco Ziletti, Felice and Giorgio Valgrisi, Girolamo Donzellini, and Claudio Textor trafficked in prohibited books and were convicted or accused of heresy, or possibly both. Diverse witnesses and commercial relations linked most of them together, usually in the context of illicit activities or heretical beliefs. It is likely that a clandestine organization including most or all of them flourished in the 1570s and 1580s, and that it was the continuation or revival of Perna's network of the 1550s. The smuggling organization can be reconstructed. Perna at the northern terminus in Basel printed heretical books and arranged contacts with publishers in other Protestant cities until his death in 1582. Bookmen like Longo and Giorgio Valgrisi went to him to learn German and to become familiar with the ways of Protestant publishing. Either they participated as a consequence of Protestant sympathies, or they converted while abroad. One or more experienced bookmen of Protestant beliefs—Longo certainly, Giorgio Valgrisi and others possibly—filled the essential but hazardous role of carrier. Longo hid the contraband titles with his legitimate merchandise and transported it to Venice, where the Valgrisi and Ziletti firms helped spirit it through the customs inspection and arranged for subsequent distribution. The carrier retailed a few items, such as the highly sought after occult titles, and the Ziletti and Valgrisi took the rest, selling some and passing the remainder on to other bookstores. Ardent Protestants arranged for hand-to-hand distribution of titles such as Calvin's *Institutes*, which the bookmen hesitated to sell through their stores. And they provided liaison with groups of Protestants in Venice and Padua in such a way as to protect the bookmen from the consequences of too much knowledge. With these arrangements the bookmen satisfied the demand for banned volumes at the height of the Counter Reformation.[45]

2. THE MARKET FOR PROHIBITED BOOKS

Despite the laws of church and state, the bookmen did import prohibited books. How did they manage it, and for whom did they procure the banned titles?

[45] Much remains unknown, and the missing Longo and last Donzellini trials may hold some answers, although the severe punishment of the men argues that they probably did not implicate others. Did Donzellini play a role in the clandestine trade after his release from prison in 1576? Since he corresponded with Perna about books in 1572, it is likely that he had a hand in the smuggling later. See Rotondò, "La censura ecclesiastica e la cultura," p. 1,449. Why didn't the Holy Office question Giorgio Valgrisi, or launch an intensive investigation with the goal of halting the smuggling? Possibly the government restrained the Inquisition with the argument that Longo's death sentence would accomplish this without disrupting the book trade.

From the reports, Longo simply packed his contraband together with his legal merchandise in Basel, and proceeded south. He had no need of secret routes or clandestine methods until he reached the Holy Office inspection at the Venetian customs house. Perhaps he evaded the inspection entirely by taking the books across the lagoon to the city in a small boat by night. A number of incidents also hint that the bookmen submitted to the inspection and emerged with their contraband intact. The inspection machinery was cumbersome and tedious, and it required much attention to detail. The law required the Inquisition representative to examine the arriving books and prepare, or have prepared, a detailed inventory. Faced with the thousands of volumes entering Venice from all over Europe, the inspectors probably took shortcuts and became careless. If the inspector examined only the books at the top of a barrel, accepted a prepared inventory after a cursory glance, or gave verbal, instead of written, approval, the system broke down. The bookmen had at their disposal several devices with which to promote carelessness. They might affix false title pages and colophons at Frankfurt or Basel, or pack the innocent titles on top of the prohibited ones. The bustle of one of Europe's great emporia obviously aided the bookmen. Possibly they bribed a customs official or an Inquisition agent, although the latter may have been well-nigh incorruptible.

In any case, the customs inspection sometimes, perhaps often, failed. The Congregation in Rome exhorted the Venetian Inquisition to exercise greater vigilance, and the local tribunal reacted typically by ordering the guild to rent a storehouse to hold imported books pending inspection.[46] Even if implemented, this probably did not stop the flow of contraband, for locked and sealed storehouses had proved vulnerable. Once entry into the city was gained, the books were practically impossible to locate. With the facilities and skills of one of the world's great publishing centers at their disposal, the bookmen could hide, falsify, and sell the books with little trouble. The Holy Office could do nothing unless the roving commissioners happened upon the volumes or a denunciation provided a lead.

The prices asked for prohibited titles indicate in a general way the volume of the illegal commerce; assuming steady demand, the greater the supply the lower the price. A bookseller in 1588 sold two prohibited occult titles, Michael Scott's *Physionomia* and Andreas Corvus's *De chiromantia*, and a banned Hegendorff legal title, for 1 ducat, 40 soldi, and 30 soldi respectively.[47] Without knowledge of the format, number of

[46] BAVa, Vaticanus Latinus 10945, ff. 118r–v, November 15, 1586; SU, Bu. 50, Orazio De Gobbio, no pag., Holy Office order of November 5, 1583.
[47] SU, Bu. 61, Giovanni Battista Capponi, ff. [29r], Capponi's testimony of June 9, 1588 [31r], testimony of the bookseller, Evangelista Dehuchino, of June 14.

pages, and condition of the volumes, a judgment is tentative, but it appears that, while the Scott sold for a high price, the other two sold for the average price of ordinary, innocent volumes printed in Venice. The prices argue that an adequate supply existed to hold prices down to reasonable levels. An adequate supply of occult titles signifies that a large number were in circulation, for the demand was high.

Since the market for prohibited titles existed, the volume of contraband depended on how many bookmen were engaged in smuggling. If Longo had toiled alone, carrying a handful of banned titles in each quarterly or bimonthly trip south, he could have imported only a few hundred volumes in the course of ten or fifteen years. The availability of prohibited titles in many stores suggests that the total volume was large and that Longo was not alone. Unusual profits enjoyed by a network of a few bookmen would tempt others, so long as the risk was not prohibitive.

Professional experience and accumulated hostility toward the papacy tended to blunt the church's teaching on the evils of heretical books and to lead the bookmen, apart from those of Protestant sympathies, to put profits ahead of obedience.[48] Their trade taught them to see books, not as threats to the established order, but as neutral merchandise whose value was determined by demand and by physical properties. The cosmopolitan structure of the book trade, including commercial relations with Protestant bookmen and visits to Frankfurt, eased the fear of heresy. Resentment and cynicism hardened the bookmen's resolve after Paul IV used economic sanctions to compel obedience to his Index and other popes threatened excommunication to enforce papal privileges. By the 1580s, many Venetian bookmen must have had difficulty in perceiving censorship in religious terms at all. They saw themselves as defending their livelihood in the face of harassment from political authorities—an attitude dear to merchants of all centuries.

Not all the bookmen engaged in the illicit commerce. Undoubtedly some disapproved, but they did not denounce their erring brothers. Even though the bookmen knew a great deal about each other's affairs, they offered information grudgingly. On the rare occasions when one bookman testified against another, as when Gaspare Bindoni testified against Longo, they reported heretical beliefs rather than trafficking in prohibited books. Both fear of reprisal and the habits of the industry inhibited free speech. The bookmen adopted a laissez-faire attitude toward violation of the Index because they did not want to encourage examination of the trade and the inevitable additional legislation. The chief danger from denunciations came from people outside the industry.

---

[48] The Venetian bookmen were by no means unique; Christophe Plantin, for example, printed both Catholic and Protestant works.

Judging from the authors and titles discovered, the bookmen offered their customers a nearly complete spectrum of banned foreign titles in the 1580s. Imprints from Basel surfaced most frequently, but the pressmarks of Geneva, Strasburg, and Zurich were also found. Each kind of contraband was brought in to satisfy a precise reader demand.

Undoubtedly, the greatest number of customers for contraband sought occult titles. Nobles and commoners, clerics and laymen, resorted to the occult arts for reasons of greed, desire for power over the elements, desire for success in love, and curiosity. The number of occult Inquisition trials increased in the 1580s, even though Rome repeatedly cautioned prudence and skepticism.[49] The punishment of occult practitioners attracted great attention; an overflowing crowd attended the public abjuration of four offenders in St. Mark's Basilica in 1580. However, despite severe civil punishment, such as the 1585 beheading of a noble for demonology, Venetian interest in the hidden knowledge grew.[50]

Some famous occult authors, like Agrippa, were banned outright, and Rule IX of the Tridentine Index prohibited all other occult titles except astrological works that preserved free will. Yet readers knew that the books were available. On one occasion a prisoner of the Holy Office repeatedly begged a fellow prisoner, a bookman, to get an Agrippa for him; how the incarcerated bookman could have executed the commission is not clear.[51] Occult titles surfaced regularly both in the Inquisition trials of those who pursued the hidden arts and in other trials.[52] Vigorous demand from a large clientele, which embraced the nobility, meant that occult titles were the most numerous of the prohibited titles smuggled into Venice.

Northern humanistic and scientific works authored by Protestants com-

---

[49] I have not counted the occult trials, but have noted that they begin to appear frequently in the 1580s. Cecchetti, *La Repubblica di Venezia*, II, p. 5, shows that occult trials increased from 199 in the cinquecento to 695 in the seicento. For a series of papal cautions, 1567–1640, see Vaticanus Latinus 10945, ff. 143^r–44^r.

[50] For the 1580 abjuration, see Stella, *Chiesa e stato*, pp. 286–88; it is also mentioned by several chroniclers. For the 1585 execution, see VM, Mss. Italiani, Classe VII, 553 (8812), "Compendio di Francesco da Molin," pp. 134–35.

[51] SU, Bu. 61, Giovanni Battista Capponi, ff. [46^v–47^r], testimony of Giovanni Battista Milledonne of June 30, 1588.

[52] In addition to the examples already mentioned, see SU, Bu. 48, Fra Ippolito da Bagno, 1581; Bu. 50, Tommaso Cazzola, 1583; Bu. 64, Domenico Canal, 1589; Bu. 64, Bernardo Morosini, 1589; Bu. 67, Giulio Ricci, 1591. Also see the inventory of Claudio Textor's books (1587) in Stella I, 180–82. Of course, Italians the length of the peninsula had banned occult works; see DTC, Roman Inquisition, Sentences and Abjurations. Mss. 1225, 1226, 1227, sentences for 1580–82. For one example of many, see Ms. 1225, ff. 209^r–15^v, sentence of Urbano di Steffano Mandolini of Ferrara, May 15, 1580, who had Agrippa and other works.

prised the next largest group of prohibited titles sought by readers. Several trials suggest that those of humanistic bent disobeyed the Index because it denied them access to much northern European scholarship. Older readers molded by Erasmian humanism in freer times especially resented the Index; since permission to hold prohibited books was practically impossible to obtain, they ignored the Index and tried to escape detection.[53] In 1574 the Inquisition interrogated a lawyer and druggist, aged either seventy-four or eighty-four, who had around eighteen prohibited titles, nearly all authored by northern humanists. Included were several titles of Erasmus, four of Melanchthon, and single works of Lefevre d'Etaples, Simon Grynaeus, Hegendorff, Andreas Osiander, and Sebastian Muenster. The man had purchased the books from booksellers on the Rialto bridge, but he would not (or could not) be more precise. Admonished by the inquisitor that prohibited books fostered evil in their readers, he answered that this was true only if the reader's intention was bad.[54] The lawyer-druggist probably alluded to St. Paul's dictum, "To all who are pure themselves, everything is pure; but to those who have been corrupted and lack faith, nothing can be pure" (Titus 1:15), a favorite humanist defense for reading pagan literature. A Venetian who served the Republic for several years as a judge before becoming a monk, possessed many commentaries on the classics by banned authors such as Celio Secondo Curione, Grynaeus, Hegendorff, Melanchthon, Peter Ramus, Joannes Rivius, and Joannes Sturm. He testified that they were necessary for his studies.[55] Banned scientific and humanistic titles, especially those of Erasmus, appeared frequently in the trials of the 1580s. As with the occult titles, the reader needed no heretical commitment to disobey the Index.

Assessing the quantity of smuggled northern Protestant religious titles, as well as the magnitude of the demand, is difficult. Nevertheless, it is clear that commentaries on, and editions of, the Bible, including those of Erasmus, made up a large part of the total—probably more than half. Even the papacy recognized the high level of Protestant biblical scholarship and attempted to counter it by encouraging Catholic efforts. But until the papal program bore fruit with the Clementine Vulgate of 1592, readers

---

[53] Readers asked repeatedly for permission to hold expurgated versions of "le cose d'Erasmo d'humanità" and Machiavelli, but Rome instructed the Venetian Inquisition to refuse them all. Vaticanus Latinus 10945, ff. 112[r] (May 19, 1576), 113[v] (May 2, 1579). Also see Rotondò, "Nuovi documenti," p. 157; and "La censura ecclesiastica e la cultura," p. 1,449.

[54] SU, Bu. 37, Marcantonio Valgolio, testimony of April 24, May 4, 8, 1574. His prohibited titles are listed in App. II.

[55] SU, Bu. 47, Fra Clemente Valvassore, ff. 44[r–v], 68[v] (his testimony of June 30, 1580, and September 5, 1581), and his written defense of February 13, 1581, paragraphs 27–31. See App. II for his prohibited titles.

sought out the editions of Bèze, Erasmus, Robert Èstienne, Oecolampadius, Osiander, and others. Not only readers of Protestant leaning, but also religious scholars and others who wanted the best texts purchased them. Other customers came from the ranks of those who, unaware of the textual variations, bought Protestant versions carrying false title pages. Perhaps the clergy were the best customers, as the example of the Franciscan monk who purchased an Erasmus New Testament from Francesco Ziletti suggests. It is likely that the demand was large enough to warrant a steady flow of such works through smuggling.

The number of Italian and foreign heretics living in Venice, Padua, and nearby areas determined the demand for Protestant doctrinal titles. Girolamo Donzellini and Claudio Textor held heretical volumes at the time of their last arrests; how many native heretics avoided detection and kept their faith alive with heretical books brought in by Longo is unknown. Many more foreign Protestants, from nine hundred to a thousand, according to a reliable estimate, lived in Venice and Padua.[56] German Protestant students at Padua, as well as a few of other nationalities, comprised two hundred of this total. Despite repeated papal demands, the Republic neither barred them entry nor enforced the law demanding a profession of faith before graduation because it feared political and commercial repercussions from German Protestant princes. Besides, the foreign students contributed approximately 30,000 ducats annually to the Venetian economy.[57] The Protestant students probably brought heretical titles into the Venetian state, for there is no evidence that the Republic examined their baggage closely, and they possibly purchased additional contraband at selected bookstores. Certainly the students disseminated heresy; for example, a group of Greeks from Crete studying at Padua between 1560 and 1568 obtained heretical books from Flemish, German, and Italian Protestants, and were converted.[58]

Another seven hundred German Protestants lived and worked in Venice. Of them, approximately two hundred merchants (including their employees and servants) lived in the Fondaco dei tedeschi; about five hundred artisans (especially bakers, tailors, and watchmakers) lived elsewhere in the city.[59] The Germans freely expressed their views and read what they pleased within the Fondaco, but the artisans outside were obliged to conform to Catholic practices. The merchants in particular, and the artisans

[56] The estimate is that of ex-nuncio Alberto Bolognetti in 1581. Stella, *Chiesa e stato,* pp. 277–79.

[57] Letter and memorandum of Nuncio Facchinetti of September 14, 1566, in *Nunziature* VIII, 105–9.

[58] SU, Bu. 27, Emmanuele Mara, Francesco Cassimati, e Francesco Gentile, testimony and documents of June 14, 1568, through August 24, 1572.

[59] Stella, *Chiesa e stato,* pp. 278–79.

to a lesser extent, probably brought from their homeland some contraband books to be distributed, and occasionally purchased Protestant works from the bookmen.

Smuggling also helped the bookmen to meet the demand for banned Italian imprints. Publishers in Basel, Geneva, and Zurich printed Ochino's works in Italian and Latin in the 1550s and 1560s; undoubtedly the Venetian bookmen smuggled some of these into the city to replenish dwindling stocks of older Venetian imprints. The same held true for other banned Italian authors. A bookstore inventory made in 1584 listed eighteen copies of the "Dialoghi del Machiavelli in ottavo"; whatever the true title, the quantity suggests that the proprietor had recently obtained a fresh supply of Machiavelli's works from somewhere.[60] After John Wolfe of London began to reprint Aretino and Machiavelli in Italian editions carrying fictitious title pages in the 1580s, Venetian bookmen could buy them at the Frankfurt fairs and smuggle them south.

The availability of prohibited titles and the existence of smuggling demonstrated the practical limits of the Inquisition's power.[61] The tribunal was able to halt the publication of prohibited titles, but it lacked the resources to search out and destroy every banned volume. It could not completely halt the clandestine importation and distribution of prohibited titles since the state would not grant it wider powers, such as the right to impose surprise house searches and to expel foreigners. The Venetian government was unwilling to disrupt its commerce for the sake of banned books or to throw its full police apparatus into the fight. The illegal book traffic could have been stopped completely only through the deployment of police-state methods characteristic of the twentieth century, a procedure beyond the conception of both church and state.

The Inquisition could, at most, hold the traffic down to an acceptable

---

[60] Giudici di Petizion, Inventari, Bu. 338, nos. 43–44, Anzollo Bonfadini, April 19, 1584, f. 4ʳ. Bonfadini, at the sign of the Diamante in San Moisè, may have been Angelo Bonfadio, who published two titles in 1582, or a relative of two Bonfadini active as small publishers in the 1590s. Possibly Bonfadini had Wolfe imprints, for the London publisher sent part of his output abroad for sale in Catholic lands. But the date on this inventory makes it doubtful. Wolfe's initial printings of Machiavelli (the *Prince* and *Discourses*, usually found bound together) were dated January 28, 1584. Woodfield believes that this was an old style date, hence 1585. See Denis Woodfield, *Surreptitious Printing in England 1550–1640* (New York City, 1973), pp. 9–10, 96–99.

[61] Possibly the Venetian experience was little different from that of other cities. Heretics confessing to the Inquisitions of Turin, Cremona, Mantua, and Ferrara, 1580–82, admitted holding Calvin's *Institutes* and *Catechism*, and titles of Hermannus Bodius, Brunfels, Curione, Melanchthon, Oecolampadius, Ochino, Francesco Negri, Vermigli, and Pierre Viret. DTC, Ms. 1225, ff. 30ʳ⁻ᵛ, 75ʳ–79ᵛ; Ms. 1226, ff. 86ʳ–87ᵛ, 255ʳ, 419ᵛ–21ʳ.

level. An evaluation of its success depends on the subject matter of the prohibited volumes and the definition of "acceptable." Many trials of the 1570s and 1580s suggest that a reader could locate banned occult, humanistic, and scriptural titles after a relatively casual search. But it is likely that Protestant doctrinal works were unavailable to all but a few determined readers willing to undergo great difficulty, expense, and risk. If far from complete success, this was no small achievement. It signified that the Holy Office, with the aid of the state, quarantined all but a few Italians against Protestant literature. And even if the Holy Office did not discover Longo's illicit activities until 1587, his execution must have given pause to others. They may have suspended smuggling until the change in the political climate in the 1590s signaled declining enforcement.

VII

VENICE AND ROME PART COMPANY

THE Venetians checked the power of the Holy Office in the 1590s. After the important trials of the 1560s, the patriciate and the papacy had agreed on the role of the Holy Office and allotted it an essential place in Venetian life. But in the 1590s, as a result of various economic, political, and ideological stimuli, the patriciate changed its attitude toward the Inquisition, a shift as fundamental as the gradual move to support the tribunal in the 1550s. The leaders of the Republic curtailed the scope of the Holy Office and exerted greater control over its operations to bring it in line with the views on ecclesiastical jurisdiction prevailing in the highest ranks of government.

The Venetian desire to alter the role of the Holy Office, and the stubborn refusal of the papacy and local inquisitors to change their ways, generated the friction. With some justice the Venetians asserted that the churchmen had failed to honor agreements on the functioning of the Holy Office and that the Republic sought changes to eradicate abuses. More to the point, widespread acceptance of Counter Reformation values and Venetian lack of supervision had allowed the growth of de facto modifications in the operation of the tribunal, especially in the Dominion. The Venetians had to adopt an aggressive stance to restore what they felt to be a proper balance.

Disputes over the Holy Office were one facet of the intense jurisdictional strife that marked the whole spectrum of Venetian-papal relations in the 1590s. On a variety of fronts the two powers were edging their way toward new understandings in their usual fashion: interminable wrangling over a series of individual cases. The Venetians strove to alter arrangements of the previous decades and militantly refused to make the compromises that had brought resolution in the past.[1] The papacy appeared to accept

---

[1] For example, Paolo Paruta, ambassador to the Holy See, on his own initiative in 1595 sought out Clement VIII and worked out a solution to the problem of sovereignty over Ceneda in which the papacy made many concessions. But to his chagrin, the Senate refused to ratify the settlement, and the dispute festered on. Gaetano Cozzi, "Paolo Paruta, Paolo Sarpi e la questione della sovranità su Ceneda,"

change, and relied on resistance and inertia to maintain the status quo. The antagonism steadily increased.

It has been argued that the rise of a new group of leaders explains Venetian jurisdictional militancy.[2] According to this interpretation, Leonardo Donà (1536–1612) was the leader of the *giovani,* a faction of patricians who came to power in the constitutional crisis of 1582–83 and attempted to turn the Republic toward a pro-French, anti-Spanish, foreign policy, to recover the Republic's historical maritime commercial position and, above all, to assert lay jurisdiction at the expense of the local church and the papacy. Although no change of leadership occurred in 1582–83, some of the *giovani* did reach the highest governmental circles in the 1590s, after death had thinned the ranks of those who had dominated the chief offices in the previous decades.[3] Then Donà did lead the Republic toward greater jurisdictional militancy, although not toward a maritime revival.

But the concept of new men with new ideas provides only a partial explanation for Venetian combativeness. Giovanni di Bernardo Donà (d. 1591—not a close relative of Leonardo) and Nicolò Da Ponte (d. 1585), powerful figures of an earlier generation, had advocated vigorous antipapal policies, but persuaded the rest of the leadership only when an overriding economic or political interest was at stake. By contrast, Leonardo Donà led the Collegio and Senate majorities in the 1590s. Moreover, Giacomo di Alvise Foscarini, Donà's chief rival, stood with Donà on most issues even though nuncios identified him as a *vecchio,* a propapal conservative.[4]

The tangle of political and economic differences did much to set the stage for jurisdictional wrangling. Conflicting claims over navigational

---

BSV, 4 (1962), 205–6. The most recent survey of Venetian-papal relations is Gino Benzoni, *Venezia nell'età della controriforma* (Milan, 1973).

[2] Cozzi, *Contarini,* pp. 1–52, is the fundamental work. Also see Aldo Stella, "Le regolazione delle pubbliche entrate e la crisi politica veneziana del 1582," in *Miscellenea in onore di Roberto Cessi,* vol. 2 (Rome, 1958), pp. 157–71; Stella, *Chiesa e stato,* pp. 3–12, 65–69; and Bouwsma, *Venice,* pp. 232–92.

[3] Lowry, "Reform of the Council of Ten," pp. 275–310, shows with a careful analysis of officeholders, before and after, the narrow limits of the reform.

[4] The somewhat older Foscarini (1523–1602) reached the ranks of the Council of Ten (1577) and Savii grandi (1580) in the same years as Donà, and the Procuratorship (1580) at the same age as Donà. Foscarini and Donà dominated governmental councils in the 1590s, and the two, plus Marino Grimani, the eventual winner, contested the ducal election of 1595. Perhaps the differences between the two were less of substance than of style. Donà always presented his views in militant language, Foscarini more moderately. Cozzi, *Contarini,* pp. 12, n. 1, 38, 86, 95, n. 1, sees Foscarini as a *vecchio;* Lowry, "Church and Venetian Political Change," pp. 346–48, provides details on his political career and wealth.

rights in the Adriatic generated endless friction. The Venetians were distressed to see neighboring Ferrara pass from the Este to the more powerful papacy in the winter of 1597–98. On the other hand, the Venetian plan to divert the Po, which the papacy correctly foresaw would silt the harbor of Goro and flood lands on the papal side of the river, angered Rome, as did the Venetian refusal to join hostilities against the Turks.[5] The papacy gradually escaped Spanish tutelage in the 1590s, but it still favored Madrid too much for Venetian comfort. No overwhelming issue, such as the Cyprus War or the discovery of heresy within the nobility, moderated Venetian jurisdictional militancy.

Of all issues in the political-economic spectrum, the development of Venetian public policy favoring secular acquisition of ecclesiastical lands probably did the most to exacerbate relations with the papacy. Economic duress lay behind the policy, for a series of reverses, especially the shift from Mediterranean to Atlantic shipping, had reduced the patriciate's historical share in European commerce.[6] The increasing cost of patrician life, from dowries to foreign embassies, drove the nobles to find new sources of revenue. Inexorably nobles and commoners turned to the land in the late cinquecento; Terraferma properties promised greater and more secure profits than other ventures.[7] The government saw the reclamation of land by laymen as the answer to the perennial problem of providing food for the city without relying unduly on imports. It also hoped to realize additional tax money from mainland properties at a time of inflation and diminishing revenue from other sources.

When the nobility and the government turned to the land, they dis-

[5] In 1600 the Republic selected Foscarini and Donà to defend the diversion of the Po (completed in 1604) against papal opposition; Collegio, Esposizioni Roma, R. 9 and 10, show that they carried out their charge.

[6] Excellent studies of Venetian economic life in the late cinquecento and the seicento have appeared in recent years. Several of the most important are collected and edited by Brian Pullan, *Crisis and Change in the Venetian Economy in the Sixteenth and Seventeenth Centuries* (London, 1968). Pullan's introduction (pp. 1–21) is particularly useful for an overview, as are Davis, *Decline of the Venetian Nobility*, pp. 34–53, and Lane, *Venice*, pp. 274–389. Also see the complementary studies of Ugo Tucci, "The psychology of the Venetian merchant in the sixteenth century," and Pullan, "The occupations and investments of the Venetian nobility in the middle and late sixteenth century," in J. R. Hale ed., *Renaissance Venice* (London, 1973), pp. 346–78 and 379–408.

[7] In addition to the above, see Daniele Beltrami, *Saggio di storia dell'agricoltura nella Repubblica di Venezia durante l'età moderna* (Venice-Rome, 1955); and *La penetrazione economica dei veneziani in terraferma. Forze di lavoro e proprietà fondiaria nelle campagne venete dei secoli XVII e XVIII* (Venice-Rome, 1961); and Aldo Stella, "La crisi economica veneziana della seconda metà del secolo XVI," *Archivio veneto*, ser. v, 58–59 (1956), pp. 17–69.

covered that the church was already there.[8] Neither the Venetians nor the papacy knew exactly how much land the church held, but contemporary estimates put the figure at anywhere from one-sixth to one-half in various regions of the Terraferma. Although many ecclesiastical institutions and individuals lived in poverty, a few were very wealthy and inevitably attracted attention. Moreover, it appears that the Republic realized little tax revenue from church properties in comparison to the profits that some ecclesiastical persons and institutions enjoyed. Inefficiency, peculation, inaccurate assessments, and the necessity of obtaining prior approval from the pope and from bishops frustrated Venetian efforts to collect taxes on church lands. But probably the extensive network of ecclesiastical exemptions most angered the Venetians. The mendicant orders claimed to be exempt, although they occasionally paid a little, but lucrative benefices held *in commendam* by foreign, i.e., non-Venetian, prelates escaped taxation. These exemptions could lead to infuriating situations, as when the Knights of Malta claimed tax exemption at the same time that they practiced piracy on Venetian shipping.

Gradually the government decided to reduce ecclesiastical land holdings. The food crisis of 1590–91, the worst of the century, brought on by a succession of bad harvests, soaring population, and diminished grain shipments from the Levant, provided the catalyst. It underscored the importance of terraferma agriculture and convinced the government that with these lands and proper legislation the city could achieve autarky in food production. At this moment the Republic launched the first attack on ecclesiastical land tenure, choosing the abbey of San Zeno of Verona as the target. Extremely large and conspicuously wealthy during a period of famine, the abbey acted as a fiscal and judicial state-within-a-state with its own bank, marketing system, and courts. A stream of complaints against the abbey from lay tenants led to senatorial scrutiny of its affairs in the autumn of 1591, when the food crisis was most severe and the papacy effectively paralyzed by a succession of conclaves.[9] In May 1592 the Senate swept away most of the fiscal and judicial structure of the abbey.[10] Clement VIII tried for nearly a year to reopen the case but was

[8] The argument that follows is based on the excellent analysis of Lowry in ch. IV, "Property and the Church: Economic Background," and ch. v, "Property and the Church: From Principle to Policy," in his "Church and Venetian Political Change," pp. 201–93. Also see Aldo Stella, "La proprietà ecclesistica nella Repubblica di Venezia dal secolo XV al XVIII," *Nuova rivista storica* 42 (1958), 50–77.

[9] Gregory XIV was elected on December 5, 1590, and died October 15, 1591. Innocent IX was elected October 27 and died December 30, 1591. Clement VIII was not elected until January 30, 1592.

[10] The majority of the Savii grandi who proposed the law to the Senate are

forced to concede in the spring of 1593. The Venetians went on to assert civil control over church lands in a series of additional cases in the 1590s.

The Republic turned practice into public policy with laws of 1602, 1604, and 1605.[11] The first severely limited the litigation rights of ecclesiastics who wished to regain possession of lands let to laymen. Many nobles had invested heavily in leasing and developing ecclesiastical properties; Leonardo Donà, for example, rented over six hundred fields from the abbey of San Zeno in Verona, and Giacomo Foscarini and other powerful patricians had made similar investments.[12] Most often they leased the land with an emphyteusis contract, in which the monastery or bishop conceded the right to cultivate the land and to enjoy the fruits for a long period of time in exchange for an annual rent, which might be very low. The Senate's law of May 23, 1602, in effect transferred ownership to lay lessees so long as they paid the rent. On January 10, 1604, the Senate decreed that its approval had to be obtained before any new churches might be built in the Dominion. The government obviously wished to prevent the foundation of new ecclesiastical institutions and to halt the expansion of existing ones. On March 26, 1605, the Senate moved to prevent the church from adding to its lands by placing severe restrictions on the bequeathal of property to church bodies. A layman might transfer land to the church for up to two years, but then the church had to sell to a layman.

The Venetians reached several goals with this policy. The government secured a larger part of the Republic's food supply by bringing additional lands under lay ownership, where they would more easily be controlled in times of distress. It also enlarged the tax base by guaranteeing lay tenancy with its accompanying tax liability. The leaders of the Republic protected their own extensive holdings in church lands and facilitated the transformation from a commercial, to a landed, patriciate. But the policy contributed heavily to the growth of Venetian-papal tension; Paul V cited Venetian refusal to repeal the land laws as partial justification for laying Venice under interdict in early 1606. Like other economic and political differences, the Republic's appetite for ecclesiastical lands helped nurture a more hostile jurisdictional climate within which the Inquisition had to act.

---

usually considered to be protectors of clerical rights: Alberto Badoer, Marcantonio Barbaro, Lorenzo Bernardo, Giacomo Foscarini, and Alvise Zorzi. Lowry, "Church and Venetian Political Change," p. 287.

[11] These are printed in Enrico Cornet, *Paolo V e la Repubblica Veneta. Giornale dal 22 ottobre 1605–9 giugno 1607* (Vienna, 1859), pp. 265, 268–69.

[12] For the holdings of various patricians, see Lowry, "Church and Venetian Political Change," pp. 210, 344 (for Donà); 347–48 (Foscarini); 362 (Giovanni Soranzo); 363 (Bernardo Tiepolo).

1. LAY JURISDICTION OVER PUBLIC MORALITY

The jurisdictional issue joined in the 1590s was whether lay or ecclesiastical authority would exercise punitive control over sinners who were simultaneously criminals. Church and state had each claimed for many years the right to regulate the moral, religious, and social lives of both clergy and laymen and to punish violators in their respective courts. But a clear jurisdictional division of responsibility often did not exist, however persuasively one side or the other argued. For two to three decades church and state organs had glossed over differences and shared jurisdiction more or less amicably. But in the last years of the cinquecento, the Venetian Republic, like other states, extended lay jurisdiction.[13]

Venetian patricians shared with Vatican prelates a faith in the use of legislation and punishment to encourage virtue in the society that they jointly led. Both pursued within Catholic paths the twin goals of social stability and spiritual salvation.[14] Fundamental accord is hardly surprising, for the same religious values had shaped both groups. The works of the extremely popular Luis de Granada strongly influenced Leonardo Donà, who attempted to follow their precepts: resist temptation, frequent the sacraments, mortify the body, pray often, read edifying literature, and do good works.[15] Contemporaries agreed that Donà lived up to these goals,[16] as did Cardinal Carlo Borromeo, whom Donà esteemed personally and whose works he annotated.[17] But Donà and Borromeo differed strongly over whether the state, by means of its legislative and judicial organs, or the church, through parish priest and Holy Office, should play the dominant role. Much of the heated jurisdictional strife of the last years of the cinquecento in Venice and elsewhere stemmed from the pursuit of the same goal of the stable society of God-fearing citizens—through different means. Had either the Roman prelates or the Venetian nobles been less sincerely desirous of the common end, or less convinced of the means of reaching it, relations would have been much smoother.

[13] Church-state jurisdictional disputes marked Milanese history, 1596–1615, and a concordat in the latter year only partially resolved them. Mario Bendiscioli, "Politica, amministrazione e religione nell'età dei Borromei," in *Storia di Milano*, vol. x, *L'età della Riforma Cattolica (1559–1630)* (Milan, 1957), 314–18, 322–28. Also see A. D. Wright, "Why the *Venetian* Interdict?" *English Historical Review* 89 (1974), 534–50.

[14] The Republic's poor relief should be kept in mind. Pullan, *Rich and Poor*, shows how ecclesiastical and state organizations worked together to alleviate misery, promote social stability, and save the souls of donor and recipient.

[15] Seneca, *Donà*, pp. 33–38.

[16] See the comments of Nuncio Bolognetti in 1580, as quoted by Cozzi, *Contarini*, p. 32, n. 1.

[17] Seneca, *Donà*, p. 123.

In addition to their commitment to the moral society, the Venetian patriciate, like other European rulers, were attracted to the theories of state absolutism. Widespread turbulence stimulated a universal desire for peace and stability, and at the end of the century only the state's authority promised to provide them. Frenchmen desperately seeking to escape the religious wars permitted Henry IV to enlarge the crown's authority in the hope that peace would follow. Jean Bodin and others provided the ideological foundation by elaborating the political doctrines that culminated in the concept of the divine right of kings. Elizabeth I and James I followed a similar path and were supported by similar theories; the petty princes of Italy and Germany aped their powerful brothers and leaned on the same ideological props. Nearly everywhere the highest authority in the state attempted to eliminate constitutional, historical, and institutional checks, and to extend its control over the total life of the citizenry.

Although a republic rather than a princedom, Venice shared in this development. At the time of the interdict Sarpi and others argued that, since states were instituted by God to govern men, governments were responsible only to God.[18] The state could direct every aspect of life in society on behalf of the public good, which was to be defined by the government. They asserted the unified, inalienable, and unlimited sovereignty of the state, over which no private interest or right, whether individual or corporate, ecclesiastical or lay, could take precedence. Sarpi concluded that the Venetian state thus had the right to determine the use of all property within its boundaries and to punish all criminals, whether clerics or laymen.

The theoretical defense legitimatized a growing practice. Years before Sarpi's eloquent treatises, the Venetian government had expanded its control over morals and social life. The Council of Ten had already empowered the Esecutori contro la bestemmia to punish blasphemers, sodomites, occult practitioners, and corrupt clergymen; beginning in the 1570s it added prostitutes, vagabonds, gamblers, and those who disturbed public order.[19] Laws designed to arrest sin were often repealed or allowed to lapse when the danger was past, but those of the 1570s and 1580s were upheld into the next century, eloquent testimony to the strain felt by the leadership trying to guide the Republic through difficult times.

Not only did the Venetians pass more laws, but they also imposed the death penalty far more frequently in the last quarter of the century. The contrast with earlier years was dramatic: in the first two decades of the cinquecento the government carried out 22 death sentences. The figure dropped to 9 for the entire period between 1520 and 1569. But it rose to

[18] Bouwsma, *Venice*, pp. 431–41.
[19] Cozzi, *Religione, moralità a Venezia*, pp. 10–11, 15, 18–19, 26–36.

22 in the 1570s, to 42 in the 1580s, and to a height of 68 in the 1590s. The state courts continued this harsh policy in the early seicento, carrying out 47 executions in the first decade and 46 in the next. All crimes punishable by death—treason, rebellion, homicide, theft, blasphemy, and sodomy—increased, but perhaps the greatest rise occurred in crimes of violence that also threatened public order. "Assassins of the street" frequently suffered capital punishment in the last quarter of the century.[20]

Whether the increase in executions reflected a growth of crime, or greater use of capital punishment to deal with the same quantity of crime, or a combination of both is difficult to determine. But certainly more frequent recourse to the death penalty and repeated affirmation of the laws testified to the leaders' real fears for the moral and social fabric of the Republic. Inevitably the state's heightened concern altered its view of the Holy Office.

Crimes such as homicide and theft presented no church-state jurisdictional conflict unless the accused was a clergyman. But a wide range of moral offenses with social consequences did, for by the 1590s the Esecutori and other civil courts occupied much of the same jurisdictional turf claimed by the Inquisition. Like the state, the Holy Office had also expanded its jurisdictional claims. After mid-century various popes asserted inquisitorial jurisdiction over sodomites, bigamists, Judaizing Christians, occult practitioners, solicitors in the confessional, and other sinners.[21] By the end of the century, the Inquisition in Rome and other Italian cities tried few accused heretics but a multitude of other offenders.[22] The Vene-

---

[20] Newberry Library, Case/MS/6A/34, "Vollume de' Giustiziati in Venezia," ff. 10–28.

[21] For papal Inquisition legislation and an analysis of the kind of inquisitorial activity in Rome, see Pastor, XIII, 213; XIV, 265–69; XVI, 309–19; XVII, 288–316, 331–333; XIX, 296–308; XXI, 192–95; XXIV, 198–202, 561–63.

[22] A Congregation of the Inquisition decree of June 4, 1580, ordered local tribunals to send annually to Rome copies of the abjurations accepted and sentences handed down. Vaticanus Latinus 10945, f. 2^r. Some of these survive in DTC, Roman Inquisition, Sentences and Abjurations. Mss. 1225 (sentences of 1580), 1226 (1581–82), 1227 (1582), 1228 (1603), 1229 (1607). The sentences are from all over Italy, for example, from Bergamo, Brescia, Casale, Como, Cremona, Mantua, Milan, Turin, Venice, Verona, Vicenza, etc., in ms. 1225. Only a minority of the sentences dealt with heresy. In ms. 1227 (1582), local Inquisitions had many cases of necromancy, witchcraft, Judaizing Christians, and repentant apostates who wished to return to Catholicism upon escaping Turkish captivity. In ms. 1228 (1603), the reported sentences involved the above offenses as well as polygamy, but practically no Protestantism. One caution should be entered; if the Venetian cases mentioned are any indication, only the results of the more notable trials were forwarded to Rome. But this would not alter the picture, for surely most heresy sentences were considered noteworthy.

tian Holy Office claimed the same broad powers but had its hands full with heretics and holders of prohibited books until the 1580s. Then the Venetian tribunal began to concentrate on other offenses. Heresy was the charge in 843 trials in the cinquecento but only 175 in the seicento. Trials dealing with necromancy, magic, and witchcraft increased from 199 to 695; blasphemy, from 65 to 146; solicitation in the confessional, from 5 to 78; and polygamy, from 5 to 17.[23] The Holy Office began to punish bookmen who disobeyed civil imprimatur and copyright laws in the last years of the 1580s, the first time that the tribunal had ventured into this area—clearly reserved to the Esecutori—since Fra Peretti was inquisitor (1557–59).[24] Ironically, the Inquisition's success in curbing heresy contributed to its loss of power, for when the state had less need of protection from heresy, it nourished its own jurisdictional ambitions and cast a hostile eye at inquisitorial expansion.

A closer look at polygamy provides some insight into the motives behind, and the results of, the state's move into a jurisdictional area claimed by diocesan courts and the Holy Office. A 1577 law of the Council of Ten lamented that certain villainous scoundrels induced women to cohabitate with them under the pretext of clandestine marriage. After enjoying the girl's favors for a while, the scoundrel discarded her by obtaining the dissolution of the "marriage" by appealing to the Tridentine decrees, which freed him to contract another union. The Council of Ten ordered the Esecutori to punish the evildoers with imprisonment, the galleys, banishment, and fines. The Esecutori was to contact the patriarchal tribunal monthly to obtain the names of malefactors.[25]

A complex situation lay behind the law. Before Trent some theologians held that an exchange of consents between the two parties (*per verba de praesenti*) without benefit of priest or witnesses constituted a clandestine

---

[23] These statistics were compiled by Cecchetti, *La Repubblica di Venezia*, II, 4–7. Because of the gap in the trials, the figures are for 1541–92, and 1616–99, respectively. Although I have not attempted a count, it is my impression that the changeover from heresy to other offenses, especially to necromancy, occurred in the 1580s. Moreover, the material in BAVa, Mss. Barberino 5195 and 5205, and Vaticanus Latinus 10945, confirms the impression that heresy was no longer the major part of inquisitorial activity in the 1590s. Also see the remark of Nuncio Antonio Maria Graziani: "Io sono certissimo della religione di questa città, et non ho bisogno di altri segni; ma andando almeno due volte alla settimana alla inquisitione, resto grandemente consolato, che non sento altro se non questa donniciola ha fatto una bagatella, et quella un'altra, et non esserci altra cosa di momento." Collegio, Esposizioni Roma, R. 6, f. 166^v, September 6, 1596.

[24] SU, Bu. 60, Roberto Mileto [i.e., Meietti], October 13, 1587; Bu. 61, Grazioso Percachino, May 5, 1588; Bu. 63, Giovanni Antonio Rampazetto e Camillo Zanelli, November 24 through December 10, 1588; Bu. 65, Domenico Farri, January 18, 1590.

[25] Cozzi, *Religione, moralità a Venezia*, pp. 16–18.

but valid marriage. These theologians argued that the contracting parties conferred the sacrament on each other. Under pressure from the French and Spanish governments, the Council of Trent decided to rule on marriage, and found itself sharply divided. The majority held that clandestine marriage had to be abolished; a substantial minority argued that it was illicit but, nonetheless, valid. In November 1563, after much debate, the Council adopted the majority position. It conceded that a clandestine union, considered in itself, was a true marriage, but it went on to establish the public forms that constituted a valid marriage in the eyes of ecclesiastical and civil authorities: proclamation of the banns, exchange of consents in the presence of a priest and two witnesses, and recording of the details in the parish register. Previous clandestine unions were nullified and had to be regularized. The Council awarded jurisdiction over marital disputes to ecclesiastical tribunals.[26] But the decree was not generally accepted or understood, especially on the popular level, and clandestine marriages continued. Faced with a confused populace, episcopal courts dealt with the situation on an ad hoc basis, sometimes handing down rulings at variance with canon law.[27] The legislation of the Council of Ten indicated that some individuals took advantage of the muddle.

Undoubtedly the government sincerely desired to preserve the honor of Venetian women. But more—or less—than virtue was at stake. In addition to "carnality," Sarpi pointed out, "stealing dowries" and "similar reasons" were common motives for bigamy.[28] Legitimacy, noble status, dowries, and inheritances all depended on the public record of a valid marriage. To preserve intact the family patrimony, Venetian nobles commonly permitted only one or two of their children to marry.[29] They had no intention of leaving open the escape hatch of a clandestine marriage.

The Venetians held as axiomatic that any dispute having financial consequences should go to a secular court because the state had a legitimate interest in the disposal of money. They held to this view in marital litigations despite the Tridentine decree.[30] But close liaison between the In-

[26] Hubert Jedin, *Crise et dénouement du Concile de Trente, 1562–1563. Une rétrospective après quatre cents ans*, trans. from the German by Ephrem Florival (Paris, 1965), pp. 156–60. The decrees are in *Conciliorum oecumenicorum decreta*, pp. 729–35.

[27] See the study based on marriage cases before the episcopal courts of Feltre and Padua in the late 1560s of Pietro Rasi, "L'applicazione delle norme del Concilio di Trento in materia matrimoniale," in *Studi di storia e diritto in onore di Arrigo Solmi* (Milan, 1941), I, 233–81.

[28] "Ma quando o per carnalità o per rubbar la dote o altri simili rispetti alcun ha preso la seconda moglie. . . ." *Scritti giurisdizionalistici*, p. 172.

[29] Davis, *Decline of the Venetian Nobility*, pp. 62–72.

[30] Rasi cites a 1566 clandestine marriage case involving a dowry in which the episcopal judge agreed that the civil court should rule. "L'applicazione delle norme," pp. 273–74.

quisition and the civil courts held the friction to a minimum in the 1570s. Indeed, members of the Avvogaria di commun, the supreme Venetian court, frequently came to the nuncio's house to discuss marital disputes and other cases before the Inquisition.[31]

Cooperation ended when the government claimed greater authority over cases involving bigamy. Disputes between the lay authorities and the Inquisition appeared first in the Terraferma in the 1580s and in Venice in the 1590s, growing more numerous in the last years of the Cinquecento and the first years of the following century.[32] As the Venetians advanced their claims more firmly, the nuncios regularly protested what they considered to be usurpations, although Clement VIII took no stand. One example can serve for many. In July 1598 the nuncio protested to the Collegio that the pope had decreed, and other states had accepted, that the Holy Office should exercise jurisdiction over accused bigamists, who violated the sacrament of matrimony, and thus committed heresy, by practicing polygamy. Leonardo Donà assured him that the lay courts punished bigamists more severely than the Inquisition. The nuncio agreed, and dropped the matter.[33]

The leadership's concern for public morality, especially for the morals

[31] Stella, *Chiesa e stato*, pp. 107, 137–38.

[32] There are nine jurisdictional disputes over matrimonial cases in Verona between 1580 and 1590, twenty-six others from the Dominion, 1590–1624, and eleven Venetian disputes 1591–1625, noted with the names of the accused bigamists in BAVa, Barberino Latino 5195, "Raccolta di alcuni negotij, e cause spettanti alla Santa Inquisitione nella Città e Dominio Veneto. Dal principio di Clemente VIII sino al presente mese di luglio MDCXXV," ff. 71ᵛ–75ᵛ. Twelve Venetian quarrels between 1592 and 1625, and twenty in the Dominion, 1590–1622 (some of them duplicates of those described in Barberino Latino 5195) are listed in Barberino Latino, 5205, identical title to Ms. 5195, ff. 17ʳ–20ʳ. (These two mss. are the same with the following exceptions: Part I and a short epilogue are nearly identical in chapter sequence and material within the two mss., but with minor variations in the organization and description of the disputes. Ms. 5195 lacks ff. 21ʳ–44ᵛ [chs. v through XII]; these can be found in Ms. 5205, ff. 13ᵛ–33ʳ. On the other hand, Ms. 5195 contains an appendix of Inquisition decrees and related disputes [ff. 66 bisʳ–109ʳ] not to be found in the other ms.) There are fourteen Venetian disputes, 1594–1628, and four Paduan disagreements, 1601–6, listed in Vaticanus Latinus 10945, ff. 132ʳ–33ᵛ. The names of the accused are not given. Sampling the years 1593–1614, Cozzi found that marriage cases ranged from 13 percent in 1606 to .8 percent in 1602 of the total caseload of the Esecutori, who tended to regularize the unions. *Religione, moralità a Venezia*, p. 38. It is interesting to note that the Republic was not the only state to claim jurisdiction over matrimony at this time. In England bigamy was an ecclesistical offense until 1603, when it became a felony.

[33] Collegio, Esposizioni Roma, R. 8 ff. 58ʳ⁻ᵛ, 67ᵛ–68ʳ (July 24, August 14, 1598). Similar protests and Venetian refusals are found in Senato, Deliberazioni Roma, R. 12, f. 54ʳ (July 31, 1598); R. 13, ff. 158ᵛ⁻ʳ (March 23, 1602); Collegio, Esposizioni Roma, R. 10, ff. 160ʳ⁻ᵛ (August 10, 1602); R. 11, 3ᵛ–4ʳ (September 6, 1602), 34ʳ⁻ᵛ (January 10, 1602 mv).

of the young patriciate on whom the future rested, was genuine, as was their belief in the rights of the state. Nevertheless, concrete political, financial, and personal motives also moved the Venetians toward civil absolutism. The state wanted to try bigamists because dowries and inheritances depended on valid unions. The ruling patricians tried to regulate gambling and prostitution to shield young nobles from financial ruin. The government wanted to remove Jews from the jurisdiction of the Holy Office because a civil court was more likely to keep in mind that the delicate rapport with the Turks partially depended on benevolent treatment of the Jews. Gradually a series of ad hoc initiatives took on the character of policy.

In every area where church and state had earlier shared jurisdiction and resolved disputes through accommodation, the government in the 1590s asserted stronger lay jurisdiction on a case-by-case basis. Many, perhaps a majority, of the blasphemers, infidels, Jews, Greek Orthodox communicants, and clergymen accused of crimes, as well as a certain number of those accused of magic and witchcraft, were tried in lay courts. They received immunity from Holy Office prosecution similar to that previously enjoyed by ultramontane scholars, German artisans, diplomats and their households, and foreign merchants.[34] Various governmental officers —the Esecutori, the Avvogadori di commun, members of the Collegio and Council of Ten, and Dominion rectors—intervened in the Inquisition with increasing frequency. The papacy protested regularly but futilely.

The Holy Office and Rome encountered many examples of what they considered to be unwarranted and high-handed lay action. In 1591 the Venetian governor of Sebenico imprisoned and expelled the inquisitor of Dalmatia and was, in turn, excommunicated by the local bishop. It was arranged that the governor would seek absolution, and the matter was smoothed over.[35] Another typical case occurred in the Dominion in 1602. The Holy Office of Capo d'Istria had already begun to examine a Jewess accused of blasphemy against the sacraments when the Venetian governor

---

[34] In 1599 the Venetian Holy Office sent to Rome a denunciation against Johann Andreas Fugger, the Venetian agent of the famous firm. Wistfully, the Roman Congregation asked under what conditions the Inquisition might proceed against Fugger? The Venetian inquisitor replied that, although no written agreement guaranteeing the immunity of merchants existed, there was no chance of prosecution. Barberino Latino 5195, ff. 88^{r-v}. In 1603, when the Republic made an alliance with the Protestant Grisons to keep the Valtelline out of Spanish and Milanese hands, the Venetians formalized the immunity from Holy Office prosecution of all foreign merchants so long as they did not import prohibited books, or act against the faith in any other way, while in Venice. See the letters of Nuncio Offredo degli Offredi of September 27, October 2, 4, 1603, in ASVa, Segretario di Stato, Venezia, F. 37, ff. 455^{r-v}, 462^v, 469^v–71^r.

[35] Barberino Latino 5195, f. 60^r.

took her into lay custody. The nuncio protested in the Collegio, but Doge Marino Grimani informed him that among the privileges granted to the Jews was the right to be tried by the state. As usual, the doge promised that the civil court would judge rigorously.[36] In Venice in 1596 the Esecutori arrested two men accused of heretical blasphemy. After finding them guilty of blasphemy, the Esecutori turned them over to the Inquisition to examine for heresy. The Holy Office found no heresy, but it had not completed its investigation when the Esecutori seized the men and immediately put them to death. Their blasphemies had been so shocking that public opinion demanded their execution. The nuncio made a token protest.[37]

Whenever the nuncio protested the state's moving into the jurisdiction of the Inquisition, the Venetians sought to pacify him with the assurance that the state's tribunals were more rigorous than the Holy Office. The evidence suggests that the state did deal more harshly with blasphemy, and possibly with other offenses, especially if the offense was public and reflected on the good reputation of the Republic. In these circumstances, even nobles were severely punished. In 1593 a group of men were denounced to the Inquisition for running through the streets at night singing hymns and litanies mixed with blasphemies and obscenities. Unable to apprehend them, the Inquisition went to the Heads of the Council of Ten, who offered a reward of 1,000 scudi for their capture. When the culprits were taken into custody, the nuncio and inquisitor asked that they be given to the Holy Office for trial. The government refused; it condemned the malefactors, including a member of the Vendramin family and possibly other young nobles, to death.[38]

[36] Collegio, Esposizioni Roma, R. 11, ff. 27^v-28^r (December 14, 1602); Senato, Dispacci da Roma, F. 49, f. 403^r (January 25, 1602 mv). Two more cases in which the Senate ordered that Inquisition suspects should be tried in lay courts are in Senato, Deliberazioni Roma, R. 12, ff. 94^{r-v} (Tolmezo, December 3, 1598), 76^r (Pordenone, October 10, 1598). Additional governmental interventions to restrict the activities of Terraferma inquisitors are found in Senato, Deliberazioni Roma, R. 13, ff. 142^{r-v} (Dalmatia, November 17, 1601), 161^v-62^r (Udine, April 6, 1602), 200^v (Conegliano, October 12, 1602).

[37] Letters of Nuncio Antonio Maria Graziani of November 14, 30, 1596, in VC, Ms. Morosini-Grimani, R. 359, "Tre volumi di lettere di Mons. Antonio Maria Gratiani dal Borgo S. Sepolcro, Vescovo d'Amelia, Scritte nella Nuntiatura sua di Venetia. 1596. 1597. 1598," pp. 104–5, 122–23. Other disputes concerning jurisdiction over blasphemy and sacrilege are to be found in Barberino Latino 5195, f. 20^v; Barberino Latino 5205, 14^v-17^r. For jurisdictional disputes over witchcraft cases, see Barberino Latino 5195, ff. 18^v-20^r; for disputes over Jews, Barberino Latino 5195, ff. 76^r-80^r; Barberino Latino 5205, ff. 20^r-22^v; Vaticanus Latinus 10945, f. 92^r. For disputes involving Greeks, see Barberino Latino 5195, ff. 80^r-82^v; Barberino Latino 5205, ff. 22^v-24^v.

[38] Barberino Latino 5205, f. 15^r. Case/MS/6A/34, f. 19, lists the decapitation in

Paul V cited the Venetian insistence on trying two clergymen in civil courts as part of the justification for laying Venice under interdict. This area was merely one of many in which the state asserted its power in the 1590s; and the case, only one of a series. Scandals and crimes involving the clergy were frequent, and the state often acted. In 1601 the Senate informed the nuncio that a group of Franciscans in Padua accused of robbery, sacrilege, attempting to poison their prior, and resisting arrest were to be tried by the lay arm. In 1602, in another case, Doge Grimani informed the nuncio that the Venetians were happy to cooperate with the Inquisition; nevertheless, secular courts would try ecclesiastics.[39] In short, the exercise of civil jurisdiction over clergymen was not unusual. What was extraordinary was the determination of Paul V to bring it to a halt.

2. THE REPUBLIC TIGHTENS ITS SUPERVISION OF THE HOLY OFFICE

Simultaneously with the assertion of lay jurisdiction over public morality, the Venetians examined more closely the internal operation of the Inquisitions in their state. The practice of conducting trials without lay participation, a longstanding habit of Dominion inquisitors, constituted the greatest abuse in the eyes of the Venetians.

The contention centered on the participation of the lay representatives, i.e., the Venetian governors in the Dominion, in "processi informativi," or information proceedings, such as denunciations, which preceded the arrest of the accused. In September 1551, at the end of a lengthy dispute over lay participation in Dominion Inquisitions, the Republic and the papacy came to an agreement. Sarpi looked upon it as a concordat, but papal apologists saw it as a concession or favor rather than a formal compact.[40] The agreement authorized the governors to be present "in everything that the Reverend Vicars and Inquisitors do."[41] Other laymen were ex-

---

December 1593 by the Council of Ten of three men, all age 20, bearing the noble names of Canal, Venier, and Trevisan. Perhaps they were part of the group.

[39] Senato, Deliberazioni Roma, R. 13, ff. 110ᵛ–11ʳ (May 8, 1601), 209ʳ (December 7, 1602).

[40] Sarpi, *Scritti giurisdizionalistici*, p. 123; *Opere*, ed. Cozzi and Cozzi, p. 1,206. Albizzi, *Risposta*, pp. 158–59. There is no agreement on the exact definition of a concordat. See Benedetto Ojetti, "Concordat," *The Catholic Encyclopedia*, IV, 196–203.

[41] "E a tutto quello, che operaranno i Reverendi Vicarij ed Inquisitori." Letter of the Capi del Consiglio dei Dieci to all the rectors in the Venetian state, September 26, 1551, in SU, Bu. 153, a packet of material entitled "Editti, lettere . . . . riguardanti il Santo Uffizio," arranged chronologically. Nuncio Ludovico Beccadelli confirmed the arrangement in the exact wording in a letter to the bishop of Belluno of October 20, 1551. Ibid. For the negotiations leading to the agreement, see the let-

cluded, although the inquisitor could call in experts, who might be laymen. In addition, the rectors were directed to meet weekly with the inquisitor and the episcopal vicar to discuss Inquisition matters. In effect, the agreement granted the provincial governors the same role played by the Tre savii in the Venetian Inquisition; when disputes arose in the following decade, the Venetians reaffirmed these terms.[42] Although the agreement of 1551 failed to make explicit reference to the various parts of an Inquisition trial, its meaning was clear: a Dominion Inquisition, like the tribunal in Venice, could take no action without the participation and concurrence of the civil representative.

With the acceptance of the Holy Office as an integral part of Venetian life, the Terraferma inquisitors had increasingly enjoyed a free hand. Their independence probably came about initially because the one or two Venetian governors in each Dominion city had many other duties to discharge. When a denouncer presented himself but the rector was unavailable, the temptation to proceed without him must have been overwhelming; the informant might fear to return at a later date, or the accused might flee. With Roman encouragement, proceeding without the lay governors became normal practice. In 1575, as a consequence of a problem that had arisen in Verona, the Congregation of the Holy Office instructed all Dominion inquisitors to examine "information witnesses" without the civil authority.[43] The instruction clearly violated the agreement of 1551. In 1589 the Congregation directed the inquisitor of Vicenza to try without civil assistance "persone Ecclesiastiche" and "persone secolari di Cologna o di altri luoghi," i.e., foreigners.[44] In 1591, on the grounds that Inquisitions were encountering difficulties, the Congregation renewed the general instruction of 1575, adding that witnesses might also be examined without the lay presence "in order not to lose the opportunity." Should the civil authorities object, the testimony could be repeated in their presence.[45] The Dominion Inquisitions followed Rome's orders. In 1597 the inquisitor of Verona reported that from 1575 to 1593 more than 460 witnesses had been examined without the presence of the lay representative. Other Dominion inquisitors reported similarly.[46] The governors had to be aware that local

---

ters of Nuncio Beccadelli and Cardinals Marcello Cervini and Girolamo Dandino of November 15, 1550 through October 19, 1551, in *Nunziature* v, 161–62, 164, 169, 173, 175–76, 221–22, 228–29, 279–81, 290, 294–95, 302–3. Paschini, *L'Inquisizione*, pp. 53–67, 78–83, deals with it extensively but not exhaustively.

[42] See the letters of Doge Girolamo Priuli to the rectors of Bergamo and Verona of May 18, and December 30, 1563, in SU, Bu. 153, "Editti, lettere. . . ." Moreover, one of the charges levied by the Venetians against Fra Peretti in 1560 was that he conducted "processi informativi" without the lay presence.

[43] Barberino Latino 5195, ff. 7[r–v].   [44] Vaticanus Latinus 10945, f. 14[r].

[45] Barberino Latino 5195, f. 7[v].   [46] Barberino Latino 5195, ff. 7[v]–8[r].

Inquisitions were acting without them and must have informed the Council of Ten, the body that oversaw the governors. But the Council ignored the situation. As the patriciate became comfortable with the Holy Office, they left far behind the prickly sensitivity of the 1550s.

A clamorous incident awakened the Venetians to the political consequences of their failure to oversee Dominion Inquisitions. In February 1591, on instructions from Pope Gregory XIV, Cardinal Giulio Antonio Santori,[47] head of the Congregation of the Inquisition, wrote to the Verona inquisitor asking about a group of Italians who had gone north to fight in the Protestant cause.[48] Rome had heard that three cavalry captains (two from Vicenza and one from Florence) had passed through Verona in December 1590 on their way to defend Geneva against the Duke of Savoy and to join the army of Henry of Navarre. The inquisitor, Fra Alberto da Lugo, went outside the tribunal to question two young Vicenzans, who confirmed the facts, but would not repeat their testimony before the Inquisition. The inquisitor did, however, find a local man who was cooperative. The witness testified before the tribunal that he and others had been solicited to join the captains, and he promised to produce additional witnesses. But that same evening, the Verona *podestà*, acting under Venetian orders, arrested Fra Alberto and seized the papers of the Holy Office. Fra Alberto was taken to Venice and thrown into a "prigione scurissima" for two or seven days.[49]

[47] Santori (1532—made cardinal 1570–1602), called Santo Severina, came to Rome as a part of the Carafa entourage, and stayed to become a key Vatican figure.

[48] There are five sources for this incident, and although they agree generally on the events they differ considerably on the motivations of the participants, especially on the terms of the settlement, and on the significance of the incident. The best and most complete documentation is to be found in VC, Ms. P D C 808, "L'Inquisizione a Venezia, documenti storici." This ms. contains copies, probably from the nineteenth century, of documents dealing with the Holy Office from 1289 through the eighteenth century. For the Verona episode, there are eight unpaginated folios of excerpts dated March 1 through May 11, 1591, copied from the Consiglio dei Dieci, Senato, and Dispacci da Roma files, as well as from the "Annali della Republica di Venezia 1591–1592." Unless otherwise indicated, this source is followed. Albizzi, *Risposta*, pp. 143–45, claims to be based on Roman Holy Office records. It is particularly useful for a report on Fra Alberto's activities in Verona, but its account of the final settlement is unreliable. Another brief papal source suffers from the same defect: Barberino Latino 5195, ff. 16ᵛ–17ʳ. In his treatise of 1613 on the Inquisition, in *Scritti giurisdizionalistici*, p. 161, Sarpi used the episode to show that if lay assistants were absent, inquisitors would misuse their office by instigating "processi secreti" against the state and good men. In his "In materia di crear novo inquisitor di Venezia" of 1622, in *Opere*, ed. Cozzi and Cozzi, p. 1,209, he used the incident to demonstrate that inquisitors used their office to turn people against their prince. He also concluded that lay jurisdiction had sustained a setback because the Venetians gave the appearance of giving way to the pope.

[49] The accounts differ on the time in prison and how dark it was; Sarpi omits it altogether.

After Fra Albetro was interrogated and his papers examined, the Heads of the Council of Ten accused him of "forming a trial against the Republic." In their judgment, he had sought to embarrass the Venetians and had used false evidence and unreliable witnesses to do it. The Heads accused him of exceeding Roman instructions by taking testimony in writing and by asking "illicit" questions. A papal source notes that these questions included, In whose pay were the soldiers, and was their armor made in Verona?[50] The Heads ordered Fra Alberto to leave the Venetian state and never return.

The Venetians reacted strongly because Fra Alberto touched the most sensitive nerve of papal-Venetian relations at that moment: contrasting policies toward Henry of Navarre. The Republic recognized Navarre as king of France; Gregory XIV opposed him, and was renewing the excommunication and making ready to dispatch subsidies and troops to aid the Catholic League at the moment when the Verona affair erupted.[51] The Republic had assured Sixtus V that it had no intention of supporting Navarre with money or troops, but it clearly favored him.[52] Indeed, rumors circulated in Rome in 1592 that the Venetians were subsidizing the Huguenot general Lesdiguières.[53] Two of the three captains were Venetian subjects; perhaps the Venetians did not want Fra Alberto to learn who were the captains' paymasters?[54]

Gregory XIV and his advisors were conciliatory. They agreed that Fra Alberto had exceeded his commission, and they promised to resolve the situation in a way satisfactory to Venice. But then the pontiff began to learn of the repercussions of the episode; the other inquisitors in the Venetian state were so frightened that those of Bergamo and Vicenza fled, and the Venetian inquisitor wanted to leave. To reassure the inquisitors and to stop the rumors, the pontiff asked that Fra Alberto be allowed to return to Verona as inquisitor. The pope promised that Fra Alberto would not exercise his office upon his return, and that he would be recalled shortly. The Venetians agreed; Fra Alberto returned to Verona, and was relieved within two to three months.[55]

Both sides probably wished to close the incident quickly and quietly. After halting the use of a Dominion Inquisition for political purposes,

---

[50] Albizzi, *Risposta*, p. 144.   [51] Pastor, XXII, 368–75.

[52] Pastor, XXI, 337, on December 15, 1589.

[53] Ambassador Paruta denied the rumor. *La legazione di Roma di Paolo Paruta (1592–1595)*, ed. Giuseppe de Leva, 3 vols. (Venice, 1887), I, 51, letter of December 26, 1592.

[54] I have not been able to learn the answer either, nor to determine if the Venetians supported Henry with money or troops at this time.

[55] VC, Ms. Cicogna 2557, "Annali 1592–1595 di Francesco Contarini," no pag., conclusion of the entry of February 18, 1594 mv.

the Venetians had nothing to gain and risked potentially embarrassing questions by prolonging the dispute. There was also the risk that the Spanish in nearby Lombardy, at that time fighting Henry IV, might conclude that the Venetians were not observing strict neutrality. The papacy also had reason to be conciliatory. Intransigence might bring the Inquisition to a standstill throughout the Venetian state. Moreover, additional publicity of the papacy's blatant use of a local Inquisition to gather political intelligence for possible use against a lay power might well produce strong reactions in other states. Finally, the incident called the Republic's attention to its failure to supervise Dominion Inquisitions, for Fra Alberto could hardly have initiated such a tactless inquiry had the lay representative been present. The incident produced no immediate change, but the Venetians remembered it.

In February 1595 the inquisitor of Bergamo began to try laymen without the participation or permission of the rector. The Venetians considered this action a "usurpation of the liberty of the state," and were inclined to summon the inquisitor to Venice. But with the case of Fra Alberto still fresh in their memories, they resolved to avoid making a martyr of the Bergamo inquisitor. They nullified the trial, held the suspects as prisoners of the state, and instructed Ambassador Paolo Paruta to discuss the matter with the Holy See. Paruto found both Pope Clement VIII and the Congregation of the Inquisition conciliatory. Probably the Verona incident was on their minds as well. The Bergamo inquisitor acknowledged his error, annulled the proceedings, and promised to begin a new trial with civil representation. The episode quickly terminated, to the satisfaction of the Republic.[56]

There is little or no evidence that the ecclesiastical members of the tribunal had taken the same liberties as their Terraferma brothers, for the Tre savii attended proceedings faithfully. Nevertheless, the Dominion cases helped to focus attention on the city's Inquisition, and the Venetian leaders concluded that the lay deputies were failing to protect secular rights from clerical encroachment. Less than a month after the affair of

---

[56] VC, Ms. Cicogna 2557, "Annali 1592–1595 di Francesco Contarini," entries of February 18, 1594 mv. and March 4, 1595. (The diarist was Francesco di Bertucci Contarini [1558–1624], who later had a brilliant diplomatic career and became doge in 1623. He served regularly in the Collegio as a Savio di Terraferma for the period covered by his diary. Lowry, "Church and Venetian Political Change," p. 331. Contarini relates a number of church-state disputes from a moderately antipapal point of view. See Cozzi, *Contarini*, pp. 31–32.) Also see the letters of Paruta of February 25, March 11, 1595, in *La legazione di Roma*, III, 63–65, 84–85, with the Republic's instructions in the footnotes. Brown, *Venetian Press*, pp. 142–43, summarizes the dispute, but from Paruta's dispatches only. Sarpi briefly mentioned this incident in his 1622 treatise on the Inquisition. *Opere*, ed. Cozzi and Cozzi, p. 1,209.

the Bergamo inquisitor, the Venetians made the important move of changing the election procedure for the Tre savii sopra eresia. The interregnum
between the death of Doge Pasquale Cicogna on April 5 and the election
of Marin Grimani on April 26, 1595, provided the opportunity. The
Venetians viewed an interregnum as an extraordinary legislative period
in which needed but politically difficult changes might be made. The
constitution provided the means with the temporary office of the Cinque
Correttori who enjoyed wide executive and legislative powers during
an interregnum. Their task was to correct errors of the previous admin-
istration and, if necessary, pass new laws to restrain the incoming doge.[57]
Since 1554 the doge had nominated candidates to serve with the Inquisition; the Correttori proposed that the Collegio, the Senate's "cabinet,"
nominate the Tre savii and the Senate vote on them. The Great Council
passed the new law by an overwhelming margin.[58]

One patrician wrote in his diary that the action had been taken because
the priests had "in a thousand ways eroded lay jurisdiction." The doge
had tended to name "good gentlemen" to the post rather than men alert
to the public interest, and, consequently, everyone was of the opinion that
a change was needed.[59] When it learned of the change, the papacy worried that the results might be "prejudicial" to the operations of the Holy
Office.[60]

[57] Donato Giannotti, *Libro della Repubblica de' Veneziani* in his *Opere*, vol. 1
(Pisa, 1819), 142. The work was composed in 1525–1527 and published in 1540.
Also see Giuseppe Maranini, *La costituzione di Venezia dopo la serrata del Maggior
Consiglio* (Venice, Perugia and Florence, 1931), pp. 275-76, n. 2.

[58] A copy of the law of April 8, 1595, is found in SU, Bu. 154, "Sommari di
leggi e decreti relativi all'Inquisizione," organized chronologically. Brief accounts
of the new law with the names of the Correttori and the vote (1,107 yes, 20 no,
and 24 abstentions) are found in VM, Mss. Italiani, Classe VII, 134 (8035), "Cronaca
Veneta di Girolamo Savina sino al MDCXV," f. 382ᵛ; and VM, Mss. Ital., VII, 73
(8265), "Cronaca Veneta Anonima ab Urbe Condita sino al 1615. Tomo II," f. 448ᵛ.

[59] "Il che è stato fatto perche li Preti hanno in mille vie intacata la iurisdition laica,
et andavano di giorno in giorno dilatando le . . . [omission] . . . poichè erano
nominati dal Prencipe boni Gentilhuomeni, et non di quel spirito, che si ricerca per
ben avertir al servitio publico a questi tempi massime, che ad ogni uno pare che sia
lecito intrar in messa alienare." VC, Ms. Cicogna 2557, entry of April 10, 1595.
This passage was first noted and quoted by Cozzi, *Contarini*, p. 31.

[60] "Et quoniam huismodi electionis mutatio in dies posset afferre praeiudicium
Sancto Officio, summus [i.e., pope or head of the Congregation] mandavit, ut se
informet de praedictis, et quid in praeteritum servatum fuerit, et qua occasione,
et quare hodie non fuerit servatum." BAVa, Barberino Latino 1370, "Decreta
Sanctae Romanae et universalis Inquisitionis Clemente VIII Pont. Max.," p. 206. The
same is to be found in Barberino Latino 1369, "Decreta Sanctae Romanae et universalis Inquisitionis fere omnia sub Clemente VIII Pont. Max." f. 92ᵛ. The two
mss. contain summaries from the papers of the Congregation of the Holy Office,

The most powerful leaders of the Republic, men whose views on ecclesiastical jurisdiction were diametrically opposed, effected the change. All procurators, the Correttori included the three contenders for the ducal crown, Marin Grimani, Leonardo Donà, and Giacomo Foscarini, as well as the less well-known Giovanni Paolo Contarini and Luca Michiel. Public opinion held Grimani to be as pious as his predecessor, and the nuncio considered him to be sympathetic to the papacy and to "cose ecclesiastiche." Unlike most patricians at this time, he made substantial bequests to the Capuchins, the Jesuits, and a number of ecclesiastical institutions. But Donà opposed every clerical prerogative, and Foscarini, who may once have been sympathetic to Rome, had by 1595 adjusted to the new atmosphere. The views of Contarini and Michiel are unknown.[61] Within three days of the death of Doge Cicogna, this heterogeneous group proposed the new law to the Great Council, which endorsed it strongly, suggesting that, indeed, the move had wide support.

The major result of the new electoral procedure was the exclusion of the few patricians, some fervent protectors of "ecclesiastical things," who had dominated the Tre savii for the past ten to fifteen years. The exclusion of Procurator Federico di Francesco Contarini (1538–1613) illustrates the change. Contarini was wealthy enough to purchase a Procuratorship in 1571 with a loan of 20,000 ducats to the state, and he later held a number of financial posts. A strong supporter of the educational aims of the Jesuits, he became involved in various religious and charitable projects.[62] First appointed a lay assistant in 1589, Contarini served all or part of every succeeding year through 1595. In 1590 he aided the negotiations between the Holy Office, Rome, and Venice that resulted in the excision of passages offensive to the Latin rite in Greek religious books, and to the Greek rite

---

with references to the originals, concerning various Italian Inquisitions as well as those of Spain and Portugal. The two mss. are identical except that Ms. 1369 contains additional material.

[61] For Grimani's political career, views, and economic activity, see Lowry, "Church and Venetian Political Change," pp. 349–51; for Foscarini, pp. 346–48. I have found little on the other two. Michiel was elected to the Council of Ten in 1581, 1583, and 1585, and became procurator in 1587. Contarini was elected to the Zonta in 1578 and to a procuratorship in 1594. Their views are unknown. Lowry, "Church and Venetian Political Change," pp. 308, 311–12. One can only speculate why the three contenders for the ducal throne agreed to limit the doge's power and, especially, why Grimani concurred. Ducal elections generated intense politicking, and this one was no exception. Perhaps relinquishing ducal nomination of lay assistants was part of the price that Grimani paid for his eventual victory. Senators hostile to ecclesiastical jurisdiction might have been willing to vote for him if Senate control over the election of the Tre savii were assured.

[62] Gaetano Cozzi, "Federico Contarini: un antiquario veneziano tra Rinascimento e Controriforma," BSV, 3 (1961), 190–220.

in Latin books. In January 1593 he played a key role in the successful papal effort to extradite Giordano Bruno.[63] The nuncio considered him to be "very pious," "of good character," and "always favorable to ecclesiastical things." In 1593 and again in 1595, the nuncio asked the pope to send Contarini letters of commendation for his work on the Holy Office, but cautioned secrecy, for Contarini would be ruined if it were learned that he was partial to the papacy. Rome sent the letters, the second at the end of May 1595.[64] The Senate held its first elections for the Tre savii in July, and did not elect Contarini. In contrast to his previous continuous service, Contarini was elected only twice more, in 1598 and 1610.[65] It is likely that the exclusion of Contarini was one of the objectives, perhaps the chief one, of the new law.

Death also thinned the ranks of those who had served frequently during the 1580s. Vido di Piero Morosini who had served in 1582–84 and 1586–90 died in 1591, and Giovanni Battista di Pietro Querini who had filled the office in 1584–85, 1587–89, and 1592–93, died in 1596.

In the first five years of their new mandate, the Collegio and Senate elected men not known to be either strongly propapal or antipapal. Turnover was frequent, and the rule against repetition enforced; perhaps the leadership wished to neutralize the office. As the new century opened and Venetian-papal tensions increased, key members of the government, some of them conspicuously hostile to ecclesiastical rights, began to be selected. The Senate elected the future doge Nicolò di Zan Gabriel Contarini (1553–1631), and Nicolò Donà in October 1600, and Leonardo Donà in October 1604.[66] These zealous upholders of lay jurisdiction had never previously served with the Holy Office.

[63] For his faithful service with the Holy Office, see the trials in SU, Bu. 65–69. For the emendation of Greek and Latin works, see Giorgio Fedalto, *Ricerche storiche sulla posizione giuridica ed ecclesiastica dei Greci a Venezia nei secoli xv e xvi* (Florence, 1967), pp. 104–7, 138–44. His speech to the Collegio of January 7, 1593, urging Bruno's extradition is printed in Vincenzo Spampanato, *Vita di Giordano Bruno con documenti editi e inediti* (Messina, 1921), II, 760–61.

[64] See the letters of Nuncio Ludovico Taverna of February 27, 1593, May 24 and June 9, 1595, in ASVa, Segretario di Stato, F. 30, ff. 59^{r-v}, F. 31, ff. 72^{v}–73^{r}, 88^{r}. They were first noted by Cozzi, "Federico Contarini," pp. 195–97.

[65] Segretario alle voci, Elezioni del Senato, R. 6 (1588–1600), f. 132^{r}; R. 8 (1606–1613), f. 104^{v}. In 1610, the nuncio wrote of Contarini: "Egli però è gentilhuomo di buona mente, et, per quello che può, aiuta il Santo Officio." Letter of Nuncio Berlinghiero Gessi of December 25, 1610, as quoted in Savio, "Per l'epistolario di Paolo Sarpi," 14 (1940), 68.

[66] Segretario alle voci, Elezioni del Senato, R. 6, f. 132^{r}, R. 7, f. 104^{v}. Contarini is the subject of Cozzi, *Contarini*. Since patronymics are not given, it is not known if Nicolò Donà was Nicolò di Giovan Battista, the brother of Leonardo, or Nicolò di Giovanni, the future doge (1618). The former was moderately antipapal (Cozzi,

The Collegio also modified the Inquisition's arrest procedure to bring it more securely under lay control. In the past, upon hearing a denunciation and deciding that sufficient evidence existed, the lay assistants had issued a verbal order to the captain (a civil police officer assigned to the tribunal), who made the arrest. In November 1602 the Collegio told the captain that he had to get a written warrant signed by at least two of the lay assistants. Moreover, if the nuncio, patriarch, their vicars, or any other prelate asked him to arrest someone, he must first seek a warrant from one of the Collegio secretaries. The Collegio charged the captain to obey the new procedure under pain of death.[67] Obviously the government was reacting to attempts by the ecclesiastical membership of the tribunal to make arrests without obtaining the approval of the Tre savii. The Congregation in Rome protested this "novelty prejudicial to the Holy Office."[68]

For more than a decade the government attempted to bring the Venetian and Terraferma Inquisitions more securely under civil supervision; yet the tribunals did not substantially change their ways. If the local tribunals could avoid attracting the attention of the state or win the approval of a lay observer who shared inquisitorial views, they could continue as before. Inquisitors often succeeded in disregarding state directives until after the interdict; only then did the patriciate carefully watch every inquisitorial move to prevent reprisals against those who supported Venetian policy during the interdict.[69] Similarly, not until 1609 and 1613 did the Republic issue comprehensive new guidelines for the conduct of the Holy Office.[70] And though extradition, as always, was difficult, the papacy succeeded in extraditing to Rome ten or more prisoners, including Bruno and Tommaso Campanella, between 1590 and 1605.[71]

Contarini, pp. 18–20, 40, 57, 73, n. 2, 104, n. 1) and the latter strongly so. Ibid., p. 140, 167, n. 1. Incidentally, Leonardo Donà was elected or appointed to so many offices between 1602 and January 1606 that it is difficult to see how he could have served in all of them. Seneca, *Donà*, p. 245, n. 1.

[67] Senato, Deliberazioni Roma, R. 13, f. 77ᵛ, November 4, 1602.

[68] Papal protests of September 6 and November 22, 1603, and January 31, 1604, are noted in Vaticanus Latinus 10945, f. 39ʳ, and Barberino Latino 5195, f. 62ᵛ.

[69] Barberino Latino 5195, ff. 1ʳ⁻ᵛ.

[70] These regulations are found in Sarpi, *Scritti giurisdizionalistici*, pp. 120–30; Albizzi, *Risposta*, passim; and Barberino Latino, 5195, ff. 2ʳ–6ʳ.

[71] The extradited prisoners were, from Venice: Giovanni Gasparo Lupi da Rovigo in 1592, Bruno in 1593, and "Frate Archangelo da Piacenza Min. Oss." in 1602; from Padua: Campanella, Giovanni Battista Clario, and Ottavio Longo in 1599; from Verona: Ercole Rota in 1597 and perhaps Fra Ludovico Petrucci in 1599; from Vicenza: Giordano Siloprochi, a Capuchin novice, in 1599. Barberino Latino 5195, ff. 17ᵛ–18ᵛ. Albizzi, *Risposta*, pp. 152–53, adds Prete Biagio da Digiuno in 1597 and Ferdinando de las Infantas in 1605, both from Venice. An unnamed relapsus

Clement VIII followed a standard procedure for most jurisdictional conflicts centering on the Holy Office. He defended ecclesiastical rights with great tenacity until the Senate put its weight behind a demand; then he gave way. But he did not always make his wishes prevail with the Congregation of the Holy Office, a body that enjoyed great independence[72] —or perhaps he did not always try hard. The Congregation sought to recover whatever had been lost in direct papal-ambassadorial negotiations once the inquisitors were out of sight of the Senate and Collegio. The Venetians were vulnerable to this tactic. Although the government enunciated lay rights in uncompromising tones and passed stern decrees, it seldom pulled out the roots of the abuse. The oligarchs who commanded the great offices had neither the time nor the opportunity to oversee enforcement by lower administrative bodies staffed by lesser nobles. And though they repeatedly stated what they claimed were unshakeable constitutional principles, they habitually resolved issues on an ad hoc basis. Hence, Donà and the other leaders changed much less than they thought. They issued new decrees and laws, but they underestimated the difficulty of modifying Counter Reformation attitudes and practices.

On the other hand, much more had changed in Venice than the pope and curia realized. A certain degree of success in maintaining the status quo on a practical level blinded them to the full significance of the shift of attitude that had occurred within the patriciate. Many Vatican prelates failed to comprehend the importance of the growth of the state's absolutist claims, or the great danger to the church of festering, unresolved jurisdictional disputes, until the interdict. Three decades of a triumphant Counter Reformation had encouraged them to see the wave of disputes of the 1590s as a passing aberration.

Clement VIII and his advisers did show a few signs of appreciating the new Venetian sensibilities. In 1604 an inquisitor, possibly from outside the Venetian state, reported a denunciation for heresy of one "Cavalier Michiel," more than likely Marchio di Benetto Michiel (1548–1606), a diplomat but not a major figure. The pope instructed the Venetian inquisitor to discuss secretly with the nuncio and patriarch what should be done, and cautioned them not to inform the lay assistants. The nuncio and patriarch decided that the patriarch should approach Michiel quietly and persuade him to confront and repent his errors. If Michiel should prove obstinate, they would await further instructions from Rome. Patriarch

---

from Gradisca (between Pordenone and Udine) was extradited in 1590. Letters of Nuncio Marcello Acquaviva of April 7, "il sabato santo" (i.e., April 21), and May 12, 1590, in ASVa, Segretario di Stato, F. 27, ff. 85^r, 97^r, 110^r.

[72] Pastor, xxiv, 198.

Matteo Zane succeeded in his delicate task, and the matter was dropped.[73] On this occasion, at least, the papacy recognized that much had changed since the 1560s.

A crisis similar to the interdict might have occurred at any moment from the mid-1590s until the death of Clement VIII on March 5, 1605, but no dispute was large enough in itself, and no position so inflexible, as to precipitate a break. Instead, a growing number of disputes accumulated bitterness until a change of personalities finally tipped the balance. From the beginning of his pontificate on May 16, 1605, Paul V demonstrated greater jurisdictional intransigence, and less political finesse, than had his predecessor. The contrast was as evident in Inquisition affairs as elsewhere. In July 1605 Paul V ordered the Venetian Holy Office to follow customary processes, specifically including the participation of the lay assistants, in proceeding against some nobles.[74] Typically, he demonstrated none of Clement's wariness. In Venice militant defenders of civil jurisdiction had steadily gained power, and by early 1603 they dominated the great offices.[75] Between 1602 and 1605, with large Senate majorities, they legislated lay rights over ecclesiastical lands and over clerics accused of crimes. Their actions would have been a sharp challenge to any pope. Paul V issued an ultimatum in late December 1605, and the Venetians elected Leonardo Donà doge. These two determined men defended the claims of their respective bodies at the interdict confrontation.

[73] Vaticanus Latinus 10945, f. 70ᵛ, March 20–May 15, 1604; Barberino Latino 5195, f. 61ʳ. For the identification, see ASV, Barbaro, "Arbori," III, p. 125.

[74] Vaticanus Latinus 10945, f. 70ᵛ, July 9, 1605.

[75] Cozzi, *Contarini*, pp. 93–100.

VIII

THE REPUBLIC PROTECTS THE PRESS

ECONOMIC differences and jurisdictional militancy spurred the Republic to scrutinize papal attempts to regulate commercial aspects of the press. Beginning in the 1580s, and increasingly in the 1590s, the Republic protected the financial health of the industry by restricting papal copyright claims. As in the 1560s, canonical works became the focal point of disputes.

1. ECONOMIC DECLINE OF THE PRESS

In early 1588 the nuncio asked the Senate for a privilegio so that a book previously published in Rome might not be reprinted in Venice without the author's permission. The Senate denied the request on the grounds that the number of Venetian presses had declined from 120 to 70, and such concessions to foreign printers would inflict further damage.[1] In May 1596 the printers' guild addressed a petition to the doge and Collegio asking for the abolition of all papal privileges on ecclesiastical works because they were destroying the Venetian press. The petitioners lamented that 125 presses had been reduced to only 40.[2]

The figures for the number of presses should be approached cautiously, especially the figure of 40 presented by the bookmen seeking governmental support in another battle over liturgical and canonical works. The figures alone cannot give a full picture of the prosperity of the industry, for 40 or 70 busy presses might produce as many volumes as 120 presses working half-time. The number of imprimaturs granted and, consequently, the number of new titles published, is a better indicator, although by no

[1] "Conoscendo che l'arte di già comincia a mancare in gran parte per altre innovationi, et in spetie per l'introduttione et ampliatione de la stampa di Roma, che non può da loro essere ben intesa, essendo quì redotta da 120 torcolani a 70." Letter of Nuncio Girolamo Matteucci of April 2, 1588, Venice, in ASVa, Segretario di Stato, Venezia, F. 26, f. 181^v. *Torcolano* or *torcolo* means an actual press, not a publishing firm, which would be a *stamperia*.

[2] "Acciò fosse levato con pernicioso disordine hora non solo perseverando ma ampliando tanto inconveniente che ci destrugge, vedendosi noi da 125 torcoli ridotti in soli 40. . . ." Petition of May 3, 1596, to be found in ASVa, Fondo Borghese IV, 224, f. 117^r; and ASVa, Segretario di Stato, Venezia, F. 32, ff. 339^{r-v}.

means an infallible one. Table 4 shows that the press had declined quantitatively since the peak period of 1560–74, but not as dramatically as the claimed decline in the number of presses. During the peak period of 1560–74, the average annual number of imprimaturs granted was 89.3. It dropped to 45.2, or 51 percent of the peak figure, during the decade 1575–84, when Venice suffered the effects of the plague. Average annual production climbed to 72.9 imprimaturs for 1585–99, i.e., 82 percent of the peak. It further climbed to 79.2 for the period 1600–1604 (90 percent of the peak figure), suggesting that the press was regaining more of the lost ground.

TABLE 4

AVERAGE NUMBER OF IMPRIMATURS ISSUED ANNUALLY
PER FIVE-YEAR PERIOD, 1550–1604

1550–54	55.2
1555–59	78
1560–64	87
1565–69	92.4
1570–74	88.6
1575–79	45.2[a]
1580–84	45.25
1585–89	81.4
1590–94	63.6[b]
1595–99	73.7
1600–04	79.2

[a] Great Plague of 1575–77   [b] Famine, 1590–91

SOURCE: Capi del CX, Notatorio, R. 14–33 and F. 1–14. Data for 1584, 1595, and 1596 are missing.

The plague of 1575–77 and the resultant economic dislocation precipitated a sharp decline in the number of books published. Death, the flight to the countryside, and the spasmodic efforts of the government to halt the plague by suspending commercial activity combined to depress the entire economy, including the press.[3] Among publishers who disappeared at this time were Lodovico degli Avanzi, who published 30 editions between 1556 and 1576, and Giovanni Bariletto, who issued 22 printings between 1560 and 1575.[4] Other publishers were succeeded by heirs who

[3] Pullan, *Rich and Poor*, pp. 315–19, 325.

[4] This and the following data are based on Pastorello, and occasionally supplemented by *STC Italian*, "Index of Printers and Publishers," pp. 757–992. It should be remembered that Pastorello's figures represent only about 50 percent of the production of the bookmen, but they are useful for making relative comparisons. The

printed much less. Giovanni Griffio published 129 editions from 1545 to 1576; the heirs of Giovanni produced one title in 1576, and Giovanni il Giovane and other members of the family published only 47 works between 1578 and 1598. Various members of the Bindoni family published 227 editions between 1508 and 1574, but only 8 other editions in the rest of the century. Several Bonelli published 56 editions between 1552 and 1576, but only 13 more books between 1579 and 1589. The Borgominieri published 19 titles between 1559 and 1575, and an additional 6 between 1583 and 1593. Sometimes the decline was less sharp: Bolognino Zaltieri published 48 works between 1555 and 1576; after a hiatus that closely paralleled the overall slump of the press, Marc'Antonio Zaltieri published 24 titles, between 1583 and 1598. Emigration contributed to the decline. In January 1578, as the plague was ending, the Senate lamented that the bookmen were leaving, taking their presses and tools with them.[5]

The disappearance of a publisher did not necessarily mean the removal of his assets from the industry, for inventory and tools could be transferred to another bookman through sale or dowry. Yet, the total number of publishers declined, and the majority of heirs printed less than had their fathers and uncles. Since a firm's chances in a highly competitive industry depended heavily on the energy and resources of its head, the new firms led by inexperienced heirs suffered. Perhaps for this reason some publishers encouraged their sons to enter the more secure professions. Giovanni Giolito, the son of Gabriel, studied law at Padua and only entered the book industry upon the death of his father in 1578.[6] Still a young man of twenty-four, he did not succeed in arresting the firm's decline. Young heirs were particularly disadvantaged in a period of economic duress.

Death, emigration, and decline were not the whole story. Some large firms, such as Gardano, Guerra, Rampazetto, Sessa, and Scoto, rebounded in the mid-1580s and continued to operate at a high level of activity into the next century. The Giunti firm, aided by its international connections,

---

Aldine and Giolito presses also declined quantitatively, but their decline began in the 1560s when the industry as a whole was still expanding. Moreover, personal reasons, such as the move to Rome in 1561 by Paolo Manuzio, and Gabriel Giolito's age, may have been the chief causes. The figures for the total production of the Aldine press by decade are: 1551–60, 211; 1561–70, 135; 1571–80, 98; 1581–90, 76; 1591–1600, 26. For the Giolito press, they are: 1551–60, 326; 1561–70, 234; 1571–80, 113; 1581–90, 96; 1591–1600, 16. The counts are based on Renouard, *Annales des Aldes*, Bongi, *Giolito*, and Camerini, "Notizia sugli Annali Giolitini," with non-Venetian editions, and a few broadsides and leaflets excluded.

[5] Senato Terra, F. 72, entry of January 11, 1577 mv; also quoted in Brown, *Venetian Press*, pp. 89–90, n. 2. Although the plague is not mentioned, it is likely that the Senate had it in mind.

[6] Bongi, *Giolito*, I, lxxiii–lxxv.

actually increased its production at the time of the plague.[7] The expansion of this major firm partially compensated for the decline elsewhere.

Some new publishing houses arose to replace those that declined and died out, especially in or about 1583. Nicolò Moretti published 37 editions between 1583 and 1599. Giovanni Battista and Paolo Ugolino published 27 editions during the same period, and Pietro Dusinelli and Giacomo Vincenzi each reached comparable figures. Domenico and Giovanni Domenico Imberti published 15 editions between 1585 and 1599. As had always been characteristic of the printing industry, and was now common throughout Venetian commerce and industry, foreigners took the places left vacant.[8] Roberto Meietti moved from Padua, where his father Paolo had been a busy publisher for fifteen years, to Venice in 1590. By the early seicento he had assumed a major role in the industry. Giovanni Battista Ciotti from Siena, who began in Venice in 1583, published a few works through 1590, and had expanded to 5 or 6 annually by the end of the cinquecento. Yet, as the production figures demonstrate, neither he nor any of the newcomers wholly succeeded in replacing the dead giants.

Perhaps most important, the plague presented a commercial opportunity to other Italian publishing centers. Some of them quickly took advantage. As Table 5 shows, other Italian presses expanded at the time of the Venetian plague. In 1555–74, the Venetian press published a little over two and one-half times as many books as the other major centers combined. But during the decade of difficulty, 1575–84, Venetian production dropped until it only equaled the total production of the other cities. The Roman and Turin presses expanded markedly at this time, and they continued to expand even when the Venetian press recovered. The Venetian bookmen regained their lead in the late 1580s, but they produced only about 15 percent more books than the other centers combined in the last fifteen years of the century.

The Roman press rose from a low position to become Italy's second largest press in the late 1580s. Roman book production had been small even in the 1560s, when the papacy had subsidized Paolo Manuzio. Manuzio printed a number of important titles, including new editions of several of the Greek fathers and the reformed liturgical works, but he never realized the profits he expected.[9] Upon his departure in 1570, only a diminished Popolo Romano press, two other presses of moderate size (the heirs of Antonio Blado and the Accolti family), and a handful of

[7] The total (new and reprint) Giunti production by decades is: 1551–60, 88; 1561–70, 90; 1571–80, 113; 1581–90, 171; 1591–1600, 101. See Camerini, *Annali dei Giunti*.

[8] Tucci, "Psychology of the Venetian Merchant," pp. 363–65.

[9] Barberi, *Paolo Manuzio*, pp. 10–14.

TABLE 5

AVERAGE NUMBER OF ANNUAL PUBLICATIONS PER FIVE-YEAR PERIOD
IN MAJOR ITALIAN PUBLISHING CENTERS, 1550–99

	Venice[a]	Total Other Centers	Rome[b]	Florence[c]	Turin[d]	Bologna-Milan-Naples[e]
1550–54	115	72	16	37	1	19
1555–59	163	64	18	16	2	27
1560–64	182	72	12	34	2	23
1565–69	193	66	16	31	6	13
1570–74	185	82	20	32	7	23
1575–79	94	82	24	27	16	14
1580–84	95	109	34	40	15	20
1585–89	170	160	65	51	19	26
1590–94	133	116	52	30	10	24
1595–99	154	122	43	28	12	38

[a] For Venice the average annual number of imprimaturs granted was multiplied by 2.09 on the supposition that 1.09 reprints (which did not need a new imprimatur) were issued for each original work. See Ch. 1, sec. 2, for justification of the multiplier. Since all figures in the table have been rounded off to the nearest whole number, the figure for "Total Other Centers" sometimes does not exactly equal the sum of the individual production of the other cities.

[b] The Roman count is based on Fernanda Ascarelli, *Le cinquecentine romane. "Censimento delle edizioni romane del XVI secolo possedute dalle biblioteche di Roma"* (Milan, 1972). Ascarelli examined the contents of fourteen Roman libraries, including the Vatican; her count can be accepted as fairly complete. As always in counting the number of publications, I have eliminated official governmental printings, such as laws, edicts, broadsides, and *motu proprii*, as well as other material too short to be considered a book or even a pamphlet. For the Roman printers, this meant the elimination of the bulk of papal pronouncements.

[c] The Florentine figures are based on a count of Florentine editions listed in the *STC Italian* multiplied by 2.06. The reason for this multiplier is that the *STC Italian* appears to list slightly less than one-half the number of publications that a census based on a number of Italian libraries turns up. For example, Ascarelli's count for 1550–99 is 2.06 times the number of Roman publications listed in *STC Italian* for the same period.

[d] The Turin count is based on the thorough census of Marina Bersano Begey, *Le cinquecentine piemontesi*, vol. 1, *Torino* (Turin, 1961). She surveyed 56 Italian and foreign libraries. The Bevilacqua press, which began in 1573, accounted for about two-thirds of the Turin production from 1575 through 1589. When Bevilacqua faltered in the 1590s, Turin production declined as well.

[e] The combined Bologna-Milan-Naples count is based on *STC Italian* multiplied by a factor of 2.06. Bologna and Milan produced roughly the same number of books, and Naples about one-half as many.

minuscule publishers carried on. But in 1576, the relocation in Rome of the Zanetti, a publishing family probably driven from Venice by the plague, greatly strengthened the Roman press. Originally from Brescia, Bartolomeo Zanetti began publishing in Venice in 1535, printing Brucioli's Bible among other works. Cristoforo printed in the 1560s and 1570s until his name disappeared in 1576; Daniele published a handful of editions in 1576 before he, too, stopped. Francesco Zanetti, their probable successor, began to publish in Rome in 1576 and produced about 170 editions through 1591. Upon Francesco's death, Luigi (or Aloyse) published about 140 more editions from 1590 through 1599. The Zanetti name did not reappear in Venice until 1596, when one Daniele, possibly a young relative, published Hebrew books.[10]

Other new publishers appeared in Rome in the late 1570s and 1580s: Giacomo Torneri, who published about 55 editions (1577–91); Giorgio Ferrari, who issued about 55 imprints (1581–98); and Bartolomeo Bonfadino, who produced about 90 works (1583–99), as well as a number of smaller printers.[11] The popes also helped. A strong patron of learning, Gregory XIII brought scholars to Rome, and Sixtus V founded the Typographia Apostolica Vaticana in 1587.

The Roman press never threatened Venetian quantitative leadership. Nevertheless, between the 1550s and the late 1580s it increased fourfold and offered some competition to the Venetians, especially in the important religious field. Situated in the center of Catholicism, the Roman printers had easy access to the many clerical authors who taught at the new colleges, served prelates, or labored in Vatican congregations. These writers could send their manuscripts anywhere, but convenience and the growing Venetian reputation for inaccuracy led many to the Roman printers. Moreover, Vatican prelates could provide subsidies for Roman publications. The Roman bookmen were not limited to religious works, for the city had regained its place, lost at the Sack of 1527, as a scholarly and literary center. The growth of the Roman press, aided by exclusive papal privileges, at a time when the Venetian bookmen were struggling, inevitably generated friction.

The Turin press also grew at the expense of the Venetian press, as a direct result of the relocation of Nicolò Bevilacqua. A native of the Trentino, Bevilacqua moved to Venice, served an apprenticeship with Paolo Manuzio, and then became one of Manuzio's ablest associates. He also operated his own press, publishing 48 titles from 1554 through 1572. Impressed by his work, Duke Emanuele Filiberto of Savoy induced him to

[10] For the production of the various Zanetti, see *STC Italian*, 984–86; and Ascarelli, *Le cinquecentine romane*, pp. 356–59.

[11] Ascarelli, *Le cinquecentine romane*, pp. 331–32, 340–41, 355.

move to Turin in late 1572 by means of substantial financial concessions. Although Nicolò died in 1573, his heirs continued to manage the Turin firm, publishing about 200 works in all fields, especially law, before the end of the century. Despite commercial harassment by Luc'Antonio Giunti, the Bevilacqua firm prospered in Turin.[12]

Competitors arose where there had been none. Luca Bonetti, who called himself a Venetian, printed for others in Florence in the 1560s. In 1571 he set up his own firm in Siena, a city that had for some time lacked a press, and from that date through 1623 published over 400 titles.[13] Since vernacular works of secular and devotional literature comprised the bulk of his list, he competed directly with the Venetians in one of their most important areas.

As the century waned, the deterioration of their workmanship rendered the Venetian bookmen less competitive. During a dispute over a papal privilege in 1595, Paolo Paruta, ambassador to the Holy See and an author of historical and political works, advised the Senate that mistakes and the inclusion of unauthorized material disfigured Venetian imprints. He feared that Venetian adamancy in the current dispute might lead to a Roman embargo on Venetian books; Roman customers would then turn to Germany and France for many of the titles currently supplied by Venice. German and French editions cost a little more, but were better corrected and more beautiful, Paruta concluded.[14] The Venetian bookmen competed because their wares were cheaper, but once readers became accustomed to better books they would not return to the inferior Venetian product.

The Venetian press faced heavy foreign competition for the important Latin scholarly market. As early as 1567 Donato Giannotti complained that Venetian publishers printed only titles of little importance and reprints, while France, Germany, and especially Plantin in Antwerp published the "good books." He advised a friend searching for a publisher for a Latin scholarly work that Lyons would serve him better than Venice, especially for accuracy.[15] Since a Latin work could be printed anywhere, an author would take into account accuracy, quality of paper and ink, and cost, as well as proximity, when choosing a printer. Because authors or their

[12] Alfredo Cioni, biographies of Giovanni Battista and Nicolò Bevilacqua in DBI, 9, pp. 794–95, 798–801; Bersano Begey, *Le cinquecentine piemontesi*, I, 462–73.

[13] Possibly Luca was the descendant of a Bonetti who published in Venice in the 1480s. Alfredo Cioni, "Luca Bonetti," DBI, 11, pp. 794–96.

[14] Letter of March 11, 1595, in *La legazione di Roma*, III, 87.

[15] Letter of September 12, 1567, Padua, in Donato Giannotti, *Lettere a Piero Vettori, pubblicate sopra gli originali del British Museum da Roberto Ridolfi e Cecil Roth, con un saggio illustrativo a cura di Roberto Ridolfi* (Florence, 1932), p. 140. Also see his letters of June 13, 15, 1567, Padua, on pp. 136–37.

sponsors often paid the printing costs for scholarly works, the presses that failed to secure manuscripts suffered a loss of revenue and, perhaps more important, a diminished reputation.

Foreign competition and waning quality also caused difficulties for the Venetian press in the highly competitive reprint market. Since bookmen paid little attention to foreign copyrights, competing printings of titles in demand, such as Cicero's *Epistolae ad familiares*, appeared in all the major centers. The rival publishers of Antwerp, Basel, Frankfurt, Lyons, Paris, and Venice tried to win buyers by producing a better product at a reduced cost, or by some trade-off between the two.

Not all the difficulties facing the bookmen resulted from their own inadequacies or the prowess of competitors. As the commercial center of Europe shifted from the Mediterranean to the Atlantic, northern readers had more money to spend on books. Similarly, as northern scholars achieved leadership, Dutch, French, and German publishers had the advantage in competing for manuscripts. Venetian maritime problems also touched the bookmen, for books, like other merchandise, had to be shipped to markets such as Spain.

The Index and Inquisition did not seriously harm the Venetian press, but they added to its burden in small ways that are difficult to measure quantitatively. The long route through prepublication censorship touched the press directly because it cost the printer time and money, although not large amounts. When the Holy Office occasionally halted or delayed the publication or sale of a title, the publisher suffered further.

The indirect effects of censorship were less tangible but possibly more serious. The Index may have contributed to the economic vulnerability of the Venetian press by making it too dependant on religious works. The increase in vernacular devotional literature compensated for the prohibitions of authors such as Aretino and Machiavelli, but even in a genuine religious revival the public could absorb only so much sacred literature. The Venetian bookmen made every effort to maintain this market by translating the seemingly inexhaustible supply of Spanish devotional authors, but the thirst had to be slaked eventually. Sooner or later, part of the reading public was certain to want something else, such as the witty pornography that Aretino did so well. The Index had eliminated this option.

Similarly, the climate of control and regulation may have dissuaded authors and publishers from attempting permissible but financially risky ventures. The Venetian bookmen of the 1540s profited from a uniquely unfettered existence; they were free to publish almost anything except overt heresy and criticism of things Venetian. Possibly the freedom of the 1540s contributed to the industry's prosperity by encouraging printers to experiment with new authors and titles; the printers could capitalize on projects with reprints and additional titles when an author or subject caught the public's fancy. When church and state combined to create the restrictive atmosphere of the Counter Reformation, the bookmen possibly became less venturesome.

Despite difficulties, the Venetian press did not collapse. Even with an absolute quantitative decline of output of about 18 percent, it remained one of the great publishing centers at the end of the century. But its percentage of the total amount of European publishing had probably declined substantially. By 1600, for example, annual Venetian production was only 50 to 55 percent of that of Paris.[16] Since the Venetian bookmen could do little about northern Europe's greater wealth, they had to concentrate primarily on maintaining or improving their position within the Italian peninsula. The Republic became convinced of the necessity of protecting the bookmen against papal regulations that aided the Roman press at Venetian expense.

2. THE ROLES OF THE PRESS

Scholar, prelate, prince, and printer expected different things of the press, and each projected his own goal onto it. Most bookmen, whether Venetian or Roman, viewed the press in fairly simple terms as a livelihood. But prelate, prince, and scholar cast the bookmen into other roles and did not understand why they refused to play their assigned parts. The differing conceptions rendered disputes doubly difficult to resolve, for often the goals were mutually exclusive.

The papacy believed that the purpose of the press was to promulgate truth, specifically, to aid the renewal of sacred learning that was approaching fruition in the last decade of the cinquecento. The humanist ideal of freeing the sources from centuries of error, and the hope that authoritative Catholic editions would wean scholars and laymen from Protestant editions, animated the revival. The papacy called scholars to Rome and provided facilities and support, enabling them to give their attention to the Vatican library and its precious codices. Gradually new editions of patristic sources, improved versions of the canonical titles, and, above all, a reformed Vulgate approached completion.

Scholars and prelates sought to ensure that the new texts would be correctly printed and widely promulgated, and older, faulty editions elim-

---

[16] In the years 1598–1600, the Parisian presses issued 313, 274, and 338 imprints. Parisian annual production rose to an average of 543 for the years 1598–1643. Henri-Jean Martin, *Livre, pouvoirs et société à Paris au XVIIe siècle*, 2 vols. (Geneva, 1969), 1, 75, 79, 473. By comparison, Venetian annual production for 1595–99 averaged 154 works, and for 1600–1604, about 166.

inated; only then would Christendom reap the benefits of their immense labors. In the 1560s the papacy relied upon exclusive privileges supported by the threat of excommunication, but it found them difficult to enforce. Nevertheless, Rome felt that something was needed to force the printers to discard old inventory and to print the new editions accurately. Those concerned with the program of renewal sought to adjust the privileges in order to render them more effective.

Giovanni Carga, a scholar and a secretary to the cardinal, made a proposal in 1576.[17] He began by lamenting the problem of printing errors in sacred and liturgical texts, offering as a sample of the printer's art a reprint of the Tridentine decrees containing 6,000 errors. According to Carga, a large number of errors inevitably distorted the meaning of a work. To ensure publishing accuracy, a Roman press should publish the first edition, with the aid of a college of editors and press correctors to be established by the papacy. All previous privilegi having been abolished, this Roman press would enjoy an exclusive, worldwide, and perpetual copyright. High papal officials, such as the Master of the Sacred Palace or deputies charged with press supervision, should authenticate the first copies. These would then be sent to princes, ordinaries, and inquisitors, who would constrain local publishers to print exact copies of the Roman text. Local bookmen would employ at their own expense correctors approved by the inquisitor or ordinary, and the civil authority would punish inaccuracy with fines.

Carga answered possible objections and extolled the benefits of his scheme. He did not believe that the designated Roman press would enjoy a monopoly because any other publisher could reprint a title, subject to restrictions to ensure accuracy. The lifting of all previous copyrights would make possible agreement among printers on such matters as paper, ink, type, and price. The Roman press would be revitalized and become first among the presses of Catholic Christendom. Last, but certainly not least, pious readers everywhere would receive evangelical truth uncontaminated by printing errors. As Carga's memorandum produced no action immediately, the problem continued to exercise scholars. About ten years later, Antonio Castelvetro, a physician from Modena, addressed to Sixtus V a

---

[17] Carga's memorandum, "Sopra un modo facile, et sicuro, di essequire in Roma, senza gravar la Camera, il Decreto della Quarta Sessione del Concilio di Trento, che ordina, *ut Sacra Scriptura quam emendatissime imprimatur*," is found in ASVa, Miscellaneorum Armarium xi, vol. 93, ff. 110ʳ–16ᵛ. I follow the printed version in Paul Maria Baumgarten, *Die Vulgata Sixtina von 1590 und ihre Einführungsbulle. Aktenstücke und untersuchungen.* Altestamentliche Abhandlungen, vol. iii, fasc. 2. (Münster, 1911), pp. 141–51. It can be securely dated because it refers to the Tridentine decree on Scripture (1546) as having been passed thirty years ago (Baumgarten, 148). Carga was in the entourage of Cardinal Benedetto Lomellino of Genoa.

treatise on the reform of the press that approached the issue from the same perspective and made similar proposals.[18]

In April 1587 Sixtus V took the first step toward bringing the fruits of the renewal of sacred learning to the public by creating the Typographia Apostolica Vaticana, an official papal press to be directed by Domenico Basa, to whom a loan of 20,000 scudi was granted. In his bull the pontiff expressed hope that the press would combat the deceit of the heretics and the "malice and ignorance" of printers by preparing and publishing new editions of the Bible, patristic sources, and Scholastic theologians. In 1588 Sixtus named a congregation to oversee the press and a group of correctors to serve it and the Vatican library.[19]

The memoranda of Carga and Castelvetro illustrated the approach to the press of the scholar, clergyman, and ruler who believed that the press should spread truth or, at least, refrain from promulgating error. To accomplish this end, the scholar, churchman, and ruler sought to supervise the press with the same authoritarian regulations imposed on other crafts. Both Carga and Castelvetro explicitly compared printers to scribes, notaries, secretaries, and minters, whom civil authorities controlled with laws and procedures designed to guarantee that professions were practiced accurately and honestly. The proposals demonstrated a limited understanding of past difficulties with papal privileges, for Carga wished to drop the threat of excommunication and some other restrictive aspects. But overall, Carga and Castelvetro simply modified the papal privileges slightly and relied on a combination of civil and ecclesiastical coercion to induce the bookmen to behave. They failed to take into account the fundamental question of the bookmen: could a profit be earned under this system?

Carga and Castelvetro did not grasp that the bookman had to sell as

---

[18] VM, Mss. Italiani, Classe XI, 1 (6958), "Trattato breve di Antonio Castelvetrj medico da Modona [sic] sopra la riforma della stampa." This is the copy used here; another copy can be found in ASVa, Fondo Borghese I, 913, ff. 743ʳ–85ʳ. Although lacking a date, internal evidence places it after April 10, 1585, the death of Gregory XIII mentioned on f. 28ᵛ, and before April 27, 1587, the founding of the Typographia Apostolica Vaticana, which surely would have been mentioned had it taken place. Tiraboschi reported that Castelvetro (d. 1612) composed his press reform proposal spontaneously, and then journied to Rome to present it to Sixtus V personally. Girolamo Tiraboschi, *Biblioteca modenese o notizie della vita e delle opere degli scrittori natii degli stati del Duca di Modena*, 6 vols. (Modena, 1781–86), I, 430; VI, 612.

[19] *Bullarium Diplomatum et Privilegiorum Summorum Romanorum Pontificum*, vol. VIII (Naples, 1883), pp. 841–47, 996; Baumgarten, *Die Vulgata Sixtina*, pp. 9–11, 16–17; Pastor, XXII, 199–201. Basa (c. 1510–96) from Cividale del Friuli, was a prominent Roman publisher over several decades. See Alfredo Cioni, "Domenico Basa," DBI, 7, pp. 45–49.

many copies as possible at the lowest attainable cost per unit if he wished to survive in the fiercely competitive trade. The bookmen needed some compensation if they were to bear the costs of a carefully printed new text. An exclusive worldwide privilege, which might be exploited by the sale of more books to the public at a high retail price or by the sale of regional rights, rewarded the original publisher. But it did nothing for the printers left out of the arrangement. Carga and Castelvetro offered the excluded printers nothing more than the right of printing the new text under strict supervision and at their own cost, including that of press correctors. Inevitably the excluded printers would be tempted to produce a less expensive, poorer quality text in an effort to undersell the exclusive edition.

In their enthusiasm for a new, improved text, scholar and prelate overlooked the problem of disposing of the older texts. The book business depended on a large inventory sold gradually over the years; whenever the papacy promulgated a new edition of a canonical work and banned the older one, it transformed an asset into a liability. What could a bookman do with hundreds or thousands of volumes? Sometimes he substituted a new title page and passed them off as new. The papacy discovered that the Giunti press had published a *Pontificale Romanum* whose title page advertised it as the new Tridentine revision, but which was only an unaltered older text. After investigation, the nuncio reported that the bookmen often engaged in this kind of fraud to sell old inventory.[20] In their many complaints against papal restrictions, the Venetian bookmen never admitted any culpability in this or any other aspect of their trade. They, too, failed to admit any goal for the press except their own.

Venetian commercial principles encouraged the printers to disobey papal rules. When the papacy sought to regulate the reproduction of works, it collided with the Venetian notion of the freedom of the press: the right to publish anything that had been published elsewhere. On the whole, the bookmen respected Venetian privileges but refused to honor foreign copyrights. When they sought Venetian imprimaturs and privileges, they sometimes explicitly mentioned that the title had been previously published elsewhere, perhaps no farther away than Verona.[21] The bookmen accepted papal designation of the original publisher of a religious work because they could do nothing about it, but they argued that they might

[20] Letters of Cardinal Tolomeo Galli and Nuncio Giambattista Castagna of June 15 and 19, 1574, in *Nunziature* xi, 204, 210.
[21] For examples, see Capi del CX, Notatorio, R. 22, ff. 28ʳ (May 18, 1568, for a title previously published in Lyons), 73ʳ (October 7, 1568, Genoa); R. 32, ff. 127ʳ⁻ᵛ (September 27, 1602, Verona), 132ʳ (October 31, 1602, Rome), 201ʳ (November 20, 1603, Treviso).

reprint the title at will without compensating the original publisher, limited only by Venetian law and their own internal arrangements. The foreign publisher or author who wished to protect his investment against Venetian infringement could only petition the Senate for a privilege, usually without success.

The Venetian nobility, like the scholars and prelates, saw the press as an industry, but a lay industry subject to civil jurisdiction. They accepted the papal claim to ban heretical books and willingly inserted the Inquisition into the civil censorship machinery, but rejected ecclesiastical regulation of other aspects of the press. As a result, the government questioned papal privileges and regarded the threat of excommunication as an invalid use of a spiritual sanction in a commercial dispute.

The bookmen offered a humanitarian argument to counter the assertion that papal privileges were needed to ensure that the world would receive the full benefit of the papacy's program of encouraging sacred learning. The bookmen contended that they fostered learning and contributed to the spread of true religion by selling their product at one-third the price charged by Roman printers holding exclusive privileges. Further, the Venetians charged that the Roman bookmen garnered illicit profits at the expense of poor students and monks.

The elevated jurisdictional rhetoric concealed pressing financial considerations on both sides. The Venetian bookmen argued for freedom of publication so that they might reprint works previously issued elsewhere without compensating the original publisher. They could charge lower retail prices if they did not have to bear the cost of careful editing and correction. Behind the sincere desire of the papacy to spread truth and arrest inaccuracy lurked the Roman bookmen and ecclesiastical patrons who stood to profit from papal privileges. Vatican prelates were as aware as Venetian patricians of the economic benefits to a city of a vigorous press, and just as ready to permit local bookmen to exploit privileges unscrupulously. The Venetian bookmen and government piously objected to any Roman monopoly on canonical works—in order to safeguard their own near monopoly.

3. DEFENDING THE PRESS

Altercation marked the history of the press in the late cinquecento. From the early 1580s to the eve of the interdict, the disputes almost always centered on papal privileges granted to Roman printers. The Republic again and again took up the cause of the bookmen, until habit became a policy of protectionism. The Venetian bookmen increasingly won the disputes, and the Republic accumulated precedents for greater state control of all aspects of the press.

In contrast to the battles of 1566–73, the Venetian government in the late cinquecento immediately and repeatedly came to the defense of the bookmen, because its leaders believed that the Venetian press was declining as a result of foreign, especially Roman, competition. In times of general economic duress, the government quickly noted the contribution of the book industry to the city's economic health and felt the loss of revenue on imported paper and exported books. Again and again the bookmen merely hinted at the potential loss of tax revenue or suggested that they would be constrained to emigrate, and the government sprang into action.

Canonical book production and, ultimately, the prosperity of the Venetian press was at stake again. After they defeated the papal privileges on the Tridentine breviary, missal, and Little Office, the Venetian bookmen captured the lion's share of European production of these works. With the decline of the Stamperia del Popolo Romano, Venice, Antwerp, and Paris divided breviary production. From the first edition of the Tridentine breviary in 1568 to the appearance of the Clementine breviary in 1602, the Venetian bookmen published 47 Tridentine breviaries (27 of them by the Giunti) and the Plantin press in Antwerp published 32; in Paris 21 printings appeared, almost all issued by Jacobus Kerver. Another 15 appeared in Rome, Lyons, Salamanca, and elsewhere. The Venetian bookmen dominated missal production even more heavily: from 1570 through 1604, they issued 86 printings; only 27 were issued in Antwerp, 20 in Paris, and another 22 elsewhere.[22] As the Clementine revisions of the canonical works neared promulgation at the end of the cinquecento, the Venetian bookmen moved to protect this lucrative market, and Roman bookmen sought to carve out a piece of it.

Economic and intellectual differences divided the Republic and papacy, but the disputants tended to employ jurisdictional language. Whenever a conflict arose, the Venetian bookmen immediately took their grievance to the government, stating it in economic terms primarily and jurisdictional terms secondarily. When the Senate took the case to Rome, it gave economic and jurisdictional arguments equal weight. A continuing dispute became overwhelmingly jurisdictional, as ambassador and prelate all but dropped the other aspects.

The first dispute surfaced in 1581. As new editions of the *Corpus juris canonici* and *Martyrologium Romanum* neared completion, the papacy prepared for their publication.[23] In *Cum pro munere* of July 1, 1580,

---

[22] The figures are compiled from Bohatta, *Bibliographie der Breviere*, pp. 31–41; and Weale and Bohatta, *Bibliographia Liturgica*, pp. 199–216.

[23] The *Corpus juris canonici* collected the medieval laws of the church, including in the edition of Gregory XIII the Decretals of Gratian, Gregory IX, Boniface VIII, and Clement V, and the *Extravagantes* of John XXII. The *Martyrologium* catalogues

Gregory XIII granted to the Stamperia del Popolo Romano, now in the hands of a consortium of Roman bookmen led by Domenico Basa, an exclusive ten-year privilege of worldwide validity, with violators subject to a penalty of 1,000 ducats and excommunication, for the *Corpus juris canonici.*[24] Before receiving the papal privilege, Basa and his associates had secured from Henry III an exclusive French privilege, which they immediately sold to a Lyons publisher.[25] The revised *Martyrologium* included not only scholarly emendations, but also the new Gregorian calendar. Since Antonio Lilio had received an exclusive papal privilege to publish the new calendar in recognition of the work done on it by his late brother, he also received a ten-year, pain of excommunication privilege for the *Martyrologium* in 1582.[26] Basa and Lilio had already moved to secure Venetian production; in December 1581, Nuncio Lorenzo Campeggi requested in the pope's name Venetian privileges for them.

The Venetians at first refused, arguing that Venetian law denied copyrights to foreign publishers. The nuncio noted that exceptions had been made. Doge Nicolò Da Ponte protested that the Venetian privileges issued for the reformed breviary and missal had gravely injured the local press. The nuncio in his dispatch amplified the reasons for Venetian reluctance: the "major publishers" (probably Luc'Antonio Giunti and his associates) and their patrician supporters objected that such privileges would so harm the Venetian press as to force the bookmen to emigrate or give up publishing.[27]

Nevertheless, the Senate conceded half of the request. It granted to Lilio a ten-year, pain of 300 ducats, Venetian privilege for the *Martyrologium*

---

the martyrs and other saints according to the order of their feast days; a historical martyrology includes a biographical sketch of each saint as well. For the preparation of the Gregorian calendar, *Corpus juris canonici*, and *Martyrologium*, see Pastor, XIX, 279–90.

[24] A copy of *Cum pro munere* is to be found in BNF, 2. 6. 178, *Corpus juris canonici*, in the volume of the *Decretum Gratiani*. . . . (Roma, In Aedibus Populi Romani, MDLXXXIII), Sigs. a2ʳ–a3ʳ.

[25] A. M. Giorgetti Vichi, *Annali della Stamperia del Popolo Romano (1570–1598)* (Rome, 1959), p. 41. Also see Alfredo Cioni, "Domenico Basa," DBI, 7, pp. 45–49.

[26] Antonio Lilio (or Giglio) was the brother of Luigi, who did most of the calendar reform. After Luigi's death in 1576, Antonio took his brother's material to Gregory XIII, and after further work, the new calendar was adopted. I have searched vainly through the Roman editions of 1583 (two) and 1586 of the *Martyrologium* for the terms of the privilege, but they are noted in the contract arranged between the Roman printers and Luc'Antonio Giunti and Giambattista Sessa. See Tenenti, "Luc'Antonio Giunti," pp. 1,035–36.

[27] Letters of Nuncio Lorenzo Campeggi of December 16, 23, 29, 30, 1581, in ASVa, Segretario di Stato, Venezia, F. 22, ff. 356ʳ, 364ʳ–65ʳ, 371ʳ, 377ʳ⁻ᵛ.

and calendar.[28] Lilio formed a Roman company with Domenico Basa and Francesco Zanetti to publish the work, and they immediately sold Venetian rights to Luc'Antonio Giunti and Giovanni Battista Sessa. Two Roman printings appeared in 1583, but these contained so many errors that they were withdrawn. An improved edition appeared in 1584, followed by the Giunti Venetian printing in 1585.[29]

Although the Senate refused to issue a Venetian privilege to the Stamperia del Popolo Romano for the *Corpus juris canonici*, the Venetian bookmen refrained from publishing the work. The Roman edition appeared in 1582, but no Venetian printing appeared before the 1595 Giunti edition. The Bevilacqua press in Turin published the work in 1588, and the Parisian bookmen persuaded Henry III to revoke the French privilege granted to Basa and the Lyons publisher, so that other French bookmen might publish it.[30] Possibly the size of the project (about 3,500 pages in 4° in the 1582 Roman printing), more than the fear of excommunication, daunted most of the Venetian bookmen. The Giunti press possessed the experience and financial resources, but perhaps Luc'Antonio decided not to antagonize the papal officials and Roman bookmen who had given him access to other ecclesiastical works. The bulk of the Venetian bookmen could not have been satisfied, for the Senate had avoided taking a stand on principle against papal privileges.

Within a few years the Republic showed signs of adopting a stronger attitude, although on a less significant matter: requests for Venetian privileges to protect noncanonical titles. Now and then a cardinal asked for a Venetian privilege on behalf of an author. The Senate judged the requests individually, obviously weighing the importance of the petitioner. In 1585, for example, Cardinal Michele Bonelli, a nephew of the late Pius V, petitioned for a Venetian privilege for the *Vita del gloriosissimo papa*

[28] A copy of the privilege is appended to Nuncio Campeggi's letter of December 30, 1581, ibid., f. 379ʳ.

[29] Tenenti, "Luc'Antonio Giunti," pp. 1,035–36; Annibale Bugnini, "Martirologio," *Enciclopedia Cattolica*, VIII, 254. The two 1583 Roman editions, both published by Domenico Basa, are in BNF, Magl. 15. 2. 195 and Magl. 12. 4. 41. The 1585 Giunti edition is listed in Camerini, *Annali dei Giunti*, item 906. To my knowledge, no other Venetian bookman published this edition for the duration of the privilege, although Pietro Dusinelli published Baronius's revision of the *Martyrologium* in 1587. *STC Italian*, 385.

[30] The 1582 Popolo Romano edition is noted in Giorgetti Vichi, *Annali della Stamperia del Popolo Romano*, pp. 93–95; the Giunti edition in Camerini, *Annali dei Giunti*, item 1001; the Bevilacqua edition in Bersano Begey, *Le cinquecentine piemontesi*, I, 154; and editions of Lyons 1584 and 1591, and Paris 1587, are listed in *STC French*, 381, and *Cambridge Catalogue*, items C2667–68. For the revocation of the French privilege, see Giorgetti Vichi, p. 48.

Pio Quinto, authored by Bonelli's secretary, Giovanni Girolamo Catena.[31] And in 1592 Cardinal Cinzio Aldobrandini, a nephew of, and secretary of state to, Clement VIII, asked for a Venetian privilege for Torquato Tasso's *La Gerusalemme conquista*, the revised version of the great poem.[32] The Senate granted both, but made it clear that these were special favors.

In 1587 Francisco de Toledo, a Jesuit scholar, diplomat, and later (1593) cardinal, requested a Venetian privilege for his forthcoming *In Joannis Evangelium commentarii*. Despite support from Leonardo Donà and the ambassador to Rome, the Senate refused, giving as reasons the alleged decline in the number of Venetian presses from 120 to 70, the lower Venetian retail price for such a volume (5 lire compared to the Roman price of 14), and the Republic's notion of freedom of publication.[33] Since the Venetians did not view Padre Toledo as politically significant, their refusal did not establish a precedent, but it did reveal a dawning awareness that the press needed help.

The next dispute concerned a matter of greater importance: the publication of the Sistine Vulgate in 1590. A Tridentine decree of 1546 had ordered the preparation of a new Bible that would meet the standards of modern scholarship, and perhaps no project meant more to the Catholic revival. Sixtus V personally did much of the editorial work on the new Vulgate. However, his enthusiasm exceeded his scholarship, and his idiosyncratic emendations earned sharp criticism from cardinals and scholars. Stung, but unwilling to abandon his work, the pontiff plunged forward, completing the new Vulgate in the spring of 1590. The bull *Aeternus ille caelestium* of April 10, 1590, granted the Typographia Apostolica Vaticana an exclusive worldwide privilege for ten years, with violators under threat of excommunication. After ten years others might print the work if they followed strictly the original edition, subject to the approval of the local ordinary or inquisitor. Older Bibles, breviaries, and missals were to be corrected according to the new Vulgate. When the printed version ap-

[31] Senato, Deliberazioni Roma, R. 6, ff. 77ᵛ–78ʳ (September 28, 1585), 129ᵛ (June 14, 1586). The book was published in Rome in 1586 and 1587, and in Mantua in 1587, but not, to my knowledge, in Venice. Pastor, xvii, 420–23; and *STC Italian*, 158.

[32] Senato, Deliberazioni Roma, R. 9, ff. 96ʳ, 97ᵛ, November 14, 1592; letter of Ambassador Paruta of December 5, 1592, in *La legazione di Roma*, 1, 31. The book was published in Rome in 1593, but not in Venice until 1609.

[33] Letters of Nuncio Girolamo Matteucci of January 2, 9, April 2, 16, 1588, in ASVa, Segretario di Stato, Venezia, F. 26, ff. 22ʳ, 39ʳ, 181ʳ⁻ᵛ (especially), 183ʳ; Senato, Deliberazioni Roma, R. 7, ff. 16ʳ, 53ʳ, March 7 and October 3, 1587. Toledo (1532–96) published his work in Rome in 1588, with Cologue editions of 1589 and 1599 following, but I have not located a Venetian edition. *Cambridge Catalogue*, items T780–82.

peared at the end of May, Sixtus sent copies to Italian and other European heads of state.[34]

The bookmen had no interest in the scholarly qualities of the new Vulgate, but they worried intensely over the directive that older breviaries and missals be corrected.[35] In a petition of June 1590 to the doge, followed by two others in August, the bookmen lamented that this provision rendered older Bibles, breviaries, and missals unsalable. They underlined the economic consequences to the city: the government would lose tax revenue on the paper imported and the books exported, and the bookmen would have to emigrate to Rome to print liturgical titles. The Roman bookmen sold their books for three times the Venetian prices, and the price would climb further if the privilege was permitted to stand. Moreover, the bookmen believed that Basa intended to use the Vulgate privilege as the opening wedge in a campaign to secure exclusive privileges for all ecclesiastical works—an accurate assessment of Basa's intentions. The petition concluded by reminding the government of the worldwide nature of Venetian book commerce.

The Senate accepted the petition and instructed Ambassador Alberto Badoer to obtain the revocation of the entire bull. In its instructions, the Senate clothed the economic argument in humanitarian garb: if the bookmen could not sell the infinite quantity of Bibles, missals, etc., in their warehouses, they stood to lose hundreds of thousands of ducats and would face starvation along with their families. They could not correct older copies because no one would buy canceled or amended volumes. The Sen-

---

[34] Only the more important studies on the Sistine Vulgate controversy, especially those with documents, are cited. *Aeternus ille caelestium* is not included in the *Bullarium*, but was discovered and printed by Baumgarten, *Die Vulgata Sixtina*, pp. 40–64. He also includes *avvisi* and other material. Excerpts relating to the Vulgate from Ambassador Alberto Badoer's dispatches of July 1 through August 27, 1590, are printed in Fridolin Amann, *Die Vulgata Sixtina von 1590. Ein quellenmässige Darstellung ihrer Geschichte mit neuem quellenmaterial aus dem venezianischen Staatsarchiv.* Freiburger theologische Studien, fasc. 10. (Freiburg im Breisgau, 1912), pp. 141–52. The Senate's instructions to Badoer and three petitions from the bookmen are printed by Johann B. Nisius, S. J., "Weitere Venezianische Dokumente in Sachen der Sixtusbibel," *Zeitschrift für Katholisches Theologie* 37 (1913), 878–89. For summary accounts, see Pastor, xxi, 208–22; and F. J. Crehan, S. J., "The Bible in the Roman Catholic Church from Trent to the Present Day," in S. L. Greenslade ed., *The Cambridge History of the Bible: The West from the Reformation to the Present Day* (Cambridge, 1963), pp. 208–11.

[35] It appears that the Venetian Inquisition promulgated and then revoked *Aeternus ille caelestium.* In addition to frequent references to the Inquisition's actions in the documents printed by Amann and Nisius, see the letters of Nuncio Marcello Aquaviva of August 4, 1590, and of the inquisitor, Fra Stefano Cento, of August 4, 18, 1590, in ASVa, Segretario di Stato, Venezia, F. 27, f. 161^r; F. 28, ff. 318^r–19^r.

ate prudently omitted the emigration threat, which might have encouraged Roman protectionism. Then the Senate advanced a jurisdictional argument: the bull was prejudicial to the temporal power that had always permitted anyone "to print, sell, and contract as he wishes, as is done in the other trades and businesses, all kinds of books after they have been on one occasion approved by the authority of the Holy Church."[36] Next the government lamented that the threat of excommunication caused spiritual anguish among the bookmen—a point not once raised by the bookmen. The Senate asked for the revocation of the bull, citing Gregory XIII's withdrawal of Pius V's missal *motu proprio* as a precedent.

In Rome Ambassador Badoer further elaborated both the economic and, especially, the jurisdictional arguments. He claimed that the Roman printers sold their Bibles for five or six ducats, in contrast to the Venetian price of one—a doubling of the alleged price difference. And in an interview with the pope, he vastly amplified the Republic's fears of ecclesiastical encroachment on civil rights. Badoer accepted the papal right to control the initial printing of a sacred text. But when the press reprinted a work for the common benefit of the world, it acted in its capacity as a lay craft (*arte laica*) and, as such, was subject to the civil authority. If the lay authority lost control of the press, no area of civil jurisdiction would be secure. Tomorrow the pope might prohibit tailors outside of Rome from making ecclesiastical vestments, and artists and sculptors from constructing religious artifacts. Before long no artisan would be permitted to build a church without a papal privilege, for the church would have spirited away whole groups of subjects from temporal jurisdiction. Six years later almost to the day, Leonardo Donà used a restrained version of this argument in the fight against the Clementine Index.[37]

[36] "Oltra il manifesto pregiudicio anchora, che ne veniriano a ricever le proprie leggi, et consuetudini del nostro temporal governo, libero per gratia del S. Dio: essendo stato sempre licito ad ogniuno di stampare, vendere, et contrattare a' suo beneplacito, come si fa nelle altre arti, et mercantie, ogni sorte di libri dopo che una volta sono stati approbati dall'auttorità di Santa Chiesa." Instruction of June 30, 1590, as printed in Nisius, "Venezianische Dokumente," p. 880.

[37] "Ma che quanto più era stampata, tanto più si divulgava a beneficio commune, et che il stamparla era di arte laica et si doveva fare di artefici laici sottoposti alla iurisdittione de' loro Principi che quando si volesse considerar in questo termine le cose, si potria anche domane ordinar che in niun locco fuori di Roma si potessore far da' sarti paramenti di chiesa di alcuna sorte nè da pitori o scultori imagini di Nostro Signore, della gloriosa Vergine, et de tutti li santi, nè da dotti Maestri Croci Calici, Tabernaculi, et tant' altre cose, perchè siano dedicate a sacro uso, anzi che si potria dire che niun altro Maestro se non chi tenesse il Privilegio potesse fabricar le chiese stesse, il che non sarebbe altro che distrugger le città intiere, et levar li sudditi alli Principi temporali. . . ." Letter of July 29, 1590, in Senato, Dispacci da Roma, F. 25, ff. 332^v-333^r; also printed by Amann, *Die Vulgata Sixtina*, p. 144. For Donà's

The dispute continued through July and August. The pontiff agreed that the bull should not be enforced, but would not revoke it. He acknowledged the validity of the criticism of his scholarship and tried to make amends by issuing tiny correction slips to be pasted over the errant passages,[38] but he could not bring himself to withdraw his Bible. While the controversy swirled, the pope's health suddenly weakened, and death intervened on August 27 to spare him the inevitable but painful decision. A few days later, the Vatican suspended the sale of the Sistine Vulgate.

The Sistine Vulgate languished until the accession of Clement VIII on January 30, 1592. While the scholars returned to their labors, the pope ordered the acquisition (at papal expense) and destruction of all printed copies of the Sistine Bible.[39] The pontiff presented a new Vulgate (generally termed the Clementine Vulgate although it still carried the name of Sixtus V) to the Typographia Apostolica Vaticana in September 1592. The promulgation bull, *Cum sacrorum Bibliorum* of November 9, granted the Typographia Apostolica Vaticana a ten-year universal privilege, with excommunication and unspecified temporal punishment threatened against violators. But it avoided any reference to the correction of breviaries and missals or to the prohibition of older Vulgates.[40] Clement VIII presented a copy to Ambassador Paolo Paruta, who relayed it to the Senate, and neither the Senate nor the bookmen mentioned it further.[41]

The government's attitude had stiffened since 1581, with the result that the economic threats of the bookmen provoked quick action.[42] The patriciate was learning to use jurisdictional arguments to protect the economic interests of the press and the Republic. It had not yet formulated a protectionist policy, but it was acquiring the habit. The Sistine Vulgate dis-

---

use of this argument in 1596, see Ch. IX, sec. 3. A prominent noble, Badoer (d. 1592) is considered to be sympathetic to the papacy by Cozzi, *Contarini*, p. 6, n. 1, 124; and by Stella, *Chiesa e stato*, p. 68. Lowry cautions against exaggerating his papal sympathies. "Reform of the Council of Ten," pp. 295–96, n. 91. I agree with Lowry, and would add that it is difficult to determine a patrician's views on the basis of stances taken in diplomatic encounters. Whatever his own feelings, the ambassador's duty was to advance the Venetian position with any available argument.

[38] See Plate 35 in *The Cambridge History of the Bible*.

[39] Senato, Deliberazioni, Roma, R. 9, ff. 105^v, 166^r (January 2, 1592 mv, and August 14, 1593); Pastor, XXIV, 224.

[40] *Bullarium Diplomatum et Privilegiorum Summorum Romanorum Pontificum*, vol. IX (Turin, 1865), pp. 636–37.

[41] Paruta's letter of December 26, 1592, in *La legazione di Roma*, I, 52–53.

[42] The government may have been unusually ready in 1590 to oppose any potential economic threat because it faced perhaps the most serious food shortage of the century and needed money to purchase grain from abroad. Pullan, *Rich and Poor*, pp. 355–56.

pute eventually yielded a substantial, though incomplete, victory for the bookmen. The papacy had again issued an exclusive ten-year privilege for a religious work, and the bookmen had honored it; but the papacy had also allowed the bookmen to sell old, uncorrected stock. Undoubtedly the outcome heartened the bookmen and encouraged further opposition to papal privileges. This dispute established a pattern for the future.

In November 1594 Clement VIII issued to Domenico Basa, still director of the Typographia Apostolica Vaticana, a ten-year universal privilege, with excommunication and 500 ducats' penalty for violators, for all canonical books that he might publish.[43] The Venetian bookmen told the Senate that they could only abandon publishing or move to Rome. The Senate immediately sent stern instructions to Ambassador Paruta, adding to the usual arguments the fear that if the papacy acquired control over sacred books it would claim jurisdiction over all titles. The Senate ordered Paruta to obtain the same satisfactory resolution secured in the Sistine Vulgate controversy.

Both the papal officials and Paruta took the matter more calmly. The pontiff was conciliatory, and the Congregation of the Index took a restricted view of Basa's privilege. Paruta reported that Basa owed large sums of money because of a bank failure, and the privilege was simply a papal gesture to help him fend off creditors. Paruta concluded that the privilege would harm the Venetian bookmen only if new editions of the breviary or missal were envisaged, but the pope had no such plans.[44]

Despite Paruta's soothing letter, the Senate continued to fulminate. This was not a question of books but of jurisdictional principle, the Senate stormed, because the papacy was attempting to rule a lay industry with the ecclesiastical weapon of excommunication. Paruta then spoke to a cardinal from the congregation that oversaw the Typographia Apostolica Vaticana. The cardinal defended papal privileges on the grounds that Rome possessed no other means of contending with printers, who through "negligence or ignorance" frustrated efforts to reform sacred texts. The congre-

---

[43] Senato, Deliberazioni Roma, R. 10. ff. 102ᵛ-4ʳ (February 18, 1594 mv), 110ᵛ (March 4, 1595), 113ᵛ (March 18); letters of Paruta of February 25, March 11, 1595, in *La legazione di Roma*, III, 65-68, 85-87. Basa's privilege of November 17, 1594, the protest of the bookmen of February 14, 1595, and some of the above Senate material are printed in *La legazione di Roma*, III, 65-66, n. 1, 67, n. 1, 85, n. 2. Brown, *Venetian Press*, pp. 140-42, describes this incident but makes several errors.

[44] Paruta was mistaken on this last point. Clement VIII had in 1593 and 1594 signified his intention to reform the breviary and missal. See Paul Maria Baumgarten, *Neue Kunde von alten Bibeln: Mit zahlreichen Beiträgen zur Kultur- und Literaturgeschichte Roms am Ausgange des sechzehnten Jahrhunderts* (Rome, 1922), p. 342.

gation sought not to restrict the liberty of the Venetian press, but to cure a disorder.

Paruta made it clear to the Senate that he believed that many of the charges leveled against the Venetian bookmen were justified. Readers had told him that Venetian books contained many mistakes, adulterations, and even frauds; indeed, all Venetian books might be prohibited if the product failed to improve. He advised the Senators not to pursue the matter, reminding them that Paul IV had banned all Venetian imprints from the papal state in 1559. He believed that a compromise on breviaries and missals could be arranged despite Basa's privilege. The Senate took Paruta's advice, and Basa went bankrupt and died in 1596.[45] The incident showed that positions had not changed, except for the growing stridency of senatorial rhetoric.

The next round followed very shortly. In late 1595 the papacy issued a revised *Pontificale Romanum*, the manual detailing procedures for conferring the sacraments of confirmation, Holy Orders, and other episcopal rites. After the usual intrigue by Roman bookmen, the papacy prohibited all previous editions and bestowed an exclusive thirty-year privilege on a group of Roman bookmen, who published it; violators were threatened with fines of 1,000 ducats and excommunication. The Giunti of Venice, who had printed at least six earlier cinquecento editions, the last in 1582, had 400 unsalable copies on their hands. Moreover, the Roman bookmen printed the new work for three scudi per copy and sold it for ten.[46] On May 3, 1596, the Venetian bookmen addressed a petition to the government objecting to this and all other papal privileges on ecclesiastical works. They charged that the privileges enabled the Roman bookmen to prosper at the expense of the Venetian presses, whose number had declined from 125 to 40.[47] On June 14 the Senate abolished all past, present, and future papal privileges; anyone attempting to use one within the Venetian state would be liable to a fine of twelve ducats per copy and confiscation.[48]

[45] Cioni, "Domenico Basa," DBI, 7, pp. 48–49. Possibly the Senate dropped this issue because it received full satisfaction from the papacy in a concurrent dispute, that of the inquisitor of Bergamo, who had conducted an unlawful trial.

[46] The privilege is found on sig. A3ᵛ of *Pontificale Romanum Clementis VIII Pont. Max. iussu restitutum atque editum* (Romae, MDXCV, Colophon: Apud Iacobum Lunam. Impensis Leonardi Parasoli, & Sociorum). I cite the BM copy, C 21, f. 13. The promulgation bull is in *Bullarium Diplomatum et Privilegiorum Summorum Romanorum Pontificum*, vol. x (Turin. 1865), pp. 246–48. Details of the intrigue and printing are given by Giovanni Battista Bandini in his memorandum (to be discussed shortly) in Giovanni Mercati, "Vecchi lamenti contro il monopolio de' libri ecclesiastici, specie liturgici," *Opere minori*, vol. ii (Vatican City, 1937), pp. 486–87.

[47] AVSa, Fondo Borghese iv, vol. 224, ff. 117ʳ⁻ᵛ. Another copy in ASVa, Segretario di Stato, Venezia, F. 32, ff. 339ʳ⁻ᵛ.

[48] Copies of the law are found in ASVa, Fondo Borghese iv, vol. 224, f. 118ʳ,

The Senate's pronouncement of June 14, 1596, seemed an enunciation of a clear policy rejecting papal privileges. In one sense it was, for from this point forward the government universally supported the bookmen in their complaints against Rome. For the moment, however, the government employed this decree only as a bargaining counter in the simultaneous dispute over the Clementine Index. Ambassador Giovanni Dolfin sought to persuade the pope to revoke the privileges, as did Cardinals Cesare Baronius, Agostino Valier, and the rest of the Congregation of the Index. But the ambassador discovered that certain "persone grandi" with a financial stake in the outcome of the dispute supported the Roman printers and blocked a papal surrender. Clement did not budge, and the Senate dropped the privilege question when it won concessions on the Clementine Index.[49] The Venetian bookmen did not print the *Pontificale* in the last years of the cinquecento.[50]

Besides the financial involvement of important personages, the papacy had another reason for continuing to issue privileges: the Venetian bookmen persistently refused to follow the new texts. In February 1601 the Congregation of the Index condemned the Venetian consortium, led by Giunti, that had monopolized Venetian missal production in the last twenty years of the cinquecento, charging them with textual deviations in a 1596 printing of the missal.[51] The promulgation bull for the Clementine missal of 1604 detailed some of the alterations discovered in this and other printings: changes in the order of the epistles and gospels to be read from the pulpit; the substitution of unauthorized texts for the introit, gradual, and offertory; and other errors.[52]

Despite the difficulty of convincing the Venetian bookmen to follow the authorized texts, one experienced Vatican scholar realized that papal privi-

and Segretario di Stato, Venezia, F. 32, ff. 340ʳ⁻ᵛ. See also ASV, Senato, Deliberazioni Roma, R. 11, ff. 68ᵛ–69ʳ. Brown, *Venetian Press*, p. 215, prints it.

[49] Letters of Ambassador Dolfin of June 22, 27, 29, July 13, 20, 1596, in Senato, Dispacci da Roma, F. 37, ff. 204ʳ⁻ᵛ, 269ʳ⁻ᵛ, 271ʳ, 281ᵛ, 295ᵛ, 324ᵛ–25ʳ; Collegio, Esposizioni Roma, R. 6, ff. 165ʳ⁻ᵛ, September 6, 1596.

[50] I do not believe that the work was published again in the sixteenth century.

[51] The condemnation embraced Luc'Antonio Giunti (whose name appeared on the faulty printing), the heirs of Melchiorre Sessa (i.e., Giovanni Battista and Giovanni Bernardo), Nicolò Miserino, Bonifacio Ciera, the heirs of Giovanni Varisco, and the Paganini firm, which included the brothers Camillo, Orazio, and Scipione. These firms had published thirty-seven of the thirty-eight extant missals printed in Venice between 1583 and 1600. However, the papacy took no concrete action against the bookmen. ASVa, Miscellaneorum Armarium iv–v, vol. 30, f. 11ʳ, a printed edict of February 17, 1601, Romae, Apud Impressores Camerales; Weale-Bohatta, *Bibliographia Liturgica*, pp. 209–16.

[52] *Bullarium Diplomatum et Privilegiorum Summorum Romanorum Pontificum*, vol. xi (Turin, 1867), pp. 88–90, paragraph 2.

leges also opened the door to substantial Roman abuses. Giovanni Battista Bandini (1551–1621), who spent most of his adult life working on the liturgical texts, had served as a corrector and later a supervisor of the Typographia Apostolica Vaticana. Between 1596 and 1598 he addressed a detailed memorandum to Clement VIII strongly urging him to drop the use of privileges.[53] Bandini reviewed the scandals, beginning with the reformed breviary, missal, and Little Office of Our Lady of the 1560s. Paolo Manuzio and his confederates had raked in thousands of scudi on these works while Pius V's privileges were honored. But they had published books of such poor quality that, in the end, many unsold copies remained. More recently, the Clementine Vulgate privilege had led the Roman publisher (the Typographia Apostolica Vaticana, i.e., Domenico Basa) to print only 2,000 copies, and he had not sold them all because of their high price. Shipping costs, customs duties, and other expenses had put them beyond the means of ultramontane customers.

Bandini next described how Paolo Blado, a Roman bookman who published official papal documents, exploited his position. Granted exclusive rights for three years to publish a new office and mass of the saints to be inserted in existing breviaries and missals, Blado had printed whole new breviaries and missals, thus forcing the customer to purchase a complete work instead of a supplementary pamphlet. Blado also refused to reprint papal bulls; hence, the bull that cost two scudi to print and sold originally for four or five soon climbed to twenty because of its scarcity. In similar fashion Blado charged pilgrims exorbitant prices for the leaflets cataloguing the indulgences to be earned in the eternal city.

Bandini strongly urged the pope to drop the use of privileges. They unjustly threatened excommunication in commercial matters, failed to work in any case, and offered great opportunities for abuse and scandal. He believed that everyone should be permitted to print canonical works as long as they followed the authorized texts, and ordinaries and nuncios could see to that.

Perhaps because of Bandini's protest, or possibly as a result of constant Venetian pressure, the papacy conceded most of the Venetian demands upon the promulgation of the Clementine revisions of the breviary and missal. The Clementine breviary promulgation bull of May 10, 1602, limited the privilege of the Typographia Apostolica Vaticana to the papal state and permitted other printers to publish the breviary if they secured

---

[53] The memorandum, from BAVa, Vaticanus Latinus 6097, ff. 85r–86r, was printed by Giovanni Mercati, "Vecchi lamenti contro il monopolio de' libri ecclesiastici specie liturgici," *Rassegna Gregoriana* 5 (1906), coll. 13–24, and reprinted in Mercati's *Opere minori*, II (Vatican City, 1937), 482–89, which is the copy cited here. On Bandini, see Paolo Prodi, "Giovanni Battista Bandini," DBI, 5, pp. 713–14.

PARTE
PRESA
NELL' ECCELLENTISS.
Conseglio di Pregadi.

Adì 14. Zugno. 1596.

In materia delli Stampatori, e Librari di questo Serenissimo
Dominio, che hanno ottenuto & otteneranno
Motu proprij.

Stampata per Antonio Pinelli
Stampator Ducale.

A S. Maria Formosa, in Cale del Mondo Nouo

13. The Senate's law of June 14, 1596, abolishing papal *motu proprii*.
Source: VC, Ms. Cicogna 3044

written permission from the ordinary or inquisitor and exactly followed the Roman edition. The bull forbade the bookmen to reprint older breviaries, but permitted them to sell, and clergymen to use, older versions if constrained by economic necessity. Finally, the papacy made the conciliatory gesture of formally revoking all earlier papal breviary privileges. Although the bull still threatened excommunication, it had eliminated most of the reasons for disobedience. The bookmen had won a clear and substantial victory. Five different Venetian bookmen took advantage of their new freedom by publishing at least twelve printings of the Clementine breviary between 1602 and 1611.[54]

The papacy followed the same policy for the Clementine missal after obtaining assurances that the Republic would compel the bookmen to meet a higher standard of accuracy. As the work neared completion, the two powers arranged for Ambassador Francesco Vendramin to forward an authenticated manuscript so that the Venetian bookmen could print it immediately. But the Congregation of the Index still worried about accuracy. In January 1603 the secretary of the Congregation presented to the ambassador a list of the "infinite number of errors" (alleged to be 5,000 or more) found in the last missals published in Venice. He severely criticized the inadequate numbers and the carelessness of the Venetian press correctors, lamented the Republic's negligence, and threatened reprisals. The ambassador and the Senate promised a remedy.[55]

The Senate kept its word. After taking the precaution of forbidding the bookmen to emigrate, it passed a sweeping press reform act on May 21, 1603.[56] The preamble lamented the decline of the industry, blaming it on avaricious bookmen who produced inferior books, on the insufficient number of proofreaders, and on emigration. A series of measures to ensure a better product followed, beginning with the appointment of official proofreaders and instructions for the performance of their duties. The law also exhorted the bookmen to pay greater attention to the quality of paper, ink, and type; established new copyright regulations; encouraged

[54] *Bullarium*, x, 788–90; Pastor, xxiv, 227–29; Bohatta, *Bibliographie der Breviere*, pp. 41–43.

[55] Letters of Ambassador Vendramin of March 2, 16, 23, 1602, January 25, February 8, 1602 mv, February 14, 1603 mv, in Senato, Dispacci da Roma, F. 48, ff. 1^v, 56^v, 73^r–74^v, F. 49, ff. 406^v–7^r, 431^{r-v}, F. 51, f. 425^{r-v}; Senato, Deliberazioni Roma, R. 13, ff. 154^r (February 23, 1601 mv), 158^r (March 23, 1602), 217^r (February 1, 1602 mv); F. 23, entry of February 23, 1601 mv.

[56] For the laws, see Brown, *Venetian Press*, pp. 217–21, documents xviii–xx, from Senato Terra, R. 72 and 73. Brown summarizes them on pp. 175–77, but was unaware of the pressure from Rome. His account also needs to be corrected: document xviii should be dated "mv," i.e., 1603; the date "1601" on p. 175 line 12 should become "1603"; and the date "1601" on p. 180 line 12 should be canceled. Brown's conclusion that these measures were not enforced is probably correct.

guild matriculation; and provided for periodic inspection of the industry as a whole.

A satisfied papacy promulgated the Clementine missal under the same terms as the new breviary in 1604. The Typographia Apostolica Vaticana printed the first edition, the Giunti produced a faithful copy, and other printings followed.

After forty years of conflict and violation the papacy had apparently abandoned the exclusive privilege. On the contrary, a final dispute erupted on the eve of the interdict, and Clement with characteristic inconsistency defended not a papal but a religious order privilege. When Pius V had decreed the adoption of the reformed Tridentine breviary and missal, he had exempted those religious orders, including the Order of Preachers, that could prove prescription of two hundred years for their own liturgical texts. The Dominicans' publisher, Giunti of Venice, enjoyed an Italian, and very nearly a European, monopoly on Dominican canonical works until the early 1590s. Giunti then lost the privilege to Giovanni Bernardo Sessa of Venice, who published them in association with Barezzo Barezzi. But in 1603 the general of the order lifted Sessa's privilege and bestowed it on a Roman publisher, Alfonso Ciacconio (or Ciacone). The latter began immediately to publish the Dominican breviary and missal, selling them throughout Italy and possibly beyond, in order to exploit his monopoly.[57] Sessa frantically petitioned the Republic for help, and the Senate took up his cause in Rome.

The Venetians took their case to the general, the pontiff, and their advisors, while Sessa hired a Roman agent to bombard the Vatican with petitions, and Ciacconio replied in kind. Two Venetian ambassadors pursued the matter continuously for more than a year but ran into a stone wall.[58] The general flatly refused to revoke Ciacconio's privilege, citing

[57] The Giunti of Venice published twelve Dominican breviaries from 1552 through 1592, and six Dominican missals from 1550 through 1590, as well as the Dominican *Caeremoniale* (1582), *Constitutiones* (1582), *Martyrologium* (1582), *Processionarium* (1560, 1572, 1590), and *Psalterium* (1551, 1583). Camerini, *Annali dei Giunti*, passim; and *STC Italian*, 387, for the 1572 *Processionarium* not noted by Camerini. Sessa and Barezzi, published three Dominican breviaries and one missal in 1596 and 1597. Bohatta, *Bibliographia der Breviere*, pp. 147–49; Weale and Bohatta, *Bibliographia Liturgica*, pp. 315–16. Very few other Dominican breviaries and missals were published while Giunti held the privilege, and none while Sessa held it. Barezzi, originally from Cremona, published at least 21 editions between 1588 and 1599, and continued to be active in the following century. Alfonso Ciacconio was the *nipote*, and editor of the works of the Spanish Dominican scholar Alfonso Chacon (Ciacconius), 1540–99.

[58] For the entire affair, see Senato, Deliberazioni Roma, R. 14, ff. 62r–v, 70v, 82v–83r, 91r, 92r, 94v–95r, 102v–3r, 107v, 111v–12r, 130v (June 21, 1603, through August 28, 1604); letters of Ambassador Vendramin of September 6, 1603, through May 1, 1604, and of Ambassador Agostino Nani of May 29 through July

the bad quality of Sessa's work and of that of the Venetian bookmen generally, and the pope would not intervene. Other reasons besides the poor quality of Venetian printing influenced the general and the pontiff. Ciacconio's enterprise, estimated to involve 20,000 scudi and many presses, meant a great deal to the city. Moreover, he basked in the protection of powerful figures, including, possibly, the Spanish ambassador.

As the dispute dragged on, pope and ambassador enunciated all the jurisdictional and economic arguments that each knew by heart. Sometimes the meetings degenerated into heated wrangling over the whole history of Venetian-papal relations. When Ambassador Vendramin protested past Venetian devotion to the Holy See, the pope charged that Venice had stolen papal land in the Romagna. The ambassador countered with the famous story of the Venetian championship of Pope Alexander III in 1177. The pope contemptuously dismissed it as a fable. Despite broad hints from two ambassadors to drop the case, the Senate pursued it with great tenacity, once threatening to bar entry into Venice of the publications of Ciacconio and other Roman printers. The cardinal-nephews shrugged when they heard this threat, because such an action would invite retaliation far more damaging to Venice than to Rome. In the end the privilege stood.[59]

The two sides probably fought over this relatively minor privilege because they saw it as a bargaining chip to use in discussions of the more important Clementine missal. The coincidence of the promulgation bull permitting all Venetian bookmen to publish the missal (July 7, 1604) and the last time that the ambassador raised the Dominican privilege (shortly before July 24) supports this supposition. In addition, so much tension strained Venetian-papal relations at this time, that any issue could ignite quarreling.

In the 1590s the Venetian government had settled into a policy of protecting the press from ecclesiastical controls, a corollary to a similar expansion of civil jurisdiction in other areas. The state's rejection of papal privileges encouraged the bookmen to resist the Clementine Index, and the patriciate to begin the process of substituting civil for inquisitorial authority over prohibited books.

31, 1604, in Senato, Dispacci da Roma, F. 51, ff. 4ʳ, 16ʳ–19ʳ, 43ʳ, 48ʳ⁻ᵛ, 116ʳ–17ʳ, 149ʳ, 167ʳ⁻ᵛ, 185ᵛ–87ᵛ, 200ᵛ–1ʳ, 214ʳ–20ʳ, 256ᵛ–57ᵛ, 279ʳ–80ᵛ, 309ʳ–11ʳ, 327ʳ, 368ᵛ–69ʳ, 381ʳ–83ʳ, 399ʳ–400ᵛ, 424ʳ–25ᵛ, 456ᵛ–57ʳ, 472ʳ⁻ᵛ; and F. 52, ff. 2ᵛ, 12ᵛ, 28ᵛ, 53ʳ–56ᵛ, 79ʳ⁻ᵛ, 126ʳ–29ᵛ, 171ᵛ, 183ʳ⁻ᵛ, 201ᵛ–2ʳ, 216ᵛ, 227ᵛ–28ʳ, 233ᵛ, 245ʳ–47ʳ, 259ʳ–60ʳ, 271ᵛ–72ʳ, 285ᵛ. It is interesting that two ambassadors of such opposed views as Vendramin, elected patriarch in 1608 and cardinal in 1615, and Nani, antipapalist and friend of Sarpi, used the same arguments, but were equally unsuccessful.

[59] Ciacconio published five Dominican breviaries and three missals between 1603 and 1615.

PARTE
PRESA
NELL' ECCELLENTISS·
Conseglio di Pregadi,

1 6 0 3. *Adi* 1 1. *Maggio.*

Con vna Terminatione delli Eccellentissimi Signori
Reformatori dello Studio di Padoua, in materia
dell' Arte de' Stampatori, & Librari.

Stampata per Antonio Pinelli,
Stampator Ducale.
A S. Maria Formosa, in Cale del Mondo Nouo.

14. The Senate's press reform law of May 11, 1603. Source: VC, Ms. Cicogna 3044

IX

THE WANING OF THE INDEX

INEVITABLY, the Republic's altered views on ecclesiastical prerogatives and its policy of asserting lay control over the press touched the Index and its enforcement. Although the gap in the records of Inquisition trials for most of the period from 1592 to 1616 renders a judgment tentative, the available information points to increased violation. In contrast to its quiet acceptance of the Tridentine Index thirty years previously, the Republic sharply challenged the terms of the Clementine revision in 1596. Increased conflict marked all phases of censorship in the decade or so before the interdict.

Possibly more heretical prohibited books entered Venice between 1592 and 1605 than at any time since the 1560s. Enlarged commercial contact with the militantly Protestant Dutch and English, a prelude to the renewal of diplomatic relations, offered new opportunities for the entry of contraband. The papacy sent a stream of warnings about these foreigners. In January 1593 Clement VIII warned the Venetians that Dutch and English ships brought in heretical titles and that English merchants distributed them. The Senate agreed to appoint someone to search the ships, but the result, if any, is unknown. Later that year the pontiff spoke to Ambassador Paruta about the Englishmen who disseminated Calvinist views in Venice. The Republic assured Rome that the merchants tended to their affairs and that the sailors stayed on their ships.[1] Despite the assurances, it is likely that heretical books entered through these avenues, for the papacy normally did not issue warnings without concrete information gleaned by its widespread diplomatic corps.

Moreover, Venetian bookmen were again smuggling prohibited titles into and out of the city. In 1594 the papacy discovered that Roberto Meietti, a publisher who always managed to stay one step ahead of the Holy Office, was distributing prohibited German titles in Rome itself. He had brought the banned books into Venice, removed their title pages, substituted innocent new ones, and then shipped the disguised works to Rome.

[1] Barberino Latino 5195, f. 53ᵛ; Collegio, Esposizioni Roma, F. 3. ff. 206ʳ⁻ᵛ, January 29, 1592 mv; letter of Paruta of July 17, 1593, in *La legazione di Roma*, 1, 265–66.

The Congregation of the Index demanded that the Venetian Holy Office proceed against Meietti and his accomplices. The Council of Ten promised that the Riformatori dello Studio di Padova would investigate; quite likely, they did little or nothing.[2] The incident suggests that Meietti judged the risk of incurring the harsh punishment that had been dealt to Pietro Longo to be slight.

Venetian refusal to follow renewed papal strictures against Hebrew books provides additional evidence of the waning enthusiasm for papal-initiated censorship. Departing from the more generous policy toward Jews and their books of Sixtus V, Clement renewed and intensified prohibitions of the Talmud and other Hebrew titles early in his pontificate, although he sometimes modified, and did not always succeed in enforcing, the decrees.[3] In Venice neither the Holy Office nor the civil courts molested the Hebrew press. At least four different Hebrew publishers, led by Giovanni di Gara, who issued at least forty-five titles between 1590 and 1600, brought about a modest revival of the Hebrew press. Asher ben Jacob Parenzo, who printed at least eleven titles between 1579 and 1598, published an appendix and commentary to the Palestinian Talmud in 1590, a work that came very close to violating the ban on the Talmud.[4]

To a limited extent, the Esecutori contro la bestemmia increased its surveillance of the press. In contrast to a single sentence handed down in the 1580s, the court levied penalties of up to fifty ducats in seven press cases, most of them involving printing a title without a privilegio, between 1592 and 1604.[5] The increase demonstrated a slightly greater lay effort to punish press law infractions, but the Esecutori in no way filled the gap in press regulation left by a waning Holy Office.

Before long the state turned its attention to the Index in order to measure it against the new standards of civil control. As the papacy pre-

[2] Letter of Paruta of November 19, 1594, in *La legazione di Roma*, II, 488–90; CX, Deliberazioni Roma, R. 3, f. 59^v, November 29, 1594. Because the Riformatori *fondo* is very incomplete for the cinquecento, I cannot confirm that they did not act. However, I have not come upon any notice that they ever punished bookmen for violations. For some information on Roberto di Paolo Meietti, who published in Venice from 1588 through 1617, see my forthcoming article, "Books for Sarpi: The Smuggling of Prohibited Books into Venice during the Interdict of 1606–1607," in Sergio Bertelli ed., *Studies in Honor of Myron P. Gilmore* (Florence, forthcoming).

[3] Baron, *History of the Jews*, XIV, 49–59; Pastor, XXIV, 218–21; Reusch, *Index*, I, 48–51.

[4] The Parenzo publication is in *STC Italian*, 657. Daniele Zanetti published twenty-five titles from 1596 through 1600, and Giovanni Bragadin four from 1590 through 1600; the figures are based on *STC Italian*. See also Amram, *Hebrews Books in Italy*, pp. 338–71.

[5] Bestemmia, Bu. 57, Notatorio Terminazioni 1582–1597, ff. 231^v–32^r, 258^r; Bu. 61, Notatorio Terminazioni 1593–1614, ff. 15^v, 20^v, 27^r, 31^r, 94^{r-v}.

pared to issue a new Index, the Republic sought changes favorable to the Venetian press, an approach pioneered in other areas of disputed jurisdiction.

1. PREPARATION OF A NEW INDEX

Years had passed since the appearance of the Tridentine Index, and both Rome and the local inquisitors felt the need for a new one. The Congregations of the Index and Inquisition had dealt with some new titles by sending out instructions and answering individual inquiries—an inadequate substitute for a comprehensive list. During the pontificate of Gregory XIII, Rome began and then dropped work on a new Index.[6] To fill the lacuna, the inquisitors of Parma and another northern Italian city drafted their own supplementary Indices in 1580 and between 1574 and 1587, respectively.[7] These local efforts were more severe, especially on secular vernacular literary titles, than the papal Index to follow, but they could have had only local validity, if the Roman Congregation permitted that.

In February 1587 Sixtus V commissioned a group of cardinals, including Agostino Valier, Girolamo della Rovere, who was Archbishop of Turin, the veteran diplomat Vincenzo Laureo, Costanzo Bucafoci da Sarno, OSF, and either Marcantonio or Ascanio Colonna, to prepare a new Index.[8] Advice came from various sources, including Antonio Castelvetro, who proposed that the task of expurgation be taken out of the hands of the Congregation of the Index and given to university faculties, especially theologians. Sixtus did not heed him, but did ask the major Catholic universities outside Italy for advice.[9]

The commission drafted and printed an Index in the spring of 1590, but then hesitated.[10] Some Vatican prelates thought it overly severe, for

---

[6] Pastor, xix, 319–21.

[7] Reusch, *Indices*, 579–92, prints the Parma Index. Joseph Hilgers discovered the other one in a BAVa ms. and printed it in his "Indices verbotener Bücher aus dem 16. Jahrhundert," *Zentralblatt für Bibliothekswesen* 20 (1903), 450–56.

[8] Letter of Ambassador Giovanni Gritti of February 7, 1586 mv, in Senato, Dispacci da Roma, F. 20, f. 567ʳ. The "Cardinal Colonna" mentioned could have been either Marcantonio or Ascanio since both later had a hand in the Index.

[9] VM, Ital. xi, 1 (6958), "Trattato," f. 16ᵛ; Pastor, xxi, 197.

[10] It is not clear how final the commission considered the printed version. Because of the variations between the three copies to be found in the BAVa, Hilgers argued that the commission had not completed its work and viewed this printing as a trial run. Hilgers, *Index*, pp. 11–13, 524–25. Reusch, on the other hand, edited the 1590 Index in his *Indices*, 448–523, from another copy discovered and reprinted in the nineteenth century. He considered it to be a completed Index, which, however, suffered the same fate as the Sistine Vulgate. Reusch, *Index*, 1, 501–32. Differences in rules and entries between the 1590 Index and the 1596 Clementine Index

it banned several Catholic theological works, including a title of Robert Bellarmine, for failing to defend papal temporal power strongly enough.[11] Alerted to the Republic's concern for the press as a result of the Vulgate discussions, Ambassador Badoer raised the subject of the new Index with Cardinals Della Rovere and Ascanio Colonna in late August. Badoer criticized the Index, arguing that the condemnation of so many titles would greatly hurt the "poor bookmen" and the banning of works of theologians like Bellarmine would generate scandal. Della Rovere asserted that the Catholic texts were to be banned only until they could be corrected. Badoer responded that it was unreasonable to prohibit an entire work if one wished only to correct a few words, and if one changed a book's argument it would no longer express its author's views.[12] The fundamental objection to expurgation could not have been more neatly stated. Two days later Sixtus V died, and the curia shelved his Index.

Badoer's intervention, although not the result of instructions from Venice, expressed the patriciate's intention to examine all aspects of papal press policy for possible adverse effect on the Venetian press. Not since 1549 had the government challenged the papal claim to judge individual titles; only the bookmen had done so. However, the nobility followed the new Index closely, challenging its contents and regulations when necessary.

The Congregation of the Index resumed work on the new Index upon Clement VIII's accession in 1592, and brought it to completion and had it printed in the summer of 1593 (see figure 15).[13] Bellarmine's book had been dropped, but a completely new feature for papal Indices had been added: lengthy appendices of vernacular authors or titles derived from various regional Indices. These lists attempted to prohibit the numerous objectionable vernacular titles that had appeared since 1564 and to rectify Tridentine omissions.

---

finally promulgated were not great, but much additional discussion had taken place in the intervening years. See below.

[11] Pastor, XXI, 197.

[12] "Ma Rovere trattò questo negotio più copertamente, diffendendo prima l'indice con diverse ragioni alle quali fu anco da me risposto, et dicendo, che li libri d'alcuni non sariano del tutto prohibiti, ma fino che fossero corretti, alchè non mi potei contenir di dire, che se si voleva correggere qualche parola, pareva quasi non ragionevole che si prohibissero tutte l'opere, ma se si voleva alterar li sensi et l'opinioni principali, non sarebbe più stata l'opera di quest'auttore. . . ." Letter of Alberto Badoer of August 25, 1590, in Senato, Dispacci da Roma, F. 25, ff. 417^{r-v}.

[13] *Index librorum prohibitorum. . . . Postea vero à Sixto V & nunc demum à Sanctissimo D. N. Clemente Papa VIII recognitus & auctus. . . .* (Romae, Apud Paulum Bladum, Impressorem Cameralem, MDXCIII). I cite the copy in BAVa, Racc. I. IV. 1649. It is not printed in Reusch, *Indices.* For the background, see Hilgers, *Index,* 13, 529–31; Pastor, XXIV, 216.

The French appendix included some 90 authors or titles, and the Dutch and German appendix about 160 entries, all outright condemnations taken from the Antwerp Index of 1570.[14] The Iberian appendices listed about 190 Spanish and 18 Portuguese proscriptions, repeated from the 1583 Index of the Spanish inquisitor-general Quiroga. The Italian appendix differed from the others by splitting its 190 author or title entries between prohibitions (about 40 percent) and expurgations (60 percent). Some of the Italian entries, such as the ban on the works of Aretino, Machiavelli, and various Italian Protestants, simply reiterated Tridentine condemnations. The new entries, many of them probably taken from the Parma Index of 1580, moved toward greater severity. For example, the 1593 Index banned the opera omnia of Nicolò Franco in place of the Tridentine condemnation of a single title, and ordered expurgation of all of Anton Francesco Doni's works in comparison to the previous ban of a single title. Few, if any, of the newly prohibited works were heretical, but, like much Italian secular literature, they abounded in anticlericalism and other material that the Counter Reformation found morally objectionable.

When Cardinal Baronius and others in Rome protested the severity of the new Index, the pontiff hesitated about promulgation. Ambassador Paolo Paruta moved to exploit Clement's indecision. Without waiting for Senate instructions, he went immediately to the pontiff to protest the Index, bringing to the task his formidable diplomatic gifts.[15] He began by noting the great commercial importance of the Venetian press, calling it the most flourishing in Europe and gracefully underlining the Republic's solicitude for it. Then he moved to the main part of his argument: the new Index was so severe that it would provoke an antipapal backlash among bookmen, readers, and scholars. It contained so many titles never previously condemned that the bookmen would suffer severe losses. Bookmen who had published, and readers who had purchased, titles approved by the Tridentine Index would be ruined. The newly condemned works were not heretical, but only marred by "trivialities," Paruta's oblique term for the anticlericalism, obscenity, and lasciviousness found in the vernacular works. Paruta played upon papal fears of scholarly rejection of the new Index; he claimed already to have heard a "universal displeasure" in Rome. If the Index were promulgated, men of

[14] The appendices are found on ff. 45ʳ–50ᵛ (Italian), 51ʳ–56ᵛ (Spanish), 57ʳ⁻ᵛ (Portuguese), 58ʳ–61ʳ (French), and 61ᵛ–69ᵛ (Dutch and German), of the 1593 Index. For comparison with previous Indices, see Reusch, *Indices*, 579–92, 432–41, 304–18, respectively.

[15] Paruta's letter of August 14, 1593, in *La legazione di Roma*, I, 296–98. Passages dealing with the Index from this and the following letters are printed by Hilgers, *Index*, 531–35. Brown, *Venetian Press*, pp. 137–40, summarizes them.

INDEX
LIBRORVM
PROHIBITORVM

Cum regulis confe&is per Patres à Tridentina Synodo
dele&os auctoritate P I I . I I I I . primum editus.

Poſtea vero à S I X T O . V . & nunc demum à Sanctiſſimo
D . N . C L E M E N T E P A P A . V I I I .
recognitus & auctus .

Inſtructione adiecta de imprimendi, & emendandi libros rationc

R O M AE , Apud Paulum Bladum , Impreſſorem Cameralem,
CVM PRIVILEGIO SVMMI PONTIFICIS.
M. D. X C I I I .

15. Title page of *Index librorum prohibitorum. . . . Postea vero à Sixto V & nunc
demum à Sanctissimo D. N. Clemente Papa VIII recognitus & auctus. . . .* (Romae,
Apud Paulum Bladum, Impressorem Cameralem, MDXCIII). Source: BAVa, Racc.
I. IV. 1649

learning everywhere, whose opinions and good will were cherished by the papacy, would disapprove.

The pope agreed to hold up promulgation while he studied the Index. But he took exception to Paruta's argument against the prohibition of vernacular texts: surely these books contained some evil to have merited condemnation. Sighing, Paruta agreed, but argued that, since one could neither force all men to be good nor eliminate all error, it would be better to ignore small transgressions lest men turn to worse. And he again emphasized the dangers of alienating the learned, who had acquired their libraries with much care and at great cost; if they could not rest secure that their shelves would not be stripped by future expansion of the Index, they would reject papal authority. Clement promised to consider Paruta's remarks, and the audience ended.

Paruta presented his arguments skillfully. He wanted the appendix of vernacular Italian titles excised because the Venetian press printed most of them, but to do this he had to question the papal claim to being the arbiter of faith and morals. Paruta screened this challenge by emphasizing the objections of Roman prelates and scholars. The pontiff feared alienating the scholars because the renewal of sacred learning depended on them. Paruta only lightly sounded the chord of Venetian commercial interests, and he did not raise the Republic's jurisdictional claims, thus avoiding jangling Clement's most sensitive nerve. Similarly, Paruta refrained from pushing the pontiff to take a stand, while providing him with arguments with which to answer the zealots within the Congregation of the Index. It was a virtuoso performance.

The Senate endorsed Paruta's position and asked him to repeat it in their name.[16] Paruta next learned that a deputation of scholars had asked the pope to soften the Index, while the Congregation pressured him to promulgate it without revision. Paruta sought out the pope to remind him of the fate of Paul IV's Index; the severity of that Index had caused Italians and ultramontanes to reject it, and Rome had had to modify and then withdraw it, at great cost to papal prestige.[17]

Clement reached a decision. In a meeting with the Congregation in January 1594, he ordered the cardinals to modify the Index. Specifically referring to Paruta's protests and drawing upon his arguments, including the possibility of loss of respect for the papacy, he overrode objections. Paruta reported with satisfaction that the list of vernacular titles would be dropped or sharply reduced.[18] The Senate instructed Paruta to express

---

[16] Senato, Deliberazioni Roma, R. 9, ff. 169ᵛ–70ʳ, August 21, 1593.

[17] Letter of September 4, 1593, in *La legazione di Roma*, I, 332–33.

[18] Letters of January 15, March 19, 1594, in *La legazione di Roma*, II, 180, 245–46.

to the pontiff Venetian gratitude for the "castration" of the Index, but one may rest assured that the tactful ambassador did not use that word.[19]

Paruta had won a significant and encouraging victory for the bookmen and the Republic. By exploiting internal Vatican opposition to the Index, he had secured modifications in the list of condemned titles. More generally, the division of opinion and pontifical accommodation to Venetian wishes showed that the winds of change were blowing through Roman corridors, however gently.

2. THE CLEMENTINE INDEX

The papacy finally published and promulgated the Clementine Index in the spring of 1596. The new Index took the form of a supplement to the Tridentine Index, and its spirit wavered uneasily between severity and moderation.

The Clementine Index reprinted the Tridentine list of condemned titles with a few variations, which usually involved the substitution of expurgation for outright condemnation. The new Index added authors and titles published since 1564, but not the appendices of vernacular works. In similar fashion, it reprinted the Tridentine censorship rules, and added eighteen paragraphs of an *Instructio*, which under the headings of Prohibition, Expurgation, and Printing added new rules and amplified, clarified, or repeated the earlier rules.[20]

Shortly after the new Index arrived in Venice, the bookmen presented their objections to the Collegio, which forwarded them to Rome.[21] The Congregation of the Index responded in June, arguing that the new Index was "easier" than those of 1559 and 1564, and the rules less burdensome to the bookmen.[22] Some easing of the censorship was possible, in the opinion of the Congregation, because fewer pernicious books circulated in Italy.

To a certain extent, the Congregation evaluated the new Index correctly, especially because it promulgated the expurgation procedures promised by the Tridentine Index. Most authors, readers, and bookmen probably preferred an expurgated version to none at all. Moreover, the new Index authorized local expurgation under the supervision of ordinary and inquisitor (paragraph one under Expurgation); in effect, the papacy

---

[19] Senato, Deliberazioni Roma, R. 10, f. 28ᵛ, March 26, 1594.

[20] For the Clementine Index, see Reusch, *Indices*, 524–78, with the *Instructio* on pp. 529–35. Reusch summarizes the rules and entries in *Index*, 1, 532–49, 560–83.

[21] Collegio, Esposizioni Roma, F. 4, ff. 500ʳ⁻ᵛ, June 21, 1596.

[22] The Congregation's "Risposta alli avertimenti di Venetia sopra il novo Indice," which clarified and interpreted some of the rules of the *Instructio*, is appended to Ambassador Giovanni Dolfin's letter of June 27, 1596, in Senato, Dispacci da Roma, F. 37, ff. 272ʳ⁻73ᵛ.

acknowledged that it could not do the entire job itself.[23] The bookmen undoubtedly preferred local expurgation, for a local clergyman could act more quickly than a Roman commission and, possibly, would be more responsive to protests over individual passages.[24] A few years before the promulgation of the Clementine Index, the Venetian publishers had begun to print expurgated versions of works, especially secular vernacular literary titles that, though not banned, had been avoided for years. To cite one example among many, Nicolò Franco's *Dialogi piacevoli*, last printed in 1559, appeared seven times (six times in Venice, once in Verona) between 1590 and 1609 in an expurgated version prepared by Fra Girolamo Gioannini da Capugnano.[25]

The Clementine *Instructio* further eased the censorship by allowing for individual expurgation. Tacitly acknowledging that local Inquisitions could not collect and expurgate all copies of a title, the *Instructio* ordered readers to correct their own according to the printed expurgated version (paragraph five under Expurgation). This rule made no provision for enforcement.[26] A few years later, the papacy went a step further by trusting the reader to expurgate according to his own understanding of the guidelines. The papacy made the concession after abandoning its project for a comprehensive *Index Expurgatorius*, of which a single volume appeared in 1607 with instructions for the correction of only fifty titles.[27] In 1608 the papacy instructed the Venetian Holy Office that it could permit "suitable and intelligent persons" to hold and expurgate "suspect books" according to the expurgation guidelines issued with the

[23] For example, the Congregation of the Index had devoted years to the expurgation of Boccaccio's *Decameron* and Castiglione's *Courtier* in the 1570s and 1580s. Of course, these two works were of extraordinary importance; nevertheless, the time and effort spent on them must have given pause to the Congregation.

[24] Although local expurgation probably became the norm, the Congregation and local inquisitors did sometimes exchange *correctii* (lists of corrections) for specific titles. It is not always possible to determine the point of origin of the expurgated version of a title. See Tedeschi, "Florentine Documents," pp. 582–84.

[25] Grendler, *Critics*, pp. 182, 218–19. The more frequent appearance of expurgated titles about 1590 suggests that the papacy permitted the Venetian bookmen to proceed with the publication of expurgated versions at about the time that the expurgation guidelines (contained in the stillborn 1590 Index) were drafted. Paruta probably objected to the appendix of Italian titles in 1593 because its more severe condemnations (prohibition in place of expurgation in some cases) would have halted the printing of expurgated vernacular titles.

[26] Rotondò, "Nuovi documenti," p. 179, doc. 21; and Tedeschi, "Florentine Documents," p. 584, note that inquisitors elsewhere did sometimes attempt to round up copies in bookstores and in private hands to introduce corrections. However, I have not found any evidence of this practice in Venice at the end of the cinquecento or in the early seicento.

[27] See Reusch, *Index*, 1, 549–59.

1596 Index. In particular, they might hold *"libri d'humanità"* if they canceled the names of heretics and their glosses.[28] With this concession, the papacy all but gave up its attempt to keep editions of the classics edited by Protestants and other kinds of banned humanistic works out of the hands of Italian scholars, at least in Venice.

But the Clementine Index balanced these relatively liberal procedures with severe guidelines for the actual expurgation (paragraph two under Expurgation). It instructed expurgators to excise heretical, erroneous, scandalous, schismatic, seditious, and blasphemous passages, as well as those offensive to pious ears. Other matter to be expurgated included ambiguous phrases that might lead souls to evil opinions; praise of heretics; passages dealing with superstition, prophecy, or divination; passages in which Fate and Fortune limited free will; anything paganistic; anything prejudicial to the good name of a neighbor, clergyman, or prince; propositions challenging ecclesiastical liberty, immunity, and jurisdiction; arguments favoring reason of state and tyranny; *facetiae* that injured another's good name; lascivious passages; and, finally, obscene pictures.

The Congregation of the Index obviously sought to strengthen the hand of the local clergyman expurgating a book for the press by giving him the longest possible list of reasons for making deletions. He had to use his own judgment on particular passages, but the *Instructio* provided him with an arsenal of prohibitions to justify his decisions. If as a result of the guidelines the local expurgator leaned toward greater rather than less severity, some curial circles would say, "So much the better."

Much of the rest of the *Instructio* repeated Tridentine rules, sometimes making them more precise. Paragraph five under Prohibition granted bishops and inquisitors authority to examine "national" Indices in order to determine whether titles included in them should be prohibited elsewhere. This restatement of a Tridentine rule sought to empower local Inquisitions to ban additional works chosen from foreign Indices, such as those of Spain and Portugal. Obviously some members of the Congregation regretted dropping the appendices of vernacular titles and wanted to leave open the possibility of adding them in the future. But when the Venetian bookmen objected, the Congregation agreed to a very narrow interpretation of this power. The Congregation stated that local Inquisitions could ban additional titles only if they were foreign, or carried counterfeit imprimaturs, *privilegi*, or imprints, and that the Congregation

---

[28] "Le dico per ordine de signori cardinali ch'ella può concedere licenze de libri sospesi, Donec corrigantur, a persone idonee et intelligenti, con la clausula, Deletis delendis: et anco de' libri d'humanità ne' quali sono postille d'Autori Heretici con far cassare i loro nomi e dette postille, che fussero cattive. Et in ciò ella si governi conforme alle Regole dell'Indice," Vaticanus Latinus 10945, f. 113ʳ, July 12, 1608.

and the Venetian Holy Office would act together. The Congregation further promised that such action would be taken "very rarely" (*rarissime volte*).[29] In effect, the Congregation agreed that the local inquisitor would not add to the Index.

The *Instructio* (paragraph five under Printing) also demanded that each printed volume carry a copy of the approval (testamur) of the bishop or inquisitor or both, a Tridentine Index rule that had never been implemented in Venice. The Congregation argued that if volumes carried these, foreign heretical printers would find it more difficult to prepare counterfeits, and Venetian publishers would not be able to circumvent local censorship.[30] If the imprimatur were printed in the front matter of each volume, the inquisitorial inspector in Venice would be able to determine at a glance whether a book could be accepted or needed careful scrutiny. A foreign Protestant printer might attempt a counterfeit imprimatur, but he would have to reproduce accurately its form, as well as several proper names. By the time a Genevan publisher, for example, succeeded in obtaining the information to make an accurate counterfeit imprimatur, the names of the Heads of the Council of Ten or inquisitor would have changed. The Congregation also sought to improve detection of Venetian violators. If a volume had to carry its imprimatur, with a date and the names of accountable officials, investigation of fraud would be easier.

Rule four under Printing demanded that a printer, upon completion of his press run but before selling it, deposit with the Holy Office a copy of the manuscript followed. The Congregation sought to make it easier for the inquisitorial reader to make sure that the approved manuscript had been faithfully followed.

The Clementine *Instructio* contained one completely novel feature: a demand that bookmen swear an oath before the bishop and inquisitor that they would obey the Index and not knowingly admit anyone suspected of heresy into their guild (paragraph six under Printing). Not in the Tridentine Index rules, but anticipated in the 1590 Index, the oath was inspired by Pius IV's demand of 1564 that all university professors and students make a profession of faith.[31] This new feature was, in fact, an

---

[29] "Al 6.o come al primo si risponde, perchè si intende de' libri forestieri, o con licentie finte, o false stampati, e rarissime volte si darà il caso, ne si farà senza giustissima causa con participatione costì del S. Officio, e auctorità delli Ss. Cardinali delle Congregatione dell'Indice." From the "Risposta alli avertimenti di Venetia sopra il novo Indice" appended to the letter of June 27, 1596, in Senato, Dispacci da Roma, F. 37, f. 273.^{r}

[30] "Risposta," in Senato, Dispacci da Roma, F. 37, ff. 272^v–73^r.

[31] Rule nineteen of the Sistine Index required bookmen to swear an oath that they would not admit anyone suspected of heresy into their guild, and that they

HABES HIC AMICE LECTOR.

P. TERENTII

COMOEDIAS VNA CVM

INTERPRETATIONIBVS

AELII Donati: GVIDONIS. Iuuenalis Cæ
nomani: IO. Calphurnii uiri apprime docti: nec
nõ & SERVII: ac Iodoci Badii ASCENSII.
Insuper & SCHOLIA ex Donati: Asperi: &
CORNVTI commentariis decerpta. Nec nõ
& ~~━━━━━━━━━━━━━━━~~ in eiuldé Terentii comœdias argumenta, Adiunctis. atcp emenda
tis dictionibus græcis: quæ deerát. appoſitis etiá
figuris aptiſſimis.

Indicata ſunt præterea diligentius carminum
genera: & in his incidentes difficultates. Corre-
cta quædá & Cóſulũ nomina: idcp ſtudio & opera

ex ueterum exemplariorum collatione.

Adhæc acceſſit copioſiſſimus & accuratiſſimus
Index tam uocũ a comentatoribus declararatũ: q̃
adagiorũ: quæ annotatũ digna uiſa ſunt. Atcp ea
quidé omnia q̃ antea unq̃ prodierint emédatiora.

M D   XXXVI

16. Title page of Erasmus ed., *Terentii comoedias.* . . . (MDXXXVI. Colophon: Venetiis per Ioannem Patavinum & Venturinum Rossinellis. MDXXXVI), with the editor's name inked out. Source: VM, 388. D. 60

attempt to return to the sterner Counter Reformation of the 1560s. When the bookmen objected that the oath subverted lay jurisdiction by turning them into ecclesiastical subjects, the Congregation of the Index responded that anyone unwilling to swear the oath wished to engage in "secret commerce" with heretics.[32] Obviously the Congregation remembered Pietro Longo and believed that contacts with ultramontane Protestant printers for the purpose of importing banned titles continued. The papacy probably believed that the oath offered hope of more effective enforcement. A bookman apprehended for dealing in prohibited titles would also face perjury charges, a serious matter with both legal and spiritual consequences.

3. STRUGGLE OVER PROMULGATION

Gone forever were the days in which the Republic accepted an Index without comment. On June 14 the Senate formally stated its opposition to the Index, specifically objecting to the oath, the authority granted to ordinaries and inquisitors to prohibit additional titles, and the requirement that printers give the Holy Office manuscripts.[33] The Senate instructed Ambassador Giovanni Dolfin to seek out the pontiff and Cardinal Valier, now the head of the Congregation of the Index, and obtain the elemination of these features. The Senate refused to publish the Index pending their removal.

The Republic and papacy negotiated simultaneously at various levels in Rome and Venice.[34] Ambassador Dolfin raised the subject of the Index

---

would faithfully reproduce the authorized texts when printing liturgical and sacred works. Reusch, *Indices*, 458.

[32] "Risposta," in Senato, Dispacci da Roma, F. 37, f. 273[r].

[33] Senato, Deliberazioni Roma, R. 11, ff. 67[v]–69[r]. The Index occupied only one-third of the instruction; the Senate also stated at length its objections to the papal press privileges, and directed the ambassador to demand that the pontiff revoke them as well. Obviously the Senate joined Index and privileges for bargaining purposes, and the ambassador raised them in tandem in his audiences with the pope through late July. One wonders whether the Senate would have compromised on the oath if the pope had made major concessions on the privileges, but Clement refused to give way on either at this time.

[34] The subsequent account is based on the following sources. For the discussions in the Collegio, see Collegio, Esposizioni Roma, R. 6, ff. 112[r]–70[v], passim (June 14 through September 13, 1596); the same can be found in ibid., F. 4, ff. 403[r]–502[r], passim, in reverse chronological order. The Senate's instructions to the ambassador are in Senato, Deliberazioni Roma, R. 11, ff. 67[v]–113[r], passim. Ambassador Giovanni Dolfin's letters of June 22 through September 21 are in Senato, Dispacci da Roma, F. 37, ff. 202[r]–409[v], passim, and F. 38, ff. 32[r]–33[v]. Three copies of the nuncio's letters on the Index exist: (1) ASVa, Segretario di Stato, Venezia, F. 32, ff. 293[r]–351[r], passim. These also include four letters on the Index of Patriarch

in his weekly audiences with the pope, met frequently with the cardinal-nephews Pietro and Cinzio (Passeri) Aldobrandini and with the cardinals Valier and Baronius. In Venice Nuncio Anton Maria Graziani and the Collegio discussed the Index—or, to be precise, they bickered and quarreled over it. The Collegio reported to the Senate, which sent instructions to the ambassador. A Venetian working committee embracing Matteo Zane, a Riformatore dello Studio di Padova who spoke for the Collegio, the nuncio, the cardinal-patriarch Lorenzo Priuli, and the inquisitor and patriarch's vicar in subordinate roles pursued detailed bargaining over terms and language.

The Congregation of the Index quickly acceded to the Venetian demands. Led by Valier, who displayed "his customary loving affection in the service of his *patria*,"[35] and Baronius, who took his habitual moderate stance on Index matters, the cardinals felt that speedy publication was worth concessions on the rules. They repeated their narrow interpretation of the power of bishops and inquisitors to prohibit additional titles, made other concessions, and agreed to revoke the oath.

The pope, however, would not compromise. Too many disputes punctuated by Venetian belligerence had eroded his original good will toward the city. Not only had he given way far too often, in his opinion, but also early in the negotiations he concluded that the Republic's position failed to show proper deference for the papal office. Clement claimed that the Venetians would rather please "two or three bookmen" than offer

---

Priuli (August 17, 24, September 7, 14) not found elsewhere. (2) VC, Mss. Morosini-Grimani, "Lettere di Mons. Gratiani," R. 358, f. 11ᵛ–97ᵛ, passim, and R. 359, pp. 1–56, passim. (3) Excerpts dealing with the Index are found in VM, Mss. Italiani, Classe VII, 414 (7809), Fra Carlo Lodoli, "In materia dell'indice tra i dispacci di Mons. Gratiani Nuntio in Venetia." Lodoli addressed his work to three Riformatori dello Studio di Padova, Carlo Ruzini, Alvise Pisani (both *Cavalieri* and *Procuratori*) and Giampiero Pasqualigo. The ms. lacks a date, but since these three held the office on September 4, 1727 (Brown, *Venetian Press*, 273), one can conclude that it dates from about that time. Spot checks indicate that Lodoli's excerpts (probably taken from the VC Morosini-Grimani copies, for it is difficult to imagine that he had access to the ASVa letters) are accurate and complete. Mario Brunetti, "Schermaglie veneto-pontificie prima dell'Interdetto. Leonardo Donà avanti il Dogado," in *Paolo Sarpi e i suoi tempi: studi storici* (Città di Castello, 1923), pp. 124–33, summarized the battle over the Index from the VC Morosini-Grimani letters only. Seneca, *Donà*, pp. 252–54, did the same, very briefly, from Collegio, Esposizioni Roma, alone.

[35] Letter of Ambassador Dolfin of July 20, 1596, in Senato, Dispacci da Roma, F. 37, f. 324ᵛ. Other ambassadors in other battles expressed similar appreciation of Valier's efforts. See, for example, Paruta's letter of January 15, 1594, in *La legazione di Roma*, II, 180. The Venetians also considered Baronius to be well-disposed toward the Republic.

the pontiff the respect due him.[36] He agreed only to suspend the oath, pending a journey to Rome for further negotiations by Patriarch Priuli.

The Collegio and Senate adopted an equally unyielding stance, focusing their opposition on the oath. Whatever benefits in enforcement the oath promised, the Congregation and papacy had made a serious tactical error in demanding it because it presented a jurisdictional issue around which opposition to the Index could coalesce. In the opinion of the nobility, the oath egregiously challenged the state's claim to rule its citizens. With the full support of the Collegio, Leonardo Donà made the most of the issue.

Donà articulated the jurisdictional argument in a long speech on July 12.[37] He began by acknowledging the papal right to prohibit books it judged to be heretical and by professing the Republic's willingness to accept the list.[38] (He could not, however, resist mentioning that the Index had undergone many changes in the past five or six years.) Then he moved to his main point: the oath intolerably undermined lay jurisdiction by transforming four to five hundred Venetian laymen into ecclesiastical subjects. He claimed that the papacy wished to take control of a lay craft, and hinted that if the bookmen swore the oath they would not be completely free to print what the state wanted. Digressing a bit, he enunciated the familiar theme of Venetian loyalty to the Holy See, contrasting it with the disobedience of the rest of the Catholic world. Returning to his main argument, Donà asserted that the Collegio unanimously agreed not to permit laymen to take this oath because, as craftsmen, they were subject to the state's authority. The church already ruled the consciences of the bookmen through the confessional; further subjugation to ecclesiastical power could not be endured. Donà repeated Alberto Badoer's argument of 1590: if the Republic gave way, the church would little by little extend its jurisdiction to cover the craftsmen who made artifacts for ecclesiastical use—chalicemakers, candlestickmakers, tailors who sewed priestly vestments. Because the Apostolic See claimed so much, secular governments had to exercise eternal vigilance lest they lose their temporal power. Doge Marino Grimani, Giacomo Foscarini, and other members of the Collegio expressed similar views, although less eloquently.

By early August the working committee had settled all differences over the *Instructio*, usually through papal concessions, except for the oath.

[36] See, for example, the audience reported by Dolfin on July 13, in Senato, Dispacci da Roma, F. 37, ff. 295^r–96^v.

[37] Collegio Esposizioni Roma, R. 6, ff. 123^{r-v}; Seneca, *Donà*, pp. 252–53, also quotes it in full.

[38] Donà did not need to challenge the contents of the Index, nor would it have been advisable. Through Paruta's timely interventions the Republic had obtained as much amelioration of the entries as it could expect.

The pope had agreed only to suspend it, and the Venetians demanded revocation. Both sides spoke vaguely of Patriarch Priuli's going to Rome for further discussions. On August 9 Nuncio Graziani asked the Collegio to promulgate the Index on the grounds that all had been settled except the oath, and Patriarch Priuli would resolve that problem shortly in Rome. Speaking for the Senate, the doge flatly refused, and the meeting degenerated into jurisdictional wrangling.

The nuncio immediately forced the issue. On August 10 he wrote Cardinal Cinzio Aldobrandini, the Secretary of State for Italian affairs, that on the following Tuesday (August 13) he and the patriarch would promulgate the Index. Bypassing the Holy Office and the lay deputies, the two men informed an assemblage of abbots and clerical deans of parochial districts that the Index was to be implemented. The nuncio and patriarch ordered confessors to question penitents to determine whether they possessed prohibited titles and to deny absolution to those who refused to destroy their banned volumes.

The Venetians were enraged. The Collegio ordered the bookmen under pain of death to disregard the Index, and summoned the patriarch, his vicar, and several priests to justify their actions. Donà stormed at this arrogant assertion of ecclesiastical power. At one point Donà asked the vicar what respect he had for the prince. The vicar answered that he respected the prince's authority very much, but as vicar he also owed allegiance to the church. Donà pounced on him: You say that you respect the prince very much? I say that he is everything, and that all other powers are accessorial.[39]

Not reasons of state but personal considerations motivated the nuncio and patriarch. Doubtlessly the nuncio initiated the premature promulgation of the Index in Venice. Throughout his nunciature Graziani manifested strong convictions of papal supremacy and zealously fought for papal rights.[40] He also wished for a speedy end to the dispute because he had heard that other states, notably Savoy, had delayed promulgation of

[39] "Come? Voi disse di ricconoscer [sic] il Principe qui per molto? Io dico che egli è il tutto, et che per il tutto bisogna ricconoscerlo, et obedirlo, et che gli altri tutti sono accessori. . . ." Collegio, Esposizioni Roma, R. 6, f. 142^v, August 16, 1596.

[40] From Sansepolcro (Tuscany), Graziani (1537–1611) was the bishop of Amelia (Umbria) from 1592. A secretary through most of his career, first to the veteran diplomat Cardinal Giovanni Francesco Commendone and later to Sixtus V, he took up his duties in Venice, his first nunciature, c. April 1, 1596. The Index was the initial dispute in his tour of duty, but many others followed until he was relieved on October 8, 1598. He never received another diplomatic assignment. His appointment demonstrated a serious failure of judgment in Rome, but was by no means the only sign of deterioration in the Vatican diplomatic service in the last decade or so of the century. On Graziani, see Pietro Amat di S. Filippo, *Biografia dei viaggiatori italiani colla bibliografia delle opere.* 2nd ed. (Rome, 1882), 1, 309–10.

the Index pending the Venetian outcome. Unfortunately for his cause, Graziani failed to comprehend Venetian sensitivity to any alleged violation of lay rights. A comparison of his letters with the transcripts of his discussions with the Collegio shows that he reported what the Venetians said accurately enough, but that he failed to perceive that they meant what they said. Even after his abortive attempt to implement the Index, he seemed unaware of the intensity of Venetian anger—or, at least, he failed to report it to Rome.

Similarly, Graziani appeared to be wholly unacquainted with Venetian political realities. In one attempt to explain his actions, he wrote that a patrician had informed him that the Collegio would have quieted down and accepted the fait accompli of the Index promulgation had not Donà stirred them to fight. If Graziani swallowed this explanation—he could have been simply using it to exculpate himself—he was totally ignorant of recent Venetian policy. The majority of the Venetian leaders held strong views on lay jurisdiction and had implemented them often in recent years.

The patriarch bore the brunt of Venetian anger, and had the most explaining to do. Priuli told the Collegio that he had felt that he could accede to the nuncio's request to promulgate the Index because the government had not objected to the Index per se and because the negotiations on the rules were nearly completed. He admitted to some confusion and misunderstanding on how close to agreement the negotiatiors were, but fervently protested his devotion to the Republic, as well as his allegiance to the pope—at a ratio of about eight to one. However, Priuli wrote to Rome that because the negotiations went so slowly and the reputation of the church was suffering, he had judged it necessary to act. He claimed that the Holy Office had often proceeded without consulting the lay assistants—a dubious assertion. He begged the pope not to consider him "troppo Venetiano," and declared his willingness to shed his blood for the pope and church.[41]

Perhaps the explanation for the patriarch's puzzling behavior can be found in his career. One of the most important noble families, the Priuli produced consecutive doges in the brothers Lorenzo (1556–59) and Girolamo (1559–67). Lorenzo di Giovanni (1538–1600) came from another, comparatively poor branch of the Priuli.[42] Nevertheless, while still very young, he was elected the Venetian ambassador extraordi-

[41] Collegio, Esposizioni Roma, R. 6, ff. 144^r–47^r, August 17, 1596; letter of Priuli of August 24, 1596, in ASVa, Segretario di Stato, Venezia, F. 32, ff. 331^r–32^r.

[42] For Priuli's career, see E. Albèri, *Le relazioni degli ambasciadori al Senato*, ser. II, vol. 4 (Florence, 1857), pp. 291–92; and Lowry, "Church and Venetian Political Change," p. 191, n. 141 (with the nuncio's comment), 359–60.

nary to Tuscany (1565–66), and then the regular envoy to the key courts of Spain (1573–76), France (1579–82), and Rome (1583–86). Upon the last appointment, the nuncio reported to Rome that Lorenzo had been elected ahead of others of greater qualifications and years because of *broglio* (intrigue), doubtlessly through the family connections. Priuli also served as *podestà* at Belluno, Brescia, and Cremona; during the infrequent pauses in his diplomatic career, he was elected Savio di Terraferma (1576, 1579, and 1582), Savio Grande (1584 and 1588), and a member of the Council of Ten in 1587. In January 1591, the Senate elected him patriarch. In short, Lorenzo Priuli was one of the most important and most politically successful nobles of his generation. A man of his connections and experience did not misjudge the political atmosphere or become confused over something as simple as the progress of negotiations.

Conflicting pressures from Rome and Venice trapped Priuli, and he elected to satisfy the papacy and to take the calculated risk of affronting the Republic. He had earlier demonstrated some sympathy for papal jurisdictional claims and church reform. Before he was chosen for his Roman ambassadorship, he was rumored to have said that the current bitter dispute (conflicting sovereignty claims over the patriarchate of Aquileia) could be settled with a little tact. As ambassador he did resolve the issue, and he obliquely criticized the intransigence of Donà, his predecessor, in his concluding *relazione*.[43] As patriarch Priuli demonstrated a commitment toward religious reform by inaugurating the convent and parish visitations that had been demanded years previously by Trent.[44]

An earthier consideration may also have obliged Priuli to serve Rome. Major foreign embassies enabled a patrician to attain political success, but the stipends did not cover the expenses. A relatively poor noble like Priuli must have been deeply in debt after holding four of them, and the patriarchate undoubtedly brought much-needed financial relief.[45] The

[43] I make no attempt to give a complete bibliography on the complex Aquileia dispute between 1580 and 1585, but the following works are essential: Pio Paschini, "La questione del feudo di Taiedo e le peripezie di un patriarca," *Memorie storiche forogiuliesi* 40 (1952–53), 76–137; Lowry, "Church and Venetian Political Change," pp. 49–52; and Seneca, *Donà*, pp. 128–41.

[44] See the letter of Nuncio Ludovico Taverna of April 13, 1594, in ASVa, Segretario di Stato, Venezia, F. 30, ff. 169ᵛ–70ʳ; Oliver M. T. Logan, "Studies in the Religious Life of Venice in the Sixteenth and Early Seventeenth Centuries: The Venetian Clergy and Religious Orders, 1520–1630," Ph.D. thesis, University of Cambridge, 1967, pp. 159, 290, n. 2.

[45] In the *decima* of 1582 Lorenzo and his two brothers declared a combined income of only 772 ducats annually, quite low for a major Venetian politician; Lowry, "Church and Venetian Political Change," p. 359. The patriarchate, by contrast, produced annual income of 9,000 ducats in 1644.

cardinal's hat (announced on June 5, 1596) promised more, but at the time of the Index controversy Priuli had not yet been formally installed, assigned a titular Roman church, or, perhaps, benefices.[46] Even though Priuli owed his patriarchate to the Senate, his pecuniary needs may have placed him in greater bondage to the papacy.

It also appears that the nuncio and patriarch acted on Vatican instruction, or at least approval, not from the pope but from Cardinal Cinzio Aldobrandini. In a letter of August 17, written before learning what had happened in Venice on the thirteenth, Ambassador Dolfin related a curious statement of the pope. At the end of a discussion of the Index, Clement had assured the ambassador of his sincere good will toward the Republic, and carefully charged him to report the sentiments accurately. Twice the pope charged him, adding at the end that Cinzio had written differently. Dolfin had quickly sought out Cinzio to tell him what the pope had said. Cinzio was angry and hostile, declaring that the pope must not cede on the Index.[47] In brief, it looks as if Cinzio had either ordered the nuncio to act, or had approved his proposal, without clearing it with the pope. In any case, Clement dissociated himself from his nephew's deed.

Cinzio's character and his rivalry with his younger cousin Pietro help to explain his action. Clement had appointed Cinzio (1551–1610), his favorite nephew, secretary of state, but Cinzio had no talent for diplomacy.[48] Impetuous, outspoken, and a rigid defender of papal claims, Cinzio soon alienated the Spanish ambassador and provoked scenes with

---

[46] HC, IV, 4.

[47] "Se così mi haveva detto, restando certa, ch'io osservo tanto diligentemente le parole dettemi da Sua Santità, che nel rappresentarle alla Serenità Vostra difficilmente posso commetter errore; cosi il Papa confesso due volte havermi detto le medesime parole, et non mi disse altro della causa perchè il Signore Cardinale S. Georgio havesse scritto diversamente. . . . sendo andato dal Signore Cardinale S. Georgio secondo il solito, et havendo dato conto di tutto quello havevo passato col Papa, et delle risposte havute, io l'ho ritrovato così duro, et così aspro in questo negotio, et tanto fermo in dir liberamente che il Papa non doveria ceder mai a questo punto. . . ." Letter of Dolfin of August 17, 1596, in Senato, Dispacci da Roma, F. 37, ff. 372^r, 373^r. This was before the news of the attempted implementation and consequent Venetian outrage arrived in Rome. When the news arrived, Dolfin, on instructions from the Senate, carefully watched the reactions of Cinzio and Pietro: Cinzio "almost laughing" ("quasi in riso"), but Pietro expressing his displeasure and asking what could be done to retrieve the situation. Letter of August 24, 1596, in ibid., f. 395^{r-v}. Incidentally, the instructions of Cinzio to the nuncio are not included in any of the three collections of the nuncio's letters. They may survive somewhere in the ASVa or BAVa, but I have not made a systematic search for them.

[48] See the articles by E. Fasano Guarini on Cinzio and Pietro respectively in DBI, 2, pp. 102–4, 107–12.

the Tuscan and Venetian envoys. By the end of 1592, the much younger Pietro Aldobrandini (1571–1621) shared the ministry. Cinzio directed relations with Germany, Poland, Transylvania, Sweden, Switzerland, and Italy (with the exception of Savoy), and Pietro managed the Savoyard and the all-important French and Spanish desks. The much abler Pietro quickly enlarged his responsibility; by 1594 some nuncios nominally under Cinzio's supervision dispatched two sets of letters, sending routine matters to Cinzio but significant issues to Pietro. Despite Clement's efforts to appear to hold them in equal esteem, Cinzio found his position harder and harder to bear, and he fled the papal court in the spring of 1598. He returned a year later to accept resignedly his secondary role. Ironically, the failed diplomat Cinzio achieved an enduring niche in history as the friend and patron of Torquato Tasso, and Pietro has been forgotten.

Cinzio's rigid presumption of papal supremacy and his failure to understand the rules of Venetian-papal diplomacy probably led him to attempt a quick victory through unilateral promulgation of the Index. The pope and the Collegio had settled into their ideological fortresses with typically strong jurisdictional speeches while they waited for a change in the political weather to induce one or the other to compromise. Cinzio and the nuncio forced the issue after the stalemate had lasted but two months, a short time by the standard of Venetian-papal disputes.

The arrogant action of the nuncio and patriarch stirred up much antipapal murmuring in Venice; "atrocious and horrendous things" were said, according to the nuncio. It also produced a quick Venetian victory on the oath. Ambassador Dolfin sought out Pietro Aldobrandini to tell him of the attempt to promulgate the Index, and the cardinal immediately grasped what had to be done. He prevailed upon the pope, not to revoke the oath, but to abide by whatever decision the nuncio and patriarch reached in the negotiations in Venice. This procedure saved face for Clement, for the resolution was now a foregone conclusion. After further skirmishing, the nuncio protesting every inch of the way, the two sides signed an agreement on September 14, 1596.

4. THE CONCORDAT

The *Dechiarationi delle regole*, or concordat, contained nine rules modifying the *Instructio*, some of them significant victories for the bookmen and Republic, others clarifications of *Instructio* provisions, and a few of little practical consequence.[49] Rule One stated that books banned by the Index

---

[49] The concordat can be found in Collegio, Esposizioni Roma, R. 6, ff. 169ᵛ–70ᵛ, September 13, 1596; in some surviving copies of the 1596 Venetian printing of the Index (see below); in Brown, *Venetian Press*, pp. 215–17; and elsewhere.

pending expurgation might be sold in unexpurgated form without restriction to those holding permissions from the ordinary or inquisitor. This rule slightly modified an *Instructio* regulation (in paragraph two under Prohibition) that limited such permissions to three years plus renewals. Rule Two of the concordat insisted on local, rather than Roman, expurgation of these suspended titles. The *Instructio* (paragraph one under Expurgation) had granted the local bishop and inquisitor authority to expurgate without indicating what Rome's role, if any, was to be.

Rule Three decreed that a publisher must present to the secretary of the Riformatori dello Studio di Padova the original manuscript of each new imprint, a repetition of a provision of the Council of Ten's press law of June 28, 1569. The secretary would then deposit the manuscript in a locked chest and keep an inventory. This rule modified the *Instructio* regulation (paragraph four under Printing) that ordered publishers to give the inquisitor the manuscript of each new imprint. It made inquisitorial access to the manuscripts conditional upon the favor of the Riformatori, a civil body, although the negotiators had agreed verbally that the inquisitor would be given a key to the chest.[50] There is no evidence that this regulation was obeyed in 1569 or 1596. But with Rule Three and the following rule the Republic reiterated its intention to maintain formal lay control over the censorship process.

The Clementine *Instructio* demanded that all books reproduce the imprimatur of the inquisitor and the ordinary (paragraph five under Printing), a Tridentine Index regulation that had long been ignored in Venice. Rule Four of the concordat demanded that the state's imprimatur (i.e., the approval of the inquisitor) be printed on the verso of the first folio of every book. The Venetians did partially implement this rule, probably to the astonishment of Rome; a minority of Venetian imprints carried the required imprimatur in the next few years.[51]

Rule Five clarified a minor point. The *Instructio* prohibited indecent woodcuts universally and profane woodcuts in religious works (paragraph three under Printing). Rule Five affirmed the former ban, but guaranteed that profane woodcuts could be used (presumably in secular works) as long as they avoided portraying "immodest acts" (*atti dishonesti*).

Rule Six required the bookmen to present the Holy Office with inventories so that prohibited titles might be removed, but "once only" (*una*

[50] See the nuncio's letter of July 13, 1596, in VM, Ms. Ital., vii, 414 (7809), ff. 16ᵛ–17ʳ.

[51] A sampling from the BNF of twenty-three new or substantially revised Venetian imprints issued in the decade 1597 through 1606 reveals that five carried the imprimatur.

volta solamente). Not in the *Instructio*, the inventory requirement re-stated a Tridentine Index rule. The "once only" provision protected the bookmen from future requests, but there is no evidence that the book-men presented any inventories in 1596.[52]

Rule Seven sharply limited the power of the inquisitor and the patriarch to prohibit titles not listed in the Clementine Index. They might ban a work only if it were "contrary to religion," published outside the Vene-tian state, or printed fictitiously within the Venetian state, i.e., in viola-tion of the Republic's press laws. The inquisitor and patriarch would exercise their power "very rarely" (*rarissime volte*), only with a very good reason (*giustissima causa*), and in consultation with the lay deputies of the Holy Office. This rule added only the restriction "contrary to religion" to the interpretation offered by the Congregation of the Index in June.

With Rule Seven the Venetians apparently permitted the papacy to con-tinue to issue new prohibitory edicts, but they obviously intended to limit the number sharply. The Venetians especially wanted to stop the papacy from overriding the state censorship machinery through post facto pro-hibitions or by imposing in-press corrections.[53] They probably succeeded, at least for a few years. For example, the Heads of the Council of Ten granted imprimaturs for a work by the Piacenza jurist Pietro Antonio Pietra (*De iure quaesito per principem non tollendo*, published in Venice by Damiano Zenaro in 1599) and for a work by Tommaso Zerola, the bishop of Minori (the *Praxis episcopalis* published in Venice by Giorgio Varisco in 1599). Rome found that the works contained "many heretical propositions" and "grave errors," and ordered inquisitors in Modena and Florence to ban them in 1600 and 1602 respectively.[54] But these works could not be prohibited in Venice, according to Rule Seven; they had been lawfully printed in accordance with Venetian press law. Indeed, the papacy did not attempt to ban them in Venice.[55]

By 1603 Rome had begun to instruct the Venetian inquisitor to notify the bookmen privately of new prohibitions, probably in order to avoid the restrictions of Rule Seven.[56] And in 1604 Rome banned a work by the

[52] Even if only token inventories were offered, they would have left some trace of their existence in the various Venetian or Vatican sources. I have found nothing.

[53] See Ch. IV, sec. 4, for some examples.

[54] Capi del CX, R. 31, ff. 156[r] (December 12, 1598), 176[r] (April 21, 1599). For the titles, see *Cambridge Catalogue*, items P769, Z138. For the prohibition letters, see Rotondò, "Nuovi documenti," 173, doc. 15; Tedeschi, "Florentine Documents," pp. 599–600, 602–3, docs. 19, 23.

[55] I have been unable to find any reference to the Pietra and Zerola works in Vaticanus Latinus 10945 or Barberino Latino 5195 and 5205.

[56] "Del che faccia diligenza privata appresso i librari, senza publicarne editto." Vaticanus Latinus 10945, f. 72[v], November 22, 1603, and subsequently.

Spanish heretic and exile Cypriano de Valera (1531–?), *Dos tratados. El primero es del Papa y de su autoridad.... El segundo es de la Missa....* (En casa de Arnoldo Hatfildo [London], 1588; reprinted Ricardo del Campo [i.e., Richard Field, London], 1599). Rome instructed the inquisitor not to publish an edict, but to contact the bookmen privately.[57]

Instead of issuing a public notice over the signatures of the lay deputies, the inquisitor presumably ordered a commissioner to advise the bookmen verbally of the prohibition. If the ecclesiastical members of the tribunal failed to inform the lay assistants, they violated Rule Seven of the concordat. Why was this semiclandestine procedure necessary? Surely a heretical work printed fictitiously in London was "contrary to religion." The papacy probably feared that the lay deputies opposed to ecclesiastical jurisdiction, who dominated the office in the last years before the interdict, would make difficulties, possibly on the grounds that the papacy attempted to ban books too frequently. The result had to be less censorship, for the bookmen certainly realized that private prohibitions lacked the authorization of the lay assistants and were unenforceable. After the interdict the papacy continued to instruct the Holy Office to issue private prohibitions to the bookmen, and admitted that it wished to avoid trouble.[58] The transformation of the patriciate forced the Holy Office and disobedient bookmen to exchange roles; now the tribunal resorted to clandestine methods to carry on its normal activities.

Rule Nine required heirs to present to the Holy Office a list of all prohibited and suspect books left to them. Insofar as can be determined, heirs had ignored the Tridentine Index version of this rule, and continued to do so after 1596.

Of course, the Holy Office did not always encounter obstacles, and it sometimes succeeded in issuing new prohibitions. In 1605 the papacy instructed the Venetian Inquisition to ban two works of Ferdinando de las Infantes, *Tractatus de praedestinatione secundum scripturam sacram et veram evangelicam lucem, divina mediante gratia* (Paris, 1601), and *Liber divinae lucis secundum divinae et evangelicae scripturae lucem in 109. Psalmi expositionem* (Cologne, 1603). The Holy Office took the author into custody, burned the books in his presence, and extradited him

---

[57] Vaticanus Latinus 10945, f. 119ʳ, March 27 and October 30, 1604. Valera is identified in Marcelino Menendez Pelayo, *Historia de los heterodoxos españoles*, vol. II (Madrid, 1880), pp. 491–97. Also see Paul J. Hauben, *Three Spanish Heretics and the Reformation: Antonio Del Corvo—Cassiodoro De Reina—Cypriano De Valera* (Geneva, 1967), pp. 108–16 and passim.

[58] "Notifichi privatamente a librari et a chi sarà di bisogno, che non devino vendere, tenere, ne leggere detto libro e tutto esequisca con prudente maniera, senza formar editto, per non causare qualche difficultà fuori di bisogno." Vaticanus Latinus 10945, f. 72ᵛ, November 28, 1609; the same on f. 115ʳ.

to Rome in 1608.[59] The Holy Office could not have done all this without the full cooperation of the lay assistants.

Rule Seven and Rule Eight (which forbade the oath) substantially diminished papal censorship authority and enhanced civil control. They best expressed the new Venetian preference for state supremacy in censorship.

In a determined rearguard action, the nuncio fought to restrict promulgation of the concordat. First he tried to persuade the Venetians to distribute it in manuscript only; then, to print only a few copies; and, finally, to issue it separately from the Index.[60] He partially succeeded, for the Senate authorized only one hundred fifty printed copies (it is not clear whether the Senate meant this to be a total figure or in addition to the copies to be included in the printed Index).[61] Nicolò Moretti published the new Index (see figure 17) in a format that placed the concordat immediately after the title page and before the promulgation letter of Clement VIII. The Tridentine Index rules, Clement's *Instructio*, and the list of prohibited titles followed. However, not all extant copies of the Moretti printing contain the concordat,[62] and none of the subsequent Venetian printings of the Clementine Index (1596, 1597, 1600, 1604 [twice], 1608, 1611, 1613, and 1616) include it.[63] Sarpi charged in 1613 that only

[59] Vaticanus Latinus 10945, f. 114ᵛ, October 1, 1605; Barberino Latino 5195, f. 18ʳ; Albizzi, *Risposta*, 153. Reusch, *Index*, II, pt. 1, p. 302, describes the works as "Molinist," but I have been unable to identify the author.

[60] See Matteo Zane's description of the final negotiations in Collegio, Esposizioni Roma, R. 6, ff. 167ʳ–69ᵛ, September 11 or 13, 1596.

[61] Senato, Deliberazioni Roma, R. 11, f. 112ᵛ, September 12, 1596.

[62] *Index librorum prohibitorum. . . .* (Venetiis, Apud Nicolaum Morettum, 1596). The *Dechiarationi delle regole* are on pp. 1–4 (Sigs. Aʳ–A1ᵛ) in the copies that contain it. However, not all extant copies of this first Venetian printing of the Clementine Index contain the concordat. For example, the following copies do: VC Op P D 6961 and 6962; BAVa Barb. Z-XIII. 109; but the Columbia University library copy, B098 In 2 1596, and Morgan Library copy, do not. The Hispanic Society of America library (New York) has two copies of the Moretti printing, one of which lacks the concordat, the other of which prints it in a nine-page appendix in a different type from the *Dechiarationi* to be found in other copies.

[63] None of the following copies of subsequent Venetian printings of the Clementine Index contain the concordat: Apud Floravantem Pratum, 1596 (Hispanic Society of America copy examined); Apud Marcum de Claseris, 1597 (VM 223. D. 201); Apud Lucium Spinedam, 1600 (New York Public Library); Apud Haeredes Dominici de Farris, 1604 (VC Op P D 6968); Apud Marcum Antonium Zalterium, 1604 (Columbia University and Morgan Library); Apud Marcum Antonium Zalterium, 1608 (New York Public Library); Apud Marcum Antonium Zalterium, 1611 (New York Public Library); Apud Marcum Antonium Zalterium, 1613 (Columbia University); Apud Marcum Antonium Zalterium, 1616 (New York Public Library).

sixty copies of the concordat had been printed; whether or not his figure was accurate, the papacy did succeed in limiting the distribution of the concordat.[64]

Thanks to Venetian intransigence and papal mishandling, the bookmen and Republic achieved a clear victory with the concordat. The logical consequence of the Republic's move to govern public morality and to protect the press, the concordat symbolized the great change that had taken place since the 1560s. Although it left intact the list of prohibited titles and the expurgation guidelines, it substantially restricted in practical ways papal and inquisitorial control of the book trade. Perhaps most important of all, it established the precedent for the state's exercising a strong voice, in some areas the dominant voice, in the operation of the Index. It built the jurisdictional platform from which Sarpi launched future challenges against papal censorship.[65]

The quarrel left hard feelings, especially in Rome. In his meeting with Ambassador Dolfin on August 30, Clement roundly condemned the Venetians for showing themselves contemptuous of papal dignity, for "wishing to declare to the world that they supported heretics," for threatening Cardinal Priuli and the nuncio, and for much else.[66] Donà answered for the Republic a week later. He defended civil jurisdiction, declared that Venice was a more religious and Catholic city than Rome, and charged that many in the Vatican stirred up trouble for the Venetian bookmen in order to aid the Roman printers, from whom they stood to profit.[67] The two sides were beyond easy reconciliation.

With the Index, as with most issues during Clement's long pontificate, the papacy wavered between accepting and rejecting the changing realities. Every aspect of the Clementine Index—the various mutations, the rules, the handling of the dispute—reflected internal Vatican tension between the old and the new. The attempt to require an oath, to include more vernacular titles, and to empower the ordinary and inquisitor to expand the Index expressed the militant Counter Reformation of the past. The pope, the nuncio, and Cinzio Aldobrandini often echoed the words of Pius V and his nuncio. On the other hand, Clement's amendment of the Index in response to Paruta's remonstrances and scholarly disapproval, the substitution of local expurgation for outright prohibition, and the con-

[64] *Scritti giurisdizionalistici*, p. 189.

[65] In his *consulti* on censorship 1613–1617, Sarpi often used the concordat, especially Rule Seven, to justify state control. See, for example, *Scritti giurisdizionalistici*, pp. 196, 207; *Opere*, ed. Cozzi and Cozzi, pp. 601, 605, 606.

[66] Letter of Ambassador Dolfin of August 31, 1596, in Senato, Dispacci da Roma, F. 37, ff. 404r–7v; for more of the same, see his letter of September 21, 1596, in ibid., F. 38, ff. 32r–33v.

[67] Collegio, Esposizioni Roma, R. 6. ff. 164v–65v, September 6, 1596.

INDEX
LIBRORVM
PROHIBITORVM

CVM REGVLIS CONFECTIS
Per Patres à Tridentina Synodo delectos.

AVCTORITATE PII IIII. PRIMVM EDITVS.

Postea vero à Syxto V. Auctus

ET NVNC DEMVM S. D. N.
CLEMENTIS PAPAE VIII.
iussu recognitus, & publicatus.

INSTRVCTIONE ADIECTA.

De exequenda prohibitionis, deq. sincere emendandi, & imprimendi Libros, ratione.

VENETIIS, Apud Nicolaum Morettum. 1596.
Cum Licentia Superiorum.

17. Title page of *Index librorum prohibitorum . . . et nunc demum S. D. N. Clementis Papae VIII iussu recognitus, & publicatus. . . .* (Venetiis, Apud Nicolaum Morettum, 1596). Source: BAVa, Barb. Z. XIII. 109

ciliatory tone of the Congregation of the Index showed that Vatican officials, and even the pontiff on occasion, bowed to change. Rome sometimes gracefully accepted eased censorship and greater state control.

5. DECLINING CENSORSHIP

The dispute over papal privileges, the concordat, and the general deterioration of Venetian-papal relations produced a cumulative ebbing of effective censorship. The decay of ecclesiastical censorship, already noticeable before 1596, was accelerated by new developments, and the interdict conflict of 1606–7 brought censorship to a standstill. Even after the two belligerents were reconciled, the Holy Office probably did not succeed in regaining its former effectiveness.

The smuggling continued as before. In August and September 1599, the Holy Office apprehended four prominent firms (Giovanni Battista Ciotti, Francesco dei Franceschi, Roberto Meietti, and the House of Sessa) importing from Germany a volume of the *Magdeburg Centuries*, a banned astronomical work, and possibly other works. The Inquisition confiscated the books, threatened the bookmen with fines of 100 ducats, and released them.[68]

The renewal of diplomatic relations with England in 1603 after a hiatus of forty-five years opened a new route for the introduction and distribution of heretical books. Ambassador Sir Henry Wotton, a fervent Protestant who judged the Venetians to be ripe for conversion, and his staff proselytized behind the shield of diplomatic immunity. Both Wotton and the Dutch ambassador sheltered Protestant ministers who announced their Sunday worship services by ringing bells and throwing open the doors. The papacy repeatedly protested, but the Venetians blandly relayed assurances given by the ambassadors that only their households attended. The frustrated papacy instructed the Inquisition to spy on the houses to find out who else participated in these provocative services.[69]

Then came the interdict. In December 1605 Paul V issued an ultimatum: if the Republic would not hand over two clergymen accused of crimes, and revoke the laws asserting secular jurisdiction over clerics accused of

---

[68] SU, Bu. 49, Libri prohibiti, no pag., documents of August 3 and September 4, 1599. This folder contains miscellaneous charred fragments, difficult to read, of several trials concerning prohibited books. The astronomical title was *Ephemerides novae annorum xxxvi incipientes ab anno mdxcv* (Frankfurt, 1599) of David Origanus (1558–1628), a follower of Copernicus. It was banned in 1603. Reusch, *Index*, II, pt. I, p. 182.

[69] K. T. Butler, "Giacomo Castelvetro, 1546–1616," *Italian Studies* 5 (1950), 24; Cozzi, *Contarini*, pp. 111, 119–20, 133; Barberino Latino 5195, ff. 83ʳ–86ʳ; Vaticanus Latinus 10945, ff. 95ʳ–ᵛ.

crimes and over ecclesiastical lands, he would excommunicate the Senate and impose an interdict on the Republic. The Venetians refused, and the pope acted on his threat in April 1606. The interdict forbade clergymen to exercise almost all priestly duties, such as celebrating mass and administering the sacraments. The Republic enjoined Venetian ecclesiastics to disobey the papacy. The majority did so willingly, others were coerced, and the Jesuits, Capuchins, and Theatines were expelled. Both the Republic and the papacy applied diplomatic pressures and made ostentatious preparations for a war that could only have enhanced the French and Spanish presences in the peninsula.

The contest to win the approval of the European public paralleled the political struggle, and the cases of the papacy and the Senate attracted enormous attention. Catholic and Protestant princes and subjects watched this first great church-state confrontation of the post-Reformation era to find portents for the future. The Senate appointed Sarpi its official theologian, and he and other clerics and laymen argued the Venetian position in pamphlets and treatises. Cardinals Baronius and Bellarmine and many other Italian papal apologists answered. Soon French Gallicans, German Jesuits, Huguenot theologians, and jurists from everywhere joined the fray.

During the struggle, the Republic adapted the prepublication censorship to its new needs. The system functioned normally for uncontroversial titles, but certain "Reverend theologians" or "seven theologians" substituted for the inquisitorial reader when antipapal tracts needed imprimaturs.[70] These were Sarpi, Fulgenzio Micanzio, Giovanni Marsilio, and the other Venetian clerical pamphleteers. They enjoyed the luxury of censoring their own books.

Some of the bookmen put their considerable skills at the disposal of the state during the interdict. Honed through years of practice, their expertise in clandestine operations gave the Republic an enormous advantage in the propaganda warfare. No bookman contributed more than Roberto Meietti, who published antipapal tracts in Venice and sent others north for printing and distribution. He also arranged for the smuggling into the Venetian state of ultramontane titles that Sarpi and the other Vene-

---

[70] For example, Sarpi's *Considerationi sopra le censure della Santità di Papa Paulo V contra la Serenissima Republica di Venetia* (In Venetia, presso Roberto Meietti, 1606) contains an imprimatur of the "Reverend theologians." This imprimatur can also be found in Capi del CX, Notatorio, R. 33, f. 157^r, August 21, 1606. Additional such imprimaturs for antipapal titles of Sarpi, Antonio Querini, Giovanni Marsilio, etc., are found in ibid., ff. 157^{r-v}, 159^{r-v}, 163^r, 167^r, 179^r. They can also be found in the printed works. On Sarpi's theological colleagues, see Gino Benzoni, "I 'teologi' minori dell'interdetto," *Archivio veneto*, ser. v, vol. 91 (1970), pp. 31–108.

tian apologists would find useful. The papacy excommunicated him in October 1606, but the action had no effect.[71]

Within a few months the Republic and papacy reached an impasse and began to extend peace feelers. Paul V softened his position, and the unanimity of the Senate started to crack. In February 1607 the Venetians accepted mediation by a French cardinal, and on April 21 the pope lifted the interdict. The Venetians handed over to the French king the accused clerics sought by Rome, but retained the laws claiming secular jurisdiction over clergymen and church lands. As was usual in Venetian-papal conflicts, much was left unsettled to ignite future disputes. Despite their claims, neither side profited from the interdict. Paul V suffered a distinct defeat because he had levied an interdict and then withdrawn it without attaining much of his goal. The Venetians could more legitimately claim a victory, but the struggle had underlined the dangers to a small state of isolation in an indifferent world. Perhaps the major outcome of the conflict was to teach the doge and the pope that they had to settle their differences in the old way of interminable negotiation, lest they become pawns of the great powers.

Despite the lifting of the interdict, the Republic did not restore the inquisitorial check on imported books for several years.[72] If a bookman could elude the Tridentine authorities and reach Venetian territory with his contraband, he need no longer worry. For example, when the Verona inquisitor wished to inspect a shipment of books from the north destined for Venice, the Republic rebuffed him.[73]

Once prohibited titles entered Venice, they could turn up anywhere. For example, the father-general of the Franciscan Conventuals visited a Venetian monastery in May 1609. During the mealtime scriptural reading, he suddenly heard passages that deviated from the Catholic Vulgate. Examining the Bible, he discovered that it was a Protestant version lacking a title page and colophon.[74] More than likely, the bookseller had torn out the pages that would identify it as a Protestant import, and then sold it to the unsuspecting friars.

As a result of the smuggling, Venetian readers had access to a broad

---

[71] Please see my forthcoming article, "Books for Sarpi," for the details of Meietti's activity.

[72] The papacy complained in 1610 and 1611 that the bookmen were unpacking German imports at the customs house without an inquisitorial presence. Vaticanus Latinus 10945, f. 118^v.

[73] Letter of Nuncio Berlinghiero Gessi of May 24, 1608, as quoted in Pietro Savio, "Il nunzio dopo l'interdetto," *Archivio veneto*, ser. v, Anno 56–57 (1955), 77, n. 1.

[74] Letter of the father-general of May 8, 1609, as quoted in Savio, "Per l'epistolario di Paolo Sarpi," 10 (1936), 26, n. 1.

range of old and new prohibited titles. In August 1608, Fra Fulgenzio Manfredi, one of the Republic's theologians during the interdict, suddenly defected to Rome. He provided the papacy with a brief list, a sampling, as it were, of the prohibited titles that circulated.[75] The nobility and the learned had Calvin's *Institutes* in Latin, and such English anti-Catholic titles as *Problema de Romanae fidei ementito catholicismo* (Cambridge, 1604), by the Puritan theologian William Perkins, and *Disputationum de Antechristo libro* (London, 1605), by the Anglican controversialist Gabriel Powel. Manfredi also reported that the majority of the nobles had Machiavelli.[76] Titles circulating among commoners and in nonlearned circles included Calvin's *Catechism* in Italian, the Psalms in Italian as printed in Geneva in 1585, a Protestant vernacular version of the New Testament, and the antipapal *Mercurio et Caronte* of Valdés.

The nuncio confirmed that "a great quantity" of prohibited books circulated, and that "he who wants them has them." But, he warned Rome, nothing could be done, for there would be great trouble with the Venetians if he were to instruct priests to preach on the subject.[77] At the same time, he counseled Rome to keep the situation in perspective. Although "many heretics and others of little piety" certainly had Protestant Bibles, heretical literature had not inundated the city.[78] The nuncio was undoubtedly correct; if Protestant books had threatened the city's traditional loyalty to Catholicism, the government would have acted. The leaders of the Republic rejected the jurisdictional claims of the papacy, but had no intention of enlisting under the Protestant banner.

Until the various censorship bars were put back into place, a process that took ten to fifteen years to accomplish, the bookmen could do pretty much as they pleased. In 1610, Roberto Meietti, still under excommunication, was secretly vending an Italian translation of the *Anticoton* (first published in 1610), the French tract attacking Pierre Coton, a Jesuit advisor to Henry IV. Although the Italian translation carried the name of a

---

[75] Savio, "Per l'epistolario di Sarpi," 10 (1936), 26–27. I have completed some of the identifications. The unfortunate Manfredi was executed as a *relapsus*. Benzoni, "I 'teologi' minori," pp. 67–68.

[76] Like other Italians, Venetians continued to be fascinated with Machiavelli and wished to reconcile him with the Counter Reformation. For example, in 1598 an unnamed noble requested permission of the Venetian Inquisition to publish a "revised and corrected" edition of Machiavelli's works. He claimed that the previous inquisitor had asked him to prepare the edition. Rome denied the request. Vaticanus Latinus 10945, f. 149ᵛ, February 21, 1598.

[77] Letter of Nuncio Gessi of February 14, 1609, in Savio, "Il nunzio dopo l'interdetto," pp. 83–84.

[78] Letter of Nuncio Gessi of June 27, 1609, in Savio, "Per l'epistolario di Sarpi," 16 (1942), 11.

Lyons publisher, the nuncio suspected that Meietti had printed it, either in Venice or abroad. The Holy Office could not act because the lay deputies refused to permit the tribunal to confiscate the title or punish Meietti.[79] In 1614, he submitted to papal authority and the excommunication was lifted. Nevertheless, Rome still advised the inquisitors of other cities to observe the prohibitions against Meietti lest "under the pretense of a change of heart he might introduce bad and pernicious books" into their jurisdictions.[80] Papal suspicions were justified, for in 1621 Meietti was selling anti-Catholic pamphlets printed in Germany in his Venetian store.[81] Nor was he the only one. In 1617 another Venetian bookman sold Aretino's *Lettere* and *Ragionamenti.*[82]

Unable to halt the traffic into Venice or to take effective action against the local bookmen, Rome could only try to stop the distribution of banned works elsewhere. The papacy admonished inquisitors in other Italian cities to scrutinize closely books arriving from Venice, and in 1614 it deputized an official in Frankfurt to draft a list of permissible books from which the bookmen might select their purchases.[83] It is unlikely that the papacy had enough local political support to force the bookmen to comply.

The prepublication inquisitorial reader also found himself ignored. Rome lamented several times between 1612 and 1614 that works with many "errors, indecencies, and notable defects" were published in Venice.[84] The papacy objected as well that the ducal secretary altered manuscripts, especially those treating of ecclesiastical jurisdiction, before issuing an imprimatur.[85]

Since papal-Venetian relations improved only marginally, if at all, as the years went by,[86] the restored censorship machinery ran at reduced speed. The Holy Office still exercised prepublication scrutiny and pur-

[79] See the letters of Nuncio Gessi of December 4, 11, 18, 25, 1610, as quoted in Savio, "Per l'epistolario di Sarpi," 14 (1940), 67–68. The Congregation of the Index formally banned the *Anticoton* in 1617, but an Italian translation has not been located.

[80] Barberino Latino 5195, ff. 52^{r-v}, July 11, 1614; Rotondò, "Nuovi documenti," p. 184, n. 2.

[81] SU, Bu. 77, Roberto Meietti.

[82] SU, Bu. 72, Giuseppe Vago da Verona.

[83] Rotondò, "Nuovi documenti," pp. 193–97, documents 37, 38, 40, and 42.

[84] Vaticanus Latinus 10945, f. 147^{v}; Barberino Latino 5195, f. 52^{v}.

[85] Vaticanus Latinus 10945, ff. 148^{r-v} (1607, 1612, and 1614); Barberino Latino 5195, ff. 49^{v}, 53^{r} (1612 and 1613).

[86] New differences, sometimes involving the Inquisition, arose between Republic and papacy in the 1620s, and these culminated in sharp conflict in 1630 and 1631. See Agostino Zanelli, "Di alcune controversie fra la Republica di Venezia e il Sant'Officio nei primi anni del pontificato di Urbano VIII (1624–1626)," *Archivio veneto*, ser. v, Anno 59 (1929), 186–235; Pastor, xxix, 175–84.

sued violators, but its powers were reduced. Consequently, the bookmen enjoyed increased freedom. Marco Ginammi, a prominent publisher, flaunted the Index by printing Machiavelli and Aretino. Under the title *De' discorsi politici, e militari libri tre, scielti* [*sic*] *fra gravissimi scrittori da Amadio Niecollucci*, he published Machiavelli's *Discourses* in 1630 and 1648.[87] "Amadio Niecollucci" might be translated (in reverse) as "Nicky Lovesgod." Ginammi also published from 1627 to 1651 no fewer than nine different titles in twenty-three printings of the works of "Partenio Etiro," who was Pietro Aretino. They were *Le Carte parlanti* (the second dialogue from part three of the *Ragionamenti*), published in 1650 and 1651; *Dell'Humanità del Figliuolo di Dio*, in 1628, 1633, 1645, and 1653; a partial edition of the *Lettere*, in 1637; *Parafrasi sopra i sette Salmi della penitenza*, in 1627, 1629, and 1635; *La Sirena, Marfisa & Angelica, poemetti*, in 1630; *Dello Specchio delle opere di Dio nello stato di natura*, in 1628, 1629, and 1635; *Vita di Maria Vergine,* in 1628, 1633, and 1642; *Vita di Santa Caterina,* in 1628, 1630, and 1636; and *Vita di San Tomaso d'Aquino*, in 1628, 1630, and 1636.[88] Ginammi probably mocked a powerless Holy Office with these transparent anagrammatic pseudonyms.

At about the same time, a group of local intellectuals rejected Christianity altogether without suffering any molestation from the Holy Office. In 1630 Giovan Francesco Loredano (1607–61) founded the Accademia degli Incogniti, a gathering of nobles and literary adventurers who pursued libertine ideas within the context of the Aristotelian naturalism taught at Padua by Cesare Cremonini (1550?–1631). Despite the receipt of several denunciations, the Holy Office ignored the men, leaving them free to write a number of books, some of which were published in Venice and later prohibited by the Index.[89] The vivid contrast between the Protestant patricians who endured prosecution in the 1560s and their libertine successors who basked in immunity in the 1630s illustrates the vast distance that the Republic had traveled in the intervening decades.

[87] The titles are listed in the *British Museum General Catalogue. Ten Year Supplement 1956–1965*, vol. 33, col. 342; and *British Museum General Catalogue*, vol. 171, col. 923, respectively.

[88] The list has been compiled from the *British Museum General Catalogue*, vol. 68, col. 868; Suzanne P. Michel and Paul-Henri Michel, *Répertoire des ouvrages imprimés en langue italienne au XVIIe siècle conservés dans les bibliothèques de France*, vol. 1 (Paris, 1967), pp. 66–68; and the catalogues of the BNF. I have examined some of the Ginammi imprints in the latter. For an overall view of seicento censorship, see Paolo Ulvioni, "Stampa e censura a Venezia nel seicento," *Archivio veneto* 106 (1975), 45–93.

[89] Giorgio Spini, *Ricerca dei libertini. La teoria dell'impostura delle religioni nel Seicento italiano* (Rome, 1950), 139–63.

X

THE IMPACT OF INDEX AND INQUISITION ON ITALIAN INTELLECTUAL LIFE

SCHOLARS since Burckhardt have agreed that the Counter Reformation destroyed the Renaissance in Italy. At the conclusion of a brief, ecstatic description of the philosophy of Giovanni Pico della Mirandola, Burckhardt wrote: "Looking at Pico, we can guess at the lofty flight which Italian philosophy would have taken had not the Counter Reformation annihilated the higher spiritual life of the people."[1] This view has prevailed through De Sanctis, Croce, and others. Discussing the impact of the Index in the second half of the cinquecento, Garin wrote: "Everything vital and new that had been produced during a century and a half of cultural effort was now being mutilated and suppressed."[2] The majority of scholars assign little value to much of the intellectual production of Italians after 1550, and tend to view those figures whose work is assessed positively (especially Tasso, Bruno, Campanella, Sarpi, and Galileo) as Renaissance men who carried on in spite of clerical repression.

Of course, scholars from Burckhardt through Garin postulate a dichotomy between a lay, secular, and modern Italian Renaissance of the late trecento and quattrocento, and a clerical, religious, and medieval Counter Reformation of the following century. Scholars of past generations have viewed the Reformers of northern Europe as lifting high the torch of modernity lit by Renaissance Italians, and Cantimori proposed that Italian Protestants had inherited Valla's mantle. All agreed that the church had blocked the path of human progress with the Counter Reformation.

Interpretations that place too much emphasis on a distinction between a secular Renaissance and a clerical Counter Reformation overlook the many similarities in the two movements. The Renaissance of the trecento

---

[1] Jacob Burckhardt, *The Civilization of the Renaissance in Italy*, trans. S.G.C. Middlemore, introd. Benjamin Nelson and Charles Trinkaus (New York, 1958), I, 210.

[2] Eugenio Garin, *Science and Civic Life in the Italian Renaissance*, trans. Peter Munz (Garden City, N. Y., 1969), p. 85.

and quattrocento was by no means as secular as once believed, for humanists from Petrarch through Ficino were profoundly pious in orthodox ways, although they rejected Scholastic modes of expression.[3] Had the Protestant heresy appeared in 1417 or 1467, Italians would have reacted little differently than they did a century later. They would have ignored it until they perceived that it threatened the institutions and beliefs held sacred by most, and then the vast majority of rulers and subjects would have joined in suppressing it. To approach the inaccurate distinction between lay Renaissance and clerical Counter Reformation from another direction, it should be remembered that ecclesiastical leaders did not foist the Counter Reformation on a protesting lay society. Rather, princes and prelates, laymen and priests, joined hands to suppress heresy.

Nevertheless, the Counter Reformation—the joint effort of church and state—profoundly oppressed cinquecento Italian intellectual life. Evidence abounds that the Index and Inquisition were effective. Within a few decades they snuffed out Protestantism in Italy except for a little clandestine activity. The Counter Reformation forced gifted men of religion, *letterati*, and scholars to flee if they held Protestant beliefs. The Index and Inquisition also hounded many who remained; the harassment of Francesco Patrizi, the imprisonment of Campanella, and the recantation forced upon Galileo are well-known incidents of repression. Further, the Index prohibited, and the Inquisition destroyed, many humanistic and scientific works needed by Italian scholars. The prepublication scrutiny, undoubtedly the most effective part of the censorship machinery, rendered difficult certain areas of speculation, such as political theory along Machiavellian lines. Italian literature lost much of its vitality when vernacular authors accustomed to writing in free, mocking, and even slanderous ways during the epoch of Aretino shifted to safer topics in the 1560s. All authors became careful self-censors.

The Index and Inquisition also stifled Erasmian humanism in Italy, a repressive effect sometimes overlooked. The abundance of Erasmus's works discovered by the Inquisition pointed to their popularity, just as their destruction demonstrated the hostility of the agents of the Counter Reformation.[4] Prelates and inquisitors from Cardinal Aleandro on loathed Erasmus's books. Erasmus believed in reform as much as some of the leading figures of the Catholic Reformation, but "the philosophy of Christ" and the Tridentine way seemed irreconcilable. Reforming circles in Rome keenly felt the importance of editions of the Bible and patristic sources

---

[3] See Trinkaus, *In Our Image and Likeness.*

[4] For additional discussion of the fate of Erasmus's works, see Marcella T. and Paul F. Grendler, "The Survival of Erasmus in Italian Libraries," in *Erasmus in English*, 8 (University of Toronto Press, 1976), pp. 2–22.

that would meet the canons of humanistic textual criticism, but they rejected the rest of the Erasmian program. His light-hearted moralism, devastating criticism of clerical sin, and faint enthusiasm for doctrine and ecclesiastical structure rendered him anathema to the Counter Reformation puritans. Above all, they could not distinguish him from the German Reformers. Yet, Erasmus had many Italian readers until the Index banned his works. Erasmian humanism grafted to the humanistic piety of the quattrocento might have profoundly changed Italian religious history had not the Index and Inquisition stamped it out.

The oppressive influence of the Index and Inquisition should not be exaggerated, for it was less strong in fields of study unrelated to religion. With a few exceptions, the censors found nothing objectionable in works of classical scholarship, history, law, literary criticism, logic, mathematics, medicine, philology, and rhetoric. Scholars carried on their study of these disciplines with little interference, making notable contributions in some cases.

Nor did the Index and Inquisition succeed in shutting off Italians from the European world of learning. A very large Paduan private library provides ample evidence that scholars in the university community there had access to many prohibited books. A Neapolitan nobleman born in 1535, Gian Vincenzo Pinelli came to study in Padua in 1558 and stayed for the rest of his life. Endowed with money, love for scholarship, and a gift for hospitality, he opened his house to scholars of the most diverse interests and backgrounds. He was Galileo's friend, host, and patron during Galileo's Paduan career (1592–1610), but Tasso, Sarpi, Sperone Speroni, and Justus Lipsius also enjoyed his hospitality; his correspondents included Paolo Manuzio and Joseph Scaliger.[5]

Scholars came to Pinelli not only for his company but also to use his library, one of the great collections of the time. Upon Pinelli's death in 1601, the library was dispersed and partially destroyed, although a significant portion of it survives in the Ambrosiana library in Milan. Fortunately, an inventory of October 7, 1604, catalogued all or most of it, a magnificent collection of about 6,500 printed volumes and about 800 manuscripts in Latin, Italian, Greek, French, Spanish, Hebrew, and Arabic, on all the subjects that interested cinquecento scholars.[6]

---

[5] On Pinelli and his library, see Adolfo Rivolta, *Catalogo dei codici pinelliani dell'Ambrosiana* (Milan, 1933), pp. xvii–lxxx; and Antonio Favaro, *Galileo e lo Studio di Padova* (Florence, 1883; rpt. Padua, 1966), II, 52–59, and passim.

[6] VM, Mss. Italiani, Classe x, 61 (6601), "Inventario della libreria di Giovanni Vincenzo Pinelli ereditata da Francesco Pinelli." Marcella Grendler is preparing a study of Pinelli's library.

The library included at least ninety prohibited titles by about forty-four different banned authors, roughly 1.4 percent of the total printed volumes.[7] Nonreligious titles authored by Protestant scholars comprised a heavy majority of the banned works. Pinelli had eight legal and political works of François Hôtman, six works of Petrus Ramus, five of Theophrastus Paracelsus, four of Konrad Gesner, and additional titles of Agrippa, Etienne Dolet, Charles Du Moulin, Sebastian Muenster, and Josias Simler. He also had Bibles printed by Protestant publishers, anti-Catholic historical works such as the *Magdeburg Centuries,* and Huguenot political treatises, including the *Vindiciae contra tyrannos* and Hôtman's *Francogallia.* Machiavelli's *Discourses, History of Florence, Asino d'oro,* and *La Clizia,* Aretino's *Ragionamenti,* Brucioli's *Dialogi,* and three titles of Ortensio Lando found a place in his library. He possessed one volume of Melanchthon's *opera,* which probably contained philosophical rather than religious titles. In short, Pinelli owned a representative sampling of nondoctrinal banned titles.

There is no sign that Pinelli entertained heretical views; on the contrary, a life full of associations with major Counter Reformation prelates, such as Cardinals Ippolito Aldobrandini (the future Clement VIII), Baronius, Bellarmine, and Carlo Borromeo, argues fidelity to Rome— except for the Index. He did not transgress through ignorance, for he owned at least four copies of the Index. Rather, he violated the church's rules for the sake of learning. Pinelli kept abreast of new titles through publishers' catalogues from Basel, Frankfurt, Geneva, Zurich, and elsewhere, and through his extensive correspondence with northern European scholars. He then asked Roberto Meietti and other Venetian bookmen to obtain the volumes for him.[8] And through Pinelli Paduan scholars and visitors from other Italian cities had access to many banned titles from abroad. Pinelli felt the same commitment to the universal world of learning as had the humanists of the past century, and he honored that commitment in the middle of the Counter Reformation.

Other individuals owned nonreligious prohibited titles. A Venetian of unknown profession who died in 1584 had Machiavelli's *Historie fiorentine* and unidentified titles of Aretino.[9] Another deceased Venetian (1602) possessed Ramus's *Institutionum dialecticarum* and Muenster's *Cosmo-*

---

[7] Please see App. II for the list of prohibited titles.

[8] Rivolta, *Catalogo,* xxxvi.

[9] Giudici di Petizion, Inventari, Bu. 338, no. 61, Ippolito Ganason, f. 3[r]. The court made inventories, which occasionally listed the titles of books, when the owners died intestate or survivors disputed the inheritance. Ganason, whose profession was not listed, owned about 140 books.

graphia. Similar nonreligious prohibited titles continued to appear in the libraries of seventeenth-century Venetians.[10] The titles found in private libraries, as well as the variety of banned works that surfaced in Holy Office trials, demonstrate that Italians obtained the prohibited books that they wanted. Even Sixtus V had nearly two dozen prohibited titles in his large library of over 1,600 volumes![11] Presumably the books were read. Even if Italians could not discuss these prohibited titles openly, they could still read, ponder, and debate their contents within limited circles. If far from complete freedom of inquiry, it was a good deal better than nothing.

Scholars have also charged that the Counter Reformation altered the direction of Italian intellectual development by discouraging some areas and fostering others. While partly true, this point of view assigns the Counter Reformation too much influence, for the Index and Inquisition were hardly solely responsible for the many and profound differences between the quattrocento and the cinquecento and, subsequently, the seicento. Great changes began to occur early in the cinquecento and became especially noticeable in the middle third of the century. Disheartened by political and military disasters, some Italians began to question the validity of a political system of small, independent city-states, the utility of the *studia humanitatis* as a guide to the active life, and their traditional

---

[10] Giudici di Petizion, Inventari, Bu. 342, no. 26, Ludovico Usper, ff. 13^{r-v}. His library totaled about 250 volumes. The library of a Venetian physician who died in 1624 contained seven prohibited titles of Gesner, Muenster, and others, among about 320 titles. Ibid., Bu. 349, no. 25, Alberto Quattrocchi, ff. 5^r, 6^v, 8^v. A very large library of about 3,500 titles catalogued in 1640 listed at least 63 prohibited titles, none of them doctrinal, of 27 different authors. Ibid., Bu. 356, no. 67, Marco Antonio Felette. Of course, some libraries of these years contained no prohibited books.

[11] They included at least a dozen legal titles of the prohibited German jurist Joannes Oldendorpius, Gesner's *Bibliotheca universalis*, Christoph Hegendorff's *Dialecticae legalis*, a historiographical treatise of Simon Grynaeus, an astrological work of Joannes Schoener, a historical work of Joannes Sleidanus, the *Adagia* and *Apophethegmata* of Erasmus, Anton Francesco Doni's *Lettere*, and Ortensio Lando's *Cathaloghi* and *Paradossi*. Cugnoni published three undated inventories, and surmised that they may date from Peretti's pontificate (1585–90) because they include some titles published at that time. As an influential prelate and former inquisitor, Peretti could probably have obtained permission to hold prohibited titles if he sought it, but one wonders what reasons he would have offered for titles far from his professional and scholarly interests. The catholicity of the banned titles and, indeed, of his entire library suggests that Peretti acquired prohibited works for personal and scholarly reasons. C. Cugnoni, "Documenti Chigiani concernanti Felice Peretti, Sisto V, come privato e come pontefice," *Archivio della Società Romana di Storia Patria* 5 (1882), 217, 221, 226, 233–35, 237, 241, 251, 256, 268, 278, 282, 290, 292, 296.

loyalty to an unreformed papacy.[12] Machiavelli, Guicciardini, and the lesser figures who followed attempted to come to grips with the new darkened conditions by questioning old values. Aside from the great achievements of the two Florentines, iconoclastic appraisal of Italian life produced little of lasting intellectual value, but it did clear the path for future innovators. This movement of criticism began long before the Index and Inquisition became effective.

Similarly, the quest for new ideas and styles in the arts and in other disciplines generated great change in Italian intellectual life. This quest proceeded in the cinquecento just as it does always. For example, Weinberg wrote: "There is no doubt but that the signal event in the history of literary criticism in the Italian Renaissance was the discovery of Aristotle's *Poetics* and its incorporation into the critical tradition."[13] The process of discovery, evaluation, and assimilation of the *Poetics* began in the 1540s, lasted through the end of the century, and exercised enormous influence on Italian literature. It is difficult to attribute to the Index and Inquisition any role in this process. Thanks to the genius of Caravaggio, Bernini, and others, Italian painters, sculptors, and architects moved from the high Renaissance style through Mannerism to the glories of the Baroque. In music, Palestrina treated Italians to polyphonic delights, and Monteverdi created the new dramatic monody. Again, it is impossible to assign the Index and Inquisition any influence in these evolutions.

Perhaps the deep, pervasive religious revival generated more change in sixteenth-century Italy than anything else, even more than did the wars. The religious revival manifested itself initially through the small groups that, before the Protestant Reformation, withdrew from the world to devote themselves to God, and then often moved back into the world to convert it. The Catholic Reformation had great success in reforming the papacy and prelacy; other Italians found salvation outside of Catholicism in the 1530s and 1540s. These two manifestations of the religious revival have been extensively studied, but the later orthodox quest for personal piety through spiritual guidance and religious activity, which was the largest part of the Italian religious revival, has not. Even after those who professed pious ways to achieve clerical advancement are discounted, an enormous number of persons of genuine religiosity remains. The cas-

---

[12] See Mario Santoro, *Fortuna, ragione e prudenza nella civiltà letteraria del Cinquecento* (Naples, 1966), and *Il concetto dell'uomo nella letteratura del Cinquecento* (Naples, 1967), and Grendler, *Critics*.

[13] Bernard Weinberg, *A History of Literary Criticism in the Italian Renaissance*, 2 vols. (Chicago, 1961), p. 349. For more on the literary achievement of the era, see Peter M. Brown, *Lionardo Salviati: A Critical Biography* (London, 1974).

cade of devotional literature coming from the Venetian presses after 1560 testified to Italy's search for salvation.

Italians exhibited religious creativity in the last forty years of the cinquecento on a level comparable to their achievements in secular fields in earlier generations. The preparation of the new Vulgate, the editing of canonical and patristic texts, the work on the *Corpus juris canonici*, the ecclesiastical histories of Baronius and others, and especially the Italian Jesuit missionary labors all manifested an authentic orthodox revival. Its effect on Italian civic, economic, moral, and social life has not been assessed, but it had to be profound.

The Index and Inquisition undeniably affected Italian intellectual developments, but were by no means the only, nor the major, influence at work. Certainly Italy altered profoundly in the cinquecento, but only a part of this great transformation can be charged to the Counter Reformation. And the Counter Reformation itself must be seen in the context of economic, intellectual, political, and religious change.

A final historiographical question has attracted little attention: when and for what reasons did the Counter Reformation end? There is some tendency to mark its closing with the Treaties of Westphalia in 1648. Jedin prefers not to assign specific limits, arguing that its medieval elements preceded the sixteenth century, and its effects persisted long after the Thirty Years' War.[14] Some Catholics of the 1960s and 1970s, committed to the *aggiornamento* initiated by John XXIII and Vatican II, share the latter view. They object that, although the Index has been abolished (1966), the Holy Office under the new name of the Congregation for the Doctrine of the Faith continues to harass daring theologians, but Catholics only.

The secular state in Venice, and possibly elsewhere in Italy as well, terminated the prime years of the Counter Reformation about 1600, whatever its total lifespan.[15] As the Counter Reformation achieved its goal of the suppression of Protestantism, the state inevitably had less need for it and withdrew support from it. Any evaluation of the strength of the Index and Inquisition in seventeenth-century Italy must be tentative because, with the exception of the Galileo tragedy, the subject has been little studied; nevertheless, it is likely that public support dwindled and that their power waned. In late seicento Naples, for example, lawyers openly criticized the Inquisition for violating procedurally the natural right of defense. They also elevated the right of philosophical inquiry to a level

[14] *Riforma cattolica o controriforma*, pp. 62–63.

[15] The Catholic Reformation also ended at the end of the sixteenth century in the judgment of Alberigo, "L'applicazione del Concilio di Trento," p. 297; and Prodi, "Riforma cattolica e Controriforma," pp. 401–4.

equal to the duty of the public authority to maintain unity, a position that would have been impossible to have conceived a century earlier.[16] The Index and Inquisition endured in Venice until the fall of the Republic in 1797, but probably never again attained the strength and effectiveness enjoyed for a few decades in the cinquecento. The era of the high Counter Reformation had ended.

[16] Vittor Ivo Comparato, *Giuseppe Valletta: Un intellettuale napoletano della fine del Seicento* (Naples, 1970), pp. 139–94.

DOCUMENTS

In editing the following documents, punctuation and accents have been revised according to modern usage, but no orthographic changes have been introduced.

DOCUMENT 1

Memorandum of the bookmen to the Tre
Savii sopra eresia, July 24, 1548

On behalf of the guild, Tommaso Giunti presented this protest against the Council of Ten's censorship decree of July 18, 1548. See Ch. III, sec. 4. Source: SU, Bu, 156, "Librai e libri proibiti 1545–1571," ff. [63^{r-v}].

Illustrissimi et eccellentissimi signori
deputati sopra gli heretici

Havendo noi stampatori et venditori de libri in questa inclita città veduta la parte presa nel Illustrissimo et eccellentissimo Consiglio di X con la Gionta publicata sotto 19 del instante ne la qual si fa comandamento che si debbino appresentar tutti i libri ne li quali sia scritta alcuna cosa contra la fede catholica. Et considerando che in questa nostra arte si ritrovano molti et diversi libri in stampa composti da authori antiqui et moderni ne li quali potria esser qualche cosa contra la fede christiana, il che a noi è incognito, et maxime tra li authori gentili, come Galeno, Porphirio, et altri medici et philosofi, tra i Macomethani, com'è Averroe, Avicena, et Alpharabio, et tra gl'Hebrei, com'è Joseph *De bello Judaico*, Rhabi Mose d'Egitto, et altri infiniti che scrivono secondo il lor ritto; i quali, non conoscendo questa verità, potriano in qualche luoco de le lor composizioni con cuoda di scorpione, non haver havuto rispetto alcuno a la nostra fede catholica. Et tamen sono in uso tra i studiosi di philosofia, astrologia, medicina, et de tutte tre le lingue, e si sono venduti liberamente inanzi che questa peste di opinione lutherana habbi cominciata a morbar il mondo. Et vendonsi anchor hora in publico ne le nostre boteghe, unde per non esser certi se tal comandamento si estendi sopra i prediti authori et altri simili, o pur solamente sopra tutti quelli che hanno scritto secondo la opinione et heresia lutherana, et sopra tutti gl'altri che hanno parlato contra la sancta madre chiesia catholica romana. Semo hora recorsi al conspetto de le Sig.rie Vostre Ecc.me, come quelli che semo prontissimi ad esseguir ogni suo comandamento, per supplicar quelle che si degnino dechiarvini in scrittura il detto comandamento, dandone il thema de le sorte de' libri de li quali si dovemo per l'avenir guardar. Per ciò che l'animo nostro è disposto ad ubedir con ogni nostra possibile diligentia a le limitationiche da sue Sig.rie ne sarà fatte, et exercitar l'arte nostra honorevolmente et senza suspetto di cader in censura alcuna, supplicando quelle che voglino fino che siano dechiarite le sorti da le quali si dovemo guardar, tenir ditto comandamento et termine in suspeso a la gratia de le qual humilmente si raccomandiamo.

(verso) 24 julii 1548. Scrittura delli librari nella supplica che li sia dechiarito la difficultà di certa parte. [Another hand] Die marti 24 julij 1548 prestat. per d. Thomas Juncta fidei.

DOCUMENT 2

Petition of the bookmen against the Index of 1554/55

As discussed in Ch. III, sec. 6, the Venetian Inquisition presented a new Index to the bookmen on March 12, 1555, and gave them three months to comment on it. By the end of June, the bookmen presented to the Inquisition three petitions protesting the new Index. One of these, probably the first, is printed here, from SU, Bu. 156, "Librai e libri proibiti, 1545–1571," ff. [60^r–62^v]. It lacks a date and is probably incomplete, for it begins without formally addressing the Inquisition, and it appears to break off abruptly.

One explanatory note on this petition may be useful. In the course of criticizing the vagueness of the Index entries, the bookmen lamented that the works of "IOANNES RICCIUS" had been banned, although he taught openly at Padua and was reputed to be a Catholic. The bookmen were seizing upon an error in the original Venetian printing of this Index, which meant to ban the works of Joannes Rivius, a German author of Protestant religious works. The counterfeit printing corrected the entry to "Rivius;" compare p. 16 ("Riccius") of the original, and Sig. B1 verso ("Rivius") of the counterfeit, in VC, both catalogued under Opusc. P D 92. Reusch, *Indices*, printed the 1554/55 Venetian Index from the counterfeit version; therefore, he reproduced the entry accurately. The Indices of 1559, 1564, and subsequently also corrected the error to ban the works of "Joannes Rivius Atthendorien." The works of "Joannes Riccius" were never again prohibited.

The Riccius-Rivius error helps to establish the date of this petition as the spring of 1555. So does the reference in the following paragraph to "quel regno [i.e., England] tornato recentemente alla obedientia della santa chiesa." The bookmen referred to the English return to Catholicism under Mary Tudor in the autumn of 1553.

Sforza printed two other petitions against this Index, one lacking a date, the other dated June 22, 1555, in his "Controriforma," pt. 2, pp. 48–52. Both differ in content from the one printed here. Sforza cited only SU, Bu. 14 (without a precise trial), as his source for the undated petition, and gave no reference for the one of June 22. (It should be remembered that the *Archivio storico italiano* published Sforza's article posthumously and after some delay; see the editors' apology, couched in vague terms, in pt. 1, p. 5.) I have been unable to locate in SU either of the two petitions printed by Sforza. However, the secretary's minute of June 22, 1555, in SU, Bu. 159, "Acta S. Officij Venetiarum 1554–1555," pt. 3, ff. 41^r–42^v, confirms that a petition matching the content of the one of that date printed by Sforza was, indeed, presented to the Holy Office and discussed. For this reason, and because Sforza normally documented his work carefully and at length, I accept as genuine the two petitions that he printed.

(60^r) Qui saranno sottoscritti li nomi di alcuni auttori, fra li molti altri simili, che sono compresi nel cathalogo, li quali auttori hanno composte diverse opere in diverse facultà non appartinenti alla fede, nè alle cose ecclesiastice, ma solamente alle leggi, alla medicina, alla philosophia, et alle traduttioni di altri auttori non prohibiti, offerendone di mostrarne anchora molti altri, se et quando ne sarà ordinato, o che altramente farà bisogno.

Conradus Gesnerus

Questo ha composto Historiam animalium
    Cathalogus plantarum
    Thesaurum Euonimi de modo distillande
    De usu pharmacopei
    Libellum experimentorum ex Galeni operibus
    De compositione medicaminum secundum locos affectos
    De urinarum differentiis indiciis, ac causis
    De lacte, et operibus lactariis
    De medicamentis simplicibus
    De compositiones medicamentorum secundum genera
    Et altre opere simili di medicina, oltra molte traduttioni di greco in latino di philosophia, et oltra La bibliotheca universale.

Appendix I

Janus Cornarius Medicus

Ha composto Libros duos de peste, et Medicinam universalem. Ha tradutto di greco in latino alcuni libri di medicina di Hippocrates, et anche le epistole del medesimo.

Item De respirationis causis librum unum Galeni
De respirationis utilitate librum unum
De respirationis difficultate libros tres
De veteri dissectione librum unum
De foetus formatione librum unum
De compositione pharmacorum libros decem
In easdem libros decem quoque commentarios
Traduxit etiam atium medicum in latinum.

Le quale soprascripte opere tutte sono di grandissimo giovamento alla medicina et in molta stima appresso li buoni medici

(60ᵛ)   *Joannes Oldendorpius*

Ha composto moltissime opere in iure, come
De sententia, et re indicata
De successionibus ab intestato
De executoribus ultimarum voluntatum
De iure naturali, gentium, et civili
De usucapione
De jure singulari
De probationibus
In leges duodecim tabularum
Locos comunes actionum
Formulas libellandi
Formulas investigandi actiones
De iure, et equitate, et molte altre opere legali simili
Lexicon iuris, et de copia verborum, et rerum.

Hier. Schurpff de santo Gallo

Ha composto molti consegli, che sono inserti in un gran volume de altri consegli tutti feudali.

Item, molti altri consegli inserti in un'altro volume, pur de consegli del cardinale Zabarella
Item, un'altro gran volume pur de consegli del medesimo auttore intitolato Consiliorum Hier.i etiam Centuria prima.

Christophorum Hegendorphinus

Ha composto una dialetica legale
Item, De compendiaria dissendi iuracivilia ratione

Item, commentarios in titulos Pandectarum Juris civilis v. 3

De jurisdictione o minimum judicum

In titulum quod quisque iuris etc.

Item, in titulum si quis ius dicenti etc.

Item, in intulum de in ius vocando

Item, in titulum si quis in ius vocatus

Item, in titulum in ius vocati, ut eant.

Item, sopra il codice di Giustiniano

(61ʳ) Le quali opere legali, oltra che non trattano di cose de la fede, sono stampate insieme con altre opere in modo che non si potriano levare chi non stracciasse o abrusciasse anche quelle altre.

Jacobus Zeglerius

Ha composto De constructione solide sphere

Item, la discrittione del paese di terra santa, e lla Soria

[Syria], della Arrabia, et dello Egitto

Item, de rebus indicis librum unum

Item, commentarium in librum secundum Historie naturalis

Plinii

Item, molte opere in mathematica

Joannes Velcurio

Ha composto quattro libri sopra la Phisica di Aristotile.

Item, super Ethica

Item, super Anima

Item, Annotationes in Titum Livium

Philippus Melanchthon

Ha fatto un tomo intiero tutto di opere di philosophia.

Item, un commentario sopra il p.°, il ii.°, il iii.°, et v.° libro dell'Ethica di Aristotile. Item, sopra la Politica del medesimo.

Ha composto un commentario de Anima

Item, una grammatica latina

Item, una greca

Item, doi libri de Rettorica

Item, quattro di Dialetica

Item, un trattatello delle misure et delle monete, et molte altre opere simili di Philophia [sic] o di humanità.

Sebastianus Munsterus

Ha composto Cosmographiam universalem

Dictionarium trium linguarum

Dictionarium lingue hebraice

Dictionarium caldaicum

(61ᵛ) Grammaticam hebream

Grammaticam Caldaicam

Horologeographiam, vel de Horologiorum compositione

Rudimenta Mathematice

Theoricam omnium planetarum

Introductionem in librum novi orbis

Decalogum Hebraicum

Item, molte altre cose di cosmographia, et de Geographia, et molte altre in hebreo, et in caldeo, che sono di grandissima utilità per chi desidera haver la cognitione di queste lingue.

Otho Brunfelsius medicus

Ha composto Herbarum volumina tria

Onomasticum medicinae

De usu pharmacopolae

Epithomen Medicorum

Locos comunes totius rei medice

De artificio ciendi aluum suppressam

De remediis omnium morborum, qui tam hominibus quam pecudibus accidere possunt opus preclarum, et multum a medicis extimatum et quasi innumerabili altre opere in medicina.

Se le S.rie V.re Reveren. et Ecc.me ne ordineranno, noi li mostraremmo come delli soprascritti, così di molti altri auttori compresi nel cathalogo opere diverse non attinenti alla religione, il privare il mondo delle quali non saria di utile ad alcuno, ma sì bene di evidentissimo danno, et di grandissimo dispiacere ad infiniti.

(62ʳ) Non è anche da tacere, che per un'altro rispetto importantissimo, la prohibitione di molti auttori in questo cathalogo col solo simplice cognome senza altra espressione delle opere loro, et senza alcuna altra circumstantia, genera grandissima confusione, intrigamento et scandalo, come, verbi gratia, si prohibisce nel detto cathalogo IOANNES RICCIUS, et non se dice altro; et tra noi librari non si conosce altro Joannes Riccius che quello che legge publice in Padua. Et par pur dura cosa che un valent'huomo, et reputato catholico, come è quello, condotto da questa Ill.ma S.ria a leggere publice in un suo studio quale, debba a questo modo, ricevere un fregio et una macchia nell'honor suo, et che havendo egli composto annotationi molto utili sopra la prattica giudiciaria papiense, che già sono imprese et publicate, et altre sue fatiche honorevoli in legge, le quali li scolari et professori di questi studii aspettano da lui alla giornata, debba senza alcuna sua colpa essere prohibito a darle fuora per colpa di un'altro che non si conosce; et che non solamente lui, ma ogni altro di tal nome et cognome habbia per l'avenire da esser notato per heretico, et prohibito perpetualmente a non dover mai mandare in luce alcuna sua compositione, per catholica et santa ch'ella sia, o habbia da essere. Et questo che noi dicemo di Ioannes Riccio si può dire anchora di moltissimi altri che nel medesimo cathalogo sono prohibiti nello istesso modo col simplice nome et cognome loro; anzi pure col nome simplicissimo come, per mostrarne alcuni, diremo degli infrascritti:

Almericus	Lentius	Marsilius de Pad.a
Alnordus	Joannes Saxo	Gaspar Ubertinus
Luscinius	Matthias Boemus	Georgius Spalatinus
(62ᵛ) Georgius Amilius	Petrus de Arragonia	
Frater Michael de Cesena	Petrus Ferrariensis	
Franc.s Lambertus	Petrus de Luna	
Durianus Novariensis	Petrus Anglus	
Didimus Faventinus	Ant.s Anglus	

Nel prohibire delli quali Inglesi così simplicemente con nota di tutti gli altri che hanno li istessi nomi, è ben da considerare che con questa generalità non si offenda tutto quel regno tornato recentemente alla obedientia della santa chiesa, maxime essendo da credere che in un regno tanto patents [sic] potrà ritrovarsi, et si ritrouverà senza dubio, o adesso o in processo di poco tempo, qualche altro Ant.o et qualche altro Pietro, li quali hora che Iddio benedetto gli ha illuminati vorrano scrivere catholicamente. Et per li tanti segni di allegrezza che ha fatto la santità di Nostro Signore nella conversione di questo regno, crediamo certo che alla sua beatitudine istessa non sia per satisfare una prohibitione così generale.

Se le S.rie V.re leggeranno le prohibitioni, et reprobationi de' libri fatte ne' tempi passati, le vederanno che o sono state prohibite le opere sole, et distintamente, o le opere insieme con li nomi delli loro auttori, et non li nomi delli auttori soli senza le opere, eccetto se per sententia declaratoria non fosse stato condennato alcuno per heretico insieme con tutti li suoi scritti et compositioni, sì come alle molte sono stati condennati alcuni heresiarchi, come fu Martin Luthero, et simili.

DOCUMENT 3

Omnibus press law of the Council of Ten, June 28, 1569

This law extended the prepublication censorship to foreign imprints, and established the inquisitorial inspection of imported books at the customs house. See Ch. IV, sec. 4, and Ch. V, sec. 1. Source: CX, Comune, R. 59, ff, 30ʳ–31ʳ, June 28, 1569.

MDLXIX *Die xxviij Junij*

(30^r) Hanno introdotto li compositori delle opere che si danno alla stampa, doppo fatte veder esse opere et ottenuta la licentia di stamparle, non solo di corregger gli errori di ortografia o fatti per trascorso di penna, ma insieme anco di mutare et aggiongere le clausule, et molte volte le carte intiere, et sì come fanno hora questo per dar maggior ornamento et perfettione alle loro opere, così per la licentia che si prendono, potriano anco mutar o aggionger cosa che alterasse la sustantia, et di buone che fussero le opere con questa aggionta et mutatione, farle diventar cattive, mescolandovi specialmente qualche passo contra la religione, il che faria riuscir vana ogni fatica et diligentia usata avanti la concessione di stampar il libro, la qual cosa essendo di quella importantia, che è ben noto ad ogn'uno di questo conseglio.

L'anderà parte che tutti quelli che per l'avvenire voranno dar alla stampa alcuna opera nova siano obligati prima che ottengano la licentia di stamparla far di essa due copie, una da esser riveduta iuxta la forma delle leggi et ordini nostri per portarla poi alla stampa, et l'altra da esser consignata ligata nell'officio delli Reformatori, perchè si possa veder dapoi stampato il libro se vi sarà stato aggionto o mutato cosa alcuna. Et si debba avvertire il compositor, o altro che porterà detta copia, che non ardisca far stampar il libro con niuna alteratione, ma in quella forma a ponto[1] che sarà la copia rimasa presso li Reformatori predetti. Et se 'l compositor giudicasse che 'l suo libro havesse bisogno d'alcuna mutatione o aggionta, non possa farlo se non con questa conditione, che sia prima veduta da uno delli Reformatori nostri, et dalli revisori (30^v) di essa opera, et da loro approbata, dovendosi parimente lassar la copia di essa mutatione o aggionta al ditto Riformator, la qual sia rimessa nel libro. Et se alcuno contrafarà alla presente deliberatione, incorrer debba in irremissibil pena de ducati cento, da esser divisa la mità all'accusator, il qual sia tenuto secreto, et il resto applicato all'Arsenal nostro. Il qual ne sia subitamente avvertito, et la cognitione de simil contrafattione sia rimessa alli Proveditori contra la biastema; i quali, conosciuta la colpa, non possano sotto debito di sacramento dar minor pena della sopradetta, ma ben possano accrescerla secondo la qualità del delitto. Li libri che resterano presso di loro Reformatori et sarano da essi giudicati degni della libraria publica siano posti nella libraria sopradetta. Delli quali il secretario a loro deputato debba tenerne particolar nota.

Et perchè non minor è il pericolo che si corre nel vender li libri che vengono condotti in questa città stampati in altri luoghi, così del Dominio nostro come alieni, è conveniente che in questi anco sia posto ordine tale

---

[1] appunto.

che habbia ad ovviar alli inconvenienti che potriano succeder. Però sia preso che non si possa da alcuno nè publicar nè vender libro di qualunque sorte stampato fuori di questa città, il quale overo sia novo overo novamente ristampato, con aggionta di espositioni o altra alteratione importante, se non haverà prima la fede delli Reformatori sopranominati, i quali, prima che la concedano, debbano farlo riveder con tutti quei modi et conditioni istesse che sono osservate da quelli che dano libri di novo alla stampa. Et non osservando li librari, o altri che vendessero libri stampati, quanto è sopradetto, cadano all'istessa pena da esser divisa come di sopra.

Et sia nell'avenire tenuto questo ordine in tutti i libri stampati altrove che sarano presentati nella Doana, o venirano per qual si voglia altra via in questa città che non possa esser aperta nè botte nè balla nè fagotto nè altra cosa ove fussero libri senza la presentia del Reverendo Inquisitore, et d'uno almeno delli presidenti dell'arte che non habbia interesse in essi libri, il quale sotto pena de ducati vinticinque debba alla presentia dell' Inquisitor sopradetto fedelmente et diligentemente far la lista, così della qualità come della quantità di essi libri. Et la copia di essa (31ʳ) lista sottoscritta di propria mano debba immediate presentar alli Reformatori, la qual sia dal Segretario loro messa in filcia di tempo in tempo, espettando ciascuno di essi librari prima che vendano, nè lascino veder ad alcuno detti libri, la licentia delli capi del Conseglio nostro di X, nella qual sia osservata quanto è sopraditto. Et la presente parte sia intimata alli stampatori et librari acciò in niun tempo possano escusarsi d'ignorantia. Et sia etiam publicata sopra le scalle de Rialto.

De parte 26

De non 1

Non sincero 1

1569 a dì 9 luglio publicata sopra le scalle de Rialto per Francesco de Simon Comandador.

INVENTORIES OF PROHIBITED TITLES
c. 1555–1604

These eleven inventories present additional documentation on the diffusion of prohibited books in Venice. The first was submitted in forced obedience to the Pauline Index, the next nine come from Inquisition trials of heretical suspects and bookmen, and the last catalogues the prohibited books in the library of Gian Vincenzo Pinelli. Some of these inventories complete the documentation for individual trials discussed previously in the text; others offer new information. In combination with inventories of prohibited titles described in the text, and those printed by Perini and Stella, this appendix presents the greatest part of such inventories found in the Inquisition trials, and all the longer ones.[1]

The Inquisition official compiling an inventory of the books of a suspect or disobedient bookman normally listed only the author (often just the surname) and a one-, two-, or three-word title. Such an abbreviated description is usually enough to identify the work, but not the printing. When the work can easily be found in the *STC French*, *STC German*, or *STC Italian*, no additional identifying reference is included; when the work was located in another reference work, it is mentioned in the footnotes. The entries in the following lists are presented in the form of short titles sufficient to locate the title in a library catalogue or bibliographical guide. When the title cannot be identified, the original entry is reproduced in quotation marks, along with a tentative identification in some cases. When the original entry included the place and/or date of publication and the format, this additional information is added to the identifications. Sometimes, then, the exact printing can be determined. Each author and title has been checked against the Tridentine Index (and the Clementine Index of 1596 in the case of the Pinelli inventory) to determine if it was prohibited or ordered expurgated. Finally, the following inventories include all the banned or expurgated titles in the libraries or bookstores of the suspects, but not the innocent volumes.

---

[1] Perini, "Ancora sul Pietro Perna," pp. 387–94, prints an annotated list of the prohibited titles discovered by the Holy Office in the possession of Francesco Stella (1549), Paolo Rosello (1551), and Pietro Cocco (1551). Stella 1, 180–82, lists the titles of Claudio Textor (1587).

INVENTORY 1

Prohibited books presented by Gabriel Giolito
to the Inquisition on August 14, 1559

Like the other bookmen, Giolito submitted prohibited books from his shop to the Holy Office in partial compliance with the Pauline Index. As the inventory demonstrates, he presented mostly books published in northern Europe, and not prohibited titles printed in Venice (see Ch. III, sec. 8). Entitled "Libri quali apresenta al'officio delle Magnifici Vostre, Gabriel Giolito libraro alla fenice," it is in SU, Bu. 156, "Librai e libri proibiti, 1545–1571," f. [88ʳ]. Although undated, it is included with other inventories of 1559. It cannot be a list submitted in September 1571 because the latter would have included Machiavelli's *Discorsi*, to which the inquisitor referred. See ibid., ff. [23ᵛ–25ʳ], which is discussed in Ch. v, sec. 1.

Italian authors

Brucioli, Antonio. "Comentaria." One of his several Biblical commentaries, all of which were published in Venice between 1541 and 1546.

Fregoso, Federigo. *Trattato della oratione.* Venice: Giolito, 1542; reprinted by Giolito in 1543. This was a posthumous orthodox work of Cardinal Fregoso (c. 1480–1541), Archbishop of Salerno and strong advocate of internal reform of the church. However, also issued with the *Trattato*, and under Fregoso's name, were vernacular translations of two of Luther's tracts: *Della giustificatione, della fede et dell'opere* and *Prefatione alla lettera di S. Paolo a' Romani.* Paul IV's Index banned what it thought was a three-part work of Fregoso. The Tridentine and later Indices noted that only part of the work was truly Fregoso's but, nevertheless, banned the tripartite book. Because of the extreme rarity of the counterfeit edition, nothing is known of how the deception was arranged or who was involved. Whether all three titles were printed and issued by Giolito, or whether the two treatises of Luther were printed separately by another bookman and then bound with the authentic Fregoso work, remains a mystery.[2]

Non-Italian authors

"Armachani." This was probably a work of Richard Fitzralph (d. 1360), Archbishop of Armach (Ireland) and often called Armachanus, who asserted that Scripture and early church tradition failed to sanction mendicancy and poverty. Innocent VI called upon him to defend his

---

[2] Reusch, *Indices*, 186, 262; *Index*, I, 382–83; Bongi, *Giolito*, I, 34–35, 50. I have not located any copies of the tripartite work; Bongi notes that copies of the *Trattato della oratione* alone are also extremely rare.

opinions, but Fitzralph died before the hearing could take place. Wycliffe, however, accepted and extended his ideas. Fitzralph's best known work was *Defensorium curatorum*, which enjoyed a number of printings as an incunable. The 1554/55 Venetian Index had banned the works of Armachanus, but Paul IV's Index permitted them. Either Giolito erred or, perhaps, the work submitted was an unknown Protestant commentary on Armachanus.[3]

"Bibliotheca." Probably Konrad Gesner, *Bibliotheca universalis.*

Castellio (Châteillon), Sébastien. *Moses latinus ex Hebraeo factus.* A Latin edition of the Pentateuch published in Basel, 1546.

"Concordantie no. testi. grecij in fo." Possibly [Xystus Betuleius (Sixt Birck)], *Concordantiae graecae Novum Testamentum* (Basel, 1546), in folio.[4]

"Dialoghi Sacrorum." Probably Castellio, *Dialogorum sacrorum*, first published in Basel, 1540, and in many subsequent editions, some lacking the author's name.

Dolet, Étienne. *Carminum.*

———. *Cato christianus.*

"Dramata sacre scriptura." Possibly the anonymous Protestant work, *Comoedie ac tragoediae aliquot ex novo et veteri testamento desumptae.* Per N. Brylingerum: Basileae, 1540.[5]

Eobanus, Helius. *Psalterium Davidis.*

"Epistolae S. Paulini." Unidentified, but probably a Protestant version.

Erasmus. *De puritate tabernaculi s. ecclesiae christianae.*

———. *Enchiridion militis christiani.*

———. *Espositione di Matheo Evangelista.* The Tomitano translation.

———. *In Novum Testamentum annotationes.*

———. *Modus orandi Deum.*

———. *Moriae encomium.*

———. *Precationes aliquot novae.*

"Grisostimj con scobis Oecolampadi." One of Oecolampadius' many editions, translations, and/or commentaries on the works of St. John Chrysostom.

"Io. benesi de civitate christiana." Unidentified.

"Io. benesi del libero arbitrio." Unidentified.

Melanchthon, Philipp. "De Anima." Either his *Commentarius de anima* or *Liber de anima recognitus.*

[3] See "Richard Fitzralph" by R. L. P. in the *Dictionary of National Biography*, vol. VIII (Oxford, 1886), pp. 194–98; Reusch, *Index*, I, 22; Hain 13672–13675; Copinger 5021–5024.

[4] *STC German*, 124; Reusch, *Index*, I, 241. Paul IV's Index listed it under its title only. Reusch, *Indices*, 183.

[5] *STC German*, 123; Reusch, *Index*, I, 137, and *Indices*, 182.

"Modus confitendi." Possibly Erasmus, *Exomologesis sive modus confitendi*, sometimes issued simply as *Modus confitendi.*[6]

"Moysis Iustifucuris." Unidentified.

"Pandecte sacre scriptura." Probably Otto Brunfels, *Pandectarum veteris et novi Testamenti*, first published in Strasbourg, 1527, an important source for Nicodemite thought.[7]

Piccolomini, Aeneas Sylvius. *Liber dialogorum de auctoritate concilii generalis ac de gestis Basilensium et Eugenii contradictione.*

"Preccatio Biblie." Quite likely Brunfels, *Precationes biblicae sanctorum patrum illustrium virorum et mulierum utriusque Testamenti*, first published in Strasbourg, 1528, and followed by many other editions and translations.[8]

Schade, Petrus (Mosellanus). No title given, but possibly his popular *Paedologia*, his only work to be banned in 1559.

INVENTORY 2

Prohibited titles in the possession of Venetian heretics
and suspects c. 1555 to c. 1567

From about 1555 through about 1567, a group of young nobles, local craftsmen, and a few foreign merchants participated in the group of interrelated conventicles led by Andrea Da Ponte, Teofilo Panarelli, and several humanist schoolmasters (see Chs. III, sec. 7; IV, sec. 2). Abjurees and witnesses in the series of Inquisition trials that broke up the conventicles testified that the members had the prohibited titles listed here. However, the Holy Office did not succeed in seizing any copies. The principle sources are SU, Bu. 32, Teofilo Panarelli e Ludovico Abioso, ff. 21ᵛ–22ᵛ (testimony of Abioso of July 8, 1568), and ff. [1ᵛ–3ʳ], testimony of Panarelli of November 23, 1571. Other titles are mentioned in the following trials: Bu. 11, Giovan Andrea Ugone (1565); Bu. 20, Antonio Loredano e Alvise Malipiero (1565); Bu. 20, Michele De Basili, Carlo Corner, e Venturino Dalle Madonette (1565); Bu. 20, Pietro Agusto (1565); Bu. 23, Silvestro, Cipriano, e Stefano Semprini, Andrea Dandolo, Marc'Antonio da Canale, Luigi Mocenigo, et al., esp. ff. 66ʳ–68ᵛ (testimony of Alvise Mocenigo of July 12, 1568); Bu. 29, Paolo Avanzo, ff. 19ʳ–20ᵛ (1568 and 1569); Bu. 32, Teofilo, Virginia, e Catherina Panarelli, Francesco Rocca libraro, Giulio Gemma, e Hieronimo de Padua (1572).

---

[6] *Bibliotheca Erasmiana*, ser. 1, 104–5.

[7] Carlo Ginzburg, *Il nicodemismo. Simulazione e dissimulazione religiosa nell'Europa del '500* (Turin, 1970), passim.

[8] Ginzburg, *Il nicodemismo*, pp. 98–102.

Beneficio di Christo.

Betti, Francesco. Unnamed work.

[Bettini, Luca.] *Oraculo della rinnovazione della Chiesa secondo la dottrina del R. P. Hieronimo Savonarola.*[9]

Brucioli, Antonio. Bible. (Mentioned twice.)

——. *Nuovo commento ne divini et celesti libri evangelici.* Venice, 1542. (This is the first volume of his *Commento al Nuovo Testamento.* Venice, 1542–44.)[10]

——. "Parabole, proverbi et sententie."[11]

Il capo finto. Nuovamente dalla lingua tedesca nella italiana tradotto e con somma diligentia corretto, et revisto. Stampato nella inclita città di Roma per gli Heredi di Marco Antonio di prati Barolitano. Nell'anno del Signore MDXLIIII.[12]

Della Rovere, Giulio. *Prediche.*

——. "Alli carcerati d'Italia." (Ms.)

Fregoso, Federigo. *Trattato della oratione.*

Ochino, Bernardino. *Catechismo.* Basel, 1561.[13]

——. "De justificatione." (Probably *Sermo . . . conversus Coelio Secundo Curione interprete: Quid sit per Christum iustificari, tum qui iustificationis modus.* Basel, 1544.)[14]

——. *Espositione sopra la Epistola di S. Paolo alli Galati.* N.p., 1546.[15]

——. "Espositione sopra li salmi." (Possibly his *La quarta parte delle prediche. . . . Psalm xliiij.* Basel? 1555?)[16]

——. *Prediche.* (Mentioned several times.)

——. "una opera . . . latina dove se trattava di Poligamia."[17]

Savonarola, Girolamo. Unnamed letters and sermons. (The Pauline Index banned, and the Tridentine Index ordered expurgated, a long list of Savonarola's works.)

Vergerio, Pier Paolo. *Discorsi sopra i fioretti di San Francesco.*[18]

[9] Although attributed to Savonarola, this work published in Venice in 1536 and 1543 was the product of a devoted follower. Reusch, *Index,* I, 370.

[10] Spini, "Bibliografia di Brucioli," p. 157.

[11] Possibly this was his *Epistole, lettioni, et evangeli, che si leggono in tutto l'anno,* printed in Venice in 1532, 1539, 1543, and once without a date. Spini, "Bibliografia di Brucioli," pp. 154–55.

[12] Perini, "Ancora sul Pietro Perna," p. 387.

[13] Karl Benrath, *Bernardino Ochino von Siena: Ein Beitrag zur Geschichte der Reformation,* 2nd ed. (Braunschweig, 1892; rpt. Nieuwkoop, 1968), p. 323, item 45.

[14] Benrath, *Ochino,* pp. 316–17, item 15.

[15] Ibid., p. 317, item 20.   [16] Ibid., p. 321, item 34.

[17] Possibly this was part of the Latin *Dialogi XXX* (Basel, 1563), as noted by Benrath, *Ochino,* p. 323, item 47.

[18] Perini, "Ancora sul Pietro Perna," p. 390.

Vermigli, Peter Martyr. *In Epistolam Pauli ad Romanos commentarii.*

———. "una lettera essortativa stampata."

Non-Italian authors

Bèze, Théodore de. *Parlamento de Protestanti . . . dinanzi al Re di Francia . . . a Poissi, il giorno 9 di settembre 1561.* Geneva, 1561.[19]

Brenz, Johann. Two unnamed titles.

Bucer, Martin. Unnamed work.

Bullinger, Heinrich. Unnamed work.

Calvin, Jean. *Catechism.*

———. *Institutes.* (Mentioned several times.)

"Un'altra espositione dell'epistole ad Romanos senza authore, ma è heretica."

Hus, John. Unnamed title in two volumes.

Luther, Martin. Four folio volumes described as "due delle questioni che hebbe con Ecclio [Eck], et due di alcuni sermoni sopra l'Evangelij. . . ."

Melanchthon, Philipp. *Loci communes theologici.*

Oecolampadius, Joannes. Treatise on the Eucharist.[20]

Psalms. (Mentioned by witnesses several times, but without precise identifications; probably Protestant editions of the Psalms.)

Rhegius, Urbanus. *Dottrina vecchia et nuova.* (Mentioned twice.)[21]

Sleidanus [Philippson], Joannes. "Historia." (Possibly *Commentariorum de statu religionis et reipublicae Carolo Quinto Caesare.*)[22]

———. Unnamed work.

"Testamento novo vulgare con le postille d'un heretico di Geneva."

"Testamento nuovo stampata in Geneva."

"Vite dei martiri."

"Vite di Giov. Huss et Hier. de Praga."

INVENTORY 3

Vincenzo Bertoldi—1570

The Venetian Holy Office arrested Vincenzo Bertoldi of Bassano, a notary aged 60, upon receipt of a denunciation alleging possession of

---

[19] *Les livres imprimés a Genève de 1550 a 1600*, pp. 45–46.

[20] Oecolampadius authored several works on the Eucharist. See Ernst Staehelin, *Oekolampad-Bibliographie*, 2nd ed. unchanged (Nieuwkoop, 1963), items 40, 52, 113, 124, 131, 140, 206.

[21] Reusch, *Index*, I, 192.

[22] This may have been the Italian translation published in Geneva, 1557. See Dennis E. Rhodes, "La traduzione italiana dei *Commentarii* di Giovanni Sleidano," *La Bibliofilia* 68 (1966), 283–87.

heretical books. The tribunal compiled this inventory of his prohibited titles on April 2, 1570, but Bertoldi died in prison before the trial had progressed far. Unlike most inventories compiled by the Inquisition, this one included fairly complete titles, and format, and in one case (the Geneva printing of Ochino's *Sermones*) the place of publication, making possible more precise identifications. Fifteen of the seventeen titles were banned. The other two ("Pie et Christiane meditatione" and the Latin New Testament) are included on the grounds that they were probably also Protestant, given the nature of the library. In general, Bertoldi owned prohibited titles very similar to those of Francesco Stella (1549), Paolo Rosello (1551), and Pietro Cocco (1551) listed by Perini, "Ancora sul Pietro Perna," pp. 387–94. Source: SU, Bu. 26, Vincenzo Bertoldi. This inventory has not been mentioned in the text.

Italian authors

Della Rovere, Giulio. *Prediche, Parte II.* 8°.[23]

Gribaldi, Mofa Matteo. *La historia di M. Francesco Spira.* Trans. Pier Paolo Vergerio. 8°.[24]

Ochino, Bernardino. *Espositione sopra la Epistola di S. Paolo alli Galati.* Augsburg, 1546. 8°.[25]

———. *Sermones.* Geneva, n.d. 8°.

———. *Sermones.* 4°.[26]

Opere catholice et Christiane di M. Hier.o Savonete, et gloria Dio. 8°.[27]

"Pie christiane epistole composte da un servo de Iddio alli fideli in Christo." 8°.[28]

"Pie et Christiane meditatione et orationi formate sopra li Epistole di S. Paulo à Romani." 8°.[29]

Sommario de la Sacra Scrittura. 16°.

Valdés, Juan de. *Alphabeto Christiano.*

Vermigli, Peter Martyr. *Dichiaratione sopra gli xii articoli della fede.* Basel, 1544. 8°.[30]

[23] Perini, "Ancora sul Pietro Perna," p. 392, notes a printing lacking place and date in the Bibliothèque Nationale, Paris.

[24] See *STC German*, 826, and *STC Italian*, 755, for a printing of Basel(?) 1551, 8°.

[25] Benrath, *Ochino*, p. 377, item 20.

[26] Ibid., pp. 375–76, lists six Geneva printings of 1543 and 1544, but all in 8°.

[27] The identity of "Hieronymus Savonen" (as listed in the Tridentine Index) eludes scholars.

[28] The Indices of 1549, 1554/55, 1559, and 1564, all prohibited this anonymous work.

[29] I have been unable to identify this title, which does not seem to be listed in the Indices.

[30] McNair, *Peter Martyr*, p. 299.

Virginio Bresciano, Giovanni Francesco [probably Cornelio Donzellini].
Le dotte e pie parafrasi sopra l'epistole di S. Paolo à Romani. (Either
Lyons, 1551, or Geneva, 1555.) 16°.[31]

Non-Italian authors

"Catechismo seu formulario per ammaestrar li fanciulli nella Religione
Christiana alli vescovi, et ministri delle chiesie della Italia." 8°. (This
may be Calvin's *Catechismo cio e formulario per ammaestrare i fanciulli ne la religion christiana, fatto in modo di dialogo, dove il ministro
della chiesa domanda è il fanciullo risponde.* [Geneva, 1545.] 8°.)[32]
Lefèvre d'Etaples, Jacques. *Commentarii in quatuor Evangelia.* (Unless
expurgated.)
Luther, Martin. "Il libro inscritto alli nobili principi Germani in esorta-
tione di correggere il stato christiano et quello in meglio reformato.
8°." (An Italian translation of the *Address to the German Nobility*.)[33]
New Testament. Latin. 16°.[34]
Rhegius, Urbanus. *Medicina dell'anima.* 8°.[35]

INVENTORY 4

Vincenzo Valgrisi—1570

The Holy Office on August 18, 1570, compiled the following inventory
of the large quantity of prohibited books discovered in the storehouse of
Vincenzo Valgrisi, publisher and bookseller (see Ch. v, sec. 1). This
inventory indicates the range and quantity of prohibited titles offered for
sale at this time. All banned titles were marked with a cross, as were titles
of Erasmus that were permitted in expurgated form and an innocent
title of Gelli. Source: SU, Bu. 14, Vincenzo Valgrisi et al., "Contro Vincentium Vadrisium," ff. [37^r-41^v].

Italian authors

Aretino, Pietro. *Canti di Marphisa.*
———. *Capitoli.*
———. *Dialoghi.* (Probably *Ragionamenti.*) 2 copies.

---

[31] Tedeschi, "Genevan Books of the Sixteenth Century," pp. 174–76.

[32] Alfred Erichson, *Bibliographia Calviniana* (Berlin, 1900; rpt. Nieuwkoop, 1960),
p. 5.

[33] *STC Italian*, 171, lists an Italian translation (Strasbourg, 1533) with a slightly
different title.

[34] Although the entry lacks additional information, one can presume that it was
a Protestant version.

[35] This could be the Italian translation published by Vincenzo Valgrisi in 1545.
See Ch. v, sec. 1, and the following inventory.

———. "Dialoghi della corte." (Unidentified.) 7 copies.

———. *Genesi.* 4 copies.

———. *Humanità di Christo.*

———. *Lettere.* 8 copies.

———. *Passione di Giesu.*

———. *Sette salmi della penitentia.* 21 copies.

———. *Vita di Maria Vergine.* 3 copies.

———. *Vita di San Tomaso d'Aquino.* 3 copies.

Boccaccio, Giovanni. *Decameron.* (Unless expurgated.) 2 copies.

Brucioli, Antonio. *Dialogi.* 3 copies.

Gelli, Giambattista. *La Circe.* (Although marked as prohibited in the inventory, the Tridentine Index had neither banned it nor ordered expurgation. The Indices of 1554/55 and 1559 had prohibited it earlier.)

Machiavelli, Niccolò. *Discorsi.* 3 copies.

———. *Historie fiorentine.*

———. *Opere.* 4 copies.

Valdés, Juan de. *Alphabeto Christiano.* 29 copies.

Non-Italian authors

Agrippa, Henricus Cornelius. *De occulta philosophia.* 7 copies.

———. *In Artem brevem Raymundi Lullij commentaria.* 5 copies.

Carion, Johann. *Chronica.* 187 copies.

Castellio [Châteillon], Sébastien. Bible. Trans. and com. S. C.

Clinch [Klinch or Mlinch], Melchior. "Sopra li decreti." (Possibly *Lectura super secundum sexti decretalium*[36] or *In praecipuos secundi l. Decretalium titulos.*)[37] 4 copies.

———. "Sopra l'instituta." (Probably *Enarrationes in IV Institutionum libros.*)[38] 4 copies.

Columna, Petrus [Galatinus]. *De arcanis Catholicae* with *I. Reuchlini de arte cabalistica.* 2 copies.

Cordier, Mathurin. Unnamed work. 16 copies.

Cousin, Gilbert. *Commentarius in omnes Luciani lucubrationes.*[39] 2 copies.

———. Unnamed work. 4 copies.

Du Moulin, Charles. *De verborum obligationibus.*[40] 3 copies.

———. *Tractatus commerciorum et usurarum.*

Eobaus Helius. *Psalterium Davidis.* 8 copies.

Erasmus, Desiderius. *Adagia.* (Unless expurgated.) 32 copies.

---

[36] *Bibliotheca instituta et collecta, primum a Conrado Gesnero, deinde . . . per Iosiam Simlerum . . . amplificata per Iohannem Iacobum Frisium* (Tiguri, excudabat Christophorus Froschoverus, MDLXXXIII), p. 600.

[37] Reusch, *Index,* I, 120.   [38] Ibid.

[39] Gesner, Simler, and Frisius, *Bibliotheca,* p. 285.

[40] Ibid., p. 137.

————. *Colloquia.* 10 copies, 2 specified as Italian translations.

————. *Institutio Christiani matrimonii.* 4 copies.

————. *Joannes Chrysostomus in Evangelium Matthaei.* (Unless expurgated.)

————. *Opera Omnia.* 9 vols. Basel, 1540. (Unless expurgated.)

————. *Proverbi.* Italian trans. of *Apophthegmata*, published by Giolito, 1550.[41] 30 copies.

————. *Testamentum novum.* Greek and Latin. (Unless expurgated.) 2 copies.

————, and Musculus, Wolfgang. *Joannes Chrysostomus commentarius in Pauli epistolas.* 6 copies. (The inventory marked other works of Erasmus, including *De conscribendis epistolis* and commentaries on Cato and Terence, as prohibited, but the Tridentine Index did not ban them.)

Gesner, Konrad. *Bibliotheca universalis*, Part I.

Holbein, Hans, and Rhegius, Urbanus. *Simulacri, historie, e figure de la morte.* Venice: Vincenzo Valgrisi, 1545.[42] This edition includes Urbanus Rhegius's *Medicina dell'Anima* and other material. See Ch. v, sec. 1. 300 copies with a false title page and 104 copies of the original.

Indagine, Joannes ab. *Chiromantia.* 7 copies.

Lagus, Conradus. *Methodica iuris utriusque traditio.* 9 copies.

Lefèvre d'Etaples, Jacques. *Commentarii in quatuor Evangelia.* (Unless expurgated.) 4 copies.

————. *Epistolae divi Pauli.* (Unless expurgated.) 4 copies.

Lycosthenes (Wolffhardt), Conradus. "Facetie." (Unidentified.) 2 copies.

Melanchthon, Philipp. *De rhetorica.* 3 copies.

————. *Grammatica.* 24 copies.

————, and Erasmus. Commentary on Terence.[43] 2 copies.

Micyllus [Moltzer], Jacobus. Commentary on Pliny, *De mundi historia.*

Musculus, Wolfgang. St. Basil, *Opera omnia.* Ed. and trans. W. M. 3 copies.

Nicodemus. *De magistri et salvatoris nostri Jesu Christi passione et resurrectione evangelium.*[44]

Oecolampadius, Joannes. *Theophylacti in quatuor Evangelia enarrationes.*[45] 6 copies.

Oldendorpius, Joannes. *Actionum juris civilis loci communes.* 7 copies.

————. *De copia verborum & rerum in jure civili.*[46] 7 copies.

---

[41] Bongi, *Giolito*, I, 278–79. [42] *STC Italian*, 208.

[43] *Bibliotheca Erasmiana*, II, 55; *STC German*, 852.

[44] The Tridentine Index banned the Gospel attributed to Nicodemus. Reusch, *Indices*, 272; Reusch, *Index*, I, 292.

[45] *Oekolampad-Bibliographie*, p. 45, item 93, and passim.

[46] Gesner, Simler, and Frisius, *Bibliotheca*, p. 480.

————. *De duplici verborum & rerum significatione.* 7 copies.

————. *De origine juris.*[47] 6 copies.

————. *Enchiridion exceptionum forensium.* 5 copies.

————. "In Paulo." (Unidentified.)

————. "Intulim juris." (Unidentified.) 6 copies.

————. *Practica actionum forensium.* 7 copies.

————. *Topica legalia.* 13 copies.

————. *Variarum lectionum aliquot ad iuris civilis interpretationem.* 6 copies.

Osiander, Andreas. *Harmoniae Evangelicae.* 7 copies.

Postel, Guillaume [Helias Pandochaeus]. Unnamed work. 31 copies.

Schoener, Joannes. *I tre libri della nativita.* (Ital. trans. of *De iudiciis nativitatem.*) Venice: Vincenzo Valgrisi, 1554.[48] 150 copies.

————. Unnamed work.

Sturm, Joannes. *Partionum dialecticarum.*

Trutfetter, Jodocus. Commentary on Terence.

————. "Vergil." (Unidentified.) 20 copies.

Vadianus [von Watt], Joachim. Unnamed work.

Westhemerus, Bartholomaeus. *Phrases seu modi loquendi divinae scripturae.*[49] 8 copies.

INVENTORY 5

Marcantonio Valgolio—1574

A lawyer and druggist originally from Brescia, Valgolio was either seventy-four or eighty-four at the time of his arrest. He owned about forty titles, nearly all humanistic, including fifteen of Erasmus. The library included the following prohibited titles, banned in most cases because the author was a northern Protestant whose *opera omnia* had been prohibited by the Tridentine Index. Valgolio defended his possession of these titles with the argument that the reader's disposition, rather than the book's content, determined the impact of a bad volume. Because of his age and possible senility, the Inquisition released him with a warning. See Ch. VI, sec. 2. Source: SU, Bu. 37, Marcantonio Valgolio.

Italian authors

Boccaccio, Giovanni. *Decameron.* (Unless expurgated.)

"Carmina ad Pasquillum." (Described as a pasquinade against Paul IV in the trial.)

[47] Ibid., p. 479.   [48] *STC Italian*, 618.   [49] Reusch, *Index*, I, 108.

Valla, Lorenzo. Unnamed work. (The Tridentine Index banned *De falsa donatione Constantini, De libero arbitrio,* and *De voluptate.*)

Non-Italian authors

Brunfels, Otto. *Epitome . . . rei medicae.*[50]

"Chiromantia." (Rule IX of the Tridentine Index issued a blanket condemnation of occult works.)

Grynaeus, Simon. *Aristotelis de virtutibus per S. G. latinitate donatus.*

Hegendorff, Christoph. *Scholia & argumenta in familiares epistolae Ciceronis.*[51]

Lefèvre d'Etaples, Jacques. *Epistolae divi Pauli.* (Unless expurgated.)

Lycosthenes [Wolffhardt], Conradus. *Elenchus scriptorum omnium.*[52]

Melanchthon, Philipp. *Commentarius de anima.*

———. "De Prosodia." (Probably *Syntaxis, sive constructio Latini sermonis, cum libello de Periodis & Prosodia.* Cologne, 1541.)[53]

———. *Moralis philosophiae epitome.*

———. *Terentius comoediae a P. M. restitutae.*

Muenster, Sebastian. *Compositio horologiorum.*

Osiander, Andreas. Unnamed work.

Spangenberg, Joannes. "Grammatica latina." (Unidentified.)[54]

Valgolio also owned about fifteen titles of Erasmus, all permitted in expurgated form. They included the *Adagia, Apophthegmata, Bellum, Catalogus lucubrationum, De duplici copia verborum,* and commentaries on Cato and other ancient authors.

INVENTORY 6

Fra Leonardo—1574

The Inquisition arrested Fra Leonardo, a priest and Canon Regular (Augustinian) at the Venetian monastery of San Salvatore, in September 1574, upon receipt of a denunciation from a fellow monk. The Holy Office discovered the listed prohibited titles in his library. Fra Leonardo admitted to having purchased them from Venetian booksellers between late 1572 and August 1574. But he denied heretical intent, arguing that his passion for "l'arte oratoria" had led him to purchase the books. When

[50] *Cambridge Catalogue,* item B2922.

[51] Gesner, Simler, and Frisius, *Bibliotheca,* p. 144.

[52] *Cambridge Catalogue,* item W248.

[53] Gesner, Simler, and Frisius, *Bibliotheca,* p. 692.

[54] It is not clear which of Spangenberg's several works on grammar and eloquence this is.

witnesses produced no evidence of heresy, the Holy Office sentenced him to penances and forbade him to preach for three years.

The titles suggest a wide religious curiosity, but not necessarily heresy. The inventory also shows that these banned works, most of which had been published in Venice some twenty to thirty years before Fra Leonardo's arrest, still circulated through the bookstores. Source: SU, Bu. 38, Fra Leonardo. This trial has not been mentioned in the text.

Italian authors

Aretino, Pietro. *Humanità di Christo.*
————. *Passione di Giesu.*
————. *Sette salmi della penitentia.*
————. *Vita di San Catherina.*
Boccaccio, Giovanni. *Decameron.* (Unless expurgated.)
Bracciolini, Poggio. *Facetiae.*
Brucioli, Antonio. New Testament "ad insignia spei (Venice) stampato del 48."[55]
Clario, Isidoro. New Testament. (The Tridentine Index banned the first edition of Venice, 1541–42.)[56]
Franco, Nicolò. *Rime.*
Gelli, Giambattista. *Capricci del bottaio.* (Unless expurgated.) 2 or 3 copies.
Ochino, Bernardino. *Prediche.*
Valdés, Alfonso de. *Mercurio et Caronte.*
Vergilius, Polydorus. *De inventoribus rerum.*

Non-Italian authors

Erasmus, Desiderius. *Colloquia.* (The inventory included five other titles of Erasmus that were banned unless expurgated: *De conscribendis epistolis, De duplici copia verborum, De praeparatione ad mortem, Paraphrasis Joannem,* and *Querela pacis.*)
Sarcerius, Erasmus. *Loci communes theologici.*

INVENTORY 7

Giovanni Battista Sanudo—1574

A lawyer with a noble name, although probably illegitimate, Sanudo was denounced for heretical opinions and blasphemy. The Inquisition

---

[55] Although not an exact reprint of the Brucioli New Testament, this edition is closer to his work than to other vernacular versions. Spini, "Bibliografia di Brucioli," p. 157.
[56] See Reusch, *Indices,* 248, and *Index,* 1, 266; *Enciclopedia cattolica,* III, 1,771.

found these prohibited books in his library, but released him with a warning upon discovering that a bitter family quarrel lay behind the denunciation. With the exception of the "Interim," the titles present a microcosm of the fairly innocuous banned titles in circulation at this time. Source: SU, Bu. 37, Giovanni Battista Sanudo. This material has not been mentioned in the text.

Italian authors

Aretino, Pietro. *Ragionamenti.*
————. Unnamed work.
Boccaccio, Giovanni. *Decameron.* (Unless expurgated.)
Fregoso, Federigo. *Trattato della oratione.*
Valdés, Alfonso de. *Mercurio et Caronte.*

Non-Italian authors

Agrippa, Henricus Cornelius. *De incertitudine et vanitate scientiarum.*
"Interim."[57]

INVENTORY 8

Fra Clemente Valvassore—1580

Born about 1530 in Bergamo, Valvassore took a degree in canon and civil law at Padua, and then served as a judge for the Republic in Belluno, Bergamo, Brescia, and Verona. In light of his "virtù et industria," the Council of Ten in 1559 conferred on him the right to practice law in the ducal palace, a privilege normally restricted to "cittadini originarii," i.e., native-born citizens below noble rank (CX, Commune, R. 24, f. 38ᵛ, August 9, 1559). Motivated partly by his desire to pursue his studies in leisure, Valvassore in or about 1574 abandoned his legal career to enter the Carthusian monastery of Sant'Andrea on the Lido. He professed his vows in 1576 or 1577. But a fellow monk denounced him for heresy, anticlericalism, and contempt for monastic ceremonies in 1580, thus initiating a long and bitter Inquisition trial. One monk defended Fra Clemente, but the other five of the tiny community corroborated the denunciation. Fra Clemente retaliated by accusing the prior and his fellow monks of ignorance, sloth, fraud, and debauchery. He charged that they could not

[57] The Tridentine Index did not list this, but the Clementine Index of 1596 banned "Interim, anno 1548 editus." See Reusch, *Indices,* 564, and *Index,* I, 522–23. The book probably discussed the religious settlement imposed by Charles V at the Diet of Augsburg in 1548. For some titles that might meet this description, see *STC German,* 349, and *Cambridge Catalogue,* items A2150, and C1360–61. Calvin also authored a work with this title (1549 and subsequently). *Bibliographia Calviniana,* p. 9 and passim.

read Latin, that their pose of "holy simplicity" disguised gross laziness and stupidity, and that the monastery had no library. He further alleged that the prior, with the aid of laymen, had embezzled monastic funds, and had so misgoverned that the community had declined from eighteen to seven during Fra Clemente's residence. When he had attempted to report the prior's misdeeds to the authorities, the prior and his cohorts had intercepted his letter, and confined him within the monastery. On the other hand, the trial revealed Fra Clemente to be an outspoken, irascible man, completely lacking in tact. After more than a year of investigation, including the use of torture once in an unsuccessful effort to discover if Fra Clemente shielded heretical accomplices, he confessed to having denied the Real Presence in the Eucharist, Extreme Unction, and the efficacy of confession and prayers for the dead. He also admitted to having called the pope "Anti-Christ." The Inquisition sentenced him to perpetual imprisonment, but also fined the prior and the denouncer for criminal misconduct.

Fra Clemente's prohibited books fell into two groups. He had been persuaded to heretical views partly through reading unnamed titles of Martin Bucer and Heinrich Bullinger, and he also confessed to a recent purchase of Pier Paolo Vergerio's *Instruttione Christiana* (Poschiavo: Dolfin Landolfo, 1549) at the bookstore of Francesco Ziletti. The Holy Office did not find these works in his library of about thirty-five titles, but did discover many humanistic works of northern Protestant scholars. Fra Clemente defended possession of these prohibited titles on the grounds that the Index banned them only because of incidental objectionable statements, or because of an unjustified blanket condemnation of the author. Informed by Aldo Manuzio il Giovane that inquisitorial permission to hold these books was extremely difficult to obtain, Fra Clemente had, nevertheless, decided to hold on to them, expurgating passages only when he felt it necessary.

Whatever the truth of Fra Clemente's assertions about his banned scholarly books, his argument must have been typical of those of humanistic tendencies. Unable to obtain permission to hold banned scholarly titles, they disobeyed the Index and tried to be discreet. If they avoided calling attention to themselves, they probably held banned books without being disturbed. Source: SU, Bu. 47, Fra Clemente Valvassore, February 7, 1580, through December 12, 1581. Ch. vi, sec. 2, very briefly mentions this trial.

Italian authors

Boccaccio, Giovanni. *Decameron.* (Unless expurgated.)
Brucioli, Antonio. *Dialogi.*

Non-Italian authors

Bible. Published by Robert Estienne, Paris, 1532.

Borrhaeus, Martinus. *Aristotelis de arte dicendi commentaria.*

——. *De censura veri & falsi.*

Cicero. *De officiis.* With commentary by Xystus Betuleius (Sixt Birck).[58]

——. *Epistolae familiares.* Commentaries by Erasmus, Melanchthon, and Joannes Rivius.

——. *Orationes.* Commentaries by Betuleius, Joachimus Camerarius the Elder, Janus Cornarius, Celio Secondo Curione, Erasmus, Christoph Hegendorff, and Michael Toxites.

Fabricius (Chemnicensis), Georgius. *In Horatium Flaccum argumenta.*

——. *Partitionum grammaticarum.*

Grynaeus, Simon. *Julii Polucis onomasticon.*

Hegendorff, Christoph. "De arte rhetorica." (Possibly *Dramata locorum tam Rhetoricorum quam Dialecticorum.* Strasbourg, 1534.)[59]

Melanchthon, Philipp. *De arte rhetorica.*

Naogeorgus [Kirchmeyer], Thomas. *Praeterea transtulit Dionis Chrysostomi orationes.*[60]

Plato. *Opera.* With epistle of Grynaeus.

Rivius, Joannes. *De rhetorica.*

——. *Tabulae trium Ciceronis de officiis.*[61]

Sallust. *De Catilinae coniuratione ac bello Iugurthino.* Ed. Joannes Rivius.

Sturm, Joannes. Unnamed work.

"Terentius cum annotationibus, argumentis, et scholiis diversorum auctorum damnatorum."

Toxites, Michael. "Tabulae partitionum oratoriarum." (Unidentified.)

Ziegler, Jacobus. *Terrae sanctae quam Palestinam Syriae descriptio.*

INVENTORY 9

Bartolomeo Chemer—1582

As mentioned in Ch. VI, sec. 1, the Holy Office discovered in the shop of Bartolomeo Chemer, a bookseller but not a publisher, several prohibited northern titles that had been imported from Frankfurt. Chemer told the tribunal that such titles sold daily in Venice, and that the customs inspection rules were impossible to obey. The Inquisition fined him six ducats.

---

[58] The inventory does not make it clear whether the commentaries on the works of Cicero were separate titles, or multiple commentaries within the covers of one volume.

[59] Gesner, Simler, and Frisius, *Bibliotheca*, p. 144.

[60] Ibid., *Bibliotheca*, p. 798.   [61] *Cambridge Catalogue*, item R605.

The trial illustrates that the bookmen continued to import and sell prohibited northern Bibles. Source: SU, Bu. 48, Bartolomeo Chemer.

Non-Italian authors

"Compendium theologiae." (The Inquisition treated this unidentified title as prohibited.)

Du Moulin, Charles. *Commentarij in consuetudines Parisiensis.*[62]

Muenster, Sebastian. *Sei libri della cosmographia universale.*[63]

New Testament. Ed. Erasmus and Théodore de Bèze.[64]

———. Ed. Robert Estienne.

———. Greek and Latin. Basel: Brylinger, n.d.[65]

INVENTORY 10

Gioachino Brugnolo—1587

The Inquisition discovered the following prohibited titles in the bookstore of Gioachino Brugnolo, bookseller and occasional publisher. He told the tribunal that he had acquired the titles from the estate of a lawyer, but then the documentation breaks off. Source: SU, Bu. 59, Gioachino Brugnolo, April 9, 1587. It is mentioned in Ch. VI, sec. I.

Italian authors

Doni, Anton Francesco. *Lettere.*

Odonus, John Angelus. *Epistolae ad Gilbertum Cognatum.*[66]

Vergilius, Polydorus. *De inventoribus rerum.*

Non-Italian authors

Erasmus, Desiderius. *Colloquia.*

———. "Colloquium de matrimonio et celibatu." (Erasmus praised marriage and attacked clerical celibacy in several colloquies; this was doubtlessly one of them. The inventory listed seven other titles of Erasmus that were banned unless expurgated: *Hieronymi opera omnia cum argumentis et scholiis D. Erasmi, Irenaeus, Opus epistolarum Hieronymi cum scholiis Erasmi, Paraphrasis in epistolam Jacobi, Paraphrasis in epistolas Pauli, Paraphrasis in evangelium Joannem,* and *Paraphrasis in evangelium Marci.*)

Hegendorff, Christoph. *Dialecticae legalis.*

---

[62] Gesner, Simler, and Frisius, *Bibliotheca,* p. 137.

[63] *STC Italian,* 455.

[64] I have been unable to identify this edition.

[65] Since Brylinger frequently printed Erasmus's New Testament, this is probably that of the Dutch humanist.

[66] Gesner, Simler, and Frisius, *Bibliotheca,* p. 400.

———. *In actiones Verrinas et in Topica Ciceronis adnotatiunculae.*

———. *Oratio in artium liberalium laudem.*[67]

———. "Scholia in partitionis oratoria." (Unidentified.)

Hutten, Ulrich von. *Cum Erasmo expostulatio.*

Lefèvre d'Etaples, Jacques. *Epistolae divi Pauli.* (Unless expurgated.)

Luther, Martin. "Ad colonias rusticorum." (Unidentified.)

———. *Ad librum A. Catharini responsio.*

———. *De libertate Christiana.*

———. "Contra Georg. Missam et alia." (Unidentified.)

Melanchthon, Philipp. *Moralis philosophiae.*

Muenster, Sebastian. *Dictionarium hebraicum.*

Oecolampadius, Joannes. *Graecae literaturae dragmata.*

Oldendorpius, Joannes. "Iuris naturalij Arenibui." (Unidentified.)

Postel, Guillaume. *De magistratibus.*

Ricius, Paulus. *De coelesti agricultura.*[68]

Schiurpff [Schurff], Hieronymus. Illegible title.

Vadianus [von Watt], Joachim. *Orthodoxa epistola an corpus Christi.*[69]

Wolfius, Hieronymus. "Prefatio." (Unidentified.)

INVENTORY 11

Gian Vincenzo Pinelli—1604

Source: VM, Mss. Italiani, Classe x, 61 (6601), "Inventario della libreria di Giovanni Vincenzo Pinelli ereditata da Francesco Pinelli." Please see Ch. x for a discussion of Pinelli.

Italian authors

Aretino, Pietro. *Ragionamenti.*

Boccaccio, Giovanni. *Decameron.* (Unless expurgated.) 5 copies.

Brucioli, Antonio. *Dialogi.*

Lando, Ortensio. *Forcianae quaestiones.*

———. *Paradossi.*

———. *Vari componimenti.*

Machiavelli, Niccolò. *Asino d'oro.*

———. *Discorsi.* 2 copies.

———. *Historie fiorentine.* 2 copies.

———. *La Clizia.*

Pomponazzi, Pietro. *De incantationibus.* Basel. (Pinelli also had Pomponazzi's *Opera* [Basel], which may also have included this banned title.)

[67] Ibid., p. 144.   [68] *Cambridge Catalogue*, item R520.

[69] Ibid., item V13.

Vergerio, Pier Paolo. *Catalogo de' libri condannati da Giovanni Della Casa.* (This is the counterfeit, with Vergerio's commentary, published in Zurich, 1549.)

Non-Italian authors

Agrippa, Henricus Cornelius. *Apologia adversus calumnias.*
———. *De incertitudine et vanitate scientiarum.*
Bible. Printer Robert Estienne. (Unless expurgated.)
———. Old Testament. Hebrew. Ed. Sebastian Muenster. Basel. (Unless expurgated.)
———. New Testament. Greek and Latin. Printer Henri Estienne. (Unless expurgated.)
Bibliander, Theorodus. *Temporum.* Basel.
Bodin, Jean. *De Republica.* (Unless expurgated.) 3 copies (2 published in Paris, 1 in Genoa).
———. *Methodus ad facilem historiarum cognitionem.* Lyons. (Unless expurgated.)
Borrhaeus, Martinus. *Aristotelis de arte dicendi commentaria.* Basel.
Carion, Johann. *Chronica.* 2 copies.
Chytraeus, David. *De lectione historiarum.* Strasbourg.
Cordier, Mathurin. *De corrupti sermonis emendatione.*
Dolet, Etienne. *Commentariorum linguae latinae.* Lyons. 2 copies.
———. *De re navali . . . dialogus de imitatione Ciceroniana.* Rome. 4°. (A Roman printing has not been located.)
Du Moulin, Charles. *In regulas cancellariae Romanae.* Lyons.
———. *Tractatus commerciorum et usurarum.* Paris.
Erasmus, Desiderius. *Colloquia.* 2 copies (Lyons and n.p.).
Estienne, Henri. *Orationes.*
Fabricius [Chemnicensis], Georgius. *Rerum Misnicarum.* Leipzig.
Flacius Illyricus, Mathias et al. *Ecclesiastica historia.* Basel.
———. *Quinta centuria.* Basel.
———. *Sesta centuria.* Basel.
Gesner, Konrad. *De lacte et operibus lactariis.*
———. "De lattibuis." Zurich. 8°. (Possibly another copy of *De lacte.*)
———. "Filosophia." Zurich. 8°. (Unidentified).
———. *Historiae animalium.*
Grynaeus, Simon. *Aristotelis Topicorum.* Ed. and com. S. G. Basel. 8°.
Hegendorff, Christoph. *Dialecticae legalis.* Basel.
Hôtman, François. "De reb. credditij." 8°. (Unidentified.)
———. *De re numaria populi romani.* 8°.
———. *Dialecticae institutionis.* 8°.
———. *Francogallia.* 8°. 3 copies (2 published in Paris, 1 in Frankfurt).

———. *Justiniani imperatoris vita.* Frankfurt. 8°.

———. *Novus commentarius de verbis juris.* Basel. Folio.

———. *Observationum in ius civile.* Folio.

———. *Quaestionum illustrium.* Paris. 8°.

Lambert, François. "Ethicei christ." 8°. (Unidentified.)

Lycosthenes [Wolffhardt], Conradus. *Similium loci communes.* Basel. 8°.

Marot, Clément. *Les oeuvres.* Lyons.

———. Unnamed title. Lyons.

Melanchthon, Philipp. Vol. 4 of *Opera.* Basel. Folio.

Muenster, Sebastian. *Cosmographia.*

———. *Organum uranicum.*

Neander, Michael, of Sorau. *Methodum in omni genere artium.* Basel.

Osiander, Andreas. *Harmoniae Evangelicae.*

Palladius, Peder. *Isagoge ad libros propheticos et apostolicos.* Wittenberg.

Paracelsus, Theophrastus (Bombast von Hohenheim). *Archidoxorum seu de secretis naturae mysteriis.* Frankfurt.

———. *Auroram philosophorum.* Frankfurt.

———. *De morbis Tartareis.* Basel.

———. *De restituta utriusque medicinae.* Lyons.

———. *De vita longa.* 2 copies (Paris and n.p.).

Petreus, Henricus. "Continguentius. pedagogi." Frankfurt. 4°. (Unidentified.)

Peucer, Caspar. *Commentarius de praecipuis divinationum generibus.* 2 copies (Frankfurt and n.p.).

Postel, Guillaume. *De orbis terrae concordia.*

Rabelais, François. *Les oeuvres.* Lyons.

Ramus, Petrus. *Collectaneae prefationes.* Paris.

———. *De Caesaris militia.* Paris.

———. "De eloquentia." Paris. (Possibly his *Scholarum rhetoricarum, seu quaestionum Brutinarum in Oratorem Ciceronis.*)

———. *Dialectica.* 2 copies (Frankfurt and Basel).

———. *Proemium mathematicum.* Paris.

———. *Scholae in liberales artes.* Venice. Folio. (A Venetian printing has not been located.)

Richier, Christophe. *De rebus Turcarum.* Paris. 4°.

Schegkius [Degen], Jacobus. *De commentariis suis in Topica Aristotelis.*

Simler, Josias. *De republica Helvetiorum.* Zurich.

———. *Vita Conradi Gesneri.* Zurich. 4°.

Sleidanus [Philippson], Joannes. *De quatuor summis imperiis.*

———. *De statu religionis et reipublicae Carolo quinto.* Strasbourg.

———. *Orationes.*

Vadianus [von Watt], Joachim. *Epitome trium terrae partium.* Zurich.

Wolfius, Hieronymus. "Enchiridion." Basel. (Unidentified.)
Zwinger, Theodor. *Methodus apodemica*. Basel.

Pinelli owned additional titles that, although not listed in the Clementine Index, would have aroused inquisitorial suspicion. He had, for example, Giordano Bruno's *De triplici minimo et mensura* (Frankfurt) and a number of occult works that might have fallen under the general prohibition of Rule IX of the Tridentine Index. Pinelli also possessed many French political works, both Protestant and Catholic, including the *Vindiciae contra tyrannos*.

BIBLIOGRAPHY

ARCHIVAL

Parma, Archivio di Stato

    Carteggio Farnesiano e Borbonico Estero, Venezia, F. 510/2 (1547–1555), letter no. 64, ff. 192–93, of Annibale Grisonio of June 29, 1549, Venice. Consulted on microfilm at the Fondazione Giorgio Cini in Venice.

Vatican City, Archivio Segreto Vaticano

    Fondo Borghese, iv, 224. Miscellaneous correspondence, mostly of Nuncio Anton Maria Graziani of 1596, Venice.

    Miscellaneorum Armarii, iv–v, 30. Printed edicts concerning book prohibitions and expurgations of the Congregations of the Index and Inquisition.

    Segretario di Stato, Venezia

Venice, Archivio di Stato

    Archivio Proprio Roma

    Arte dei libreri, stampatori e ligadori

    Capi del Consiglio dei Dieci, Lettere di Ambasciatori a Roma

    Capi del Consiglio dei Dieci, Notatorio

    Collegio, Esposizioni Principi

    Collegio, Esposizioni Roma

    Collegio, Notatorio

    Consiglio dei Dieci, Comune

    Consiglio dei Dieci, Deliberazioni Roma

    Consiglio dei Dieci, Secrete

    Dieci Savii sopra le Decime in Rialto, Condizione di Decima

    Esecutori contro la bestemmia

    Giudici di Petizion, Inventari

    Indice 303, "Indici alfabetico, cronologico, e geografico dei Processi del Santo Uffizio 1541–1794."

    Santo Uffizio

    Segretario alle voci, Elezioni del Maggior Consiglio

    Segretario alle voci, Elezioni del Senato

    Senato, Deliberazioni Roma

    Senato, Dispacci da Roma

    Senato, Terra

MANUSCRIPTS

Basel, Universitätsbibliothek

Mss. Frey-Grynaeus, ii. 4, letters 163, 164, 166, 169, 171, 176, 179, 182; ii. 19/11, letters 45, 47, 56; ii. 23 1/11, letters, 302, 304, 305. Letters of Girolamo Mercuriale, Padua, to Theodore Zwinger, Basel, August 5, 1573, through June 4, 1582.

Ms. G. 1. 70, ff. 60^{r-v}, letter of Ludwig Iselin to Basil Amerbach, February 19, 1588, Venice.

Chicago, Newberry Library

Case/MS/6A/34, "Vollume de' Giustiziati in Venezia."

Dublin, Trinity College

Mss. 1224–28, Roman Inquisition, Sentences and Abjurations from Rome and elsewhere, 1564–68, 1580, 1581–82, 1582, 1603.

Florence, Biblioteca Nazionale Centrale

Ms. Magliabecchiana ii. iv. 19, "Diario di Firenze dal 1536 al 1555."

Florence, Biblioteca Riccardiana

Ms. 2131, "Ricordi istorici di Michelangelo Tenagli."

Vatican City, Archivio Segreto Vaticano

Fondo Borghese, i, 913, ff. 743^r–85^r, "Sommario delli petitioni per la proposta della riforma della stampa. Antonio Castelvetri Medico."

Vatican City, Biblioteca Apostolica Vaticana

Barberino Latino 1369, "Decreta Sanctae Romanae et universalis Inquisitionis fere omnia sub Clemente VIII Pontifex Maximus."

Barberino Latino 1370, "Decreta Sanctae Romanae et universalis Inquisitionis Clemente VIII Pontifex Maximus."

Barberino Latino 5195, "Raccolta di alcuni negotij, e cause spettanti alla Santa Inquisitione nella Città e Dominio Veneto. Dal principio di Clemente VIII sino al presente mese di luglio MDCXXV."

Barberino Latino 5205, "Raccolta di alcuni negotij e cause spettanti alla Santa Inquisitione nella Città e Dominio Veneto. Dal principio di PP. Clem. VIII sino al presente mese di luglio MDCXXV."

Vaticanus Latinus 10945, "Anima del Sant'Offitio spirata dal Sopremo Tribunale della Sacra Congregatione raccolta dal Padre Predicatore F. Giacomo Angarano da Vicenza l'anno del Signore MDCXLIV."

Vaticanus Latinus 12141, "Sixtus Quintus Pontifex Maximus."

Venice, Archivio di Stato

Marco Barbaro, "Arbori dei Patritii veneti." 7 vols.

Venice, Biblioteca Marciana

Mss. Italiani, Classe vii, 73 (8265), "Cronaca Veneta Anonima ab Urbe Condita sino al 1615. Tomo II."

Mss. Italiani, Classe vii, 134 (8035), "Cronaca veneta di Girolamo Savina sino al MDCXV."

Mss. Italiani, Classe VII, 414 (7809), Fra Carlo Lodoli, "In materia dell'indice tra i dispacci di Mons. Gratiani Nuntio in Venetia."

Mss. Italiani, Classe VII, 519 (8438), Niccolò Trevisan, "Cronaca di Venezia al 1585."

Mss. Italiani, Classe VII, 553 (8812), "Compendio di me Francesco da Molin de Missier Marco delle cose, che reputero degne di venerne particolar memoria, et che sucederanno in mio tempo si della Republica Venetiana e di Venetia mia Patria come anco della special mia persona."

Mss. Italiani, Classe VII, 808 (7296), "Annali di 1545-1546."

Mss. Italiani, Classe VII, 925-928 (8594-8597), Marco Barbaro, "Arbori dei Patritii veneti." (This is a shorter version than the Venice, Archivio di Stato, copy.)

Mss. Italiani, Classe VII, 1279 (8886), "Avisi notabili del Mondo, et deliberazioni più importanti di Pregadi, dal 4 marzo 1588 al 25 febbraio 1588 (mv)."

Mss. Italiani, Classe VII, 2500-2502 (12077-12079), "Privilegi veneziani per la stampa concessi dal 1527 al 1597, copiati da Horatio Brown."

Mss. Italiani, Classe X, 61 (6601), "Inventario della libreria di Giovanni Vincenzo Pinelli ereditata da Francesco Pinelli."

Mss. Italiani, Classe XI, 1 (6958), "Trattato breve di Antonio Castelvetrj medico da Modona [sic] sopra la riforma della stampa."

Mss. Latini, Classe X, 285 (3180), Alvise Contarini, "Delineatio Historiae, quae res gestas Venetorum complectitur, nulla diligentia contexta, iterum expolienda et debitis coloribus exornanda in quatuordecim libris distincta."

Venice, Museo Civico Correr

Ms. Cicogna 2552, "Annali delle cose della Repubblica di Venezia dall' anno 1541-1548."

Ms. Cicogna 2557, "Annali 1592-1595 di Francesco Contarini."

Ms. Cicogna 3044, "Elenco di stampatori e librari tanto veneti che forestieri et di quelli ad istanza de quali si pubblicarono libri in Venezia."

Mss. Morosini-Grimani, R. 358-360, "Tre volumi di lettere di Mons. Antonio Maria Gratiani dal Borgo S. Sepolcro, Vescovo d'Amelia, Scritte nella Nuntiatura sua di Venetia. 1596. 1597. 1598."

Ms. P (Provenienze) D (Diverse) C 808, "Copie di documenti tratti dall'Archivio di Stato relative all'Inquisizione a Venezia (secc. xiii-xviii)."

Ms. P D C 2118, "Ricevuto 1571-1580." Miscellaneous business records of Giulio Michiel.

PRINTED WORKS

Primary Sources

Albèri, E. *Le relazioni degli ambasciadori veneti al Senato.* Ser. i, vol. 3. Florence, 1853.

——. *Le relazioni degli ambasciadori veneti al Senato.* Ser. ii, vol. 4. Florence, 1857.

[Albizzi, Francesco.] *Risposta all'Historia della Sacra Inquisitione composta già dal R. P. Paolo Servita.* . . . Edizione seconda corretta. . . . [Rome, 1678].

Alunno, Francesco. *Le ricchezze della lingua volgare . . . di sopra il Boccaccio novamente ristampate.* . . . In Vinegia nell'anno MDLI. In Casa de' Figliuoli di Aldo.

Annales Camaldulenses. Ed. J. B. Mittarelli and A. Costadini. Vol. 9. Venice, 1773.

Basil, St. *The Letters and Address to Young Men on Reading Greek Literature.* Trans. Roy J. Deferrari and Martin R. P. McGuire. Vol. iv. Loeb Classical Library. London and Cambridge, Mass., 1934.

"The *Beneficio di Cristo.*" Trans. and introd. Ruth Prelowski, in *Italian Reformation Studies in Honor of Laelius Socinus,* ed. John A. Tedeschi. Florence, 1965, pp. 21–102.

Bernardino da Siena, St. *Le prediche volgari inedite, Firenze 1424, 1425 —Siena 1425.* Ed. P. Dionisio, O.F.M. Siena, 1935.

Boccaccio, Giovanni. *Boccaccio on Poetry: Being the Preface and the Fourteenth and Fifteenth Books of Boccaccio's "Genealogia Deorum Gentilium" in an English Version with Introductory Essay and Commentary.* Trans. Charles S. Osgood. Princeton, N. J., 1930.

Botero, Giovanni. *Della ragion di stato con tre libri Delle cause della grandezza delle città, due Aggiunte e un Discorso sulla popolazione di Roma.* Ed. Luigi Firpo. Turin, 1948.

Bruni, Leonardo. *Leonardo Bruni Aretino Humanistisch-Philosophische Schriften mit einer Chronologie seiner Werke und Briefe.* Ed. and introd. Hans Baron. Leipzig-Berlin, 1928.

Bullarium Diplomatum et Privilegiorum Summorum Romanorum Pontificum. Vol. vii, Naples, 1882. Vol. viii, Naples, 1883. Vol. ix, Turin, 1865. Vol. x, Turin, 1865. Vol. xi, Turin, 1867.

Caesar, Julius. *C. Iulli Caesaris Comentarii Ab. Aldo. Manuccio.* . . . Venetiis, MDXXCIIX, Apud Aldum.

Castellani, C. "Documenti circa la persecuzione dei libri ebraici a Venezia." *La Bibliofilia* 7 (1905–6), 304–7.

Catechismo, cioè istruttione, secondo il decreto del Concilio di Trento, a' parocchi. . . . In Venetia, MDLXVII, Appresso Aldo Manutio.

Catechismus, Ex Decreto Concilii Tridentini, ad parochos. . . . Romae, In Aedibus Populi Romani, apud Paulum Manutium, MDLXVI.

Conciliorum oecumenicorum decreta. Ed. J. Alberigo, P-P. Joannou et al. Freiburg im Breisgau, 1962.

Concilium Tridentinum: diariorum, actorum, epistularum. Nova Collectio edidit Societas Goerresiana. Vol. III, *Diariorum pars tertia, volumen Prius*, ed. Sebastian Merkle. 2nd ed. Freiburg im Breisgau, 1967.

————. Vol. VIII, *Actorum Pars Quinta*, ed. Stephan Ehses. Freiburg im Breisgau, 1964.

————. Vol. XIII, *Tractatuum pars altera prius ex collectionibus Vincentii Schweitzer*, ed. Hubert Jedin. 2nd ed. Freiburg im Breisgau, 1967.

Conti, Natale. *Delle historie de' suoi tempi . . . Parte Prima. . . . tradotta da Giovan Carlo Saraceni.* . . . In Venetia, Appresso Damian Zenaro, 1589.

Cornet, Enrico. *Paolo V e la Repubblica Veneta. Giornale dal 22 ottobre 1605–9 giugno 1607.* Vienna, 1859.

Cugnoni, C. "Documenti Chigiani concernanti Felice Peretti, Sisto V, come privato e come pontefice." *Archivio della R. Società Romana di Storia Patria* 5 (1882), 1–32, 210–304, 542–89.

Decretum Gratiani. . . . Roma, In Aedibus Populi Romani, MDLXXXIII.

Dolce, Lodovico. *Le trasformationi di M. Lodovico Dolce di nuovo stampate.* . . . In Venetia, Appresso Gabriel Giolito de' Ferrari e Fratelli, MDLIII.

Doni, Anton Francesco. *I Marmi.* . . . In Vinegia per Francesco Marcolini MDLII. Colophon: MDLIII.

(Erasmus, Desiderius). *Espositione letterale del testo di Matteo Evangelista di M. Bernardin Tomitano.* In Venetia, per Gio. dal Griffo, nel 1547.

————. *Ordinatione del Matrimonio de Christiani, per Desiderio Erasmo Roterodamo, opera veramente utile non solo ai maritati, ma a tutti quelli, che desiderano vivere secondo la christiana dottrina; hora del latino tradotta, e primieramente stampata.* In Vinetia per Francesco Rocca et fratelli, 1550.

Erizzo, Sebastiano. *Le sei giornate di messer Sebastiano Erizzo.* Ed. Gaetano Poggiali. Londra [Livorno], 1794.

Fontana, Bartolomeo. "Documenti vaticani contro l'eresia luterana in Italia." *Archivio della R. Società Romana di Storia Patria* 15 (1892), 71–165, 365–474.

Gaeta, Franco. "Documenti da codici vaticani per la storia della Riforma in Venezia." *Annuario dell'istituto storico italiano per l'età moderna e contemporanea* 7 (1955), 5–53.

Gesner, Konrad; Simler, Josias; and Frisius, Joannes Jacobus. *Bibliotheca instituta et collecta, primum a Conrado Gesnero, deinde . . . per Iosiam Simlerum . . . amplificata per Iohannem Iacobum Frisium.* Tiguri, excudabat Christophorus Froschoverus, MDLXXXIII.

Giannotti, Donato. *Lettere a Piero Vettori, pubblicate sopra gli originali del British Museum da Roberto Ridolfi e Cecil Roth, con un saggio illustrativo a cura di Roberto Ridolfi.* Florence, 1932.

————. *Opere.* Vol. 1. Pisa, 1819.

Ginzberg, Carlo. *I costituti di Don Pietro Manelfi.* Florence and Chicago, 1970.

Gozzi, Niccolò Vito di. *Dello stato delle republiche secondo la mente di Aristotele.* . . . In Venetia, MDXCI, Presso Aldo.

Index Librorum Prohibitorum

> *Catalogo di diverse opere, compositioni, et libri; li quali come heretici, sospetti, impij & scandalosi si dichiarano dannati, & prohibiti in questa inclita citta di Vinegia.* . . . In Vinegia, alla bottega d'Erasmo di Vincenzo Valgrisi, MDXLIX.
>
> *Cathalogus librorum haereticorum.* . . . Venetiis Apud Gabrielem Iulitum de Ferraris, et Fratres, MDLIIII.
>
> *Index auctorum, et librorum, qui ab Officio S. Rom. & universalis Inquisitionis caveri ab omnibus, et singulis in universa Christiana Republica mandantur.* . . . Venetiis, Presb. Hieronymus Lilius, & socij excudebant, Die XXI Iulij, MDLIX.
>
> *Index librorum prohibitorum, cum regulis confectis per Patres a Tridentina Synodo delectos, auctoritate Sanctiss. D. N. Pij IIII, Pont. Max. comprobatus.* Venetiis, MDLXIIII.
>
> *Index librorum prohibitorum.* . . . *Postea vero à Sixto V & nunc demum à Sanctissimo D. N. Clemente Papa VIII recognitus & auctus.* . . . Romae, Apud Paulum Bladum, Impressorem Cameralem, MDXCIII.
>
> *Index librorum prohibitorum . . . et nunc demum S. D. N. Clementis Papae VIII iussu recognitus, & publicatus.* . . . Venetiis, Apud Nicolaum Morettum, 1596.

Indice copioso, e particolare, di tutti li libri stampati dalli Gioliti in Venetia, fino all'anno 1592. N.p., n.d.

Kristeller, Paul Oskar, ed. "Francesco Patrizi da Cherso, 'Emendatio in libros suos novae philosophiae.'" *Rinascimento*, ser. 2, vol. 10 (1970), 215–18.

Lando, Ortensio. *Commentario delle più notabili & mostruose cose d'Italia, & altri luoghi.* . . . In Venetia, Appresso Giovanni Bariletto, MDLXIX.

————. *Paradossi cioè, sententie fuori del comun parere.* . . . In Venetia, MDXLV.

Le Roy, Louis. *Della vicissitudine o mutabile varietà delle cose nell'universo.* . . . In Venetia, MDXCII, Presso Aldo.

Livy, Titus. *Historiarum ab Urbe condita libri qui extant XXXV.* . . . Venetiis, MDXCII, Apud Aldum.

Martyrologium Romanum . . . Gregorii XIII Pont. Max. iussu editum . . . . Romae, Ex Typographia Dominici Basae, MDLXXXIII. Colophon: Romae Excudebat Franciscus Zannettus Anno MDLXXXIII Sexto kal, Junii.

Martyrologium Romanum ad novam kalendarii rationem, et ecclesiasticae revitatem restitutum. Gregorii XIII Pont. Max. iussu editum . . . Auctore Caesare Baronio. . . . Romae, Ex Typographia Dominici Basae, MDLXXXVI.

Masini, Giulio. *Sacro arsenale overo prattica dell'Officio della Santa Inquisitione.* Di nuovo corretto, & ampliato. . . . In Bologna, MDCLXXIX, Per Gioseffo Longhi.

Mattioli, Pietro Andrea. *De i discorsi . . . nelli sei libri di Pedacio Dioscoride Anazarbeo, della materia medicinale.* . . . MDLXXXV, In Venetia, Appresso Felice Valgrisio.

Mercati, Angelo. *I costituti di Niccolò Franco (1568–1570) dinanzi l'Inquisizione di Roma esistenti nell'Archivio Segreto Vaticano.* Studi e Testi, 178. Vatican City, 1955.

Mercati, Giovanni. "Vecchi lamenti contro il monopolio de' libri ecclesiastici, specie liturgici." *Opere minori.* Vol. II, pp. 482–89. Studi e Testi, 77. Vatican City, 1937.

Missale Romanum Ex Decreto Sacrosancti Concilij Tridentini restitutim Pii V Pont. Max. iussu editum. Cum Privilegiis. Venetiis, Apud Ioannem Variscum, Haeredes Bartholomei Faleti, & Socios, MDLXXI.

Muzio, Girolamo. *Lettere catholiche del Mutio Iustinopolitano.* In Venetia, Appresso Gio. Andrea Valvassori, detto Guadagnino, MDLXXI.

Niero, Antonio. "Decreti pretridentini di due patriarchi di Venezia su stampa di libri." *Rivista di storia della Chiesa in Italia* 14 (1960), 450–52.

Nisius, Johann B. "Weitere Venezianische Dokumente in Sachen der Sixtusbibel." *Zietschrift für Katholisches Theologie* 37 (1913), 878–89.

Novellieri minori del Cinquecento: G. Parabosco—S. Erizzo. Ed. Giuseppe Gigli and Fausto Nicolini. Bari, 1912.

Nunziature di Venezia. Vol. I (1533–1535), ed. Franco Gaeta. Istituto Storico Italiano per l'età moderna e contemporanea. Fonti per la Storia d'Italia. Rome, 1958.

———. Vol. II (1536–1542), ed. Franco Gaeta. Rome, 1960.

———. Vol. V (1550–1551), ed. Franco Gaeta. Rome, 1967.

Nunziature di Venezia. Vol. VI (1552–1554), ed. Franco Gaeta, Rome, 1967.

———. Vol. VIII (1566–1569), ed. Aldo Stella. Rome, 1963.

———. Vol. IX (1569–1571), ed. Aldo Stella. Rome, 1972.

———. Vol. XI (1573–1576), ed. Adriana Buffardi. Rome, 1972.

Officium B. Mariae Virginis nuper reformatum et Pii V Pont. Max. iussu editum. . . . Romae, In Aedibus Populi Romani, MDLXXI.

Officium Beatae Mariae Virginis nuper reformatum Pij V Pont. Max. iussu editum. Venetiis Apud Iunctam, Permittente Sede Apostolica, MDLXXXI.

Officium hebdomadae sanctae ad Missalis, & Breviarij reformatorum rationem. Pii V Pont. Max. iussu restitutum. . . . Venetiis, Ex bibliotheca Aldina, 1573.

Orano, Domenico. *Liberi pensatori bruciati in Roma dal xvi al xviii secolo. (Da documenti inediti dell'Archivio di Stato in Roma).* Rome, 1904; rpt. Livorno, 1971.

Panigarola, Francesco. *Lettioni sopra dogmi fatta da F. Francesco Panigarola minore osservante alla presenza, e per commandamento del Ser.mo Carlo Emanuelle Duca di Savoia, l'anno MDLXXXII in Turino.* . . . In Venetia, Presso Pietro Dusinelli, MDLXXXIIII.

———. *Prediche quadragesimali . . . predicate da lui in San Pietro di Roma, l'anno 1577.* . . . In Venetia, Appresso Pietro Miloco, MDCXVII.

Paruta, Paolo. *La legazione di Roma di Paolo Paruta (1592–1595).* Ed. Giuseppe de Leva. 3 vols. Venice, 1887.

Piccolomini, Paolo. "Documenti del R. Archivio di Stato in Siena sull'eresia in questa città durante il secolo XVI." *Bullettino senese di storia patria* 17 (1910), 3–35.

Plato. *Laws.* Trans. R. G. Bury. 2 vols. Loeb Classical Library. London and New York, 1926.

———. *The Republic.* Trans. Paul Shorey. 2 vols. Loeb Classical Library. London and New York, 1930–35.

Pontificale Romanum Clementis VIII Pont. Max. iussu restitutum atque editum. Romae, MDXCV. Colophon: Apud Iacobum Lunam, Impensis Leonardi Parasoli, & Sociorum.

Priuli, Girolamo. *I diarii di Girolamo Priuli.* Vol. 4, ed. Roberto Cessi. Rerum Italicarum Scriptores, n. s., vol. 24, pt. 3. Bologna, 1938.

Prosatori volgari del Quattrocento. Ed. Claudio Varese. La Letteratura Italiana, Storia e Testi, vol. 14. Milan and Naples, 1955.

Reusch, Franz Heinrich, ed. *Die Indices Librorum Prohibitorum des Sechzehnten Jahrhunderts.* Tübingen, 1886; rpt. Nieuwkoop, 1961.

Roseo, Mambrino. *Delle istorie del mondo parte terza. Aggiunte da M.*

M. R. da Fabriano alle istorie di M. Giovanni Tarcagnota. In Venezia, Appresso i Giunti, MDLXXXV.

Rotondò, Antonio. "Nuovi documenti per la storia dell'Indice dei libri proibiti (1572–1638)." *Rinascimento,* ser. 2, vol. 3 (1963), 145–211.

Salutati, Coluccio. *Epistolario di Coluccio Salutati.* Ed. Francesco Novati. Vol. IV, pt. 1. Fonti per la Storia d'Italia, Epistolari secolo xiv–xv. Rome, 1905.

Sanuto, Marino. *I Diarii di Marino Sanuto.* Vol. 29. Venice, 1890.

Sarpi, Paolo. *Opere.* Ed. Gaetano and Luisa Cozzi. La Letteratura Italiana, Storia e Testi, vol. 35, tomo 1. Milan-Naples, 1969.

———. *Scritti giurisdizionalistici.* Ed. Giovanni Gambarin. Bari, 1958.

Savio, Pietro, ed. "Per l'epistolario di Paolo Sarpi." *Aevum* 10 (1936), 3–104; 11 (1937), 13–74, 275–322; 13 (1939), 558–622; 14 (1940), 3–84; 16 (1942), 3–43, 105–138.

Tedeschi, John A. "Florentine Documents for a History of the *Index of Prohibited Books.*" In *Renaissance Studies in Honor of Hans Baron,* ed. Anthony Molho and John A. Tedeschi, pp. 577–605, Florence, 1971.

Tolomei, Claudio. *De le lettere di M. Claudio Tolomei.* Vinegia, Appresso Gabriel Giolito de' Ferrari, MDXLVII.

Tomitano, Bernardino. *Oratione seconda de l'eccellente M. Bernardino Tomitano, alli medesimi signori.* N.p., n.d. [dedicatory letter of Padua, March 20, 1556].

Valier, Agostino. *Dell'utilità che si può ritrarre dalle cose operate dai veneziani libri xiv, del Cardinale Agostino Valerio Vescovo di Verona.* Tradotti dal latino ed illustrata da Monsignor Niccolò Antonio Giustiniani. Padua, 1787.

Vairus, Leonardus. *De Fascino libri tres. . . .* Venetiis, MDXXCIX, Apud Aldum.

Vegius, Mapheus. *Maphei Vegii Laudensis . . . opera . . . quarum prior de educatione liberorum lib. vi. . . . Pars prima.* Laudae (Lodi), Ex Typographia Bertoeti, MDCXIII.

PRINTED WORKS

Secondary Sources

Albanese, F. *L'inquisizione religiosa nella Repubblica di Venezia. Ricerche storiche e raffronti.* Venice, 1875.

Alberigo, Giuseppe. "Girolamo Aleandro." DBI, 2, pp. 128–35.

———. "Daniele Barbaro." DBI, 6, pp. 89–95.

———. "Studi e problemi relativi all'applicazione del Concilio di Trento in Italia (1945–1958)." *Rivista storica italiana* 70 (1958), 239–98.

Allen, T. W. "Horatio Brown." In *The Dictionary of National Biography, 1922–1930*, pp. 120–23. Oxford, 1937.

Allgemeine Deutsche Biographie. 56 vols. Leipzig, 1875–1912.

Amann, Fridolin. *Die Vulgata Sixtina von 1590. Eine quellenmässige Darstellung ihrer Geschichte mit neuem quellenmaterial aus dem venezianischen Staatsarchiv.* Freiburger theologische Studien, fasc. 10. Freiburg im Breisgau, 1912.

Amat di S. Filippo, Pietro. *Biografia dei viaggiatori italiani colla bibliografia delle loro opere.* 2nd ed. Rome, 1882.

Amram, David W. *The Makers of Hebrew Books in Italy: Being Chapters in the History of the Hebrew Printing Press.* Philadelphia, 1909.

Ascarelli, Fernanda. *Le cinquecentine romane: "Censimento delle edizioni romane del XVI secolo possedute dalle biblioteche di Roma."* Milan, 1972.

———. *La tipografia cinquecentina italiana.* Florence, 1953.

Barberi, Francesco. *Paolo Manuzio e la Stamperia del Popolo Romano (1561–1570) con documenti inediti.* Rome, 1942.

Baron, Salo Wittmayer. "The Council of Trent and Rabbinic Literature." In *Ancient and Medieval Jewish History: Essays by Salo Wittmayer Baron*, ed. Leon A. Feldman, pp. 353–71, 555–64. New Brunswick, N. J., 1972.

———. *A Social and Religious History of the Jews.* 2nd ed. rev. Vol. xiii, *Inquisition, Renaissance, and Reformation.* Vol. xiv, *Catholic Restoration and Wars of Religion.* New York, London, and Philadelphia, 1969.

Battistella, Antonio. "La politica ecclesiastica della Repubblica Veneta." *Archivio veneto*, ser. 2, vol. 16 (1898), 386–420.

———. *Il S. Officio e la riforma religiosa in Bologna.* Bologna, 1905.

Baumgarten, Paul Maria. *Neue Kunde von alten Bibeln: Mit zahlreichen Beiträgen zur Kultur- und Literaturgeschichte Roms am Ausgange des sechzehnten Jahrhunderts.* Rome, 1922.

———. *Die Vulgata Sixtina von 1590 und ihre Einfürungsbulle: Aktenstücke und untersuchungen.* Altestamentliche Abhandlungen, vol. iii, fasc. 2. Munich, 1911.

Beloch, Julius. "La popolazione di Venezia nei secoli XVI e XVII." *Nuovo archivio veneto*, n.s., 3 (1902), 5–49.

Beltrami, Daniele. "Lineamenti di storia della popolazione di Venezia dal Cinquecento al Settecento." In *Storia dell' economia italiana.* Vol. i, *Secoli settimo-diciassettesimo*, ed. Carlo M. Cipolla, pp. 501–31. Turin, 1959.

———. *La penetrazione economica dei veneziani in terraferma. Forze di lavoro e proprietà fondaria nelle campagne venete dei secoli XVII e XVIII*. Venice-Rome, 1961.

———. *Saggio di storia dell'agricoltura nella Repubblica di Venezia durante l'età moderna*. Venice-Rome, 1955.

Benayahu, Meir. *Haskamah u-reshut bi-defuse Venetse'ah (Copyright, Authorization and Imprimatur for Hebrew Books Printed in Venice)*. Jerusalem, 1971.

Bendiscioli, Mario. "Politica, amministrazione e religione nell'età dei Borromei." In *Storia di Milano*. Vol. x, *L'età della Riforma Cattolica (1559–1630)*, pp. 1–350. Milan, 1957.

———. "Vita sociale e culturale." In *Storia di Milano*. Vol. x, *L'età della Riforma Cattolica (1559–1630)*, pp. 353–495. Milan, 1957.

Benrath, Karl. *Bernardino Ochino von Siena: Ein Beitrag zur Geschichte der Reformation*. 2nd ed. Braunschweig, 1892; rpt. Nieuwkoop, 1968.

Benzoni, Gino. "I 'teologi' minori dell'interdetto." *Archivio veneto*, ser. v, vol. 91 (1970), 31–108.

———. *Venezia nell'età della controriforma*. Milan, 1973.

Bersano Begey, Marina. *Le cinquecentine piemontesi*. Vol. i, *Torino*. Turin, 1961.

Bietenholz, Peter G. *Basle and France in the Sixteenth Century: The Basle Humanists and Printers in Their Contacts with Francophone Culture*. Geneva and Toronto, 1971.

Bloch, Joshua. "Venetian Printers of Hebrew Brooks." *Bulletin of the New York Public Library* 36 (1932), 71–92.

Bohatta, Hanns. *Bibliographie der Breviere, 1501–1850*. Leipzig, 1937; rpt. Stuttgart-Nieuwkoop, 1963.

———. *Bibliographie des livres d'heures (Horae B.M.V.) Officia, Hortuli Animae, Coronae B.M.V., Rosaria und Cursus B.M.V. des XV und XVI Jahrhunderts*. Vienna, 1909.

Bongi, Salvatore. *Annali di Gabriel Giolito de' Ferrari da Trino di Monferrato, stampatore in Venezia*. 2 vols. Rome, 1890–97; rpt. Rome, n.d.

Bonnant, Georges. "Les index prohibitifs et expurgatoires contrefaits par des protestants au XVIe et au XVIIe siècle." *Bibliothèque d'Humanisme et Renaissance* 31 (1969), 611–40.

Bouwsma, William J. *Venice and the Defense of Republican Liberty: Renaissance Values in the Age of the Counter Reformation*. Berkeley and Los Angeles, 1968.

Boyle, Leonard E. *A Survey of the Vatican Archives and of Its Medieval Holdings*. Toronto, 1972.

Bozza, Tommaso. *Scrittori politici italiani dal 1550 al 1650. Saggio di bibliografia*. Rome, 1949.

Bremme, Hans Joachim. *Buchdrucker und Buchhändler zur Zeit der Glaubenskämpfe: Studien zur Genfer Druckgeschichte 1565–1580*. Geneva, 1969.

Brown, Horatio. "The *Index Librorum Prohibitorum* and the Censorship of the Venetian Press." In *Studies in the History of Venice* (2 vols.), II, 39–87. London, 1907.

———. *The Venetian Printing Press 1469–1800: An Historical Study Based upon Documents for the Most Part hitherto Unpublished*. London, 1891; rpt. Amsterdam, 1969.

Brown, Peter M. *Lionardo Salviati: A Critical Biography*. London, 1974.

Brunetti, Mario. "Schermaglie veneto-pontificie prima dell' Interdetto. Leonardo Donà avanti il Dogado." In *Paolo Sarpi e i suoi tempi: studi storici*, pp. 119–42. Città di Castello, 1923.

Bugnini, Annibale. "Martirologio." *Enciclopedia Cattolica*, VIII, 243–58.

Burckhardt, Jacob. *The Civilization of the Renaissance in Italy*. Trans. S.G.C. Middlemore, introd. Benjamin Nelson and Charles Trinkaus. 2 vols. New York, 1958.

Buschbell, Gottfried. *Reformation und Inquisition in Italien um die Mitte des XVI Jahrhunderts*. Paderborn, 1910.

Busino, Giovanni. "Italiani all'Università di Basilea dal 1460 al 1601." *Bibliothèque d'Humanisme et Renaissance* 20 (1958), 497–526.

Butler, K. T. "Giacomo Castelvetro, 1546–1616," *Italian Studies* 5 (1950), 1–42.

Cabrol, Fernand. "Breviary." In *The Catholic Encyclopedia*, II, 768–77.

———. "Divine Office." In *The Catholic Encyclopedia*, XI, 219–20.

Calenzio, Generoso. *La vita e gli scritti del Cardinale Cesare Baronio della Congregazione dell'Oratorio, Bibliotecario di Santa Romana Chiesa*. Rome, 1907.

Camaiani, Pier Giorgio. "Interpretazioni della Riforma cattolica e della Controriforma," in *Grande antologia filosofica*, ed. M. F. Sciacca. *Parte III: il pensiero della Rinascenza e della Riforma (Protestantesimo e Riforma cattolica)*. Vol. VI, 329–490. Milan, 1964.

Camerini, Paolo. *Annali dei Giunti. Volume I, Venezia, Parte I e II*. Biblioteca Bibliografica Italica, nos. 26, 28. Florence, 1962–63.

———. "Notizia sugli Annali Giolitini di Salvatore Bongi." *Atti e memorie della R. Accademia di scienze, lettere ed arte in Padova. Memorie della Classe di scienze morali*, n.s., 51 (1934–35), 103–238.

Campana, Lorenzo. "Monsignor Giovanni della Casa e i suoi tempi," *Studi storici* 16 (1907), 3–84; 17 (1908), 145–282, 381–606; 18 (1909), 325–513.

Cantimori, Delio. *Prospettive di storia ereticale italiana del Cinquecento*. Bari, 1960.

————. "La Riforma in Italia." In *Questioni di storia moderna*, ed. Ettore Rota, pp. 181–208. Milan, 1948.

————. *Storici e storia.* Turin, 1971.

————. *Studi di storia.* Turin, 1959.

Cantù, Cesare. *Gli eretici d'Italia. Discorsi storici.* 3 vols. Turin, 1865–66.

Carcereri, L. "Cristoforo Dossena, Francesco Linguardo e un Giordano, librai processati per eresia a Bologna (1548)." *L'Archiginnasio* 5 (1910), 177–92.

Casali, Scipione. *Annali della tipografia veneziana di Francesco Marcolini da Forlì.* Forlì, 1861; rpt. Bologna, 1953, with a new introd. by Luigi Servolini.

Catalogue of Books printed on the Continent of Europe, 1501–1600, in Cambridge Libraries. Compiled by H. M. Adams. 2 vols. Cambridge, 1967.

The Catholic Encyclopedia. 15 vols. London, 1907–12.

Cecchetti, Bartolomeo. *La Repubblica di Venezia e la Corte di Roma nei rapporti della religione.* 2 vols. Venice, 1874.

Cessi, Roberto. "Bartolomeo e Camillo Zanetti, tipografi e calligrafi del '500." *Archivio veneto-tridentino* 8 (1925), 174–82.

Chaix, Paul; Dufour, Alain; and Moeckli, Gustave. *Les livres imprimés à Genève de 1550 à 1600.* Rev. ed. by Gustave Moeckli. Geneva, 1966.

Chojnacki, Stanley. "Crime, Punishment, and the Trecento Venetian State." In *Violence and Civil Disorder in Italian Cities 1200–1500*, ed. Lauro Martines, pp. 184–228. Berkeley, Los Angeles, and London, 1972.

Church, Frederic C. *The Italian Reformers 1534–1564.* New York, 1932.

Cicogna, Emmanuele A. *Delle iscrizioni veneziane.* 6 vols. Venice, 1824–53.

Cioni, Alfredo. "Domenico Basa." DBI, 7, pp. 45–49.

————. "Giovanni Battista Bevilacqua." DBI, 9, pp. 794–95.

————. "Nicolò Bevilacqua." DBI, 9, pp. 798–801.

————. "Daniel Bomberg." DBI, 11, pp. 382–87.

————. "Luca Bonetti." DBI, 11, pp. 794–96.

Comba, Emilio. *I nostri Protestanti.* Vol. 11, *Durante la Riforma nel Veneto e nell'Istria.* Florence, 1897.

Comparato, Vittor Ivo. *Giuseppe Valletta: un intellettuale napoletano della fine del Seicento.* Naples, 1970.

Cozzi, Gaetano. "Cultura politica e religione nella 'pubblica storiografia' veneziana del '500." BSV, 5–6 (1963–64), 215–94.

————. *Il doge Nicolò Contarini: Ricerche sul patriziato veneziano agli inizi del Seicento.* Venice-Rome, 1958.

Cozzi, Gaetano. "Federico Contarini: un antiquario veneziano tra Rinascimento e Controriforma." BSV, 3 (1961), 190–220.

———. "Paolo Paruta, Paolo Sarpi e la questione della sovranità su Ceneda." BSV, 4 (1962), 176–237.

———. *Religione, moralità e giustizia a Venezia: vicende della magistratura degli Esecutori contro la bestemmia.* Padua [1969].

———. "Rinascimento Riforma Controriforma." In *La storiografia italiana negli ultimi vent'anni.* Atti del I Congresso nazionale di scienze storiche organizzato dalla Società degli storici italiani con il patrocinio della Giunta centrale per gli studi storici, Perugia, 9–13 ottobre 1967 (2 vols.), II, 1,191–1,247. Milan, 1970.

Crehan, F. J. "The Bible in the Roman Catholic Church from Trent to the Present Day." In *The Cambridge History of the Bible: The West from the Reformation to the Present Day,* ed. S. L. Greenslade. Cambridge, 1963.

Davari, Stefano. "Cenni storici intorno al Tribunale dell' Inquisizione in Mantova." *Archivio storico lombardo* Anno 6 (1879), 547–65, 773–800.

Davis, James C. *The Decline of the Venetian Nobility as a Ruling Class.* Baltimore, 1962.

Davis, Natalie Z. "Holbein's *Pictures of Death* and the Reformation at Lyons." *Studies in the Renaissance* 3 (1956), 97–130.

De Benedictis, Luigi. *Della vita e delle opere di Bernardino Tomitano: studio.* Padua, 1903.

De Frede, Carlo. "L'estradizione degli eretici dal Dominio veneziano nel Cinquecento." *Atti dell'Accademia Pontaniana,* n.s., 20 (1970–71), 255–86.

———. *La prima traduzione italiana del Corano sullo sfondo dei rapporti tra Christianità e Islam nel Cinquecento.* Studi e materiali sulla conoscenza dell'oriente in Italia, 2. Naples, 1967.

———. "Tipografi, editori, librai italiani del Cinquecento coinvolti in processi d'eresia." *Rivista di storia della Chiesa in Italia* 23 (1969), 21–53.

De Roover, Raymond. "The Business Organisation of the Plantin Press in the Setting of Sixteenth-Century Antwerp." *De Gulden Passer* 34 (1956), 104–20.

Dictionnaire de théologie catholique contenant l'exposé des doctrines de la théologie catholique. 15 vols. Paris, 1908–50.

Dizionario biografico degli Italiani. Rome, 1960–.

Droz, Eugénie. *Chemins de l'hérésie: Textes et documents.* Vols. II and III. Geneva, 1971 and 1974.

Elton, G. R. *Policy and Police: The Enforcement of the Reformation in the Age of Thomas Cromwell.* Cambridge, 1972.

Emerton, Ephraim. *Humanism and Tyranny: Studies in the Italian Trecento.* Cambridge, Mass., 1925.

Enciclopedia cattolica. 12 vols. Vatican City, 1949–54.

Enciclopedia filosofica. 4 vols. Rome-Venice, 1957.

Erichson, Alfred. *Bibliographia Calviniana. Catalogus chronologicus operum Calvini. Catalogus systematicus operum quae sunt de Calvino: cum indice auctorum alphabetico.* Berlin, 1900; rpt. Nieuwkoop, 1960.

Favaro, Antonio. *Galileo e lo Studio di Padova.* 2 vols. Florence, 1883; rpt. Padua, 1966.

Febvre, Lucien, and Martin, Henri-Jean, et al. *L'apparition du livre.* 2nd ed. rev. Paris, 1971.

Fedalto, Giorgio. *Ricerche storiche sulla posizione giuridica ed ecclesiastica dei Greci a Venezia nei secoli xv e xvi.* Florence, 1967.

Fenlon, Dermot. *Heresy and Obedience in Tridentine Italy: Cardinal Pole and the Counter Reformation.* Cambridge, 1972.

Firpo, Luigi. "Correzioni d'autore coatte." In *Studi e problemi di critica testuale.* Convegno di studi di filologia italiana nel centenario della Commissione per i Testi di Lingua. 7–9 aprile 1960, pp. 143–57. Bologna, 1961.

————. "Esecuzioni capitali in Roma (1567–1671)." In *Eresia e Riforma nell'Italia del Cinquecento*, pp. 309–42. Florence and Chicago, 1974.

————. "Filosofia italiana e Controriforma." *Rivista di Filosofia* 41 (1950), 150–73, 390–401; 42 (1951), 30–47.

————. "Il processo di Giordano Bruno." *Rivista storica italiana* 60 (1948), 542–97; 61 (1949), 5–59.

Fiumi, Luigi. "L'Inquisizione Romana e lo Stato di Milano: Saggio di ricerche nell'Archivio di Stato." *Archivio storico lombardo*, Anno 37, ser. 4, vol. 14 (1910), fasc. 25, pp. 5–124; fasc. 26, pp. 285–414; fasc. 27, pp. 145–220.

Fontana, Pierina. "Per la storia della censura pontificia. Il primo caso di sequestro di un libro a stampa." *Accademie e biblioteche d'Italia* 5 (1932), 470–75.

Fragnito, Gigliola. "Cultura umanistica e riforma religiosa: il *De officio boni viri ac probi episcopi* di Gasparo Contarini." *Studi veneziani* 11 (1969), 75–189.

Gaeta, Franco. *Un nunzio pontificio a Venezia nel Cinquecento (Girolamo Aleandro).* Venice-Rome, 1960.

Galiffe, J.B.G. *Le refuge italien de Genève aux XVIme et XVIIme siècles.* Geneva, 1881.

Garin, Eugenio. *Science and the Civic Life in the Italian Renaissance.* Trans. Peter Munz. Garden City, New York, 1969.

Gilbert, Felix. "Cristianesimo, Umanesimo e la Bolla 'Apostolici Regiminis' del 1513." *Rivista storica italiana* 79 (1967), 976–90.

———. "Venice in the Crisis of the League of Cambrai." In *Renaissance Venice*, ed. J. R. Hale, pp. 274–92. London, 1973.

Ginzberg, Carlo. *Il nicodemismo: Simulazione e dissimulazione religiosa nell'Europa del '500.* Turin, 1970.

Giorgetti Vichi, A. M. *Annali della tipografia del Popolo Romano (1570–1598).* Rome, 1959.

Greenslade, S. L., ed. *The Cambridge History of the Bible: The West from the Reformation to the Present Day.* Cambridge, 1963.

Grendler, Marcella T. and Paul F. "The Survival of Erasmus in Italian Libraries." In *Erasmus in English* 8 (University of Toronto Press, 1976), pp. 2–22.

Grendler, Paul F. "Books for Sarpi: The Smuggling of Prohibited Books into Venice during the Interdict of 1606–1607." In *Studies in Honor of Myron P. Gilmore*, ed. Sergio Bertelli. Florence, forthcoming.

———. *Critics of the Italian World 1530–1560: Anton Francesco Doni, Nicolò Franco, & Ortensio Lando.* Madison, Milwaukee, and London, 1969.

———. "The Destruction of Hebrew Books in Venice, 1568." In *Proceedings of the American Academy for Jewish Research*, vol. 45.

———. "Francesco Sansovino and Italian Popular History 1560–1600." *Studies in the Renaissance* 16 (1969), 139–80.

———. "The Roman Inquisition and the Venetian Press, 1540–1605," *The Journal of Modern History* 47 (1975), 48–65.

Grosskurth, Phyllis. *John Addington Symonds: A Biography.* London, 1964.

Guarini, E. Fasano. "Cinzio Aldobrandini." DBI, 2, pp. 102–4.

———. "Pietro Aldobrandini." DBI, 2, pp. 107–12.

Gundersheimer, Werner L. "Crime and Punishment in Ferrara, 1440–1500." In *Violence and Civil Disorder in Italian Cities 1200–1500*, ed. Lauro Martines, pp. 104–28. Berkeley, Los Angeles, and London, 1972.

Hale, J. R., ed. *Renaissance Venice.* London, 1973.

Hauben, Paul J. *Three Spanish Heretics and the Reformation: Antonio Del Corvo—Cassiodoro De Reina—Cypriano De Valera.* Geneva, 1967.

Hierarchia Catholica medii et recentioris aevi. Ed. C. Eubel et al. 6 vols. Munich, 1913–35; Pavia, 1952–58; rpt. Padua, 1960–68.

Hilgers, Joseph. "Bücherverbot und Bücherzensur des sechzehnten Jahrhunderts in Italien." *Zentralblatt für Bibliothekswesen* 28 (1911), 108–22.

————. "Censorship of Books." In *The Catholic Encyclopedia*, III, 519–27.

————. *Der Index der Verboten Bücher*. Freiburg, 1905.

————. "Indices verbotener Bücher aus dem 16. Jahrhundert." *Zentralblatt für Bibliothekswesen* 20 (1903), 444–56.

Hirsch, Rudolf. "Bulla Super Impressione Librorum, 1515." *Gutenberg-Jahrbuch*, 1973, pp. 248–51.

————. "Pre-Reformation Censorship of Printed Books." *Library Chronicle* 21 (1955), 100–105.

————. *Printing, Selling and Reading 1450–1550*. Second printing with a supplemental annotated bibliographical introduction. Wiesbaden, 1974.

Hubert, Friedrich. *Vergerios publizistische Thätigkeit nebst einer bibliographischen Übersicht*. Göttingen, 1893.

Index Aureliensis. Catalogus librorum sedecimo saeculo impressorum. Baden-Baden, 1962–.

Jedin, Hubert. *Crise et dénouement du Concile de Trente, 1562–1563: Une rétrospective après quatre cents ans*. Trans. from the German by Ephrem Florival. Paris, 1965.

————. *A History of the Council of Trent*. Trans. E. Graf. Vol. I. London, 1957.

————. *Papal Legate at the Council of Trent: Cardinal Seripando*. Trans. F. C. Eckhoff. St. Louis and London, 1947.

————. *Riforma cattolica o Controriforma? Tentativo di chiarimento dei concetti con riflessioni sul Concilio di Trento*. Trans. Marola Guarducci. 2nd ed. Brescia, 1967.

Jung, Eva-Maria. "On the Nature of Evangelism in 16th-century Italy." *Journal of the History of Ideas* 14 (1953), 511–27.

Kaufmann, David. "Die Verbrennung der Talmudischen Litteratur in der Republik Venedig." *Jewish Quarterly Review* 13 (1901), 533–38.

————. "Die Vertreibung der Marranen aus Venedig im Jahre 1550." *Jewish Quarterly Review* 13 (1901), 521–32.

Kingdon, Robert M. "Patronage, Piety, and Printing in Sixteenth-Century Europe." In *A Festschrift for Frederick B. Artz*, ed. David H. Pinkney and Theodore Ropp, pp. 19–36. Durham, N. C., 1964.

————. "The Plantin Breviaries: A Case Study in the Sixteenth-Century Business Operations of a Publishing House." *Bibliothèque d'Humanisme et Renaissance* 22 (1960), 133–50.

Labalme, Patricia H. *Bernardo Giustiniani: A Venetian of the Quattrocento*. Rome, 1969.

Lami, Giovanni. *Catalogus codicum manuscriptorum qui in Bibliotheca Riccardiana adservantur*. Livorno, 1756.

Lane, Frederic C. *Venice: A Maritime Republic.* Baltimore and London, 1973.

Laven, P. J. "The *Causa Grimani* and its Political Overtones." *Journal of Religious History* 4 (1967), 184–205.

Logan, Oliver M. T., *Culture and Society in Venice 1470–1790: The Renaissance and Its Heritage.* London, 1972.

———. "Grace and Justification: Some Italian Views of the Sixteenth and Early Seventeenth Centuries." *Journal of Ecclesiastical History* 20 (1969), 67–78.

———. "Studies in the Religious Life of Venice in the Sixteenth and Early Seventeenth Centuries: The Venetian Clergy and Religious Orders, 1520–1630." Ph.D. thesis, University of Cambridge, 1967.

Lopez, Pasquale. *Inquisizione stampa e censura nel Regno di Napoli tra '500 e '600.* Naples, 1975. This came to my attention too late to use.

———. *Sul libro a stampa e le origini della censura ecclesiastica.* Naples, 1972.

Lowry, Martin J. C. "The Church and Venetian Political Change in the Later Cinquecento." Ph.D. thesis, University of Warwick, 1970–71.

———. "The Reform of the Council of Ten, 1582–3: An Unsettled Problem?" *Studi veneziani* 13 (1971), 275–310.

Mackie, J. D. *The Earlier Tudors 1485–1558.* Oxford, 1952.

McNair, Philip. *Peter Martyr in Italy: An Anatomy of Apostasy.* Oxford, 1967.

——— and Tedeschi, John A. "New Light on Ochino." *Bibliothèque d'Humanisme et Renaissance* 35 (1973), 289–301.

Maranini, Giuseppe. *La costituzione di Venezia dopo la serrata del Maggior Consiglio.* Venice, Perugia, and Florence, 1931.

Marchi, Gino. *La Riforma Tridentina in diocesi di Adria nel secolo XVI col sussidio di fonti inedite.* Rovigo, 1946.

Marciani, Corrado. "Editori, tipografi, librai veneti nel Regno di Napoli nel Cinquecento." *Studi veneziani* 10 (1968), 457–554.

———. "Il testamento, e altre notizie, di Federico Torresani." *La Bibliofilia* 72 (1971), 165–78.

Martin, Henri-Jean. *Livre, pouvoirs et société à Paris au XVIIᵉ siècle.* 2 vols. Geneva, 1969.

Maselli, Domenico. "Per la storia religiosa dello Stato di Milano durante il dominio di Filippo II: l'eresia e la sua repressione dal 1555 al 1584." *Nuova rivista storica* 54 (1970), 317–73.

Menchi, Silvana Seidel. "Spiritualismo radicale nelle opere di Ortensio Lando attorno al 1550." *Archiv für Reformationsgeschichte* 65 (1974), 210–77.

Menendez Pelayo, Marcelino. *Historia de los heterodoxos españoles.* Vol. II. Madrid, 1880.

Mercati, Angelo. *Il sommario del processo di Giordano Bruno, con appendice di documenti sull'eresia e l'inquisizione a Modena nel secolo XVI.* Studi e testi, 101. Vatican City, 1942.

Michel, Suzanne, and Michel, Paul-Henri. *Répertoire des ouvrages imprimés en langue italienne au XVIIe siècle conservés dans les bibliothèques de France.* Vol. I. Paris, 1967.

Molmenti, Pompeo. *La storia di Venezia nella vita privata, dalle origini alla caduta della repubblica.* 5th ed. 2 vols. Bergamo, 1911.

Monter, E. William. "Crime and Punishment in Calvin's Geneva, 1562." *Archiv für Reformationsgeschichte* 64 (1973), 281–87.

———. "La sodomie à l'époque moderne en Suisse romande." *Annales: Economies, Sociétés, Civilisations* 29 (1974), 1,023–33.

Morozzo della Rocca, Raimondo, and Tiepolo, Maria Francesca. "Cronologia veneziana del Cinquecento." In *La civiltà veneziana del Rinascimento,* pp. 197–249. Florence, 1958.

New Catholic Encyclopedia. 15 vols. New York, 1967.

Nicolini, Benedetto. *Aspetti della vita religiosa politica e letteraria del Cinquecento.* Bologna, 1963.

———. *Ideali e passioni nell'Italia religiosa del Cinquecento.* Bologna, 1962.

Ojetti, Benedetto. "Concordat." In *The Catholic Encyclopedia,* IV, 196–203.

Olivieri, Achille. "Il *Catechismo* e la *Fidei et doctrinae . . . ratio* di Bartolomeo Fonzio, eretico veneziano del Cinquecento." *Studi veneziani* 9 (1967), 339–452.

Panella, Antonio. "L'introduzione in Firenze dell'Indice di Paolo IV." *Rivista storica degli archivi toscani* 1 (1929), 11–25.

Paschini, Pio. "Daniele Barbaro letterato e prelato veneziano nel Cinquecento." *Rivista di storia della Chiesa in Italia* 16 (1962), 73–107.

———. "La questione del feudo di Taiedo e le peripezie di un patriarca." *Memorie storiche forogiuliesi* 40 (1952–53), 76–137.

———. *Tre ricerche sulla storia della Chiesa nel Cinquecento.* Rome, 1945.

———. *Venezia e l'inquisizione romana da Giulio III a Pio IV.* Padua, 1959.

Pastor, Ludwig von. *The History of the Popes.* Trans. F. I. Antrobus et al. 40 vols. London and St. Louis, 1898–1953.

Pastorello, Ester. "Di Aldo Pio Manuzio: Testimonianze e Documenti." *La Bibliofilia* 67 (1965), 163–220.

———. *Tipografi, editori, librai a Venezia nel secolo XVI.* Florence, 1924.

Perini, Leandro. "Ancora sul libraio-tipografo Pietro Perna e su alcune figure di eretici italiani in rapporto con lui negli anni 1549–1555." *Nuova rivista storica* 51 (1967), 363–404.

———. "Note e documenti su Pietro Perna libraio-tipografo a Basilea." *Nuova rivista storica* 50 (1966), 145–99.

Pesenti, Giulio. "Libri censurati a Venezia nei secoli XVI–XVII." *La Bibliofilia* 58 (1956), 15–30.

Pettas, William A. "The Cost of Printing a Florentine Incunable," *La Bibliofilia* 75 (1973), 67–85.

Pollard, Graham, and Ehrman, Albert. *The Distribution of Books by Catalogue from the Invention of Printing to A. D. 1800 Based on Material in the Broxbourne Library*. Cambridge, 1965.

Pommier, Edouard. "Notes sur la propagande protestante dans la République de Venise au milieu du XVIe siècle." In *Aspects de la propagande religieuse*, pp. 240–46. Geneva, 1957.

———. "La société vénitienne et la Réforme protestante au XVIe siècle." BSV, 1 (1959), 3–26.

Popper, William. *The Censorship of Hebrew Books*. New York, 1899.

Prodi, Paolo. "Silvio Antoniano." DBI, 3, 511–15.

———. "Giovanni Battista Bandini." DBI, 5, pp. 713–14.

———. *Il Cardinale Gabriele Paleotti (1522–1597)*. 2 vols. Rome, 1959–67.

———. "Riforma cattolica e Controriforma." In *Nuove Questioni di Storia Moderna*. Vol. 1, pp. 357–418. Milan, 1964.

Pullan, Brian, ed. *Crisis and Change in the Venetian Economy in the Sixteenth and Seventeenth Centuries*. London, 1968.

———. "The Occupations and Investments of the Venetian Nobility in the Middle and Late Sixteenth Century." In *Renaissance Venice*, ed. J. R. Hale, pp. 379–408. London, 1973.

———. *Rich and Poor in Renaissance Venice: The Social Institutions of a Catholic State, to 1620*. Cambridge, Mass., 1971.

———. "Service to the Venetian State: Aspects of Myth and Reality in the Early Seventeenth Century." *Studi secenteschi* 5 (1964), 95–148.

———. "Wage-Earners and the Venetian Economy, 1550–1630." In Pullan, ed., *Crisis and Change*, pp. 146–74.

Putnam, George H. *The Censorship of the Church of Rome*. 2 vols. New York and London, 1906.

R.L.P. "Richard Fitzralph." In the *Dictionary of National Biography*. Vol. VII, pp. 194–98. Oxford, 1886.

Rasi, Pietro. "L'applicazione delle norme del Concilio di Trento in materia matrimoniale." In *Studi di storia e diritto in onore di Arrigo Solmi* (2 vols.) I, 233–281. Milan, 1941.

Renouard, A. A. *Annales de l'imprimerie des Alde, ou Histoire des trois Manuce et de leurs éditions.* 3rd ed. Paris, 1834; rpt. Bologna, 1953.

Reusch, Franz Heinrich. *Der Index der Verbotenen Bücher: Ein Beitrag zur Kirchen- und literaturgeschichte.* 2 vols. in 3 parts. Bonn, 1883–85; rpt. Darmstadt, 1967.

Rhodes, Dennis E. "Roberto Meietti e alcuni documenti della controversia fra Papa Paolo V e Venezia." *Studi secenteschi* 1 (1960), 165–74.

———. "La traduzione italiana dei *Commentarii* di G. Sleidano." *La Bibliofilia* 68 (1966), 283–87.

Ridolfi, Roberto. *The Life of Niccolò Machiavelli.* Trans. Cecil Grayson. Chicago, 1963.

Rill, G. "Pietro Bertano." DBI, 9, pp. 467–71.

Riondato, E. "Bernardino Tomitano." *Enciclopedia filosofica*, IV, 1,228–30.

Rivolta, Adolfo. *Catalogo dei codici pinelliani dell'Ambrosiana.* Milan, 1933.

Romanin, Samuele. *Storia documentata di Venezia.* 2nd ed. unchanged. 10 vols. Venice, 1912–21.

Rosa, M. "Pomponio de Algerio." DBI, 2, p. 361.

Rose, Constance H. "New Information on the Life of Joseph Nasi, Duke of Naxos: The Venetian Phase." *Jewish Quarterly Review* 60 (1969–70), 330–44.

Rose, Paul Lawrence. "The Accademia Venetiana: Science and Culture in Renaissance Venice." *Studi veneziani* 11 (1969), 191–242.

Ross, James B. "The Emergence of Gasparo Contarini: A Bibliographical Essay." *Church History* 31 (1972), 1–24.

———. "Gasparo Contarini and His Friends." *Studies in the Renaissance* 17 (1970), 191–232.

Roth, Cecil. *The History of the Jews in Italy.* Philadelphia, 1946.

———. *History of the Jews in Venice.* Philadelphia, 1930.

Rotondò, Antonio. "La censura ecclesiastica e la cultura." In *Storia d'Italia.* Vol. V, *I documenti*, pp. 1,397–1,492. Turin, 1973.

———. Review in *Rivista storica italiana* 72 (1970), 752–55.

Santoro, Mario. *Il concetto dell'uomo nella letteratura del Cinquecento.* Naples, 1967.

———. *Fortuna, ragione e prudenza nella civiltà letteraria del Cinquecento.* Naples, 1966.

Santosuosso, Antonio. "The Life and Thought of Giovanni Della Casa, 1503–1556." Ph.D. thesis, University of Toronto, 1972.

———. "Religious Orthodoxy, Dissent and Suppression in Venice in the 1540s." *Church History* 42 (1973), 476–85.

Sartori, Antonio. "Documenti padovani sull'arte della stampa nel sec.

XV." In *Libri e stampatori in Padova. Miscellanea di studi storici in onore di Mons. G. Bellini—tipografo editore libraio*, pp. 111–231. Padua, 1959.

Sartori, Claudio. "Una dinastia di editori musicale. Documenti inediti sui Gardano e i loro congiunti Stefano Bindoni e Alessandro Raverii." *La Bibliofilia* 58 (1956), 176–208.

Savio, Pietro. "Il Nunzio a Venezia dopo l'interdetto." *Archivio veneto*, ser. v, anno 56–57 (1955), 55–110.

Scaduto, Mario. "Lainez e l'indice del 1559: Lullo, Sabunde, Savonarola, Erasmo." *Archivum historicum societatis Jesu* 24 (1955), 3–32.

Schmitt, Charles B. *Gianfrancesco Pico della Mirandola (1469–1533) and His Critique of Aristotle*. The Hague, 1967.

———. "Gianfrancesco Pico della Mirandola and the Fifth Lateran Council." *Archiv für Reformationsgeschichte* 61 (1970), 161–78.

Schnitzer, Joseph. *Savonarola*. Trans. Ernesto Rutili. 2 vols. Milan, 1931.

Scholderer, Victor. "Printers and Readers in Italy in the Fifteenth Century." *Proceedings of the British Academy* 35 (1949), 25–47.

Sella, Domenico. "Crisis and Transformation in Venetian Trade." In Pullan, ed., *Crisis and Change*, pp. 88–105.

———. "The Rise and Fall of the Venetian Woollen Industry." In Pullan, ed., *Crisis and Change*, pp. 106–26.

Seneca, Federico. *Il Doge Leonardo Donà: la sua vita e la sua preparazione politica prima del Dogado*. Padua, 1959.

Sforza, Giovanni. "Riflessi della Controriforma nella Repubblica di Venezia." *Archivio storico italiano* 93 (1935), pt. 1, pp. 5–34, 189–216; pt. 2, pp. 25–52, 173–86.

Short-title Catalogue of Books printed in France and of French Books printed in other countries from 1470 to 1600 in the British Museum. London, 1924; rpt. London, 1966.

Short-title Catalogue of Books printed in the German-speaking countries and German Books printed in other countries from 1455 to 1600 now in the British Museum. London, 1962.

Short-title Catalogue of Books printed in Italy and of Italian Books printed in other countries from 1465 to 1600 now in the British Museum. London, 1958.

Spampanato, Vincenzo. *Vita di Giordano Bruno con documenti editi e inediti*. 2 vols. Messina, 1921.

Spini, Giorgio. "Bibliografia delle opere di Antonio Brucioli." *La Bibliofilia* 42 (1940), 129–80.

———. *Ricerca dei libertini: La teoria dell'impostura delle religioni nel Seicento italiano*. Rome, 1950.

———. *Tra rinascimento e riforma: Antonio Brucioli*. Florence, 1940.

Staehelin, Ernst. *Oekolampad-Bibliographie*. 2nd ed. unchanged. Nieuwkoop, 1963.

Stella, Aldo. *Anabattismo e antitrinitarismo in Italia nel XVI secolo: Nuove ricerche storiche*. Padua, 1969.

———. *Dall'Anabattismo al Socinianesimo nel Cinquecento veneto: Ricerche storiche*. Padua, 1967.

———. *Chiesa e stato nelle relazioni dei nunzi pontifici a Venezia. Ricerche sul giurisdizionalismo veneziano dal XVI al XVIII secolo*. Studi e testi, 239. Vatican City, 1964.

———. "La crisi economica veneziana della seconda metà del secolo XVI." *Archivio veneto*, ser. v, 58–59 (1956), pp. 17–69.

———. "Guido da Fano eretico del secolo XVI al servizio dei re d'Inghilterra." *Rivista di storia della Chiesa in Italia* 13 (1959), 196–238.

———. "L'orazione di Pier Paolo Vergerio al Doge Francesco Donà sulla riforma della chiesa (1545)." *Atti dell'Istituto Veneto di scienze, lettere ed arti: Classe di scienze morali, lettere ed arti* 128 (1970), 1–39.

———. "La proprietà ecclesiastica nella Repubblica di Venezia dal secolo XV al XVIII." *Nuova rivista storica* 42 (1958), 50–77.

———. "Le regolazione delle pubbliche entrate e la crisi politica veneziana del 1582." In *Miscellanea in onore di Roberto Cessi*. Vol. 2, pp. 157–71. Rome, 1958.

———. "Utopie e velleità insurrezioniali dei filoprotestanti italiani (1545–1547)." *Bibliothèque d'Humanisme et Renaissance* 27 (1965), 133–82.

Stow, Kenneth R. "The Burning of the Talmud in 1553, in the Light of Sixteenth Century Catholic Attitudes toward the Talmud," *Bibliothèque d'Humanisme et Renaissance* 34 (1972), 435–59.

Tacchi Venturi, Pietro. *Storia della Compagnia di Gesù in Italia narrata col sussidio di fonti inedite*. Vol. 1, pt. 1, *La vita religiosa in Italia durante la prima età della Compagnia di Gesu*. 2nd ed. enlarged. Rome, 1930.

Tedeschi, John A. "La dispersione degli archivi della Inquisizione Romana." *Rivista di storia e letteratura religiosa* 9 (1973), 298–312.

———. "Genevan Books of the Sixteenth Century." *Bibliothèque d'Humanisme et Renaissance* 31 (1969), 173–80.

———. Review in *The Journal of Modern History* 44 (1972), 259–62.

Tenenti, Alberto. "Luc'Antonio Giunti il giovane, stampatore e mercante." In *Studi in onore di Armando Sapori* (2 vols.) II, 1,021–60. Milan, 1957.

Tentori, P. "Giorgio Arrivabene." DBI, 4, pp. 324–25.

Thurston, Herbert. "Missal." In *The Catholic Encyclopedia*, x, 354–57.

Tinto, Alberto. *Annali tipografici dei Tramezzino*. Annali della tipografia veneziana del Cinquecento, 1. Venice-Rome, 1968.

Tiraboschi, Girolamo. *Biblioteca modenese o notizie della vita e delle opere degli scrittori natii degli stati del Duca di Modena.* 6 vols. Modena, 1781–86.

Toke, Leslie A. St. L. "Little Office of Our Lady." *The Catholic Encyclopedia*, IX, 294–95.

Tramontin, Silvio. "La visita apostolica del 1581 a Venezia." *Studi veneziani* 9 (1967), 453–533.

Trinkaus, Charles. *In Our Image and Likeness: Humanity and Divinity in Italian Humanist Thought.* 2 vols. Chicago, 1970.

Tucci, Ugo. "The Psychology of the Venetian Merchant in the Sixteenth Century." In Hale, ed., *Renaissance Venice*, pp. 346–78.

Ulvioni, Paolo. "Stampa e censura a Venezia nel seicento." *Archivio veneto* 106 (1975), 45–93.

van der Haeghen, F. *Bibliotheca Erasmiana.* Ghent, 1893; rpt. Nieuwkoop, 1961.

Weale, W. H. Iacobus, and Bohatta, Hanns. *Bibliographia Liturgica. Catalogus Missalium Ritus Latini ab anno MCCCCLXXIV impressorum.* London, 1928.

Webster's New International Dictionary. 2nd ed. unabridged. Springfield, Mass., 1961.

Weinberg, Bernard. *A History of Literary Criticism in the Italian Renaissance.* 2 vols. Chicago, 1961.

Woodfield, Denis. *Surreptitious Printing in England 1550–1640.* New York, 1973.

Woodward, William H. *Vittorino da Feltre and Other Humanist Educators.* Cambridge, 1897; rpt. New York, 1963, with a foreword by Eugene F. Rice, Jr.

Woolf, S. J. "Venice and the Terraferma: Problems of the Change from Commercial to Landed Activities." In Pullan, ed., *Crisis and Change*, pp. 175–203.

Wright, A. D. "Why the *Venetian* Interdict?" *English Historical Review* 89 (1974), 534–50.

Zaccaria, Francescantonio. *Storia polemica della proibizioni de' libri.* Rome, 1777.

Zanelli, Agostino. "Di alcune controversie fra la Republica di Venezia e il Sant'Officio nei primi anni del pontificato di Urbano VIII (1624–26)." *Archivio veneto*, ser. v, 59 (1929), 186–235.

Zille, Ester. *Gli eretici a Cittadella nel Cinquecento.* Cittadella, 1971.

INDEX

The index includes substantive material in the footnotes but not references to scholarly works. The appendices are indexed but not individual titles in the inventories of prohibited books in Appendix II. Passing references to Inquisition, papacy, prohibited books, and Venice, to be found on almost every page, are not indexed; substantive references are. The designation "publisher" or "Hebrew publisher" behind a name indicates one active in Venice. Others are identified by location.

Library of Congress Cataloging in Publication Data

Grendler, Paul F.
 The Roman Inquisition and the Venetian press, 1540–1605.

 Bibliography: p.
 Includes index.
  1. Inquisition. Venice.   2. Press—Italy—Venice.   3. Counter-
Reformation.   I. Title.
BX1723.G73   274.5'31   76-45900
ISBN 0-691-05245-X